FINNEGANS WAKES

Tales of Translation

PATRICK O'NEILL

Finnegans Wakes

Tales of Translation

UNIVERSITY OF TORONTO PRESS
Toronto Buffalo London

ISBN 978-1-4875-4199-6 (cloth)   ISBN 978-1-4875-4201-6 (EPUB)
                                 ISBN 978-1-4875-4200-9 (PDF)

Library and Archives Canada Cataloguing in Publication

Title: Finnegans wakes : tales of translation / Patrick O'Neill.
Names: O'Neill, Patrick, 1945– author.
Description: Includes bibliographical references and index.
Identifiers: Canadiana (print) 20210278730 | Canadiana (ebook) 20210278749 |
    ISBN 9781487541996 (cloth) | ISBN 9781487542016 (EPUB) |
    ISBN 9781487542009 (PDF)
Subjects: LCSH: Joyce, James, 1882–1941 – Translations – History and
    criticism. | LCSH: Joyce, James, 1882–1941. Finnegans wake.
Classification: LCC PR6019.O9 Z78116 2022 | DDC 823/.912–dc23

We wish to acknowledge the land on which the University of Toronto Press
operates. This land is the traditional territory of the Wendat, the Anishnaabeg,
the Haudenosaunee, the Métis, and the Mississaugas of the Credit First
Nation.

This book has been published with the help of a grant from the Federation
for the Humanities and Social Sciences, through the Awards to Scholarly
Publications Program, using funds provided by the Social Sciences and
Humanities Research Council of Canada.

University of Toronto Press acknowledges the financial support of the
Government of Canada, the Canada Council for the Arts, and the Ontario Arts
Council, an agency of the Government of Ontario, for its publishing activities.

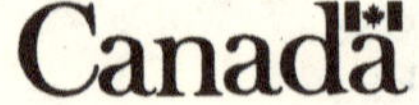

For Trudi,
as always

Contents

Acknowledgments

For assistance, support, and general encouragement of various kinds over the years in matters Joycean, thanks are due to Marcelo Zabaloy in Argentina; Dieter Fuchs in Austria; Geert Lernout and Dirk Van Hulle in Belgium; Alfonso Gumucio in Bolivia; Vitor Alevato do Amaral, Dirce Waltrick do Amarante, Noélia Borges, Caetano Galindo, Laura Puntini de Izarra, Larissa Lagos, Sérgio Medeiros, Daiane Oliveira, Donaldo Schüler, Afonso Teixeira Filho, and Barry Tumelty in Brazil; Marie-Christine Aubin, the late Mark Boulby, Tim Conley, Beth Coward, Amal Eldiaby, the late Michael Groden, Duru Güngör, Na'ama Haklai, Margaret Maliszewska, Brian and Christy O'Neill, and Colin Wright in Canada; Congrong Dai, Arleen Ionescu, and Zhiyao Zhang in China; John Christiansen, Peter Laugesen, and Karl Emil Rosenbæk in Denmark; Cristina Burneo Salazar in Ecuador; Päivi Koivisto-Alanko and Lauri Niskanen in Finland; Philippe Blanchon and Hervé Michel in France; Tamar Gelashvili in Georgia; Ulrich Blumenbach, Friedhelm Rathjen, Christine Schönmetzler, and Wolfgang Teichgräber in Germany; Ágota Bozai and Ferenc Takács in Hungary; Ronan Crowley, Anne Fogarty, John Kearns, Jim and Cora Lawler, and Alan Titley in Ireland; Yehuda Vizan in Israel; Massimo Bacigalupo, the late Rosa Maria Bollettieri Bosinelli, Orlando Mezzabotta, Enrico Terrinoni, and Serenella Zanotti in Italy; Tatsuo Hamada and Eishiro Ito in Japan; Younghee Kho in Korea; James Ramey and Juan Díaz Victoria in Mexico; Erik Bindervoet and Robbert-Jan Henkes in the Netherlands; Leif Høghaug and Bjørn Tysdahl in Norway; Ricardo Silva-Santisteban in Peru; Krzysztof Bartnicki, Katarzyna Bazarnik, and Tadeusz Szczerbowski in Poland; Mihaela Manolache and Erika Mihálycsa in Romania; Andrey Rene in Russia; Borivoj Gerzić and Siniša Stojaković in Serbia; Marissa Aixàs and María Teresa Caneda Cabrera in Spain; Bertil Falk in Sweden; Fritz Senn and his colleagues Ruth Frehner and

Ursula Zeller at the Zurich James Joyce Foundation in Switzerland; Zeynep Atayurt, Umur Çelikyay, and Ceren Kuşdemir Özbilek in Turkey; Boriana Alexandrova, Christian Lloyd, Adam Roberts, and Robert Weninger in the UK; and Kimberly Devlin, James Elkins, Carol Kealiher, Derek Pyle, Bonnie Kime Scott, Jolanta Wawrzycka, and Michelle Woods in the USA.

My best thanks are gratefully offered, as always, to my wife Trudi, who has been unfailingly supportive of my various literary enthusiasms, Joycean and otherwise, over the years.

FINNEGANS WAKES: TALES OF TRANSLATION

Introduction

Latin me that, my trinity scholard, out of eure sanscreed into our eryan. (FW 215.26–7)

It is universally acknowledged that James Joyce's *Finnegans Wake* (*FW*) is an untranslatable text. And yet, as of this writing, no fewer than sixteen complete (would-be) translations of it exist in thirteen different languages altogether: French (Lavergne 1982; Michel 2004), German (Stündel 1993), Japanese (Yanase 1993; Hamada 2012), Dutch (Bindervoet and Henkes 2002), Korean (Kim 2002), Portuguese (Schüler 2003), Polish (Bartnicki 2012), Greek (Anevlavis 2013), Spanish (Zabaloy 2016), Turkish (Sevimay 2016), Italian (Mazza 2018; Schenoni, Terrinoni, and Pedone 2019), quasi-Latin (Roberts 2019), and Serbian (Stojaković 2020). At least thirteen further complete renderings have been announced as under way for anticipated publication in the 2020s, in Portuguese (Amarante et al., Galindo, Teixeira Filho, Garcia Ferreira, Alves), Norwegian (Høghaug), Finnish (Lindholm), Russian (Rene), Turkish (Çelikyay), German (Blumenbach), Hungarian (Bozai), Georgian (Gelashvili), and Chinese (Dai). The favourite single chapter of translators, as it was of Joyce himself, the eighth chapter (*FW* I.8), originally published in 1928 as *Anna Livia Plurabelle* (*ALP*), exists in no fewer than thirty-five complete versions and a further thirty-four partial or fragmentary versions, in twenty-six different languages altogether. The inclusion of partial and fragmentary renderings from other chapters of *FW* brings the total number of languages involved to well more than thirty, including such perhaps unexpected languages as Galician, Guarani, and Irish – not to mention Latin and Ancient Egyptian. The present work charts the international history of these renderings of and from *Finnegans Wake*.

While it will be convenient to continue to refer to "translations," as if translations were possible after all, *Finnegans Wake* can indeed not be translated, it can only be rewritten – and thereby hangs a tale, indeed multiple tales, for rewritings will inevitably differ both from the original and among themselves; the nature and degree of their differences both within individual target languages and across multiple target languages invite and encourage exploration; and *all* rewritings, with their multiple differences, may interestingly be seen as constituting together with the original text a *Wake* macrotext that is in principle both a continuation of Joyce's original work and, as new renderings continue to appear, a continually expanding source of, in principle, inexhaustible intertextual and macrotextual pleasure. The macrotext thus involves both *extension*, in that it extends the number of (rewritten) texts of *Finnegans Wake* in existence, and *expansion*, in that it enables readings of those rewritten texts that in principle contribute to the continued expansion of the *Finnegans Wake* universe.

Joyce's own iconic French rendering of *Anna Livia Plurabelle* in 1931 and, especially, his no less iconic Italian rendering of the same text in 1940 already suggested *Wake* translation as a process not of reproduction or replication or clarification but rather of both extension and expansion in the sense suggested here – and thus also implicitly suggested the concept of a *Wake* macrotext. Genetic studies, as is well known, have demonstrated their value in helping to cope with the multiple readerly challenges of *Finnegans Wake* by extending the concept of the literary text backwards in time to include its various beginnings. The concept of a *Wake* macrotext, focusing on post-textual rather than pre-textual matters, extends the concept of the literary text forwards in time, to include its multiple and multilingual translations – some of which will of course be more successful and some less successful in doing translational justice to Joyce's extraordinary text.

Translations necessarily involve translators, and translators of *Finnegans Wake* include some very remarkable people, with a great variety of personal and cultural and linguistic backgrounds, and who inevitably leave their distinctive personal stamp on their individual extensions of Joyce's text. It is of course the case that the role of the translator, traditionally all too often undervalued or even ignored altogether, is a fundamentally important element in the generation of a reader's response to the translated text. While this is true of any translated literary text, in the case of *Finnegans Wake* the translator's role will be entirely crucial – and will almost certainly generate at various points in the translated text readerly responses entirely different from those generated for readers of Joyce's original text. A dominant concern of the present work is thus, on the one hand, the essential untranslatability of *FW*, and, on the other, the apparently irrepressible temptation for would-be translators to continue transfiguring, transposing, rewriting, recreating, and thus extending it. In the process, it presents something of the tale of their trials, their occasional tribulations, their occasional triumphs – and their occasional distinctive quirks.

The central question with regard to a translation of *Finnegans Wake* is whether and how such a possibility can be envisaged in the first place.[1] As Fritz Senn felicitously puts it, "the text's potential is in inverse ratio to its translatability" (1998, 192). Some translators, especially but not only the earlier translators, therefore attempt essentially to explain what Joyce's text is taken to really mean behind the surface verbal pyrotechnics. These are in principle what Gerald Parks calls *semantic* translations, "exclusively concerned with the transferral of meanings," as opposed to *pragmatic* translations, which attempt "to re-create the overall effect of the original in another language" (1992, 198). The latter approach is exemplified in the comment of the Italian translator Luigi Schenoni that "translating *Finnegans Wake* is to give your interpretation of the work, one of the infinite possible ones, in your own language" (1982a, 4). Overlappings between the two approaches are of course also multiply in evidence.

Finnegans Wakes: Tales of Translation assumes that it is both productive and pleasurable to consider *all* would-be translations of the ultimately untranslatable *FW* as contributing to a *FW* macrotext and explores just some of the multifarious interlingual pleasures that such a macrotext can provide. And while there is certainly lots of fun to be had with *Finnegans Wake* the original text, there is arguably even more fun to be had with *Finnegans Wake* the macrotext. The expanding universe of *Finnegans Wake*, that is to say, involves not just a corresponding increase but an exponential increase in the pleasures of *Finnegans Wake* – which is, of course, essentially what Joyce would have envisaged his original text as making possible.

The nine decades of the survey presented may conveniently be seen as very broadly divided into three periods: the early years (1930s–1960s), the middle years (1970s–1990s), and what we might call the boom years (2000s–2020s), with the 2020s, though barely begun, already promising multiple new and multiply interesting renderings to come. The story told begins with a chapter providing a strictly chronological listing of renderings of and from the *Wake* in more than thirty languages, thus

---

1 Discussions of the translatability of *Finnegans Wake* are numerous, and include among many others Senn (1967c; 1984, 39–56; 1998), Knuth (1972), Eco (1978, 1996), Blumenbach (1990, 1998), Topia (1990), Parks (1992), Milesi (1998), Versteegen (1998), and Bosinelli (2000).

suggesting the overall contours of the continuing polyglot extension and potential continuing expansion of the original text. Subsequent chapters, elaborating and enlarging on that initial listing, are devoted to individual decades, beginning with Joyce's own involvement in translational experiments in the 1930s. Within individual decades, the presentation is organized by individual languages, arranged (with occasional minor strategic deviations) by the earliest rendering to appear in the particular language. The organization by individual languages also allows a reader who is primarily interested in renderings in a particular language to follow the overall translational fortunes of *FW* in that language throughout the nine decades covered.

Short excerpts from individual renderings, collected with the assistance of many helpful colleagues in various countries (and whose assistance is gratefully acknowledged), are quoted in many cases. Typically, these excerpts involve the opening and/or closing lines of the *Wake* and/or the opening and/or closing lines of *ALP*. Brief commentaries are offered on many of these excerpts in various languages, their purpose being to illustrate that there is indeed an enormous amount of fun to be had with a macrotextual *Finnegans Wake*. The comments are of course the work of a reader whose native language is English and whose grasp of other languages will undoubtedly vary significantly in depth and insight and agility from one language to another – much as any one reader's grasp of the language of *Finnegans Wake* will undoubtedly likewise vary significantly from one page to another, one line to another, one word to another. In some other cases brief excerpts quoted are left without commentary of any kind, these examples being presented for the general interest and macrotextual amusement of like-minded readers.[2]

Complete *Wake* translations that appeared after the present work had gone to press are noted on page 332.

---

2 References to *Finnegans Wake* occur in one or more of three forms, depending on the particular context: chapter 8, the *ALP* chapter, is thus variously 196.1–216.5 (indicating both pages and lines), 196–216 (indicating pages only), or I.8 (indicating book I, chapter 8). The first three books of *FW* are divided into chapters (I.1–8; II.1–4; III.1–4), while the fourth (IV) consists of a single chapter.

Chapter One

Wake in Progress: 1930s to 2020s

The following is a chronology of the international growth of what we may think of as an expanding multilingual *Finnegans Wake* (*FW*) universe, constituting a progressive polyglot extension into more than thirty languages to date of an already extravagantly polyglot original text. Full details of all renderings mentioned will be found in the concluding bibliography.

1923   Joyce writes a first sketch (*FW* 380–2) in March 1923.[1]
1924   April: The first published fragment of *Work in Progress* (*FW* 383–98), as Joyce called the preliminary stages of *Finnegans Wake* until its publication in 1939, appears in Paris in the *transatlantic review.*
1925   October 1: first printed version of what would become *Anna Livia Plurabelle* (*ALP*) appears in Paris (as "From Work in Progress") in Adrienne Monnier's journal *Le Navire d'Argent*, 2.5 (1 October 1925): 59–74.
1927   April: "Opening Pages of a Work in Progress," *transition* 1 (April 1927): 9–30. Corresponds to I.1 (*FW* 3–29). The serial publication in *transition* of *Work in Progress* continues for eleven years until April–May 1938, finally including all but the last of the seventeen chapters of *FW*.
1928   October 29: *Anna Livia Plurabelle* published in New York by Crosby Gaige.

---

1 An earlier version of this chronology, here revised and considerably extended, appeared in my book *Impossible Joyce* (O'Neill 2013). For a chart describing the composition of *Finnegans Wake* during the first ten years, see Ellmann (1982, 794–6). For a detailed discussion of the process of composition, and for details of the many serial incarnations of *Work in Progress* between 1924 and 1938, see Crispi and Slote (2007, 485–94).

1929 Georg Goyert, translator of the German *Ulysses* (1927), begins work early in the year on a complete German *ALP*, the first translation of that text to be undertaken in any language – but it will not be the first to be published (see 1933).

1929 July 20: Joyce, writing in German, asks Goyert to send him a few pages of his German *ALP* so that he can ascertain if a translation of it is even a possibility – "ob überhaupt eine Übersetzung davon möglich ist" (*L* 3, 191).

1929 Summer: *Tales Told of Shem and Shaun* (*FW* 152–9, 282–304, 414–19) separately published in Paris by the Black Sun Press, with a preface by C.K. Ogden.

1929 August: Joyce records the closing pages of *ALP* (corresponding to *FW* 213.11–216.5) for Ogden's Orthological Institute.

1929 November 22: Joyce writes to Harriet Weaver that the French poet Léon-Paul Fargue and he are to meet the following day "to set to work to put Alp into French, the last eight pages" (*L* 1, 287). This plan comes to nothing, however, and Fargue has no further involvement.

1929 December: Joyce invites his young fellow Dubliner Samuel Beckett to undertake a French translation of the opening pages of *ALP* (rather than the closing pages as envisaged with Fargue).

1930 April: Beckett and his French friend Alfred Péron begin work on their French rendering of *ALP*.

1930 *Haveth Childers Everywhere* (*FW* 532–54) separately published in Paris by Babou and Kahane and in New York by Fountain Press.

1930 August: The Czech writer and artist Adolf Hoffmeister obtains Joyce's somewhat reluctant permission to undertake a Czech team translation of *ALP*.

1930 Late September: Beckett and Péron's French translation of *ALP* submitted to Joyce for his approval, which was initially forthcoming.

1930 October 16: Beckett and Péron's translation of *ALP*, under the title "Anna Lyvia Pluratself" (*FW* 196.1–201.20), reaches page-proof stage for Georges Ribemont-Dessaigne's avant-garde journal *Bifur*.

1930 November: Joyce abruptly instructs Beckett and Péron to withdraw their rendering as "not yet perfect" – and begins instead to coordinate a French team translation himself.

1931 May 1: Joyce's own French team translation (Joyce et al. 1931) of the opening and closing pages of *ALP* (*FW* 196–201, 215–16) appears in Paris in the *Nouvelle Revue Française*: Beckett and Péron's initial version of 1930 here reworked and extended by Paul Léon, Eugene Jolas, and Ivan Goll, under Joyce's supervision; further reworked by Joyce, Léon, and Philippe Soupault; and finally revised by Jolas and Adrienne Monnier.

1931   Summer: Joyce collaborates with C.K. Ogden on an experimental Basic English rendering of the closing pages of *ALP*.

1931   October: Ogden's "Anna Livia Plurabelle in Basic" (*FW* 213.11–216.5) appears in Ogden's own journal *Psyche*.

1931   An excerpt (*FW* 197.16–199.10) from the forthcoming Czech *ALP* (see 1932), signed by Adolf Hoffmeister and Vladimír Procházka as translators, appears in the Prague journal *Literární noviny*.

1932   *Two Tales of Shem and Shaun* (*FW* 152–9, 414–19) separately published in London by Faber and Faber.

1932   March: C.K. Ogden's 1931 translation into Basic English of the closing pages of *ALP* (*FW* 213–16) reprinted in Paris in Eugene Jolas's journal *transition*.

1932   Complete Czech *ALP* – the first complete published translation of *ALP* in any language – by Maria Weatherall, Vladimír Procházka, and Adolf Hoffmeister, published in Prague.

1933   Complete German translation of *ALP* reportedly finished by Georg Goyert and reportedly approved by Joyce – but because of the increasingly unstable political situation in Germany published in part only in 1946 (*FW* 196–8, 213–16), and in full only in 1970.

1933   Japanese version of the opening and closing pages of *ALP* (*FW* 196, 213–16) by Junzaburo Nishiwaki published in Tokyo.

1934   *The Mime of Mick, Nick and the Maggies* (*FW* 219–59) separately published in The Hague by the Servire Press.

1937   *Storiella As She Is Syung* (*FW* 260–75, 304–8) separately published in London by Corvinus Press.

1937   Joyce proposes to an initially reluctant Nino Frank that they undertake an Italian translation of the same pages from *ALP* earlier translated into French.

1938   Joyce and Frank's Italian *ALP* completed early in the year.

1939   May 4: *Finnegans Wake* published in London by Faber and Faber and in New York by Viking Press.

1940   February 15: Joyce and Frank's Italian "Anna Livia Plurabella" (*FW* 196.1–201.20) appears in Rome in the journal *Prospettive* – but silently emended by Ettore Settanni, without authorization, and misleadingly attributed to Joyce and Settanni without any mention of Frank.

1940   December 15: Joyce and Frank's Italian "I fiumi scorrono" (*FW* 215.11–216.5), attributed in this case to Joyce, Frank, and Settanni, appears in Rome in the journal *Prospettive*.

1941   January 13: Joyce dies of a perforated ulcer in Zurich. The next five years, unsurprisingly in an increasingly war-torn Europe, see no attempts at all to translate any part of *FW*.

1940s   Ivan Goll rumoured during the mid-1940s to be working on a German rendering of or from *FW* – but no such translation ever appeared.

1946   Excerpts from Goyert's German *ALP* (see 1933) appear both in Salzburg in the journal *das silberboot* and in Munich in the affiliated journal *Die Fähre* (*FW* 196–8, 213–16).

1946   July: Reported plan (subsequently abandoned) for a French team translation of *FW*, involving Philippe Soupault, Raymond Queneau, Eugene Jolas, Stuart Gilbert, and Samuel Beckett.

1948   Brief excerpts (from *FW* 3, 196, 216, 419) in French translation by Michel Butor.

1949   Further excerpts in French translation by Michel Butor (from *FW* 627–8) in Maria Jolas's *James Joyce Yearbook*.

1950   French translation by André du Bouchet of excerpts from the final chapter, including the closing pages, in the journal *L'Âge Nouveau* (*FW* 619, 624, 625–8).

1951   French translation of the closing pages (*FW* 627–8) by Maxime Chastaing et al. in the journal *Roman*.

1956   Anonymous Serbian rendering of an excerpt from *ALP* in the Belgrade journal *Mlada kultura*.

1957   French versions by André du Bouchet in the *Nouvelle Revue Française* of excerpts from the final chapter (from *FW* 604–28), including revised versions of his 1950 translations.

1957   Portuguese translations by the Brazilian poets (and brothers) Haroldo and Augusto de Campos of seven excerpts in the *Jornal do Brasil* (from *FW* 3, 159, 196, 214–16, 556, 561, 627–8).

1959   December: Polish translation by Jerzy Strzetelski of excerpts from *ALP*, including its opening and closing pages (*FW* 196–8, 206–7, 215–16).

1960   March: German translation by Guido Meister of *FW* 627.34–628.16 and other excerpts in his translation of Jean Paris's *James Joyce par lui-même* (1957).

1961   German translation by Fritz Senn of more than thirty brief excerpts from *FW* in the German translation of Richard Ellmann's *James Joyce* (1959) by Albert Hess et al.

1961   November 10: German translation in a radio program of selected excerpts by Arno Schmidt, subsequently published in Schmidt's *Der Triton mit dem Sonnenschirm* (1969).

1961   Italian versions of more than forty pages of excerpts by Juan
       Rodolfo Wilcock, conceived of as an outline introduction to *FW*
       (*FW* 3, 33–4, 104–9, 112, 169–70, 179, 182–4, 185, 187–8, 189–91,
       196, 206–7, 219–22, 249, 258–9, 306–8, 384, 543–5, 558–9, 572–5,
       599–606, 626–8).
1961   Italian translation by Mario Diacono of a brief excerpt (*FW* 107–8).
1962   French translation by André Coeuroy of more than thirty brief
       excerpts from *FW* in his translation of Richard Ellmann's *James
       Joyce* (1959).
1962   French translation, slightly abbreviated, of *FW* I.1 and IV by
       André du Bouchet in his volume *Finnegans Wake*, which also
       contains Joyce's 1931 French team translation of *ALP*.
1962   June: Extensively annotated Spanish translation of the opening
       page (*FW* 3.1–24) by Salvador Elizondo.
1962   December: Eleven excerpts in Portuguese translation (from *FW*
       3, 143, 159, 189, 196, 214–16, 226, 556, 559, 561, 627–8) by Au-
       gusto and Haroldo de Campos (see 1957) appear in book form
       as *Panaroma do Finnegans Wake*.
1964   French translation of excerpts (from *FW* 3, 44, 169–71, 384, 627–
       8) by Daniel Castelain.
1964   November: Hungarian translation in the Yugoslav journal *Híd* of
       excerpts (from *FW* 8–10, 169–95, 196–216, 627–8) by Endre Bíró.
1964   Italian translation by Piero Bernardini of more than thirty brief
       excerpts from *FW* in his translation of Richard Ellmann's *James
       Joyce* (1959).
1965   Slovak translation by Jozef Kot of the opening two pages (*FW*
       3–5) in the journal *Slovenské pohľady*.
1965   Romanian translation by Ion Biberi, from Joyce's French *ALP*,
       of *FW* 200.16–19.
1966   Japanese team translation led by Masayoshi Osawa of the open-
       ing two paragraphs of I.7 (*FW* 169–70).
1966   Czech rendering by Zdeněk Urbánek of two passages from *FW*
       about HCE in a detailed analysis of Joyce's verbal technique
       (Sonja Bašić 2004, 194).
1967   German translation by Wolfgang Hildesheimer in a radio
       program of the opening two pages of *ALP* (*FW* 196–7), subse-
       quently published as Hildesheimer 1969.
1967   December 10: German translation by Klaus Reichert in a radio
       program of excerpts from the closing pages (*FW* 619.20–620.2,
       626.35–628.16).
1967   French translation by Philippe Lavergne of I.7 (*FW* 169–95) in
       the journal *Tel Quel*.

1968   French translation by Philippe Lavergne of I.1 (*FW* 3–29) in the journal *Change*.

1968   Japanese translation by Masayoshi Osawa and Junnosuke Sawasaki of excerpts, including the closing pages (*FW* 206–7, 418–19, 627–8).

1968   March: Portuguese translation by Manuel Lourenço of the opening page (*FW* 3).

1968   German rendering by Manfred Triesch of various excerpts from *FW* in his translation of Anthony Burgess's *Here Comes Everybody* (1965).

1969   German translation by Arno Schmidt of selected excerpts (*FW* 30–1, 39, 63–4, 142, 166–7, 175, 182–4, 244–5, 259, 308, 403–6).

1969   German translation by Wolfgang Hildesheimer, with commentary, of the opening pages of *ALP* (*FW* 196–7).

1969   Galician translation of an excerpt (*FW* 216) by Leopoldo Rodríguez.

1970   Three separate complete German translations of *ALP* by Wolfgang Hildesheimer, Hans Wollschläger, and Georg Goyert, respectively, published in a single volume edited by Klaus Reichert and Fritz Senn.

1970–2 Japanese translation by Masayoshi Osawa et al. of the first twelve pages of *ALP* (*FW* 196–208), serialized in seven numbers of the Japanese journal *Kikan Paedeia* between 1970 and 1972.

1971   Japanese translation by Yukio Suzuki et al. of *FW* I.1–3 (*FW* 3–74), the most extensive translation from *FW* in any language to that date.

1971   Portuguese translation of sixteen excerpts (from *FW* 3, 13, 143, 157–9, 182–4, 189–90, 196, 202, 206–7, 214–16, 226, 244, 556, 559, 561, 627–8) by Augusto and Haroldo de Campos appear in an expanded second edition of their *Panaroma do Finnegans Wake*.

1971   Spanish translation of the first two paragraphs (*FW* 3.1–14) by Juan Benet.

1971   Spanish translation by Ricardo Silva-Santisteban in the journal *Creación y crítica* of the closing pages (*FW* 626–8).

1972   Italian translation by Gianni Celati of excerpts from I.1 (*FW* 8–10).

1972   Polish translation by Maciej Słomczyński of "The Ballad of Persse O'Reilly" (*FW* 44.22–47.29) and an excerpt from II.4 (*FW* 398–9).

1973   Polish translation by Maciej Słomczyński of the opening and closing pages of *ALP* (*FW* 196–202, 215–16).

1973   French translation by Stephen Heath and Philippe Sollers of *FW* 593.1–594.9, 596.34–598.16, 626.35–628.16.

1974   Luigi Schenoni begins work on a planned complete Italian translation of *FW*.

1974   Italian translation by Luigi Schenoni of Bygmester Finnegan episode (*FW* 4.18–5.4).

1974   Spanish rendering by Mario Monteforte Toledo of excerpts from *FW*.

1975   Italian version by Anthony Burgess of the first two paragraphs (*FW* 3.1–14).

1975   Hungarian rendering by Miklós Szentkuthy of *FW* 628.16, 3.1–3 and of the final paragraph of *ALP* (*FW* 215.31–216.5).

1976   Italian translation by Luigi Schenoni of the prankquean vignette (*FW* 21.5–23.15).

1977   Russian translation by Andrey Sergeev of "The Ballad of Persse O'Reilly" (*FW* 44.22–47.29).

1977   Italian translation by Luigi Schenoni of the Mutt and Jute (*FW* 15.29–18.16) and O foenix culprit episodes (*FW* 23.16–29.36).

1977   Italian translation by Luigi Schenoni of opening pages of I.2 (*FW* 30.1–32.19).

1978   Italian translation by Luigi Schenoni of the cad with a pipe episode (*FW* 35.1–42.16).

1978   Italian translation by Luigi Schenoni of the opening lines (*FW* 3.1–10).

1978   Series of German radio programs over a twelve-month period includes German translations by Uwe Herms (*FW* 17, 18, 66, 68), Ulrich Sonnemann (*FW* 429–30, 431), Erich Fried (*FW* 403–4), Peter von Haselberg (*FW* 593), and Fritz Senn (*FW* 176–7).

1978   Japanese translation by Masayoshi Osawa et al. of five excerpts (*FW* 169–70, 206–7, 418–19, 593, 627–8).

1978   Croatian rendering by Nada Šoljan of brief excerpts from *FW* reported by Sonja Bašić (2004, 181–2).

1979   Italian translation by Luigi Schenoni of the museyroom vignette (*FW* 8.9–10.23).

1979   Italian translation by Luigi Schenoni of an episode from I.3 (*FW* 55.3–62.25).

1979   French version by Simonne Verdin in the *Courrier du Centre International d'Études Poétiques* (Brussels) of the closing pages (*FW* 627–8).

1979   Joyce and Frank's original Italian "Anna Livia Plurabella," edited by Jacqueline Risset and purged of Settanni's emendations of 1940, appears in Milan in Joyce's *Scritti italiani*.

1982   February: Italian translation by Luigi Schenoni of an episode from I.4 (*FW* 85.20–86.31).

1982   June: Italian translation by Luigi Schenoni of the first four chapters (*FW* I.1–4), until October 1982 the most extensive translation from *FW* in any language to that date.

1982   Catalan version by Josep-Miquel Sobré of an excerpt from *FW* III.3.

1982   October: Complete French version by Philippe Lavergne of *FW*, the first complete rendering in any language.

1982   Italian translation by Piero Bernardini of more than thirty brief excerpts from *FW* in his translation of Richard Ellmann's *James Joyce* (1982).

1982   Italian translation of the opening three pages of Book IV (*FW* 593.1–595.29) by Roberto Sanesi.

1982   Complete Japanese team translation of *ALP* led by Masayoshi Osawa.

1982   Polish translation by Tomasz Mirkowicz of the first six paragraphs (*FW* 3.1–5.12).

1982   Spanish translation by Enrique Castro and Beatriz Blanco of more than thirty brief excerpts from *FW* in their translation of Richard Ellmann's *James Joyce* (1982).

1982   Spanish version of the opening and closing pages of *ALP* (*FW* 196–7, 213–16) by Ricardo Silva-Santisteban.

1982   April: Spanish rendering by Mario Monteforte Toledo of excerpts from *FW*.

1983   Roberto Sanesi's Italian translation (1982) of the opening three pages of Book IV (*FW* 593.1–595.29) appears in book form as *Il risveglio di Finnegan*.

1983   German translation of *FW* 4–5 by Wilhelm Füger.

1984   German translation by Robert Weninger, with extensive commentary, of "The Mookse and the Gripes" (*FW* 152–9).

1984   Polish translation by Ewa Krasińska of more than thirty brief excerpts from *FW* in her translation of Richard Ellmann's *James Joyce* (1982).

1985   French translation of the opening pages of *ALP* (*FW* 196–201) by Samuel Beckett and Alfred Péron, completed in 1930, finally published after more than half a century.

1985   Special issue of the Viennese literary journal *Protokolle* contains German excerpts translated by Christian Enzensberger (*FW* 241), Erich Fried (*FW* 403–4), Uwe Herms (*FW* 17, 55, 68), and Robert Weninger (*FW* 152–9).

1985   Complete Korean *ALP*, translated by Chong-keon Kim.

1985   Complete Polish *ALP*, translated by Maciej Słomczyński.

1986   German translation by Harald Beck of the opening pages (*FW* 3–5).

1986   Italian translation by Luigi Schenoni of the closing pages (*FW* 627.9–628.16).

1986   Anonymous Serbian rendering of the opening of the final chapter (*FW* 593–4) in the Belgrade journal *Delo*.

1987   German translation by Harald Beck of *FW* 5–7.

1987   German excerpts translated by Klaus Schönmetzler (*FW* 3–5, 152–9, 169–75, 383–4, 414–15, 605–6, 626–8).

1987   Swedish adaptation by Georg and Gösta Friberg of John Cage's song text "The Wonderful Widow of Eighteen Springs" (1942) based on *FW* 556.1–22.

1988   Further Spanish excerpts (see 1982) translated by Ricardo Silva-Santisteban (*FW* 3.1–5.29, 196.1–197.17, 213.11–216.5, 626–8).

1989   October: *Finnegans Wake Deutsch*, edited by Klaus Reichert and Fritz Senn, containing collected excerpts from *FW* (about a quarter of the original text in all) in German translation by various hands, including Harald Beck (*FW* 3.1–11.28), Ulrich Blumenbach and Reinhard Markner (*FW* 619.20–628.16), Ingeborg Horn (*FW* 126.1–168.14), Kurt Jauslin (*FW* 3.1–5.29), Friedhelm Rathjen (*FW* 3.1–14, 30.1–47.32, 152.15–159.18, 383.1–399.36, 414.16–419.10, 627.24–628.16), Klaus Reichert (*FW* 619.20–620.2, 626.35–628.16), Wolfgang Schrödter (*FW* 3.1–4.17), Helmut Stoltefuß (*FW* 30.1–38.8), Dieter Stündel (*FW* 383.1–399.36, 619.20–620.2), Robert Weninger (*FW* 152.15–159.18, previously published in 1984), a seminar group of the Goethe-Universität, Frankfurt, led by Klaus Reichert (*FW* 169.1–195.6), the three previously published translations of *ALP* (see 1970) by Georg Goyert, Wolfgang Hildesheimer, and Hans Wollschläger, respectively, and Arno Schmidt's previously published versions of selected passages (see 1969). The volume provides as many as four different German translations of certain passages.

1989   Portuguese translation by Lya Luft of more than thirty brief excerpts from *FW* in her translation of Richard Ellmann's *James Joyce* (1982).

1980s In the late 1980s the Spanish novelist Ramón Buenaventura reportedly considered undertaking a rendering of *FW*, but the plan was eventually abandoned.

1980s In the late 1980s the Swedish poet Jan Östergren reportedly considered undertaking a rendering of *FW*, but the plan was eventually abandoned.

1990   Italian translation by Luigi Schenoni of *FW* 104.1–112.27.

1990   Portuguese translation by Arthur Nestrovski of an excerpt from I.7 (*FW* 193–5).

1991   First volume (*FW* I–II) of Naoki Yanase's complete Japanese translation of *FW*.

1991   Italian translation by Luigi Schenoni of *FW* 117.9–125.23.

1991   Complete Spanish translation of *ALP* by Ricardo Silva-Santisteban.

1992   German translation of excerpts (*FW* 282–7) by Friedhelm Rathjen.

1992   Hungarian translation by Endre Bíró (see also 1964) of substantial excerpts (from *FW* 8–10, 35, 152–9, 169–95, 196–216, 226, 261–2, 414–21, 499–501, 627–8).

1992   May: German translation by Dieter Stündel of *FW* 309–21.

1992   June: Compendium of renderings in various languages of and from *ALP* in the Argentinian psychoanalytical journal *Conjetural*.

1992   June: Spanish translation of opening pages and final paragraph of *ALP* (*FW* 196.1–199.12, 215.31–216.5) by Luis Chitarroni and C.E. Feiling.

1992   June: Spanish rendering of opening pages of *ALP* (*FW* 196.1–198.16) by Leónidas Lamborghini.

1992   June: Spanish rendering of Ogden's Basic English *ALP* by C.E. Feiling.

1992   Complete Spanish team translation of *ALP* led by Francisco García Tortosa.

1993   Annotated Galician translation of the first two chapters (*FW* 3–47) by Alberte Pagán.

1993   Complete German rendering of *FW* by Dieter Stündel as *Finnegans Wehg*.

1993   Second volume (*FW* III–IV) of Naoki Yanase's complete Japanese version of *FW*.

1993   Abridged and much simplified Spanish version of *FW* by Víctor Pozanco.

1994   German translation by Friedhelm Rathjen of various excerpts from *FW* in his translation of Anthony Burgess's *Here Comes Everybody* (1965).

1995   German translation by Friedhelm Rathjen of excerpt from III.4 (*FW* 555–63).

1995   Separate publication of Friedhelm Rathjen's *Der Mauchs und der Traufen*, a German translation of "The Mookse and the Gripes."

1996   Compendium by Rosa Maria Bosinelli of renderings of and from *ALP*, including Joyce's French and Italian, Beckett's French, Ogden's Basic English, and a new Italian translation of *FW* I.8 by Luigi Schenoni.

1996   Polish translation by Jacek Malicki of two fragments (*FW* 6.29–7.15, 306.11–308.36).

1996   Polish translation of closing page (*FW* 628) by Maciej Słomczyński.

1996   Complete Romanian translation of *ALP* by Felicia Antip.

1996–9 Russian translation by Henri Volokhonsky of some forty pages of excerpts from the first seven chapters (*FW* 3–171), appearing in six separate issues of the St. Petersburg journal *Mitin*.

1997   Danish translation by Peter Laugesen of excerpts from *FW* 618–28.

1998   Polish translations by Adam Królikowski from *FW* 3.1–24, 4.1–17, 4.18–5.12.

1998   Portuguese translation by Arthur Nestrovski of the opening paragraphs of I.5 (*FW* 104.1–112.27).

1998   Romanian translation by Laurent Milesi of final pages of *ALP* (*FW* 213–16).

1998   Nevzat Erkmen, translator of *Ulysses* into Turkish (1996), reportedly begins work on a planned complete Turkish rendering of *FW*.

1999   Italian translation by Luigi Schenoni of opening pages of I.7 (*FW* 169.1–171.28).

1999   Polish translations by Adam Królikowski from *FW* 5.13–29, 5.29–6.12, 6.13–28.

1999   Two different Danish translations by Peter Laugesen of *FW* 171.12–28.

1999   Portuguese translation by Donaldo Schüler of *FW* I.1, the first volume of an eventual five-volume complete translation.

1999   Additional Portuguese excerpts (*FW* 292, 449) translated by Haroldo de Campos, more than forty years after the first version of *Panaroma do Finnegans Wake* (1957).

1999   June: Sérgio Medeiros translates *FW* 189.28–190.9 into Guarani.

2000   Portuguese translation by Donaldo Schüler of *FW* I.2–4.

2000   Russian translation in book form by Henri Volokhonsky of excerpts from the first seven chapters (*FW* 3–171), previously published in the journal *Mitin* from 1996 to 1999.

2000   Russian translation by Konstantin Belyaev of an excerpt from *ALP* (*FW* 209–12).

2000   Slovenian translation by Andrej Skubic of selected excerpts (*FW* 30–4, 380–2, 604–6, 611–12, 615–19).

2000   Spanish translation by Ricardo Silva-Santisteban of some thirty-six pages of selected excerpts (*FW* 3.1–4.17, 185.27–190.9, 196.1–216.5, 418.11–419.8, 619.20–628.16).

2000   Czech translation by Tomáš Hrách of *FW* 74.16–19, 177.31–178.7, 188.9–24, 189.28–190.9, 201.5–6, 627.33–628.16.

2001   March: Italian translation by Luigi Schenoni of I.1–4 (reprinted from 1982) and I.5–8.

2001   Polish translation by Jacek Malicki of opening pages (*FW* 3–7).

2001   Portuguese translation by Donaldo Schüler of *FW* I.5–8.

2001   Complete Swedish translation of *ALP* by Mario Grut.

2001   Further excerpts in Portuguese translation by Haroldo and Augusto de Campos (from *FW* 3, 13, 143, 157–9, 182–4, 189–90, 196, 202, 206–7, 214–16, 226, 244, 556, 559, 561, 627–8) appear in a fourth edition of *Panaroma do Finnegans Wake*.

2002   April: Complete Dutch translation of *FW* by Erik Bindervoet and Robbert-Jan Henkes.

2002   Complete Korean translation of *FW* by Chong-keon Kim.

2002   Portuguese translation by Donaldo Schüler of *FW* II.1–4.

2002   Swedish translation by Mario Grut of "The Ondt and the Gracehoper" (*FW* 414.22–419.8).

2002   An anonymous newspaper obituary (Anon. 2002) of the Egyptian Joyce scholar Taha Mahmoud Taha, translator of *Ulysses* into Arabic in 1982, indicates that he had also completed an Arabic translation of *FW* – which, though advertised, may have remained unpublished.

2003   The Russian translator Henri Volokhonsky refers vaguely in a radio interview to the existence of an Albanian rendering of some part of *FW* – but no such translation appears to exist.

2003   October: French translation, slightly abbreviated, of *FW* IV and I.1 by André du Bouchet, reprinted from his 1962 rendering.

2003   Portuguese translation by Donaldo Schüler of *FW* III–IV, completing his five-volume translation of *FW*.

2003   Russian translation by Dmitry Smirnov of "Three quarks for muster Mark" (*FW* 383.1–14).

2003   Polish translation by Arkadiusz Łuba of selected excerpts from *FW*.

2004   Polish translation by Krzysztof Bartnicki of *FW* I.1 and IV in the journal *Literatura na Świecie*.

2004   Complete Catalan version of *ALP* by Marissa Aixàs, together with other excerpts (*FW* 8–10, 15–18, 182–6).

2004   February: Italian translation by Luigi Schenoni of *FW* II.1–2 (*FW* 219–308).

2004   June: Abridged and simplified Japanese translation of *FW*, including roughly half of the original text, by Kyoko Miyata.

2004   Complete online French translation of *FW* by Hervé Michel, as *Veillée Pinouilles*.

2005   Online French translation of some eighty pages of excerpts by Michel Chassaing.

2005   Polish version by Krzysztof Bartnicki of "The Mookse and the Gripes" (*FW* 152–9).

2006   Finnish version by Miikka Mutanen of the opening pages (*FW* 3–10).

2007   June: Spanish version by Juan Díaz Victoria of *FW* 3.1–24.

2007   Hungarian version by Ágota Bozai of the opening pages (*FW* 3–5).

2007   Spanish version by Leandro Fanzone of selected excerpts (*FW* 159, 215–16, 627–8).

2008   Japanese translation by Tatsuo Hamada of *FW* I.2–4 and IV.

2008   Portuguese version of *FW* I.1 by Afonso Teixeira Filho.

2008   August: Spanish version by Juan Díaz Victoria of *FW* 4.18–5.12, 5.26–6.28.

2008   Irish version by Alan Titley of the opening lines (*FW* 3.1–6).

2008   Hungarian rendering by Ágota Bozai in the online journal *Kalligram* of *FW* 3.1–3, 115.20–35, 213.29–216.5 (with László Kuroli), 627.1–628.16.

2009   Danish rendering by Peter Laugesen of the opening pages of I.8 (*FW* 196.1–201.4).

2009   Finnish version by Miikka Mutanen of the opening pages continued (*FW* 10–15).

2009   April: Japanese version by Tatsuo Hamada of *FW* I and IV.

2009   Complete Portuguese version of *ALP* by Dirce Waltrick do Amarante.

2009   Online Spanish translation of I.1 (*FW* 3–29) by Juan Díaz Victoria.

2010   Italian rendering by Orlando Mezzabotta of the prankquean episode (*FW* 21–3) posted on YouTube.

2010   Revised and heavily annotated Spanish rendering by Juan Díaz Victoria of *FW* 3.1–4.17, 8.9–10.23.

2011   Italian translation by Luigi Schenoni of *FW* II.3–4 (*FW* 309–99) appears posthumously.

2012   February: Complete Polish translation of *FW* by Krzysztof Bartnicki, as *Finneganów tren*.

2012   October: Japanese version by Tatsuo Hamada of *FW* II and III.

2012   Krzysztof Bartnicki's musical cryptogram *Da Capo al Finne*.

2012   German translation by Friedhelm Rathjen of *Tales Told of Shem and Shaun* (*FW* 152–9, 282–304, 414–19).

2012   German translation by Friedhelm Rathjen in his *Winnegans Fake* of more than two hundred pages of excerpts from *FW* (I: 3, 6, 11–13, 22–9, 30–47, 58, 92–3, 102–3, 104–11; II: 219–24, 229, 250, 257–9, 260–1, 276, 307–8, 316, 336–7, 342, 353, 371–82, 383–99; III: 410–12, 420–8, 433–40, 448–73, 483–527, 531–40, 555–63, 564–82, 582–90; IV: 627–8).

2012   Danish translation by Peter Laugesen of *FW* 196.1–201.4 (reprinted from 2009).

2012   December: Chinese version by Congrong Dai of *FW* I.1–8.

2013   A very free Finnish verse transcreation of *FW* I.1 by the poet Hannu Helin published in Turku.

2013   March: First instalment of an online Spanish rendering of *ALP* by Eduardo Lago.

2013   April: Complete Greek translation of *FW* by Eleftherios Anevlavis.

2013   June: *Finn's Hotel* published by Danis Rose's Ithys Press.

2013   Separately published Dutch translation of *ALP* by Erik Bindervoet and Robbert-Jan Henkes (reprinted from their 2002 translation of *FW*), with extensive commentary – and "basic Dutch" renderings (88–9, 131–2) of Ogden's Basic English *ALP*.

2013   French rendering by Philippe Blanchon of Ogden's Basic English *ALP*.

2013   Portuguese translation by Caetano Galindo of the prankquean vignette (*FW* 21–3).

2013   Spanish translation of *Finn's Hotel* by Pablo Ingberg.

2013   November: Italian translation of *Finn's Hotel* by Ottavio Fatica.

2013   December: Swedish version by Bertil Falk of *FW* I.1.

2014   October: Fully revised version of Tatsuo Hamada's complete Japanese translation of *FW*.

2014   Italian translation by Vittorio Santangelo of more than thirty brief excerpts from *FW* in his translation of Richard Ellmann's *James Joyce* (1982).

2014   Portuguese translation by Adriano Scandolara of the closing and opening lines (*FW* 626.29–628.16; 3.1–5.12).

2014   Serbian translation by Siniša Stojaković of *FW* I.

2014   March: Greek translation of *Finn's Hotel* by George-Icaros Babassakis.

2014   June: Portuguese translation of *Finn's Hotel* by Caetano Galindo.

2014   October: German translation of *Finn's Hotel* by Friedhelm Rathjen.

2014   November: German translation by Friedhelm Rathjen of *FW* II.4 ("Mamalujo") and of two earlier versions of the chapter.

2014   Romanian translation of *Finn's Hotel* by Mihai Miroiu.

2014   French translation by Marie Darrieussecq of five early sketches later largely incorporated in *FW* II.4.

2014   Krzysztof Bartnicki's musical cryptogram *F_nnegans a_e: Suite in the Key of Ш*.

2015   Krzysztof Bartnicki and Marcin Szmandra's rolodex *Finnegans Meet*.

2015   French translation by Philippe Blanchon, with commentaries, of a selection of the poems in *FW*.

2015   German translation by Friedhelm Rathjen of *FW* I.2 ("Earwicker") and of four earlier versions of the chapter.

2015   Hebrew translation by Yehuda Vizan of *FW* 44–5, 196, 627–8.

2015   A projected new Portuguese translation of *FW* by Eclair Antonio Almeida Filho is announced in Brazilian newspapers – but later indefinitely postponed.

2015   Polish translation of *Finn's Hotel* by Jerzy Jarniewicz.

2016   January: Publication in book form of Juan Rodolfo Wilcock's 1961 Italian rendering of selected excerpts from *FW*.

2016   January: Turkish translation by Umur Çelikyay of *FW* I.1–8.

2016   Complete Turkish translation of *FW* by Fuat Sevimay.

2016   Online Italian translation by Orlando Mezzabotta of *FW* I.1.

2016   Portuguese translation by Caetano Galindo of the opening pages of I.5 (*FW* 104.1–107.35).

2016   February: Final instalment of a complete online Spanish translation of *ALP* by Eduardo Lago, begun in March 2013.

2016   Complete French translation of *ALP* (and also of *FW* 627.6–628.16 and 3.1–8.8) by Philippe Blanchon.

2016   French translation of *FW* 196.1–199.33 by Ludivine Bouton-Kelly and Tiphaine Samoyault.

2016   June: Complete Spanish translation of *FW* by Marcelo Zabaloy.

2016   Online Russian translation by Andrey Rene of *FW* I.1–2 and 196.1–201.20.

2016   June: Spanish rendering by Juan Díaz Victoria of *FW* 279.

2016   October: Heavily annotated Spanish rendering of *FW* I.1 by Juan Díaz Victoria published in book form.

2016   November: Spanish rendering of *FW* 44.24–47.32 by Juan Díaz Victoria.

2016   Norwegian translation by Leif Høghaug of *FW* 3.1–10.24.

2017   January: Italian translation by Enrico Terrinoni and Fabio Pedone of *FW* III.1–2, continuing Luigi Schenoni's translation of the first twelve chapters.

2017   Online Russian translation of *FW* I.1–4, 7–8, with extensive commentary, by Andrey Rene.

2017   October: Turkish translation by Umur Çelikyay of *FW* II.1–4.

2017   Serbian translation by Siniša Stojaković of *FW* III–IV.

2017   Italian rendering by Orlando Mezzabotta of the opening and closing pages of *ALP* (*FW* 196.1–201.20, 215.11–216.5) posted on YouTube.

2017   Italian translation by Luigi Marrozzini of *FW* 627.33–628.16.

2017   Norwegian translations by Leif Høghaug of *FW* 13.33–19.19
and *FW* 44.22–47.29.

2017   Russian rendering by Elena Genyevna Fomenko of *FW*
593.1–595.30.

2018   January: Jure Godler posts on YouTube a Slovenian rendering
of *FW* 4.18–6.12.

2018   Complete Italian translation of *FW* by Giuliano Mazza.

2018   Portuguese rendering by Dirce Waltrick do Amarante of a series
of excerpts suggesting a possible narrative thread through *FW*.

2018   Russian translation by Andrey Rene of *FW* I.1–8, in book form
(without commentary) and online (with extensive commentary).

2018   September: Orlando Mezzabotta posts on YouTube a rendering
in Ancient Egyptian hieroglyphics of the last and first lines of
the *Wake* (*FW* 628.15–16, 3.1–3).

2018   October: Orlando Mezzabotta posts on YouTube a rendering in
Ancient Egyptian hieroglyphics of the first and last lines of *ALP*
(*FW* 196.1–9, 216.3–5).

2018   Norwegian translation by Leif Høghaug of *FW* 169.1–174.4.

2018   Georgian translation by Tamar Gelashvili of *FW* I.8.

2019   February: Adam Roberts's *Pervigilium Finneganis* appears online, a complete quasi-Latin machine rendering of *FW*.

2019   April: Appearance in a single annotated volume (Milan: Mondadori) of an Italian rendering of *FW* III.3–4 and IV by Enrico
Terrinoni and Fabio Pedone.

2019   April: Appearance in six matching volumes of the complete
Italian Mondadori *Finnegans Wake*, translated by Luigi Sche-
noni (*FW* I–II) and by Enrico Terrinoni and Fabio Pedone (*FW*
III–IV).

2019   December: Online Portuguese translation by Caetano Galindo
of the Mutt and Jute dialogue (*FW* 15.29–18.30).

2019   December: Online Portuguese translation by Vitor Alevato do
Amaral of *FW* 474.1–3.

2019   December: Russian translation by Andrey Rene of *FW* II.1–4, in
book form (without commentary) and online (with extensive
commentary).

2020   March: Portuguese version by Leide Daiane de Almeida Oliveira of *FW* I.5.

2020   April: Friedhelm Rathjen publishes an introduction to *FW* for
German readers, including numerous excerpts from his own
previous translations.

2020   April: Siniša Stojaković's Serbian rendering of *FW* II appears,
completing his Serbian *FW*.

2020   October: Georgian rendering by Tamar Gelashvili of *FW* I.1–8.

Translations announced as forthcoming in the 2020s:

2020s? Anticipated appearance of Congrong Dai's Chinese rendering of *FW* II.

2020s? Anticipated appearance of Juan Díaz Victoria's heavily annotated Spanish rendering of *FW* I.1, I.2, I.8, and II.2 – to be followed at some indefinite future point by his likewise heavily annotated rendering of the complete *Wake*.

2020s? Anticipated appearance of a Portuguese rendering by Dirce Waltrick do Amarante of "The Ondt and the Gracehoper."

2020s? Anticipated appearance of a Danish rendering by Peter Laugesen of one of the following chapters: *FW* I.1, I.8, IV.

2020s? Anticipated appearance of *FW* III–IV of Umur Çelikyay's planned complete Turkish translation of *FW*.

2020s? Anticipated appearance of *FW* III–IV of Andrey Rene's planned complete Russian translation of *FW*.

2020s? Anticipated appearance of a complete Portuguese team translation of *FW*, coordinated by Dirce Waltrick do Amarante and involving eleven different translators altogether.

2020s? Anticipated appearance of a complete Finnish rendering of *FW* by Juhani Lindholm.

2020s? Anticipated appearance of a complete Norwegian rendering of *FW* by Leif Høghaug.

2020s? Anticipated appearance of a complete Portuguese rendering of *FW* by Caetano Galindo.

2020s? Anticipated appearance of a complete Portuguese rendering of *FW* by Afonso Teixeira Filho.

2020s? Anticipated appearance of a complete Portuguese rendering of *FW* by Luis Henrique Garcia Ferreira.

2020s? Anticipated appearance of a complete Portuguese rendering of *FW* by Vinícius Alves.

2020s? Anticipated appearance of a general revision by Siniša Stojaković of his complete Serbian rendering of *FW*.

2020s? Anticipated online appearance of a complete Hungarian rendering of *FW* by Ágota Bozai.

2020s? Anticipated online appearance of a complete German rendering of *FW* by Ulrich Blumenbach.

2020s? Anticipated appearance of a complete Georgian rendering of *FW* by Tamar Gelashvili.

Chapter Two

The 1930s

1 Beckett's French ALP, *Joyce's French* ALP, *Ogden's Basic* ALP
2 Goyert's German ALP, *Weatherall's Czech* ALP, *Nishiwaki's
Japanese* ALP

The history of *FW* translations – strategically assuming the possibility
of such translations in the first place – begins in these early years with
renderings of *ALP*, which occupies a very special place in *FW* studies,
having clearly been Joyce's own favourite chapter, and one on which he
reportedly spent an extraordinary sixteen hundred hours in the writing, which is to say, roughly eighty hours per page, or more than three
hours for every single line (Higginson 1960, 4). Separately published
more often than any other complete chapter of *FW*, *ALP* also occupies
a particularly special place in the discussion of *FW* translations. Not
only was *ALP* the first *Wake* text to be attempted by translators, it has
also long been the favourite chapter of *FW* for translators in many languages, crucially including Joyce himself. Close to seventy renderings
of and from it, complete or abbreviated, partial or fragmentary, in more
than twenty languages, currently exist.[1]

The story of the international translatorial response to *FW* starts
with those renderings from *ALP* in which Joyce himself was involved
in one way or another. One of the two master texts in the history of
ALP translations is Joyce's own 1931 French team translation of the
opening and closing pages – and the other is his 1940 rendering, with
Nino Frank, of the same pages into Italian. Those two dates provide

---

1 See appendix 2 for a complete listing of international renderings of and from *ALP*.

appropriate bookends for what one might think of as the heroic age of
ALP translation.[2]

1 Beckett's French *ALP*, Joyce's French *ALP*, Ogden's Basic English *ALP*

Very soon after the original *ALP* appeared in book form on 29 October
1928, published in New York in a deluxe limited edition of eight hundred copies by Crosby Gaige, Joyce, after the concentrated development
of that text in ever greater degrees of complexity over the preceding five
years, became increasingly interested also in the possibility of its translation. He evidently discussed the possibility of a German translation
with Georg Goyert, translator of the German *Ulysses* (1927), soon after
the appearance of the English *ALP*, for Goyert, apparently at Joyce's
instigation (Rathjen 2012b, 291), undertook in early 1929 already to
produce a complete German rendering of *ALP*, though his translation
was plagued by delays from the start. Joyce's enthusiasm for the project
was clear from the beginning, as witnessed by his enquiry on 20 July
1929 already as to whether or not Goyert was finding a translation to be
possible in the first place (*L* 3, 191). Goyert for whatever reason failed
to respond to the enquiry – and that failure may well have contributed to Joyce's decision shortly afterwards to explore the possibility of
a translation himself, for just four months later, on 22 November 1929,
we find him writing to his English patron and benefactor Harriet Shaw
Weaver that the French poet Léon-Paul Fargue and he were actually to
meet the following day "to set to work to put Alp into French, the last
eight pages" (*L* 1, 287). Since Goyert's translation (to which we shall
return), though eventually completed in 1933, did not appear in print
until more than forty years later, the history not just of *ALP* translations but of *FW* translations in general may in a more productive sense
be seen as beginning with that letter of November 1929 from Joyce to
Harriet Weaver.

Born in Paris, and six years older than Joyce, Léon-Paul Fargue (1876–
1947), who had begun his poetic career as a member of the Symbolist
circle before going on to become a prominent representative of French
Cubism, was already a firmly established figure in the Parisian literary
scene by 1929, with almost a dozen published volumes of poetry to
his credit. Famous for his scintillating wit and his love of extravagant
and sophisticated wordplay, he was reportedly even already regarded

---

2 The discussion of Joyce's French *ALP* draws on material originally presented in my
   book *Trilingual Joyce: The Anna Livia Variations* (O'Neill 2018).

in some circles as the greatest living French poet. A friend and collaborator of Joyce's foremost French champion Valery Larbaud, he had become a member of the enthusiastic group of French writers, critics, and translators surrounding Joyce as early as 1920, and he was significantly involved in both the translation and promotion of the French *Ulysses* of 1929 (Ellmann 1982, 522, 562–3). Reportedly fascinated by Fargue's linguistic brilliance both in conversation and in his writings, Joyce was clearly keen to enlist his services as a translator of *ALP* (Bataillard 2014, 241). His letter to Harriet Weaver proved to be premature, however, for although the two men did indeed discuss the possibility of Fargue's involvement (Ellmann 1982, 618–19), the plan, for whatever reason, came to nothing, and no more is heard of any further involvement on Fargue's part, though Joyce and he continued to be close associates throughout the years of Joyce's stay in Paris.[3]

Beckett's French ALP

The plan of a French translation was by no means abandoned as a result of the failed plan to involve Fargue, and at some point during the following month already (Bair 1978, 95) Joyce, "with his secondary passion for extending other languages as he had extended English" (Ellmann 1982, 632), invited his young fellow Dubliner Samuel Beckett (1906–89), then in his early twenties, to undertake an experimental French translation of the opening pages (rather than of the closing pages initially envisaged with Fargue).

Beckett's French *ALP*, for its part, occupies an intriguing place in any discussion of Joyce's own French *ALP*. Just days after the appearance in book form of *Anna Livia Plurabelle* on 29 October 1928, the recently graduated twenty-two-year-old Beckett arrived in Paris to take up his teaching duties at the École Normale Supérieure, having been selected by Trinity College Dublin, as part of a standing inter-university exchange agreement, to spend two years as *lecteur d'anglais* at that institution. Beckett immediately became an enthusiastic member of the circle of admirers surrounding Joyce – who one year later, in December 1929, invited him to undertake a French translation of the opening pages of *ALP*. The invitation was conveyed by Joyce's Parisian friend Philippe Soupault (1897–1990), who by now, at the age of thirty-two, was already

---

3 Willard Potts's mistaken assertion (1979, 85n) that Fargue assisted in the French translation of *ALP* is evidently based on Joyce's letter to Harriet Weaver announcing the planned collaboration (*L* 1, 287), which remained unrealized.

a force to be reckoned with in French literary circles as one of the founders, with André Breton, of the much-discussed and much-publicized Surrealist movement.

The proposed translation was intended to appear in the avant-garde literary journal *Bifur*, recently founded and still edited by the writer and artist Georges Ribemont-Dessaignes (1884–1974). Soupault's role in the matter was a double one, acting on behalf of Joyce in soliciting the translation and on behalf of the journal in overseeing its progress (Knowlson 1996, 115). According to Beckett's biographer Deirdre Bair, "Beckett was delighted by the opportunity, but still not sure of his command of French, and he asked Alfred Péron to assist him. He brought him to meet Joyce, and Péron passed Joyce's test and became Beckett's collaborator" (1978, 95). Péron, born in 1904, had graduated in Classics in 1924 from the École Normale Supérieure, went on to study English language and literature, and spent two years (1926–8) as an exchange *lecteur* of French at Trinity, where Beckett, just two years younger than he, was one of his language students (Pilling 2006, 237). The two young men quickly struck up a close and lasting friendship. Bair reports that Péron's two years at Trinity had also had the significant advantage that they "had given an Irish cast to his English, which delighted Joyce" (1978, 95).

Beckett and Péron began work on the translation towards the end of April 1930 and continued to work on the task during the summer, meeting several times a week to work on the dauntingly complex text (Knowlson 1996, 115). The task began in fact to seem insuperable as the work progressed, and Beckett was increasingly tempted to tell Soupault that it simply could not be done (Cronin 1996, 119). In a progress report of 5 July 1930, he was nonetheless able to inform Soupault that two large single-spaced typed pages of the translation were ready (Aubert 1985, 417). Relations with Soupault, almost a decade older than Beckett, had obviously deteriorated sharply, for when Péron, as a good Parisian, made arrangements to leave Paris on vacation for most of August, a clearly disgruntled Beckett wrote to his Irish friend the poet Thomas MacGreevy (1893–1967) shortly afterwards, on 7 July 1930, that he did not want to continue working on the translation alone – or to sign a contract with "that bastard Soupault." He continued to worry particularly about Joyce's anticipated reaction, fearing that the master might be disgusted "by the chasm of feeling and technique between his hieroglyphics and our bastard French" (Ackerley and Gontarski 2006, 13).

They persevered with the task, however, and since Beckett had to return to Dublin in mid-September to take up a lectureship in French at Trinity for which he had successfully applied earlier that year (Pilling 2006, 25), Péron was entrusted with the final polishing of the manuscript, at this stage rather extravagantly entitled "Anna Lyvia Pluratself," which he duly presented to Joyce in late September 1930 (Pilling 2006, 26). "Joyce seemed satisfied with it and sent it to the printer" (Bair 1978, 112). The manuscript, which translated the equivalent of the first six pages of the future chapter I.8 of *Finnegans Wake* (*FW* 196.1–201.20), reached the page-proof stage for *Bifur* by mid-October. In early November, however, Joyce abruptly and unexpectedly instructed the two young men, no doubt to their considerable dismay, to withdraw their rendering. Eugene Jolas reports that the translation "had even been announced for appearance in a coming issue. I mentioned this fact to Joyce, who seemed disturbed. 'The translation is not yet perfect,' he said. 'It should be withdrawn.' ... In reality, this version was already quite remarkable, when one considers the almost insuperable difficulties involved" (Maria Jolas 1949, 172). There is an interesting development here in Joyce's thinking about translation and translatability. In June 1929, in correspondence with Georg Goyert, he was still wondering if a translation of *ALP* was even possible in the first place (*L* 3, 191); by November 1930, seventeen months later, he evidently not only considered that *ALP* was indeed translatable – but that even a "perfect" translation of it was a possibility.

Several reasons have been suggested for what Beckett and Péron no doubt saw as a completely ruthless intervention on Joyce's part. First, Joyce's comment to Jolas indicates his opinion that the translation did indeed still leave something to be desired. Second, Joyce very likely realized the desirability of a strategic move away from a small experimental journal whose continued survival was doubtful – and which did in fact very soon cease publication. Third, as Megan Quigley observes, he likely saw the commercial value of becoming involved himself and having his own name rather than those of two as yet unknown young men associated with the translation (2004, 479).

Perhaps the most important reason of all for Joyce's decision to have Beckett and Péron withdraw their rendering, however, was a significantly increased interest on his own part in the possibilities of translation as related to the ongoing compositional process of *Finnegans Wake* itself, which would of course continue for close to another decade. Daniel Ferrer and Jacques Aubert write that a new development in the 1920s was that foreign languages, long a part of Joyce's private life, "invade, and become active in, his actual writing. How could he then fail to take part in such an experiment ... ? Was he not, after all, engaged in a 'Work in Progress' which was nothing less than generalized translation – translation raised to its ultimate power?" (1998, 180–1). Joyce, in short, wanted to become involved in the endeavour himself.

He decided in fact to coordinate a team translation – and to extend it by including those final paragraphs of *ALP* previously discussed with Fargue and on which he had declared to Harriet Weaver that he was "prepared to stake everything" (*L* 3, 163).

Joyce's French ALP

Philippe Soupault, in an introduction to the resulting team translation, which was published on 1 May 1931 in the *Nouvelle Revue Française* (Joyce et al. 1931), offers a detailed account of the complex process of its development. First of all, there was Beckett and Péron's "first attempt," as Soupault, whose relations with Beckett clearly continued to be strained, condescendingly called it. A first revision followed, during which that initial version was reviewed by Paul Léon, Eugene Jolas, and Ivan Goll, under Joyce's own supervision (Soupault 1931, 633). In a third stage, Soupault was enlisted to meet with Joyce and Léon every Thursday at 2:30 p.m. in Léon's apartment. "They sat for three hours at a round table ... and while Joyce smoked in an armchair Léon read the English text, Soupault read the French, and Joyce or one of the others would break into the antiphony to ask that a phrase be reconsidered" (Ellmann 1982, 632). In a statement that further irritated Beckett, Soupault asserted that the team "rejected, with Mr Joyce's approval, everything that seemed contrary to the rhythm, the meaning, or the transformation of the words and then tried to suggest a new translation." In a fourth stage, the resulting draft, which was arrived at in early March 1931 after fifteen three-hour meetings, and which by that stage also included the rendering of the final pages, was sent to Eugene Jolas and Adrienne Monnier, both of whom contributed further suggestions, which were then considered at two further and final meetings. "The completed version," writes Richard Ellmann, "is even more than the French translation of *Ulysses* a triumph over seemingly impossible obstacles" (1982, 633).

It has variously been observed that Joyce's French team translation, crucial as it was to be in the history of *Finnegans Wake* translations, was in essence very much an amateur undertaking. Joyce himself had recently been heavily involved in extensive revisions of Goyert's 1927 German rendering of *Ulysses* (Mitchell 1976, 56–8), but not a single one of the other seven participants had previously demonstrated any particular interest at all in the practice or possibilities of literary translation. Neither Beckett nor Péron had any previous experience as a translator. Soupault's well-deserved reputation was purely as a poet. Paul Léon (1893–1942), an émigré Russian Jew, was a lawyer, man of letters, and author of a biography of Benjamin Constant. Eugene (or Eugène) Jolas (1894–1952), writer, critic, and influential editor of the journal *transition*, was born in the United States to immigrant parents of French and German origin who returned to Alsace-Lorraine when he was two years old (Pilling 2006, 235). He grew up in Alsace, wrote in both English and French, and was an enthusiastic promoter of Joyce's work.[4] Ivan (or Yvan) Goll (1891–1950), born in Alsace-Lorraine and thus a German citizen, was a successful bilingual poet in French and German who also wrote in English. Adrienne Monnier (1892–1955), born in Paris, was a writer and publisher as well as a successful bookseller. Together, under Joyce's direction, and given the impetus of his already powerful influence in French literary circles, they essentially founded the international field of *Finnegans Wake* translation, which would continue to grow from strength to strength over the next century.

Beckett much later confirmed to the French Joyce scholar Jacques Aubert, on 16 September 1983, that the final published version (Joyce et al. 1931) was in fact arrived at without any further input from either Péron or himself. Beckett, whose attitude towards the onerous task of translation has been characterized as "an act as much of literary masochism as reverence" (Ackerley and Gontarski 2006, 206), was clearly deeply disappointed with what in his view amounted to an entirely high-handed rejection of their work on Joyce's part and "could not help but consider it a personal affront" (Bair 1978, 113). While the two young men's names do indeed figure as the first two names in the published (and otherwise alphabetical) list of seven translators in addition to Joyce himself – and whom Joyce jokingly referred to as the "Septuagint"[5] – Péron's name, adding insult to injury, was misspelled as "Alfred Perron." Joyce's own enthusiasm for the result of the team project was obvious. He reports to Harriet Weaver on 4 March 1931, possibly tongue in cheek, possibly not, that "the French translation of A.L.P. is now finished and I think it must be one of the masterpieces of translation" (*L* 1, 302).[6]

Writing in 1982, before Beckett and Péron's rendering was yet separately available in print, Ellmann suggested that perhaps the most important thing about Beckett and Péron's contribution was that

---

4   "Beckett's relations with Jolas seem to have been prickly (on Beckett's part at least), perhaps because Jolas was so close to Joyce" (Pilling 2006, 235).

5   Joyce uses the phrase in a letter of 23 April 1931 to Sylvia Beach (Banta and Silverman 1987, 167).

6   On Beckett and Péron's rendering of *ALP* and its relationship to Joyce's team translation, see also McMurren (2002), Quigley (2004), Mooney (2011), O'Neill (2016, 2018), Milaneschi (2019).

"although it was much changed in the course of revision by others, it demonstrated that a translation was feasible" (1982, 803). Definitively sidelined by Joyce's "official" team translation, their version disappeared from general view for more than half a century, until it was published for the first time in 1985 by Jacques Aubert under the translators' original title "Anna Lyvia Pluratself" (Aubert 1985, 417–22), making it available for comparison with the *Nouvelle Revue Française* version.[7]

Very likely as a combined result of Soupault's superciliously dismissive comments and Ellmann's rather muted endorsement, some critics have been quick to suggest that Beckett and Péron's rendering is much weaker than that of the team translation organized and led by Joyce. Kim Allen thus suggests that "Beckett's strengths lie in his keeping the translation fairly literal," while "his weakness is that he does not play as much with the French language as the reader might like and the text might require" (2000, 430). Sinéad Mooney similarly asserts that "it is not hard to see why Beckett and Péron's version was deemed inadequate by Joyce. Their version loses the vividly spoken quality of the original's pair of gossipy washerwomen, and is written in rather mannered French." Their version, she adds, "privileges 'sense,' in the limited sense in which it is possible to use the term of *Anna Livia Plurabelle*, over the differing morphological richness of the original" (2011, 44) and "compares ill with the increasing semantic plenitude and compression of the *Nouvelle Revue française* version" (2011, 45).

In fact, however, Eugene Jolas was quite right in suggesting that Beckett and Péron's version "was already quite remarkable, when one considers the almost insuperable difficulties involved" (Maria Jolas 1949, 172). A detailed comparison of Beckett's and Joyce's respective renderings shows that the earlier version is far from being merely a rough first draft, as Soupault suggests, or merely a demonstration that a translation was indeed feasible, as Ellmann suggests. It is in fact a sophisticated translatorial achievement in its own right, preliminary only in the sense that it precedes Joyce's team translation. In the case of quite a few passages, phrases, coinages, wordplays, and conceits, indeed, as I have argued elsewhere (O'Neill 2018 passim), and as Blair McMurren also demonstrates (2002), Beckett's rendering is by no means inferior and is in some instances even arguably superior to the team-translated version that officially supplanted it.

---

7 John Pilling's assertion (2006, 91, 226) that Beckett and Péron's rendering was first published in Algiers in 1943 in Soupault's *Souvenirs de James Joyce* is mistaken. What Soupault in fact reprinted in that work was Joyce's own team-translated French *ALP*.

Alfred Péron was later, in June 1939, to give the first radio talk on *Finnegans Wake*, just a month after its appearance. He joined the French Resistance in 1940 and recruited Beckett to it in September 1941. Their cell was infiltrated and betrayed, Péron, who was Jewish, was arrested by the Gestapo in August 1942, and in February 1943 he was deported to the notorious Mauthausen concentration camp in Austria. Fatally weakened by his treatment there, he died in Switzerland on 1 May 1945, just forty years of age, and only two days after his liberation from the camp by the Swiss Red Cross. Beckett had been warned just in time by a telegram sent at considerable personal risk by Péron's wife Maya ("Mania") about the betrayal of the cell and managed to make a hurried escape from Paris even as other members of the cell were already being rounded up by the Gestapo.[8]

The opening lines of the 1928 text of *ALP* (corresponding to *FW* 196.1–11) read as follows:

O / tell me all about / Anna Livia! I want to hear all / about Anna Livia. Well, you know Anna Livia? Yes, of course, we all know Anna Livia. Tell me all. Tell me now. You'll die when you hear. Well, you know, when the old cheb went futt and did what you know. Yes, I know, go on. Wash quit and don't be dabbling. Tuck up your sleeves and loosen your talk-tapes. And don't butt me – hike! – when you bend. Or whatever it was they threed to make out he thried to two in the Fiendish park.

Beckett and Péron, whose version, though completed in 1930, appeared in print only in 1985, render these opening lines as follows:

Ô dis-moi tout d'Anna Livia! Je veux tout savoir d'Anna Livia. Eh bien, tu connais Anna Livia? Évidemment, tout le monde connaît Anna Livia. Dis-moi tout. Dis-moi vite. Alors, tu sais, quand le vieux gaillarda fit krach et fit ce que tu sais. Oui, je sais, et après? Lave tranquillement, et ne bats pas l'eau comme ça. Retrousse tes manches et délie ta langue. Et ne me bouscule pas – ho! – quand tu te penches. Ou quel quel que fût le tréfleuve qu'il aurait trouvé dans le parc de l'Inphernix. (Beckett and Péron 1985; qtd. Bosinelli 1996, 155)

Dispensing with the introductory typographical delta of the 1928 *ALP*, Beckett and Péron's rendering begins with a particularly striking

---

8 Cronin (1996, 328–9, 346); Knowlson (1996, 314–15); Ackerley and Gontarski (2006, 431–2); Pilling (2006, 237).

conceit, their "Ô" not only replicating the "O" of the original but suggesting the delta after all in the form of the diacritical circumflex. Since Joyce obsessively added more and more river names and water-related terms in succeeding revisions of the original *ALP*, amounting eventually to the names of at least a thousand rivers, translators are of course challenged to do likewise. It is therefore particularly serendipitous that in at least one romanized version of Chinese, *ô* means "lake." Given this splendid beginning, it is interesting to discover, as I have pointed out elsewhere (O'Neill 2018, 44), that the circumflex is actually not to be found in Beckett and Péron's original text at all but is instead a subsequent silent addition by the editor of the 1985 printed version, Jacques Aubert.

Other rivers evoked, even at this very early stage, include the Scottish Dee and Irish Moy ("dis-moi"), the Croatian Sava ("savoir") and Swiss Emme ("évidemment"), the Scottish Cona and Japanese Onna ("connais, connaît"), and the Indian Sai ("sais"). The old cheb who went futt in Joyce's original, evoking the central European Cheb and South American Futa, becomes a "gaillarda," a "dirty old brute" who went bust ("krach"), evoking in the process the Italian Arda and French Krach. The punning evocation of Dublin in the original "don't be dabbling" is lost in favour of "ne bats pas l'eau comme ça" ("don't keep thrashing the water like that"). "Retrousse les manches" ("roll up your sleeves"), one washerwoman advises the other, evoking the English Channel (La Manche), "et délie ta langue" ("and loosen your tongue").

Joyce's original formulation, "Or whatever it was they threed to make out he thried to two in the Fiendish park," by far the most complicated sentence so far, evokes the three watchers in the trees delightedly putting together their version of the story, soon to be spread enthusiastically abroad, of what HCE "tried to do to the two" young women in the renamed Phoenix Park. It is rendered by Beckett and Péron as "Ou quel quel que fût le tréfleuve qu'il aurait trouvé dans le parc de l'Inphernix," departing quite radically from Joyce's original with something like "or what whatever the triple stream or three-leaved clover was that he was supposed to have found," where the initial doublet "quel quel" may be read as hinting at the presence of the two temptresses, while the stuttering sequence "quel quel que" provides an early example of HCE's stutter, employed throughout *Finnegans Wake* as suggestive of his guilty conscience. The *tré-* of "tréfleuve" may similarly be read as hinting at the three (*trois*) watchers in the trees.

There now also appears, however, to be the distinct hint of a quite unexpected reference to the patron saint of the Irish, St. Patrick, whose reputation, though now long since sanctified, was likewise, during his own lifetime, subject at one point to malicious rumour, and also to the three-leaved shamrock or clover (*trèfle*, from the Latin *trifolium* "three-leaved") he reportedly used to demonstrate the unity of the Trinity. But the portmanteau coinage "tréfleuve" certainly also includes *fleuve* ("river"), evoking the less strictly theological concerns of HCE and the forbidden "river" (or rivers) he may, his interest piqued, have peeked at in the park. Appropriately for the aquatic context, the past participle "trouvé" ("found") duly evokes the French river Ouve.

Thus Beckett and Péron's rendering ("Beckett's French" for short). Joyce's team translation ("Joyce's French" for short) renders the same opening lines as follows (with departures from Beckett's French marked in **bold** here):

> O, dis-moi tout d'Anna **Livie**! Je veux tout savoir d'Anna **Livie**! Eh bien! tu connais Anna **Livie**? **Bien sûr** tout le monde connaît Anna **Livie**. Dis-moi tout, dis-moi vite. **C'est à en crever!** Alors, tu sais, quand le vieux gaillarda fit krach et fit ce que tu sais. Oui, je sais, et après, **après**? Lave tranquillement **ton linge et ne patauge pas tant**. Retrousse tes manches et délie **ton battant**. Et ne me **cogne pas avec ta caboche, hein**! Ou **quelque** fut le tréfleuve **que le triplepatte qu'on dit** qu'il **trouva** dans le parc de l'Inphernix. (Joyce et al. 1931, 633; qtd. Bosinelli 1996, 3)

Joyce's French, likewise dispensing with the original typographical delta, begins by renaming Anna Livia as "Anna Livie," suggesting the river of life (*la vie*) itself and playing translingually on the Irish *Life* /'lɪfə/, anglicized as *Liffey*. Most of the river names in Beckett and Péron's version reappear, though the Swiss Emme is replaced by no fewer than three rivers, the Sûre and Syr of Luxembourg and the homonymous Central Asian Syr. The English original's "You'll die when you hear," no doubt inadvertently overlooked in Beckett's French, becomes "C'est à en crever!," suggesting a literal "You'll burst" and a colloquial "You'll die," while evoking the English river Ver. Beckett's "gaillarda" who "fit krach" for the cheb who went futt is taken over unchanged, and the evocation of Dublin in the original "don't be dabbling" disappears in Joyce's French as it did in Beckett's. The Beckett rendering "ne bats pas l'eau comme ça," however, is improved by an alliterative and assonantal wordplay, "ne patauge pas tant" ("don't splash so much"), evoking in passing the French Tauge and Korean Patong rivers. Beckett's "délie ta langue" ("loosen your tongue") is made more complex as "délie ton battant" ("untie the tongue of your bell"), while completing a wordplay on *patauge / pas tant / battant*.

Joyce's French team version of the statement "Or whatever it was they threed to make out he thried to two in the Fiendish park" provides a further elaboration of the Beckett and Péron rendering that is even less amenable to linear back-translation. One possible reading of Joyce's rendering, "Ou quel que fut le tréfleuve que le triplepatte qu'on dit qu'il trouva," would be "Or whatever the triple stream or three-leaved clover or triple whatever it was they say he found." Clearly building on Beckett's rendering, Joyce's team version, with its "triplepatte," more definitely introduces the once-maligned St. Patrick ("-patte"), while simultaneously suggesting *tripatouiller* ("to grope sexually") and offering *patte* ("paw") as a translingual pun on "pawing" someone, a stage HCE may or may not have succeeded in reaching but may certainly have envisaged. His guilty conscience plays an even more noticeable role in the extended stuttering "quel que ... que ...qu' ... qu'" that runs through this version. Joyce's team rendering, in which the Ouve still appropriately flows ("trouva"), dispenses oddly enough with any more specific reference to the two young women, and thus obscures the details of the alleged misdeed, translatorial attention focusing instead ("tré-," "triple-") on the perceived threat posed by the three observers of what may or may not have happened.

Joyce's French adopts Beckett and Péron's suggestion of the "infernal" setting of the encounter, whatever it may or may not have involved, with both versions electing for "le parc de l'Inphernix," combining Phoenix and the *Inferno* (one of Beckett's lifelong favourite works) to hint ominously at the appropriateness of Dantesque retribution – while simultaneously introducing the Irish river Erne and the nix or water nymph excluded in Joyce's original preference for "Fiendish" rather than "Phoenix." This is the first of several occasions where Joyce's team translation incorporates a particularly felicitous turn of phrase from Beckett's earlier version. Readers are invited both by Beckett's "quel quel" and by Joyce's "quelque" to detect not only an echo of HCE's guilty stutter but also a translingual aquatic pun on the German *Quelle* ("spring, well").[9]

While Beckett and Péron's *ALP* limited itself to the opening pages (corresponding to *FW* 196.1–201.20), Joyce's team translation also included the closing paragraphs (corresponding to *FW* 215.1–216.5). The final paragraph of *ALP* includes the following lines (corresponding to *FW* 215.31–5, 216.3–5 – though with two changes in the latter text, "Tom

---

9 For a more extended comparison of Beckett's and Joyce's French renderings of the opening sentences of *ALP*, see O'Neill (2018, 40–66 passim).

Malone" becoming "Thom Malone" and "the liffeying waters" becoming "thim liffeying waters"):

> Can't hear with the waters of. The chittering waters of. Flittering bats, fieldmice bawk talk. Ho! Are you not gone ahome? What Tom Malone? Can't hear with bawk of bats, all the liffeying waters of. Ho, talk save us! My foos won't moos. I feel as old as yonder elm. A tale told of Shaun or Shem? ... Tell me, tell me, tell me, elm! Night night! Telmetale of stem or stone. Beside the rivering waters of, hitherandthithering waters of. Night!

These lines are rendered as follows in Joyce's French team translation:

> N'entends pas cause les ondes de. Le bébé babil des ondes de. Souris chauve, trottinette cause pause. Hein! Tu n'es pas rentré? Quel père André? N'entends pas cause les fuisouris, les liffeyantes ondes de. Eh! Bruit nous aide! Mon pied à pied se lie lierré. Je me sens vieille comme mon orme même. Un conte conté de Shaun ou Shem? ... Dis-mor, dis-mor, dis-mor, orme. Nuit, nuit! Contemoiconte soit tronc ou pierre. Tant rivièrantes ondes de, couretcourantes ondes de. Nuit. (qtd. Bosinelli 1996, 29)

Joyce's French washerwoman is unable to hear (*entendre*), for good reason (*pour cause*), because of (*à cause de*) the chatter (*causer* "to chat") of the waves – waves (*ondes*) rather than waters to accommodate a dactylic "ondes de" and a reference to the French river Onde. The chittering waters now produce a "bébé babil," the stammering baby-like "prattling" of the stuttering waves. In a scene evocative of *Alice in Wonderland*, and blurring the boundaries of species, an occasional "bald mouse" ("souris chauve"), or perhaps it is just a discombobulated bat (*chauve-souris*) forgetting that it can fly, scurries along (*trottiner* "to scurry along") as if on wheels (*trottinette* "scooter"), sometimes causing a pause ("cause pause"), perhaps by baulking talk, and sometimes, on the contrary, just stopping to chat (*causer*). The scenario plays on the colloquial phrase *on entendrait trotter une souris*, colloquially, "you could hear a pin drop" – but literally, "you could hear a mouse trotting."

The speaker, substituting "hein!" ("hey!") for "ho!" and the Chinese river Hei for the Chinese noun *ho*, asks "Tu n'es pas rentré?" ("Haven't you gone back?") but is misheard as referring to an otherwise undocumented Père André, possibly a priest, Father André, possibly just an old man, Old André, who owes his name and his existence, like Tom Malone, entirely to the exigencies of rhyme. One can't hear because of (*à cause de*) the chatter (*causer* "to chat") of the "fuisouris," mice (*souris*) scurrying and scattering (*fuir* "to flee"), and the liffeying waves. God

(*Dieu*) may not save us, but "noise" (*bruit*) may. Meanwhile, in a play on *lier* ("to bind") and *lierre* ("ivy"), and strengthening the note of Ovidian metamorphosis, "Mon pied à pied se lie lierré" ("My foot to ivied foot is bound"). As Joyce's original "I feel as old" rhymes with "a tale told" in English, "Je me sens vieille" ("I feel old") rhymes with "un conte conté" ("a tale told") in his French rendering. Similarly, "yonder elm" becomes a French "mon orme même" ("my own elm"), evoking the African Mono and French Orme, facilitating the corresponding rhyme on "Shaun ou Shem," and implying that the speaker is in fact already well on the way to transformation into the elm.

The Indian Tel and American Elm evoked in "Tell me, tell me, tell me, elm!," with its sustained play on /l/ and /m/, are replaced in Joyce's French by the Scottish Dee and Indian Mor (conflated with *moi* "me") and the French river Orme in "Dis-mor, dis-mor, dis-mor, orme," with its corresponding play on /r/ and /m/ suggesting the uninterrupted background murmuring of the river. Serendipitously, the Scottish Dee takes its name from a British Celtic *deva* ("goddess"), while the Irish adjective *mór* ("great") and the Scandinavian noun *mor* ("mother") translingually combine to evoke Anna (Hungarian *anya* "mother," Turkish *anne* "mother") as fluvial Great Mother, the river of rivers on its widening way to the sea (Breton *mor*, Cornish *mor*, Welsh *môr* "sea"). "Contemoiconte," while allowing for hints of the Irish Moy and French Onde, is a quite literal rendering of "tell" (*conter*) and "tale" (*conte*), as "tronc ou pierre" is of "stem or stone," though the echo of "Shem or Shaun" is abandoned in favour of the two Canadian rivers Grand Tronc and Pierre. The "rivering" and "hitherandthithering waters" become "rivièrantes ondes" ("rivering waves") and, drawing on the verb *courir* ("to run"), while playing on nasal vowels, "couretcourantes ondes" ("runandrunning waves").

Ogden's Basic English ALP

Within little more than a month of the appearance in May 1931 of Joyce's French *ALP*, we find him collaborating during the summer with C.K. Ogden on a Basic English rendering of the closing pages. Charles Kay Ogden (1889–1957), who was born in Lancashire and had been a student of Classics at Cambridge, was an English linguist, philosopher, and eccentric with a keen interest in literature and psychology. His co-translation from the German of Ludwig Wittgenstein's *Tractatus Logico-Philosophicus* was published in 1922, the same year as *Ulysses*, and during the following year he was co-author with I.A. Richards of the influential study *The Meaning of Meaning* (Richards and Ogden 1923).

Ogden began working in the mid-1920s on what was to be his best-remembered undertaking, namely, the development of what he called "Basic English," a radically simplified subset of standard English with a vocabulary strictly limited to 850 words, including only eighteen permissible verbs. Basic English was designed in principle to be an international auxiliary language adequate for all day-to-day purposes – ultimately in the idealistic but entirely forlorn hope, following the catastrophe of the Great War but preceding innumerable further wars, that its contribution to international understanding might conceivably help to provide an eventual route towards world peace. His *Basic English: A General Introduction* was published in 1930.

One of Ogden's central concepts, to which he gave the name "orthology," involved the intersection and interaction of psychology, philosophy, and linguistics, and in 1927 he founded the Orthological Institute in Cambridge to promote Basic English and to train teachers of English who planned to employ the method for foreign learners. The Institute was equipped with sophisticated recording machines by the standard of the day, and part of Ogden's program was to organize recordings by contemporary writers (one of whom had already been George Bernard Shaw) as a further teaching tool.

Joyce had made Ogden's acquaintance through Sylvia Beach and had agreed in early 1929 to record the closing pages of *ALP* (corresponding to *FW* 213.11–216.5) for Ogden's Institute. "The idea was Ogden's," Joyce later wrote to Mrs. Herbert Gorman (*L* 3, 203). The recording, which lasts about eight and a half minutes, took place in Cambridge in August 1929. Though still only in his mid-forties, Joyce's eyesight was already so weak by this stage that the pages had been prepared for him in half-inch-high letters, which he nonetheless had considerable difficulty in reading and had to be prompted in a whisper throughout (Ellmann 1982, 617).[10] Sales of the resulting gramophone record proved to be disappointing (*L* 3, 203).

On the occasion of the recording Joyce reportedly indicated to Ogden that he would also be interested in principle to see to what extent the complex textual effects he was aiming to achieve in *ALP* might transfer to the extremely rigid confines of Basic English. During Joyce and Nora's stay in London from May to September 1931 in order to satisfy British residency requirements for their planned marriage, Joyce reportedly collaborated with Ogden (though to a still undetermined degree) on the experiment. The result appeared, with a very brief introductory

---

10 On Joyce's delivery on this occasion, see Curtin (2009, 273–7).

note by Ogden, in *Psyche*, Ogden's own journal of experimental psychology, in October 1931 and was reprinted in Paris in Eugene Jolas's more widely distributed journal *transition* in March 1932.[11]

Basic English was never intended to be a language capable of generating complex literary effects. Its name suggests as much, being an acronym for a very down-to-earth descriptor, "*B*ritish, *A*merican, *S*cientific, *I*nternational, *C*ommercial" (McArthur 1992, 107). It is thus, as Susan Shaw Sailer asserts, "a completely inadequate tool for translating *Finnegans Wake*" (1999, 866). Ogden's curiosity-driven rendering was thus essentially a linguistic rather than a literary experiment, and Joyce's highly complex text inevitably suffers greatly in the highly reductive process. Sailer identifies two major and inevitable shortcomings in Ogden's procedure. First, "where multiple possibilities for signification arose, as they did continuously, Ogden decided what the passage's 'simple sense' was on the basis of the inflections that Joyce gave to his reading" (Sailer 1999, 854) – but, as Sailer convincingly points out, this was a highly unreliable criterion to begin with, since Joyce, because of his by now extremely weak eyesight, had in fact "to be prompted in a whisper throughout" (1999, 854). Second, and even more damaging, Ogden is "forced to combine silliness with distortion" (Sailer 1999, 864) in his translation, because he sees the "simple sense" of Joyce's language as merely one of transmitting semantic information, innocent of any literary or poetic connotations.

The two projects, Joyce's flamboyantly polysemous original *ALP* and Ogden's rigidly reduced Basic English *ALP*, were in fact diametrically opposed, but the experiment was certainly not without linguistic interest: "Ogden tried to limit the vocabulary of the English language to 850 words, whereas Joyce kept pushing back all linguistic boundaries. But no matter how different their projects were, they both showed a keen interest in each other's extreme experiment" (Van Hulle 2004, 78). Van Hulle agrees with Sailer that Ogden's inevitably reductive and even disabling aim was "to retrieve unambiguous, familiar meaning from Joyce's language," undoing in the process those aspects that do not strictly belong to its purely semantic communication, and thus constituting a rigorous, even crippling, domestication of Joyce's text (Van Hulle 2004, 81, 83). For Harry Levin, anticipating both Sailer and Van Hulle, Ogden's problem as a translator, as opposed to the challenges facing Joyce's own French and later Italian translations, "was not to imitate the suggestiveness of the original, but to reduce it to direct

---

11 Ogden's *ALP* is also reprinted by Bosinelli (1996, 141–50).

statement. Hence he is forced to ignore harmonies and conceits, and to rule out ambiguities, sometimes rather arbitrarily. There is not much left" (1960, 196). Despite that assessment of the translational results, however, Levin considers the juxtaposition of "Ogden's language of strict denotation and Joyce's language of extreme connotation" as being of considerable interest in that "both are reactions against our modern Babel" (1960, 197). Sam Slote writes in similar vein: "While it might seem that Ogden's aims for Basic English are the inverse of Joyce's *Wake*, both aim towards a universalizing patois that begins from English. Joyce complicates English, whereas Ogden refines and simplifies it" (Slote 2019, 78).[12]

Given this inevitable weakness as a translation, one of the most intriguing questions with regard to Ogden's rendering is the actual degree to which Joyce himself was involved. The purpose of the Basic English version, Ogden modestly wrote in 1931, was merely "to give the simple sense of the gramophone record made by Mr Joyce, *who has himself taken part in the attempt*; and the reader will see that it has generally been possible to keep almost the same rhythms" (emphasis mine). In some places, "the sense of the story has been changed a little, but this is because *the writer took the view* that it was more important to get these effects of rhythm than to give the nearest Basic word every time" (emphasis mine). Joyce also rejected the use of explanatory footnotes of any kind, and in this way "the simplest and most complex languages of man are placed side by side" (Ogden 1931, 95; 1932a, 259). The April 1932 issue of *Psyche* contained Ogden's further "Notes in Basic English on the *Anna Livia Plurabelle* Record" (1932b, 86–95). Joyce himself appears to have collaborated also in the production of these notes (McHugh 2016, 213n).

Ogden's *ALP* begins with his rendering of the following lines from Joyce's *ALP* (corresponding to *FW* 213.11–18 – with one change in the latter text, "since eye" becoming "senne eye," thus adding rhe name of three more rivers, the Belgian Senne, French Seine, and Welsh Senni):

Well, you know or don't you kennet or haven't I told you every telling has a taling and that's the he and the she of it. Look, look, the dusk is growing. My branches lofty are taking root. And my cold cher's gone ashley. Fieluhr? Filou! What age is at? It saon is late. 'Tis endless now since eye or erewone last saw Waterhouse's clogh. They took it asunder, I hurd thum sigh. When will they reassemble it? O, my back, my back, my bach! I'd want to go to Aches-les-Pains.

---

12   See also Franke (2008); Schotter (2010); Loukopoulou (2013); Quigley (2015, 138–46).

Ogden's rendering:

Well are you conscious, or haven't you knowledge, or haven't I said that every story has an ending and that's the he and the she of it. Look, look, the dark is coming. My branches high are taking root. And my cold seat's gone grey. *'Viel Uhr? Filou!* What time is it? It's getting late. How far the day when I or anyone last saw Waterhouse's clock! They took it to pieces, so they said. When will they put it together again? O, my back, my back, my back! I would go then to Aix-les-Pains. (qtd. Bosinelli 1996, 142)

Perhaps the most immediately striking thing about Ogden's version of this passage is the disappearance of the numerous river names so carefully integrated into the original text by Joyce over the years he spent composing and recomposing *ALP*: Yuno, Kennet, Taling, Root, Cher, Ashley, Saône, Erewon, Hurd, and Ache all vanish, while the aquatic implications of German *Bach* ("stream") and French *bains* ("baths") are almost entirely invisible. Fourteen aquatic references in the original eight lines are thus reduced to two, "well" and "Waterhouse," while the rippling effect of Joyce's opening sentence is approximated only roughly. Minor poetic effects are achieved with "my branches high" and "how far the day." The play on "eye or erewone" is abandoned in "I or anyone," while the intriguing phrase "And my cold cher's gone ashley" is reduced to a determinedly mundane and far less than intriguing "And my cold seat's gone grey." Much else has also necessarily gone grey.

A second example is provided by the closing lines of *ALP* (corresponding to *FW* 215.31–5, 216.3–5 – with two changes in the latter text, the earlier "Tom Malone" becoming "Thom Malone" and the earlier "the liffeying waters" becoming "thim liffeying waters"):

Can't hear with the waters of. The chittering waters of. Flittering bats, fieldmice bawk talk. Ho! Are you not gone ahome? What Tom Malone? Can't hear with bawk of bats, all the liffeying waters of. Ho, talk save us! My foos won't moos. I feel as old as yonder elm. A tale told of Shaun or Shem? ... Tell me, tell me, tell me, elm! Night night! Telmetale of stem or stone. Beside the rivering waters of, hitherandthithering waters of. Night!

Ogden's rendering:

No sound but the waters of. The dancing waters of. Winged things in flight, field-rats louder than talk. Ho! Are you not gone, ho! What Tom Malone? No sound but the noise of these things, the Liffey and all its waters of. Ho, talk safe keep us! There's no moving this my foot. I seem as old as that tree over there. A story of Shaun or Shem but where? ... Say it, say it, tree! Night night! The story say of stem or stone. By the side of the river waters of, this way and that way waters of. Night! (qtd. Bosinelli 1996, 148, 150)

The final lines of *ALP*, with their aquatically rippling dactylic rhythm, are one of the poetic highpoints of *Finnegans Wake*. In Basic English, the dactylic rhythm of the original is fitfully retained, but rhyming plays on "chittering/flittering" and on "bawk/talk" are abandoned. Given the *a priori* restrictions, the very specific "bats" becomes a very unspecific but rhyming "winged things," the hyponym necessarily yielding to a hyperonym. Fieldmice, for purely linguistic reasons, become perhaps more threatening "field-rats." The rhyming "my foos won't moos" is replaced by the minor poetic effect of "There's no moving this my foot," abandoning the suggestion of an Ovidian metamorphosis. The rhyming play on "yonder elm" and "Shaun or Shem" is more or less adequately replaced by the rhyming "over there" and "but where?" The sonorous "Tell me, tell me, tell me, elm! ... Telmetale of stem or stone" becomes a pedestrian and unnecessarily reduced "Say it, say it, tree!" and an alliterative "The story say of stem or stone," while the splendid "rivering waters of, hitherandthithering waters of" is likewise reduced to "river waters of, this way and that way waters of." Joyce, as mentioned, wrote to Harriet Weaver that he was prepared to stake everything on the final lines of *ALP* (*L* 3, 163); he would scarcely have said the same for those lines as refigured in Basic English.

One must of course assume that, in the interests of the specific experiment with the rigid constraints of Basic English, Joyce himself was fully prepared to accept these almost debilitating simplifications – just as later he would be found prepared to abandon many of the same carefully collected river names and aquatic effects in his Italian rendering of *ALP*. His French rendering of *ALP* just weeks before his collaboration with Ogden was clearly intended not to replicate but to extend the original text, to continue working on it and complexifying it by taking maximum advantage of the specific resources of the French language. The same approach would later be even more flamboyantly true of his Italian translation. In the case of Ogden's *ALP*, however, the central point of the exercise for Joyce was clearly not at all to embellish or extend or even retain at least some of the intricacies of the original text but simply to establish just how much would inevitably be lost.[13]

---

13 Ogden's *ALP* has been translated into Spanish (Feiling 1992), Dutch (Bindervoet and Henkes 2013), and French (Blanchon 2013).

2 Goyert's German *ALP,* Weatherall's Czech *ALP,* Nishiwaki's Japanese *ALP*

Before Joyce's planned collaboration with Fargue, and his subsequent invitation to Beckett, and his collaboration with Ogden, the German translator Georg Goyert, apparently on Joyce's personal invitation, had already begun work early in 1929 on what was intended to be a complete German *ALP* – and was in fact the first would-be complete rendering of that text to be undertaken in any language. Because of the increasingly fraught political circumstances in Hitler's Germany, however, Goyert's complete rendering would not actually appear in print until more than forty years later, in 1970. It is appropriate to discuss it in the context of the 1930s, however, because of Joyce's personal involvement – including the intriguing possibility that Joyce may even have played some part in its production, as he appears to have done in the case of Ogden's *ALP*. He would in principle have had ample opportunity to do so when Goyert's rendering, eventually completed four years after its inception, was submitted to him in 1933 for his authorial approval.

Goyert's German ALP

Georg Goyert (1884–1966), born in the northern German city of Witten, in the Ruhr Valley, and just two years younger than Joyce, studied English, French, and German at the University of Marburg, spent a year teaching German in France, obtained his doctorate in 1910 with a dissertation on the French novelist Pierre Loti, qualified as a *Gymnasiallehrer* or high-school teacher, and spent thirty years teaching English and French in his home town of Witten. He was simultaneously a highly prolific and well-respected translator from both French (Flaubert, Balzac, Rimbaud, Maupassant, Camus) and English (Faulkner, Whitman, Lawrence, Joyce), as attested to by the fact that the website of the Deutsche Nationalbibliothek currently lists roughly three hundred works under his name.[14]

By 1929 he was already well established especially as Joyce's authorized German translator, having by then translated all of *A Portrait of the Artist as a Young Man* (in 1926), *Ulysses* (in 1927), and *Dubliners* (in 1928). The initiative to translate *ALP* appears to have come primarily from Joyce (Rathjen 2012b, 291), and one may assume that the Swiss Rhein Verlag, which had published all three of these previous Joyce translations by Goyert, would also have been interested, at least in principle. From the beginning, Joyce

---

14 See also Schulte (1990); Ahrens (2017); Barlach et al. (2017).

continued to display a lively interest in the progress of the translation, asking Goyert for a preliminary progress report as early as 20 June 1929, in order, as he put it himself, to establish at least in principle if a translation was even possible (*L* 3, 191). For whatever reason, Goyert does not seem to have responded to this request from the master, for we find Joyce writing to him again more than two years later, on 9 October 1931, observing that he had still not seen any of the German translation (*L* 1, 307). And still a further year later, on 22 October 1932, we find Joyce contacting Goyert a third time to see how the endeavour was progressing (*L* 3, 262).

Goyert's repeated (and probably embarrassed) failure to respond was very likely due to the fact that, as a professional translator, he had been heavily occupied with other commitments over the intervening three years, producing during that period published translations of no fewer than seven substantial literary works (including, for example, D.H. Lawrence's *Sons and Lovers*) in addition to his no doubt rigorous full-time duties as a senior German high-school teacher. Joyce's third enquiry does appear to have had something of a catalytic effect, however. A letter of 17 March 1933 from Paul Léon to Harriet Weaver asserts that Ivan Goll was now engaged in a German translation of *ALP* (*L* 3, 270), but the trilingual Goll, who had also been one of the contributors to Joyce's French *ALP*, seems in fact to have been taking advantage of his previous experience as a translator of *ALP* to become engaged in working over Goyert's now finally completed version before its submission to Joyce. Goll's involvement will probably have been at the invitation of Daniel Brody, director of the Rhein Verlag of Zurich.

By the end of March 1933 the German *ALP* was reportedly finished, reportedly submitted to Joyce, and reportedly given the seal of approval by the master. Maria Jolas in 1949 reported information to this effect that she had obtained from Daniel Brody, reporting Brody's statement in her own translation: "Goyert translated *Anna Livia Plurabelle* from the chapter which appeared under this title at Faber & Faber's. The translation was worked over by Mrs Brody and myself and after having been okayed by Ivan Goll and, I think, by Larbaud, finally received Joyce's placet too" (Maria Jolas 1949, 173; Senn 1998, 188).[15]

---

15   The publisher Daniel Brody (1883–1969), born in Budapest, was both proprietor and director of the Rhein Verlag from 1929. Being Jewish, he emigrated from Hitler's Germany in 1936. His wife, Desirée "Daisy" Spitz (1889–1979), born in Vienna, was a literary translator who in 1925 produced the first German version of Sinclair Lewis's controversial novel *Babbitt* (1922). Valery Larbaud (1881–1957), a noted linguist, studied German and English at the Sorbonne, and also spoke Italian and Spanish in addition to his native French.

Seven years passed, and by then no doubt highly pleased by the news that his and Nino Frank's Italian version of *ALP* was shortly to appear in the Roman journal *Prospettive* (the greater part of it appeared on 15 February 1940), but obviously disappointed that the German *ALP* had still not appeared, Joyce wrote to Brody, whose enforced wanderings had by now taken him to the Hague, on 10 January 1940, enquiring about Goyert's still unpublished rendering. He clearly implied his personal approval of the rendering, while disavowing any political implications: "Do you think it would be possible to publish the version you have in Holland? After all it is only about rivers and washerwomen" (*L* 3, 464). Because of the turmoil of the times, however, which also saw Brody well-advisedly abandon the Netherlands for the greater safety of Mexico in 1942, Goyert's *ALP* was to remain unpublished for several more years, appearing partially only in 1946 (after Joyce's death) and in full only in 1970 (after Goyert's own death), together in the latter case with two further and much later German versions, translated respectively by two already well-known figures in the German literary world, Wolfgang Hildesheimer and Hans Wollschläger.

Goyert's translation (Reichert and Senn 1970, 141–64) has suffered by the comparison with these two later versions – both of which had, of course, the advantage of several further decades of acquaintance with the intricacies and extravagances of *Finnegans Wake*. Goyert's rendering was for the most part not very linguistically daring, and Fritz Senn points out that there are long stretches in it that do not deviate from entirely normal German – but, as he justifiably observes, this is hardly surprising, since "it took some time of maturation for translators to interfere with morphology or syntax the way Joyce did" (1998, 190). There are occasional striking exceptions to this relatively unexciting norm, however, giving rise to what is undoubtedly the most intriguing question with regard to Goyert's translation – as it is with regard to Ogden's rendering of the closing pages – namely, the degree to which Joyce himself may possibly have had a hand in shaping its final version.

Admittedly, no documentary evidence in support of this possibility has come to light. Despite the lack of such evidence, however, there are at least three plausible reasons for thinking that Joyce in 1933 might indeed have had a hand in the German *ALP*. First, he was almost certainly still elated with the success of the 1931 French *ALP*, on which he had already collaborated intensively, triumphantly demonstrating to himself and to others that *ALP* was indeed translatable. Second, while his German was not at all as strong as his French or Italian, it was certainly more than adequate after five years spent living in Zurich, from 1915 to 1920, and given his demonstrated disappointment with

Goyert's 1927 *Ulysses*, which needed more than six thousand alterations in preparing the 1930 second edition on which Joyce laboriously collaborated (Mitchell 1976, 56–8), it would hardly have been surprising if he had thought it advisable to cast a wary eye over the German *ALP* before giving it his formal approval. Third, given both of these factors, together with his obsessive need to continually complexify his own ongoing *Work in Progress*, it would again have been highly surprising if he had *not* made at least occasional adjustments to Goyert's *ALP*. While none of this constitutes proof of involvement on Joyce's part, and while Goyert's rendering of *ALP* is indeed considerably less sophisticated as a whole than those of his two later German competitors, occasional flashes of unexpected humour, unusually ingenious wordplay, or sudden flaunted linguistic extravagance are suggestively reminiscent of the translatorial freedoms Joyce allowed himself in both his French rendering and, even more so, his later Italian rendering of *ALP*.

Goyert's rendering of the opening sentences of *ALP* includes the following lines (corresponding to *FW* 196.1–7, 9–11):

Oh! Erzähle mir alles über Anna Livia! Alles will ich von Anna Livia wissen! Du kennst doch Anna Livia? Aber natürlich, wir alle kennen Anna Livia. Erzähle mir alles, erzähl's mir sofort. Lachst dich kaputt, wenn du es hörst. Na, du weißt doch, als der alte Holdrio hopps ging und tat, was du weißt. ... Oder was alles sie ihm zu beweisen sich erdreisten, was er in Pfuinix-Park zu entzweien versuchte. (Reichert and Senn 1970, 141)

Like Beckett's and Joyce's French *ALP*s, Goyert's rendering ignores the opening typographical delta. Joyce's "O" is reductively rendered as "Oh!," foregrounding the exclamatory over either the aquatic or the suggestion of circularity implicit in Joyce's text. Goyert uses the verb *erzählen* to translate Joyce's "tell me," thus arguably evoking the importance of storytelling (the primary meaning of *erzählen* being "to tell a story") and thus of fictionality. While Joyce's washerwoman wants "to hear all" about Anna Livia, Goyert's washerwoman wants to "know" all (*wissen*), just as Beckett's and Joyce's own French renderings had opted for *savoir* ("to know"). The use of *wissen* allows for a supplementary aquatic hint of the English river Wissey. That the German conjunction *aber* ("but") is coincidentally also a homonym of the Welsh noun *aber* ("estuary") is a splendidly Joycean example of linguistic serendipity. The Canadian Duke River and the Austrian Enns appear in "du kennst" and the French Enne in "kennen," all likewise without any need of special translatorial ingenuity.

Goyert's rendering already shows a predilection for strongly marked dactylic rhythms, his "Er- | *zähle* mir | *alle*s, er- | *zähl*'s mir so | *fort.* | | *Lachst* dich ka- | *putt,* | | *wenn* du es | *hörst*" constituting a sprightly dactylic rendering generally evocative in tone of German children's rhymes. Laughter is more in evidence than any hint of death in his "Lachst dich kaputt," suggesting "You'll laugh yourself to bits." The Portuguese Mira ("mir alles") and Nigerian Kapu ("kaputt") put in discreet fluvial appearances. The old cheb who went futt is for Goyert "der alte Holdrio" ("the old rake"), an epithet that allows for the evocation of a Spanish *río* ("river"), and as for the nature of his reported fall from grace, Goyert has it that he simply "hopps ging" ("went bust") – and is able to take advantage of the convenient fact that "du weißt" ("you know") effortlessly evokes the German river Weiss.

The complex formulation "Or whatever it was they threed to make out he thried to two in the Fiendish park" becomes Goyert's "Oder was alles sie ihm zu beweisen sich erdreisten, was er in Pfuinix-Park zu entzweien versuchte." This rendering, serendipitously invoking the German Oder, back-translates roughly as "or whatever they are being bold enough to claim that he tried to get from the two of them," where "sich erdreisten" ("to be bold") includes a punning reference to *drei* ("three") and "entzweien" to *zwei* ("two"). The verb *entzweien*, meanwhile, literally means "to break asunder, break in two," but is here pressed into punning service as meaning to "get something from" (*ent-*) a specific two (*zwei*).

Finally, Goyert's text is clear as to the swinish nature of our malefactor's behaviour: the park is the "Pfuinix-Park," with the phoenix (German *Phönix*) conflated with a German *pfui*, a conventional exclamation of disgust. The fact that the name of the park ends in "-nix" suggests the possible presence of a German *Nixe* ("water nymph"), or even two of them, such mythical beings not at all out of place in a text awash in water. That the name of the real Dublin park shares this ending can be taken as constituting just one further example of Wakean serendipity.

The strongest feature of Goyert's rendering throughout is undoubtedly its consistent musicality, for the most part strongly favouring dactylic rhythms, as in Joyce's original. Just a few lines later, the washerwoman's disgust at the appalling state of HCE's shirt, "And the dneepers of wet and the gangres of sin in it!" (*FW* 196.18), becomes Goyert's "Welche Neiße der Pleiße und Gangeräne der Sünde stecken da drina, o yemen, o je!" In this amusing variation, Goyert, sacrificing the Dnieper, suggests "What disgusting wetness and gangrene of sin are in it, oh dear, oh dear!" Here he conflates, first, *Nässe* ("wetness") and the Polish river Neisse; second, *Pleite* ("disaster") and the

German river Pleisse; third, the English *gangrene* and the Indian river Ganges; fourth, *da drinnen* ("inside there") and the Serbian river Drina; and, finally, a jocular *ojemine oje* ("oh dear, oh dear") and, highly unexpectedly, the Middle Eastern country of Yemen – the geographical joke here being that there *are* no permanent rivers in that country. The rhythm once again closely matches that of the original, even improving on Joyce's dactylic tetrameter by humorously expanding it to a double tetrameter: "Welche | *Neiß*e der | *Pleiß'* und Gang'- | *rä*ne der | *Sün*de | | *stec*ken da | *drin*a, o | *yem*en, o | *je!*"

The tricky statement "It was put in the newses what he did, nicies and priers, the King fierceas Humphrey" (*FW* 196.20–2) generates the rendering "In den Zittigen las Majadas Wasser tat, niedliche Weibsen und tolle Kärle, Staarkanwalt gegen Humphrey." Goyert here opens his unusually adventurous version with a punning play on the standard German sentence *In den Zeitungen las man ja das, was er tat* ("One could after all read in the newspapers what he did"), where *Zeitungen* ("newspapers") becomes a Swiss German "Zittigen," allowing passing access to the Philippine river Iti; *las man ja das* becomes a quasi-Spanish "las Majadas," pronounced as if it were German while playing on the real Spanish noun *majada* ("dung"), an unambiguous evaluation of HCE's nefarious doings. As to *was er tat* ("what he did"), it is evidently connected with "Wasser" ("water"), hinting at HCE's alleged voyeurism in the park, possibly spying on two young women discreetly relieving themselves in the bushes.

One might well be tempted to see Joyce's own hand at work here, partly because of the flaunted deformation of standard German, quite unlike Goyert's practice in general, and partly because of the Swiss-German term *Zittigen*. Joyce spent five years in Zurich before moving to Paris, and *FW*, as Fritz Senn has shown on various occasions, has a number of examples of his playful interest in Swiss German usage. The interlingual technique is also similar to Joyce's many variations on the question "How are you today, my fair sir?" elsewhere in *FW*, beginning with "Come on, fool porterfull, hosiered women blown monk sewer?" (*FW* 16.4), in this case allowing translingual access to the French *Comment vous portez-vous aujourd'hui, mon blond monsieur?*

To take another example, Joyce's "Gammer and gaffer we're all their gangsters" (*FW* 215.14–15) becomes the entirely unexpected "Chef und Schäferin haben uns geschaffen." Goyert's quite remarkable rendering here, rejecting any invocation of a German *Oma, Opa*, and offspring, literally suggests that "chief and shepherdess created us." Behind this apparently quite wrong-headed German phrase one may detect a multiple alliterative play on *Chef* ("chief"), *Chefin* ("boss lady"), *Schäfer* ("shepherd"), *Schäferin* ("shepherdess"), *schaffen* ("to create"), and *Schaf* ("sheep"), resulting cumulatively in an implied "Boss man and boss lady created us – and, treating us like sheep, have turned us into sheep." Privileging playful alliteration over any semblance of semantic fidelity, this version is much the nearest Goyert's rendering comes to the untrammelled translatorial freedom in which Joyce would later repeatedly indulge in his Italian *ALP*. One might certainly be tempted once again to wonder if Joyce's own hand had played some role here.

Goyert's rendering of the closing page of *ALP* contains the following lines (corresponding to *FW* 215.31–5, 216.3–5):

> Ich hör nicht wegen des Wassers von. Des Wassergeschwassers von. Fleddernder Flug, Feldmaus pfiff schrill. Ho! Bist du nicht derheim gegangen? Was? Den Leim gegangen? Ich hör nicht vor Mäuse Gewisper liffeylaufenden Wassers von. Ho, rett uns die Red! Mein Fus ist wie Mus. Ich fühl so alt wie jener Baum. Eine alte Mär von Shem und Shaun? ... Sag mir, sag mir, sag mir, Baum! Nacht, nacht! Berichtegeschichte von Stein und Staun. Neben den flüssernden Wassern von, den hinundherrinnenden Wassern von. Nacht! (qtd. Reichert and Senn 1970, 164)

Matching dactyls with Joyce's "Can't hear with the waters of," Goyert's washerwoman can't hear "wegen des Wassers von" ("because of the water of"), the water (*Wasser*) and all its sloshing sibling (*Geschwister*) waters. The "flittering bats" in the growing dusk and growing disorientation are left unidentified, evoked only obliquely by their activity: drawing on Middle High German *vlederen* ("to flutter"), modern German bats (*Fledermäuse*) here engage alliteratively in "fleddernder Flug," a flight (*Flug*) that is not only fluttering (*flatternd*) but also, highly unexpectedly, and etymologically unrelated, plundering and pillaging (*fleddernd*). The German river Eder puts in a hinted appearance. A field mouse (a *Feldmaus* rather than a *Fledermaus*), instead of bawking talk, "squeaked shrilly" (*pfiff schrill*), perhaps seeing itself as the intended object of this pillaging flight. There is no talk of baulking talk. Joyce's delight in unexpected linguistic coincidence is well known: fluttering *Fledermäuse* in "fleddernder Flug," frightening *Feldmäuse*, offers a splendid example of such a coincidence.

Goyert's dialectally tinged "Bist du nicht derheim gegangen?" ("Haven't you gone home?"), a perfect trochaic tetrameter, misheard as having to do with the phrase *auf den Leim gegangen* ("fallen into a trap"), elicits "Was? Den Leim gegangen?" ("What? Trapped?"). Tom Malone has disappeared – not, of course, that he was ever there. The speaker can't hear for the mouse whisperings ("Gewisper") of the liffey-running ("liffeylaufend") waters. "May talk (*Rede*) save us (*rette uns*)! My foot (*Fuss*) – partially amputated for the sake of an eye rhyme – is like mush (*Mus*)" – in this case a process of deliquescence rather than vegetable metamorphosis.

In "Ich fühl so alt wie jener Baum," the elm (*Ulme*) is altered to a hyperonymous "Baum" ("tree"), while the verb *sich fühlen* ("to feel") is treated by a confused and weary speaker as if it were intransitive rather than reflexive. The "tale told" of Shaun or Shem becomes "eine alte Mär" ("an old tale") of "Shem und Shaun," suggesting an assonance between "Baum" and a "Shaun" pronounced as if it were German.

Unusually for Goyert, his combination of a repeated "sag mir" for "tell me" and the generic "Baum" ("tree") for "elm" abandons the musicality of Joyce's original. Compounding the loss, Joyce's "telmetale" is rendered by a rhyming but ponderous "Berichtegeschichte," literally "tell (*berichte*) story (*Geschichte*)." The rendering of "stem or stone" as a plural "Stein *und* Staun" allows alliteration to distort the sense of the original, with "Staun" conflating German *Stein* and English *stone* in order to capture a compensatory slant rhyme with "Baum" and an eye-rhyme with "Shaun." This attempted strategy, however, manages to eliminate Joyce's "stem" altogether.

Goyert recovers his touch again in the final sentence. "Beside the rivering waters of, hitherandthithering waters of. Night!" (*FW* 216.4–5) becomes "Neben den flüssernden Wassern von, den hinundherrinnenden Wassern von. Nacht!" As darkness finally falls, Joyce's "rivering" waters are even arguably improved upon by Goyert, become more comprehensively "flüssernd," conflating *Fluss* ("river"), *fließen* ("to flow"), and *flüstern* ("to whisper"), while Joyce's concluding dactylic tetrameter ("*hitherand-* | *thith*ering | *waters of.* | *Night!*") is matched exactly, both semantically and metrically, by Goyert's own concluding and rhyme-enhanced dactylic tetrameter: "*hin*undher- | *rin*nenden | *Wassern von.* | *Nacht!*"

Excerpts from Goyert's rendering have been analysed at somewhat greater length here than will be the case for most other renderings, mainly because of the possibility that Joyce himself may have had a hand in it. But are we any closer to determining if Joyce actually did play some role in its final shaping? It is difficult to disagree with Fritz Senn's assertion that in the end we simply don't know (1998, 188). While the few examples discussed here do not by any means constitute proof of any personal involvement on Joyce's part, however, they may at least serve to confirm it as remaining an intriguing possibility.

It is of course in principle quite unfair to Goyert to suggest the attribution of the occasional unusually striking passage to Joyce and all the rest, by implication, to a much less adventurous Goyert. The argument for doing so, on the other hand, is precisely the degree of deviation of the more adventurous passages from a relatively unadventurous norm on the whole. And if Joyce *did* involve himself to any degree in Goyert's translation beyond merely giving it his official stamp of approval, it would certainly not be surprising, given the character of his French translation of just a few years previously, not to mention the flaunted linguistic pyrotechnics of the later Italian extravaganza, if the results were to tend towards the more flamboyant end of the translational spectrum. Meanwhile, while Goyert was of course unfamiliar with Beckett's French rendering, which remained unpublished until 1985, he was almost certainly familiar both with Joyce's French team translation and with Ogden's Basic English rendering. Seasoned translator as he already was from both French and English, it is reasonable to assume that he will have been keeping up with both the *Nouvelle Revue Française* and *transition* during the early 1930s, before the Nazis had yet tightened their repressive grip on the German literary scene.

Weatherall's Czech ALP

Other than his central involvement in the French *ALP*, his involvement to at least some degree in the Basic English *ALP*, and his possible involvement in the German *ALP*, Joyce was personally involved also in one further version in the early 1930s, though in this case only to the extent of giving his (evidently rather reluctant) permission to undertake the translation (*L* 3, 201). The result, remarkably, and unexpectedly, was a complete and very early Czech *ALP*, the work of three young translators, Maria Weatherall, Vladimír Procházka, and Adolf Hoffmeister. It was published in Prague in 1932 by the avant-garde Odeon publishing house, founded in 1925 by the young Jan Fromek (1901–66), in a limited bibliophile edition of three hundred copies – and thus had the distinction of being the first complete rendering of *ALP* to be actually published in any language, despite the fact that Georg Goyert had undertaken his ill-fated German translation roughly a year earlier than the Czech trio. A pre-publication excerpt (*FW* 197.16–199.10), with an accompanying commentary, had already appeared the previous year in the Prague journal *Literární noviny* (Literary news) over the names of Hoffmeister and Procházka as translators – though making it clear that a preliminary version had been prepared by their collaborator Maria Weatherall for detailed discussion by the team as a whole. Weatherall, whose name (as a Czech "Weatherallová") is listed first of the three translators, thus enjoys the additional distinction of being the first (and for well more than half a century the only) female translator of any part of *FW*.[16]

Adolf Hoffmeister, however, was clearly the leading spirit of the project. He recounts in a later article how, as a twenty-eight-year-old, he rather apprehensively approached Joyce in Paris in 1930 and obtained the distinctly reluctant permission to undertake the Czech translation (Woods 2005). Twenty years younger than the master, and feeling almost as if he were once again a schoolboy facing a particularly intimidating oral examination, he nervously explained to Joyce that the proposed translation would in fact be undertaken not just by himself alone but by a three-person team. Hoffmeister (1902–73), a multitalented Czech artist and writer, was himself to be the chief translator; Vladimír Procházka (1895–1968) was a young economist at the Charles University in Prague with a strongly developed interest in literary translation; and Maria Weatherall, née Isakovicsová (1897–1972), was a Prague native who had married an Englishman, Robert Weatherall (1899–1973), and had recently completed a doctorate in modern English literature at the Charles University. She and her husband – subsequently a biology teacher at both Rugby and Eton – later collaborated in translating the work of the Czech writer Karel Čapek into English. Hoffmeister also named an expected fourth translator, Vítězslav Nezval, who does not seem to have taken any further part in the project, presumably because of the pressure of other commitments. Nezval (1900–58), a prolific avant-garde poet and writer, was in fact deeply involved in numerous other projects already. A personal friend of Philippe Soupault, he was soon to gain a degree of celebrity in Prague literary circles as one of the founders of the Surrealist movement in Czechoslovakia.

Interestingly, given Joyce's enthusiasm for the French translation and eagerness to see how the German rendering was progressing, his permission for the proposed Czech translation was granted, according to Hoffmeister, only with considerable reservations – almost certainly because Czech, unlike French and German, was not a language of which Joyce could feel himself to be in control.[17] The task of translation would

---

16 The next rendering by a female translator, Ingeborg Horn's German version of *FW* I.6, did not appear until 1989, fifty-seven years later.

17 Hoffmeister was struck by the accuracy of Joyce's pronunciation of Czech names, however. Joyce's sister Eileen had married a Czech, František Schaurek, in 1915, and Joyce shared their apartment for some months in Trieste in 1919–20 (Ellmann 1982, 384–5, 471), undoubtedly using the opportunity to strike up some preliminary acquaintance with at least the pronunciation of Czech.

not by any means be easy, he warned Hoffmeister sternly, it would in fact be very difficult, even extremely difficult – and Hoffmeister reports elsewhere that the three valiant translators, permission eventually obtained, did indeed work on the Czech rendering in minute detail, sentence by sentence and word by word, for "more than six months, and the book is barely over thirty pages long altogether" (1979, 136).

That Hoffmeister will almost certainly have become familiar with Joyce's 1931 French team translation of *ALP* is suggested by some of the quite bold translatorial decisions he and his team made even at this very early stage. In an afterword to the published translation, Hoffmeister pointed out certain linguistic and cultural adjustments his fellow translators and he had felt it necessary to undertake, noting for example that the demotic Dublin English of Joyce's gossiping washerwomen had sometimes been rendered by appropriate touches of colloquial Prague German; that references to Dublin and Ireland had on occasion been replaced by corresponding references to Prague and Czechoslovakia; and that the numerous rivers incorporated in Joyce's original had frequently tended in Czech to become Czech, Balkan, Polish, and Russian rivers (Mánek 2004, 190).

As for undertaking anything beyond *ALP*, however, "the complete *Work in Progress* will never be translated," Hoffmeister wrote, "because no one would be able to translate it, taking into account the average life-span." Moreover, "our translation will never be a precise mirror of the original. But ... we are clear that we have attempted a translation of beautiful poetry, one which extends the vault of the sky over the world of man" (trans. Mánek 2004, 190). While Hoffmeister was unduly pessimistic regarding the future appearance of complete translations of what would eventually become *Finnegans Wake*, the complete Czech *ALP* produced by the three adventurous young Prague translators represents, according to the Czech critic Josef Grmela, "one of the top creative performances in the whole history of Czech translation" (2004, 41). Since Goyert's complete German *ALP* did not appear in print until 1970, the Czech *ALP* remained the only complete published translation of *ALP* available in any language for very nearly the next forty years. It was reprinted in the Prague journal *Dialog* in 1965, and a new edition appeared in 1996, prefaced by a Czech translation of Michel Butor's 1957 essay on *FW*, and published by Dauphin in the Czech city of Liberec.[18] "With the notable exception of Zdeněk Urbánek's translation

---

18 On the Czech rendering of *ALP*, see Mánek (2004), Woods (2005), Paris (2017), Amaral (2019), Vichnar (2020).

of the 'HCE' *Finnegans Wake* passages, published in *Světová literatura* (World literature) magazine during the mid-60's thaw, Hoffmeister's effort [Weatherall, Procházka, and Hoffmeister 1932] is still the only extant *Finnegans Wake* fragment in Czech" (Vichnar 2020, 151).

It is possible that Hoffmeister, despite his expressed doubts as to the feasibility of any translation of the entire *Wake*, may have actually continued to work on an as yet unpublished rendering of at least some parts of it. John Banville's memoir *Prague Pictures: Portrait of a City* records a pregnant moment in a Cold War literary cafe: "That haughty-looking chap with the cockerel's crest of silver hair had been engaged for twenty years on a Czech translation of *Finnegans Wake*, and was known to be a police informer" (2003, 10). Michelle Woods suggests in personal correspondence that the reference may in fact have been to Hoffmeister, who in later years became a compromised figure because of his collaboration with the repressive political regime.

The opening sentences of the Czech *ALP*, quoted here from the 1996 edition, and unusually involving a four-line introductory typographical delta, include the following lines (corresponding to *FW* 196.1–7, 9–11):

Ó / pověz mi všechno / o Anně Livii! Chci slyšet všechno / o Anně Livii! Nu tak, znáš Annu Livii? / Ovšem, všichni známe Annu Livii. Pověz mi všechno. Povídej hned. Je to k chcípnutí. Tak tedy víš, jak se ten starej chlop zjančil a co proved. ... Tak ať už to bylo, co chtělo, co se lidi potrojčili nadělat z toho, co on se podvojil udělat v Čertovce. (Weatherall, Procházka, and Hoffmeister 1932, rpt. 1996, 28)

These opening lines, retaining and extending the introductory typographical delta, suggest, roughly, "O, tell me (*pověz mi*) all (*všechno*) about Anna Livia! I want (*chci*) to hear (*slyšet*) all about Anna Livia! Well (*nu tak*), you know (*znáš*) Anna Livia? Of course (*ovšem*), we all (*všichni*) know (*známe*) Anna Livia. Tell me all (*pověz mi všechno*). Tell me (*povídej*) now (*hned*). It is to die (*je to k chcípnutí*)." That last sentence crisply reshapes Joyce's original "You'll die when you hear" as just "You'll die." Fluvial implications already appear with the triple evocation of the Italian river Po – and while the innocuous interjection *ovšem* literally means no more than "of course," in the wonderful world of a macrotextual *Wake* it serendipitously also evokes none other than Shem, son of ALP.

The phrase "Well, you know, when the old cheb went futt and did what you know" (*FW* 196.6–7) is rendered as "Tak tedy víš, jak se ten starej chlop zjančil a co proved," roughly "Well (*tak tedy*), you know (*víš*) how (*jak*) the old chap (*ten starej chlop*) apparently (*zjevně*) finished up (*vyančil*), and (*a*) what (*co*) he did (*proved*)." The locution "zjančil," rendering "went futt," conflates the verb *vyančil* ("finished") and the adverb *zjevně* ("apparently"), while the old cheb becomes an old "chlop," suggesting perhaps just a harmless old geezer. The Czech river Cheb and the South American Futa disappear – but are promptly replaced by the Polish Lake Chłop, explaining in the process HCE's new Czech epithet.

The particularly convoluted final phrase "Or whatever it was they threed to make out he thried to two in the Fiendish park" (*FW* 196.9–11) is adroitly rendered: "Tak ať už to bylo, co chtělo, co se lidi potrojčili nadělat z toho, co on se podvojil udělat v Čertovce." This formulation suggests, roughly, "Or whatever it was (*tak ať už to bylo*) that he wanted (*co chtělo*) – or whatever it was that the three people (*lidi*) tried to make (*nadělat*) of what (*z toho*) he came to do (*udělat*) to the two in the diabolical park (*v Čertovce*)." The invented plural verb "potrojčili" conflates *počit* ("to try") and *trojče* ("triplet"), while the likewise invented singular verb "podvojil" conflates *pojít* ("to come to") and *dvojče* ("twin").[19] The Italian river Po reappears, twice.

The particularly pleasing rendering of the "Fiendish park," finally, involves no less a personage than the Devil himself (Czech *čert* "devil"), with HCE's dubious deed now seen as taking place "v Čertovce," literally, in the "diabolical" park, allowing for a doubled transcultural reference that includes not only the "fiendish" Phoenix Park in Dublin but also the small park on Kampa Island in central Prague, formed at the confluence of the Vltava river and a tributary known as the Čertovka or "Devil's Brook." The reference is a doubly appropriate one in the narrative context of *ALP*, since Prague washerwomen traditionally gathered on the Čertovka, originally a mill race, to wash their laundry, taking advantage of its several flour mill wheels (O'Neill 2013, 176).

Nishiwaki's Japanese ALP

One further translational effort of these early years deserves honourable mention, even though in this case Joyce himself, to my knowledge, had no personal involvement in it. Given his delight in more exotic languages, however, he will no doubt also have been highly pleased by the fact (if we can assume his awareness of it) that the opening page

---

19 My thanks to Michelle Woods for helpful responses in personal correspondence to linguistic and cultural queries.

and the closing four pages of *ALP* (*FW* 196.1–19, 213.11–216.5) also appeared in Japanese translation in Tokyo as early as 1933, the work of Junzaburo Nishiwaki, who was later to become one of the most celebrated of modern Japanese poets (Hirata 2014). Nishiwaki (1894–1982) was enduringly fascinated by European languages from his student years already, enhancing his study of Economics at Keio University in Tokyo by also studying English, German, Latin, and Greek – with his linguistic enthusiasm reportedly extending even to writing his undergraduate Economics thesis entirely in Latin. One can only wonder what the reaction of the Japanese thesis examiners may have been.

An enthusiastic Europhile as well as a gifted linguist, Nishiwaki continued his studies of English and French in the early twenties as a visiting student at New College, Oxford, where he used the opportunity to immerse himself in contemporary European modernism and experimented with writing poetry himself in English, French, and Latin. Given these interests, he was very likely familiar with Joyce's 1931 French team translation of *ALP*. He was certainly familiar with Ogden's Basic English version, and his own rendering of *ALP* was reportedly facilitated by drawing on Ogden's version for assistance (Ito 2004).

Poet, literary critic, painter, and subsequently for almost forty years a professor of English at Keio University, Nishiwaki was nominated four separate times for the Nobel Prize in Literature. Compared by specialists in Japanese literary studies to Eliot, Rilke, and Valéry, he is regarded by some as possibly the greatest Japanese poet of the twentieth century (Hirata 2014). His later translations from English included Chaucer's *Canterbury Tales* and a reportedly acclaimed version of Eliot's *The Waste Land*.

Chapter Three

The 1940s and 1950s

1 Joyce's Italian ALP
2 Other Voices: German, French, Serbian, Portuguese, Polish

1 Joyce's Italian *ALP*

As the 1930s are marked especially by Joyce's iconic French rendering of the opening and closing pages of *ALP*, so the 1940s are marked by his at least equally iconic and far more flamboyant Italian rendering of the same pages, undertaken on this occasion in collaboration with the young Italian writer Nino Frank (1904–88), later to become well known as a film critic, who had been introduced to Joyce in 1926 by Ivan Goll.[1] The then twenty-two-year-old Frank, who had fled Mussolini's Italy for Paris earlier that year, held a position as the Paris agent of the Italian journal *900: Cahiers d'Italie et d'Europe*, recently founded by Massimo Bontempelli and Curzio Malaparte. In 1937 Joyce, presumably still highly pleased with the success of the French *ALP* – and no doubt further encouraged both by the appearance of the Czech *ALP* in 1932 and his presumed perusal of Goyert's German *ALP* in 1933 – proposed to Frank, much to the latter's apparent initial dismay, that they jointly undertake a matching Italian version of *ALP* (Frank 1979, 96; Ellmann 1982, 700). Cheerfully ignoring Frank's protest that the task was impossible, on the grounds that the Italian language simply did not lend itself to puns, least of all to Joycean puns, Joyce insisted, perhaps quizzically, "We must do the job now before it is too late; for the moment there is

---

1 The discussion of Joyce's Italian *ALP* draws on material originally presented in my book *Trilingual Joyce: The Anna Livia Variations* (O'Neill 2018).

at least one person, myself, who can understand what I am writing. I don't however guarantee that in two or three years I'll still be able to" (Frank 1979, 96; Ellmann 1982, 700).[2]

Frank allowed himself, reluctantly, to be persuaded. As he reports, Joyce and he then met for fifty or so hours over some twenty-four meetings: "two afternoons a week for a good three months," completing "a dozen lines an afternoon" (Frank 1979, 96). "I read and interpreted the text on my own, after which Joyce explained it to me word by word, revealing to me its various meanings, dragging me after him into the complex mythology of his Dublin. Then began the slow tennis of approximations, we tossed short phrases to each other like slow-motion balls through a rarefied atmosphere. In the end our procedure resembled incantation" (1979, 97).

The Italian *ALP* was completed early in 1938 (Bosinelli 1996, 54), and Frank, by then an enthusiastic convert to the project, reports that Joyce was once again delighted with the result. A year later, and at Joyce's insistence, Frank gave a public reading of the Italian text during a party celebrating Joyce's fifty-seventh birthday, on 2 February 1939 – the occasion on which Joyce, with an unbound advance copy of *FW* already in hand (it appeared officially only three months later, on 4 May 1939), also publicly announced for the first time its long-withheld title. Frank reports (1979, 98) that Joyce was so pleased with the translation that he even insisted that Frank, somewhat to his embarrassment since not everyone in the group understood Italian, should declaim it not just once, but twice.

The Italian *ALP* appeared in print in two parts, in two separate issues of the Roman journal *Prospettive*, edited by Curzio Malaparte (1898–1957) and Alberto Moravia (1907–90). The first and longer part, entitled "Anna Livia Plurabella," corresponding to *FW* 196.1–201.20, appeared on 15 February 1940 – and it appeared with no mention at all of Nino Frank, but rather as a "traduzione italiana di James Joyce e Ettore Settanni." And thereby hangs another translatorial tale, for the said Settanni played a distinctly shadowy role in the production of the Italian *ALP*.

Settanni, journalist and writer, and a native of Capri, probably came to Joyce's attention in 1933 with a short volume in Italian on modern novels and novelists, *Romanzo e romanzieri d'oggi*, which contained a brief chapter on Joyce's work, mainly on *Ulysses*, celebrated as the work

---

2　Nathan Halper helpfully glosses: "We may dismiss this. (He was being funny.)" (1967, 224).

of an exceptional avant-garde writer. Having, like Frank, abandoned Mussolini's Italy for Paris, Settanni attracted some favourable attention there in 1937 with a novel, originally written in Italian and published in French translation as *Les hommes gris*, with a preface by Valery Larbaud praising its sophisticated use of interior monologue. A collection of novellas, *Amour conjugale*, was to appear in 1939, while a number of popular travel books on Capri helped to pay the bills. Settanni appears to have used his still available connections in Italy to help place the Italian *ALP* in Malaparte's journal – while taking the opportunity both to exclude any mention of Frank and to alter Joyce and Frank's translation, without any prior authorization, by a number of textual emendations.

Both Frank's exclusion and the unauthorized emendations seem to have been designed primarily to avert possible recriminations in Mussolini's Italy, including the risk of having the journal suppressed. Frank was still persona non grata with the authorities because of his earlier anti-fascist activities, and the omission of his name was quite likely at the urging of the editors, or at least with their support. Settanni's emendations, meanwhile, were clearly intended to defuse the potential charge of Joyce's more extreme sexual and political extravagances. *Prospettive* was already viewed with suspicion by the fascist authorities (Risset 1973, 47), so to this extent, as Rosa Maria Bosinelli suggests (1998a, 175), Settanni's role as censor was in principle a not entirely unreasonable one.

Fifteen years later, in 1955, Settanni republished the *Prospettive* version of the Italian *ALP* together with a commentary by himself in which he very belatedly revealed Frank's role as translator, while claiming at the same time to have also in fact been involved himself, together with Nino Frank and (allegedly) Benjamin Crémieux, in the translation of the opening pages (1955, 27).[3] Frank's 1979 version of events, however, rejects this claim out of hand, vigorously asserting instead (with no mention of Crémieux) that Settanni arrived on the scene only after the translation had in fact already been completed. His version of

---

3 Settanni's memory seems to have been at fault here, for Bosinelli observes that this is the only extant reference to any possible involvement on Crémieux's part (1996, 57). Crémieux (1888–1944), a French novelist, scholar of Italian literature, and translator of Pirandello into French, figured among Joyce's Paris acquaintances and published one short article on his work (1929). Joyce had enlisted his assistance in 1924 in his successful bid to bring Italo Svevo's novel *La coscienza di Zeno* (1923) to world notice (*L* 1, 211; Ellmann 1982, 560). Like Péron and Beckett, Crémieux became actively involved in the French Resistance. Arrested in 1943, he was murdered in Buchenwald concentration camp in 1944.

Settanni's alleged involvement is emphatic: "a dozen slight modifications, most of them absurd, had been made in our text," modifications which, he says, neither Joyce nor he liked (1979, 102).

While Frank was understandably furious with Settanni's manoeuvrings, whatever their motivation might have been (1979, 101–2), Joyce, obviously highly elated by the public appearance of *ALP* in his beloved Italian, remained uncharacteristically tolerant of Settanni's meddling with his text – and serenely undisturbed by the lack of recognition of Frank. He writes very blandly to Frank on 13 March 1940: "Settanni writes me from Capri that he thought it as well to soften certain passages. Please obtain a copy of the review and note the variants in the margin. In that way I will have our original text. Settanni writes me that your name does not appear for reasons you will understand at once. But it will not always be kept hidden, I trust" (*L* 3, 469; Ellmann's translation).

The final paragraphs of the Italian *ALP*, "I fiumi scorrono" (The rivers run), corresponding to *FW* 215.11–216.5, appeared in *Prospettive* on 15 December 1940. This time the translation was attributed to "James Joyce, Nino Frank e Ettore Settanni," possibly suggesting that Frank may have meanwhile had the opportunity to convey his thoughts on the matter to Settanni in suitably unvarnished terms. Joyce himself was never to see this second part in print, since the December issue did not in fact appear until a few weeks after his death in January 1941 (Bosinelli 1998b, 197). For almost forty years, from 1940 until 1979, the only published version of the Italian *ALP* was the version as emended by Settanni. Jacqueline Risset, in an article in *Tel Quel* in 1973, republished that version, whereupon Nino Frank, clearly still anxious to set the record straight even after more than thirty years, sent her the original, unamended version (Risset 1984, 5), which Risset subsequently published in 1979 in a volume of Joyce's collected writings in Italian, the *Scritti italiani*, edited by Gianfranco Corsini and Giorgio Melchiori (*SI* 197–214; Risset 1979).

Richard Ellmann, surprisingly, implies that the Italian *ALP* is essentially Frank's rather than Joyce's work, referring to Joyce's role merely as "helping Nino Frank with the Italian translation" (1982, 633). This is presumably based on Frank's report that Joyce "asked me to try to transpose into Italian, with his help," the same excerpts as translated in the French *ALP* (1979, 96). Frank goes on, however, to recount Joyce's obvious subsequent delight in playing with the Italian language as he had already done with English: "thus I can say without any false modesty that Joyce is responsible for at least three-quarters of the Italian text; for the most part I served as guinea pig and fellow worker" (1979,

96). Joyce, for his part, seems to have been in no doubt at all as to the importance of his own contribution, repeatedly referring with obvious pleasure in correspondence during March and April 1940 to the translation as *his* own achievement. Thus while in a letter to Nino Frank he collegially refers to "our translation" ("la traduzione nostra"; *L* 3, 468), other letters unambiguously refer to the translation as having been essentially his own work (*L* 1, 410, 412; *L* 3, 469, 470).

As for the original progress of that translation, and Joyce's specific role in it, Frank reports having quickly been struck by the fact "that the rhythm, the harmony, the density and consonance of the words were more important to him than the meaning, and that, for example, having written one thing [in English], Joyce scarcely hesitated to put down something completely different in Italian, as long as the poetic or metrical result was equivalent" (1979, 97). As for rhythm, when Frank on one occasion objected that Joyce's proposed version sacrificed the original rhythm, Joyce reportedly replied that he liked the new arrangement better (Ellmann 1982, 700). Fritz Senn sensibly urges caution with regard to such authorial statements taken out of context. "That for Italian *ALP* Joyce decreed a priority of sound over sense has often been perpetuated. I do not doubt that Joyce said something to this effect and has been correctly reported, but I am not sure that this was meant to be an overall rule; it looks much more like a strategic decision for certain cases. ... An out of context authorial dictum easily becomes a dogmatic rule" (1998, 188–9).

The specifically Italian nature of the translation has been emphasized by several Italian critics. "The ideal reader of this text is undoubtedly an Italian reader," writes Bosinelli. "Joyce privileged a pragmatic attitude to translation as a cross-cultural transferral of the reverberations of meanings inscribed in the original composition. He wanted to trigger associative chains for Italian readers according to a principle of equivalence, not of 'faithfulness'; in other words, the Italianized text aims to provide a similarity of reading experience even at the expense of semantic equivalence" (Bosinelli 1998b, 195). Serenella Zanotti concurs: "Joyce recast his text for readers of Italian culture (multilingual elements are drastically reduced) and additionally abandoned most of the fluvial allusions which abounded in the original because he was more interested in exploring the musicality and the creative potential of the Italian language" (Zanotti 2001, 422).

Umberto Eco calls Joyce's Italian version "a most particular case of rewriting, taken to extremes" (2001, 107). He describes *FW* as "a plurilingual text written as an English-speaker conceived of one. It seems to me therefore that Joyce's decision to translate himself was based on the idea of thinking of the target text (French or Italian) as a plurilingual text the way a French- or Italian-speaker might have conceived of one" (2001, 108). In the Italian version, Joyce "found himself having to render a language that lends itself to puns, to neologisms, and agglutination, as well as English does (which has the advantage of an abundance of monosyllabic terms) into a language like Italian, which resists the formation of agglutinative neologisms" (Eco 2001, 108–9). Noting Joyce's rejection in Italian of many of the originally included river names, Eco observes: "No longer playing with the idea of rivers (perhaps the oddest and most punctilious idea in this punctilious and extravagant book), he was playing with Italian instead" (2001, 115).[4]

The Italian *ALP*, Jacqueline Risset writes, is "an exploration of the furthest limits of the Italian language," a sustained play on "the essentially plural quality" of Italian, in which the multiple intersecting layers of the language are "understood not as fixed stratifications, but as moving planes." In Joyce's Italian, "viewed as an aggregate of strata, of reservoirs, polyglottism is transformed into 'plurilinguism,' ... dialects, tones, lexical levels merging together in a contradictory co-presence" (Risset 1984, 3, 4) – a technique that Joyce himself acknowledged having learned from Dante (Settanni 1955, 29–30).[5]

This play with the rich plurality and multiple levels of the Italian language itself, written and spoken, from its highest literary expression in the work of Dante to its multiple and competing local and regional dialects and colloquial usages, involves especially Triestine, Venetian, and Tuscan idioms and turns of phrase (Risset 1973, 48, 52). Corinna del Greco Lobner is particularly struck by the number of Tuscan idioms and sayings (1989, 38). Serenella Zanotti asserts that the language Joyce wanted his washerwomen to speak is closer to Triestine than it is to any other dialect (2001, 423), and she aptly observes that his continued predilection for the Triestine form of Italian is similar to his predilection for the Dublin form of English (2002, 303–4). Lobner adds Friulian and Roman dialects to the list, while observing that idiomatic and humorous turns of phrase, popular sayings and wordplays, proverbs, and tongue-twisters are all welcome grist to Joyce's linguistic mill (1986,

---

4 While the Italian translation does exclude a number of the originally included river names, as Eco asserts, it actually also includes a considerable number of evocations of new rivers (O'Neill 2018, 194).

5 Mary Reynolds demonstrates convincingly that Joyce "saw himself as Dante's disciple particularly in the area of linguistic innovation" (1981, 202) – and Beckett pointed out as early as 1929 the similarities between Dante's and Joyce's use of language (1972, 18). On Dante in *ALP*, see Reynolds (1981, 203–5) and Risset (1984, 9).

84). The cumulative result, as Risset writes, is nonetheless "a *poetic language* with three levels: rhythm, syntactic structure, phonic texture" (1984, 7; emphasis in original).

From the first words of his Italian rendering, in which the opening "O" of the English original, so carefully and significantly positioned, is simply ignored, it is clear that fidelity to the letter of the original text is far less important for Italian Joyce than the *authorial* as opposed to the *translatorial* impulse: not so much to make the original text helpfully available in another language as to *continue* the text by other means, in other words, in another language (Risset 1984, 6). For Rosa Maria Bosinelli, there are even points where, given that Joyce was continuing to work on the final version of *FW* at the same time as he was working on the Italian rendering of *ALP*, "one might formulate the hypothesis that it was the Italian version that influenced the 'original' rather than the other way round" (1998a, 175). The French critic Louis Gillet, writing in 1941, goes even further, so impressed by the Italian *ALP*, "an outstanding *tour de force*," that he even prefers it to the original and "cannot too strongly advise beginners to read *Finnegans Wake* in the Italian text" (1979, 193).[6]

The opening lines of Joyce and Frank's original Italian *ALP* (corresponding to *FW* 196.1–11), as first published by Jacqueline Risset in 1979, are as follows:

> Raccontami di Anna Livia. Tutto sapere vo' di Anna Livia. Beh, conosci Anna Livia? Altro che, conosciamo tutte Anna Livia! Dimmi tutto, e presto presto. Roba da chiodi!
>
> Beh, sai quando il messercalzone andò in rovuma e fe' ciò che fe'? Si, lo so, e po' appresso? Lava pulito e non sbrodolare! Rimboccamaniche e scioglilinguagnolo. Ma la zucca per te se mai ti pieghi! O cosa mai fece bifronte o triforo in quell'infenice di porco nastro? (qtd. Bosinelli 1996, 2–3)

From 1940 until 1979, however, as mentioned, the *Prospettive* version, emended by Ettore Settanni without Joyce's authorization, was the only available text of Joyce's Italian *ALP*. Its opening lines, with Settanni's emendations (given here in **bold**), are as follows:

> Raccontami di Anna Livia. Tutto **vo' sapere** di Anna Livia. Beh, **la** conosci Anna Livia? Altro che, conosciamo tutte Anna Livia. Dimmi tutto, e presto

---

6 On Joyce's Italian *ALP*, see Settanni (1955), Risset (1979, 1984), Lobner (1986), Rombi (1987), Eco (1996; 2001, 106–17), Zanotti (2002, 2004, 2013), Svevo (2011, 49–58), Harman (2019).

presto. **Roba d'altro mondo!** Beh, sai **allorché** il messercalzone andò in rovuma e fe' ciò che fe'. Sí, lo so, e po' appresso? Lava, **sbrigati** e non sbrodolare. Rimboccamaniche e sciogliolinguagnolo. **Se mai ti pieghi la zucca è per te**. O cosa mai fece bifronte o triforo in quell'infenice di porco nastro? (Joyce and Settanni 1940, 13)

While Joyce's English *ALP* is at pains to locate the opening "O" exactly on the page and in the text, in Italian, as mentioned, he chooses simply to omit it altogether, opting instead for the urgent rhythm of an unadorned "Raccontami di Anna Livia" ("Tell me about Anna Livia"). That formulation, moreover, asks merely to be told about Anna Livia, rather than to be told *all* about her. The rendering "Tutto sapere vo'" once again indicates a desire, as in his French, to "know" (*sapere*) rather than to "hear" (*sentire*) all about her, and the departure from the original is once again fluvially motivated. While the invitation "Raccontami" ("tell me") succeeds in evoking the American Raccoon River, the Irish Lough Conn, the Welsh Teme, and the English Tame and Thames (Tamigi in Italian), the declaration that "Tutto sapere vo' di Anna Livia," now clarifying that "I want to know *all* (*tutto*) about Anna Livia," contributes the Indian Tut once again, the Japanese Tosa, and the Sape River of the Solomon Islands. Settanni emends "tutto sapere vo'" to "tutto vo' sapere" – possibly on the grounds that the latter is a rather more normal word order in colloquial Italian, namely, the linguistic level suggested by the colloquial *vo'* for the formal *voglio*. The change, retaining the Tut and the Sape, but abandoning the Japanese Tosa in favour of the English Tove, also succeeds in introducing what to the ear of an English speaker (though not necessarily to that of an Italian speaker) is a double dactyl: "*tut*to vo' | *sa*pere."

Joyce's Italian specifies that the "we" who "all know Anna Livia" is feminine: "conosciamo tutte" rather than "conosciamo tutti." Fluvially, his "Beh, conosci Anna Livia? Altro che" ("Well, you know Anna Livia? Of course, what else?"), contributes evocations of the Behy of County Kerry, Lough Conn again, the Japanese Ono, and two English rivers, the Alt and the Roch. Settanni's emendation to "Beh, la conosci Anna Livia?" ("Well, you know Anna Livia?") is able to add the English Bela and Philippine Laco. For a reader of today, blessed with hindsight and familiarity with *FW* as opposed to just *ALP*, the colloquial "altro che" also allows for a serendipitous early glimpse of ALP's dubious consort HCE, lightly disguised as CHE.

The anapaestic rhythm of "Tell me all. Tell me now" changes in Joyce's Italian to the likewise urgent trochees of "Dimmi tutto, e presto presto," with the urgency increased by a colloquial "presto presto" ("quickly, quickly") for the English "now." The Turkish Dim, Scottish Dee, Dutch Diem, Sudanese Immi, and Indian Tut, meanwhile, are all suggested in "dimmi tutto" ("tell me all"). In the most radical departure so far from the English text, "You'll die when you hear" loses both its overt reference to death and its implied reference to laughter. Joyce's vigorous and highly idiomatic Italian ejaculation "Roba da chiodi!," introducing a change of tone, translates roughly as an exclamatory "Unbelievable!" while evoking the Nigerian river Bada and, visually, the Thai river Chi. Joyce no doubt encountered the particular expression during his Triestine years: Serenella Zanotti notes the Triestine variant *roba de ciodi* (2001, 424). Settanni, possibly concerned that Italian readers other than northerners might not understand the idiosyncratic exclamation, opted for a more generally understandable but still idiomatic "Roba d'altro mondo!," invoking the "other world" ("altro mondo") to suggest "unreal, unheard of," and likewise evoking the Nigerian Bada, dropping the Thai Chi, but adding the English Alt and Nigerian Ndo. Both variants evoke the Russian Ob and Nigerian Oba, while Italianizing the name of the Irish river Robe.

As for the old cheb, "well," exclaims the Italian washerwoman, approximately, "you know when the old so-and-so went crazy and did what he did?" More specifically, HCE is now "il messercalzone," an epithet combining *mascalzone* ("scoundrel"), *cazzone* ("penis, prick"), and the archaic Florentine *messere* ("master"). While the original old cheb went futt, his Italian counterpart "andò in rovuma," suggesting with exemplary concision that he went to the dogs (*andò in rovina*), that he suffered a bad fall (*rovina*), that he came to his ruin (*rovina*), and that all of this was connected in some likewise unspecified way with a bush (*rovo*) of some sort as he notoriously "did what he did" ("fe' ciò che fe'"), the identity of the miscreant now once more discreetly adumbrated in the relative pronoun *che*. Settanni's emendation of the opening "Beh, sai quando" to "Beh, sai allorché" leaves the surface meaning unchanged ("Well, you know when") while pointedly managing to include the incriminating CHE yet one more time. That streams of some sort may also have been involved is amply evident from the subliminal presence of the Irish Behy (an Italianized Irish river flowing from an English-language "well"), the Indian Sai, the Ando of the Solomon Islands, the Romanian Șercaia ("mes-serca-lzone"), the German Alz, the Rovuma of Mozambique, and the American Santa Fe. Settani's emendation of "quando" to "allorché" abandons the Ando in favour of the German Aller and its English namesake, while the impatient response "Si, lo so, e po' appresso?" ("Yes, I know, and what then?") contributes the Italian Po.

The washerwoman's poetically phrased professional advice "Lava pulito e non sbrodolare" might initially seem to mean no more than "Do your washing neatly and quickly," with *pulito* suggesting "cleanly" in standard Italian, "properly" in Triestine (Zanotti 2001, 423), and *sbrodolare* a colloquial term for "to prolong, to drag out." Since the likewise colloquial phrase *dare una pulita* means "to give a lick and a promise," however, while the primary meaning of *sbrodolare* is actually "to soil," the sober advice is simultaneously undermined by an implied and rather less professional "Give it a quick lick and a promise – and at least don't get it any dirtier." Settanni's emendation of "Lava pulito" to "Lava, sbrigati" reduces the advice to an unambiguously sober "Just do your washing and hurry up." The punning presence of Dublin in "dabbling" once again disappears.

The phrase "Rimboccamaniche e scioglilinguagnolo" shows the Italian Joyce at his most exuberantly baroque. Umberto Eco argued that since Italian, as compared to English, is relatively lacking in monosyllabic forms, Joyce here and elsewhere deliberately opts for the other extreme of inventing extravagant polysyllables – in which Italian, if anything, is even more lacking (1996, xvi). The first example of this produces, visually, two sesquipedalian monsters at once. "Rimboccamaniche," however, is in fact rather less than monstrous, being merely a humorously telescoped version of a standard Italian *rimbocca le maniche* ("tuck up your sleeves"). "Scioglilinguagnolo," however, as Bosinelli observes (1998b, 196), is a more complex creation, a portmanteau word arguably combining *scioglilingua* ("tongue twister"), *lingua* ("tongue"), *linguaggio* ("language"), and, incorporating an aquatic touch, *rigagnolo* ("stream"). The literal implication, entirely appropriate for our Wakean washerwomen, is thus something like "Roll up your sleeves and wring out the stream of language." "Rimboccamaniche," meanwhile, also serendipitously contains the element *-bocca-*, a homophone of Italian *bocca* ("mouth") and thus immediately anticipating *lingua* ("tongue"). Aquatic overtones are also not lacking, meanwhile, represented by both the English river Cam and the English Channel, known in Italian as the *Canale della Manica*, the word *manica* meaning both an "inlet" and a "sleeve." The plural *maniche*, meanwhile, allows another fugitive glimpse of HCE as CHE. The Chinese Li, English Lin, Scottish Ling, Corsican Guagno, Philippine Agno, and Portuguese Olo all flow in the tongue-twisting "scioglilinguagnolo."

An Italian *zucca* is a "pumpkin," meanwhile, and the jocular warning "Ma la zucca per te se mai ti pieghi!," evoking in passing the Romanian Mala and Lazu and the English Uck and Sem, translates roughly as "But keep your big fat head to yourself when you're bending over!" Settanni achieves one of his occasional stylistic improvements by rearranging the order of these two clauses, abandoning the Mala, and accentuating the rhythm of what in English prosody is a truncated dactylic dimeter: "*Se mai ti | pieghi la | zucca è per | te.*" The exclamation "hike!" disappears.

As for the business in the park, watchers and watched are introduced with a crisp formulation that once again deviates flamboyantly from the original English. The first phrase, "o cosa mai fece," simply means "or whatever it was he did"; the second plays much more polyvalently on the Italian architectural terms *bifronte* ("double-fronted") and *triforo* ("having three openings"), evoking the Tanzanian river Foro while suggesting HCE's two-faced (*bifronte*) behaviour relating to two girls as observed from three vantage points. Sexualized details of female anatomy are of course also discreetly adumbrated. Joyce's description of the location of the encounter as "quel'infenice di porco nastro," playing on *infelice* ("unfortunate") and *fenice* ("phoenix"), suggests "that unfortunate phoenix park of ours," while evoking the Chinese Fen and Indian Feni as well as the watery English noun *fen*. The phrase *parco nostro* ("our park"), however, is humorously rearranged into "porco nastro," which not only invokes the Romanian Porcu, Italian Orco, Scottish Cona, and Canadian Nass rivers, as well as the German adjective *nass* ("wet"), but also roundly characterizes HCE's offence as that of a complete swine (*porco*), while evoking a blasphemous *pater noster* ("our father") – and suggestively contributing a hint of incest to the affair. Settanni emends Joyce's "quel'infenice di porco nastro" to "quell'infenice di porco nastro," the change from "quel'" to "quell'" effectively emphasizing the translingual reference to German *Quelle* ("spring, well") while hinting at the English river Ellen.

The following lines (corresponding to *FW* 215.31–5, 216.3–5) are taken from Joyce and Frank's rendering of the final paragraph of *ALP*:

> Non odo più per le acque di. Le chiacchiericcianti acque di. Nottole qua, topi là fan pian. Oh! Non sei andata a casa? Che Renata la Masa? Non odo più il nottolio, le liffeyanti acque di. Rio ci scampi! Al mio piè ledra v'è. Mi sento vecchia come l'elmo tasso. Fiaba detta di Gionni e Giace? ... Dimmi, dimmi, dimmi, olm! Nottenot! Dimmifiaba d'alberoccia. Presso le frusciacque di, le quinciequindi acque di. Not! (qtd. Bosinelli 1996, 28–9)

The same lines with Settanni's emendations, once again indicated in **bold**:

> Non odo più per le acque di. Le chiacchiericcianti acque di. Nottole qua, topi là fan **piano**. Oh! Non sei andata a casa? Che Renata **La** Masa? Non

> odo più **per** il nottolio, le liffeyanti acque di. **Lio** ci scampi! Al mio piè ledra
> v'è. Mi sento vecchia come **l'olmo** tasso. Fiaba detta di **Gionno e Giaco**? ...
> **Diddmi**, dimmi, dimmi, olm! Nottenot! Dimmifiaba d'alberoccia. Presso
> le frusciacque di, le quinciequindi acque di. **Notte**! (qtd. Risset 1973, 62)

Joyce's Italian speaker, now evoking the Nigerian Odo, can no longer hear with the waters that "chatter" (*chiacchierare* "to chatter, gossip"), more or less (the Italian suffix *-iccio* operating like the English suffix *-ish*), and "curl" (*riccio* "curl, curly"), lapping in tiny waves. Creatures of the night (*notte*), bats (*nottole*) and, with species boundaries blurred, perhaps even owls (*nottole*) on the one hand, mice (*topi*) and perhaps even rats (*topi*) on the other, go softly rather than baulking talk: "Nottole qua, topi là fan pian." Settanni, without altering the sense, normalizes the final spondee "fan pian," echoing that of the original "bawk talk" (and the French "cause pause"), to a pedestrian "fan piano."

The washerwoman's question, "Non sei andata a casa?" ("Haven't you gone home?"), introduced by an "Oh!" that puns on French *eau* ("water"), elicits the counterquestion "Che Renata la Masa?," with linguistic confusion now inventing a Renata, named either for her mother Tommasa, colloquially "Masa," or an also generically confused version of her father Tommaso (whose family name may or may not have been Malone), colloquially "Maso." Lobner (1989, 41) sees the name of this transgendered Tom Malone, in which the vowel *a* now occurs five times, as one example of a sustained strategy throughout the Italian *ALP* that "ensures the predominance of the vowel *a*, an indicator in Italian of feminine gender," a strategy that begins with the elimination of Joyce's original opening "O."

Renata unleashes something of a fluvial deluge: the German Rhine, disguised in Polish as the Ren, is tumultuously joined by the Norwegian Rena, Canadian Ena, African Nata, Indonesian Tala, Russian Lama, Dutch Maas, and the Japanese Asa. One can no longer hear the bats (*nottole*) or see the rolling (*rotolio*) of their swooping flight or hear the liffeying waters, or even those of the Nigerian Oli. May God (*Dio*) and the river (Spanish *río*) together save us (*scampare* "to save"), but just look here (*vi*), even if short-sightedly (*miope*), at the ivy (*l'edera*) growing on my foot ("al mio piè"). That final sentence allows access to the Canadian Edra Creek, Algerian Dra, and central European Drave. The Ovidian context of the invitation, meanwhile – the fleeing nymph Daphne transformed into a laurel tree (Greek *daphnê*) to avoid Apollo's all-too-amorous attentions – allows implied supplementary access at a linguistic remove to Kentucky's Laurel River and Australia's Apollo Bay.

Settanni makes one actual correction to Joyce's text, changing "Non odo piú il nottolio" to "Non odo piú *per* il nottolio," now, with the washerwoman's vision and hearing confused, arguably more appropriately meaning "I can no longer hear *because of* the bats' swooping flight." Other than adding a capital letter to Renata La Masa's name, he also adjusts Joyce's "Rio ci scampi" to "Lio ci scampi," conflating the conventional phrase *Dio ci scampi* ("God save us") and the Chinese river Li, while playing also on the first-person pronoun *io*, which doubles in Italian for the English noun *ego*, to suggest a humorous dig, perhaps, at the rather less than modest Joyce, "May our ego (*l'io*) save us."

The washerwoman feels "vecchia come l'elmo tasso," playing first on *elmo* ("helmet") for *olmo* ("elm") in order to evoke the American river Elm, then on *adesso* ("just now") and *tasso* ("yew") and the Indian river Tasso, and implicitly on space ("yonder") and time ("just now"); she feels "old like that elm just now." Corinna del Greco Lobner has observed that as well as the arboreal play on elm and yew, the combination of a possibly military *elmo* ("helmet") and *tasso* suggests a passing Italian cultural reference to Torquato Tasso (1511–95), whose epic *Gerusalemme liberata* (1574) celebrates the fight to reconquer Jerusalem during the First Crusade (1989, 83).

The "tale told of Shaun or Shem" becomes an Italian fairy tale (*fiaba*) evoking the Ghanaian river Fia and told of "Gionni e Giace," pet forms of *Giovanni* and *Giacomo*, Italianized versions of the given names of John Joyce and James Joyce, as also of Shaun and Shem. Settanni emends Joyce's "vecchia come l'elmo tasso" to "vecchia come l'olmo tasso," rescuing the elm (*olmo*) for challenged Italian readers while exchanging the American river Elm for the South Sudanese river Lol. He likewise alters Joyce's "Gionni e Giace," which evokes the English river Onny and the Nigerian Acha, to what he presumably sees as a more reasonable "Gionno e Giaco," thus hinting instead at the Japanese Ono and Brazilian Iaco, while diminishing as a result the sense of increasing confusion, linguistic and otherwise.

Joyce's phrase "Dimmi, dimmi, dimmi, olm!," evoking the Scottish Dee, Turkish Dim, Dutch Diem, and Sudanese Immi, adheres closely to both the semantic meaning and the trochaic rhythm of the original, with *olmo* ("elm") reduced to a monosyllabic "olm" for the purposes of that rhythm. The German river Notte – serendipitously a homograph of Italian *notte* ("night") – continues to flow in "Nottenot," now accompanied by the Finnish Teno and American Eno. The conflated "dimmifiaba," with the *fiaba* ("tale") watered by the Ghanaian Fia, anticipates the later conflation in *Finnegans Wake* of "tell me tale" to "telmetale." "Stem or stone" generates a new Italian conflation, "alberoccia" conjoining *albero* ("tree") and *roccia* ("stone") while evoking the Romanian Apele Albe, Angolan Bero, and English Roch. The "rivering waters," finally, become, evoking the Belarussian Usha, a likewise conjoined "frusciacque," literally "rustling (*frusciare* 'to rustle') waters (*acque*)," while the "hitherandthithering waters" become the "quinciequindi acque," literally, while evoking the English Quin,"waters from here (*quinci*) and from there (*quindi*)." Settanni's emendation of the opening "dimmi" to "diddmi" spoils the effect of repetition, possibly in an attempt to include the noun *detto* ("tale"), while his alteration of "Not!" to the more conventional "Notte!" undoes Joyce's choice of a final monosyllable (O'Neill 2018, 170–9 passim).

Even these very brief excerpts support Jacqueline Risset's assertion that the Italian *ALP* "cannot really be called – in the usual sense of the word – a translation at all; for what takes place is a complete rewriting, a later elaboration of the original, which consequently does not stand opposite the new version as 'original text,' but as 'work in progress'" (1984, 3) – and, she adds, "a more daring variation on it" (1984, 6). Serenella Zanotti similarly writes that the Italian translation was done when Joyce "was out of the writing process and thus tended to recreate rather than to reproduce the original text" (2001, 422). A primary focus of interest for students of Joyce in translation, indeed, has been that Joyce, especially in the Italian version, emerges as being much less interested in producing a translation aiming at semantic fidelity to the original than in *extending* that text by providing a parallel original text. Bosinelli argues that Joyce functions essentially as author of the Italian *ALP* while he is rather a collaborator and supervisor of the French version (1996, 46). The Italian *ALP*, she argues, should more properly be regarded as an autonomous parallel text, a recreation or rewriting rather than a translation in any traditional sense. As she puts it, Joyce's Italian *ALP* is not so much a translation as "the last page of great prose that Joyce left us shortly before dying" (Bosinelli 1998b, 197).

2 Other Voices: German, French, Serbian, Portuguese, Polish

Other than Joyce's extravagant Italian *ALP*, and despite the appearance of the complete *FW* in 1939, the 1940s, unsurprisingly in the expanding devastation of world war, saw very little in the way of further attempts at translation of Joyce's extremely complex text – though Goyert's German *ALP*, thirteen years after its completion, finally made a partial appearance. The 1950s, however, began to see the tentative emergence of some interesting new voices, especially in French, but also in Serbian, in Portuguese, and in Polish – all three of these languages new entrants to the *FW* macrotext.

Goyert (German, 1946)

Goyert's German *ALP*, reportedly finished as early as 1933, and apparently in the hands of the Rhein Verlag from that date, remained unpublished even partially until 1946, when the opening and closing pages (*FW* 196–8, 213–16) appeared in Salzburg in Ernst Schönwiese's literary journal *das silberboot* and also in Munich in the affiliated journal *Die Fähre*, edited by Hans Hennecke and Herbert Burgmüller. These two journals, one Austrian, the other German, jointly aimed to introduce German-language readers to the best of contemporary writing both inside and outside of German-speaking Europe, almost all of that writing having been proscribed under the twelve years of the Nazi regime.

The partial publication of the German *ALP* in *das silberboot* seems to have taken place, interestingly, through the good offices of the prominent Austrian novelist Hermann Broch (1886–1951), well-known author already of *Die Schlafwandler* (1932; *The Sleepwalkers*) and *Der Tod des Vergil* (1945; *The Death of Virgil*), both of which already clearly demonstrated the impact of *Ulysses*. A devoted admirer of Joyce's work, Broch was also the author of the influential study *James Joyce und die Gegenwart* (1936; *James Joyce and the Present Age*), based on a lecture he had given in Vienna in 1932 to mark both Joyce's fiftieth birthday and the tenth anniversary of the appearance of *Ulysses*. Ernst Schönwiese reports (1986, 420) that Broch had evidently obtained a copy of the original manuscript of the German *ALP* from Daniel Brody, editor of the Rhein Verlag, as early as 1935 and had passed it on to Schönwiese for publication in *das silberboot* as soon as the political situation began to seem likely to allow such publication, even in part.

There was also a more personal connection between Broch and Joyce. Broch was Brody's main German-language author at the Rhein Verlag, and at Brody's prompting following the March 1938 annexation of Austria by Nazi Germany, Joyce in June 1938 had been instrumental in helping Broch (who, like Brody, was Jewish) to emigrate from Vienna to Paris, en route to the USA.[7]

Goll (German)

Rumours also apparently continued to circulate in German literary circles during the 1940s that the poet and novelist Ivan Goll was working on a partial or possibly even a complete German rendering not just of *ALP*

---

7 *L* 3, 424; Ellmann 1982, 709; Bowker 2011, 499.

but of *FW*. Born of French-speaking Jewish parents in Alsace-Lorraine, which at that time was part of the German Empire, Goll (1891–1950) studied law at the University of Strasbourg, lived in Berlin briefly before escaping to Switzerland in 1914 to avoid conscription, lived in Zurich from 1914 to 1919, in Paris from 1919 to 1939, and in New York from 1939 until 1947, before returning first to France and then to Germany.

Goll was a co-founder of the Surrealist movement and was associated with the Dadaists of Zurich, where he also became acquainted with Joyce. He functioned as the Paris representative of the Rhein Verlag and was an enthusiastic champion of Georg Goyert's 1927 German translation of *Ulysses*. In 1930 he played a part as one of the "Septuagint" involved in Joyce's French team translation of *ALP*, and in 1933 he also appears, as mentioned, to have been involved in a final revision of Georg Goyert's German *ALP* before its submission to Joyce himself. Probably as a result of this latter involvement, he was rumoured during the mid-1940s, by which time he was writing mainly in German rather than in French as previously, to be working on a German rendering of *FW* – but any such translation, if it was indeed ever undertaken, or even envisaged, failed to materialize.

Soupault et al. (French)

Rumours of a possible French version of *FW* were apparently also circulating in French literary circles during the mid-forties. Philippe Soupault had just recently published his *Souvenirs de James Joyce* (1943), in which he discussed in some detail Joyce's involvement in the French translation of *ALP*. This may have had an at least temporary catalytic effect in some quarters, for John Pilling interestingly (though without further details) reports the existence of a letter of 15 July 1946 from Harriet Weaver to Lionel Munro, Joyce's former solicitor and in 1946 Weaver's fellow administrator of the Estate of James Joyce, "expressing satisfaction with Philippe Soupault, Raymond Queneau, Eugene Jolas, Stuart Gilbert and Samuel Beckett as the translation team for a French *Finnegans Wake* and saying it would be a mistake to hurry them." Regrettably, however, as Pilling confirms, "the plan was subsequently dropped" (2006, 98).

The suggestion of such a possible translatorial collaboration is an intriguing one. Since the poet and novelist Queneau (1903–76) was at this time an editor at Gallimard (Pilling 2006, 77), and since Gallimard had already been the publisher of the French translation of *Ulysses* in 1929, the reported plan presumably involved Gallimard as potential publisher – and may consequently have well been Queneau's original initiative. He was fascinated by Joyce, especially by *Ulysses*, at this time, and his burlesque novel *On est toujours trop bon avec les femmes* (*We Always Treat Women Too Well*), published under the pseudonym Sally Mara, and humorously involving several characters sharing the names of characters in *Ulysses*, appeared in 1947. Given the brilliance and Joycean experience of the proposed translation team, it is a matter of great regret that nothing at all appears to have come of the proposed undertaking.

Butor (French, 1948, 1949)

Two years later, however, on a much more modest scale, and seventeen years after the appearance of Joyce's French *ALP* in the *Nouvelle Revue Française*, brief excerpts (from *FW* 3, 196 and 419) appeared in French translation by Michel Butor (1926–2016) in 1948, in an influential article on Joyce's overall oeuvre. The young Butor, who had graduated in philosophy from the Sorbonne just the previous year, would go on to establish himself as a major French novelist over the course of the next decade, with *Passage de Milan* (1954), *L'emploi du temps* (1956; *Passing Time*), and *La modification* (1957; *A Change of Heart*).

In the first rendering of any part of *FW* other than *ALP*, Butor renders the three-line opening (*FW* 3.1–3) as follows:

> cours de la rivière dépassé celui d'Ève et d'Adam de déviation de rivage en courbe de baie nous reporte par un *commodius vicus* de recirculation jusq'au château d'Howth et ses environs.

Aiming in 1948 at novice readers of the *Wake* understandably seen as needing just a preliminary notion of the complexities of Joyce's text, Butor limits himself to a perceived basic denotative meaning, expressed in a grammatically correct target-language phrase, his "cours de la rivière" a literal "course of the river." Butor's rendering emphasizes what he sees as the biblical implication of the opening phrase, intimating that the meaning of the river and its course is in some sense more important than that of (*dépassé celui d'*) Eve and of Adam, and thus of the biblical myth of origin. The coastal swerve becomes a "déviation," a diversion or departure from an implied regulated norm, as opposed to the gentle "courbe" or "curve" of the bay. The cryptic evocation of Commodus and Vico is retained by simply italicizing "commodius vicus" as if it were Latin and thus appropriate to leave untranslated. HCE's initials are also retained, discreetly rearranged as CHE in the "château d'Howth et ses environs."

Butor also provides a French version of the following lines from the opening of the *ALP* chapter (*FW* 196.1–7):

O / Dites-moi tout à propos / d'Anna Livia! Je veux tout entendre / à propos d'Anna Livia. Bien vous connaissez Anna Livia? Oui bien sûr nous connaissons tous Anna Livia. Dites-moi tout. Dites-moi maintenant. Vous allez mourir quand vous l'entendrez. Vous savez quand le vieux type devint futt et fit ce que vous savez.

While preserving Joyce's original "O" and the typographical delta, Butor limits his rendering once again to a basic explanatory reading in perfectly normal French. His washerwoman wants to "hear" ("entendre") all about Anna, rather than "know" all about her as in Joyce's French and Italian renderings. "You're going to die when you hear" ("Vous allez mourir quand vous l'entendrez"), she promises, reminding her listener of when the old chap ("le vieux type") went futt "and did what you know." Fluvial evocations, serendipitous or otherwise, include the Scottish Dee, Irish Moy, Indian Tut, Italian Po, Chinese Nu, French Endre, Scottish Cona, Belgian Our, and African Save.

A further fragment in Butor's translation appeared in 1949 in Maria Jolas's *James Joyce Yearbook* (177–8). Fritz Senn (1967c, 229) reprints Butor's rendering of the final page, including of the following lines (*FW* 627.34–628.4, 15–16):

I am passing out. O bitter ending! I'll slip away before they're up. They'll never see. Nor know. Nor miss me. And it's old and old it's sad and old it's sad and weary I go back to you, my cold father, my cold mad father, my cold mad feary father, till the near sight of the mere size of him, the moyles and moyles of it, moananoaning, makes me seasilt saltsick and I rush, my only, into your arms. ... A way a lone a last a loved a long the

Butor's translation:

Je disparais. O amère fin! Je vais glisser avant qu'ils ne se soient levés. Ils ne verront jamais. Ni ne sauront. Ni ne me tromperont. Et c'est vieux et vieux et c'est triste et vieux, c'est triste et lourd je retourne vers vous, mon père froid, mon froid père fou, mon froid père fou et terrible, jusqu'à ce que la proche vue de sa grandeur, ses môles et ses vagues, grognant et grognantes m'aient rendu boue de la mer toute raide de sel, et je me précipite, mon unique, entre vos bras. ... Un chemin un solitaire un dernier un aimé le long de

Once again the rendering is a straightforward one, understandably concentrating on conveying the apparent primary meaning. In the process, several connotations disappear: the "moyles and moyles" become "the piers (*môles*) and the waves (*vagues*)," without reference either to miles or to the Sea of Moyle and its legend of the magically transformed Children of Lir; "moananoaning" becomes "moaning, groaning" (*grognant*), without reference to Manannán mac Lir, legendary god of the sea; "seasilt saltsick" becomes "seasilt (*boue de la mer*) all stiff with salt (*toute raide de sel*)." Joyce's haunting final line of the *Wake* is rendered quite literally but multiplies the number of syllables and ends in a preposition (*de*) rather than a definite article. It should of course be borne in mind that this is the first translation of these particular lines in any language.

du Bouchet (French, 1950)

The 1950s saw further French interest in *FW*, especially on the part of the young poet André du Bouchet (1924–2001). A rendering by him of excerpts from the final chapter (*FW* 619, 624, 625–8) appeared in Paris in 1950, very shortly after Butor's rendering, in the journal *L'Âge Nouveau*, under the title "Dans le sillage de Finnegan," literally "in Finnegan's wake" (in the maritime sense). Fritz Senn (1967c, 230) once again reprints the rendering of the final page, including the following lines (*FW* 627.34–628.4, 15–16):

Je m'en vais. O fin amère! Je vais m'esquiver avant qu'ils soient levés. Ils ne verront jamais. Ni ne sauront. Ni ne regretteront. Et c'est vieux et vieux c'est triste et vieux c'est triste et las je m'en retourne vers toi, mon père froid, mon père fou et froid, mon père furieux et fou et froid, jusqu'à ce que sa taille si haute que je vois de si près, ses crilomètres et ses crilomètres, ses sangloalanglots, me malselle et me mersalle et je me rue, mon unique, dans tes bras. ... Un chemin un seul enfin aimée le long du!

For du Bouchet, "the near sight of the mere size of him" thus becomes "sa taille si haute que je vois de si près"; "the moyles and moyles of it" becomes "ses crilomètres et ses crilomètres," conflating cries (*cris*) and *kilomètres* rather than miles; "moananoaning" becomes an evocative long sobbing ("sangloalanglots"); while "makes me seasilt saltsick" becomes an equally evocative "me malselle et me mersalle," conflating *mal de mer* and *sel* ("salt") and *salé* ("salty"). The final line becomes "a way a lone at last loved along the" – and concludes with an exclamation mark.

Further French renderings by du Bouchet of excerpts from the final chapter (from *FW* 604–28), including revised versions of his 1950 translations, appeared in the *Nouvelle Revue Française* in 1957 under the revised title "Les veilles des Finnegans," a now pluralized "Finnegans' exequies," with the funeral sense now primary. A further revised version of his rendering from the final chapter, including the above lines, appeared in 1962 in his volume *Finnegans Wake*, to which we shall return.[8]

Chastaing (French, 1951)

A French rendering of the closing pages (*FW* 627.9–628.16) by a third French translator, Maxime Chastaing (1913–97) of the École Normale Supérieure, and two collaborators, Armand Jacob, a colleague, and Arthur Watt, an English-speaking exchange student, appeared in the journal *Roman* in 1951. Chastaing, a graduate of the Sorbonne, and one of whose early teachers had been Jean-Paul Sartre, was to become a noted literary philosopher with a special interest in the area of phonosemantics. His career was interrupted by five years of imprisonment in Germany during the Second World War.[9]

Anonymous (Serbian, 1956)

Rather surprisingly, an anonymous Serbian rendering of an (unspecified) excerpt from the *ALP* chapter (*FW* I.8) reportedly appeared in the Belgrade literary journal *Mlada kultura* (New culture) in 1956 (Josipović 2011, 101).

Campos and Campos (Portuguese, 1957)

Of fundamental importance for subsequent Brazilian interest in the translatability of *FW*, a first Portuguese translation of any part of Joyce's text appeared in 1957, when seven excerpts (from *FW* 3, 159, 196, 214–16, 556, 561, 627–8) rendered by the young Brazilian poets (and brothers) Augusto de Campos and Haroldo de Campos appeared in the São Paulo daily newspaper *Jornal do Brasil*. These renderings would appear together with other excerpts and further materials in book form in 1962, under the title *Panaroma do Finnegans Wake*, and to which we shall return.

---

8 Fritz Senn (1967c, 230–1) reprints du Bouchet's 1950, 1957, and 1962 renderings of the final lines (*FW* 627.34–628.16).

9 On Chastaing's rendering, see Aubert (1967: 217–18).

Strzetelski (Polish, 1959)

A first Polish translation of any part of *FW*, finally, appeared in 1959, in the form of a rendering by Jerzy Strzetelski (1924–94), a professor of English at the Jagiellonian University of Krakow, of selected excerpts from *ALP*. The translation included its opening and closing pages (*FW* 196.1–197.4, 198.9–14, 206.35–207.11, 215.31–216.5) and appeared in the Polish literary journal *Twórczość* (Creativity) as excerpts from "*Noc opłakiwania Finnegana*," literally "The night (*noc*) of Finnegan's mourning (*opłakiwanie*)," emphasizing the nocturnal and funereal character of the event.[10]

Strzetelski's rendering of the opening sentences of *ALP* (quoted by Szczerbowski 2000, 69, 74) includes the following lines (*FW* 196.1–3, 5–7, 9–11):

> O / mów mi wszystko / o Annie Livii! ... Mów mi wszystko. Mów mi teraz. Umrzesz, gdy uslyszysz. Otóż, jak stary drab poszedł po to i uczynił co wiesz. ... O cokolwiek było, o czym chcieli się dowiedzieć, czy on troił dwoje w szatańskim parku.

Here the washerwoman wants to hear all (*wszystko*) about Anna Livia, and she wants to hear it now (*teraz*), fluvially evoking the Mow river of Papua New Guinea and the English Ter. "You'll die when you hear" (*Umrzesz, gdy uslyszysz*), she promises her partner, and proceeds to tell how the old scoundrel (*stary drab*) "went for it" (*poszedł po to*) and did (*uczynił*) "what you know" (*co wiesz*), evoking in passing the Italian Po and German Wies. Or whatever it was (*o cokolwiek było*) about what they wanted (*o czym chcieli się*) to work out (*dowiedzieć*) for themselves, namely, if "he tripled the two" (*czy on troił dwoje*) in the "satanic park" (*w szatańskim parku*). The verb *troił* here, literally "tripled," plays not only on the three (*trzy*) watchers but also, interlingually, on the English *tried* – as in whatever he may have "tried to do" to the two (*dwa*) in the now "satanic" park, thus "tripling the two" by the addition of himself to the pair.

Strzetelski is also reported (Ćwiąkała 1971, 94) to have translated an excerpt from "The Mookse and the Gripes" in 1959. Katarzyna Bazarnik describes that rendering as, unsurprisingly, essentially explanatory (2017).

---

10 On Strzetelski's Polish renderings, see Ćwiąkała (1971), Szczerbowski (2000), Bazarnik (2017).

Chapter Four

The 1960s

*1 Italian; 2 French; 3 Spanish; 4 Portuguese; 5 Hungarian;
6 German; 7 Romanian; 8 Slovak; 9 Czech; 10 Japanese;
11 Galician; 12 Swedish*

The 1960s saw greatly increased interest in the possibilities of translating *FW*, with efforts made in at least ten languages. The most substantial results were Juan Rodolfo Wilcock's 1961 Italian rendering of some forty pages, André du Bouchet's 1962 French version of two full chapters (I.1, IV), and Philippe Lavergne's French rendering also of two full chapters, I.7 in 1967 and I.1 in 1968.

Briefer renderings appeared in Spanish by Salvador Elizondo (1962), in Portuguese by the Campos brothers (1962) and by Manuel Lourenço (1968), in Hungarian by Endre Bíró (1964), in Romanian by Ion Biberi (1965), in Slovak by Jozef Kot (1965), in Czech by Zdeněk Urbánek (1966), in Japanese by a team led by Masayoshi Osawa (1966 and 1968), in Galician by Leopoldo Rodríguez (1969), and in German by Arno Schmidt (1969) and by Wolfgang Hildesheimer (1969). The more than thirty excerpts from *FW* employed by Richard Ellmann mostly as chapter epigraphs in his *James Joyce* (1959) were translated into German by Fritz Senn (in Hess et al. 1961), into French by André Coeuroy (1962), and into Italian by Piero Bernardini (1964).

Lavergne's two chapters would later expand into a complete French *Finnegans Wake* in 1982, while Arno Schmidt's ten pages or so had originally been planned as part of a complete German rendering, though that project was abandoned at an early stage. Hungarian, Romanian, Slovak, and Galician all appeared for the first time among renderings. Rumours circulated in Sweden of a rendering by Erik Lindegren being under way, but no fragment of it, if it did indeed exist, has been found in print.

1 Italian

Wilcock (Italian, 1961)

In 1961, twenty years after Joyce's pioneering Italian rendering of *ALP*, an Italian translation appeared of some forty pages altogether of Joyce's text, the largest selection to that date of translated excerpts from *FW* in any language, translated and annotated by Juan Rodolfo Wilcock (1919–78) – who, as it happens, and like Joyce, was not a native Italian.[1] An Argentinian poet, critic, and translator, son of an English father and an Italian-speaking Swiss mother, Wilcock was born in Buenos Aires and graduated from the University of Buenos Aires in civil engineering. A friend of Jorge Luis Borges and other major Argentinian authors, he was already well known as a writer in Spanish by the mid-1950s, at which point the increasingly fraught political situation in Argentina impelled him to relocate to Italy, where he spent most of the rest of his life, writing primarily in Italian.

His renderings of 1961, intended as a very brief but representative introduction to *FW* for Italian readers, appeared as "Frammenti scelti da *La veglia di Finnegan*" (Selected excerpts from *FW*) in the final volume of a three-volume collection of Joyce's complete works, *Tutte le opere di James Joyce*, edited by Giacomo Debenedetti and published in Milan by Mondadori. The renderings appeared in book form fifty-five years later, in January 2016, edited by Eduardo Camurri and published by the small and recently established house of Giometti & Antonello in Macerata. After a preface by Camurri, the collection includes facing-page versions of the relevant excerpts from Joyce's original text, Beckett's "Dante ... Bruno . Vico .. Joyce" in Italian translation, and five short journalistic pieces on Joyce written by Wilcock in the 1960s and 1970s.[2] Wilcock's rendering of the title, "La veglia di Finnegan" ("Finnegan's wake" in the funeral sense), has in the meantime become the most generally accepted Italian title.[3]

---

1 Wilcock translates the following excerpts: *FW* 3.1–20, 33.14–34.4, 104.1–109.36, 112.9–27, 169.1–170.9, 179.9–32, 182.30–184.10, 185.14–26, 187.28–188.19, 189.28–191.4, 196.1–24, 206.29–207.14, 219.1–222.17, 249.5–33, 258.19–259.10, 306.7–308.27, 384.6–20, 543.13–545.22, 558.26–559.31, 572.7–575.7, 599.25–606.12, 626.33–628.16.

2 On Wilcock's renderings, see Camurri (2016), Bugliaro (2017).

3 Other Italian versions of the title occasionally encountered in Joyce criticism include *La sveglia di Finnegan* ("Finnegan's awakening") and *La veglia dei Finnegan* (a plural "Finnegans' wake").

Unsurprisingly in view of the early date of Wilcock's rendering, Serenella Zanotti observes that his translating strategy "seems to be more concerned with making the plot clear than with re-creating Joyce's verbal architectures" (2006, 5). In his own introduction to the 1961 collection of excerpts – which in principle anticipates such later endeavours as Anthony Burgess's *A Shorter Finnegans Wake* (1966) – Wilcock states his conviction that Joyce's irreducibly polysemous text is entirely impossible to translate and freely acknowledges that his renderings are in consequence intended only to convey some approximate sense of what he understands to be the general drift of it (O'Neill 2013, 289).

Wilcock's rendering (1961, 1129) of the opening lines (*FW* 3.1–3) reads:

> corso del fiume oltre Adamo ed Eva dallo scarto della riva alla piega della baia ci riporta lungo un commodo vico di ricircolazione al castello di Howth e dintorni.

Aiming in 1961 at novice Italian readers of the *Wake*, Wilcock limits himself to an explanatory paraphrase, his "corso del fiume" literally meaning "course of the river." Joyce's "Eve and Adam" is reversed to a more conservatively familiar Adam and Eve. The swerve of shore becomes a "scarto della riva," an unplanned swerve as opposed to the calmer "piega" ("turn, fold") of the bay. Commodus and Vico are clearly present; Joyce's alliterative effects are ignored; and HCE's initials are humorously rearranged as CHE in the rather minimalist rendering "al *c*astello di *H*owth *e* dintorni."

Wilcock's rendering of the first page continues with the following lines (*FW* 3.4–10), offered here without commentary for readers' general interest:

> Sir Tristano da oltre il mare piccolo, violista d'amori, non era ancora riarrivato da Nord Armorica, in questa parte dello scabroso istmo d'Europa Minore, a brandibattere la sua guerra penisolata; né si erano le alte rocce accanto al fiume Oconee esagerate fino ai gorghi della contea di Laurens mentre il loro numero si raddublinava continuamente; né la voce dal fuoco aveva risoffiato mishe mishe al tauf tauf tuseipetrizio;

Wilcock's rendering (1961, 1147–8) of the opening of the *ALP* chapter (I.8) includes the following lines (*FW* 196.1–7, 9–11):

> Oh / raccontami tutto di / Anna Livia! Voglio sapere tutto / di Anna Livia. Dunque, conosci Anna Livia? Ma sí, certo, noi tutte conosciamo

Anna Livia. Dimmi tutto. Dimmi subito. Roba da non crederci, vedrai. Dunque, sai, quando il vecchio perse la bussola e fece quel che sai. ... Ma non so bene che cosa dicono che egli abbia fatto a quelle due in quell'infenice parco.

Here Joyce's opening "O" is rendered as an exclamatory "Oh," reducing the connotative potential for circularity as well as weakening the pun on French *eau* ("water"). The Italian washerwoman wants to know (*sapere*) all rather than hear all and is promised "stuff" (*roba*) she wouldn't believe (*da non crederci*), especially about when the old fellow (*il vecchio*) "lost his bearings" (*perse la bussola*) and did "what you know" (*quel che sai*). "But I don't really know (*non so bene*)," she admits, "what they say (*che cosa dicono*) that he had done (*che egli abbia fatto*) to those two (*quelle due*) in that unfortunate (*infelice*) Phoenix (*fenice*) park." The three watchers in the trees remain unmentioned. A generous number of fluvial evocations includes the American Raccoon and Indian Tut, the Sape of the Solomon Islands, and the English Dun, Turkish Dim, Irish Robe (Italian *Roba*), and Indian Sai.

Wilcock's rendering (1961, 1173–4) of the final page includes the following lines (*FW* 627.34–628.4, 15–16), once again offered here without commentary for readers' general interest:

Ora trapasso. O amara fine! Me ne andrò prima che si siano alzati. Non mi vedranno. Né sapranno. Cosí non mancherò. Ed è vecchia e vecchia è triste e vecchia è triste e stanca che retorno a te, il mio freddo padre, il mio freddo folle padre, il mio freddo folle fiero padre, finché la mera prossimità della tua immensità, moli e moli gemaurorando, mi sedimenta, mi dà il mal di mare, e mi getto, oh mio solo, nelle tue braccia. ... Lontana sola infine amata lungo il

Diacono (Italian, 1961)

An Italian translation by Mario Diacono of a two-page excerpt from I.5 (*FW* 107.8–108.36) also appeared in 1961, in the journal *La Tartaruga* (The tortoise). Born in Rome in 1930, Diacono graduated from the University of Rome, where he studied modern Italian literature under the poet Giuseppe Ungaretti. The writer, poet, artist, art critic, and editor Diacono taught Italian for some years at the University of California at Berkeley in the 1960s and at Sarah Lawrence College in New York in the 1970s. During the 1970s and 1980s he divided his time between Italy and the United States and operated art galleries variously in Bologna, Rome, and Boston (Lo Pinto 2013). His translation, though brief, is regarded as being of significant importance for Italian writing in the 1960s (Zanotti 2006, 1).[4]

Bernardini (Italian, 1964)

In 1964, Piero Bernardini translated Ellmann's *James Joyce* (1959), including its more than thirty excerpts from *FW*, into Italian.

2 French

du Bouchet (French, 1962)

André du Bouchet (1924–2001) has been called "one of the world's greatest contemporary poets," though "almost totally unknown to the general public" (Kirkup 2001). Born in Paris, he emigrated with his parents at the outbreak of the Second World War from France to the United States, where the family lived from 1941 to 1948. Du Bouchet studied English at Harvard, and after graduation he taught English in the United States for some time before returning to France. Author of more than twenty volumes of poetry, he was also a translator from Russian (Mandelstam, Pasternak), German (Hölderlin, Celan), and English (Shakespeare, Faulkner – and Joyce, later including, in 1973, *Giacomo Joyce*).

In 1962, continuing the task he had begun a dozen years earlier, in 1950 already, in his mid-twenties, André du Bouchet produced a slightly abbreviated rendering of the first and last chapters of the *Wake* in his edited volume *Finnegans Wake*, which also reprinted for the first time, after three decades, Joyce's 1931 French team translation of *ALP*. The volume, sharing its title with Joyce's *Wake*, contains some sixty pages altogether of excerpts from *FW*, beginning with du Bouchet's rendering of *FW* IV, followed by Joyce's rendering of *ALP*, and followed in turn by du Bouchet's rendering of *FW* I.1. Also containing a substantial introduction by Michel Butor,[5] du Bouchet's volume almost immediately surpassed Wilcock's collection of Italian excerpts as the most substantial volume in any language of renderings

---

4 A report (Del Pozzo 1982, 156) that one "Mario Di Giacomo" translated *FW* 107–8 into Italian in 1970 is an error. The mistaken reference is in fact to Mario Diacono, whose 1961 translation (*FW* 107.8–108.36) was reprinted in Naples in 1970. It was reprinted a second time in 1988.

5 Butor's introduction had previously appeared as "Esquisse d'un seuil pour Finnegan" in the *Nouvelle Revue Française* n.s. 5, no. 60 (1957): 1033–53.

from *FW*.[6] Du Bouchet's rendering, moreover, is considered to be consistently of exceptional quality – as Jacques Aubert writes, the work not just of a translator but also, and inevitably in du Bouchet's case, the work of a poet (1967, 220).[7]

Aubert also writes that du Bouchet was initially tempted to translate the entire *FW* (1967, 219). Other than the first and final chapters, however – which were republished (without Joyce's team translation of *ALP*) in 2003 – no further renderings by him appeared.

Du Bouchet's rendering (1962, 55) of the opening lines (*FW* 3.1–3) reads as follows:

> courrive passé notre Adame des courbes de la côte aux bras de la baie nous rame par commode vicus de recirculation vers Howth, Château et Environs.

Here "courrive" (*courir* "to run") effectively conflates the river and its restraining banks, with English *river* and French *rivière* both deriving from the Latin *ripa* ("riverbank"), whence also French *rive* ("bank"). The formulation "passé notre Adame" might initially appear to have abandoned Eve, but on closer examination she is to be found not only hidden in the opening "cour*rive*" but also amalgamated with her Adam, who, as "notre Adame" ("our Adam") is also, preserving the ecclesiastical reference, "Notre Dame," male shading into female as the Liffey shades into the Seine and Dublin into Paris. The *cour-* of the opening *courrive* reappears in the pluralized and overtly sexualized "courbes" ("curves") of the coast, melting into and becoming one with the "bras" ("arms") of the bay. Suddenly, we appear to be passengers in a boat on the river, who are not just "brought" back but rather rowed (*ramer*, "to row") back, not without difficulty (*ramer*, "to strain"), and by means of a *rame*, which, as a noun, is not only an "oar" but also a "ream" of the paper on which *FW* is written (O'Neill 2013, 37–58 passim). Commodus and Vico are both present, as are HCE's initials in their original order – while Joyce's "Howth Castle and Environs" becomes, slightly less specifically, "Howth, with its Castle and Environs."

Du Bouchet's rendering continues (*FW* 3.4–9):

---

6 On du Bouchet's French renderings, see Aubert (1965, 1967), Senn (1967c, 229–31), Van Laere (1968), Topia (1990).

7 In Aubert's words, "la qualité exceptionelle de ces pages est celle d'une création authentique. Ses choix, ses décisions, ont été ceux d'un poète. Il ne pouvait en être autrement" (1967, 220).

Sire Tristam, violeur d'amores, d'oultre la manche mer, n'avait à corps ravivé du Nord de l'Armorique ès bords d'icel huisthme hérisé d'Europe mineure pour reluivreferre sa guerre péniseulte: marmerocs de sommesci-eur le long du calme Oconee ne s'étaient pour lors exagerés en gorgios de Laurens County doublin l'arrombe de mot en mot:

Du Bouchet's rendering here is particularly impressive, as I have suggested elsewhere (O'Neill 2013, 63–121 passim). His Sire Tristram arrives "d'oultre la manche mer," where Old French *oultre* on the one hand means simply "beyond" (Latin *ultra*) but in the context of du Bouchet's phrase also generates echoes of modern French *outre-Manche* ("cross-Channel"), *outremer* ("overseas"), not to mention *adultère* ("adultery, adulterous, adulterer"). The "manche mer" in question is not only *mince* ("small, slender") like the Irish Sea but extends the reference to the English Channel (*la Manche*), across which Tristram will also have originally sailed, on his way from Brittany to Cornwall. The formulation "n'avait à corps ravivé" suggests that, though "revived" (*ravivé*) "in body" (*à corps*) "once again" (*encore*), Sire Tristram had neither "yet arrived" (*n'avait encore arrivé*), nor arrived "once again" (*encore*). His mission "to wielderfight his penisolate war" becomes "pour reluivreferre sa guerre," suggesting all of "to polish up" (*faire reluire*) one's weapons (*fer* "iron, sword"), "to give battle" (*livrer bataille*), "to make war" (*faire la guerre*), and to fight wildly (*ivre* "intoxicated") again (*relivrer bataille*) and again (*refaire la guerre*).

"Topsawyer's rocks" becomes du Bouchet's "marmerocs de sommescieur," where "marmerocs" conflates Greek *mármaros* and French *roc*, both meaning "rock," and "sommescieur" combines Latin *summa* ("topmost"), French *scieur* ("sawyer"), and French *somme* ("nap, forty winks") to provide an approximate rhyming equivalent (in French phonetics) of "Tom Sawyer" as well as suggesting a dozing Tom who might well emulate Tim Finnegan in tumbling from his perch. As for "doublin their mumper all the time," du Bouchet's "doublin l'arrombe de mot en mot" conflates *leur nombre* ("their number") and *larron* ("thief"), while "de mot en mot" (literally, "from word to word") doubles as translingually echoing the English "more and more." Oddly, and presumably inadvertently, du Bouchet's rendering omits the third clause in the sequence, "nor avoice from afire bellowsed mishe mishe to tauftauf thuartpeatrick." (*FW* 3.9–10).

Du Bouchet's rendering (1962, 53–4) of the final page of the *Wake* includes the following lines (*FW* 627.34–628.4, 15–16), revised from their original appearance in his rendering of 1950:

Je trépasse. O fin amère! Je m'esquiverai avant qu'ils soient levés. Ils ne verront jamais. Ni ne sauront. Ni me regretteront. Et c'est vieux et vieux c'est triste et vieux c'est triste et lasse que je retourne vers toi, mon père froid, mon père fou et froid, mon père furieux et fou et froid, jusqu'à ce que rien que sa taille que je vois de si près, ses crilomères et ses crilomères, ses sangloalanglots, me malselle et me mersalle et je me rue, mon unique, dans tes bras. ... Le chemin l'unique l'ultime l'aimé le long du[8]

The "crilomètres" of du Bouchet's 1950 renderings (kilomètres from miles from moyles), are here adjusted to "crilomères," conflating French *cris* ("cries"), *mer* ("sea") – and potentially *mère* ("mother"), as if the sea were finally being seen both as "cold mad feary father" and as maternal haven. The 1950 rendering of the final line, "Un chemin un seul enfin aimée le long du!," literally, "a way a lone at last loved along the!" with a concluding exclamation mark, now deletes the exclamation mark and opts for the masculine definite article throughout. The result is an alliterative, and much more mellifluous, "Le chemin l'unique l'ultime l'aimé le long du," literally, "the way, the lone, the last, the loved, along the."

Coeuroy (French, 1962)

In 1962, André Coeuroy translated Richard Ellmann's *James Joyce* (1959), with its more than thirty excerpts from *FW*, into French. François Van Laere observes (1968, 130) that many lines of *FW* thus first appeared in French in Coeuroy's (largely unsung) renderings.

Castelain (French, 1964)

A French translation of five excerpts (from *FW* 3, 44, 169–71, 384, 627–8) by Daniel Castelain (born 1937) appeared in Paris in 1964 in the bilingual literary journal *Two Cities*, founded and edited by the Mauritian poet and psychoanalyst Jean Fanchette (1932–92).[9]

Lavergne (French, 1967, 1968)

Michel Butor, in an interview with Jacques Aubert in January 1967, called with some urgency for a French rendering of *FW* that would

---

8 Fritz Senn (1967c, 230–1) reprints du Bouchet's 1950, 1957, and 1962 renderings of the final lines (*FW* 627.34–628.16).

9 On Jean Fanchette and the journal *Two Cities*, see Stella (2011).

attempt to accomplish in French what Joyce had achieved in English –
while immediately volunteering that he had no plans at all to attempt
this task himself (1967, 216).[10] The attempt, however, was in fact already
under way, undertaken by Philippe Lavergne (born 1935), whose rendering of the "Shem" chapter (I.7; *FW* 169–95) appeared in Philippe
Sollers's avant-garde journal *Tel Quel* in the summer of 1967, followed
by his rendering of the opening chapter (*FW* 3–29) in the journal *Change*
in 1968. These two chapters would in due course expand into what
would prove to be Lavergne's complete French version of *FW*, to which
we shall return.[11] French readers would have to wait well more than a
decade, however, before that complete rendering would eventually appear, timed with a shrewd eye to the value of publicity by the publisher
Gallimard to do so in 1982, the first complete rendering in any language
thus scheduled to appear in the centenary year of Joyce's birth.

3 Spanish

Elizondo (Spanish, 1962)

A first Spanish translation of any part of *FW* also appeared in June 1962,
in the form of a heavily annotated rendering of the opening page by
the young Mexican poet, novelist, playwright, and journalist Salvador Elizondo (1932–2006). Born the son of a diplomat in Mexico City,
he spent his childhood and school years in Germany, California, and
Mexico, before completing an undergraduate degree in literature at the
University of Ottawa, followed by further studies at Cambridge, the
Sorbonne, Perugia, and the National Autonomous University of Mexico (UNAM), where he subsequently spent twenty-five years as a faculty member. Elizondo is regarded as having been perhaps the most
original Mexican writer of his generation, noted for his innovative and
experimental work. He was also a lifelong reader of Joyce – which even
led him momentarily into what might have become a life of crime: he
records in his published diaries having as an eighteen-year-old stolen
one hundred pesos from his mother in order to acquire a copy of *FW*
(Price 2009).

In 1962, the twenty-nine-year-old Elizondo founded and edited a
very short-lived literary journal bearing the provocative title *S.Nob*,

---

10   "Il faut donc essayer de faire à partir du français ce que Joyce a fait à partir de
     l'anglais (je précise tout de suite que je n'envisage pas de m'en charger" (1967, 216).

11   For a contemporary reaction to Lavergne's first published chapter, see Van Laere
     (1968, 129–33).

poking titular fun – in a manner reminiscent of Flann O'Brien – at the typical hispanophone pronunciation of an initial *s* before a consonant, as in, for example, /əs'nɔb/ rather than /snɔb/. One of its rather more serious aims was to introduce Mexican readers to challenging foreign writing, and in the first issue, published in June 1962, Elizondo published his own translation of the first page of the *Wake* (*FW* 3.1–24). He had originally planned to translate the complete 628-page text with the help of his friend and fellow writer Fernando del Paso, but the plan was abandoned when del Paso's command of English soon proved to be inadequate for the task (Price 2009).

Elizondo's heavily annotated exegetic rendering of the first page of the *Wake* included six pages of detailed notes for Joyce's twenty-four lines, the notes thus running to roughly nine times the length of the passage translated. Having found it necessary to employ this degree of detail in completing just the first page, any residual ambition Elizondo might have had to undertake the entire annotated translation on his own was also abandoned (Vázquez 2017). His rendering was reprinted thirty years later, in 1992, in a volume of his own literary essays, *Teoría del infierno y otros ensayos*. In June 2006, forty-four years after its initial publication, it was reprinted once again, in the Mexican literary journal *Casa del tiempo*.

Elizondo's rendering of the opening lines (*FW* 3.1–3), omitting the notes here:

> riocorrido más allá de la de Eva y Adán de desvío de costa a encombadura de bahía trayéndonos por un cómodio vícolo de recirculación otra vuelta a Howth Castillo y Enderredores.

Elizondo's "riocorrido" conflates the river (*río*) and its course (*recorrido*) beyond (*más allá de*) Eve and Adam's, with Joyce's order of the names retained. The swerve of shore becomes a "desvío" ("deviation") while the bend of bay is an "encombadura" ("curve, bend"). Commodus and Vico are clearly present; alliteration is ignored; while HCE's initials are retained by conflating "en derredores" ("environs") to produce "Howth Castillo y Enderredores."

His rendering continues (*FW* 3.4–10), once again omitting the notes here:

> Sir Tristram, violer d'amores, habiendo cruzado el corto mar, había pasancor revuelto de Nortearmórica, de este lado del estrecho istmo de Europa Menor para martibatallar en su guerra peneisolar; ni habían las rocas del alto psawrrador, esparcidas a lo largo del arroyo Oconee, exagerádose

a sí otras mismas a los gorgios del Condado de Laurens mientras iban dubliando todo el tiempo su mendiganancia; ni una voz salida del fuego surgía diciendo mishe mishe a tauftauf tuespetrarricio;

Elizondo's version of these three clauses has several notable points of interest. Sir Tristram's arriving "pasancor" not only renders "passencore" but suggests the Spanish *ancora* ("anchor") of seafaring vessels. His rendering of "this side" as "de este lado," literally "from this side," is unusual in envisaging the action as proceeding *from* rather than towards the scraggy isthmus under discussion. His "alto psawrrador" conflates *alto* ("high") and *aserrador* ("sawyer") as well as a muted echo of Tom Sawyer. Rendering "to wielderfight" as "para martibatallar" suggests to battle (*batallar*) like Mars (*Marte*) – or perhaps like a martyr (*mártir*). As for those "doublin their mumper," Elizondo takes a bleak view of such activity, seen as involving merely doubling the amount of financial "gain" (*ganancia*) they can make from "begging" (*mendigante*). His rendering of "thuartpeatrick," finally, as "tuespetrarricio" duly includes a Latin *tu es* ("thou art"), a Latin Petrus, and a Spanish Patricio – but it also hints at abandoning peat in favour of rice (Spanish *arroz*), possibly imported at this point to suggest an implied interlingual pun on "paddy" fields. Peat bogs and paddy fields – the latter so called, incidentally, from the Malay *pādī* ("rice plant") rather than from any putative Irish connection – are also linked by their shared dependance on water, entirely appropriate to the immediate context of baptism (O'Neill 2013, 119–20).

4 Portuguese

Campos and Campos (Portuguese, 1962)

Seven excerpts (from *FW* 3, 159, 196, 214–16, 556, 561, 627–8) in Portuguese translation by the two Brazilian poets (and brothers) Augusto de Campos (born 1931) and Haroldo de Campos (1929–2003) had appeared in 1957, as mentioned, in the São Paulo daily newspaper *Jornal do Brasil*. These renderings, augmented by four additional excerpts (from *FW* 143, 189, 226, 559) and a number of annotations and commentaries, were reprinted as a separate small volume in December 1962 under the cover title *Panaroma do Finnegans Wake*. "Finnicius Revém" was also employed as an internal title – which was later to be adopted, in an overt act of literary homage, by Donaldo Schüler, as the title of his complete Portuguese rendering of *FW* almost four decades later (2003). The passages from *FW* 214–16 and 627–8 are jointly translated; *FW* 189 is translated by Haroldo de Campos; and the remaining eight are the work of Augusto de Campos.[12] Fellow Brazilian *Wake* translator Dirce Waltrick do Amarante praises the Campos translation particularly for its verbal musicality (2009, 30).

Haroldo de Campos, born in São Paulo and a law graduate of the University of São Paulo, was by the late fifties already a well-known poet and literary theorist in Brazil. Together with his younger brother Augusto, who was also a lawyer by training, he founded the literary group Noigandres in 1952, which was instrumental in introducing concrete poetry into Brazilian letters. Haroldo's subsequent and extensive work as a translator – an activity he theorized as "transcreation" – was to include Homer's *Iliad* and Ezra Pound's *Cantos* as well as works by Dante and Goethe and modern poetry in several languages.[13]

Augusto de Campos renders the opening lines (*FW* 3.1–3) as follows:

riocorrente depois de Eva e Adão do desvio da praia à dobra da baía de-volve-nos por um cômodo vicus de recirculação de volta a Howth Castle Ecercanias.

Campos renders "riverrun" as a single word, "riocorrente" ("river-running"), while simultaneously evoking the river (*rio*) as perennially recurrent (*reocorrente*). Eve and Adam, as "Eva e Adão," retain their Joycean order. The "swerve" of shore is rendered as "desvio," a term that literally means a going off the road, an unplanned diversion or deviation, and thus readable as suggesting the opposition of this uncontrolled waywardness and the more restrained curve of the bay. The "bend of bay," meanwhile, is rendered as "dobra da baia," where "dobra" not only means "fold" or "turn" but is also closely related to *dobre* ("double") and *dobradura* ("doubling"), thus suggesting the identity rather than the opposition of "swerve" and "bend." Commodus and Vico are clearly identifiable, while HCE's initials are humorously retained by combining *e cercanias* ("and environs") to produce "Howth Castle Ecercanias." The phrase *de volta a* translates, entirely appropriately, the English adverbial phrase *back to* – but in the wonderful world of the *FW* macrotext there

12 A second edition, in 1971, added another five excerpts (from *FW* 13, 157–9, 182–4, 189–90, 202, 244); Haroldo de Campos independently added two more (*FW* 292, 449) in 1999; and a fourth edition, in 2001, almost fifty years after the original renderings, added yet one more (from *FW* 206–7), thus amounting to nineteen translated excerpts altogether, rendering some twenty pages of *FW*.

13 On Haroldo de Campos, see casadasrosas.org.br/centro-de-referencia-haroldo-de-campos/haroldo-de-campos.

are undoubtedly readers who will recall that the name of the cinema in which Joyce was not very successfully involved in opening in Dublin in December 1909 was none other than the Volta.

The translation of the opening page continues with the following lines (*FW* 3.4–9):

Sir Tristão, violador d'amôres, através o mar breve, tinha pazencore revoltado de Norte Armórica a êste lado do áspero istmo da Europa Menor para relutar sua guerra penisolada: nem tinham os calhaus do altom sawyerrador pelo rio Oconee sexagerado aos górgios de Laurens County enquanto êles iam dublando os bebêbados todo o tempo:

The second clause here humorously suggests that sex and booze are at the root of the matter. It back-translates roughly as "nor had the rocks (*calhaus*) of the top sawyer (*alto serrador*) Tom Sawyer on the river Oconee sexaggerated themselves to the gorgios of Laurens County while they went (*iam*) doubling (*dublando*) the number of babies (*bebês*) all the time while drunk (*bêbado*)."

The opening sentences of *ALP* as rendered once again by Augusto de Campos include the following lines (*FW* 196.7, 9–11):

Ah / fala-me de / Ana Lívia! Quero ouvir tudo / sôbre Ana Lívia. Bem, você conhece Ana Lívia? Mas claro, todo mundo. Fala-me tudo. Quero ouvir já. É de matar. Ora, você sabe, quando aquêle malandro fêz baque e fêz o que você sabe. ... Ou que diabo foi que trentaram duescobrir que êle tresandou fazendo no parque de Duendix.

Campos's opening "Ah," abandoning the generic French *eau* ("water") for the specific French river Aa, may be seen as also evoking, serendipitously, the Sumerian *a* ("water"). His speaker wants to hear (*ouvir*) all about Anna Livia's affairs, and is promised that the news will be a killer (*é de matar*), especially insofar as it concerns when "that good-for-nothing" (*aquêle malandro*) "went bang" (*fêz baque*) and "did what you know" (*fêz o que você sabe*). As for the business in the park, the speaker herself admits not knowing "what the devil (*que diabo*) it was that the three (*três*) of them were trying (*tentar*) to find out (*descobrir*) about what he was doing (*fazendo*) to offend (*tresandar*) the two (Italian *due*) in the spooky (*duende*) Phoenix park." Rivers evoked include the English Fal and African Fala, French Ouve, Brazilian Claro, Ugandan Ora, and English Trent.

From the final lines of *ALP*, jointly rendered by Augusto and Haroldo de Campos (*FW* 215.31–5, 216.3–5):

Não ouço por causa das águas de. O bebêbalbúcio das águas de. Sibilan-
tes morcegos, ratas da vala. Fala. Cala. Como é! Você não foi pra casa?
Que João José? Não ouço por causa da asa dos morcegos, tôdas as livi-
antes águas de. Ah, fala salva-nos! Planta dos pés pesa. Sinto-me tão calma
como aquêle olmo. Um conto contado de Shaun ou Shem? ... Fala-me, fala-me, fala-me álamo! Noite noite! Fala-me-fala de planta ou pedra. As
riocorrentes águas de, as indo-e-vindo águas de. Noite!

Rhyming and assonantal play are pervasive in this particularly poetic
rendering. The washerwoman cannot hear "because of the waters of"
(*por causa das águas de*), the "baby (*bebê*)-babbling (*balbúcio*) of the waters
of. Whistling bats (*morcegos*), mice (*ratas*) in the ditch (*vala*). Speak (*fala*).
Be silent (*cala*)." Tom Malone metamorphoses into another unknown,
identity lost in a misunderstood exchange, the new name generated
not just by rhyme, but inexplicably in reverse, "você não" generating
"João José" in this topsy-turvy world: "What? You haven't gone home?
What João José? What John Joseph?" The speaker can't hear because of
(*por causa de*) the noise of bats' wings (*asa*) and all the livvying waters
of. "Talk save us! The sole (*planta*), singular, of my feet (*pés*), plural,
is heavy (*pesa*)," as if the two feet had already coalesced into a single
sole, and that sole (*planta*) already metamorphosed into a plant (*planta*).
She does not feel "as old," but rather "as calm (*calma*)," she says, "as
yonder elm (*olmo*)," the noun *olmo* poetically rather than semantically
generating the adjective *calma*. The elm (*olmo*) itself promptly changes
in the general confusion into a poplar (*álamo*). "Speak to me, speak to
me, speak to me, poplar. Tell me (*fala-me*) a tale (*fala*) of plant or stone
(*pedra*). By the river-running (*riocorrentes*) waters of, the going and coming (*indo-e-vindo*) waters of. Night!"

Lourenço (Portuguese, 1968)

Manuel António dos Santos Lourenço (1936–2009), born in the Portuguese town of Sintra, near Lisbon, was a philosopher, writer, and translator of Wittgenstein. He taught at Oxford, the University of California
at Santa Barbara, and the University of Innsbruck before finally taking
up a chair of philosophy at the University of Lisbon. One of his particular literary interests was Portuguese experimental poetry, and it was in
this context that his Portuguese translation of the opening page of the
Wake (FW 3.1–24) appeared in Lisbon in the journal *O tempo e o modo* in
March 1968, five years after the Campos brothers' pioneering *Panaroma
do Finnegans Wake*.
Lourenço's rendering of the opening lines (FW 3.1–3) reads:

corrio depois de Eva e Adão, ergue-se do braço da praia até à curva da baía, traz-nos por um commodius vicus de recirculação de novo a Howthe Castelo Earredores.

Here the one-word "corrio" conflates *correr* ("to run") and *rio* ("river"). Eve and Adam, domesticated as a Portuguese Eva and Adão, retain their Joycean order, while the river "rises" (*ergue-se*) from the "arm" (*braço*) of the strand (*praia*) towards the "curve" (*curva*) of the bay (*baía*). Commodus and Vico are clearly present, and HCE's initials are saved by the strategy of combining *e arredores* ("and environs") to produce "Howthe Castelo Earredores." Howth acquires its epenthetic final vowel presumably because the consonantal ending *-th* before a following consonant was felt to be intolerable to a Portuguese ear.

His translation continues (*FW* 3.4–10):

Dom Tristram, ladcim'pre do estreito mar, violer d'amores, não tinha passancore rechegado da Armórica do Norte a este lado do ossudo istmo da Europa Menor para relutar o seu penisolado combate: nem as rochas de Pedro Sawyer se tinham dublixagerado, pela corrente do Ocone, até aos gorgios do Condado de Laurens enquanto que elas continuavam a dublinar o seu nâmero: nem uma voz vinda do fogo tinha rugido mishe mishe para tauftauf tuespetrício:

This version devotes specific attention to the contracted phrase "fr'over": the compressed "ladcim'pre do estreito mar" suggests an arrival on this side (*lado*) from "over the surface of" (*lá de cima de*) and from "across" (*sobre*) the expanse of the "narrow" (*estreito*) sea. The rendering of "passencore" as "passancore" once again, as in the case of Elizondo's Spanish version previously discussed, suggests the anchor (Portuguese *âncora*) of sailing ships, whether sailing for love or for war. Tom Sawyer as top sawyer is replaced by an extratextually suggested Peter Sawyer, renamed a Portuguese Pedro. Saints Peter and Patrick are conflatedly if abradedly present in "tuespetrício" as Latin Petrus and Portuguese Patrício, and even the necessary peat is translingually detectable ("-pet-").

5 Hungarian

Bíró (Hungarian, 1964)

Some fifteen pages of excerpts in Hungarian translation by Endre Bíró, introducing one more new macrotextual language, appeared in 1964. Born in Budapest of Jewish parentage, Miklós Endre Bíró (1919–88) overcame two decades of institutionalized anti-Semitism before eventually becoming a biochemist at Eötvös Loránd University in Budapest, where his work would eventually win international recognition. He had completed the translation of the *FW* excerpts some years earlier than 1964, but due to the then prevailing political situation, they could not be published in Hungary. They were instead published in Yugoslavia, together with an essay on *FW*, in the expatriate avant-garde literary monthly *Híd* (Bridge), a magazine for ethnic Hungarians living in Yugoslavia. The translations and the essay were subsequently reprinted in the 1970s in a Paris-based literary journal founded by Hungarian intellectuals who had fled Hungary in 1956, *Magyar Műhely* (Hungarian workshop), and they finally appeared in book form in Budapest in 1992, four years after the translator's death, under the title *Finnegan ébredése*, literally, "Finnegan's awakening." Bíró's renderings are regarded as having had a significant impact on postmodern Hungarian prose.[14]

Péter Egri, who praises Bíró's rendering for its "witty puns, ingenious telescopings of words and musical onomatopoeic distortions of syllables," reprints a short passage from the closing lines of *FW*, which, he believes, should also appeal even to the reader who speaks no Hungarian because of "the musicality of its sounds" (1967, 235). The passage quoted includes *FW* 628.12–16:

> We pass through grass behush the bush to. Whish! A gull. Gulls. Far calls. Coming, far! End here. Us then. Finn, again! Take. Bussoftlhee, mememormee! Till thousendsthee. Lps. The keys to. Given! A way a lone a last a loved a long the

> A fű nem hű, a csalit csak csal. Oh bár! Egy sirály. Sirályok. Távoli kiáltok. Jön, messze. Itt vége. És minket. Fenn megént! Vedd. Simogágyd őt, rámemorolj. Végezerig. Jkk! A kulcsai. Vedd! El, egyedül, egy végső, szeretett útján a (Bíró 1964, 1256)

6 German

Meister (German, 1960)

Guido Meister's March 1960 translation of Jean Paris's *James Joyce par lui-même* (1957) includes renderings of four excerpts from the *Wake*, including

---

14   On Bíró's Hungarian renderings, see Goldmann (2006), Anon. (2018a).

three passages from *ALP* (*FW* 196.1–11, 197.7–18, 200.23–32), and the final lines (*FW* 627.34–628.16). The excerpts appear to have been translated from Joyce's original rather than from any intermediate French version.

Meister's German rendering (152–3) of the opening lines of *ALP* (*FW* 196.1–7, 9–11):

O sag mir alles von Anna Livia! Ich will alles wissen von Anna Livia. Nun, du kennst Anna Livia? Ja, natürlich, wir alle kennen Anna Livia. Sag mir alles. Sag mir's jetzt. Es ist dein Tod, wenn du's hörst. Nun, du weißt, als der alte Kerl futschging und tat, was du weißt. ... Oder was immer sie auszumachen dreiten, er versuchte es zweifalls im Feindigs Park.

As in Goyert's rendering in 1933, Meister ignores the opening typographical delta. The unadorned opening "O" puns appropriately on French *eau* ("water") while implicitly introducing the notion of circularity. Also as in Goyert's rendering, his washerwoman wants to know (*wissen*) rather than hear (*hören*) all about Anna. It will be the death of you (*es ist dein Tod*), when you hear, her colleague warns, namely, about when the old geezer (*Kerl*) went to pieces (*futschging*). Fluvial evocations include the Austrian Enns ("kennst"), French Enne ("kennen"), and the German Weiss ("weißt") and Oder, none requiring any particular effort on the translator's part. The final sentence, requiring rather more effort, suggests something like "Or whatever it was that the three (*drei*) of them were threatening (*drohten*) to figure out (*auszumachen*), he tried (*versuchte*) it twice (*zweifach*) during his fall (*Fall*) from grace in a Phoenix Park that is also the abode of the Enemy (*Feind*), the Devil himself."

Meister's rendering (156) of Anna Livia's final monologue includes the following lines (*FW* 627.34–628.4, 15–16):

Ich verschwinde. O bitteres Ende! Ich will mich fortstehlen, ehe sie erwachen. Sie werden nichts sehen. Und nichts wissen. Und mich nicht vermissen. Und alt und alt und traurig und alt und traurig und müde kehre ich zurück zu dir mein kalter Vater, mein kalter wilder Vater, mein kalter wilder furchtbarer Vater, bis der nahe Anblick seiner blossen Grösse, seiner Moilen-Moilenweite, stöhnächzend, mich seesüchtig und salzsiech macht und ich mich in deine Arme, du mein Einziger, stürze. ... Ein Weg ein allein ein letzt ein Lieb ein entlang der

Senn (German, 1961)

The more than thirty excerpts from *FW* contained in Richard Ellmann's *James Joyce* (1959) amounted altogether, in terms of number of lines, to more than six full pages of Joyce's text.[15] Ellmann's book appeared in German translation in 1961 (Hess et al. 1961), with Fritz Senn (born in Basel in 1928) responsible for the translation of the excerpts from *FW*. The same excerpts, in Senn's renderings, would later be contained in the new and revised edition of Ellmann's biography in 1982.[16]

Senn (1967c, 232) quotes the final page (*FW* 627.34–628.16) from his own translation (Hess et al. 1961, 678), which includes the following lines (*FW* 627.34–628.4, 15–16):

Ich scheide hinaus. O bittres ende. Ich gleit hinaus bevor sie auf sind. Sie werden's nicht sehn. Noch wissen. Noch mich missen. Und 's ist alt und alt 's ist traurig und alt 's ist traurig und müde kehr ich zu dir, mein kalter vater, mein kalter irrer vater, mein kalter irrer schauriger vater, bis die nahsicht deines anblicks, dessen mühsame meilenweite, stöhnundtönend, mich seeschlamm salzsiech macht und ich treibe, mein einziger, in deine arme. ... Einweg allein zuletzt zuliebst entlang dem

Reichert (German, 1967)

The German Joyce scholar Klaus Reichert (born in Fulda in 1938) produced a German rendering of excerpts from the closing pages (*FW* 619.20–620.2, 626.35–628.16), delivered as part of a radio program of the Norddeutscher Rundfunk on 10 December 1967, under the title "Soft Morning, City," and subsequently published in Reichert's own volume of *Wake* essays *Vielfacher Schriftsinn* (1989d) and in Reichert and Senn's *Finnegans Wake Deutsch* (1989, 271–3, 320).

His rendering includes the following lines (*FW* 627.34–628.4, 15–16) from Anna Livia's final monologue:

Verscheid ich aus. Ach bittres ende! Ich mach mich ab bevor sie aufs. Sie werns nicht seen. Noch wissen. Noch mich vermissen. Und 's ist alt und

---

15 The following are the excerpts in question, rearranged here in the order in which they occur in Joyce's text: *FW* 4.1–3, 4.7–8, 26.25–7, 55.3–5, 115.21–36, 118.28–31, 120.9–14, 155.16–17, 171.4–6, 171.12–18, 175.27–8, 176.19–31, 179.24–9, 184.3–7, 185.27–186.9, 188.9–11, 188.13–17, 190.10–191.4, 192.20, 213.11–19, 219.1–6, 226.12–13, 237.11–12, 244.28–9, 301.14, 417.32–418.1, 423.14–18, 423.21–3, 423.25–31, 423.35–424.1, 473.22–4, 621.29–31, 627.13–628.16.

16 Ellmann's *James Joyce* (1959) was also translated into French by André Coeuroy in 1962 and into Italian by Piero Bernardini in 1964. Ellmann's new and revised edition of 1982 was translated into Italian by Piero Bernardini once again in 1982, into Spanish by Enrique Castro and Beatriz Blanco in 1982, into Polish by Ewa Krasińska in 1984, into Portuguese by Lya Luft in 1989, and into Italian again by Vittorio Santangelo in 2014.

alt ists trist und alt ists trist und erschöpft kehr ich zurück zu dir, mein
kalter vater, mein kalter irrer vater, mein kalter irrer fürchticher vater, bis
die nahsicht seines ahnblicks schon, die mühlen und mühlen davon, stöhn-
erdröhnend, mich seeschlick salzschlecht macht und ich stürz, mein einziger, in deine arm. ... Da hin da lein da letzt da liebt da lang m

Hildesheimer (German, 1967, 1969)

A German rendering by Wolfgang Hildesheimer (1916–91) of the opening two pages of I.8 (*FW* 196–7), with an introduction and commentary, was also broadcast in 1967 by the Norddeutscher Rundfunk and
also by the Sender Freies Berlin as part of a German radio series of
presentations on *FW*. A revised version of both the translation and the
substantial introduction appeared in print in 1969, marking the thirtieth anniversary of the appearance of *FW*. A further revised version
of this rendering appeared as part of his complete translation of *ALP*
published in 1970, to which we shall return.

Triesch (German, 1968)

In 1968 a German rendering by Manfred Triesch of various excerpts
from *FW* appeared in his translation of Anthony Burgess's *Here Comes
Everybody* (1965).

Schmidt (German, 1969)

In 1969, marking the thirtieth anniversary of the original appearance of
FW, some ten pages of selected excerpts, with extensive commentary,
appeared in German translation by the novelist Arno Schmidt (1914–
79).[17] The excerpts had originally been translated in 1960.

Born in Hamburg as the son of a police officer, on whose death he
moved as a fourteen-year-old with his mother to her home town near
Görlitz in eastern Germany, Schmidt attended secondary school and
subsequently a trade school in Görlitz. Initially employed in a clerical
position in a local textile firm, he was conscripted in 1939 to serve in
the German artillery and engineering corps. Released from British cap-
tivity in 1945, and living in considerable poverty, he began his literary

---

17 The translated excerpts in question are *FW* 63.20–64.21; 175.5–28; 182.28–184.10;
    244.1–245.4; 259.1–10; 403.1–406.21. These excerpts, supplemented by five further
    excerpts translated by Schmidt in 1960 (*FW* 30–1, 39, 142, 166–7, 308), appeared in
    1984 and were subsequently reprinted by Reichert and Senn (1989, 276–319).

endeavours with translations of Edgar Allan Poe, James Fenimore Cooper, and other English-language writers. His own earliest works of fiction, in the late forties and early fifties, quickly established him as an aggressively experimental writer. He settled in the late 1950s in the isolated hamlet of Bargfeld on the northern German Lüneburg Heath, which was eventually to become nothing short of a place of pilgrimage for his increasing numbers of admirers. Schmidt also wrote and broadcast widely and polemically on a number of both German and English authors. A literary autodidact, aggressively opinionated, and a determined solitary, he has come to be regarded by many as one of the most important modern German writers.

Having begun an intensive study of Joyce's work in the mid-fifties (Weninger 2012, 72), Schmidt made his name in German Joyce circles in 1957 with a scathing attack in a national newspaper, the *Frankfurter Allgemeine Zeitung*, on Georg Goyert's then thirty-year-old translation of *Ulysses*, eliciting an indignant response from Goyert, by then in his early seventies, who vigorously protested that his translation had after all been officially approved by Joyce himself. Schmidt then went on to translate Stanislaus Joyce's *My Brother's Keeper* (1959) and George Harris Healey's edition of *The Dublin Diary of Stanislaus Joyce* (1962). He appears to have read *FW* – which he referred to as *Finnegans Totenwacht* ("Finnegan's funeral wake") – for the first time in early 1960 (Rathjen 2009, 127), immediately translated some fifteen pages from it, and in typically idiosyncratic fashion came to understand it (or at least provocatively claimed to understand it) to be essentially a sustained 628-page polemic by Joyce against his brother Stanislaus. "According to Schmidt, James Joyce believed his brother had cuckolded him with Nora in Trieste during one of James's trips to Ireland, and *Finnegans Wake* was his form of revenge" (Weninger 2012, 72).

Whatever one may think of this remarkably reductive approach to Joyce's extremely complex text, Schmidt was obviously – and almost in spite of himself – immediately fascinated by *FW* and even made separate approaches to no fewer than six different West German publishers offering to translate the entire work over the space of three years at a very modest monthly stipend of 500 West German marks. He was forced to abandon the plan on being unable to obtain the agreement of any one of them, given the understandable likelihood at the time of dire financial consequences for any publisher.

A twenty-minute CD exists of a November 1961 radio essay by Schmidt in which he discusses *FW* and its translatability, while including a number of sample translated excerpts (Schmidt 2006). The essay was published in 1969 in a volume entitled *Der Triton mit dem*

Sonnenschirm ("the triton with the parasol," namely, Joyce), humorously adapting a phrase from the *Wake*: "how parasoliloquisingly true-toned" (*FW* 63.20), which also included most of his renderings from the *Wake*, amounting to the equivalent of roughly ten pages of Joyce's text.[18] Supplemented by a further five excerpts that first appeared in a facsimile edition of the actual typescript of his partial *Wake* translation (Schmidt 1984), they were reprinted twenty years later in Reichert and Senn's *Finnegans Wake Deutsch* (1989, 276–319). These are apparently the only examples of Schmidt's renderings that exist.

Schmidt's translations are not only fatally undermined in principle by his determinedly biographical reading of the text, but also distinctly idiosyncratic and, as has variously been argued, essentially much less translations than exercises in generating his own texts based on Joyce's originals. Among German Joyce scholars, Jörg Drews writes, however, that "despite all the objections which can be raised against these pages, they are ravishingly musical and rhythmical pieces of prose" (1977, 6). Fritz Senn writes that if a complete German rendering of *FW* were to have been undertaken in these years by anyone, Schmidt would have been the one person most obviously qualified to do so (1978b, 3). Klaus Reichert similarly finds that Schmidt's renderings potentially demonstrate just as powerful a command of the German language as Joyce's command of English and considers the missed opportunity of a complete rendering by Schmidt as an irreparable loss not just for German Joyce studies but for German literature as a whole (1989a, 16).[19]

Schmidt, for his part, was soon to achieve something close to literary cult status in Germany as the author of the massive and clearly *Wake*-inspired meganovel *Zettel's Traum* (1970; translated by John E. Woods as *Bottom's Dream*) – where the overtly ungrammatical presence of the apostrophe in the German title may certainly be read as a humorous intertextual reference to the *Wake*'s ostensibly ungrammatical absence of a similar titular apostrophe. *Zettel's Traum* indeed, as Jörg Drews writes, "can be considered the book with which Schmidt entered into competition with Joyce's *Finnegans Wake*" (1977, 7). Published by

---

18 *Der Triton mit dem Sonnenschirm: Großbritannische Gemütsergetzungen* (1969) contains, among pieces on several other writers, four essays on *Finnegans Wake*: "Der Triton mit dem Sonnenschirm. Überlegungen zu einer Lesbarmachung von *Finnegans Wake*"; "Das Buch Jedermann. James Joyce zum 25. Todestag"; "Kaleidoskopische Kollidier-Eskapaden"; "Der Mimus von Mir, Dir & den Mädies." See also Schmidt (1960, 1961, 1975, 1984, 2006).

19 "Es ist kaum auszudenken, welches Werk dadurch der deutschen Literatur verlorengegangen ist" (Reichert and Senn 1989, 16).

Stahlberg Verlag in Stuttgart in an edition of two thousand, the physically massive novel measures 17 inches high, 13 inches wide, 3 inches thick, and weighs 20 lbs. The text is an offset facsimile of the original 1,330-page typescript, corresponding to 5,320 pages in normal format. It cost 345 German marks to buy, an enormous sum at the time – and it sold out almost immediately. Schmidt's entirely extravagant book, followed by several others in similar vein before his untimely death in 1979, spurred the almost immediate formation among his admirers of an "Arno-Schmidt-Dechiffriergesellschaft," a vigorous and well-funded literary society devoted exclusively to the "deciphering" of Schmidt's works, especially the extraordinary later works. For many modern German readers, indeed, Arno Schmidt is unquestionably "the German Joyce" – the Joyce, that is to say, specifically of *Finnegans Wake*.[20]

Schmidt's renderings include a translation of the following lines (*FW* 30.11–22):

We are told how in the beginning it came to pass that like cabbaging Cincinnatus the grand old gardener was saving daylight under his redwoodtree one sultry sabbath afternoon, Hag Chivychas Eve, in prefall paradise peace by following his plough for rootles in the rere garden of mobhouse, ye olde marine hotel, when royalty was announced by runner to have been pleased to have halted itself on the highroad ... Forgetful of all save his vassal's plain fealty to the ethnarch Humphrey or Harold stayed not to yoke or saddle but stumbled out hotface as he was ...

Schmidt's version:

Wir vernehmen daselbst, wie es im Anfang geschah, daß – darin dem Kohl-Bauer Cincinnatus gleich – der große alte Gärtner das Tageslicht baß nützte, unter seinem Rotholzbaum (Sequoia immer-gigantea), und der Sabbath-Nachmittag war schwül, gleichsam Chevy-Jagd-Vorabend, und er schritt, in paradiesischem Vor-Falls-Frieden, dem Pfluge nach, rüsselnd und rodend, im Hinter-Garten von Mob-Haus, der altbekannten Seefahrer-Gaststätte, als durch einen Läufer verkündet wurde, einem Mitglied des Königlichen Hauses habe es gefallen, draußen auf der Landstraße zu halten ... Indem er über seiner offenbaren Vasallenpflicht als Lehnsmann

---

20 On Schmidt's renderings of excerpts from *FW*, see Anon. (1968), O'Neill (1974), Drews (1977), Senn (1978b), Rathjen (1995c, 2005, 2009, 2010, 2015b, 2019, 2020a), Hildesheimer (2006), Schmidt (2006), Eichhorn (2015). On Schmidt's overall reception of Joyce, see Drews (1977), Weninger (1982), Rathjen (2019, 2020a).

des Königs schlechthin Alles vergaß, versäumte Humphrey oder Harold sich nicht lange mit jochen und satteln; sondern stolperte hinaus, erhitzten Gesichts wie er war ... (Reichert and Senn 1989, 281)

Roughly back-translated:

We learn there how it came about in the beginning that, like the cabbage-farmer Cincinnatus, the great old gardener was putting daylight to better use, under his redwood tree (Sequoia ever-Gigantea), and the sabbath afternoon was sultry, as if on the eve of Chevy Chase, and he was striding, in paradisal pre-fall peace, after his plough, rooting and uprooting, in the back garden of Mob House, the well-known sailors' inn, when it was announced by a runner that a member of the Royal Household had been pleased to halt on the roadway. Completely forgetting everything but his clear feudal duty as a vassal of the king, Humphrey or Harold did not long delay with yoking and saddling, but stumbled out hot in the face as he was ...

Here Schmidt's grand old gardener was not just saving daylight but "putting daylight to better use"; his "Sequoia immer-gigantea" interlingually blends the technical names of *Sequoiadendron giganteum* (the giant redwood) and *Sequoia sempervirens* (the "evergreen" coast redwood); "Hag Chivychas Eve" is simplified (and loses HCE's initials) as merely "the eve of Chevy Chase"; rather than following his plough for rootles, HCE is alliteratively "rüsselnd und rodend" ("rooting and uprooting"); the specifically Dublin location of the "olde marine hotel" is lost as merely "the well-known sailors' inn"; and royalty is reduced to "a member of the Royal Household." The humorously quasi-Linnaean nomenclature of the redwood and the likewise humorously alliterative "rüsselnd und rodend" demonstrate Schmidt's evident translatorial willingness to improve on Joyce's text where it suits his own translatorial purposes.[21]

7 Romanian

Biberi (Romanian, 1965)

Arleen Ionescu reports that Romanian writers from the 1930s to the 1960s were in general much more familiar with French than with

---

21 For a detailed analysis (in German) of Schmidt's translatorial practice, see Senn (1978b).

English literature and culture, and that as a result Romanian translations of English-language texts were not infrequently made from a previous French translation rather than from the original (2012, 279–83). One noted Romanian writer and critic, for example, Ion Biberi (1904–90), whose own Joyce-inspired novel *Proces* appeared in 1935, produced a detailed critical study in the same year of Joyce's work, in which he cites (without translating) a passage from *ALP* taken not from the English but from Joyce's own French team rendering in the *Nouvelle Revue Française* in May 1931. In a second article on Joyce's use of interior monologue that appeared in 1965, a full thirty years later, Biberi returns to the same passage from *ALP*, this time translating a brief excerpt into Romanian, and doing so once again not from the original but from the French *ALP* (Ionescu 2012, 279–80).

The excerpt (which ends in an incomplete sentence) corresponds to *FW* 200.16–19 in Joyce's English *ALP*:

Anna Liv? As chalk is my judge! And didn't she up in sorgues and go and trot doon and stand in her douro, puffing her old dudheen, and every shirvant siligirl or wensum farmerette walking the pilend roads

Joyce's French team translation (Joyce et al. 1931) reads as follows:

Anna Livie que Gieu me juge! Et ne s'est-elle pas insorguée et mise a descendre à golo, puis à se tenir sur sa portenza tirant sur sa vieille bouflarde, et toutes les servantes à têtes de linottes, toutes les garcieuses fermierettes qui cheminaient sur les raderoutes de l'île

Biberi's Romanian version (Biberi 1965, 128; qtd. Ionescu 2012, 282):

Anna Livia, să mă ierte Giermnezeu! Nu s-a insorgat ea oare, începând să scoboare din abundapă şi să se oprească la portenţă, trăgând din chipă, şi toate servitoarele tâmpe, toate fermieretele graţilele care mergeau pe rad-drumurile insulei

Ionescu (2012, 282–3) repeats some of Biberi's own explanations for his choices: "Giermnezeu" rendering Joyce's French "Gieu" by conflating the French river Gier and *Dumnezeu* ("God"); "insorgat" conflating the French Sorgue and Joyce's French "insurgée"; "abundapă" rendering "à golo" by conflating *abundenţa* ("abundance") and *apă* ("water"); "portenţă" conflating Italian *porta* ("door") and Italian *partenza* ("setting out"); and so on. Ionescu asserts that despite the fact that Biberi produced his translation at a time when scholarship on *FW* was still very scant and imprecise, particularly in Romania, his rendering deserves to be considered an excellent one (2012, 283).[22]

Biberi's very brief rendering is the first Romanian translation of any part of *FW* to appear in print. Arleen Ionescu's suggestion elsewhere (2004, 217) that an anonymous Romanian rendering of an excerpt from Joyce's French *ALP* appeared in the journal *Cuvântul* in November 1931 is mistaken. The item in question is merely a brief notice of the appearance in Paris of the French *ALP*, with general comments on the difficulty of the language.[23]

8 Slovak

Kot (Slovak, 1965)

A Slovak translation by the writer Jozef Kot (born 1936) of the opening two pages (*FW* 3–5) appeared in Bratislava in the journal *Slovenské pohľady* (Slovak views) in 1965, under the title "Finnegannovo prebúdzanie," literally "Finnegan's awakening."

9 Czech

Urbánek (Czech, 1966)

Sonja Bašić reports a 1966 Czech translation by Zdeněk Urbánek in *Světová literatura* (Prague) of two passages from *FW* about HCE in a detailed analysis of Joyce's verbal technique (2004, 194).

10 Japanese

Osawa et al. (Japanese, 1966, 1968)

After Junzaburo Nishiwaki's version of the opening and closing pages of *ALP* (*FW* 196, 213–16) in 1933, no other Japanese rendering appeared for more than thirty years. In 1966, a Japanese team translation led by Masayoshi Osawa (1928–2020), professor of English at Chuo University in Tokyo, appeared of the opening two paragraphs of I.7 (*FW* 169–70), followed by further excerpts (*FW* 206–7, 418–19, 627–8) in 1968.

---

22 My thanks to Arleen Ionescu for further helpful advice in personal correspondence.

23 My thanks to Mihaela Manolache of the National Library of Romania for kindly sending me an electronic copy of the very brief item in question (Anon. 1931).

Eishiro Ito (2004) reports that the Osawa team's procedure for dealing with the multiple meanings of each Joycean phrase was to render the (apparent) surface meaning in readable Japanese text, while using endnotes to explain associated levels of meaning.[24]

11 Galician

Rodríguez (Galician, 1969)

Another new language made its entry into the *Wake* universe when the final paragraph of *ALP* (*FW* 215.31–216.5) appeared in Galician translation by Leopoldo Rodríguez in 1969 (in an article on the theoretical difficulty of translating *FW*) in the Galician literary journal *Grial* (Grail), published in Vigo, Spain. This was the first Galician rendering of any part of *FW* – and remained the only one until the appearance of Alberte Pagán's translation of the first two chapters in 1993, almost a quarter of a century later.

Rodríguez's Galician rendering, as reprinted by Francisco García Tortosa (1992, 119), includes the following lines (*FW* 215.31–5, 216.3–5):

> Non podo oir ren por mor das augas de. As correntes augas de. Os voantes morcegos, a barulleira charla dos ratos campesios. Ouh! ¿Te non fuches prá casa? ¿Qué Thom Malone? Non podo oir ren por mor do berrar dos morcegos, tódalas transparentes e Liffeyeiras augas de. ¡Ouh, conversa, sálvanos! Meu pé xa non voltará a selexar máis nunca. Síntome tan vella como o olmo de acolá. ¿Un conto contado de Shaun ou Shem? ... Dice-me, dice-me, dice-me, olmo. ¡Noitenoite!, contamenconto de cañota ou de pedra. Unda as rioeiras augas de, deiquiedacolá augas de. ¡Noite!

The Galician washerwoman can hear nothing with the noise (*mor*) of the waters (*augas*) of. Bats (*morcegos*) are flying (*voantes*) and bawling (*berrar*), field mice (*ratos campesios*) are making a racket (*barulho*). "Aren't you going home?" she asks, eliciting the now inexplicable reply "What Thom Malone?" Talk (*conversa*) save us, indeed, for "my foot will never be the same again." Tell me tale (*contamenconto*) of cane (*cañota*) or stone (*pedra*), by the rivering (*rioeiras*) waters of, waters from here (*deiqui*) and from there (*dacolá*). The simultaneous appearance of bats and mice is serendipitous – and even more obviously appropriate than

---

24 Masayoshi Osawa's team in the 1960s included Shigeru Koike, Junnosuke Sawasaki, and Motoi Toda.

it is in Joyce's original, for bats are "blind mice" in both Portuguese and Galician: *morcego* in both languages share the same etymological derivation as Spanish *murciélago*, originally *mur ciego* ("blind mouse") (Coromines 2012, 383).

12 Swedish

Lindegren

Among renderings of or from *FW* that might have been, but subsequently failed to materialize, is a possible version by Erik Lindegren (1910–68), a Swedish author, poet, and translator who by the late 1960s was generally considered to be modern Sweden's foremost experimental poet. His many translations included works of T.S. Eliot, Graham Greene, Dylan Thomas, and William Faulkner from English; Rainer Maria Rilke from German; and Saint-John Perse and Paul Claudel from French. Bertil Falk (2008, 143) reports a rumour once circulating in Sweden that Lindegren spent a period of time, probably in the early sixties, working on a Swedish rendering of a fragment from *FW*. The rendering, however, if it did once actually exist, does not seem to have ever appeared in print.[25]

---

25 My thanks to Bertil Falk for carrying out library research on this matter in Sweden – and for eventually confirming in personal correspondence that no published *FW* translation by Lindegren appears to exist.

Chapter Five

The 1970s

*1 German; 2 Japanese; 3 Spanish; 4 Italian; 5 Polish; 6 French;
7 Hungarian; 8 Russian; 9 Croatian*

Interest continued to be strong in the 1970s, with at least nine languages represented, including Russian and Croatian for the first time in each case. The most substantial results were in German and Japanese. Three separate complete German translations of *ALP* by Wolfgang Hildesheimer, by Hans Wollschläger, and by Georg Goyert, respectively, appeared in a single volume in 1970, and a Japanese translation by Yukio Suzuki et al. of *FW* I.1–3 appeared in 1971, the most extensive translation from *FW* in any language to that date. Briefer renderings appeared in Japanese by Masayoshi Osawa et al. (1970–2, 1978), in Spanish by Juan Benet (1971), by Ricardo Silva-Santisteban (1971), and by Mario Monteforte Toledo (1974), in Italian by Gianni Celati (1972) and by Anthony Burgess (1975), in Polish by Maciej Słomczyński (1972, 1973), in French by Stephen Heath and Philippe Sollers (1973) and by Simonne Verdin (1979), in Hungarian by Miklós Szentkuthy (1975), in Russian by Andrey Sergeev (1977), and in Croatian by Nada Šoljan (1978). Luigi Schenoni began work in 1974 on a planned complete Italian translation of *FW*, excerpts from which appeared in 1974, 1976, 1977, 1978, and 1979. Joyce and Frank's original Italian "Anna Livia Plurabella," without Settanni's unauthorized emendations of 1940, also appeared in 1979.

1 German

The 1970s opened with a major German contribution to the field of *ALP* translations, and thus also to that of *FW* translations in general, in the form of a Suhrkamp volume, edited by Klaus Reichert and Fritz Senn, containing three separate complete German renderings of *ALP*, by Wolfgang Hildesheimer, by Hans Wollschläger, and by Georg Goyert, whose complete original version of 1933 finally appeared in print after almost forty years. German thus became the first (and for more than twenty years the only) language to boast three separate complete renderings of *ALP*. Moreover, with a substantial introduction by Reichert, followed by the text of Joyce's original *ALP*, the three German *ALP*s, Ogden's Basic English *ALP*, and Joyce's own team-translated French *ALP*, the volume, which appeared in 1970, was by far the most significant contribution in any language to *ALP* and to *FW* translation studies as of that date.

The concept of a complete German rendering of the *Wake*, not just of *ALP*, had been in the air by that time for at least a decade. Possibly as a result of Arno Schmidt's promotional efforts, the Rhein Verlag of Zurich, the publisher of Goyert's translations of Joyce's earlier works, including *Ulysses*, is reported to have toyed briefly in the early 1960s with the possibility of a complete German rendering of *FW*, before abandoning it as financially impractical (Senn 1978b, 3). Some years later, in 1965, a resolution was adopted at an international congress of literary translators held in Hamburg that an annotated German rendering of *FW* should be undertaken as a matter of urgency (Senn 1967b, 216). In 1967 the Suhrkamp Verlag of Frankfurt am Main, which had meanwhile bought the translation rights for Joyce's work from the Südwest-Verlag, the successor of the Rhein Verlag, announced a new edition of Joyce's complete works in new German translations, and in 1969 Suhrkamp decided to explore the feasibility of eventually including in that edition a complete German rendering of *FW*.

To begin with, the plan was to commission two separate exploratory translations of *ALP* by Hildesheimer and Wollschläger, respectively, with the two translators under instructions from Siegfried Unseld, the director of the Suhrkamp Verlag, not to consult with each other. Their renderings duly appeared in the 1970 volume. Klaus Reichert later commented that the most interesting aspect of the two renderings is the degree to which they differ, both in their approach and in their results, with Hildesheimer concentrating on reproducing as nearly as possible the semantic layerings of the original and Wollschläger preferring to concentrate rather on reproducing Joyce's experiments in sound and rhythm – and eventually with hardly a single line in either rendering identical with the corresponding line in the other.[1]

---

1 "Diese 1970 erschienenen Übersetzungen sind insofern beispielhaft, als sie ent-
   gegengesetzte Wege gehen: Hildesheimer versuchte, in geradezu archäologischer

Hildesheimer's German ALP

Wolfgang Hildesheimer (1916–91), born of Jewish parents in Hamburg, had departed Hitler's Germany as a seventeen-year-old with his parents in 1933, travelling initially to England and then to Palestine, where his parents had decided to settle and where, initially with a view to a career in theatrical stage management, he completed an apprenticeship as a carpenter, cabinet maker, and stage decorator. Returning to England, he studied painting and stage design in London between 1937 and 1939, at which point he was posted back to Palestine as a British information officer. Returning to Germany after the war, he served from 1946 to 1949 as an interpreter for the American occupying forces during the Nuremberg War Crimes Trials.

While continuing throughout his life to exhibit his own paintings and sculptures (with considerable success), his first literary works began to appear in the early 1950s, to favourable critical reaction. After moving permanently to the small town of Poschiavo in southern Switzerland in 1957, he became one of the first German writers to experiment with the exciting new form of theatre later dubbed the Theatre of the Absurd (Esslin 1969, 224–6). He was awarded a number of literary prizes for his work during the fifties and sixties, especially the prestigious Büchner Prize in 1966 for his novel *Tynset* (1965), and achieved critical and popular success in 1977 with his bestselling biography *Mozart*. Previous translations by him included Sheridan's *School for Scandal* and Shaw's *Saint Joan*. Until his death in Poschiavo in 1991 he also served as one of the trustees of the Zurich James Joyce Foundation.

Among a number of radio features Hildesheimer wrote during the sixties, his rendering of the opening two pages of *ALP* (*FW* 196–7), with an introduction and commentary, was broadcast in 1967, as mentioned, as part of a German radio series of presentations on *FW*. A revised version of both the translation and the substantial introduction appeared in print in 1969, marking the thirtieth anniversary of the appearance of *FW*. A further revised version of that rendering appeared as part of his complete *ALP* translation of 1970. In a letter to fellow German writer Alfred Andersch, Hildesheimer "explicitly referred to his 'translation' as a 'vertical adaptation' rather than a direct word-for-word translation,

---

Abtragungs- und Rekonstruktionsarbeit, die Sinnschichten der Vorlage wiederzugeben; Wollschläger versuchte, vor allem einen rhythmisch-lautlichen Duktus zu finden. Das Ergebnis war, daß kein Satz der einen Fassung mit dem entsprechenden der anderen identisch ist" (Reichert 1989a, 16–17). For comparative discussions (in German) of the two renderings, see Reichert (1989d, 70–95), Blumenbach (1990, 32–40).

stressing that one is sometimes 'forced to find equivalents instead of translating literally'" (Weninger 2012, 75).[2]

A comparison of Hildesheimer's earlier and later renderings of *ALP* is of some interest. His 1969 version of the opening lines (*FW* 196.1–11) is as follows:

O / sag mir alles von / Anna Livia! Ich muß alles wissen / von Anna Livia. Na, du kennst Anna Livia. Gewiß, wir alle wissen von Anna Livia. Sag mir alles. Sag es mir gleich. Du kugelst dich, wenn du's hörst. Na, du weißt, als der alte Eiersack fehltrat und tat was du weißt. Ja, weiter, weiter, ich weiß. Etsch los und spree mich nicht an. Krempel hoch, laß die Redseele locker. Und steiß mich nicht – halt's Brett wenn du riffelst! Oder was das wohl war, was die drei sich erdachten, was den zweien er tat, da im Viechspark.

His version of the same lines in 1970, with his emendations in **bold** here:

O / sag mir alles von / Anna Livia! Ich muß alles **hören** / von Anna Livia. Na, **ihr kennt** Anna Livia? **Aber ja**, wir alle **kennen** Anna Livia. Sag mir alles. Sag es mir gleich. Du kugelst dich, wenn du's hörst. Na, du weißt, als der alte **Kjärl** fehltrat und tat, was du weißt. Ja, weiter, **das weiß ich**. Etsch los und spree mich nicht an. Krempel hoch, laß die Redseele locker. Und steiß mich nicht – **halt!** – wenn du riffelst. Oder was das wohl war, was die **Drei** sich erdachten, was den **Zweien** er tat, da im Viechspark. (qtd. Reichert and Senn 1970, 67)

In both versions the opening "O" captures the pun on French *eau* and suggests the notion of a circular structure. The German washerwoman wants to "know" (*wissen*) all about Anna Livia in 1969, but wants to "hear" (*hören*) all about her in 1970. She addresses her colleague in the informal singular (*du kennst*) in 1969, evoking the Austrian river Enns, but in the informal plural (*ihr kennt*) in 1970, evoking the English river Kent. In both versions, Hildesheimer's "Du kugelst dich, wenn du's hörst" humorously refers again to the concept of circularity, suggesting, colloquially, "You'll be doubled up," while a *Kugel* is literally a sphere, and any straight-line itinerary on the surface of a sphere returns to its point of origin. In 1969 the old cheb who went futt is an old bollocks (*Eiersack*), but in 1970 he is rather more restrainedly an old "Kjärl," a

---

2   On Hildesheimer's rendering, see Hildesheimer (1969), Gerber (1971), Reichert (1972), Blumenbach (1990, 32–40).

possibly disreputable old fellow (*Kerl*), but one whose epithet now reveals Scandinavian roots that may even suggest the noble blood of an earl (Norwegian *Jarl*) – or, of course, merely the inherited instincts of a pillaging Viking raider. In both versions, going futt, he "took a false step" (*fehltrat*).

In both versions, Hildesheimer's "Etsch los" combines a German *jetzt los* ("now just get on with it") and the Italian river Adige, known in German as the Etsch, while the warning "spree mich nicht an" combines a German *sprüh mich nicht an* ("don't splash me") and the German river Spree, thus also briefly enabling another doubling, as Berlin on the Spree stands in for Dublin on the Liffey. The specific reference to Dublin in Joyce's "dabbling" is compensated for by the translingual implication that residents of that city are also more often than not on the spree. The pointedly germanized "Etsch" rather than "Adige" will undoubtedly evoke for many German readers the fourfold fluvial associations of the anthem *Deutschland über alles*, which once (in a verse no longer included) celebrated the German homeland as stretching "from the Maas to the Memel, from the Etsch to the Belt."

The brisk instruction "krempel hoch" is a colloquial "roll 'em up," while "laß die Redseele locker" is based on a combination of *Seele* ("soul") and a back-formation from *redselig* ("chatty"), resulting in something like "let loose your love of gossip." As for the instruction "don't butt me ... when you bend," Hildesheimer humorously chooses to see "butt" as referring to a collision of rear ends rather than heads: his "Und steiß mich nicht ... wenn du riffelst" achieves the effect adroitly by a miscegenation of the verb *stoßen* ("to bump into") and the noun *Steiß* ("buttocks"), while "wenn du riffelst" suggests "when you're scrubbing" – his washerwomen thus presumably bending away from each other to scrub the clothes on the riverbank before turning back again to rinse them in the water. Joyce's "hike!" becomes "halt's Brett" ("hold onto your washboard") in the earlier version and a simpler and more accurate "halt!" ("whoa!") in 1970.

Joyce's final sentence reporting the dubious events in the dubious park is considerably simplified. The earlier and later renderings are identical (other than for a more standard use of capitals in 1970) and begin by evoking the serendipitously available river Oder. Opting for plain speaking, the rendering chooses to dispel some of the indeterminacy surrounding whatever happened in the park by including equally plain reference to the "three" ("die Drei") as well as the "two" ("den Zweien"). Hildesheimer's version, "Oder was das wohl war, was die Drei sich erdachten, was den Zweien er tat" back-translates as "or whatever it was that the three of them worked out for themselves that he did to the two." As for the park in question, it is simply the "Viechspark" ("swinish park"), with the phoenix disgustedly metamorphosed into a *Viech* ("swine, dirty animal"), a German colloquialism reserved for those who commit disgusting acts.

Hildesheimer's final paragraph of *ALP* includes the following lines (*FW* 215.31–5, 216.3–5), not part of the 1969 rendering:

> Hör nicht vor Wassern von. Die schliddernden Wasser von. Fliddermäus fledern, Feldratz rascht rausch. Hee! Bist du nicht heimgangen? Wen ein-fangen? Hör nicht vor Rattenrascheln, all am Liffeylauf Wasser von. Her, red steh uns bei! Mein Gebein gräbt sich ein. Ich fahl mich alt wie drüb die Ulme. Eine alte Mär von Shem und Shaun? ... Zähl mir, zähl mir, zähl mir, Elm! Nacht Nacht! Zähl mir Schicht von Stein und Stamm. Bei den flissernden Wassern von, den hinundherwissernden Wassern von. Nacht! (qtd. Reichert and Senn 1970, 96–7)

Here Hildesheimer's speaker, matching Joyce's dactyls, can't hear "vor Wassern von" ("for waters of"), waters slipping and sliding (*schliddern* "to slip, slide"). Rhyming "Fliddermäus fledern" allitera-tively, bats (*Fledermäuse*) fluttering and flittering. A field mouse (*Feld-maus*), compelled by alliteration to become a "Feldratz" ("field rat"), races (*rast*) and rustles (*rauscht*) out (*raus*) quickly (*rasch*). The question "Bist du nicht heimgangen?" ("Haven't you gone home?") is misheard as having to do with *einfangen* ("to catch, capture"): "Wen einfangen?" ("Catch *whom*?"). Nothing can now be heard above the rustling (*Ra-scheln*) of rats (*Ratten*), rather than fluttering bats, along the course of the Liffey ("Liffeylauf"). "Come (*her*), Lord (*Herr*), let talk (*Rede*) stand us in good stead ('steh uns bei'). My legs ('Gebein') are digging them-selves in (*gräbt sich ein*), are taking root."

"I feel as old as yonder elm" is rendered as "Ich fahl mich alt wie drüb die Ulme," with the verb *sich fühlen* ("to feel") conflated with the adjective *fahl* ("pale, wan"), while "drüb" conflates *drüben* ("yonder") and, given the failing light, *trüb* ("dim"). The "tale told" of Shaun or Shem becomes "eine alte Mär" ("an old tale") "von Shem und Shaun." The "elm" of "Tell me, tell me, tell me, elm!" is rendered as "Zähl mir, zähl mir, zähl mir, Elm," where "Elm" conflates German *Ulme* and English *elm*, while "zähl mir" is an apocopated version of *erzähle mir* ("tell me"), replicating Joyce's original play on /l/ and /m/. The rendering "Zähl mir Schicht," conflating *Schicht* ("layer") and *Geschichte* ("story"), points, appropriately for the context, to all his-tory (likewise *Geschichte*) as a layering of stories about other stories. "Stem or stone," meanwhile, becomes a reversed "Stein *und* Stamm" ("stone and stem"). The "rivering" waters, finally, once again match-ing Joyce's dactyls, are *flissernd*, conflating *Fluss* ("river"), *fließen* ("to flow"), and *flüstern* ("to whisper"), while the "hitherandthithering" waters run "hinundher" (colloquially, "hither and thither," literally, "thither and hither"), "wissernd," a conflation of *Wasser* and *wispernd* ("whispering").

Wollschläger's German ALP

Hans Wollschläger (1935–2007), born in the town of Minden, near Han-over in northern Germany, and subsequently a long-term resident of Bamberg in Bavaria, was originally a student of music, specializing in church organ music, before turning to literary pursuits, rather as Hildesheimer had turned from painting to literature. The polymath Wollschläger was a novelist, historian, essayist, and prize-winning translator, who translated numerous works from English to German, including Oscar Wilde's *An Ideal Husband* as well as novels of William Faukner, Raymond Chandler, and Dashiell Hammett. In the late 1960s, together with Arno Schmidt, he translated the complete works of Edgar Allan Poe, and he was later also one of the editors of a complete critical edition of the works of Karl May, a popular German writer of iconic sta-tus. His musical interests continuing, he also composed three complete symphonies, though none of them appears to have been performed. His collected writings are to be issued in a twelve-volume edition by the Wallstein Verlag of Göttingen.

Five years after his rendering of *ALP*, Wollschläger was to become very highly regarded in German Joycean circles for his award-winning translation of *Ulysses* (1975), on which he was in fact already also engaged while undertaking the translation of *ALP* and which was widely regarded as replacing Georg Goyert's version of almost half a century before. His *Ulysses* translation, as it happens, was much later, after Wollschläger's death, to become a literary *cause célèbre* in German publishing circles. A planned revision for the Suhrkamp Verlag of the 1975 rendering, undertaken after more than thirty years and involving a decade of highly detailed work on the part of a team of translators and advisors led by the German Joyce scholar Harald Beck, was ready for publication in 2018 – only to have general publication abruptly blocked by an unanticipated copyright challenge by Wollschläger's legal heir. Despite sustained and vehement objection on the part of the German-language Joyce community, only two hundred copies of the revised translation were allowed to be published for deposit in libraries and research institutes.

Wollschläger's opening lines of *ALP* (*FW* 196.1–11) read as follows:

O / erzähl mir alles von / Anna Livia! Ich will alles hören / von Anna Livia. Ach, du kennst Anna Livia? Ja doch, klar, wir alle kennen Anna Livia. Erzähl mir alles. Erzähl's mir jetzt. Dich trifft der Schlag, wenn du's hörst. Also, du weißt doch, wie der alte Sack futtsch ging und tat, was du weißt. Ja, ich weiß, mach weiter. Wasch nur flott und laß das Gedabble. Stock auf die Ärmel und lockre die Stimmstrippen. Und bocks mich nicht – aua! – wenn du dich bückst. Also was denn auch ilmer sie ausdrifteln wollten, daß er's bezwockt hätt im Faunix-Park. (qtd. Reichert and Senn 1970, 101)

Both Hildesheimer's and Wollschläger's German versions want to be "told" all about Anna Livia, with Hildesheimer opting for the neutral verb *sagen*, Wollschläger preferring the less neutral verb *erzählen*, the former implying primarily the transfer of information (the primary meaning of *sagen* being "to say"), the latter evoking the importance of storytelling (the primary meaning of *erzählen* being "to tell a story") and thus of fictionality. Wollschläger's speaker, like the later Hildesheimer's, wants to "hear" (*hören*) all rather than know all. Like the earlier Hildesheimer, however, Wollschläger has his washerwoman address the other by the singular pronoun *du*. River names are already well represented: the Austrian Enns ("kennst"), French Enne ("kennen"), and Swedish Klar ("doch klar"), while the implied aquatic reference in Joyce's interjection "well" is well echoed by Wollschläger's interjection *ach* evoking several German and Austrian rivers named Ach and Ache. The German river Weiss is triply present.

"You'll die when you hear" is rendered by Wollschläger as "Dich trifft der Schlag," literally "You'll have a stroke," on hearing about the "old geezer" ("der alte Sack"), who simply "lost it" ("futtsch ging"). The second washerwoman is advised to "just wash quickly" ("Wasch nur flott") and "leave off the dabbling" ("laß das Gedabble"), with the formulation retaining the reference to the English Wash while also hinting obliquely at Dublin. The phrase "stock auf die Ärmel" conflates the German verb *aufstecken* ("to tuck up") and hinted references to such bodies of water as the German river Stockach and the French Étang du Stock in achieving an audible translingual echo of the English *tuck*. Wollschläger's "lockre die Stimmstrippen" plainly suggests "loosen your vocal cords," while "bocks mich nicht ... wenn du dich bückst" (roughly, "don't bang into me when you bend over") both saves the original alliteration linking butting and bending and also associates the English verb *butt* with the German noun *Bock* ("goat"). The invented verb "bocks" manages to include the goat, the German verb *boxen* ("to box"), and a fluvial nod to the American Box Creek. The exclamation "aua!" translates literally as "ouch!" – and we may note that German *aua* is an almost exact homophone of the Irish *abha* ("river"), while simultaneously invoking two separate Aua rivers, one in Canada and one in Sudan.

The complex final sentence is rendered as "Also was denn auch ilmer sie ausdrifteln wollten, daß er's bezwockt hätt." This back-translates roughly as "Or whatever it was they wanted to cobble together that he was intending to do," where the phrase *was auch immer* ("whatever") is made to act as host for the German river Ilm, the verb *austüfteln* ("to cobble together") is made to incorporate a dialect form *dri* ("three"), and "bezwockt" is a combination of *bezweckt* ("intended") and a dialect form *zwo* ("two"). The park in question, meanwhile, is the "Faunix-Park," with the phoenix now conflated with a sex-obsessed satyr (German *Faun*), a fluvial hint of the Irish Faughan River, and a translingual historical reminder (English *fawn*) that the Phoenix Park was once a deer park.

From Wollschläger's final paragraph of *ALP* (*FW* 215.31–5, 216.3–5):

Kaum hör ich mehr bei den Wassern der. Den schütternden Wassern der. Fleddernd Gewisch, Felldmäus' vergraulen 's Geplausch. Ho! Warst du noch nicht davon? Was, Richter John? Kaum hör'ch mehr beim graulen Gemausel, all die liffeygen Wasser der. Ho, hör redd uns! Die Füß so müß. Alt ist es mir wie yonner Stamm. Ein' Flußtermär von Shaun oder Shem? ... Raun mir, raun mir, raun mir, Baum! Nacht Nacht! Mehrmirmär von Stamm und Stoan. Zuseiten den flüssernden Wassern der, lispelndundwispernden Wassern der. Nacht! (qtd. Reichert and Senn 1970, 133)

Wollschläger's "Kaum hör ich mehr bei den Wassern der" ("I can hardly hear any more with the waters of") is structured as a triple dactyl: "*Kaum* hör ich | *mehr* bei den | *Wassern* der." These waters, no longer gently lapping or whispering, are now pouring (*schütten*) along furiously, shattering (*erschütternd*) in their impact. A play on *Fledermaus* ("bat") and *Flederwisch* ("feather duster") suggests unnamed feathery things whizzing and whishing (*wischen*) about, fluttering (*flatternd*) and possibly even plundering (*fleddernd*). "Felldmäus'," meanwhile, field mice (*Feldmäuse*) comfortable in German fur (*Fell*) as opposed to shivering French "bald mice" (*chauves-souris*) put paid (*vergraulen* "to scare off") to any chit-chat ("Geplausch"), bawk talk.

In Wollschläger's rendering, the washerwoman's "Warst du noch nicht davon?" ("Weren't you gone already?"), misheard, elicits "Was,

Richter John?" ambiguously meaning either "What? Judge John?" or "What? John Richter?" or both. Little can be heard (*hören* "to hear"), listening (*horchen* "to listen") to the bawling (*graulen*) of the grey (*grau*) hordes of mice ("Gemausel") at their scheming (*Gemauschel*), by the liffeying ("liffeygen") waters. "Hear (*höre*), Lord (*Herr*), speak to us (*rede uns*), save us (*rette uns*). My feet (*Füße*) are so idle (*müßig*), so futile (*müßig*), like mush (*Mus*)."

"I feel as old as yonder elm" is rendered as "Alt ist es mir wie yonner Stamm," with Joyce's elm (German *Ulme*) become a less specific "Stamm" ("stem"). The adjective "yonner" conflates German *jener* ("that") and English *yonder*, while the "tale told" of Shaun or Shem becomes a "Flußtermär," a tale (*Mär*) conflating *Fluss* ("river") and *flüstern* ("to whisper"). Joyce's play on /l/ and /m/ in "Tell me, tell me, tell me, elm" becomes a play on /r/ and /m/ instead in "Raun mir, raun mir, raun mir, Baum," which also emphasizes the assonance of *raunen* ("to whisper") and the hyperonymous *Baum* ("tree"). Joyce's conflated "telmetale" is rendered by Wollschläger, continuing the play on /r/ and /m/, as "mehrmirmär," literally "more (*mehr*) me tale (*Mär*"), while the tale of "stem or stone" becomes one of "Stamm und Stoan," the latter invention conflating German *Stein* ("stone") and English *stone*. The "rivering" waters, finally, are "flüssernd" for Wollschläger, conflating *Fluss* ("river"), *fließen* ("to flow"), and *flüstern* ("to whisper"), while the "hitherandthithering" waters are now "lispelndundwispernd," the river *lispelnd* ("whispering") and *wispernd* ("whispering").[3]

Hildesheimer, Wollschläger, Goyert

Hildesheimer's rendering appears under the untranslated title "Anna Livia Plurabelle." Wollschläger's appears under the more baroque "Anna Livia Plurabelle / parryotphrosed myth brockendootsch," humorously characterizing his rendering as parroted from Joyce's English, paraphrased into prose with bits (*Brocken*) of broken German, thus putting into practice Joyce's suggestion of "swobbing broguen eeriesh myth brockendootsch" (*FW* 70.4). Goyert's version appears as "Anna Livia Plurabella," and since it was not part of the Suhrkamp plan to establish if a German rendering of the entire *FW* could be considered a possibility, it is printed in a smaller font as an appendix, serving essentially just as background material to the two modern renderings. While

---

3 On Wollschläger's rendering, see Gerber (1971), Reichert (1972), Blumenbach (1990, 32–40).

this is not an unreasonable procedure in the context of the Suhrkamp plan, for many readers it may well convey the impression that Goyert's version is of an inferior quality. While Goyert's rendering undoubtedly lacks to a considerable degree the sophistication of the two later versions, however, it also, as I have suggested in a previous chapter, has its own significant claims to our favourable attention.

Hildesheimer's rendering, as commentators have observed, tends in general to make Joyce's text rather easier for the German reader, while Wollschläger's version is in many instances even more complicated than Joyce's original. Friedhelm Rathjen also observes that Wollschläger's rendering follows Joyce's text more closely than does Hildesheimer's (Rathjen 2020b, 86n6). Despite the generally recognized high quality of both renderings, however, the Suhrkamp Verlag eventually decided against the daunting prospect (both financially and otherwise) of undertaking a complete German *Wake*. When a Suhrkamp edition of Joyce's collected works in German translation appeared in a six-volume study edition in 1987, edited by Klaus Reichert and Fritz Senn, it did indeed include a final volume dedicated entirely to *FW* – but the text was Joyce's original text, as if a complete German rendering were simply not something that could reasonably be envisaged (O'Neill 2005, 56–7).

German (1977–8)

Over the course of twelve months, from December 1977 to November 1978, the German broadcasting network Norddeutscher Rundfunk presented a series of six radio programs on *FW*. Five of these programs involved German translations of very brief excerpts from the *Wake*, together with an extensive commentary in each case. The translators involved included Uwe Herms (*FW* 17, 18, 66, 68), Ulrich Sonnemann (*FW* 429–30, 431), Erich Fried (*FW* 403–4), Peter von Haselberg (*FW* 593), and Fritz Senn (*FW* 176–7).[4] Some of the contributions later appeared in print: Herms (1985), Fried (1985), Sonnemann (1995).

2 Japanese

Suzuki et al. (Japanese, 1971)

Japanese was strongly represented during the seventies. A significant publishing event occurred in 1971, when the first three chapters of

---

4   This information is taken from Friedhelm Rathjen (2012b, 296–300).

the *Wake*, more than seventy pages altogether (*FW* 3–74), appeared in Tokyo in a Japanese team translation led by Yukio Suzuki, a professor of English at Waseda University in Tokyo. Published under the title *Finnegan tetsuya-sai* ("Finnegan's wake"), and running to 245 pages of Japanese text, this was the most extensive rendering from *FW* to that date not only in Japanese but in any other language. It was also the most substantial move beyond the pages of *ALP* of any rendering in any language to that point.[5]

Eishiro Ito (2004) reports that Suzuki's translation employed essentially the same procedure as had the Japanese team translation led by Masayoshi Osawa of the opening two paragraphs of I.7 (*FW* 169–70) in 1966, followed by further excerpts (*FW* 206–7, 418–19, 627–8) in 1968. That procedure involved rendering the most immediately apparent surface meaning in readable standard Japanese, while using notes to explain related overtones and levels of meaning.

Osawa et al. (Japanese 1970–2, 1978)

Masayoshi's Osawa's Japanese team was in the meantime continuing their work, and their translation of the first twelve pages of *ALP* (*FW* 196–208), serialized in seven numbers of the Japanese journal *Kikan Paedeia* (Paedeia quarterly) between 1970 and 1972, was appearing at the same time as Suzuki's team rendering of the first three chapters. Their rendering of five further excerpts (*FW* 169–70, 206–7, 418–19, 593, 627–8) was to appear in the journal *Sekai no Bungaku* (World literature) in Tokyo in 1978.[6]

3 Spanish

Silva-Santisteban (Spanish, 1971)

In Spanish, a rendering of the final pages (*FW* 626–8) by the Peruvian poet and academic Ricardo Silva-Santisteban appeared in the journal *Creación y crítica* (Creation and criticism), published in Lima, in 1971.

---

5 Members of Yukio Suzuki's team included Ryo Nonaka, Koichi Konno, Kayo Fujii, Tazuko Nagasawa, and Naoki Yanase. On the translation, see Suzuki (1983).

6 Members of Masayoshi Osawa's team included Kyoko Ono, Shigeru Koike, Junnosuke Sawasaki, and Kenzo Suzuki in 1970–2, joined by Motoi Toda in 1978.

Benet (Spanish, 1971)

The Spanish novelist Juan Benet (1927–93), meanwhile, is one of the few translators of *FW* who undertook a rendering of selected lines in order to demonstrate that trying to do so is in fact a pointless undertaking. Benet is regarded by some critics as one of the most significant Spanish writers of the twentieth century. He is widely noted for his complex and experimental style and is often mentioned in the international company of such writers as Proust, Joyce, and Faulkner. Benet, a civil engineer by profession, and who made his mark as a novelist in the 1960s, insisted that literature should be more about style than about telling stories or framing persuasive arguments, and Joycean echoes have frequently been noted in his work. While acknowledging the presence of such echoes, however, Benet also openly stated his provocative opinion that Joyce was in fact essentially just a minor writer obsessed by the possibilities of stylistic detail. Benet, as Marisol Morales Ladrón observes, clearly "failed to understand the implications of Joycean aesthetics" (2004, 441).

Benet demonstrated a particularly negative attitude towards *Finnegans Wake*. In his prologue to a 1971 Spanish translation of Stuart Gilbert's *James Joyce's Ulysses* he reportedly produced a Spanish rendering of the first two paragraphs of the *Wake* (*FW* 3.1–14) – but only in order to demonstrate that Joyce's much-lauded text is not only untranslatable but also not worth the effort of attempting to do so in the first place. Darío Villanueva quotes Benet's commentary, which asserts that if one discounts the "cryptogrammatical" Joycean overlay, all that remains is a *cuadro de costumbres*, a mere uninspired description of local day-to-day happenings, involving the not very interesting dream of an innkeeper obsessed by trivial details, by his growing children, and by a wife he no longer finds desirable.[7]

Monteforte (Spanish, 1974)

Excerpts from *FW* in Spanish translation by the Guatemalan writer and politician Mario Monteforte (1911–2003) appeared in Mexico City in 1974 in a cultural supplement, *La cultura en México*, of the Mexican political weekly *Siempre!*.

---

7 "si se le despojara de su investidura criptogramática, quedaría reducido a un cuadro de costumbres, el sueño de un tabernero que está obsesionado por las pequeñas cosas que le rodean, un negocio, unos hijos y una mujer que ya no le atrae" (Benet 1971, 19; quoted by Villanueva 1993, 7).

4 Italian

Celati (Italian, 1972)

An Italian translation by Gianni Celati (born 1937) of excerpts from the Willingdone Museyroom vignette (*FW* 8–10) appeared in 1972 in the journal *Il Caffè*, in a form of Italo-Wakese based on the Venetian dialect.[8] Celati, born in the northern Italian town of Sondrio, graduated from the University of Bologna with a doctoral thesis on *Ulysses* supervised by the Italian scholar and translator of English literature Carlo Izzo (1901–79). Celati's first book, *Comiche* (1970), introduced by Italo Calvino, had just appeared. Subsequently the author of numerous novels, he taught at the University of Bologna, and also in the United States at Cornell and Brown universities. Authors he has translated from English include Swift, Melville, and Mark Twain; authors he has translated from French include Stendhal, Céline, Perec, and Barthes. Crowning his translatorial career at the age of seventy-six, his new rendering of *Ulysses* (the fourth Italian version of that text) appeared in 2013.[9]

Schenoni (Italian, 1974–82)

Meanwhile, Italian translations of almost a dozen mostly short excerpts from *FW* by Luigi Schenoni, amounting to more than thirty pages in all, appeared between 1974 and 1982, most but not all of them taken from *FW* I.1, as part of his planned complete rendering of *FW*, on which he would work unremittingly for the next three decades – and the first four chapters of which (*FW* I.1–4) would appear in the Joyce centenary year of 1982.[10]

Burgess (Italian, 1975)

An Italian version of the first two paragraphs (*FW* 3.1–14) by the British novelist Anthony Burgess (1917–93) appeared in the *Times Literary Supplement* in 1975. While the rendering is only fourteen lines long,

---

8 On Celati's rendering, see Del Pozzo (1982, 156), Zanotti (2006, 1), Sullam (2017, 6).

9 *Ulysses* was translated into Italian by Giulio de Angelis in 1960, by Bona Flecchia in 1995, by Enrico Terrinoni and Carlo Bigazzi in 2012, and by Gianni Celati in 2013.

10 The excerpts in question appeared in 1974 (*FW* 4.18–5.4), 1976 (*FW* 21.5–23.15), 1977a (*FW* 15.29–18.16, 23.16–29.36), 1977b (*FW* 30.1–32.19), 1978a (*FW* 35.1–42.16), 1978b (*FW* 35.1–36.34), 1978c (*FW* 3.1–10), 1979a (*FW* 8.9–10.23), 1979b (*FW* 55.3–62.25), 1982a (*FW* 85.20–86.31).

Burgess's involvement is arguably of particular interest especially for English-language Joyceans.

Like two previous translators of *FW* into Italian, Joyce himself in 1940 and Juan Rodolfo Wilcock in 1961, Burgess was not an Italian. By 1975 he had accumulated substantial Joycean credentials, having already written three books on *Wake*-focused aspects of Joyce's work. In the first, *Here Comes Everybody: An Introduction to James Joyce for the Ordinary Reader* (1965), Burgess sets out to make Joyce's works accessible to those who, he says, have been scared off by the aura of difficulty created by academic Joyceans. In the second, *A Shorter Finnegans Wake* (1966), he reduces Joyce's text by two thirds, his aim being to provide what he considered to be the gist of the text by giving the reader lengthy extracts from the *Wake* connected by short pieces of running commentary. In the third, *Joysprick: An Introduction to the Language of James Joyce* (1973), he takes on the subject of Joyce's language itself. Subsequently, in 1982, to celebrate the centenary of Joyce's birth, the BBC commissioned a musical version from him of Joyce's *Ulysses*, entitled *The Blooms of Dublin*.

Burgess, who was born John Anthony Burgess Wilson in Manchester in 1917, graduated from Victoria University of Manchester in 1940 with a degree in English language and literature, though having originally planned to study music. After six years in the British Army, working mainly in the Royal Army Educational Corps (RAEC), and a further eight years as a teacher in England, he joined the British Colonial Service and was posted to Malaya as an education officer. His first published novels, dating from 1956, were based on his experiences in Malaya. After a further posting in Brunei, he returned to England in 1959 and became a full-time writer. A trip to Leningrad in 1961 inspired the Russian-based teen slang Nadsat used in his best-known novel, *A Clockwork Orange* (1962), which was adapted into a controversial film by Stanley Kubrick in 1971.

Burgess, who also lectured on linguistics at the University of Birmingham in the later 1940s, had considerable competence not only in several European languages, but also in Malay and Persian. He reportedly translated a selection of English literature into Malay and Eliot's *The Waste Land* into Persian, though both of these renderings remained unpublished. Extraordinarily prolific, by 1975 he was already the author of some twenty novels (to which he added another thirty or so before his death). He was also by that time the composer of several dozen musical works, including two full-length symphonies, and was a regular writer of cheerfully opinionated articles as literary critic for both the *Observer* and the *Guardian* newspapers.

The brief translation was a collaborative venture with Burgess's second wife, who, as it happens, was an Italian. Liana Burgess (1929–2007) was born Liliana Macellari in Civitanova on the Italian Adriatic coast, reportedly taught herself English initially by reading the intricately written novels of Henry James (Hawtree 2017), and later studied at the University of Bologna, the University of Paris, and Mount Holyoke College in the United States. Fascinated, like Burgess, with languages and linguistics, she subsequently lectured in linguistics at King's College, Cambridge, and became an award-winning translator from English into Italian, including works of Henry James, Thomas Pynchon, and Lawrence Durrell as well as an acclaimed version of Burgess's own *Malayan Trilogy* (1956–9). Burgess married Macellari in 1968 after the death of his first wife, and shortly afterwards they left England and lived in Malta, Rome, and the United States, before eventually settling in Monaco, where Burgess would eventually be a co-founder of the Princess Grace Irish Library.

Burgess and his new wife, as enthusiastic fellow linguists, began to work on the *FW* translation soon after they wed. He wrote in one of his columns in the *Times Literary Supplement* in 1970 that "our preliminary work on this is already showing, as it was bound to, that the resultant book – if it ever appears – will be less a translation than a sort of free Italian fantasy on Joyce's themes." Moreover, "the translation is bound to move away more and more from the Liffey to the Tiber, and Joyce will end as truly Giacomo. The book will be a ghost of what Joyce might have written had he conceived *Finnegans Wake* in Italian" (1970, 1025). It is clear that Burgess at this point was thinking of a relatively extended translation, perhaps even of the entire *FW* – or, rather more likely, perhaps, of some version of his own *Shorter Finnegans Wake*.

Writing in *American Scholar* two years later, in 1972, Burgess reports once again that he and his wife were continuing to work on translating "the text of *Finnegans Wake*" into Italian: "Our working title, by the way, is 'pHorbiCEtta': *forbicetta* means 'earwig'; there you see Humphrey Chimpden Earwicker's initials sticking out of the word; he addresses the world, *orbi*; he is both pope and insect" (1972, 141). Three years later still, in the 1975 *TLS* piece, Burgess writes, distancing himself with asperity from those numerous contemporary Italian authors whom he considers to be more interested in politics than in literature, that "an Englishman will, notoriously, do things with a foreign language that a native speaker would be shocked to dream of doing, and I have no shame in twisting the language of Dante into the first Italian oneiroglott" (1975, 1296).

Two different obituaries in major British newspapers following Liana Burgess's death in 2007 suggest that it may in fact have been she rather than Burgess himself who "began an ambitious translation of James Joyce's *Finnegans Wake* under the title 'pHorbiCEtta'"(Anon. 2007; Hawtree 2007). Her role is significantly downplayed, however, in Burgess's 1975 account, and her name does not appear as having been involved in the translation. Moreover, and distinctly oddly, Burgess, deliberately or otherwise, makes no reference at any point to the fact that Joyce himself had emphatically preceded him by more than three decades in "twisting the language of Dante" into an even earlier "oneiroglott," namely, that of the Italian "Anna Livia Plurabella" published in *Prospettive* in 1940. No reference is made either to the 1961 Italian rendering of some forty pages from *FW* by Juan Rodolfo Wilcock.

Repeating that he uses "the provisional title *pHorbiCEtta*, which has HCE addressing the same world as His Holiness but still ending up as a *forbicetta* or earwig" (1975, 1296), Burgess then presents the fourteen lines so far produced, the result, relatively slight though it may be physically, of what he describes as nothing less than "murderous labour." Though Burgess – and his wife to a finally indeterminate degree – spent several years of intermittent work on the project, the translation does not seem to have progressed beyond the opening fourteen lines. A file in the Anthony Burgess Foundation Archives in Manchester entitled "pHorbiCEtta" (and available online) contains only draft material related to the opening page of *FW*, with no suggestion that any further continuation of the translation was undertaken – a not particularly surprising fact given the frenetic pace of Burgess's other continuing endeavours both literary and non-literary.[11]

Burgess's rendering of the opening three lines (*FW* 3.1–3) is as follows:

filafiume, dopo da Eva ed Adamo, da giro di riva a curva di baia, ci riconduci per un vico giambattistamente comodo di ricirculazione al Chestello di Howth e dintorni.

Burgess's alliterative one-word "filafiume" is literally "flowriver," while Eve and Adam retain their Joycean order. His "giro" and "curva" are "turn" and "curve," respectively, and the phrasing, for the ear of an English speaker, constitutes a pleasing dactylic tetrameter: "da | *gi*ro di | *ri*va a | *cur*va di | *ba*ia." Burgess makes sure that his readers

---

11   The file is available at https://archiveshub.jisc.ac.uk/data/gb3104-ab/ab/arch/a/ pho/1.

will not miss the reference to Giambattista Vico (and to Commodus) by making his "vico" not just "comodo" but "giambattistamente comodo." HCE's initials are not only present but doubly present by replacing *castello* ("castle") with "*che*stello," thus economically achieving a double CHE.

The rendering continues (*FW* 3.4–10):

Signore Tristano, violatore d'amori, d'attraverso il mare corto, non aveva ancora gettato dell' Amorica del Nord sul cisistmo scosceso dell' Europa Minore per rimuovere la sua guerra penisulata; neppure i sassoni tomsawyereschi huckfinneschi sul ruscello Oconee ci erano esagerati ai gorghi gorgolianti di Laurens County (Gorgia) quando sempre sempre dubilavano il loro proprio Dublino; neppure una voce di fuocofuori aveva soffiettato mishe mishe a tauftauf tu es Pietrorbiera;

Here Signore Tristano had not yet dropped anchor (*gettato ancora*) again (*ancora*) to "renew" (*ri-muovere*) his penisolate war. Nor had the "sassoni tomsawyereschi huckfinneschi" exaggerated themselves to the "gorghi gorgolianti" ("gurgling whirlpools") of a Laurens County now situated not in Georgia but in "Gorgia," a land presumably of gorges as well as whirlpools – and whose inhabitants speak with a noticeable accent (Italian *gorgia* "burr, brogue"). Here *sassoni* means "large stones" but also puns on *Sassoni* as meaning "Saxons," which in Irish and Scottish usage, as "Sassanachs," means "English" and may thus perhaps be taken as indicating the irremediable foreignness of the rocks in question, albeit adjectivally qualified as both "tomsawyereschi" and, for good measure, "huckfinneschi" as well, which is to say, "à la Tom Sawyer and Huck Finn," the latter permitting a passing reference also to Joyce's Finn. The expansive phrasing here is reminiscent of his similarly expansive "giambattistamente comodo," suggesting in both cases a putative system of what one might call infixed annotation. The presence of peat is flamboyantly celebrated in "tu es Pietrorbiera," conflating a Latin *tu es* ("thou art"), an Italian *Pietro*, a likewise Italian *torbiera* ("peatbog"), and a definite hint of a papal greeting to the city and the world, *urbi et orbe*, adding up to an Italian Pope Peter Peatbog – and lacking any hint of an Irish Patrick.

Joyce and Frank (Italian, 1979)

The Italian seventies ended with the long-delayed appearance in 1979 of Joyce and Frank's original Italian version of *ALP*, stripped of Settanni's 1940 emendations and edited by the French scholar of Italian studies Jacqueline Risset, in a volume devoted to Joyce's collected early writings in Italian, the *Scritti italiani*, edited by Gianfranco Corsini and Giorgio Melchiori and published by Mondadori in Milan.

5 Polish

Słomczyński (Polish, 1972, 1973)

In 1972, in a volume of his Polish translations of selected excerpts from Joyce's work as a whole, Maciej Słomczyński, whose celebrated Polish translation of *Ulysses* had appeared in 1969, published a rendering of "The Ballad of Persse O'Reilly" (*FW* 44.22–47.29) and an excerpt from II.4 (*FW* 398–9). The following year, in 1973, he published two translated excerpts from *ALP*, the opening and closing pages (*FW* 196–202, 215–16), in the literary monthly *Literatura na Świecie* (Literature in the world). Słomczyński's complete rendering of *ALP*, to which we shall return, would appear only twelve years later, in 1985.

6 French

Heath and Sollers (French, 1973)

A collaborative French translation by the English literary critic and theorist Stephen Heath of the University of Cambridge and the French novelist, literary theorist, and *FW* enthusiast Philippe Sollers (born 1936 in Bordeaux) of excerpts from the final chapter (*FW* 593.1–594.9, 596.34–598.16, 626.35–628.16) appeared in 1973 in the avant-garde literary journal *Tel Quel*, founded and edited by Sollers himself.[12]

Their rendering (1973, 23–4) includes the following lines (*FW* 627.34–628.4, 15–16):

Je passe. O fin amère! Je filerai avant qu'ils se lèvent. Ils ne verront jamais. Ne sauront jamais. S'en rendront pas compte. Et c'est vieille et vieille, c'est triste et vieille c'est triste et fatiguée que je reviens à toi, mon froid fou férieux vieux vie père, jusqu'à voir simplement de près sa grandeur, des moilieux, des moilieux, gémoinissonnant, mal de mer vaisselle et je cours, mon unique, dans tes bras. ... Allez voie le seul dernier l'aimé le long le

---

12 On Heath and Sollers's rendering, see Topia (1990).

Verdin (French, 1979)

A French version by the Belgian Mallarmé scholar Simonne Verdin of excerpts from the closing pages (*FW* 627–8) appeared in Brussels in 1979 in the *Courrier du Centre International d'Études Poétiques* of the Belgian Bibliothèque Royale.

Her rendering (1979, 25) also includes the following lines (*FW* 627. 34–628.4, 15–16):

> Je vais à vau-l'eau. Oh, l'amère fin! Je filerai avant qu'ils soient levés. Ils ne verront jamais. Ni sauront. Sans regret. Et c'est vieux et vieux, c'est triste, et vieille et triste et lasse je retourne à toi, mon père froid, mon père froid, fou, mon père froid, fou, d'effroi. D'être contre, nêtrencontre, lui, et les lieues et les lieues de lui, chantenchantaimant, me fasse annaluviale en mal de sel et je cours, mon unique, dans tes bras! ... Au large seule et lasse l'élue le long du

7 Hungarian

Szentkuthy (Hungarian, 1975)

Ágota Bozai (2008) records a Hungarian rendering by Miklós Szentkuthy of the closing line and opening lines (*FW* 628.16, 3.1–3), which appeared in 1975 in Irén Fejér's Hungarian translation from the Polish of Egon Naganowski's study *Telemach w labiryncie świata: o twórczości Jamesa Joyce'a* (1962). Szentkuthy's version, as quoted by Bozai, reads as follows:

> Az út, az egy, a csók, a táv, a // vízverte útmeder túl Ádámén és Éváén partkanyartól öbleívig recirkulálva viciusszal, visszavisz bennünket kényelmesen Howth Castle-ig (és környékére).

Miklós Szentkuthy (1908–88), a native of Budapest, frequently referred to as "the Hungarian Joyce," was a writer of experimental novels, influenced by *Ulysses*, in the 1930s already, including the 1,225-page meganovel *Prae* (1934), but was silenced by the Stalinist regime in the 1940s (Egri 1967, 234). The prolific author subsequently of numerous novels, essays, and translations (including of Swift, Dickens, Mark Twain, and others), his Hungarian rendering of *Ulysses*, which appeared in Budapest in 1974, is regarded by many as a masterly translation. With his own works now widely translated, he has increasingly come to be seen as one of the most significant authors of modern Hungarian literature.

Writing on Szentkuthy's markedly flamboyant Hungarian *Ulysses*, outjoycing Joyce in numerous instances, Erika Mihálycsa demonstrates that Szentkuthy, whose library is known to have contained copies of *Anna Livia Plurabelle* and *Haveth Childers Everywhere*, was clearly familiar with *Work in Progress*, renderings from which he is variously reported to have attempted (2012, 87). Mihálycsa writes elsewhere that, intriguingly, it is indeed "a leitmotiv of Szentkuthy scholarship that he tried his hand at the *Wake* (probably prior to his translation of *Ulysses* – possibly in the late 1930s–40s, when he was closely following Joyce's work). To my knowledge, the translation has not been retrieved – it is possible that it is lurking in his archive (amounting to several hundred thousand pages)."[13]

Ferenc Takács of Eötvös Lorand University in Budapest confirms that two renderings by Szentkuthy appear in the Hungarian translation of the Naganowski book: *FW* 628.16, 3.1–3 as above and the closing paragraph of *ALP* (*FW* 215.31–216.5) (Szentkuthy1975, 142 and 158). Takács believes that these are the only renderings by Szentkuthy that have appeared in print, though agreeing with Mihálycsa that other renderings may exist in manuscript form.[14]

8 Russian

Sergeev (Russian, 1977)

The earliest recorded Russian rendering of any part of the *Wake* is a translation by the writer and translator Andrey Sergeev (1933–98) of "The Ballad of Persse O'Reilly" (*FW* 44.22–47.29), which appeared under the likewise punning title "Ballada o Khukho O'V'orttkke" in Moscow in 1977 in an anonymously compiled volume on twentieth-century Western European poetry. The translated title plays on *okh* ("oh"), *ukho* ("ear"), and *ukhovertka* ("earwig"). The poet Joseph Brodsky reports in an interview having found Sergeev's rendering "incredibly exciting" (Volkov 1998, 86). Sergeev also translated Robert Frost's poetry into Russian.[15]

---

13 My thanks to Erika Mihálycsa for providing this information in personal correspondence. A request to the Szentkuthy archive in Budapest for further information remained unanswered.

14 My thanks to Ferenc Takács for confirming these details in personal correspondence.

15 On the general Russian context in which Sergeev's rendering appeared, see Alexandrova (2015, 132; 2020,144–6).

9 Croatian

Šoljan (Croatian, 1978)

Sonja Bašić (2004, 181–2) reports a Croatian rendering by Nada Šoljan in 1978 of brief excerpts from *FW*, under the title "Bdijenje Finnegana," literally a singular "Finnegan's wake." First delivered as a radio talk, the rendering appeared in Zagreb in *Zbornik Trećeg programa Radio Zagreba* (Proceedings of Radio Zagreb's Third Program). This was the first Croatian rendering of any part of *FW* – and appears to be even still the only rendering in that language.

Chapter Six

The 1980s

*1 Italian; 2 French; 3 Japanese; 4 Spanish; 5 Catalan;
6 Polish; 7 German; 8 Korean; 9 Serbian; 10 Swedish*

The Joyce centenary year of 1982 provoked a very vigorous response in at least ten languages, of which Catalan and Swedish were new to the *FW* firmament. Luigi Schenoni's Italian rendering of the first four chapters of the *Wake*, the longest translation (*FW* 3–103) in any language to that date, appeared in June 1982, while October 1982 ushered in a whole new era in *Wake* translation studies, namely, a complete translation of the entire *FW*, in French, by Philippe Lavergne. Three new complete renderings of *ALP* also appeared, in Japanese by Masyoshi Osawa et al. (1982), in Korean by Chong-keon Kim (1985), and in Polish by Maciej Słomczyński (1985). Briefer renderings appeared in Catalan by Josep-Miquel Sobré (1982), in Italian by Roberto Sanesi (1982, 1983) and Luigi Schenoni (1986), in Polish by Tomasz Mirkowicz (1982), in Spanish by Ricardo Silva-Santisteban (1982, 1988) and by Mario Monteforte Toledo (1982), in Serbian anonymously (1986), and in Swedish by Georg Friberg and Gösta Friberg (1987). The 1982 revised edition of Ellmann's *James Joyce* was translated into Italian by Piero Bernardini (1982); into Spanish by Enrique Castro and Beatriz Blanco (1982); into Polish by Ewa Krasińska (1984); and into Portuguese by Lya Luft (1989). All four translations included renderings of the numerous excerpts from *FW* employed by Ellmann as chapter epigraphs.

The 1980s also saw a concerted burst of activity among German translators. Briefer renderings appeared in German by Wilhelm Füger (1983), Robert Weninger (1984), Erich Fried (1985), Uwe Herms (1985), Harald Beck (1986, 1987), and Klaus Schönmetzler (1987a, 1987b), while the important compendium *Finnegans Wake Deutsch* (1989) included full chapters by Friedhelm Rathjen (I.2, II.4), Ingeborg Horn (I.6), Klaus Reichert et al. (I.7), Dieter Stündel (II.4), and the three previously published German *ALP*s of Goyert, Hildesheimer, and Wollschläger, as well as briefer renderings by Harald Beck, Ulrich Blumenbach and Reinhard Markner, Kurt Jauslin, Friedhelm Rathjen, Klaus Reichert, Wolfgang Schrödter, Helmut Stoltefuß, Dieter Stündel, Robert Weninger, and Arno Schmidt. This volume, which includes renderings of roughly one-quarter of *FW* altogether, provides as many as four different German translations of certain passages.[1]

Meanwhile, in 1985, Beckett and Péron's French translation of the opening pages of *ALP* was finally published, after more than half a century. In the late 1980s both the Spanish novelist Ramón Buenaventura and the Swedish poet Jan Östergren reportedly considered undertaking renderings of *FW*, but in each case the plan was eventually abandoned.

1 Italian

Schenoni's Italian H.C.E. *(1982)*

The intrepid Italian translator Luigi Schenoni (1935–2008), "the first in the world to have translated one hundred pages" of *FW* (Del Pozzo 1982, 155), was born in Bologna, graduated in English at Bocconi University in Milan in 1959, and acquired his first copy of *FW* in 1960 (Gramigna 1982, 11). He worked for some fifteen years as a technical and commercial translator for an engineering firm in Bologna before deciding in the early seventies to turn his talents to the more exciting challenge of undertaking a complete Italian translation of *FW* – which, as he told at least one interviewer, had immediately fascinated him (Grisi 1982, 1064).

Schenoni began working seriously on his translation in 1974, using evenings, early mornings, and weekends while continuing with his regular employment. Eventually, in January 1981, he resigned from the latter in order to devote himself more fully to the Italian transfiguration of the *Wake* (Del Pozzo 1982, 156). After almost two decades of work and several excerpts published in the 1970s, a heavily annotated rendering of the first four chapters, with Joyce's original text on facing pages, appeared in June 1982, marking the Joyce centenary year and published in Milan by Arnoldo Mondadori Editore under the title *Finnegans Wake:*

---

1 In the present chapter, *Finnegans Wake Deutsch* will be referred to parenthetically as *FWD*.

H.C.E. It was greeted with considerable critical excitement in Italian literary circles, including also the award of a major literary prize, the Premio San Girolamo. Corinna del Greco Lobner writes: "His monumental effort to translate *Finnegans Wake* into Italian ... initiated an experiment in linguistic metamorphosis many found amusing and most found exceptionally brilliant" (2008, 434). One of his earlier promoters had been Umberto Eco, who had brought Schenoni's ongoing work to the attention of a more general audience in 1978 in *L'Espresso*, one of the most widely circulated Italian weekly news magazines, under the eye-catching title "Come si dice in italiano tumptytumtoes?" (How do you say tumptytumtoes in Italian?). Schenoni was happy to answer that particular question: "dumptydumdita" (*FW* 3.21).

Schenoni's approach is informed throughout by a lively sense of humour. He faced one translational problem peculiar to Italian – in which only foreign words, and very few of those, begin with the letter *h*, which is also always mute. Dealing with HCE is the most obvious case in point, though Schenoni is frequently happy to turn the difficulty to humorous advantage. In finding the appropriate initials for HCE in a phrase such as "this man of hod, cement and edifices" (*FW* 4.26–7), for example, he has no compunction about humorously prefixing a silent *h*, comically out of place, to a standard Italian word, resulting in an outlandish combination of letters normally quite impossible in that language: thus in this case, embellishing *sparviero* ("hod") with an initial silent *h*, "quest'uomo di hsparviero, cemento ed edifici." In each such case the Italian text humorously reminds the reader that this is a translation of a text that is quite untranslatable by any more normal translatorial practices.

Schenoni firmly asserted in interviews, however, that his aim was not at all to rewrite the *Wake* as flamboyantly as Joyce had done in his Italian rendering of *ALP* – and he even admitted that he was one of the apparently very few people who in fact did not like the result of Joyce's rewriting. His own aim, rather, was to strive for translational fidelity, in the sense of being as faithful as possible to the *spirit* of the original text (Federici 1982, 8; Silver and Torrealta 1983, 21) – not with any intention of succeeding in producing the one and only completely accurate Italian rendering, but rather just to offer his own personal interpretation of the text, just one such among the infinite number of possible versions (Gramigna 1982, 11).[2]

---

2 "cioè darne nella mia lingua la mia personale interpretazione, una tra le infiniti possibili" (Gramigna 1982, 11).

Schenoni mentioned to several interviewers that he preferred to think of his translation as essentially a *ricreazione,* a re-creation (Schenoni 2003, 225; 2004b). Rosa Maria Bosinelli, comparing Italian renderings of the *Wake,* finds Schenoni's translation in particular "quite successful in often maintaining the rhythm and sound effects of the original, in inventing words that evoke similar chains of associations, in finding brilliant solutions to puns and cultural references, in trying to construct a text that asks of the reader the same kind of efforts as Joyce's 'ideal reader affected by an ideal insomnia'" (1990, 151). Schenoni's translation, she adds, is a demonstration that the Italian language can be reinvented and manipulated just as well as English can (1990, 151).

Responding to interviewers' questions regarding his translatorial procedure, Schenoni asserted that he had decided not to begin with selected excerpts from more accessible parts of the text, such as from *ALP*, but had decided instead simply to begin with the first word and proceed undeviatingly line by line in the (eventually unrealized) hope of at some point reaching the final word (Federici 1982, 8).[3] His preferred working method, staunchly traditional, was to write in longhand, always with two sheets of A4 paper side by side on his desk, the right-hand page for tentative translational solutions, the left for extensive notes of all kinds (Del Pozzo 1982, 156). His approach to translation, as Serenella Zanotti has observed (2006, 3), was essentially philological: the published translation of 1982 accordingly contains one hundred pages of translation, followed by a good seventy pages of such notes. It is preceded by a detailed fifty-page introduction by Giorgio Melchiori (1920–2009), the most eminent Italian Joyce scholar of the day.

Unlike some later translators – Krzysztof Bartnicki in Polish, for example, or Congrong Dai in Chinese – who have reported finding the process of translating the *Wake* to be mentally exhausting or personally traumatic or both, Schenoni cheerfully informed interviewers that he found the process both gratifying and even exhilarating (Gramigna 1982, 11). Thoroughly fascinated by the task, he recalled working sixteen-hour days for an entire month on one occasion without leaving his apartment even once. Various reports (apocryphal or otherwise) were by then already circulating concerning his obsessive day-and-night devotion to the task, sustained largely by copious supplies of pasta provided by an obliging and conveniently available housekeeper aunt (Del Pozzo 1982, 156).[4]

---

3 He appears, however, to have deviated quite soon from this principle: the next excerpt to appear in print, in 1986, was a rendering of the closing pages (*FW* 627–8).

4 On Schenoni's Italian rendering, see Eco (1978), Del Pozzo (1982), Gramigna (1982), Grisi (1982), Schenoni (1984, 1990), Lobner (1989, 2008), Bosinelli (1987, 1990), Parks (1992), Zanotti (2006).

We have two different versions by Schenoni of the opening three lines (*FW* 3.1–3), one from 1978 and one from 1982:

fiume che scorre passato Eva ed Adamo da baia sinuosa a costa frastagliata ci porta per mezzo di un più commodo vico di ricircolo di nuovo a Howth Castle ed Environs. (1978)

fluidofiume passato Eva ed Adamo da spiaggia sinuosa a baia biancheggiante ci conduce con un più commodus vicus di ricircolo di nuovo a Howth Castle Edintorni. (1982)

A comparison of the two renderings is instructive. The earlier "fiume che scorre" ("river that runs") employs a relative clause; the later version succeeds both in using a single word and in retaining the alliteration of the original with "fluidofiume" ("flowriver"). Both versions reveal distinctly sexualized overtones. The earlier version contrasts the smoothness of a "baia sinuosa" ("curving bay") and the roughness of a "costa frastigliata," where the "swerve of shore," at least if we take actual Irish geography into consideration, has become a quite untenably "jagged coast." In the later version, the roles are reversed, implied gender and all: the adjective "sinuosa" ("curving, sinuous") is now transferred from the bay to a coast that is no longer romantically rugged but rather a peacefully curvaceous "spiaggia" ("strand, beach"), while the bay is now portrayed as "biancheggiante" (literally, "whitening"), not only suggesting the white crests of the waves but also connoting both "shining brightly" and "going grey," evocatively refiguring the bay both as youthful lover and as aging father to the embraced and embracing coast (O'Neill 2005,186–7). Meanwhile, abandoning the translingual "Howth Castle ed Environs" of the earlier version, Schenoni later translates "and environs" as "e dintorni," but serendipitously combined as "Edintorni," a happy coinage that splendidly evokes the Garden of Eden – and thus Eve and Adam once again, standing in as avatars respectively of ALP and HCE (O'Neill 2005,190–1). Even more splendidly, since the biblical name Eden has been seen as related to the Akkadian *edinu* ("plain") (McKenzie 1965, 211), the reader is happily allowed to think of Joyce's Dublin as one of the "cities of the plain," its unnatural wickedness crying to heaven for vengeance.

We also have two interestingly different versions of Schenoni's rendering of the next half-dozen lines (*FW* 3.4–10). The 1978 rendering is as follows:

Sir Tristram, violatore d'amores, d'oltre il mar piccolo, era passencore riarrivato dall'Armorica del Nord su questo lato dell'istmo scabroso dell'Europa Minore per wielderbattere la sua guerra peneisolata: né i roccoglioni del tommiglior sawyergantino presso l'Oconee si altrerano ingigantiti fino ai giorgi della contea di Laurens, continuando a raddublinare il loro mammero; né voce da fuoco aveva mugghiato mishe mishe al tauftauf tuseitorbizio. (1978c, 79)

His 1982 rendering of the same lines is as follows:

Sir Tristram, violista d'amores, da sopra il mar d'Irlanda aveva passencore riraggiunto dall'Armorica del Nord su questa sponda l'istmo scosceso d'Europa Minore per wielderbattere la sua guerra penisolata: né le topsawyer's rocks presso il fiume Oconee s'altrerano ingrandite fino ai gorgi della Laurens County mentre continuavano a raddublinare per tutto il tempo il loro mùmpero: né 'navoce da 'nfoco aveva soffiorato mishe mishe al tauftauf tuseipeatrizio: (1982, 3)

Schenoni's later version of these lines is consistently less flamboyant than his earlier rendering. Limiting ourselves to the more obvious changes, we find that Sir Tristram, from being a "violatore d'amores" ("violator of love") becomes a "violista d'amores" ("violist of love"), while his penisolate war changes from a "peneisolata," including "pains" (*pene*) as well as "penis" (*pene*) to a "penisolata," free of any pains. "Top sawyer's rocks" are a particularly flamboyant "roccoglioni del tommiglior sawyergantino" in 1978, where the rocks have metamorphosed into "roccoglioni," a combination of *rocche* ("rocks") and *coglioni* ("testicles"), while Tom Sawyer reveals himself as a translingual sawyer not only already "superior" (*migliore*) but also in the process of "rising" (*ergente*) even further. In 1982 this formulation disappears in favour of an untranslated "topsawyer's rocks." The earlier gorgios are doubling "il loro mammero," apparently doubling not only their *numero* ("number") but also the number of ladies who become a *mamma*, while later they simply double, slightly Italianized, a quite indefinite "il loro mùmpero." As for the fiery pronouncement, the early "tuseitorbizio" conflates an Italian *torba* ("peat, turf") and *Patrizio*, humorously emphasizing Patrick's connections with Irish bogs, while excluding any reference to the biblical Peter. The later "tuseipeatrizio" restores peat, Peter, and Patrizio alike to their Joyce-allotted roles.[5]

A full fourteen years after the appearance of his 1982 rendering of *FW* I.1–4, Schenoni's separate translation of *ALP* (to which we shall return)

---

5 For a more detailed compararison of these two renderings, see O'Neill (2013, 63–121 passim).

appeared in 1996. This was followed five further years later, and for Mondadori once again, by *FW* I.5–8 in 2001 (including a revised version of his *ALP* translation) and, after another three years, by *FW* II.1–2 in 2004. Schenoni's intention to provide a complete Italian version of *FW* was unfortunately thwarted by his untimely death in 2008, though his rendering of *FW* II.3–4 would still appear posthumously in 2011. The task of completing the full Mondadori *Wake* would be taken up several years later by Enrico Terrinoni and Fabio Pedone.

Sanesi (Italian, 1982)

An Italian rendering of the opening three pages of Book IV (*FW* 593.1–595.29) by the Milanese poet Roberto Sanesi (1930–2001) also appeared in 1982, in the literary review *Nuova Rivista Europea* under the title "Il risveglio di Finnegan" (literally, "Finnegan's awakening" or "Finnegan's revival"). Sanesi, a highly accomplished and prolific poet, who taught at the universities of Parma and Verona, has been described as one of the most remarkable Italian writers of his generation (Gooding 2001). As a translator from English, Sanesi is reportedly best known for his Italian renderings of T.S. Eliot's complete works and of Milton's *Paradise Lost*. He also translated selected works of Shakespeare, Marlowe, Coleridge, Blake, Yeats, and Lewis Carroll.

In 1983 Sanesi published a very small volume also entitled *Il risveglio di Finnegan* and containing the same three translated pages of the *Wake*. Published in Milan by the art publisher Severgnini, and just twelve pages long, it appeared in seventy-five signed, numbered, and illustrated copies and now commands high prices among collectors. Giuliana Bendelli, who observes that Sanesi regarded Joyce's poetics as being close to his own, remarks that "this was, and still is, the first Italian translation of this part of *FW* – and it curiously appeared just as Mondadori had published the first volume of the official translation of *FW* by Luigi Schenoni" (2014, 149).

2 French

Lavergne's French Wake *(1982)*

Philippe Lavergne's French *Finnegans Wake*, the first complete rendering (if slightly abbreviated in places) of Joyce's extraordinary text in any language, appeared in Paris in October 1982. Two individual chapters of his translation had appeared in 1967 and 1968 already, but the French publisher Gallimard, evidently with a businesslike eye to the anticipated market for such an endeavour, saw fit to delay the publication of the entire rendering by more than a decade, until the Joyce centenary year of 1982. The strategy was clearly an effective one, for "much to everyone's surprise, the first edition was sold out in a few days" (Attridge and Ferrer 1984, 9).

Lavergne (born 1935), a telecommunications engineer by profession, having discovered the *Wake* at the age of seventeen, won the Prix Langlois of the Académie Française thirty years later for his rendering of it. An early interviewer in *Le Monde* described him as a shy and retiring man, determined to avoid publicity, fascinated by mathematics, numerology, parapsychology, and astrology, and reportly also competent in a dozen or so languages (Jauffret 1982). His continued reluctance to grant interviews quickly turned him into something of a man of mystery – and eventually led some journalists to the flippant conclusion that there actually was no such person as "Philippe Lavergne." The possibility that the translator might in fact have been a different Philippe altogether (namely, Philippe Sollers), was also, likewise flippantly, occasionally suggested (Meltz 2003).

Lavergne appears also to have been an enthusiastic admirer of the Parisian free radio station Carbone 14, which had begun its provocatively and aggressively counterculture programming in December 1981. Lavergne's translation is in fact dedicated to the Carbone 14 team – and specifically to one of the presenters, Jean-Yves Lambert, who would later became a well-known comedian, changing his surname for greater comic effect to Lafesse (literally, "Arse"). The dedication was clearly intended to make the point that the French *Wake* would undoubtedly have a similarly provocative and intellectually liberating effect on its readers. For more conservative readers (and non-readers), it may alternatively have suggested that the whole thing should be treated as largely a hoax (Meltz 2003).

Lavergne's rendering was received in literary circles with nothing short of general stupefaction, both in France and elsewhere. Opinions were immediately divided as to its merits – and even as to whether such an undertaking should ever have been contemplated in the first place. The rendering, not at all surprisingly for a pioneering first complete translation of Joyce's massive and massively intimidating text, is very much a normalizing version – and has thus been subject to the same kind of reactions as has, for example, Goyert's German *ALP*. Deviating only relatively infrequently from good plain standard French, his version is largely couched in essentially explanatory terms, designed to demonstrate to French readers what Joyce's text is really all about, what it is really saying under cover of the verbal pyrotechnics. To this end, the translation is accompanied by more than six hundred explanatory footnotes and preceded by a four-page introduction, dated July 1982, discussing the main characters and their intersecting roles. The decidedly idiosyncratic introduction begins by comparing *FW* and the starship *Enterprise* in the popular television series *Star Trek* – and ends with the relationship between the seventeen chapters of *FW* and sura 17, "The Night Journey," of the Koran.

One notable feature of Lavergne's rendering involves his valiant attempts, not by any means always persuasive, to find specifically Irish answers to textual conundrums. When the Mookse leaves "Ludstown" (*FW* 152.28–9), for example, a footnote explains that this is "no doubt the abbreviation of Leopardstown, with its race course" (1982, 165n68; my translation). Since Leopardstown is a Dublin suburb, and since the Mookse is specifically associated with London (founded according to legend by one Lud) while the Gripes is associated with Dublin (alias "Dubville," *FW* 153.18), the footnote is not only factually inaccurate in its real-world reference but also succeeds almost immediately in confusing the relationship between the two characters and the two cities alike in the fictional world.[6] As many critics have observed, Lavergne also indisputably cuts corners and takes easy ways out on numerous occasions.

Critics in general, while acknowledging the heroic scale of Lavergne's achievement, tended (and still tend) to share the opinion expressed by Derek Attridge and Daniel Ferrer: "Unfortunately, the result of his heroic enterprise is disappointing in its lack of inventiveness (especially if it is compared with the Italian translation)" (1984, 13n11), the latter being Schenoni's 1982 version of *FW* I.1–4. Lavergne's fellow translators, similarly, while likewise admiring the scale of the pioneering undertaking, have in general been relatively disappointed by his rendering. Francisco García Tortosa, in introducing his own 1992 Spanish version of *ALP*, observes that Lavergne's rendering of *FW* consists largely of attempting to *explain* Joyce's text, that he tends to do so primarily in terms of Joyce's own biography, that he tends to limit himself to the most immediately obvious levels of the textual allusions, and that overall he loses much of the text's profundity and rhythm.[7] Naoki Yanase, whose complete Japanese *Wake* appeared in 1993, finds Lavergne's version to be only a poor substitute for the original. "First of all, there is

---

6 On Lavergne's somewhat eccentric annotational practice, see Conley (2012, 2017).

7 "Ha elegido, entre los innumerables niveles narrativos, aquel que se refiere a la biografía de Joyce, y de las alusiones se ha quedado con las más inmediatas y anecdóticas, perdiendo en el camino profundidad y ritmo" (García Tortosa 1992, 115–16).

no adventure to it. ... In the parts he couldn't handle, he simply left the original as it was, and in so many other places, passages have been omitted entirely. Perhaps it is a failing of the French language, I really don't know" (Stephens 2000, 22). Haroldo de Campos, in an appreciative review of Donaldo Schüler's 1999 Portuguese rendering of *FW* I.1, refers to Lavergne's version, by contrast, as a mere watered-down explanatory retelling (1999b). Bindervoet and Henkes, whose Dutch rendering of the *Wake* appeared in 2002, comment with a similar lack of enthusiasm in a newspaper interview that Lavergne's rendering "consists of a sort of paraphrase with an occasional wordplay here and there" (Evenhuis 2002).[8] Hervé Michel, whose own online French *Wake* appeared in 2004, comments less than enthusiastically that while Lavergne's version cannot fairly be said to constitute an actual betrayal of the original, its besetting weakness is that it rewrites Joyce's text all too smoothly in all-too-normal French, with Joyce's linguistic pyrotechnics only rarely in evidence.[9]

While his translation certainly represented a monumental achievement, and is by no means without its successes, there is some temptation to agree with one early reviewer's unkind but amusing quip that for Lavergne "the translating of the *Wake* was indeed a labor of love, but so was the monster for Dr Frankenstein" (Benstock and Benstock 1985, 231). Lavergne's *Wake* nonetheless continues to deserve great credit as the first complete rendering, not just in French but in any language, of Joyce's notoriously untranslatable text. The next complete renderings (Yanase's Japanese, Stündel's German) would not appear for another decade.[10]

While Lavergne's translation as a whole is very much a normalizing one, the same can certainly not be said of his rendering (1982, 9) of the three-line incipit, which is decidedly flamboyant:

> erre revie pass'Evant notre Adame d'erre rive en rêvière nous recourante via Vico par chaise percée de recirculation vers Howth Castle et Environs.

8　The comment in the original Dutch is that Lavergne's rendering "uit een soort navertelling bestaat met hier en daar een woordspeling."

9　"La traduction de Philippe Lavergne ne trahit pas l'original mais le comprend presque trop en reconstituant une narration plutôt surréaliste dans un texte en bon français. On y trouve rarement la conflagration de significations que Joyce opère au niveau des mots" (2004).

10　On Lavergne's French rendering, see Aubert (1982), Jauffret (1982), Sollers (1982), Cortanze (1983), Debons (1983), Rabaté (1983), Benstock and Benstock (1985), Vouvé (1985), Topia (1990), Holland (2010), Conley (2012; 2017, 72–90).

The rendering begins by portraying the slow drift (*erre*, "momentum") of a "rivi-ère" recomposed into "erre revie," where "erre" also invokes *errer* ("to rove, wander, stray"), and "revie" evokes a life (*vie*) to be relived (*re-vie*), reseen (*revue*), dreamed (*rêvée*) and redreamed (*rerêvée*). Though his errant river's Irishness is evoked by "erre," which includes *Éire*, Lavergne also provides it with the necessary textual permit (*passavant*) with which it passes in front of (*passe devant*) the French "notre Adame," once again Eving our Adam (*Evant notre Adame*) as in André du Bouchet's 1962 rendering. Lavergne chooses to ignore both swerve of shore and bend of bay, focusing instead on a river meandering both physically ("erre rive" or "wanderriver") and mentally ("rêvière" or "dreamriver"), which "nous recourante," sweeping us back on its current (*courant*) as if in a seventeenth-century French dance, the *courante*. That process of recirculation takes place "via Vico," invoking both the philosopher and Dublin's Vico Road, while the emperor Commodus gives way to the commode in "commodius" by way of a cheeky evocation of the "chaise percée," the toilet seat as site per se of *éternel retour* (O'Neill 2013, 54–5).

Lavergne's rendering of the opening page (*FW* 3.4–10) continues as follows – and is still distinctly flamboyant:

> Sire Tristram, violeur d'amoeurs, manchissant la courte oisie, n'avait pâque buissé sa derrive d'Armorique du Nord sur ce flanc de notre isthme décharné d'Europe Mineure pour y resoutenir le combat d'un presqu'Yseul penny: ni près du fleuve Oconee les roches premières ne s'élaient exaltruées en splendide Georgi Dublin de Laurens Comptez en doublant ses membres tout le temps: nulle voix humaine n'avait dessouflé son micmac pour bêptiser Patrick:

Lavergne's Sire Tristram arrives (or will arrive) "manchissant la courte oisie," which suggests *franchissant la Manche* ("crossing the English Channel") while wearing his heart on his sleeve (*manche*) in the name of knightly courtesy (*courtoisie*). The term *courtoisie*, meanwhile, puns on the French adjective *court* ("short") and the English noun *sea*. Lavergne's "n'avait pâque buissé sa derrive" seriously stretches the limits of French in a complexly tortured series of water-related puns. Taken together, they suggest that Tristram had not yet "passed over" (*pâque* "Passover"), whether by "steamship" (*paquebot*) or otherwise, but had "only" (*n'avait pas que*) managed to work out (*puiser* "to draw water, to derive an idea") the general "drift" (*dérive*) of his eventual course towards an arrival (*arrivée*), though one as yet only approximately "derived" (*dérivée*) from his calculations. The point of his arrival is "pour y resoutenir le combat," both to continue (*soutenir*) and to resolve (*ré-soudre*) the anticipated struggle. In a once again distinctly idiosyncratic rendering, that struggle is "le combat d'un presqu'Yseul penny," the struggle, whether by penis (*pénis*) or pen (*penne* "feather, quill") or both, and alone (*seul*) if necessary, for both peninsula (*presqu'île*) and Iseult – even if each, ungallantly, is worth "little more than a single penny" (*presqu'un seul penny*).

As for "avoice from afire," Lavergne, noting the potentially privative prefix, considers it "nulle voix humaine" ("no human voice"), the formulation evoking an appropriately ecclesiastical atmosphere by playing on the similarly named organ stop (vox humana) that can evoke the sound of a singing choir. This voice "n'avait dessouflé son micmac," with "dessouflé" conflating *souffler* ("to blow") and *soufflet* ("bellows"), while the words spoken are just pure *micmac* ("trickery") to impress the gullible and "pour bêptiser Patrick," where the invented "bêptiser" conflates *baptiser* ("to baptize") and *bêtise* ("nonsense, stupidity"), in a baptism that is thus "thwarted."

Lavergne's rendering (1982, 209) of the opening sentences of *ALP* contains the following lines (*FW* 196.1–7, 9–11):

O / Tellus, dis-moi tout sur / Anna Livia! Je veux tout savoir d'Anna Livia! / Mais connais tu Anna Livia? Oui, bien sûr, nous connaissons tous, Anna Livia. Dis-moi tout. Dis-moi maintenant, c'est à mourir lorsque tu l'entendras. Non tu sais lorsque le vieux, et crac, fit ce que tu sais. ... Ou quoi que ce fût que l'on essaya de découvrir qu'il ait bien pu faire à Fiendish Park.

Homer's *Odyssey* famously begins with an invocation of the muse of poetic narrative: "Tell me, O Muse, of the man of many turns." Lavergne's "O Tellus, dis-moi tout sur Anna Livia!" humorously and translingually calls in mock-Homeric vein on Mother Earth herself, whom the Romans called Tellus (*tellus* meaning "earth, land"), to "tell us" all about her affairs as Anna Livia, the river of rivers – and, by serendipitous implication, as the Irish fertility goddess Ana. The parodic introduction of a goddess as Muse raises the question as to how legitimate such unforced deviations from Joyce's original may be considered – while Joyce himself had no qualms at all about gleefully introducing many such unforced deviations. Lavergne's "c'est à mourir lorsque tu l'entendras" offers a plain French rendering of "You'll die when you hear," while evoking in passing the Belgian Our, French Endre, and Algerian Dra.

As for the final sentence, Lavergne's version is a markedly simplified one, apparently feeling the need to state in no-nonsense terms the essential meat of the matter, rendering it straightforwardly in plain French. The rendering thus avoids any direct reference either to the watchers or the watched, either to the three or the two, focusing instead on the subsequent circulation of the story: "Ou quoi que ce fût que l'on essaya de découvrir qu'il ait bien pu faire," roughly, "Or whatever it might have been that they were trying to reveal that he may have done." Avoiding the temptation to delve any further into the "fiendish" nature of Earwicker's park, Lavergne opts for an untranslated "Fiendish Park," duly identified in a footnote as the Phoenix Park.

Lavergne's rendering (1982, 232) of the final paragraph of I.8 includes the following lines (*FW* 215.31–5, 216.3–5):

J'entends pas avec les eaux de. Au fil des eaux murmuriantes de. Froissements d'elles des chaudes souris des champs en contre-chant. Ho! N'es-tu pas rentrée chez toi? Quel André Chémois? J'entends pas avec tous ces cris et battements des liffeyantes eaux de. Ho, parole, sauve qui peut! Mes pieds se moussent. Je me sens aussi vieille que l'orme là bas. Sons ces contes de Shaun ou Shem? ... Orme moi l'histoire de Stem et Stone. Près des ondes eaux de vie errante et revierrantes eaux de. La Nuit!

Lavergne's speaker can't hear with "les eaux de" ("the waters of"), evoking the French river Aude, waters that are now "murmuriantes," sometimes grumbling (*murmuriant*) and sometimes laughing (*riant*), but always murmuring (*murmuriant*). Their rustlings (*froissements*) and those of surrealistic "hot mice" ("chaudes souris"), who may in fact be bats (*chauve-souris*) or water shrews (*souris d'eau*) or fieldmice (*souris des champs*), sound in rhyming counterpoint ("en contre-chant"). The washerwoman's query, "N'es-tu pas rentrée chez toi?" ("Haven't you gone back home?"), now elicits the response "Quel André Chémois?" referring to a supposed André Chémois, whose name punningly rhymes with *chez moi* ("at my place") rather than *chez toi* ("at your place") and is identical with the medical term *chémois* ("chemosis"), a disease of the eye. The many years of debilitating eye problems that plagued Joyce are obliquely evoked.

One cannot hear with all the cries ("cris") and "flutterings" ("battements") of the liffeying waters. Let speech ("parole") save those who may be saved in these linguistically treacherous waters, the exclamation "ho" punning on Chinese *ho* ("river") and French *eaux* ("waters"). Meanwhile, playing on an invented verb based on *mousse* ("moss") and the actual verb *mousser* ("to foam"), "Mes pieds se moussent" ("My feet are foaming as they turn into moss"), and the speaker feels "aussi vieille que l'orme là bas" ("as old as yonder elm"). Focusing closely on the increasing element of confusion in Joyce's text, Lavergne goes on ("Sons ces contes de Shaun ou Shem?") to introduce a rhyming play on the noun *sons* ("sounds") and the verb *sont* ("are") while suggesting "Are these tales of Shaun or Shem?" Continuing to exploit the possibilities of linguistic confusion, he transforms the noun *orme* ("elm") into a verb in asking to be told ("orme moi") the story ("l'histoire") of "Stem et Stone," the metamorphosis of the brothers thus orthographically confirmed.

Lavergne's formulation "Près des ondes eaux de vie errante et re-vierrantes eaux de. La Nuit!" builds his translation of the "rivering" and "hitherandthithering waters," finally, on a complex combination of *ondes* ("waves"), *eaux* ("waters"), *eau-de-vie* (punning on Irish *uisce beatha* "water of life," otherwise whiskey), the present participle *errant* ("wandering"), and *rivière* ("river"), resulting in something like "by the waves, wandering like the drunken waters of life itself, the wandering rivering waters."

Lavergne's rendering (1982, 650) of the final page of the *Wake* includes the following lines (*FW* 627.34–628.4, 15–16):

> Je m'éteins. O fin amère! Je vais m'esquiver avant qu'ils soient levés. Il ne verront jamais. Ni ne sauront. Ni me regretteront. Et c'est vieux et vieux et triste et vieux et c'est triste et lasse que je m'en retourne vers toi mon père froid mon père froid et fou mon père froid et furieux jusqu'à ce que la simple vue de sa simple taille, tous ses crilomètres et ses crilomètres ses sangloalanglots me malvasent et me selcoeurent, et je me presse mon unique dans tes bras. ... Au large vire et tiens-bon lof pour lof la barque au l'onde de l'

The most striking sequence here is provided by Lavergne's final words, which, on a decidedly maritime note, and deviating sharply once again from the generally normalizing tone of his overall rendering, break free of Joyce's text ("A way a lone a last a loved a long the") altogether. Lavergne's rendering suggests, roughly, "Take to (*virer*) the open sea (*large*) and hold (*tiens-bon*) the boat (*barque*) on course on the wave (*onde*) face to the wind (*lof pour lof*) along the ..." The English *along* is translingually signalled by the ostentatiously ungrammatical formulation "au l'onde."

Lavergne's *Wake*, as noted, has come in for a considerable amount of criticism on various levels. This should certainly not be allowed to detract from the fact, however, that his rendering was the first complete version of Joyce's untranslatable text to appear anywhere in any language – and thus opened a whole host of new interpretive possibilities in readers' encounters with the *FW* macrotext.

3 Japanese

Osawa's Japanese ALP *(1982)*

In the centenary year of 1982, a first complete Japanese *ALP* also appeared, the product of a team of six led by Masayoshi Osawa (1928–2020), a professor of English at Chuo University in Tokyo, who was later to serve as the first president of the James Joyce Society of Japan, founded in 1989. Osawa and individual members of his team had been working in a relatively leisurely fashion on translating *ALP* for at least fifteen years, since the mid-sixties, and one excerpt (*FW* 206–7) had already appeared in Japanese in 1968, while the first twelve pages (*FW* 196–208), translated by Osawa and members of his team, had appeared between 1970 and 1972, serialized in seven numbers of the quarterly journal *Kikan Paedeia* (Paedeia quarterly).[11]

4 Spanish

Monteforte (Spanish, 1982)

One interesting case in Spanish in the 1980s was that of the Guatemalan writer, dramatist, and politician Mario Monteforte Toledo (1911–2003), a law graduate of the Universidad de San Carlos, Guatemala, who also studied at the Sorbonne in Paris and later at the National Autonomous University of Mexico (UNAM). Born in Guatemala City, he played important political roles in two successive national governments between 1946 and 1951, serving first as ambassador to the United Nations and later as vice-president of Guatemala. When the second democratic government was overthrown by a military coup in 1954, Monteforte went into a more than thirty-year exile, first in Mexico, where he became a prominent professor of Latin American political studies at UNAM, and later in Ecuador, returning to Guatemala only in 1987. He is regarded as one of the most important Guatemalan novelists, and a national foundation for the propagation of Guatemalan literature and culture was created in his name in 1999.

As a student in Paris, at the Sorbonne, Monteforte reportedly met Joyce in Sylvia Beach's bookshop in 1933. Joyce's work proved to be of foundational importance for his own aesthetics, and years later, among other translations of French, Italian, and English poetry, he reportedly

---

11 Members of Masayoshi Osawa's team in 1982 included Kyoko Ono, Shigeru Koike, Junnosuke Sawasaki, Kenzo Suzuki, and Motoi Toda.

translated some fifty pages of *FW* (Gumucio 2011), though most of them do not seem to have appeared in print. Some of the pages appeared in Mexico in 1974, as mentioned, in a cultural supplement, *La cultura en México*, of the political weekly *Siempre!*, and Monteforte's rendering was highly praised as an example of his exceptional literary powers (Gumucio 2011).[12] Eight years later, in April 1982, some further pages of Monteforte's translation appeared in Cuenca, in Ecuador, in recognition of the Joyce centenary year, in the journal *El guacamayo y la serpiente*. In an accompanying essay, Monteforte observes that his favoured translatorial approach to the untranslatable *FW* is to regard Joyce's text as essentially a libretto and himself as an invited performer of it, his role being to bring the libretto to vibrant life in Spanish (Burneo 2004, 22).[13]

Silva-Santisteban (Spanish, 1982, 1988)

In 1982, the Peruvian translator Ricardo Silva-Santisteban (born 1941) provided a Spanish version of the opening and closing pages of *ALP*, which appeared in Lima in the journal *Cielo abierto*. In 1988, Silva-Santisteban's *Anna Livia Plurabelle y otros textos del Finnegans Wake*, privately published in Lima in an edition of two hundred copies, includes his renderings of 1971 (*FW* 626–8) and 1982 (*FW* 196.1–197.17, 213.11–216.5) as well as the opening pages (*FW* 3.1–5.29). His complete rendering of *ALP*, to which we shall return, would appear in Mexico City in the journal *Biblioteca de México* in 1991.

Buenaventura (Spanish)

The Spanish novelist Ramón Buenaventura, born in Tangiers, Morocco, in 1940, is an award-winning translator from both French (Rimbaud) and English (F. Scott Fitzgerald, Sylvia Plath, Philip Roth, Anthony Burgess). He translated Burgess's *The Kingdom of the Wicked* (1985) into Spanish in the late 1980s, at which time Burgess reportedly encouraged him to read *FW*. Having done so, Buenaventura initially proposed to

---

12 "Su conocimiento profundo de las lenguas le permitía traducir tanto a Pessoa como a Joyce. Como recuerda Jorgenrique Adoum: 'Una muestra insólita de su talento literario fue el artículo "Finnegans Wake: Presentación y algunas páginas," publicado en *La cultura en México*, suplemento de *Siempre*': se trata de nueve cuartillas de su traducción de la obra de Joyce" (Gumucio 2011).

13 My thanks to Alfonso Gumucio in Bolivia, to Cristina Burneo Salazar in Ecuador, and to Juan Díaz Victoria in Mexico for kindly responding to requests for information on Monteforte's renderings. All efforts to track down the actual texts involved have so far been unavailing.

undertake a complete translation, but was unable at that time to reach a financial agreement with his publisher, Alfaguara of Madrid (Rosado 2016). The plan was abandoned – and some years later Buenaventura even went so far as to publish a newspaper article asserting that *FW* is not only untranslatable but in fact essentially incomprehensible (Buenaventura 1993).[14]

5 Catalan

Sobré (Catalan, 1982)

The centenary year also witnessed the first appearance of one more new language in the *Wake* universe. A Catalan version of an excerpt (*FW* 538.18–539.8) from the Yawn chapter (*FW* III.3), by the Catalan scholar and translator Josep-Miquel Sobré (1944–2015), also known by the Spanish form of his name as Josep Miquel Sobrer, appeared in a volume of critical essays on Joyce edited by Joan Ramón Masoliver, who had befriended Joyce in Paris in the 1930s. The rendering also appeared in a special issue of the Catalan journal *El Eco de Sitges* in December 1982 (Iribarren 2004, 454) – and is reprinted by Francisco García Tortosa (1992, 121–3), who speaks highly of its quality.

Sobré, a native of Barcelona, translated a number of English titles into Catalan, including works by H.G. Wells, Sylvia Plath, and Ian Fleming, as well as poetry by John Donne among others, and translated a number of works by Catalan writers into English. He taught at a number of North American universities, including finally at Indiana University in Bloomington.

Sobré's rendering includes a Catalan version of the following lines:

> I should tell you that honestly, on my honour of a Nearwicked, I always think in a wordworth's of that primed favourite continental poet, Daunty, Gouty and Shopkeeper, A.G., whom the generality admoyers in this that is and that this is to come. (*FW* 539.4–8)

Sobré's version, as reprinted by García Tortosa:

> Us hauria de dir que, de debò, pel meu honor de Neantisoreta, sempre penso amb el dídacvalor d'aquell favorit poeta europeu de primera,

---

14 This assertion was vigorously contested in the next issue of the same newspaper, *El mundo*, by the Spanish translator of *Anna Livia Plurabelle*, Francisco García Tortosa (1993).

Donant, Golleta i Xespir, S.A., a qui la gent admonirá en això que és i el que vindrá.

The name games here begin with Neantisoreta, playing on French *néant* ("nil") and Catalan *tisoreta* ("earwig"), while "dídacvalor" conflates *didáctic* ("didactic") and *valor* ("worth") in gesturing rather desperately towards Wordsworth. "Daunty" (Dante) becomes a mere "donor" (*donant*); "Gouty" (Goethe) is rendered in alcoholic terms by Spanish *gollete*, the "neck" of a bottle, possibly to be followed by a Catalan *galeta* ("cookie"); while "Shopkeeper" (Shakespeare as citizen of Napoleon's nation of shopkeepers) is rather more recognizable in Catalan than in English as "Xespir." The admired George Moyers, Lord Mayor of Dublin in the 1880s, disappears without trace.

6 Polish

Mirkowicz (Polish, 1982)

A Polish rendering of the opening pages (*FW* 3.1–5.12) by the Warsaw translator and writer Tomasz Mirkowicz (1953–2003) appeared in 1982 in the journal *Literatura na Świecie* (World literature). Katarzyna Bazarnik describes this version as rendering the multilingual complexity of the *Wake* in imaginative ways (2017).

Mirkowicz's opening lines (*FW* 3.1–3) read as follows:

rzekirzyg, obok Ewy i Adama, od wcięcia wybrzeża do zakola zatoki, prowadzi nas przez commodius vicus recorsolacji na powrót do Howth Castle i Edyficjów.[15]

Here the opening "riverrun" is rendered as a one-word "rzekirzyg"; Eve and Adam retain their Joycean order; "from swerve of shore to bend of bay" is rendered equally alliteratively as "od wcięcia wybrzeża do zakola zatoki"; Commodus and Vico are as evidently present as in Joyce's original; and we are brought back to "Howth Castle i Edyficjów," retaining HCE's initials by seeing the environs as consisting mainly of edifices – not inappropriately for HCE as a "man of hod, cement, and edifices" (*FW* 4.26–7).

---

15   Quoted here from an online blog by Krzysztof Bartnicki.

Słomczyński's Polish ALP *(1985)*

The year 1985 was a particularly important one for the multilingual extension of *ALP*, witnessing not only the complete Korean translation by Chong-keon Kim and also the eventual publication, after more than half a century, of Beckett and Péron's "Anna Lyvia Pluratself," but also a complete Polish rendering, the work of Maciej Słomczyński.

Słomczyński (1922–98) was a multitalented Polish writer, born in Warsaw to an English mother and an American father, though reportedly taking his surname from his Polish stepfather. Having joined the Polish resistance movement in the early 1940s, he was arrested, escaped, and fled to the West, serving with the American forces in France before returning to Poland in 1947 (Anon. 2017). A long-time resident of Krakow, and the author eventually of several novels under his own name, he also produced a by all accounts very successful series of detective novels, translated into more than a dozen languages, under the two pseudonyms Joe Alex and Kazimierz Kwaśniewski. He was also an extremely productive translator, whose output over the years included Polish renderings of Shakespeare's complete works as well as of individual works by Chaucer, Milton, Swift, Faulkner, Lewis Carroll, Nabokov, and various others.

He was also the central figure in Polish Joyce circles for at least the last thirty years of his life, having after twelve years of work produced a translation of *Ulysses* in 1969 that was an instant literary sensation, with an unusually large first edition of forty thousand copies reportedly selling out completely within days. Fritz Senn reported as early as 1967 that Słomczyński was also already working on what was intended to be a complete Polish translation of the *Wake* (Senn 1967c, 229). Słomczyński himself reportedly asserted that Polish was the ideal language in which to undertake a rendering of the *Wake*, in that the Polish language allegedly enjoyed a lexicon double the size of that of English (Van Laere 1968, 127). François Van Laere quotes Jacques Aubert's comment of those years that the planned complete Polish *Wake* was likely to be the only complete rendering of *FW* ever to appear.

Słomczyński's ambition to provide a complete translation, however, was to remain unfulfilled. With his Polish *Ulysses* triumphantly completed, he published a Polish version of "The Ballad of Persse O'Reilly" (*FW* 44–7) as well as an excerpt from II.4 (*FW* 398–9) in 1972, followed by a Polish rendering of the opening and closing ages of *ALP* (*FW* 196–202, 215–16) in 1973. Twelve years later, in 1985, his complete translation of *ALP* appeared, followed a decade later, in 1996, just two years before his death, by a rendering of the final page of the *Wake*. No other renderings appeared.

Fritz Senn writes reminiscently that Słomczyński was not only an entertaining character, but also "an original, full of ideas and projects" – including on one occasion a proposal to Senn that the two of them should "do a film script of the *Wake* for his friend Roman Polanski" (2007, 99). The scheme, alas, designed to make them all rich, came to nothing. Senn also reports that Słomczyński, among other eccentricities, claimed to have had a secretary in Krakow "who had typed the whole of the *Wake* in reverse, so he could read it, literally, backwards as well, from 'eht' to 'nurrevir'" (2007, 99).

Słomczyński's *ALP*, like his *Ulysses*, was also an immediate popular success, the entire edition of some thirty-three hundred copies once again selling out immediately on publication (Szczerbowski 2000, 88). Jolanta Wawrzycka reports that initially, given his already long-standing Joycean reputation, his rendering of *ALP* "went largely unchallenged by the Polish scholars and translators, though the late 1990s and 2000 brought a few new sophisticated and critical voices" (2004a, 227). One of the criticisms raised at that later point was that the surprisingly enthusiastic popular reaction to Słomczyński's *ALP* may to a considerable degree have in fact been the result of a publisher's marketing strategy that strongly emphasized the sexual boldness of Joyce's text, presenting it, appropriately illustrated to make the point, as if it were in fact likely to be primarily of interest to readers in search less of the niceties of literary experimentation than of straightforward erotic stimulation.

Tadeusz Szczerbowski disputes as a result that Słomczyński's rendering can in fact be called a translation in the first place, classifying it as transgressive on the grounds that the translator deliberately set out to vulgarize Joyce's text with potential sales in mind: "the difference between *intentio auctoris* and *intentio traductoris* is so striking that the term *translator* seems improper here. ... Possibly he simplifies Joyce in good faith to make the extremely difficult text accessible to the reader. This is why he replaces the previous context full of subtle allusions by vulgar references. One way or the other, his *Anna Livia Plurabelle* is not any more James Joyce's because of many differences. Being too original, the Polish book is not a translation" (2000, 91).[16] Fritz Senn, however, considers the result to be "a beautiful *ALP*" (2007, 99).

---

16 My thanks to Tadeusz Szczerbowski of the Pedagogical University of Cracow for kindly sending me a photocopy of Słomczyński's Polish *ALP*. On Słomczyński's rendering, see Brown (1991), Bazarnik (1999), Szczerbowski (2000), Wawrzycka (2004a, 2004b).

Słomczyński's translations of Shakespeare also came in for criticism in some quarters eventually as being too loose. For all that, in a tribute to him as a translator, Jolanta Wawrzycka writes of him as "in many respects a genius-translator and in every respect a giant figure in Poland's reception of Anglo-Saxon and American literature" (2004b, 143).

Słomczyński's rendering of the opening sentences of *ALP* includes the following lines (*FW* 196.1–7, 9–11):

O / mów mi wszystko / o Annie Livii! Chcę słyszeć wszystko o Annie Livii. No cóż, znasz Annę Livię? Tak, oczywiście, wszyscy znamy Annę Livię. Wszystko mów. Zaraz mów. Skonasz usłyszawszy. No cóż, wiesz, kiedy ten stary kiep futtknął się i zrobił to, co wiesz. ... Mów, o czym po padło, co im się troiło z tego, co wtroił tym dwóm w Pieklix parku.

Słomczyński's rendering of "tell me all" as "mów mi wszystko" fluvially evokes the river Mow of Papua New Guinea, while "Zaraz mów" ("Tell me now") adds the Eritrean Zara. His "Skonasz usłyszawszy" ("You'll die when you hear") evokes the Russian Ona, the Canadian Nass, and, for good measure, reminds us of the German adjective *nass* ("wet"). The old cheb is unsympathetically seen not just as an old chap but as "ten stary kiep" ("this old fool"). As for the reported events in the park, the phrase "co wtroił tym dwóm," suggesting "what he tried to do to the two," manages to include disguised reference to both the three (*trzy*) and the two (*dwa*) as well as playing simultaneously and interlingually ("wtroił") on the English *try*. Amusingly, whatever it was that happened in the "fiendish park" is located by Słomczyński as having happened "w Pieklix parku," in a park where one might well witness infernal goings-on (*piekło* "inferno") – as in the translingual combination offered here of HCE's regrettable "peeks" and his two temptresses' spied-upon "leaks."

7 German

Füger (German, 1983)

A German rendering of an excerpt from I.1 (*FW* 4.18–5.5) by Wilhelm Füger (1936–2017), Joyce scholar and professor of English at the Free University of Berlin, appeared in the *James Joyce Broadsheet* in October 1983.

Schmidt (German, 1984)

The early eighties also saw the reappearance in 1984 of Arno Schmidt's experimental translations made in 1960 and first published in his 1969 volume on Joyce, *Der Triton mit dem Sonnenschirm*. The reissue, marking Schmidt's seventieth birthday five years after his death, took the form of twenty-four sheets containing a facsimile of Schmidt's original (and idiosyncratic) typescript, which was published to accompany a bibliophile full-colour facsimile edition of his original working copy of *FW*, heavily annotated in Schmidt's own handwriting and with multiple underlinings, arrows, marginal notes, and exclamation marks in various colours throughout. Published in Zurich by Haffmans Verlag, it appeared in 1,001 numbered copies at the very substantial price of 500 German marks. It continues to command high prices from antiquarian booksellers online. The translations were subsequently reprinted in Reichert and Senn's *Finnegans Wake Deutsch* (276–319).

Weninger (German, 1984)

A German translation of "The Mookse and the Gripes" (*FW* 152.15–159.18) by Robert Weninger also appeared in book form in 1984, the seven pages of the translated text, "Der Muhkus und Der Trauben," preceded by more than two hundred pages of commentary. The translated fable was reprinted (without the commentary) in *FWD* (116–23). Weninger reportedly spent six years working on the rendering, largely completed while a graduate student at the Goethe University of Frankfurt am Main, under the direction of Klaus Reichert. Subsequently a Germanist by profession, and author also of *The German Joyce* (2012), Weninger taught at universities in both the United States and the United Kingdom before an eventual appointment to the chair of German at King's College London.[17]

His version of the fable of "The Mookse and the Gripes" includes a rendering of the following lines (*FW* 152.18–20, 28–30, 153.9–11):

Eins within a space and a wearywide space it wast ere wohned a Mookse. The onesomeness wast alltolonely, archunsitslike, broady oval, and a Mookse he would a walking go (My hood! cries Antony Romeo) ... and set off from Ludstown *a spasso* to see how badness was badness in the weirdest of all pensible ways. ... And, I declare, what was there on the yonder bank of the stream that would be a river, parched on a limb of the olum, bolt downright, but the Gripes?

---

17 On Weninger's version, see Weninger (1985). For comparative discussions (in German) of several German renderings of "The Mookse and the Gripes" (Weninger 1984; Horn 1989; Rathjen 1989), see Blumenbach (1990, 40–3). The discussion is broadened to include Schönmetzler (1987a) and Stündel (1993) by Friedhelm Rathjen (2009, 131–9).

Weninger's version (*FWD* 116–17):

Einst war einall und alts ein raomfassend all es hallte darinmalls äre-
wohnte ein Muhkus. Die einsamalleinkeit alltuhallein war, hörschter-
sitzstill, weitgehgend owal, und ein Muhkus der paszieren geht (Mei
Huot! Antrom Reiser fleht) ... und machte sich dann *a spatzo* von Götzwill
auf um zu sehen wie schlechtigkeit schlechtigkeit war im seltlichsten aller dünklichsten weiten. ... Und, so dekläre ich, was befand sich dort auf
jenem ufer dieses bächleins das einst ein fluß würde, sohrgehockend auf
einem limbus des olim, tiefe zugerichtet, wenn nicht der Traubenichts?

Enzensberger (German, 1985)

A German rendering of an excerpt (*FW* 241.1–26) by a seminar group of
university students led by the literary critic and theorist Christian Enzensberger (1931–2009), professor of English at the Ludwig Maximilian
University of Munich, appeared in a special issue of the Viennese literary journal *Protokolle* in 1985.[18] Enzensberger's many translations from
English included *Alice's Adventures in Wonderland* and *Alice through the
Looking-Glass* as well as Beckett's *More Pricks Than Kicks*.

Fried (German, 1985)

A German rendering of an excerpt (*FW* 403.1–404.3) by the poet Erich
Fried (1921–88), with detailed commentary, also appeared in *Protokolle*
in 1985. It had originally been delivered as part of a radio program,
"Werkstatt *Finnegans Wake*, 4," broadcast by the Norddeutscher Rundfunk on 18 April 1978 (Rathjen 2012b, 296).

Herms (German, 1985)

A rendering of four excerpts (*FW* 17, 18, 66, 68) by the German writer
Uwe Herms (born 1937), with detailed commentary, likewise appeared
in *Protokolle* in 1985. It had also originally been delivered as part of a
radio program, "Werkstatt *Finnegans Wake*, 2," broadcast by the Norddeutscher Rundfunk on 13 December 1977 (Rathjen 2012b, 296–7).

---

18 The first issue of the Viennese literary journal *Protokolle*, in 1985, contained several
    German renderings from *FW*, including by Uwe Herms (*FW* 17, 18, 66, 68), Robert
    Weninger (*FW* 152.15–159.18), Christian Enzensberger (*FW* 241.1–26), and Erich
    Fried (*FW* 403.1–404.3).

Beck (German, 1986, 1987)

A German rendering of the opening pages by the Joyce scholar Harald Beck appeared in 1986 (*FW* 3–5) and 1987 (*FW* 5–7) in the journal *Bargfelder Bote*, and the rendering was extended in 1989 to include *FW* 3.1–11.28 (*FWD* 27–35).[19] Born in Munich in 1951, and a collaborator on Hans Walter Gabler's critical edition of *Ulysses*, Beck, who studied English and German at Bonn and Munich, also translated *Dubliners* and the "Penelope" chapter of *Ulysses*. He subsequently spent ten years co-ordinating a team of colleagues preparing a detailed revision for the Suhrkamp Verlag of Hans Wollschläger's 1975 German version of *Ulysses* – before publication was eventually blocked by a legal challenge inexplicably not foreseen by the publisher.

Beck's incipit (*FWD* 27):

> flußlauf vorbei an Ev' und Adams vom küstenknick zum bug der bucht bringt uns auf kommodem vicus zirkel wieder zurück zu Howth Castells Engrer umgebung.

Beck's "flußlauf" is a literal one-word "riverrun," passing from the alliterative "küstenknick," suggesting an abrupt coastal distortion, to the likewise alliterative bend of the bay ("bug der bucht"). Commodus and Vico are clearly identifiable in what is now implied to be a potentially vicious circle ("vicus zirkel"). In order to retain HCE's initials, Beck plays on a humorous subversion of standard German orthographical usage by capitalizing the adjective "engrer" ("nearer") while leaving uncapitalized the noun "Umgebung" ("surroundings, environs") and all other nouns mentioned.

Schönmetzler (German, 1987)

Some twenty-three pages of excerpts from *FW* in German translation by Klaus Schönmetzler appeared in 1987, privately published in a twenty-page booklet of photocopied typescript.[20] Schönmetzler (1949–2017), born in the Bavarian town of Bad Aibling, was a German writer, music critic, and local historian. A slightly extended version of his rendering

---

19 The *Bargfelder Bote* (Bargfeld messenger) is a publication devoted specifically to the work of Arno Schmidt and its wider environs. Modelled in general terms on *A Wake Newslitter*, it has published a number of items on Joyce, especially on *FW*.

20 The excerpts rendered include *FW* 3.1–5.29, 152.16–159.18, 169.1–175.28, 383.1–384.32, 414.16–415.22, 605.4–606.12, 626.20–628.16.

of the opening pages (*FW* 3.1–6.1) appeared, also in 1987, in the journal *Bargfelder Bote*.[21]

Schönmetzler (1987a, 2) renders the opening lines as follows:

> flußvoran, nach Eve und Adam, vom Küstenkreis zum Buchtenband, und bringt uns auf commodestem vicus rezirkulatorisch zurück zu Howth Castle samt seiner Ebene.

Here the one-word "flußvoran," echoing the original dactylic "riverrun," literally means "riveronwards, riveron." The river passes after Eve and Adam from an alliterative curve, literally "circle" (*Kreis*), of coast (*Küste*) to a likewise alliterative ribbon (*Band*) of bay (*Bucht*), and brings us by a comfortable (*kommod*) and untranslated vicus in a process of recirculation (*rezirkulatorisch*) back to an untranslated Howth Castle and, in order to save HCE's initials, its "plateau," its "plain" (*Ebene*).

Schönmetzler's version (1987a, 5) of the fable of "The Mookse and the Gripes," the title of which he translates as "Der Muhks und Der Traube," includes a rendering of *FW* 152.18–20, 28–30, 153.9–11 that may be compared with Robert Weninger's 1984 rendering of the same lines quoted above. Schönmetzler's version:

> Einst war imall im weitenbreiten Raum, da wohnte ein Muhks. Die Einssamkeit war allzuöde und archontensitzam, breitgehend oval, und das Wandern war des Muhkens Lust, hallo! (Meinjott, schreit Antony Romeo) ... Und er brach auf aus Laudon a spasso um zu sehen, wie schlecht die Schlechtigkeit war auf dem unheimlichsten aller möglichen Wege. ... Und, ich beschwör's, was war da auf dem andern Ufer jenes Strömleins, das ein Fluß sein wollte, dürrehängend an dem Ast des Olums, pfeilgerad abwärts, anderes als der Traube?

Reichert and Senn (Finnegans Wake Deutsch, *1989*)

These German-language creative energies led in 1989 to the important volume *Finnegans Wake Deutsch* (*FWD*), edited by Klaus Reichert, Joyce scholar and professor of English at the Goethe University of Frankfurt am Main, and Fritz Senn, Joyce scholar par excellence and director of

---

21 On Schönmetzler's renderings, see Blumenbach (1990, 43–5). My thanks to Christine Schönmetzler for kindly sending me an electronic copy of her late husband's 1987 booklet. She suggested in personal correspondence that probably only a few copies of it were produced, for sale in the family bookshop.

the Zurich James Joyce Foundation. The two had already very successfully collaborated as editors of the likewise important *Anna Livia Plurabelle* volume of 1970.

In German the traditional title of *FW* in other than Joycean circles is *Finnegans Totenwache*, literally, "Finnegan's wake," the funeral wake (*Wache*) for a dead person (*ein Toter*) – but serendipitously hinting also, as in the original English title, at the states of being awake (*wach*) and of awakening (*erwachen*). Reichert and Senn, however, choose to employ instead a bilingual title that mirrors the (apparently) ungrammatical absence of an English apostrophe in the original title by the equally ungrammatical presence of a capitalized (rather than lower-case) German adjective (*deutsch* "German").

The particularly rich volume contains collected excerpts from *FW* (about a quarter of the original text in all) in German translation by various hands, including Harald Beck (*FW* 3.1–11.28), Ulrich Blumenbach and Reinhard Markner (*FW* 619.20–628.16), Ingeborg Horn (*FW* 126.1–168.14), Kurt Jauslin (*FW* 3.1–5.29), Friedhelm Rathjen (*FW* 3.1–14, 30.1–47.32, 152.15–159.18, 383.1–399.36, 414.16–419.10, 627.24–628.16), Klaus Reichert (*FW* 619.20–620.2, 626.35–628.16), Wolfgang Schrödter (*FW* 3.1–4.17), Helmut Stoltefuß (*FW* 30.1–38.8), Dieter Stündel (*FW* 383.1–399.36, 619.20–620.2), Robert Weninger (*FW* 152.15–159.18, previously published in 1984), a seminar group of the Goethe University of Frankfurt am Main led by Klaus Reichert (I.7; *FW* 169.1–195.6), the three previously published translations of *ALP* (1970) by Georg Goyert, Wolfgang Hildesheimer, and Hans Wollschläger, and Arno Schmidt's previously published 1969 versions of selected passages, supplemented by five new passages previously published in 1984 (*FW* 30–1, 39, 142, 166–7, 308). *Finnegans Wake Deutsch* provides as many as four different German translations of certain passages.[22]

Other than some of the individual renderings published in the early 1980s in such journals as the Viennese *Protokolle* and which appeared too late to be included, *Finnegans Wake Deutsch* contained all the German renderings from *FW* in existence as of the late 1980s. Those renderings amounted in all to roughly one-quarter of Joyce's text, with some major excerpts presented in as many as four different versions. While a major achievement in the field of *Wake* translations, it was nonetheless still far from being a complete German rendering of the *Wake*. One of its contributors, however, was Dieter Stündel, who had already been

---

22 On the various German renderings in *FWD*, see Reichert (1989a), Blumenbach (1990, 1998), Rathjen (2009, 2010), Reisinger (2015).

working since 1974 on exactly such a project. His *Finnegans Wehg* would appear to great media fanfare in 1993 – and thereby hangs another tale, to which we shall return.

Reichert (German, 1989)

The German team translation of the "Shem" chapter (I.7; *FW* 169.1–195.6) by a seminar group of the Goethe University of Frankfurt am Main, led by Klaus Reichert, first appeared in *FWD* (132–58). The translation was the result of two years of collective work. Reichert describes the general procedure: "A seminar participant would prepare an excerpt at home, which would then be discussed and edited by the group, a process allowing for both continuity and homogeneity, while endeavouring also not to lose completely the particular input and insights of the individual translator."[23]

Blumenbach and Markner (German, 1989)

A German rendering (*FWD* 262–70) of the closing pages (*FW* 619.20–628.16) was the work of Ulrich Blumenbach and Reinhard Markner, both then university students in Berlin. Blumenbach (born 1964 in Hanover and a long-term resident of Basel) was to become a prize-winning professional translator from English to German, focusing especially on several works by David Foster Wallace.[24]

The Blumenbach and Markner rendering of the final page includes the following lines (*FW* 627.34–628.4, 15–16):

Ich scheide dahin. O bittres Ende! Ich gleit hinaus, eh sie auf sind. Sie werdens nie sehn. Noch wissen. Noch mich missen. Und es ist alt und alt ists irr und alt ists irr und traurig kehr ich zu dir, mein kalter Vater, mein kalt wirrer Vater, mein kalt wirr feuriger Vater, bis der Nahnblick seiner bloßen Größe, seine Moylen um Moylen, jamanaandernd mich seeschlick salzsiechtig macht, und ich stürze, mein einziger, in deine Arme. ... Zuwegs allein zuletzt alliebst zulängs dem

---

23 "Jeweils ein Teilnehmer übersetzte einen Abschnitt zu Hause vor, der dann im Kollektiv diskutiert und redigiert wurde. Dadurch wurde so etwas wie Kontinuität und Homogeneität hergestellt, ohne daß jedoch die einzelnen Stimmen in ihrer Eigenart, ihrer Emphase, ihrer Skansion gänzlich getilgt wurden" (Reichert 1989a, 17).

24 On Blumenbach's work as a translator of the *Wake*, see Senn (2007, 97, 101). For a brief comparative discussion (in German) of several German renderings of Anna Livia's final monologue, see Blumenbach (1990, 43–5).

Horn (German, 1989)

Ingeborg Horn's German rendering of the more than forty-page chapter I.6 (*FW* 126.1–168.14), the result of two years of work, appeared as the longest single translation in *FWD* (73–115). Born in 1958 in Hamburg, Horn studied philosophy and Classics at the Ludwig Maximilian University of Munich before moving to the Austrian Salzkammergut, near Salzburg, to begin a career as a freelance writer. Her version (*FWD* 99–100) of the fable of "The Mookse and the Gripes," the title of which she leaves untranslated, includes a rendering of the same lines (*FW* 152.18–20, 28–30, 153.9–11) as translated by Weninger and by Schönmetzler, quoted above in both cases.

Horn's version:

> Einst wast inmal ein raum und ein schwerweiter raum ist das gewüsten ere wohned ein Mookse. Die einssamkeit wast allzuleinsam, erzunsitzgleich, breithin oval, und ein Mookse der möcht' eins walken gehen (My hood! schreit Antony Romeo) ... und machte sich auf von Ludstown *a spasso* um zu sehen wie bösenis wäre bösenis im dem weirdesten aller pensiblen wege. ... Und, Ich deklariere, was war da auf der jenseitigen uferbank von dem bächlein, von diesem möchtegernfluß, ausgedörrt an einem schwanken ast der olume, wenn nicht der Gripes?

Jauslin (German, 1989)

Kurt Jauslin's rendering (*FWD* 36–8) of the opening pages (*FW* 3.1–5.29) includes the following version of the opening three lines:

> Flußfloß furbay Eva' und Adams dahein vom Klippenrand zur verschlungenen Bucht und er bringt uns wieder in lässigem Circel zurück über Commodus und Vico nach Hoth Castle samt Einzugskreis.

Jauslin's "Flußfloß," combining "river" (*Fluß*) and "flowed" (*floß*) in a one-word "riverflowed," replicates he alliterative effect of the original "riverrun." His invented "furbay" then conflates the German verb *fuhr* ("travelled"), the preposition *bei* ("by"), the adverb *vorbei* ("past"), and, in translingual anticipation of the river's ultimate destination, the English noun *bay*. The river's progress is further specified as "dahein," conflating *dahin* ("onwards") and the suggestion that the river is both going "home" (*heim*) to the sea and simultaneously, as Dublin's own river, is already "at home" (*daheim*). This rendering speaks of the river's progress from a "rocky cliffedge" (*Klippenrand*), presumably (though not in geographical actuality) Howth, to a "winding" bay (*zur verschlungenen Bucht*), bringing us, courtesy of Commodus and Vico, back to Howth again in a lazy (*lässig*) circle (*Zirkel*). The circle is clearly a vicious one, for the variation "Circel" of the standard *Zirkel* adventurously invokes the specific viciousness of Circe, who turns men into swine, and gestures intertextually also to the "Circe" episode in *Ulysses*. Jauslin's "Hoth Castle samt Einzugskreis" changes the gloss to "with catchment area." The spelling "Hoth" – a spelling also to be found in the original *Wake* (*FW* 4.11) – is readable as not only suggesting for German readers the correct pronunciation of the tricky foreign diphthong, but also as reflecting the inevitable abrasions, onomastic and otherwise, effected by history and time.[25]

Rathjen (German, 1989)

Friedhelm Rathjen produced German renderings of six separate passages, roughly fifty pages altogether, in *FWD*.[26] Born in 1958 in Lower Saxony, and a long-term resident of Schleswig-Holstein in northern Germany, the German writer, translator, and independent scholar Rathjen has subsequently written widely especially on Joyce, Beckett, and Arno Schmidt and on the literary connections between the three. He writes, edits, and self-publishes an entire literary series of works under the title *Edition ReJoyce*, more than eighty volumes of which have already appeared. He has translated works by Joyce, Melville, Mark Twain, Gertrude Stein, and Anthony Burgess among many others. He began to translate excerpts from *FW* in 1984, in his mid-twenties (Rathjen 2012b, 7) – and continued to translate further excerpts, to which we shall return, for much of the next forty years.

Rathjen's 1989 rendering of the opening three lines of *FW*:

Flußgefließe schleunigst Ev' und Adam passiert vom Strandgestreun zum Buchtgebeug führt uns im commundiösen Wickelwirken des Rezirkulierens zurück zur Burg von Howth con Entourage.

Here "Flußgefließe," literally "riverflowings," replicates the alliterative effect of "riverrun." Unlike the slow drift of, for example, Lavergne's lazy river, Rathjen's proves to be rushing past, as indicated

---

25 On Jauslin's rendering, see also Kosta (2013).

26 The excerpts translated by Rathjen include *FW* 3.1–14, 30.1–47.32, 152.15–159.18, 383.1–399.36, 414.16–419.10, 627.24–628.16. They appeared in *FWD* 44, 45–63, 124–31, 220–37, 256–61, 275.

by the German superlative "schleunigst" ("at great speed"). This decision has less to do with geography, even literary geography, than with the attempt to imitate Joyce's apparent inclusion of the name Stephen in "past Eve and," here "-st Ev' und."[27] Joyce's "swerve of shore" becomes Rathjen's doubly alliterative "Strandgestreun," suggesting, literally, a scattering (*streuen* "to strew, to scatter") of beach (*Strand*), followed by the bending (*Gebeug*) of the bay (*Bucht*). The river's course leads us (*führt uns*) by a "process of enfolding" (*Wickelwirkung*), that also enfolds a heavily disguised Vico (*wickeln* "to enfold"). Rathjen's characterization of that process as "commundiös" not only suggests the presence of Commodus but also suggests the universality of the process (German *kommun*, "common," Latin *mundus* "world"). One challenge faced by German translators of the *Wake* is that there are very few words beginning with *c* in German, complicating the search for HCE's initials. Saving the initials, Rathjen's "Burg von *Howth con Entourage*" germanizes Howth Castle as the "Burg von Howth" and adjusts the geographical "environs" to a personal "Entourage," thus adding a French tower (*tour*) to his Irish castle.

Rathjen's version (*FWD*124–25) of the fable of "The Mookse and the Gripes," the title of which he translates as "Der Mauchs und Der Traufen," includes a rendering of the same lines (*FW* 152.18–20, 28–30, 153.9–11) as translated by Weninger, by Schönmetzler, and by Horn, quoted above in all three cases.

Rathjen's version:

Eins war womal in weitem Raum und das gar ein leerweiter Raum rin wondge ein Mauchs. Die Einseinkeit war allzuleinig, archuntischlich, breitlich üval, und ein Mauchs er pflegte spazieren zu gehen (Mein Hut! schreit Antonius Romeo) ... und machte sich *a spasso* von Ludsstadt auf zu sehen wie Schlechtigkeit Schlechtigkeit war in der gespinsten aller löblichen Weisen. ... Und, so verkünd ich, was war da anderes am jenseitigen Ufer des Wässerchens das ein Fluß sein würde, röstend auf einem Absteigast der Olume, pfeilsteil abrecht, als der Traufen?

Rathjen's rendering (*FWD* 275) of the final page includes the following lines (*FW* 627.34–628.4, 15–16):

---

27 My thanks to Friedhelm Rathjen for confirming this information in personal correspondence.

Ich entfleuße. O bittres Ende! Ich entschlüpfe bevor sie auf sind. Sie werden's nie sehen. Noch wissen. Noch mich vermissen. Und's ist trübe und trübe es ist bejahrt und trübe es ist bejahrt und benommen und geh zurück zu dir, mein kühler Vater, mein kühler vernarrter Vater, mein kühler vernarrter beklommener Vater, bis das dichte Angesicht seines schlichten Ausgehmaßes, dieser Moylen um Moylen, rumornunmurrnd, mich seetang macht salzkrang und ich mich stürze, mein einzigs, in deine Arme. ... Ein Weg ein samer ein letzter ein liebster entlang der

Schrödter (German, 1989)

Wolfgang Schrödter's rendering (*FWD* 39–43) of the opening pages (*FW* 3.1–4.17) includes his version of the three-line incipit:

Flußeslauf Seit' Eve und Adams von der Krümmung der Küste zur Biegung der Bucht bringt uns in einem commoden Rezirkulus viciosus zurück zu Howth Castle und Ergebungen.

Here the one-word "Flußeslauf" combines "river" (*Fluß*) and "course" (*Lauf*) as "river's course." The formulation "Seit' Eve und Adams" conflates geographical space (*Seite*, the "side" of the river), historical time (*seit* "since"), and the literary "page" (*Seite*) on which our story of space and time will be written. Preserving Joyce's alliterative pairs, swerve of shore becomes bend (*Krümmung*) of coast (*Küste*), and bend of bay becomes turn (*Biegung*) of bay (*Bucht*). Commodus and Vico are present in a comfortable (*kommod*) but vicious process of recirculation, a *Rezirkulus viciosus* that brings us back to "Howth Castle und Ergebungen," a formulation that preserves HCE's initials by replacing geographical environs by memories of historical *Ergebungen* ("surrenders").

Stoltefuß (German, 1989)

Helmut Stoltefuß contributes a rendering (*FWD* 64–72) of an excerpt from the opening of I.2 (*FW* 30.1–38.8), including the following lines (*FW* 30.11–18):

We are told how in the beginning it came to pass that like cabbaging Cincinnatus the grand old gardener was saving daylight under his redwoodtree one sultry sabbath afternoon, Hag Chivychas Eve, in prefall paradise peace by following his plough for rootles in the rere garden of

mobhouse, ye olde marine hotel, when royalty was announced by runner
to have been pleased to have halted itself on the highroad ...

Stoltefuß's version:

Uns wird berichtet wie am anfang es zu pass kam, daß wie der cappesköp-
fende Cincinnatus der große alte gärtner tageslicht unter seinem sandel-
baum sammelnd an einem schwülen sabbathnachmittag, Hex' Cickecack
Ev', in präsündfalltiger paradiesiger pracht beim verfolgen seines pfluges
nach würzelchen im hintergarten des mobhouse, euer altes marinehotel,
als das gerücht ausgestreut wurde von einem läufer, und es hatte geruht,
sich gehalten zu haben auf der hochstraße ...[28]

8 Korean

Kim's Korean ALP *(1985)*

Osawa's Japanese *ALP* of 1982 was followed three years later by a Korean *ALP*, the work of Chong-keon Kim. Born in 1935, Kim, who served
for many years as a professor of English at Korea University in Seoul,
has long been regarded as the central figure in the field of Korean Joyce
translations. He won a Korean PEN prize as Translator of the Year for
his acclaimed translation of *Ulysses* in 1968, on which he had already
spent six years, and then went on over the next twenty years to add
translations of *Dubliners*, *Exiles*, *Portrait*, and the collected poems, as
well as *ALP*, which appeared in 1985 (O'Neill 2005, 88–9).[29]

9 Serbian

Anonymous (1986)

An anonymous Serbian rendering of an excerpt from *FW* 593–4 is reported as having appeared in 1986 in the Belgrade literary journal *Delo*
(Work) (Josipović 2011, 101). The only previous Serbian rendering,
an anonymously translated excerpt from *ALP* in the Belgrade journal
Mlada kultura (New culture), had reportedly appeared thirty years earlier, in 1956.

---

28 Stoltefuß's version of these lines may be compared with that of Arno Schmidt
    (1969), as already quoted.
29 On Kim's renderings of Joyce, including *ALP*, see Kim (1990).

10 Swedish

Friberg, Östergren

Swedish made a first appearance in the *Wake* universe when in 1987 a Swedish adaptation by Georg and Gösta Friberg of John Cage's song text "The Wonderful Widow of Eighteen Springs" (1942), based on *FW* 556.1–22, appeared in the Stockholm literary journal *Lyrikvännen* (Poetry lover). Gösta Friberg (1936–2018) was an award-winning Swedish poet, writer, and translator.

The Swedish poet and translator Jan Östergren (1940–99), born in Lund, reportedly considered undertaking a complete rendering of *FW* in the late 1980s in collaboration with the poet and translator Tommy Olofsson (born 1950), whose Swedish translation of *A Portrait of the Artist as a Young Man* also appeared in 1988. The plan was eventually allowed to lapse.[30]

---

30 My thanks to Bertil Falk for providing this information in personal correspondence – and for energetically conducting research in Sweden on both of these items.

Chapter Seven

The 1990s

*1 Portuguese; 2 Italian; 3 Japanese; 4 Spanish; 5 Hungarian;
6 German; 7 Galician; 8 Polish; 9 Romanian; 10 Danish;
11 Russian; 12 Guarani*

The early 1990s saw the appearance of a complete Japanese *Wake* by Naoki Yanase (1991, 1993), a complete German *Wake* by Dieter Stündel (1993), and an abridged Spanish *Wake* by Víctor Pozanco (1993). The decade also saw substantial renderings in Hungarian by Endre Bíró (1992) and in Russian by Henri Volokhonsky (1996–9).

Renderings of individual chapters included complete Spanish *ALP*s by Ricardo Silva-Santisteban (1991) and by Francisco García Tortosa (1992); an Italian *ALP* by Luigi Schenoni (1996); a Romanian *ALP* by Felicia Antip (1996); a Galician rendering of *FW* I.1–2 by Alberte Pagán (1993); and a Portuguese rendering of *FW* I.1 by Donaldo Schüler (1999). A Spanish version of Ogden's *ALP* by C.E. Feiling (1992) also appeared.

Briefer renderings appeared in Italian by Luigi Schenoni (1990, 1991, 1999); in Portuguese by Arthur Nestrovski (1990, 1998) and by Haroldo de Campos (1999); in German by Friedhelm Rathjen (1992, 1994, 1995) and by Dieter Stündel (1992); in Spanish by Luis Chitarroni and C.E. Feiling (1992) and by Leónidas Lamborghini (1992); in Polish by Jacek Malicki (1996), by Maciej Słomczyński (1996), and by Adam Królikowski (1998, 1999); in Danish by Peter Laugesen (1997, 1999); in Romanian by Laurent Milesi (1998) – and in Guarani by Sérgio Medeiros (1999).

1 Portuguese

Nestrovski (Portuguese, 1990, 1998)

Arthur Nestrovski (born 1959 in Pôrto Alegre) is a Brazilian writer, musician, and professor of literary studies at the Pontifical Catholic University of São Paulo. A Portuguese translation of the closing two pages of I.7 (*FW* 193.31–195.6) by Nestrovski, then at the University of Iowa, appeared in the *James Joyce Quarterly* in 1990. The passage translated includes the following lines (*FW* 193.31–6):

MERCIUS (of hisself): *Domine vopiscus!* My fault, his fault, a kingship through a fault! Pariah, cannibal Cain, I who oathily forswore the womb that bore you and the paps I sometimes sucked, you who ever since have been one black mass of jigs and jimjams, haunted by a convulsionary sense of not having been or being all that I might have been [...]

Nestrovski's version (1990, 475):

MERCIUS (de seu mesmo): *Domine vopiscus!* Minha culpa, tua culpa, meu reino por uma culpa! Pária, Caim, canibal, eu, que abjurei solenemente o ventre que te concebeu e o seio onde algumas vezes mamei, tu que desde então tens sido sempre uma missa negra de frevos e delirium tremens, obcecado por um sentimento convulsivo de não teres sido ou não seres tudo o que eu poderia ter sido [...]

A Portuguese rendering ("Mamafesta") by Nestrovski of the opening paragraphs of I.5 (*FW* 104.1–112.27) appeared in the newspaper *Folha de São Paulo* on Bloomsday 1998. The rendering includes the opening lines (*FW* 104.1–5):

In the name of Annah the Allmaziful, the Everliving, the Bringer of Plurabilities, haloed be her eve, her singtime sung, her rill be run, unhemmed as it is uneven! / Her untitled mamafesta memorialising the Mosthighest has gone by many names at disjointed times.

Nestrovski's version:

Em nome de Annah, a Mandalamaya, a Viveterna, a Portadora de Plurabilidades, santificado seja o vosso sono, venha voz morena, seja fluente a vossa abordagem, assim naquela como no seu! / Sua mamafesta sem título, memorializando o Altissíssimo já recebeu diversos nomes nas mais variadas épocas.

2 Italian

Schenoni (Italian, 1990, 1991, 1996, 1999)

Among ongoing planned complete translations, Italian renderings by Luigi Schenoni continued to appear, in 1990 (*FW* 104.1–112.27), in 1991 (*FW* 117.9–125.23), and in 1999 (*FW* 169.1–171.28). His major rendering in the 1990s was of *Anna Livia Plurabelle* in 1996, a revised version of which would appear in 2001, and to which we shall return.

Bosinelli (Italian, 1996)

In 1996, the Italian Joyce scholar Rosa Maria Bollettieri Bosinelli (1949–2016), professor of English and translation studies at the University of Bologna, edited a valuable compendium of renderings of *ALP*. The volume included an introduction by Umberto Eco and a long essay by Bosinelli, as well as Joyce's English, French, and Italian *ALP*s, Ogden's Basic English *ALP*, Beckett and Péron's *Anna Lyvia Pluratself*, and a new Italian translation of *FW* I.8 by Luigi Schenoni (which would later appear in revised form in 2001 in his rendering of *FW* I.5–8).[1]

3 Japanese

Yanase's Japanese Wake: Fineganzu ueiku *(1991, 1993)*

As Eishiro Ito writes (2004), the history of translating *FW* into Japanese can be traced back to the year 1933 and Junzaburo Nishiwaki's partial rendering of *ALP*. Further partial translations by a team led by Masayoshi Osawa of Chuo University, and with slightly varying memberships, appeared in 1966, 1968, and 1970–2. The major accomplishment of these years in Japanese was a rendering of the first three chapters of *FW* in 1971 by a different team, this time led by Yukio Suzuki of Waseda University. Osawa's team translated five further excerpts in 1978, and

---

1 My thanks are due to the late Rosa Maria Bosinelli for kindly sending me a copy of her excellent compendium.

their efforts culminated in a complete Japanese rendering of *ALP* in the Joyce centenary year of 1982.

Twenty years after the Suzuki team translation of the first three chapters in 1971, the early 1990s saw the publication of a first complete Japanese *FW*, translated by Naoki Yanase (1943–2016). It appeared in Tokyo in two separate volumes, the first (*FW* I–II) in 1991 and the second (*FW* III–IV) in 1993 – and was reissued complete in a three-volume paperback edition (*FW* I, II, III/IV) in early 2004. It bore the title フィネガンズ・ウェイク, romanized as *Fineganzu ueiku*, and this interlingual title – rather than Suzuki's 1971 title *Finnegan tetsuya-sai* (Finnegan's wake) – would later also be used for Japanese renderings of the *Wake* by both Kyoko Miyata (2004a) and Tatsuo Hamada (2009, 2012, 2014a).

Born in Nemuro in northern Japan, Yanase studied English language and literature at Waseda University in Tokyo and spent some years as a professor of English at Seijo University, also in Tokyo. Christopher Stephens reports that Yanase "began to establish himself as a translator of forbidding English books in Tokyo in the 1970s. In the meantime, he earned his living as a university professor" (2000, 22). His translations include *Alice in Wonderland* and *Through the Looking Glass* as well as several dozen other works, and he was a member of Suzuki's team at Waseda University that translated the first three chapters of the *Wake* in 1971. He subsequently left the Suzuki group and began to translate *FW* alone in 1986, in his early forties, giving up his university teaching post in order to concentrate on the task, and eventually taking seven and a half years of almost constant work to finish the complete translation.

Yanase's rendering remained the only complete Japanese translation of *FW* for almost twenty years, until Tatsuo Hamada's version of 2012 – though an abbreviated and simplified version by Kyoko Miyata appeared in 2004. Yanase's translation reportedly proved to be a great publishing success, with sales in excess of fifty thousand copies by the year 2000 already (Stephens 2000, 22). These figures do not of course necessarily imply that each of these copies was actually read by its enthusiastic purchaser. Writing of the general reaction of Japanese readers, Eishiro Ito suggests that many if not most of Yanase's readers were in fact likely to complain rather that it was far too difficult to read, because of the highly complex use of the Japanese language employed by Yanase to suggest the multilayered meanings of Joyce's text. While Ito numbers himself among those who would consider this rendering a masterpiece both of translation and of Japanese literature, possibly even the greatest work of modern Japanese literature, "probably most readers would give up reading Yanase's translation in the first few pages" (Ito 2004).

The writing system of Japanese is a particularly complex one, the overall system composed in fact of three separate and distinct systems of writing. Japanese sentences typically contain both *kanji* and *kana*. The former are ideograms, originally adopted from Chinese many centuries earlier, while the latter consist of two different but related syllabic systems, *hiragana* and *katakana*, used for different stylistic purposes. There are several thousand *kanji*, perhaps even as many as fifty thousand, each of which has in principle an intrinsic semantic meaning or range of meanings – but many of which also have not only more than one possible reading but also more than one contextually varying pronunciation. An unfamiliar or alternate pronunciation is indicated by superscript *kana* (known in this context as *furigana* "glosses") written in a miniature font above the particular *kanji*.

This orthographic complexity, particularly involving the use of *furigana*, affords the translator a very considerable degree of flexibility in constructing shades of polysemy. One commentator on Yanase's rendering writes that the Japanese translator "made constant use of *furigana* to add new layers of meaning to words written in *kanji*. *Furigana* allowed him to emulate – while not literally reproducing – the puns, double-entendres and allusions that fill every sentence of Joyce's original text. Indeed, *furigana* enabled Yanase to layer meanings in an even more elaborate fashion than Joyce could within the phonetic constraints of the English language" (Anon. 2004). Yanase himself is reported to have considered Japanese the ideal language for translating *FW* and felt sure that Joyce would not only have embraced it as such but would even have been jealous of Japanese for all the things it is capable of doing beyond the capabilities of English (Stephens 2000, 22).

The opening lines of Yanase's rendering (*FW* 3.1–3), as romanized by Eishiro Ito (2004), read as follows:

Senso, Evu-Adamu-reihaitei wo sugi, kuneru kishibe kara wankyokusuru wan e, conmodou-senu megurimichi wo Vico shi, megurimodoru eichi shii ii wa taru Howsu-jo to sono shuen.

Ito provides the following analysis of these lines. Two opening *kanji* or Chinese characters 川走 semantically combine 川 (*kawa* "river") and 走 (*hashi* "run") while their pronunciation as individual characters also evokes for Japanese readers the noun *senso* ("war"), anticipating the numerous conflicts presented in *FW*. Three characters 礼盃亭 (*reihaitei*) then evoke both the church of Adam and Eve and HCE's tavern, by combining 礼拝堂 (*reihaido* "chapel"), 盃 (*hai* "cup, chalice"), and 亭 (*tei* "bower, tavern"). The string 今も度失せぬ (*konmodou-senu*) echoes the original "commodius" as implying the name of a Roman emperor, while 巡り路 (*megurimichi*) combines "vicious circle" and "circular road." The two characters 媚行 combine Vico's name phonetically and "love action" semantically. 巡り (*meguri* "to circulate") reoccurs in 巡り戻る (*megurimodoru* "to recirculate"). The characters 栄地四囲委蛇 (*eichi shii ii*) combine to evoke "HCE" phonetically while literally, and serendipitously, meaning "the glorious land by the mild waters," namely Howth Castle (*Howsu-jo*). The characters 周円 (*shuen*) suggest "environs" semantically while phonetically implying 終焉 (also pronounced *shuen*) meaning "ending" or "death," thus suggesting the circular structure of *Finnegans Wake*.

Another commentator (Anon. 2004), using slightly different conventions of romanization, notes the degree to which the translation retains the order of the original English phrasing: "riverrun (*sensou*), past Eve and Adam's (*Ibu to Adamu reihaitei wo sugi*), from swerve of shore (*kuneru kishibe kara*) to bend of bay (*wankyoku suru wan e*), brings us (*meguri michi*) by a commodius (*wo konmo do usenu*) vicus (*bikou shi*) of recirculation (*meguri modoru wa*) back to Howth Castle (*eichi shi ii taru Housu Jou*) and Environs (*to sono shuuen*). This commentator notes that the phrase *konmo do usenu* for "commodius" also roughly means "won't get flustered this time," while *bikou* as a transliteration of "vicus" also means, among other things, "to follow."

Takashi Okuhara, meanwhile, once again using slightly different conventions of romanization, comments on the same lines: "We find HCE in the opening lines in the phrase 'Howth Castle and Environs', and Yanase renders it into 'Eichi-shii-ii-taru housujou-to sono shuuen.' Here he creates the epithet 'Eichi-shii-ii-taru' by using 6 Chinese characters (栄地四囲委蛇) with no accepted meaning. But each character seems to have something to do with the context. '栄' means 'prosperity', '地' 'land', '四囲' 'all around', '委蛇' 'the state of meandering.'" Combining all of these, Okuhara suggests, "Yanase could argue that he tries to conjure up a vague topographical picture in the neighbourhood of 'Howth Castle and Environs' with big Finnegan looming before us, lying along the meandering Liffey, with his head resting on Howth's cape" (2000, 8). Eishiro Ito (2004) notes that in the following paragraph Sir Tristram's name (as romanized) becomes a hexasyllabic "Torisutoramu" for Yanase – as it also will later for Kyoko Miyata (2004a).

In a later review of Congrong Dai's Chinese rendering of Book I of *FW*, Sheng Yun, commenting sympathetically on the huge difficulties Dai reported having, suggests that as far as translators in any language are concerned, *FW* "is like the curse of the pharaohs: the first translator of the Japanese edition suddenly went missing, the second went mad, and it took a third to finish the job" (2014). An Italian variant of the same story is presented by Matteo Bugliaro, according to whom the first Japanese translator suddenly dropped dead (2017). Eishiro Ito, responding in personal correspondence to a query concerning such assertions, reports that variants of this colourful story are also current in Japan – but, happily, he asserts, are merely a hyperbolic statement of the difficulty of translating the *Wake*. Ito confirms that despite the undoubted difficulty of the task, no Japanese translator of *FW* appears (to date) either to have lapsed into insanity or to have dropped dead of the effort.[2]

4 Spanish

Silva-Santisteban's Spanish ALP *(1991)*

The Peruvian poet, editor, essayist, and translator Ricardo Silva-Santisteban (born 1941 in Lima), a professor of comparative literature at the Pontifical Catholic University of Peru, is the editor of several literary anthologies as well as of several works on the history of translation in Latin America. His translations into Spanish include the work of Stéphane Mallarmé from French and a collection of English Romantic poetry from English.

He published a Spanish translation of the closing pages of *FW* (626–8) in the Peruvian journal *Creación y crítica* in 1971; provided a Spanish version of the opening and closing pages of *ALP* (*FW* 196–7, 213–16) in 1982; added a rendering of the opening pages of the *Wake* (*FW* 3–5) in 1988; and produced a complete rendering of *ALP*, published in Mexico City in the journal *Biblioteca de México* in 1991.

His opening sentences of *ALP* (1991) include the following lines (*FW* 196.1–7, 9–11):

> ¡Oh, / cuéntame todo sobre / Anna Livia! Quiero oír todo / sobre Anna Livia. Bien, ¿tu conoces a Anna Livia? Por supuesto, todo el mundo la conoce. Dímelo todo. Dímelo ya. Es el acabose. Bien, ya sabes, cuando el viejo hizo futt y hizo lo que sabes. ... Triataba de hacer no sé que cosa en el Infernix Park.

Here Joyce's opening "O" is an exclamatory "Oh," the focus on exclamation somewhat diminishing the implication of circularity. His

---

2 On Yanase's Japanese rendering, see Okuhara (2000), Stephens (2000), Anon. (2004), Ito (2004). My thanks to Eishiro Ito for his repeated assistance with Japanese linguistic and cultural matters.

"cuéntame todo sobre / Anna Livia!" ("tell me all about Anna Livia") evokes the English river Tame and, more faintly, the Thames (Spanish *Támesis*). "You'll die when you hear" becomes the colloquial formulation "Es el acabose," which promises an experience that will be "the absolute limit," and since the verb *acabar* means "to finish," constitutes also an implied reference to death. The old cheb who went futt is simply "el viejo" ("the old guy") who also went futt in Spanish. The rendering of the final sentence, "Triataba de hacer no sé que cosa en el Inférnix Park," radically simplifies Joyce's complex utterance, resulting in a very bland "I don't know what sort of thing (*no sé que cosa*) he was trying to do in the Infernix Park." The opening "triataba" arguably conflates *trataba* ("he was trying") and English *tree*, readable as perhaps suggesting that HCE himself was skulking in the trees; given the unambiguously singular verb, it is difficult to read the suggestion of Spanish *tres* ("three") or a hispanicized English *three* as referring to the otherwise unmentioned three watchers; and the two girls disappear altogether. The name "Inférnix Park" conflates *fénix* (phoenix) and "inferno" – possibly, as in Joyce's (and Beckett's) French "parc de l'Inphernix," referring to Dante's *Inferno* and the appropriateness of hellish retribution.

His closing lines of *ALP* include the following (*FW* 215.31–5, 216.3–5):

No escucho con las ondas de. Las cantarinas ondas de. Volantes murciélagos, ratones charlanchillan. ¡Ei! ¿No fuiste a tu casa? ¿Que no viste a Tomasa? No escucho con los chillidos de los murciélagos, todas las liffeyantes ondas de. Ei, ¡salvanos ruido! Mis pies no se mueven. Me siento tan vieja como aquel olmo. ¿Un cuento contado de Shaun o Shem? ... ¡Dímelo, dímelo, olmo! ¡Noche! Cuentamecuento de tronco o piedra. Al lado de las rientes ondas de, de las galopantes y lejanas ondas allende de. ¡Noche!

Here Silva-Santisteban's version substitutes babbling (*cantarinas*) waves (*ondas*) for chittering waters (*aguas*). His bats (*murciélagos*) are flying about (*volantes*), his mice (*ratones*) simultaneously chatter (*charlan*), squeak, and even screech, thanks to the fact that the verb *chillar* may refer either to the squeaking of mice or the screeching of birds, an ambiguity exploited here to reflect the ambiguity of Joyce's "bawk." The rendition thus suggests something like "I can't hear with the waves of. The babbling waves of. Flying bats, chattering mice squeak, screech." The washerwoman's "¿No fuiste a tu casa?" and the presumed response "¿Que no viste a Tomasa?" retranslates roughly as "You haven't gone home?" and the confused "You haven't seen Tomasa?," where "fuiste" (literally, "went") rhymes with "viste" (literally, "saw") and "tu casa" (literally, "your home") with "Tomasa," a feminine form of *Tomás* ("Thomas"), a glance perhaps at the now departed Thom Malone. One "can't hear with the shrieking (*chillido*) and squeaking (*chillido*) of the bats, the liffeying waves of," with a slant rhyme in passing on the invented "liffeyantes" and "ondas" ("waves"). The formulation "Ei, ¡sálvanos ruido!" substitutes noise (*ruido*) for talk: literally, "Noise save us!" Joyce's "my foos won't moos" is simplified as "Mis pies no se mueven" ("My feet won't move"). The appeal to the elm (*olmo*) back-translates literally as "Tell me tale (*cuéntamecuento*) of stem (*tronco*) or stone (*piedra*). By the side (*al lado*) of the laughing (*rientes*) waves of, the rushing (*galopantes*) and faraway (*lejanas*) waves on the other side (*allende*) of. Night!"

Conjetural *(1992)*

A richly informative special issue of the Argentinian psychoanalytical journal *Conjetural* devoted entirely to versions of *ALP* appeared in Buenos Aires in June 1992, edited by Jorge Jinkis. The 140-page volume featured on its front cover a photograph of Livia Schmitz, wife of Italo Svevo, with flowing waist-length hair, recalling Joyce's comment that he had thought of her as one of the models for Anna Livia. The volume includes the complete original text of *FW* I.8; two partial Spanish renderings of that chapter, one by Luis Chitarroni and C.E. Feiling, the other by Leónidas Lamborghini; the complete text of Joyce's Italian *ALP* of 1940; most of the first page of Juan Rodolfo Wilcock's Italian *ALP* of 1961; the complete text of the Portuguese renderings from *ALP* in the Campos brothers' *Panaroma do Finnegans Wake* of 1962; the complete text of Joyce's 1931 French team translation of *ALP*; the opening pages and final paragraph of Wolfgang Hildesheimer's 1970 German *ALP*; C.K. Ogden's Basic English *ALP* of 1931 and a Spanish translation of it by C.E. Feiling; and three comparative passages from the English *ALP*, taken respectively (as in Edmund Wilson's *Axel's Castle*) from the renderings published in *Navire d'Argent* (1925), in *transition* (1927), and in the 1928 volume *Anna Livia Plurabelle*. Commentaries (in Spanish) follow by Anthony Burgess (translated from *A Shorter Finnegans Wake*), Juan Rodolfo Wilcock, the Campos brothers, Jacqueline Risset, and the Argentinian novelist and psychoanalyst Luis Gusmán.[3]

---

3 The entire volume, *Conjetural* 24, is accessible online, at http://www.conjetural
 .com.ar/revistas/24.pdf.

Chitarroni and Feiling (Spanish, 1992)

The opening pages and final paragraph of *ALP* (*FW* 196.1–199.12, 215.31–216.5) appeared in Luis Chitarroni and C.E. Feiling's Spanish translation in 1992 in the journal *Conjetural*. Chitarroni (born 1958) is an Argentinian literary critic, editor, and experimental novelist; Carlos Eduardo Feiling (1961–97) was an Argentinian novelist and poet until his untimely death in his mid-thirties.

Their rendering of the opening sentences of *ALP* includes the following lines (*FW* 196.1–7, 9–11):

¡Oh / cuéntame todo sobre / Anna Livia! Quiero saberlo todo / sobre Anna Livia. Bien, ¿conoces a Anna Livia? Sí, desde luego, todas conocemos a Anna Livia. Cuéntamelo todo. Cuéntamelo ya. Cuando lo oigas te vas a quedar de una pieza. Bien, tú sabes, cuando ese don crápula se atrevió e hizo lo que hizo. ... Sea lo que fuere lo que trestaron de averiguar que él trestó de hacerles a dos en el Parque Inférnix.

Here "You'll die when you hear" is rendered by a colloquial "Cuando lo oigas te vas a quedar de una pieza" ("You'll be flabbergasted when you hear"), namely, the story of how the old swine ("ese don crápula") was daring enough ("se atrevió") to do what he did. Whatever it was (*sea lo que fuere*) that the three (*tres*) were trying (*trataran*) to establish (*averiguar*) that he was trying (*trató*) to do to the two (*dos*) in the infernal Phoenix Park. The unexpected repetition of *tres* in "trestó" might suggest to some readers that the three in the trees might well share an ambition with the deplorable old swine regarding the two in question.

Their rendering from the final lines of *ALP* (*FW* 215.31–5, 216.3–5):

No puedo oírte por las aguas de. Las chismosas aguas de. Revoloteo de murciélagos, chillido de ratones. ¡Eh! ¿No te fuiste a casa? ¿Qué fue de Rabassa? No te puedo oir por los murciélagos, las viviliffeantes aguas de. ¡Ea, que la charla nos salve! Mis pies están duros. Me siento tan vieja como aquel olmo. ¿Un cuento de Shaun o Shem? ... ¡Cuéntame, cuéntame, cuéntame, olmo! ¡Noche, noche! ¡Cuéntamecuento de tallo o piedra! Junto a las riberantes aguas de, las deaquíparallantes aguas de. ¡Noche!

"I can't hear you with the waters of," one washerwoman says to the other, "the gossipy (*chismosas*) waters of." Bats are flying about (*revoloteo*), mice are squeaking (*chillido*). "Didn't you go home (*a casa*)?," she asks, eliciting the confused but rhyming reply, "What was that about Rabassa?," a name never yet or otherwise mentioned. The waters are both "alive" (*vivas*) and liffeying. "Talk (*charla*) save us. My feet have gone hard (*duro*), are immobile." The elm (*olmo*), she hopes, may tell a tale (*cuento*), a tale of stem (*tallo*) or stone (*piedra*), on the banks (*riberas*) of the waters of, the waters rivering ("riberantes") from here (*de aquí*) to there (*para allá*), to who knows where.

C.E. Feiling, as mentioned, also translated Ogden's Basic English *ALP* into Spanish in the same volume of *Conjetural*.

Lamborghini (Spanish, 1992)

The opening pages of *ALP* (*FW* 196.1–198.16) in a Spanish rendering by Leónidas Lamborghini (1927–2009) also appeared in the 1992 number of *Conjetural*. His version was based on the rendering by Luis Chitarroni and C.E. Feiling in the same issue, transposed by Lamborghini into a more popular idiom based on the colloquial speech of Buenos Aires.

Lamborghini, a native of Buenos Aires, was forced as a young man to abandon his university studies for financial reasons and turned his energies to journalism and poetry instead. After publishing several collections of his own poetry, he left Argentina with his family in political protest in 1977, returning only in 1990. He is known for the radical experimentalism of his work and is considered by some to be one of the most important Argentinian poets of the later twentieth century.

His rendering of the opening sentences of *ALP* includes the following lines (*FW* 196.1–7, 9–11):

> ¡O / cuéntame todo sobre / Anna Livia! Quiero saberlo todo, / oírlo todo acerca. Lábiamelo con tu labia. Bien, ¿la conoces? Sí, por supuesto, todas conocemos a Anna Livia. Entonces, dale, cuéntamelo todo. Ya. Ya. Rabiento de ganas de saberlo. Cuando lo sepas te vas a caer redonda. Bien, tú sabes lo que ese viejo craputón se atrevió a hacer. ¡Y lo hizo! ... Sea lo que fuere lo que trestaron de averiguar que él trestó de hacerles a dos en el Parque Inferfénix.

The washerwoman now wants to know (*saber*) all and everything about Anna Livia: "Give me all the gossip (*labia*). I'm going crazy ("rabiento") with wanting (*ganas*) to know." Well, the other replies, "When you do know (*cuando lo sepas*) you'll fall over in a heap (*caer redonda*)," hearing about what the old swine ("craputón") was daring enough (*se atrevió*) to do – "and he did it!" As to what happened in the park, Lamborghini is content just to repeat Chitarroni and Feiling's account, other than expanding "el Parque Inférnix" to "el Parque Inferfénix," making the phoenix (*fénix*) more obvious and incorporating an apposite example of HCE's guilty stutter.

García Tortosa's Spanish ALP *(1992)*

A complete Spanish translation of *ALP*, with an extensive commentary, by Francisco García Tortosa and two colleagues from the University of Seville, Ricardo Navarrete Franco and José María Tejedor Cabrera, also appeared in 1992. García Tortosa, born in 1937 in the southern Spanish city of Murcia, taught English at the universities of Salamanca and Santiago de Compostela before moving to the University of Seville in 1976, where he established a reputation as the central figure in Spanish Joyce studies during more than the next three decades. He is widely regarded as the foremost Spanish authority on Joyce, and his publications also include his 1999 translation, with María Luísa Venegas Lagüéns, of *Ulysses*.

In his detailed 126-page introduction to the *ALP* translation, García Tortosa describes the process adopted by the three-man team. "Separately, each one translated a few lines. Then, in weekly meetings, and in sessions that lasted between two and three hours, we examined the three versions; and word by word, phrase by phrase, we opted for the most appropriate, or if none of the three satisfied us, searched for a fourth solution" (my translation).[4] The procedure is markedly similar to that employed by Joyce himself and his team in preparing the French *ALP* published in 1931.

The complete Spanish *ALP*, the most significant example of *Wake* translation in that language to that date, was greeted with enthusiasm by those readers who appreciated its thoroughgoing attempt to produce the sort of text Joyce himself might have produced had he originally been writing in Spanish rather than in English. The Joyce scholar José Carnero González, for example, wrote with great enthusiasm that any lover of literature ought to feel gratitude for the publication of this impeccably executed book (1992, 245). The literary critic and theorist Darío Villanueva, in the major newspaper *ABC*, similarly considered the volume an extraordinary accomplishment (1993, 7).

---

4 "Cada uno hacía la traducción de unas cuantas líneas por separado. Después, en reuniones semanales, y en sesiones que duraban entre dos ys tres horas, confrontábamos las tres versiones, y palabra por palabra y frase por frase nos decidíamos por la más apropiada o buscábamos, si ninguna de las tres nos satisfacía, una cuarta solución" (García Tortosa 1992, 125).

Other readers were less willing to invest so heavily in responding to the considerable demands of the resulting reading experience. The Spanish poet, novelist, and translator Ramón Buenaventura wrote that while the attempt to translate the *Wake* was certainly a laudable one, Joyce's text, translated or not, simply remained just as unreadable and untranslatable as ever (1993). The Mexican critic Alejandro Toledo, in a sharply worded piece, also found the translation unreadable, considering what he saw as the unnecessarily complicated work of "el profesor tortuoso" ("Professor Tortuous") to be nothing less than a "tortura" ("torture") to read (2003) – especially, in this particular (transatlantic) critic's view, because of García Tortosa's allegedly excessive employment of Peninsular Spanish regionalisms. Cristina Burneo, writing as an Ecuadorean, similarly regrets what she sees as the unnecessarily overt peninsular character of Tortosa's Spanish (2004, 22). The Galician translator Alberte Pagán, who himself translated the first two chapters of the *Wake* into Galician in 1993, was among those who considered that even for Spanish readers who were also capable of working with Joyce's English the translation was considerably more difficult to read than the original (2000, 147).[5]

García Tortosa's team rendering of the opening sentences of *ALP* includes the following lines (*FW* 196.1–7, 9–11):

O / dímelo to de / Anna Livia! Quiero oírlo to / de Anna Livia. Bueno, conoces a Anna Livia? Sí, claro, tol mundo conoce a Anna Livia. Cuéntamelo to. Cuéntamelo ya. Te vas a morir cuando te enteres. Bueno, ya sabes lo del viejo calandrajo ganforro que hizo lo que sabes. ... O lo que tresaran soltar que intrestó doser en el Parque Findio.

After an unadorned "O," as in Joyce's original, García Tortosa's "dímelo to de / Anna Livia!" ("Tell me all about Anna Livia"), evoking in passing the Scottish Dee, Turkish Dim, Dutch Diem, English Mel, and Australian Todd, achieves a sense of immediate urgency with "dímelo to," where "to" is both a colloquial contraction of *todo* ("all") and an urgent Spanish interjection meaning "come on!" (García Tortosa 1998, 209). His "Te vas a morir" translates literally as "you're going to die," while "cuando te enteres" may be rendered as "when you find out" (*enterar* "to find out") and read as evoking the river Ando of the Solomon Islands and the river Ente of Tuscany.

---

5 On García Tortosa's Spanish rendering, see Carnero González (1992), Buenaventura (1993), Glaister (1993), Villanueva (1993), Antolin Rato (1994), Lobner (1994), García Tortosa (1998), Pagán (2000: 147), Toledo (2003).

The old cheb who went futt is "el viejo calandrajo ganforro" ("the rascally old rogue") who "hizo lo que sabes" ("did what you know"), as in Joyce's English. A veil of reticence is drawn over the details of how HCE "went futt," merely referring obliquely to "lo del calandrajo" ("the business of the old rogue"), but compensates generously in terms of fluvial references by suggesting all of the Chilean Río Bueno, African Save ("sabes"), Scottish Cala, Indian Andra, Algerian Dra, Ugandan Drajo, Liberian Jo ("calandrajo"), and finally the Chinese Gan and Tanzanian Foro ("ganforro").

As for what may have happened in the park, García Tortosa's compressed rendering, "O lo que tresaran soltar que intrestó doser," suggests, roughly, "or whatever the three settled on spreading about (*soltar* "to release") that he was interested in trying to do to the two of them," where "tresaran" conflates *transaron* ("they settled on"), *tres* ("three"), and the French river Aran; "intrestó" conflates *tres* ("three"), *intentó* ("tried"), and *interés* ("interest"); and "doser" conflates *dos* ("two") and *hacer* ("to do"). The two girls are present only as a numeral (*dos*), ungendered and incorporated into the verb *hacer* ("to do"), the doing (whatever it may or might have been) more important than those who may or might have been its object. The three watchers, however, not only present but doubly present, acquire a correspondingly greater significance – while the repetition of *tres* is readable as suggesting a similarity between their unspoken desires and those of the deplorable HCE.

Whatever took place did so in "el Parque Findio," a name that (while evoking the German river Inde) heavily disguises the phoenix (Spanish *fénix*) while nonetheless invoking its "outlandish" origins as *indio* (literally "Indian," colloquially merely "foreign"). It also identifies HCE with Finn, who (though the theory is now discredited) was once also considered by some scholars of Celtic studies to have had foreign origins, specifically (as in HCE's case) Scandinavian.

García Tortosa's team rendering of the final paragraph of *ALP* includes the following lines (*FW* 215.31–5, 216.3–5):

No oigo con las aguas de. Las cojijosas aguas de. Aleteantes murciélagos, garla de guarros guarenes. Fu! No te vas a casa? Que Thom Malone se casa? No oigo con el pandeo de pandiques, todas las linfas de fina lifia. Fu, el parlosanto nos guarde! Mis pies no se moven. Me siento tan vieja como aquel olmo. Cómo, un cuento que cuenta de Shaun y de Shem? ... Dime, dime, dime, dagame! La noche noche! Táblame de rocas o raigones. Junto a las ondas riberas de, másallámurmurantes olas de. La noche!

These final lines are a good example of the complexity of García Tortosa's rendering. His washerwoman "can't hear with the waters of," waters that are now "muttering" (*cojijosas*) to themselves. Bats (*murciélagos*) are fluttering (*aleteantes*), as one might expect them to do. The following phrase, however, "garla de guarros guarenes," suggesting a replacement of the noise of mice by something like the "chatter of filthy piglets," introduces a distinct element of surprise. The change from squeaking mice to squealing pigs is clearly motivated, however, less on biological grounds than by the temptation of a sustained alliterative play on the noun *garla* ("chatter"), the adjective *guarro* ("filthy"), the noun *guarro* ("hog"), the noun *guarín* ("piglet"), and, for good measure, the name of the Venezuelan river Guarenas. The combination of pigs and water, meanwhile, humorously offers a supplementary hint of the biblical Gadarene swine (*puercos gadarenos*), which, possessed by demons, rush lemming-like down a steep cliff and plunge into the sea (Matthew 8, 28–32).

The question and response "No te vas a casa? Que Thom Malone se casa?" is roughly "Aren't you going home? Thom Malone is getting married?" with a change to the present tense, and where "a casa" ("home") is a perfect rhyme for "se casa" ("is getting married"). Readers may possibly conclude that at some previous point the washerwomen must have been gossiping about Thom Malone and his marital chances. The exclamation "Fu," meaning, roughly, "good heavens!" includes a fluvial reference to the Chinese river Fu.

The washerwoman's complex "No oigo con el pandeo de pandiques, todas las linfas de fina lifia" suggests, roughly, "I can't hear with the uproar of this mad gang, all the waters (*linfas*) of lovely (*fina*) Livia." Here "pandeo" (literally, "bulging") suggests an "eruption" of *pandemonio* ("uproar"), "pandiques" is a conflation of *pandilla* ("gang") and French *panique* ("panic"), *linfa* is a poetic term for water, related etymologically to *ninfa* ("nymph"), *fino* (literally, "fine, subtle") in the context suggests "lovely," while "lifia" conflates "Liffey" and "Livia," and the phrase "linfas de fina lifia" substitutes an alternative wordplay for Joyce's "liffeying waters." In the phrase "Fu, el parlosanto nos guarde! Mis pies no se moven" the Chinese river Fu reappears; "parlosanto" plays on *Padre Santo* ("Holy Father") and *parloteo* ("chatter"); "se moven" conflates Spanish *se mueven* ("they move"), English *move*, and the river Ove of medieval Spain (the modern river Eo), to suggest "Holy chatter protect us! My feet won't move."

The washerwoman's "Tell me, tell me, tell me, elm" is transposed into an unexpected "Dime, dime, dime, dagame!" – unexpected in that the dagame is a tropical American lemonwood tree, unlikely ever to be found on the less than tropical banks of the Liffey. Its alliterative appearance also permits that of the Daga river of South Sudan. "Tel-metale of stem or stone" becomes "Táblame de rocas o raigones," with "táblame" conflating *háblame* ("speak to me") and *tabla* ("riverbed"), while "stem or stone" is alliteratively reversed as "stones" (*rocas*) or "roots" (*raigones*). The rivering waters become "ondas riberas," conflating Spanish *riberas* ("banks") and Joyce's "rivering," while the hither-andthithering waters become the "másallámurmurantes olas," waves (*olas*) over yonder (*más allá*) that murmur and mutter and gossip, all three meanings implied by the verb *murmurar*.

Pozanco's Spanish Wake (1993)

In 1993 an abridged and simplified Spanish version of the entire *FW* appeared, translated by the well-known Spanish poet Víctor Pozanco, who was born in 1940 in Biarritz and studied English at the Sorbonne and Spanish in Barcelona. As well as numerous volumes of poetry, Pozanco, based for many years in Barcelona, had already more than a hundred translations of English-language authors to his credit by 1993, including among many others Donne, Dickens, Beckett, and Burgess. In the introduction to his abbreviated *Wake*, which is approximately half the length of the original, Pozanco observes that nothing he had previously attempted to translate in his thirty years as a professional translator came anywhere close to being as difficult, and he acknowledges that his shorter rendering is much less an attempt at a translation in any normal sense than an attempt merely to "make intelligible" (1993, 11) what he considers to be the central narrative thread.

Though several commentators praised Pozanco's courage in undertaking the daunting task, his abbreviated rendering, conceived along the general lines of Anthony Burgess's *Shorter Finnegans Wake*, was not at all a critical success, being so harshly criticized by Spanish-language reviewers that it was eventually withdrawn by the publisher, Editorial Lumen of Barcelona – and in ironic consequence is by now a highly priced bibliographical rarity. While García Tortosa's *ALP* of the previous year had encountered criticism in some quarters as being unreasonably difficult as a result of its carefully (or even obsessively) worked complexity, Pozanco's rendering was heavily criticized by many – in some cases quite savagely – as being on the contrary both all too arbitrary in its selective reductions of Joyce's text and, in general, far too simplified, limiting itself essentially to the most obvious surface meaning and, as at least one fellow translator puts it, in the process resulting in a debilitating flattening and trivializing of Joyce's text (Pagán 2000,

147).[6] For all the negative criticism, however, much of it undoubtedly warranted, Pozanco's rendering is certainly also not without its occasional distinctly successful moments.

His rendering of the opening lines (*FW* 3.1–3) reads as follows:

> río que discurre, más allá de Adam and Eve, desde el recodo de la orilla a la ensenada de la bahía, nos trae por un comodius vicus de circumvalación de vuelta al castillo de Howth y Environs.

Joyce's conflated "riverrun" is here expanded to include an explanatory relative clause, Pozanco's "río que discurre" literally a "river that flows." Compensating for the arguably unnecessary expansion, the Spanish verb *discurrir* has a particularly apposite range of connotations, including not only "flowing," but also "meditating, pondering, reflecting, discoursing, speaking," all of them perfectly suited to the gossipaceous Anna Livia we encounter throughout the *Wake*. "Eve and Adams" is restored to an untranslated "Adam and Eve." The "swerve" of shore becomes a "recodo," a more pronounced "sudden turn" that is alleviated in the "ensenada" ("cove, enclosure") of the bay, while "commodius" and "vicus" are both left untranslated, presumably on the grounds that they are also closer to Latin than to English in the original. The easy translational solution of "recirculación" is interestingly avoided in favour of "circumvalación," which does double duty as meaning not only "encirclement" but also "circumvallation, surrounding by a wall," thus anticipating the walled "castillo de Howth y Environs." HCE's initials are discreetly adjusted to CHE.

The opening sentences of Pozanco's *ALP* include the following lines (*FW* 196.1–7, 9–11):

> ¡OH, / cuéntamelo todo / Anna Livia! Quiero saberlo todo / de Anna Livia. Porque sabéis quién es Anna Livia, ¿no? Claro que sí; todos sabemos quién es Anna Livia. Cuéntamelo todo; ahora mismo. Te va a dar algo cuando lo oigas. Ya sabes, cuando el viejo anduvo riorriendo, se mojó e hizo lo que hizo. ... Fuese lo que fuese lo que intentasen descubrir que les hiciera a aquellas dos en Phoenix Park.

After a primarily exclamatory "OH," Pozanco's washerwoman's "cuéntamelo todo" ("tell me all of it") fluvially evokes the English Tame and Mel and, more faintly, the Thames (Spanish *Támesis*). The

---

6 On Pozanco's Spanish rendering, see also Antolín Rato (1994), Ors (2010), Calero (2016).

perhaps inadvertent omission of the preposition *de* ("about") after "todo" in Pozanco's second line momentarily achieves the effect of the washerwoman addressing Anna Livia herself directly rather than (or as well as) speaking to her counterpart on the other bank. She wants to know all (*saberlo todo*) rather than just hearing all. "You do know who Anna Livia is?" elicits the answer "Claro que sí" ("Yes, of course"), evoking the Brazilian Claro and Swedish Klar. "Te va a dar algo," his washerwoman promises, literally, "it's going to give (*dar*) you something (*algo*)," the implication clearly being something surprising, something to laugh about, "cuando lo oigas ("when you hear"), summoning up the South Sudanese river Adar as well as the Ando of the Solomon Islands. The reference to death goes unheard.

The old cheb who went futt is just "el viejo" ("the old fellow"), who, in a humorously idiomatic formulation, "anduvo riorriendo, se mojó e hizo lo que hizo" – literally, "went laughing (*riendo*) and playing about down by the river (*río*), got himself all wet (*se mojó*), and did what he did." Whether he got all wet by going too close to the river or by peeing his pants (*se mojó*) or both or otherwise is left discreetly unspecified.

As for what may have happened in the park, Pozanco's version opts for plain but very carefully phrased Spanish, suggesting the necessity of conveying the nuances of the matter with the exactness of a legal document, but with the repeated use of subjunctive forms ("fuese, fuese, intentasen, hiciera") simultaneously underscoring the element of narrative uncertainty. His "Fuese lo que fuese lo que intentasen descubrir que les hiciera a aquellas dos," suggests, roughly, "whatever it may have been (*fuese lo que fuese*) they may have tried (*intentasen*) to uncover (*descubrir*) that he may have done (*hiciera*) to those two," the gender of the two revealed in the feminine form of the adjective *aquellas*. No specific reference to the three watchers is to be found, however, constituting a sharp departure from Joyce's English. Pozanco clarifies soberly that Joyce's "fiendish park" is really Dublin's Phoenix Park.

Pozanco's rendering of the closing sentences of *ALP* includes the following lines (*FW* 215.31–5, 216.3–5):

No oigo con las aguas de. Las lacrimógenas aguas de. Obscenos chillidos de vertiginosos murciélagos. ¿No te vas en casa? ¿Qué tal con el pulgar? No oigo con estos muchiélagos, sobrevolando el Liffey. Salve, que nos salven las salvas de la conversación. Así no me saldrá cardenillo en los pies. Me siento tan vieja como aquel olmo. ¿La historia de un idiota contada por Shaun o Shem? ... Dímelo, dímelo, dímelo, olmo. ¡Noche noche! Dime si tallo o piedra. Junto a las riocirculantes aguas de, las vagamundas aguas de la. ¡Noche!

Pozanco's washerwoman "can't hear with the waters of," waters flamboyantly if surprisingly described as "lacrimógenas" (literally, "tear-inducing"), presumably introduced less for the sense, though tears and the French *lac* ("lake") as well as the Nigerian Imo and Canadian Ena do indeed contribute aquatic references, than for the dactylic rhythm. The next phrase, "Obscenos chillidos de vertiginosos murciélagos" ("obscene squeaks and screeches of giddy bats"), exploits the ambiguity of the noun *chillido*, referring to either a squeak or a screech. The fieldmice, meanwhile, perhaps frightened off by the obstreperous bats, are nowhere to be heard or seen. The washerwoman's "¿No te vas en casa?" and the odder than usual reply "¿Qué tal con el pulgar?" retranslate rather unexpectedly, and changing to the present tense, as "Aren't you going home?" and "How are things with the thumb?" where the mysterious query regarding the addressee's "thumb" (*pulgar*), though readable as suggesting a previous work-related injury, a result perhaps of over-enthusiastic scrubbing, is more obviously motivated by the fortuitous similarity of Thom Malone's given name (and a possible interlingual play on "Tom Thumb"), while his family name is allowed to disappear.

The speaker can't hear with all the many "muchiélagos," a humorous conflation of *muchos* ("many") and *murciélagos* (bats), that are flying over (*sobrevolando*) the Liffey. Her "Salve, que nos salven las salvas de la conversación" plays, again flamboyantly, on *salve* (meaning both "Greetings!" and, appropriately for the quasi-religious overtones of Joyce's original, evoking the Latin *Salve Maria* ("Hail Mary"), with which *salva* (meaning both "salvo" and "solemn promise"), and *salvar* ("to save") combine to suggest something like "Hail Mary! May talk (*conversación*), in salvos of solemn promises, save us!"

The washerwoman's discovery that her "foos won't moos" becomes Pozanco's "Así no me saldrá cardenillo en los pies." Here, no doubt remembering that a rolling stone gathers no moss, the translator clearly discovers moss in Joyce's "moos," but rather than rendering it by the standard Spanish *musgo* ("moss"), he humorously transforms the moss into verdigris (*cardenillo*), suggesting that "That way (*así*) there will be no verdigris growing (*salir* to 'grow') on my feet." While *musgo*, like Joyce's "moos," would have evoked various North American Moose Rivers, "cardenillo" summons up the South American Cardenillo instead. Joyce's "Tell me, tell me, tell me, elm" becomes, playing likewise on /l/ and /m/, a literal and pleasingly dactylic "Dímelo, dímelo, dímelo, olmo," asking for a tale of stem (*tallo*) or stone (*piedra*). The rivering waters are "riocirculantes," while the hitherandthithering waters become "las vagamundas aguas," vagabond waters that wander (*vagar* "to wander") the world (*mundo*).

5 Hungarian

Bíró (Hungarian, 1992)

A Hungarian translation of substantial excerpts by Endre Bíró, amounting altogether to roughly sixty-five pages from the *Wake*, together with a substantial introduction and annotations, and including the translated excerpts that had originally appeared in 1964 in the Yugoslav journal *Híd*, appeared in book form in 1992 in Budapest, under the title *Finnegan ébredése* (Finnegan's awakening). The original four excerpts of 1964 are augmented by a further six.[7]

The opening lines of *ALP* (*FW* 196.1–7, 9–11) are rendered by Bíró as follows:

Ó / mondj el mindent Anna / Líviáról! Mindent tudni akarok Anna Líviáról. / Hát te ismered Anna Líviát? – Persze, mindenki ismeri Anna Líviát. Mondj el mindent, rögtön mondj el mindent. – Meghalsz ha meghallod! Hát tudod, mikor az ura, az a vén kos kilett és azt a tudodmit csinálta. ... – Hogy mi a csuda vót, amit megpróbáltak kitudni, hogy mit próbált a Fujnix parkba.

Even a reader without Hungarian may detect the presence of a number of fluvial evocations in Bíró's rendering. After a diacritically adorned "Ó," where the presence of the diacritic arguably reduces the implication of circularity, his "mondj el mindent" ("tell me all") evokes the Iranian Mond, the American Elm, and the German Inde, quickly followed by the English Tud ("tudni") and the Canadian Persse Lake ("persze"). His "Maghalsz ha meghallod!" ("You'll die when you hear"), indulging in an alliterative play involving the verbs *meghal* ("to die") and *hall* ("to hear"), manages in passing to evoke the Romanian Mag and the English Ham ("ha m-") as well as the Australian Halls Creek, soon followed by the Russian Ura ("ura"). His version of the final sentence reveals no obvious reference to either the "three" (Hungarian *három*) in the trees or the "two" (Hungarian *kettő*). His location of HCE's fall from grace "a Fujnix parkba" appears to echo the sober

---

7 Bíró's 1964 renderings included excerpts from *FW* 8–10, 169–95, 196–216, 627–8. The 1992 publication included all of these and also excerpts from *FW* 35, 152–9, 226, 261–2, 414–21, 499–501. My thanks to Erika Mihálycsa for kindly providing me with the details of Bíró's renderings. A four-page excerpt (*FW* 170.9–174.4) from the "Shem" chapter in Bíró's rendering appears online in an anonymous 2013 Wikipedia article (in Hungarian) on *FW* (Anon. 2013a).

distaste expressed by Goyert's German "Pfuinix-Park." Unusually, and in an explanatory gesture that arguably oversimplifies, Bíró's rendering employs dashes throughout to indicate a change of speaker.

Bíró's rendering of the closing paragraph of *ALP* includes the following lines (*FW* 215.31–5, 216.3–5):

> Nem hallom a vizektől. A csacsogó vizektől. Tipegő egerek, sikongó denevér szoúk. – Hahó! Nem mentél haza? – Miféle tata? – Nem hallom a kuviktól, a csobogó vizeknek.– Há! Zsivaj segíts! – Nem moccan a lábam. Olyan agg vagyok, mint ott az a szilfa. – Egy mesét Shemről vagy Shaunról, mondd? ... Namondd, namondd, namondd lomb!– Éj, éj!– Mondmesemond fáról vagy kőről. A folyongó vizeknek, csirridecsörroda vizeknek. Partján. – Éj!

Bíró's washerwoman "can't hear" ("Nem hallom") "with the waters" ("a vizektől"), with creeping ("tipegő") mice (*egerek*) and the screaming ("sikongó") of bats (*denevérek*). The misheard question, "Are you not gone ahome?" becomes a Hungarian "Nem mentél haza?" ("Didn't you go home?"), but her listener, having heard not *haza* ("home") but *tata* ("daddy"), responds, understandably, "Miféle tata?" ("What kind of a daddy?"). "Noise (*zsivaj*) help us (*segíts*)!," the first speaker exclaims, "My feet (*a lábam*) won't move (*nem moccan*)." She feels as old as that elm (*szilfa*) over there – an elm that also seems to be in the process of losing its identity, since within a few words it becomes just unspecified "greenery" (*lomb*). "Tell (*mond*) me a tale (*mese*) of tree (*fa*) or stone (*kő*)," she urges, "by the bank (*part*) of the rivering ("folyongó") waters (*vizeknek*), waters hither (*ide*) and waters thither (*oda*)." To which her partner, as identified by Bíró's dash, responds, "Night!" (*Éj!*).

6 German

Rathjen (German, 1992, 1994, 1995)

German renderings by Friedhelm Rathjen also continued to appear, in 1992 (*FW* 282–7) and in 1995 (*FW* 555–63). In 1994 he translated Anthony Burgess's *Here Comes Everybody* (1965), superseding the earlier German translation of that text by Manfred Triesch (1968). Burgess's text contains numerous excerpts from *FW*, which Rathjen translated using for the most part the versions (including his own) that had appeared in Reichert and Senn's *Finnegans Wake Deutsch* (1989). Also in 1995, his rendering of "The Mookse and the Gripes" (*FW* 152.15–159.18), reprinted from *Finnegans Wake Deutsch* (1989, 124–31), appeared in book form as *Der Mauchs und der Traufen* (1995b).

Stündel's German Wake: Finnegans Wehg *(1993)*

The year 1993 saw the appearance of a first – and controversial – complete German rendering of *FW*, the work of Dieter Stündel, born in 1947 in Siegen, a freelance radio journalist, and translator also of Lewis Carroll's *Alice in Wonderland* and *Sylvie and Bruno* among other works. After earning a master's degree in German and English at the University of Cologne, Stündel completed doctoral studies at the University of Siegen in 1974 with a dissertation on the later work of Arno Schmidt, whose difficult and highly idiosyncratic writings had by then already earned him in some circles the title of "the German Joyce" – and who in the early 1960s, as mentioned, had also briefly intended to undertake a complete translation of *FW*. Coming to Joyce in Schmidt's wake, through the idiosyncratic interpretive lens suggested by Schmidt, and beginning work immediately on graduating in 1974 already, Stündel subsequently spent an appropriately Joycean seventeen years on a likewise highly idiosyncratic transposition of Joyce's text.[8] Fritz Senn, while acknowledging Stündel's "courageous and diligent attempt to translate the whole of the *Wake*," comments understatedly that "it did not have, to put it humanely, an enthusiastic reception" (2013, 872).

Stündel seems to have intended at one point to use the title *Finnegans wach* (Finnegans awake), but his rendering eventually appeared under the title *Finnegans Wehg*, conflating German *Weh* ("woe, ache, grief, labour pains") and *Weg* ("way") and a rhyming interlingual echo /ve:k/ of the English *wake*, together with a hint of the German verb *wecken* ("to wake someone up") and a fainter residual hint of the adjective *wach* ("awake"). The lack of an apostrophe in Stündel's German title (as opposed to Joyce's English title) is necessarily reductive, producing an unambiguously singular "Finnegan's." The conflated *Wehg* might also be seen as humorously self-reflexive, hinting at the translator's own "labour pains" as he struggles to find a "way" through the dense and thorny thickets of Joyce's text. The translation appeared in Darmstadt in 1993, published by the Jürgen Häusser Verlag, in a highly priced oversized format, weighing several kilos, and clearly intended to emulate the similar physical monumentality and eccentricity of Arno Schmidt's meganovel *Zettel's Traum* – Stündel's entering into competition with Schmidt thus in one sense echoing Schmidt's earlier entering

---

8 Stündel's pre-publication rendering of the "Mamalujo" chapter (II.4; *FW* 383.1–399.36) and of two excerpts from the final chapter (*FW* 619.20–620.2, 628.6–16) originally appeared in Reichert and Senn's *Finnegans Wake Deutsch* (1989, 238–55, 274), and a further excerpt (*FW* 309–21) appeared in the journal *Schreibheft* (1992, 143–56).

into competition with *Finnegans Wake*. A more conventionally sized and priced paperback version appeared later in the same year from a different publisher, the Zweitausendeins Verlag of Frankfurt am Main. Both editions carried Joyce's original text on facing pages.

The resulting achievement was a significant media event, greeted with major fanfare in the non-specialist German literary press – invariably mentioning as newsworthy curiosities the extravagant format and price and frequently reporting Stündel's claim (perhaps humorously intended, perhaps not) that he had created as many as fifty thousand new German words in the course of the translation. The rendering was harshly criticized by reviewers and critics, however, on the grounds of a pervasive and debilitating arbitrariness, with Joyce's text serving very largely, in the opinion of many, as little more than a springboard for the translator's own (and frequently ungainly) verbal athletics, reducing the level of complexity and allusiveness, gratuitously increasing the number of sexual references, and ignoring in many cases the original's rhythm and musicality.[9]

Stündel's opening lines (*FW* 3.1–3) read as follows:

> Flußflaufs vorbei an Adam und Eva von KüstenKurven zur BuchtBiegung führt uns durch einen kommodien Ouikuß der Rezierkuhlation zurück nach Haus Castell und Emccebung.

In "Flußflaufs," the course (*Lauf*) of the river (*Fluß*) takes it sibilantly past Adam and Eve, from alliterative curves (*Kurven*) of coast (*Küste*) to an alliterative bend (*Biegung*) of bay (*Bucht*), leading us by a comfortable (*kommod*) "Ouikuß" of "Rezierkuhlation" back to "Haus Castell und Emccebung." Here "kommodien" (rather than *kommoden*) hints not only at comfort and Commodus but also at an element of comedy (*Komödie*); "Ouikuß" for "vicus" is a Franco-German "yes-kiss," evoking Vico while sexualizing the process of recirculation à la Molly Bloom; and "Rezierkuhlation" includes an expected *Rezirkulation*, but potentially also, and much less expectedly, *Zier* ("ornament"), *Kuh* ("cow"), and a hint of *kühl* ("cool"). All of this leads us (*führt uns*) not to Howth but, playing on a quasi-German mispronunciation of the name, to a German *Haus*, namely, "Haus Castell" – which in normal German usage would mean "the House of Castell" – and also to its "Emccebung,"

---

9 On Stündel's German rendering, see Rathjen (1992b, 1993, 1995c, 1999, 2005), Drews (1993, 1998), Fuld (1993), Senn (1993, 1995b, 1998, 2007), Winkler (1993), Laederach (1995), Bockelmann (2002), Cersonsky (2011), O'Neill (2013).

humorously implicating the solidity of the *Umgebung* ("surroundings, environs") in the realms of Einsteinian relativity, courtesy of the iconic formula $e = mc^2$. The House of Castell, meanwhile, is a still flourishing Bavarian noble family whose status as counts of the Holy Roman Empire dates back to the year 1200 (Anon. 2020c).

These opening lines concisely demonstrate Stündel's compulsion to force as many verbal and cultural puns as possible into his rendering, whether they contribute any meaningful new element of textual sense or not. The results may vary: "Rezierkuhlation" clearly diminishes Joyce's text in creating entirely unnecessary textual noise; "Ouikuß" is dubious at best; the German House of Castell is likewise dubiously present only because a weak verbal pun makes its presence possible; while "Emccebung," on the other hand, is a splendid coinage that arguably enriches the text and affords a generous measure of readerly pleasure. Meanwhile, Eve and Adam revert to Adam and Eve; alliteration is preserved and even enhanced; Commodus and Vico are both identifiably present; Howth is far less identifiable, if at all; and HCE's initials are retained.

Stündel's rendering of the opening sentences of *ALP* include the following lines (*FW* 196.1–7, 9–11):

Eau / sag mir alles über / Anna Livia! Ich will alles über / Anna Livia wissen. Also, kennt ihr Anna Livia? Ja freilich, wir alle kennen Anna Livia. Sag mir alles. Sag's mir jetzt. Du stirbst vor Lachen, wenn du's hörst. Also, du weißt doch noch, als der alte KNaabbe fotzging und das tat, was du weißt. ... Oder was war es bloiß ach, was die Draige sich ausdachten, was er mit den Zwaithgen im Föhlnix Park versyrchda.

Here Stündel's opening French "Eau" for Joyce's "O" has been severely criticized as reductive, both as unnecessarily and humourlessly explaining Joyce's pun, while abandoning the visual implications, and stressing merely the aquatic to the exclusion of other punning implications (Drews 1993, 153; 1998, 430). Stündel's choice might also be understood, however, as merely reversing the directionality of Joyce's pun, with Joyce's "O" implying *eau* among its other punning possibilities, Stündel's "Eau" implying "O" and thus providing access at one remove to the same possibilities. Arguably, his choice more immediately draws attention to the water itself as being invited to tell all about Anna Livia, reminding readers that the two washerwomen are also a dual manifestation of ALP and that the entire episode is therefore (and reminiscent of Molly Bloom) also an implied soliloquy, the flowing river chattering and murmuring to itself.

Stündel's washerwoman wants to know (*wissen*) all about Anna Livia, allowing for an evocation in passing of the English river Wissey. "You'll die when you hear" is rendered as an almost literal "Du stirbst vor Lachen, wenn du's hörst" ("You'll die laughing when you hear it"). The old cheb who went futt becomes "der alte KNaabbe," conflating "der alte Knabe" ("the old chap") and the German river Naab. HCE having reportedly gone futt, Stündel is gleefully specific that he "fotzging," the inclusion of *Fotze* ("cunt") narrowing the area of doubt as to the general nature of the reported behavioural lapse.

As for what happened in the park, Stündel's "Oder was war es bloiß ach, was die Draige sich ausdachten, was er mit den Zwaithgen ... versyrchda" suggests a surface meaning of "or whatever was it that the three (*drei*) of them made out (*ausdachten*) that he was trying (*versuchte*) to do with the two (*zwei*) of them." Rivers flow: the German Oder and Ach, the Burmese Loi ("bloiß"), Algerian Dra ("Draige"), and New Zealand's Waitiki ("Zwaithgen"), the latter two also suggesting heavily encrusted references to the *drei* ("three") and the *zwei* ("two"), while "versyrchda" conflates *versuchte* ("was trying") and the Syr and Sûre rivers of Luxembourg. The park itself becomes the "Föhlnix Park," conflating a thinly concealed German *Phönix* ("phoenix") and the American Fohl Creek. For many if not most German-speaking readers, the coinages "Draige" and "Zwaithgen" here will be perceived as doing violence to the German language without any compensatory generation of additional meaning.

Fritz Senn aptly summarizes Stündel's overall translational strategy: "*Finnegans Wehg* does not exude the enticing charm of the original and turns reading into an obstacle race across unwieldy conglomerates of letters. As far as can be made out – for the translator refrained from comments – a basic meaning was made out for each sentence, the cues taken from Roland McHugh's *Annotations*, and this was rendered into German. The resulting German sentence was then enriched by an overlay which is not thematically determined by the context, but by whatever phonetic possibilities there were at hand" (2007, 97).

Every translator of *FW* necessarily attempts to recuperate as much as possible of Joyce's flaunted polysemy. Different translators demonstrate different procedures for accomplishing this aim. Stündel's *Wehg* adopts a variety of procedures that are all his own. The most obvious peculiarity is its handling of German orthography. Here, to take some random examples, single letters are arbitrarily doubled (*kalte* to "kallte"); unvoiced consonants become voiced (*tranken* to "drahnken"); voiced consonants become unvoiced (*legte* to "leckte"); short vowels become long (*altes* to "ahltes"); long vowels become short (*wieder* to "widder"); vowels mutate into other vowels (*warm* to "worm"; *klopfte* to "klupfte"); adjectives are tortured into becoming pseudo-nouns (*hübschen* "pretty" becoming a grotesque "Hüppschön," conflating – but why? – *hübsch* "pretty," *hüpfen* "to hop," and *schön* "beautiful"). Only rarely do these orthographic variations involve any suggestion of an altered meaning beyond the surface deformation, and when they do, the new meaning evoked is often totally bereft of any observable textual relevance, as when *legte* ("laid") becomes "leckte" ("licked") or the adverb *wieder* ("again") becomes the noun "widder" ("ram"). There are occasional exceptions, as in the case of the early "Emccebung," but in the vast majority of cases such orthographic changes appear to be made simply because it is phonetically *possible* to do so.

That such verbal deformation, meaningful or otherwise, is going to be central to Stündel's rendering is made abundantly clear on his title page already, where *Finnegans Wehg* is described in a subtitle (already an unusual step) not as *eine Übersetzung des Werkes von James Joyce* ("a translation of the work of James Joyce") but as "Kainnäh ÜbelSätzZung des Wehrkeß fun Schämes Scheuß." There is no obvious Joycean reason for the flaunted deformation of standard German at this point, since the phrase is not yet a rendering of anything that Joyce wrote. It consequently makes the immediate point that a similar process of (humorous?) deformation will be at the heart of the next 628 pages of Stündel's text. The reader might well be expecting an *Übersetzung* at this point, but the notion is immediately undermined, with the *Übersetzung* deformed almost beyond recognition as an "ÜbelSätzZung" – conflating *übel* ("bad"), *Sätze* ("sentences"), and *Zunge* ("tongue, language") – while simultaneously claiming, despite the deformation, to be "not a bad one" (*keine üble*). Cain and Abel unexpectedly appear as "Kain-" and "Übel-," foreshadowing not only the fraternal strife of Shem and Shaun but also the textual struggle to come between the onslaught of James Joyce's astonishing *Werk* and the cheeky (*kess*) translatorial *Wehr* ("defence") to be mounted against it by Dieter Stündel. The text itself is advertised already not as "von James Joyce" but as "fun Schämes Scheuß," promising fun, which is certainly good, while allowing (humorously? self-ironically?) for the reading that the translated Joyce might well be overcome by shame (*Scham*) at having become something close to a monster (*Scheusal*). Dr. Frankenstein strikes again.

Stündel's version is clearly driven throughout by the ambition to achieve an unrelentingly self-reflexive text. The evident translatorial intention to keep readers permanently on their interpretive toes, to prevent them from yielding to any comfortable illusion of familiarity with the text and its operations, can be seen as a worthy ambition in a Wakean context – but to have that point repeatedly and relentlessly made in almost every single line of every single one of 628 pages quickly becomes self-defeating and far less than fun. Stündel's central objective is clearly to stress the irreducible foreignness, the otherness, the unreasonableness, of Joyce's text. While he succeeds extremely well in this ambition as far as his own rendering is concerned, it is very debatable whether the cumulative result has much to do with Joyce anymore, or whether it provides its readers with anything approximating a similar reading experience. His rendering, as numerous German-language critics have asserted, is consequently characterized overall by a pervasive and debilitating arbitrariness. This is accompanied, moreover, by an equally arbitrary and almost obsessive tendency to invent excretory and sexual transpositions even where they are entirely unmotivated by any contextual necessity.

As an overall result, it must be said that Stündel's version, in which the translator's visibility is completely unmissable, vastly increases the noise of *Finnegans Wake*. As Fritz Senn has observed, "Stündel's technique differs from most others who, usually, for their necessary substitutions, try to keep the context in mind," while Stündel "appears to proceed by free semantic expansion" (1998, 191). As for the 628-page relentlessness of Stündel's atomistic fragmentation of Joyce's text, Senn comments wrily that this translator certainly "does not choose the easy path (he sometimes comes on like Sisyphus taking on a complementary order of stones for the next ascent)" (1998, 191). The Dutch *Wake* translators Erik Bindervoet and Robbert-Jan Henkes, discussing previous translations of *FW*, comment in a newspaper interview that Stündel "took every word apart in order to squeeze in as many wordplays as possible, mostly alluding to sexual organs. 'It would drive you crazy'" (Evenhuis 2002; my translation).[10] Nonetheless, however, as Robert Weninger collegially observes, Stündel's rendering, for all its faults, remains even still the only complete version of *FW* in German (2012, 93).

Emily Cersonsky, finally, while acknowledging the deficiencies of Stündel's rendering, interestingly employs what I have elsewhere called a "transtextual" reading (O'Neill 2005, 10–12), a reading that "strives towards an understanding of the translation as on an even keel with the original, taking stock of how even a 'bad' translation might

---

10   The Dutch translators are reported as suggesting that Stündel "elk woord apart had genomen om daar zoveel mogelijk woordspelingen in te wringen die voornamelijk op geslachtsdelen doelen. Beide laconiek: 'Je kunt het ook te gek maken'" (Evenhuis 2002).

enrich, expand, and emend Joyce's meaning" (Cersonsky 2011, 192). Her argument advocates specifically "for the usefulness and interest of even this flawed (un)translation in conjunction (side-by-side) with the English original because all translations are 'flawed' in different ways, and Stündel's particular iniquities illuminate and balance many of the aspects of Joyce's work, which would be impossible to stress in a single text" (2011, 199).

7 Galician

Pagán (Galician, 1993)

Alberte Pagán, born in Galicia in northern Spain in 1965, studied Spanish and English at the University of Santiago de Compostela. His meticulously annotated Galician rendering of the first two chapters of the *Wake* (*FW* I.1–2) appeared in 1993 – and still remains the most substantial Galician rendering of any part of *FW*.[11] This was the first complete translation of the first two chapters (as opposed to Pozanco's abridged Spanish translation) in any of the languages of the Iberian Peninsula. The title *Finnegans Wake* is translated as *Velório de Finnegans*, a plural "Finnegans' wake" in the funeral sense. Since *FW* is frequently referred to in the Iberian Peninsula as "el *Finnegans*," however, much as English-speaking readers refer to "the *Wake*," Pagán's title can also be taken as self-reflexively implying, humorously, either "the wake in the *Wake*" or "the wake of the *Wake*." Pagán later, in 2000, produced a book-length study (in Galician) of the *Wake*, which also contained much of the 1993 translation, copiously annotated. A film critic and author of several studies on experimental film, he subsequently established a reputation in Galicia primarily as a maker of experimental films.

Pagán's rendering of the opening lines (*FW* 3.1–3), quoted from the 2000 edition, reads:

> recorrio passando Eva e Adán de cámbio de beira a curva de baía, trainos por um cómodus vicus de recirculación de volta ao Castelo Howth e Extramuros.

Here "recorrio" conflates *correr* ("to run") and *rio* ("river"), while also suggesting *recórrer* ("to travel") and *recordar* ("to remember"). The

---

11   The only other extant Galician rendering appears to be the brief excerpt from the final lines of *ALP* (*FW* 216) translated by Leopoldo Rodríguez in 1969. My thanks to Teresa Caneda Cabrera of the University of Vigo for confirming this information.

centrality of remembering and repetition is underlined by the strategic deployment of *re-* as the first syllable of, by implication, the entire 628-page text. Joyce's "from swerve of shore to bend of bay" is reshaped, with interlinked alliteration, as "from change (*cámbio*) of shore (*beira*) to curve (*curva*) of bay (*baía*)." Eve and Adam, Commodus, and Vico are all replicated without difficulty, while the "Castelo Howth e Extramuros," saving HCE's initials, glosses Joyce's "Environs" as, literally, "what lies beyond its walls." The phrase "de volta" ("back") will for some readers once again recall the name of the cinema Joyce unsuccessfully attempted to establish in Dublin in 1909.

8 Polish

Malicki (Polish, 1996)

In May 1996, Jacek Malicki (born 1946) translated two fragments (*FW* 6.29–7.15, 306.11–308.36) into Polish under the title "Przebudzenie Finnegana" (Finnegan's awakening) in the Polish journal *Gnosis*.

The first fragment includes his rendering of the following lines (*FW* 6.33–5):

From Shopalist to Bailywick or from ashtun to baronoath or from Buythebanks to Roundthehead or from the foot of the bill to ireglint's eye he calmly extensolies.

Malicki's version:

Od Listyzakupów do Posiadłościj lub od strojupopiołów do przysięgibarona lub od Kuptebrzegi do Zaokrąglgłowę lub od stopy rachunku do gniewnegobłysku oka on spokojnie rozlegleleży.

The passage exemplifies the (often insuperable) difficulties faced by translators in deciding what to do with the specifically Irish implications of such terms as "Shopalist" and "ireglint's eye." Malicki's "Listyzakupów" for "Shopalist" combines *listy* ("letters") and *zakupów* ("shopping") as if suggesting an epistolary shopping list, but abandons any reference to Chapelizod, a name traditionally associated with Iseult and serendipitously also containing the initials of both HCE and ALP. His "gniewnegobłysku oka" combines *gniewne* ("angry"), *błysku* ("flash"), and *oka* ("eye") to suggest quite literally an eye glinting with anger – but it understandably ignores the reference to Ireland's Eye, the small uninhabited island directly north of Howth.

Królikowski (Polish, 1998, 1999)

Polish renderings of the first four pages of the *Wake* (*FW* 3.1–24, 4.1–17, 4.18–5.12, 5.13–29, 5.29–6.12, 6.13–28) by the Warsaw writer Adam Królikowski appeared over six issues of the journal *Magazyn Literacki* in 1998 and 1999.[12]

His rendering of the first three lines (*FW* 3.1–3) reads as follows:

rzekobieg, pokąt Adama i Ewy, od wybrzuszenia brzegu do odtoczenia zatoki, przenosi nas wikiańskim wszechmodem w kole wiecznego powrotu do Zamku Howth i Okolic.

Here "rzekobieg" achieves a one-word conflation of the corresponding vocabulary elements, *rzeka* ("river") and *bieg* ("run"); Adam and Eve revert to their traditionally gendered relationship; alliteration is abandoned; Vico is present in "wikiańskim"; Commodus has disappeared; and HCE's initials likewise disappear in the literal Polish rendering of "Howth Castle (*zamek*) and Environs (*okolica*)."

9 Romanian

Antip's Romanian ALP (1996)

A complete Romanian translation of *ALP* appeared in Bucharest in 1996 in the journal *Lettre Internationale*, the work of Felicia Antip (1927–2013), journalist, literary critic, and translator also of Paul Auster and Elie Wiesel. Antip's rendering appears under the title "Veghea lui Finnegan: Anna Livia Plurabelle," the Romanian noun *veghea* deriving from Latin *vigilia* and thus suggesting "Finnegan's wake" in the funeral sense. The translation, together with a brief introduction, appeared under the cover title "Să ne jucăm de-a Joyce," literally, "Let's play some Joyce," clearly suggesting the lots of fun to be had at the Joycean game ("un joc à la Joyce") that is *Finnegans Wake*.

The Romanian writer and academic Adrian Oţoiu, citing Antip's introduction, duly reports that "Felicia Antip, a lifelong reviewer of English literature, declares that her translation was meant as a game" (2004, 203), and discusses the implications of this approach: "Her rendering of Joyce's 'Wakese' shuns complex philological strategies and opts instead for a restitution of the passages' fluency. Joyce's often obscure word

---

12 My thanks to both Krzysztof Bartnicki and Katarzyna Bazarnik for separately carrying out bibliographical research on Królikowski's renderings.

coinages have been turned into more palatable calembours or even sacrificed altogether." However, he concludes, "Antip's version might be less faithful to the multilayered intertextuality of the original, but it has the right sound and rhythm – fast-paced, succulent, bawdy and boisterous" (2004, 203).

Arleen Ionescu later asserts that Antip's knowledge of Joyce and understanding of *FW* were in fact very basic. Antip does not seem to be aware, for example, that the names of many rivers flow through *ALP* (Ionescu 2014a, 208). Antip herself not only cheerfully admits in her brief introduction that she consciously consulted neither of Joyce's own renderings of *ALP* but also, as Ionescu puts it, uses the introduction to present a general "apologia for the mistakes she would playfully commit in her translation." In the process, "she did not shy away from gratuitously adding to Joyce's semantic webs and, arguably, she did so not in keeping with the re-creative, adaptive manner of Joyce's own linguistic and cultural recastings," arguing instead that "the lilt and the texture of words were more important for [Joyce] than the meanings" (Ionescu 2014a, 207).

Adrian Oțoiu, meanwhile, reported in 2004 that the dust jackets of several volumes published by the Bucharest publishing house RAO had long been advertising a Romanian version of *FW*, "but such an event seems more like wishful thinking, since none of Romania's major translators appears to be engaged in this project" (2004, 203). Ten years later, Arleen Ionescu writes optimistically that the cultural situation in Romania has changed significantly and that by 2014 "there are great expectations that Romanians will soon have a Romanian *Finnegans Wake*" (2014a, 210). Six years later still, however, in May 2020, Ionescu advises in personal correspondence that there is in fact still no complete Romanian rendering of the *Wake*.[13]

Antip's Romanian rendering of the opening sentences of *ALP* includes the following lines (*FW* 196.1–7, 9–11):

O / spune-mi totul despre Anna Livia! Vreau să aud totul despre Anna Livia. / Ei, o știi pe Anna Livia? Da, sigur, o știm cu toatele pe Anna Livia. Zi-mi tot. Zi-mi acum. O să mori când o să auzi. Păi, știi, când pezevenghiul de babalâc a luat-o razna și a făcut ce știi. ... Sau cum naiba îi spune la ce au tăiat ei firul în trei să priceapă că a încercat ei în doi în parcul Necurat.

---

13 My thanks to Arleen Ionescu for detailed information in personal correspondence. On the Romanian reception of Joyce's work in general, see Oțoiu (2004), Ionescu (2004, 2012, 2014a, 2014b).

Here "spune-mi totul" ("tell me all") evokes the American Spoon River and the Indian Tut. "O să mori când o să auzi" ("You'll die when you hear") adds the central European Mur and the Ando of the Solomon Islands. For Antip's Romanian, the old cheb who went futt is a complete moral bankrupt, nothing short of a "pezevenghiul de babalâc," not just an "old crock" (*babalâc*) but one who turns out also, rather surprisingly, to be an old "pimp" (Turkish *pezevengi*) living disgracefully off immoral earnings. Since this characterization does not seem to be supported by other evidence, Antip's readers will presumably see it as a reflection either of HCE's perennially guilty conscience or of a subliminal desire on his part that remains unspoken in other renderings. The statement offers fluvial access to the Thai Pai and the Ugandan Alla.

As for the events in the park, Antip's "Sau cum naiba îi spune la ce au tăiat ei firul în trei să priceapă că a încercat el în doi" appears to suggest, roughly, "Or however it is that the three of them spin the yarn they were being good at making up about what he was trying to do to the two of them." References to both the "three" (*trei*) and the "two" (*doi*) are overt and undisguised, and the fact that water was involved is revealed in the conflation ("priceapă") of *se pricepe* ("to be good at") and *apă* ("water") as well as by the presence of the eastern European river Sau. Earwicker's dubious deed takes place in "parcul Necurat," the "Unclean park," the term *necurat* ("unclean") one traditionally used in euphemistic and apotropaic reference to witches and, shades of Dublin's Bram Stoker, vampires.

Antip's rendering of the closing sentences of *ALP* includes the following lines (*FW* 215.31–3, 216.3–5):

Nu mai aud nimic din cauza apei. A apei care murmură. Lilieci fâlfâitori, şoareci de câmp rozători stau la şezători. Ho! Nu te duci acasă? Şi ce-i cu Thom Malone? ... Spune-mi, spune-mi, spune-mi, ulmule! Noapte noapte! Spune-mi, zi-mi despre lemn sau piatră. Lângă apele curgătoare ale, apele de aici şi apele de acolo. Noapte!

Milesi's Romanian ALP (1998)

Two years after Felicia Antip's rendering, a competing Romanian translation of the final pages of *ALP* (*FW* 213–16) by Laurent Milesi, then teaching at the University of Cardiff in Wales and subsequently at Fudan University in Shanghai, appeared in 1998. Adrian Oţoiu contrasts Antip's and Milesi's versions, "each starting from a different philosophy" (2004, 203). Milesi's translation "shows a better awareness of the intricacies of the text and adopts a complex strategy for its 'naturalization' and localization. In his prefatory note, Milesi outlines the four types of adaptation mobilized by this strategy. A 'topographical adaptation' replaces the original fluvial toponyms with Eastern European rivers. A 'cultural adaptation' inserts Romanian contexts (references to Dante are replaced by allusions to Mihai Eminescu).[14] The 'linguistic adaptation' converts the book's Irish voice into a Romanian-based idiom that is both synchronic (pluridialectal) and diachronic (ranging from Slavonic archaisms to French neologisms). The 'contextual adaptation' takes advantage of homophonous, homographic and paronymic opportunities offered at the lexical level, plays on diacritics, telescopes words and proliferates puns, always aiming both at the highest level of ambiguity and the highest congruity with the 'water' theme, while keeping the whole tightly anchored in the Danubian space. The result is an extremely densely wrought network of allusions that betrays a trained philologist's ear. It is a brilliant if somewhat demanding demonstration made with that kind of linguistic intuition that is sometimes the advantage of the non-native" (2004: 204).

Unlike Felicia Antip, Milesi, a French native fluent in Italian and Romanian as well as English (Ionescu 2014, 207), is fully cognizant of Joyce's French and Italian renderings of *ALP*. He writes of his own translation: "The overall approach could best be defined as a cross between the aesthetics behind Joyce's own transposition of this chapter into Italian (and French to a minor extent), with its reliance on musicality, its cultural adaptations, and the shift from a polyglottal to a pluridialectal level of creation, and my own critical awareness of the inbuilt problematic of translation of and in *Finnegans Wake*" (1998, 201). Arleen Ionescu notes in particular Milesi's treatment of the numerous river names in *ALP*: "Milesi not only displaces the geographical palette of river names to bring them closer to a Romanian cultural landscape, but echoes Joyce's tendency to keep, meaning not to translate, the original toponyms. Milesi's choice is to preserve the locale at the cost of a higher degree of foreignness in the target language" (2014a, 208).

Milesi's rendering of the closing sentences of *ALP* includes the following lines (*FW* 215.31–5, 216.3–5):

Nu aud de ape de. Cîrîitoarele ape de. Fîlfîitori lilieci, şoareci-de-cîmp gurăie chiţăie. Ho! N-ai ajuns acasă? Care Yon Coasă? Nu aud de chiţ de lilieci, toate liffiitoarele ape de. Ho, vorbă, stai-ne de ajiutor! Picioapele-mi

---

14   The Romantic poet Mihai Eminescu (1850–89) is generally regarded as the most outstanding literary figure of Romania (Milesi 1998, 201).

nu se mooşchiă. Mă simt bătrînă ca saalca acotlon. O storie spusă de Shem sau Shaun? ... Spune-mi, spune-mi, spune-mi, saalcă! Noapte noapte! Spune-mi despre stem sau stone. Lîngă rîurrîndele ape de, aicişiacolîndele ape de. Noapte!

Joyce's "Can't hear with the waters of" becomes Milesi's "Nu aud de ape de," evoking the Chinese Nu and French Aude. The washer-woman's original "Are you not gone ahome?" becomes a literal "N-ai ajuns acasă?" but now elicits the confused response "Care Yon Coasă?" ("Which Yon Coasă?") where "Yon" conflates Romanian *Ion* ("John") and the French river Yon, while "Coasă" conflates the Romanian river Coasa and the noun *coasă* ("hay making"). Joyce's Thom Malone is thus humorously transformed into Milesi's "John Hayfield." Talk (*vorbă*) may or may not stand us in good stead (*stai-ne de ajiutor*), but introduces the Romanian river Jiu. That the speaker's "foos won't moos" becomes "Picioapele-mi nu se mooşchiă," the "feet" (*picioare*) now appropriately conflated with "water" (*ape*), perhaps even that of the American river Moose, and they still won't move (*nu se muta*). She feels as old (*bătrîn*) as that tree over there (*acotlon*), a tree that is no longer an elm (*ulm*), but rather a willow (*salcie*), conflated ("saalca") with the French Aa, Indian Saal, and German Saale. "Tell me, elm!" is accordingly transformed into "Spune-mi, saalcă!" and "Telmetale of stem or stone" into "Spune-mi despre stem sau stone," leaving the two nouns untranslated, with "stem sau stone" slant-rhyming with "Shem or Shaun" and evoking the American Stone River.

10 Danish

Laugesen (Danish, 1997, 1999)

Born in Copenhagen in 1942, and a long-term resident of the Danish city of Aarhus, the poet, playwright, and translator Peter Laugesen is the award-winning author of more than fifty collections of poetry and is considered to be one of the central figures of modern Danish literature. He has also translated Gertrude Stein from English and Emil Nolde and Novalis from German – and in his spare time he has been working on and off since the mid-1990s on a possible Danish rendering of *FW*, which he first encountered in 1960 or thereabouts.

A Danish translation of excerpts from the closing pages (from *FW* 618–28) by Laugesen appeared in 1997. Entitled *ALP-Traum*, it appeared in a printed program for a theatre performance of excerpts from *FW* 618–28 in Danish translation, delivered by a pair of female actors at the Betty Nansen

Theatre in Copenhagen.[15] The title plays on three German meanings: "ALP's dream" and "dreaming of ALP" and *Alptraum* ("nightmare").

Two different Danish versions of *FW* 171.12–28 by Laugesen then appeared in the Copenhagen journal *Passage* in 1999 under the title "Vågn op igen, Finn!" (Wake up again, Finn! – which is to say, an invitation to "wake up" in Danish). The passage describes in glimmering rainbow colours the lowness of Shem as illustrated even by his completely perverted taste in alcohol, rejecting as he does any normal honest-to-goodness drink:

> Instead the tragic jester sobbed himself wheywhingingly sick of life on some sort of a rhubarbarous maundarin yellagreen funkleblue windigut diodying applejack squeezed from sour grapefruice (*FW* 171.15–18)

Laugesen's two versions:

> I stedet hulkede den tragiske klown sig selv skummetmælkende dødssyg på en eller anden slags rabarberisk munderin gulgrøn funkelblå vindigo æblesjuft presset af sur druesjus

> I stedet hulkede den tragiske klovn sig selv mælkeskummende søsyg på en eller anden afart af rabarberisk munderin gulgrøn funkelblå vindigo æblemos presset af sure druer i sjus

11 Russian

Volokhonsky (Russian, 1999, 2000)

The only Russian translation of any part of *FW* before the mid-1990s was a rendering in 1977 of "The Ballad of Persse O'Reilly" (*FW* 44.22–47.29) by Andrey Sergeev. A significant new contribution was made in the later 1990s, when renderings of roughly forty pages of excerpts from the first seven chapters (*FW* 3.1–171.28), translated by the poet Henri (or Anri) Volokhonsky (1936–2017), appeared in six separate issues of the Saint Petersburg journal *Mitin* between 1996 and 1999. A collected edition of the same excerpts appeared in book form in the Russian city of Tver in 2000.[16]

---

15 My thanks to Peter Laugesen for confirming this information.
16 My thanks to Tadeusz Szczerbowski of the Pedagogical University of Cracow for kindly sendng me an electronic copy of Volokhonsky's *Weik Finneganov*.

Volokhonsky, who was born in what was then Leningrad, previously and subsequently Saint Petersburg, graduated from the Leningrad Chemical-Pharmaceutical Institute with a degree in biochemistry. He began writing as an underground poet in the 1950s and was eventually the author of some twenty volumes of poetry altogether. He emigrated to Israel in 1973 and later, in 1985, to Germany. After ten years in Munich, working as a translator for Radio Free Europe, he moved to Tübingen in the Black Forest in 1995, where he spent the rest of his life (Anon. 2018c).[17] Boriana Alexandrova writes that "today he is regarded as a major figure in Russian literature, known for his poetry, songs, and translations of chiefly classical and religious texts." As of 2015, Alexandrova continues, "his 'attempt at a partial transposition' of *Finnegans Wake* is the most substantial piece of translation of Joyce's text currently available in Russian" (2015, 137). That situation, however, was very soon to change, with the first instalment of Andrey Rene's complete online Russian *Wake*-in-progress appearing in 2016 already. Alexandrova also notes that Volokhonsky's renderings of the *Wake* constituted, oddly enough, his only attempts at translating from English (2015, 166n47).

Volokhonsky's translations appeared under two different Russian titles – or two variants of the same title – giving rise to some particularly interesting linguistic implications. For his excerpts from *FW* in the journal *Mitin*, Volokhonsky (or possibly the journal editor) employed the title Из Финнеганова Уэйка (*Iz Finneganova Weika*), where *iz* means "from" and "weik" is a transliteration of the English *wake*; the collected edition of 2000, however, appeared as Уэйк Финнеганов (*Weik Finneganov*). Andrey Rene informs me in personal correspondence that the name *Finneganov*, depending on word order, can be read as having either an adjectival or a nominal function. In the title *Iz Finneganova Weika*, given the word order, *Finneganov* functions primarily as an adjective, suggesting "From a Finneganian Wake," and the title is thus readable as referring to either a singular "Finnegan's Wake" or a plural "Finnegans' Wake." In the title *Weik Finneganov* on the other hand, given the new word order, the nominal meaning of *Finneganov* is now primary and the title thus a singular "Finnegan's Wake" – but with the adjectival meaning ("A Finneganian Wake")

---

17 Volokhonsky was the older brother of the award-winning Russian translator Larissa Volokhonsky (born 1945), who since the 1980s, together with her American husband Richard Pevear, has translated Tolstoy, Dostoevsky, Pushkin, Chekhov, and Pasternak into English.

even still resonating to imply the possibility also of a plural "Finnegans' wake."[18]

In a very brief introductory paragraph to *Weik Finneganov*, which had also appeared in the first instalment of *Iz Finneganova Weika*, Volokhonsky modestly presents his text as a series of "experiments in fragmentary arrangement in the Russian alphabet."[19] The primary purpose of the rendering, on which he had worked for five years, he writes, was "to open up for our young writers opportunities reached in the West that far surpass anything known in Russia."[20] Because of the difficulty of the task, he writes, he thought it appropriate to abandon the usual term *translation* and replace it with the broader term *arrangement*.[21]

Boriana Alexandrova writes that Volokhonsky's rendering itself is primarily explanatory: "Volokhonsky consistently overlooks the narrative, semantic, and phonological simultaneity of Joyce's text: he rarely attempts to either convey the linguistic and cultural multivalency of the Wakese, or to devise similarly expansive Russophonic alternatives. His translatorial methodology primarily stresses elucidation through linguistic domestication: that is, stripping away most of the multilingual complexity of Joyce's text in an apparent effort to 'clarify' what the translator deems to be the core meaning embedded in the Wakese" (2015, 140).[22]

Volokhonsky's rendering of the opening three lines (*FW* 3.1–3) reads as follows:

бег реки мимо Евы с Адамом, от берой излучины до изгиба залива просторным пространством возратных течений приносит нас вспять к замку Хаут и его окрестностям.

In the following transliteration I follow Alexandrova's corrections of what she takes to be misprints in both the published versions,

---

18 An unambiguously singular "Finnegan's wake," meanwhile, would be *Weik Finnegana* – though the popular song "Finnegan's Wake," as Rene informs me, is usually called *Pominki po Finneganu*, using an alternative prepositional construction. My thanks to Krzysztof Bartnicki, Colin Wright, and particularly Andrey Rene for their advice in personal correspondence on the linguistic inricacies of this matter.

19 "opyty otryvochnogo perelozheniya rossiyskoyu azbukoy."

20 "otkryt' dlya nashikh molodykh sochiniteley dostignutyye na Zapade vozmozhnosti, daleko prevoskhodyashchiye vse izvestnoye v Rossii."

21 "Imenno poetomu prishlos' otkazat'sya ot obychnogo termina *perevod* i zamenit' yego boleye shirokim *perelozheniyem*."

22 For a detailed analysis of Volokhonsky's rendering, see Alexandrova (2015, 137–46; 2020, 147–56).

reading "beregovoy" for "beroy" and "vozvratnyh" for "vozratnyh" (2015, 141):

Beg reki mimo Evy s Adamom, ot beregovoy izluchiny do izgiba zaliva prostornym prostranstvom vozvratnyh techeniy prinosit nas vspyat' k zamku Haut i ego okrestnostyam.

The opening "beg reki" offers an overtly explanatory two-word "run (*beg*) of the river (*reká*)." Alexandrova writes indeed that Volokhonsky's text of these opening lines "offers a linear narrative in near-standard Russian" (2015, 141). In her reading, which I follow with some minor adjustment, "the run (*beg*) of the river (*reká*) past (*mimo*) Eve with Adam (*Evy s Adamom*), from (*ot*) coastal (*beregovoy*) swerve (*izluchin*) to (*do*) bend (*izgib*) of bay (*zaliv*), through the commodious (*prostorniy*) space (*prostranstvo*) of the returning (*vozvratnyh*) flow (*techenie*) brings us (*prinosit nas*) again (*vspyat'*) to Howth castle (*zamok*) and its (*ego*) environs (*okrestnosti*)." Here Commodus, Vico, and the Vico Road are all missing; the "commodius vicus of recirculation" as suggested in human and historical affairs is flattened; Howth, in deference to Russian phonetics, is renamed as "Haut"; and HCE's initials have disappeared. Alexandrova also suggests that the term *okrestnosti* primarily implies the castle's walls rather than the surrounding territory.

Volokhonsky's rendering continues (*FW* 3.4–10):

Сэр Тристрам с виолой д'аморе из-за ближнего моря прибыл назад пассажиром транспорта Северной Арморики на эту сторону изрезанного перешейка в Европу Малую дабы самолично вести пенисолированную войну на полуострове: не то чтобы возмышенные горы у потока Окони раздувались до прожорливых горджиев графства Лоренс, а те все время в тисме дублинировали вдвое: не то чтобы глас огня вздувал миш миш для поперечного виски:

Sér Tristram s violoy d'amore iz-za blizhnego morya pribyl nazad passazhirom transporta Severnoy Armoriki na étu storonu isrezannogo peresheyka v Evropu Maluyu daby samolichno vesti pe-nisolirovannuyu voynu na poluostrove: ne to chtoby vozmyshennyye gory u potoka Okoni razduvalis' do prozhorlivykh gordzhiyev grafstva Lorens, a te vse vremya v tisme dublinirovali vdvoye; ne to chtoby glas ognya vzduval mish mish dlya poperechnogo viski:

Even a very limited knowledge of Russian allows one to identify the presence here of some obvious pleasures. The opening phrase, for example, clearly allows for a contextually appropriate play on the legendary minstrel

Sir Tristram's relationship not only to music and love but also to the sea, the phrase "s violoy d'amore" serendipitously anticipating his fateful voyage over the "neighbouring (*bliznhi*) sea (*more*)." The final phrase, meanwhile, intriguingly ending with the word *viski*, suggests an unexpected memory of Tim Finnegan's love of the liquor, with Peter, Patrick, peatricks, and biblical echoes alike all disappearing in favour of the apparently discombobulating pleasures of whiskey: "not so much (*ne to chtoby*) did a voice (*glas*) from a fire (*ogon'*) blow out (*vzduvat'*) mish mish athwart (*poperechnyy*) whiskey (*viski*)."

Alexandrova also writes of Volokhonsky (2015, 146) that "in an interview for Radio Svoboda, given three years after the publication of *Weik Finneganov*, he explains that he 'doesn't understand' how any of the other *Wake* translations he was vaguely aware of at the time were at all possible to execute. Here Volokhonsky alludes to a French translation done in Joyce's lifetime, and an Albanian translation, but he does not discuss either with any specificity; and he adds that he has 'heard that there is something like a German translation,' but 'how that was done, I don't understand. This text is incredibly difficult to translate. What I have done is not a translation in the classical sense, but it is an exercise around [translation].'"[23] Volokhonsky is obviously very vague as to whatever other translations might exist. The French translation is presumably Joyce's own 1931 team translation, but the "Albanian" translation mentioned, which neither I nor various correspondents have succeeded in identifying, is presumably just a mistake – possibly involving a vague memory of having heard of the early Czech translation of *ALP* (Weatherall, Procházka, and Hoffmeister 1932). Several German renderings were of course available by 2003 – by which time Volokhonsky had been living in Germany for almost two decades.

12 Guarani

Medeiros (Guarani, 1999)

For Bloomsday 1999 celebrations in São Paulo, the Brazilian scholar and poet Sérgio Medeiros of the Federal University of Santa Catarina in Florianópolis, Brazil, with the assistance of some Paraguayan colleagues, rendered an excerpt from *FW* into Guarani, an indigenous South American language widely spoken especially in Paraguay, but also in Argentina and Brazil (Amarante 2018, 14n2).[24]

---

23 Alexandrova gives the following reference for the interview: Volchek, "Stikhi i pesni Anri Volokhonskogo," 21 July 2003, http://www.svoboda.org/content/transcript/24200160.html.

24 My thanks to Sérgio Medeiros for kindly sending me an electronic copy of his rendering.

Guarani, which is recorded as having some five million native speakers, is certainly one of the more exotic languages into which a rendering of any part of the *Wake* has been attempted. It is a member of the large South American Tupian language family rather than the Indo-European family of languages, with any member of which it reportedly shares very few features. Among features that might arguably be helpful for a translator of the *Wake*, it is an agglutinative language, like Turkish, for example. Possibly less helpful features might include the lack of either a definite article or any grammatical gender. Joyce would undoubtedly have relished the translational challenge involved.

The passage chosen (*FW* 189.28–190.9):

Sniffer of carrion, premature gravedigger, seeker of the nest of evil in the bosom of a good word, you, who sleep at our vigil and fast for our feast, you with your dislocated reason, have cutely foretold, a jophet in your own absence, by blind poring upon your many scalds and burns and blisters, impetiginous sore and pustules, by the auspices of that raven cloud, your shade, and by the auguries of rooks in parlament, death with every disaster, the dynamatisation of colleagues, the reducing of records to ashes, the levelling of all customs by blazes, the return of a lot of sweetempered gunpowdered didst unto dudst but it never stphruck your mudhead's obtundity (O hell, here comes our funeral! O pest, I'll miss the post!) that the more carrots you chop, the more turnips you slit, the more murphies you peel, the more onions you cry over, the more bullbeef you butch, the more mutton you crackerhack, the more potherbs you pound, the fiercer the fire and the longer your spoon and the harder you gruel with more grease to your elbow the merrier fumes your new Irish stew.

Medeiros's Guarani version:

Husamenta: So'o ne retûha, itakuapegua pyahu, ohekáva mba'e vai ñe'ê porã apytépe, nde, rekéva ore pay jave ha rekaru'yva rovy'a aja, nde ndekuaarekópe, hesakuaitépe eréva'ekue hosue jekuaaraê' ne pore'yetépe, hesapyso, yaváicha rehykuavova nde ytaku pupu ári. Tyryrukue ha mbae'e kaigue, ai péu ha péu hape, amo arai yryvu oipotáre ne ã ha ha'ûvo chiã oúva grajasgui, mano sarambipa, mbokapu guasu javeguakuéra rehe téra ryrúgui oikopa tanimbu, opa teko ombokusugue tata rendy atyra marangatúva ojevy yvy timbo vevére. Oikopa tepoti ramo aga araka'eve oike'yva ne andai apyra'y yvytúre. (Ha aña retã, Ha ja oúma ña ne re'ôngue ñoty! Ha mba'asy, asaîmba, ajavy che ñeha'â) reikyty kytyvérô zanahoria, rembo'i mbo'ivérô nabo, reipiro pirovérô papas, membyesay sayvérô sevói rejuka jukayerõ guéi remyangu'i ngh'ivérõ cancros, rejoso josóverô ka'avo, rehapy hetaverô jepe'a, ipukuve ne kuimbe. Ha hetave ty'ái ne rembi'u rykuépe, heta hetave tata nde aópe, iñandyve ha imbareteve, otimbo rory kyre'yve nde japepo pyahu irlandapegua.

Not too surprisingly, the uninterrupted flow of Joyce's seventeen-line sentence is subdivided into four more manageable separate sentences. The result will still remain almost completely incomprehensible for most readers – certainly including the present would-be reader, who can manage to decipher or at least guess at the meaning of only a small handful of words: *nde*, as suggested by the initial repetition, evidently means "you," while borrowings from Spanish help with *zanahoria* ("carrot"), *nabo* ("turnip"), and *papas* ("potatoes"), and the final word, "irlandapegua," presumably means "Irish stew." There are of course paragraphs and even pages of the original *Wake* where the yield would hardly be hugely better. It is pleasing in the context to discover elsewhere that the first-person-singular pronoun in Guarani, serendipitously, is *che* – as if in anticipation of hosting a Bloomsday text relating to HCE and his environs.

Chapter Eight

The 2000s

*1 Czech; 2 Russian; 3 Slovenian; 4 Swedish; 5 Italian;
6 Dutch; 7 Korean; 8 Portuguese; 9 French; 10 Japanese;
11 Catalan; 12 Irish; 13 Finnish; 14 Hungarian; 15 Spanish;
16 Danish; 17 Polish*

The 2000s saw the appearance of a complete Dutch *Wake* by Erik Bindervoet and Robbert-Jan Henkes (2002), a complete Korean *Wake* by Chong-keon Kim (2002), a complete Portuguese *Wake* by Donaldo Schüler (2003); an abridged Japanese *Wake* by Kyoko Miyata (2004); a complete French *Wake* by Hervé Michel (2004); an Italian rendering of *FW* I.1–8 and *FW* II.1–2 by Luigi Schenoni (2001a, 2004a); and a Japanese rendering by Tatsuo Hamada of *FW* I.1–8 and IV (2009).

Translations of individual chapters included a Swedish *ALP* by Mario Grut (2001); reprinted French versions of *FW* IV and I.1 by André du Bouchet (2003); a Polish translation of *FW* I.1 and IV by Krzysztof Bartnicki (2004); a Catalan *ALP* by Marissa Aixàs (2004); a Portuguese version of *FW* I.1 by Afonso Teixeira Filho (2008); a Spanish rendering of I.1 by Juan Díaz Victoria (2009), and a Portuguese *ALP* by Dirce Waltrick do Amarante (2009). Other substantial translations included Henri Volokhonsky's reprinted Russian rendering of excerpts from *FW* 3–171 (2000); some thirty-six pages of excerpts in Spanish by Ricardo Silva-Santisteban (2000); and some eighty pages of excerpts in French by Michel Chassaing (2005).

Briefer renderings appeared in Czech by Tomáš Hrách (2000); in Russian by Konstantin Belyaev (2000) and by Dmitry Smirnov (2003); in Slovenian by Andrej Skubic (2000); in Polish by Jacek Malicki (2001), by Arkadiusz Łuba (2003), and by Krzysztof Bartnicki (2005); in Portuguese by the Campos brothers (2001); in Swedish by Mario Grut (2002); in Finnish by Miikka Mutanen (2006, 2009); in Spanish by Juan Díaz

Victoria (2007, 2008) and by Leandro Fanzone (2007); in Hungarian by Ágota Bozai (2007, 2008); in Irish by Alan Titley (2008); and in Danish by Peter Laugesen (2009). Dutch, Irish, and Finnish appeared in each case for the first time in the *Wake* macrotext.

1 Czech

Hrách (Czech, 2000)

David Vichnar notes (2020, 151n8) that "in the late 1990s, Tomáš Hrách, a talented young translator of Beckett's trilogy, announced the intention of producing, over the course of ten years, a full Czech version of *Finnegans Wake*. An intention backed up by Hrách's masterful translation of the *Wake* passages quoted in the Czech translation of Harold Bloom's *The Western Canon*.[1] That intention was thwarted by his premature tragic death in June 2000, aged 33." Hrách reportedly died after an accidental fall from a balcony. The passages quoted by Bloom are *FW* 74.16–19, 177.31–178.7, 188.9–24, 189.28–190.9, 201.5–6, 627.33–628.16.

Anonymous (Czech, 2009)

An anonymous Czech rendering of the opening three lines (*FW* 3.1–3) appears in the 2009 Czech Wikipedia page for *Finnegans Wake*, which notes that the traditional Czech title is *Plačky nad Finneganem*, literally, "crying over Finnegan, weeping for Finnegan, mourning for Finnegan." The opening three lines appear as follows:

> protéká za Evou a Adamem od pobřežního pokroucení k zahnutí zálivu,
> přináší nám od commodia vica koloběh zpět ke hradu Howth a okolí.

Here the Czech "protéká" achieves a one-word conflation of *proud* ("river") and *útěk* ("run"). Eve and Adam retain the revised order of Joyce's original, while "from swerve of shore to bend of bay" becomes a pleasingly alliterative "od pobřežního pokroucení k zahnutí zálivu." Commodus ("commodia") and Vico ("vica") are both identifiably present, while HCE's initials disappear in a literal "ke hradu Howth a okolí."

---

1 Harold Bloom, *Kánon západní literatury*, trans. Ladislav Nagy and Martin Pokorný (Prague: Prostor, 2000), 439–46.

2 Russian

Belyaev (Russian, 2000)

Anna Livia took her first tentative steps in Russian in the year 2000, in the form of five pages from *ALP* (*FW* 196.1–5, 209.18–212.19) translated by the Ukrainian poet, translator, and essayist Konstantin Belyaev, born in 1971 in Sosnivka, in the Lviv province of Ukraine. His rendering appeared, together with the original text, in the Russian literary journal *Soyuz Pisatelei* (Writers united), published in the Ukrainian city of Kharkov, as part of a richly annotated article on translating the *Wake*. Belyaev uses the title "Pominki po Finneganu" (a singular "Finnegan's wake," in the funeral sense), which is the traditional Russian rendering of the title.

Belyaev and Volokhonsky were working on their respective Russian renderings more or less simultaneously. Comparing their renderings, Boriana Alexandrova writes that in his commentary "Belyaev goes to great lengths to detail his very particular and deliberate vision of what a *Finnegans Wake* translation should look like. He concerns himself not only with how the text should be handled by the translator but also with how it should be shaped and presented for the reader, whom Belyaev frequently invites to participate in the process of literary invention" (2015, 147). Belyaev's Russian *ALP* "bears little resemblance to Volokhonsky's largely monolingual, unannotated, and scarcely referenced transposition. By contrast, Belyaev retains the multilingualism of Joyce's text with remarkable resourcefulness and richness, and displays a far more textually involved and informed translatorial approach, which draws extensively on existing *Wake* scholarship" (2015, 153).[2] Nor does he hesitate to criticize quite severely Volokhonsky's rendering, which, he asserts, as quoted by Alexandrova, simply "tumbles along, for the most part conveniently inaccurately, without making an effort to incorporate the various metatextual meanings" (2015, 148).

Belyaev's rendering of the opening lines of *ALP* (*FW* 196.1–6):

O / rasskazhi mne vsë pro / Annu Liviyu! Khochu uslyshat' vsë pro / Annu Liviyu. Ty chto zhe, znaesh' Annu Liviyu? Eshchë by, vse my znaem Annu Liviyu. Rasskazhi vsë-vsë. Rasskazhi skorey. Umrësh', kak uslyshish'.

---

2 For a detailed textual analysis of Belyaev's rendering, see Alexandrova (2015, 147–59; 2020, 157–68).

Belyaev evokes the Serbian river Rashka no fewer than four times in the first six lines, beginning with his "O / rasskazhi mne vsë pro / Annu Liviyu" ("O / tell me all about Anna Livia") and ending with the promise that "You will die" ("umrësh'") "when you hear" ("kak uslyshish'").

Smirnov (Russian, 2003)

A Russian translation by Dmitry Smirnov of "Three quarks for muster Mark" (*FW* 383.1–14), reportedly completed in 1999 already, appeared in 2003 in a collection of Joyce's poems in Russian translation (Alexandrova 2015, 162n18; 2020, 144, 146).

3 Slovenian

Skubic (Slovenian, 2000)

A richly annotated Slovenian translation by Andrej Skubic of selected excerpts from *FW* also appeared in 2000, under the title "Finneganovo bdenje" (literally, "Finnegan's vigil"). An award-winning Slovene novelist, playwright, and translator, Skubic was born in Ljubljana in 1967. He studied Slovenian and English at the University of Ljubljana, where he earned a doctorate in sociolinguistics. He lives in Ljubljana and works as a freelance writer and translator. His translations into Slovenian include Flann O'Brien's *At Swim-Two-Birds* and *The Third Policeman* as well as anthology selections from Samuel Beckett. The selection from the *Wake* includes *FW* 30.1–34.29, 380.6–382.27, 604.28–606.7, 611.4–612.15, 615.12–619.19.

A very brief sample, from *FW* 30.11–15:

We are told how in the beginning it came to pass that like cabbaging Cincinnatus the grand old gardener was saving daylight under his redwoodtree one sultry sabbath afternoon, Hag Chivychas Eve, in prefall paradise peace ...

Izvemo, kako se je vse začelo, ko se je kot koleravbarski Cincinat imenitni stari vrtnik popridnoletnočasil med begunijami neko soparno sabatno popoldne, na Hag Chevychase Eve, v predjabolčnem paradižnem pokoju ...

For a reader armed only with what can be gleaned from a Slovenian vocabulary list, this offers a potentially interesting experiment in (seriously challenged) reading. Cincinnatus (or Cincinat), to begin with, appears to be associated specifically with kohlrabi (*kolerabar*) and possibly also with rhubarb (*rabarbara*), rather than just common or garden cabbage (*zelje*), while the grand (*imenitni*) old (*stari*) gardener (*vrtnik*) appears to have been pottering away in summer time (*poletni čas*) at his begonias (*begonije*) rather than under his redwood tree that sabbath (*sabatno*) afternoon (*popoldne*), Hag Chevychase Eve, in the paradise peace (*v paradižnem pokoju*) that reportedly obtained before (*prej*) the business with the apple (*jabolko*). While an amusing and personally pleasing experiment in reading in the dark, so to speak, my reading is also most likely an entirely inadequate one – but such, after all, to make the point once again, is very often (if not even usually) the fate of the reader of *FW* in any language, however accomplished the particular reader may be in the particular language involved.

4 Swedish

Grut's Swedish ALP *(2001)*

The year 2001 saw the appearance of a complete Swedish rendering of *ALP* by Mario Grut (1930–2007), a journalist and translator from both French and English, published as a separate volume by the Ellerström publishing house in the Swedish city of Lund. Grut had long been fascinated by *FW* and was reportedly still continuing in his mid-seventies, up until his death in 2007, to work on Swedish renderings of its opening and closing pages. While Grut's work reportedly encountered occasional criticism among Swedish readers as either not adequately reflecting the complexity of Joyce's text, or as doing unacceptable violence to the Swedish language, or both, Bertil Falk, a fellow Swedish translator of *FW*, argues forcefully that Grut's rendering deserves major credit as a genuinely pioneering endeavour in the Swedish language (2008, 149; 2013, 8–9).

Grut's rendering of the opening sentences of *ALP* includes the following lines (*FW* 196.1–7, 9–11):

> Å / berätta allt om / Anna Livia! Jag vill höra allt / om Anna Livia. Känner du Anna Livia? Så klart, gör vi alla. Berätta allt. Berätta nu. Du kommer att dö när du hör det. Du vet när gubbstrunten fick fnatt och gjorde det där, du vet. ... Eller vad tre nu påstred han försöktu sig två i Fiendix Park.

Grut's rendering opts for "Å," pronounced /o:/, and arguably challenging even Beckett and Péron's French "Ô" as a splendidly felicitous rendering of Joyce's opening "O," managing to incorporate ALP's own initial, Joyce's "O" in diacritical form, the delta suggested by the typographical shape of an upper-case *A*, the Swedish *å* ("river"), the Sumerian *a* ("water"), the French *eau* ("water"), and the several western European rivers named Aa. His "berätta allt" ("tell all") includes an evocation of the English river Alt, but also serendipitously evokes the Scottish Gaelic noun *allt* ("stream"), a fluvial evocation very likely lost on many readers (possibly including even the translator) – an excellent example of the capacity of *Finnegans Wake*, whether in the original or in translation, to generate retrospectively individual meanings for individual readers. The Swedish text promises that "Du kommer att dö när du hör det" ("You'll die when you hear it"), adding in passing a reference to the Danish river Omme and oblique hints of the English Doe and Colombian Nare. The "old cheb" becomes "gubbstrunten," the "good-for-nothing (*strunt*) old geezer (*gubb*)."

The complex statement "Or whatever it was they threed to make out he thried to two in the Fiendish park" becomes for Grut's Swedish "Eller vad tre nu påstred han försöktu sig två i Fiendix Park," with the speaker wondering, roughly, "or what the three (*tre*) were now maintaining that he was trying his hand at doing to the two in the Fiendix Park," where "påstred" conflates *påstå* ("to maintain") and *tre* ("three") and "försöktu sig två" conflates *försöka sig på* ("to try one's hand at") and *två* ("two") as well as changing the regular past-tense verb ending *-te* into a *-tu* that likewise evokes the English *two*. The watchers' readiness to tell tales is firmly established. Grut's "Fiendix Park," conflating Dublin's Phoenix Park and Joyce's "Fiendish park," repeats the suggestion of the park as a potentially hostile place where one might well encounter an enemy (Swedish *fiende*) – or perhaps, as here, even three (*tre*) of them, lurking in interlingual trees (Swedish *träd*, English "trees").

Grut (Swedish, 2002)

Mario Grut continued his Joycean labours by providing a Swedish rendering of "The Ondt and the Gracehoper" (*FW* 414.22–419.8) in 2002. It appeared, under the title *Maran och gracehoppet*, as a tiny duodecimo booklet of sixteen pages, published in Lund by Ellerström.[3] La Fontaine's fable of the ant and the grasshopper is most commonly known in Swedish as *Myran och gräshoppan*. Grut's variation on Joyce's variation is ingenious: Swedish *myra* means "ant," *myran* "the ant," while *mara* means "nightmare"; *grace* /gra:s/ means "grace, charm," while

---

3 My thanks to Bertil Falk for kindly sending me a copy of this rendering.

gräshoppa is a "grasshopper"; *hoppa* is "to jump" and *hoppas* "to hope"; while *-et*, finally, is the postpositional neuter definite article.

In the opening line of Joyce's fable, "The Gracehoper was always jigging a jog, hoppy on akkant of his joyicity" (*FW* 414.22–3). This is rendered by Grut as "Gracehoppet jimmade jämt och jazzade, joy som ett ja som han var" (2002, 5), thus very roughly: "The gracehoper was always (*jämt*) jimming and jazzing, a joy like (*som*) a (*ett*), well (*ja*), like the joy he indeed (*ja*) was." Here the sequence of five *j*s plays amusingly on the difference in pronunciation between Swedish *j* /j/ and English *j* /dʒ/, while "jimmade" and "joy som" make clear the relationship to Joyce's own "joyicity."

As for the Ondt, "the Ondt was a weltall fellow, raumybult and abelboobied, bynear saw altitudinous wee a schelling in kopfers" (*FW* 416.3–4). In Grut's rendering, "Maran var en färserad typ, bredbystad och muskellös, nästen i höjd med en örtug i koppar." The suggestion, broadly, is that the "nightmare Ondt-ant was a stuffed-shirt type (*färserad* 'stuffed')," broad (*bred*) in the bust (*byst*) and, depending on how you saw it, either muscular (*muskulös*) or free (*loss*) of any muscle (*muskel*) at all, close (*näst* "next") in height (*höjd*), almost (*näst*), to "a year's-worth fistful of coppers (*koppar*)." The final phrase plays on *öre*, a Swedish "cent"; *år*, a "year"; *åra*, an "oar"; and *årtag*, the amount of water displaced by the "pull of an oar."

5 Italian

Schenoni (Italian, 2001)

Luigi Schenoni laboured, with interruptions, on his Italian translation of *FW* for almost thirty-five years until his death, aged seventy-three, in 2008. His rendering of I.1–8 appeared in 2001, as part of which his *Finnegans Wake: H.C.E.* of 1982 reappeared under the title *Finnegans Wake: Libro Primo I-IV* (2001a), accompanied by a matching volume containing his new rendering of *Finnegans Wake: Libro Primo V-VIII* (2001b). During the almost twenty years between 1982 and 2001 several scattered excerpts from Schenoni's translation in progress had appeared, amounting to roughly forty pages altogether, and in 1996 including the entire text of I.8.[4] His rendering of *FW* II.1–2 (*FW* 219–308) appeared in February 2004.

4　The excerpts in question appeared in 1986 (*FW* 627.9–628.16), 1990 (*FW* 104.1–112.27), 1991 (*FW* 117.9–125.23), 1996 (the complete text of I.8), 1999 (*FW* 169.1–171.28).

The lengthy twenty-year gap between the original appearance of I.1–4 in 1982 and that of I.5–8 in 2001 is explained by the fact that the continuing work on the *Wake* was accompanied by Schenoni's simultaneous work as a busy freelance literary translator for a number of Italian publishers. During those two decades he translated, by his own account, some fifty novels from English, by such writers as John Updike, Charles Bukowski, Robert Coover, and many others (Schenoni 1990). He observes in an introductory note to the later *Wake* volume that the translation of I.5–8 alone took ten of those years (2001b, v). The volume, which includes a revised version of his 1996 rendering of I.8, also contains more than 220 pages of detailed notes, and concludes with an essay, "Il sogno di H.C. Earwicker," a translation of Edmund Wilson's 1939 essay "The Dream of H.C. Earwicker."[5] Schenoni's 2001 rendering of the opening lines of I.8 (*FW* 196.1–7, 9–11):

O / dimmi tutto di / Anna Livia! Voglio sentire tutto / di Anna Livia. Be', conosci Anna Livia? Sì, certo, Anna Livia la conosciamo tutti. Dimmi tutto. Dimmel ora. Creperai quando sentirai. Be', sai, quando il vecchio chebscalzone fece foutsco e combinò quello che sai. ... O qualunque cosa fosse che hanno trescato di affermare che tontò con quelle due nel Fistolpark.

Unlike Joyce's own Italian rendering of *ALP*, Schenoni preserves the aquatic pun on French *eau*, while his "dimmi tutto" ("tell me all") goes on to afford us glimpses of the Turkish Dim, Dutch Diem, Sudanese Immi, and Indian Tut. As for "You'll die when you hear," Schenoni avoids Joyce's extravagant "Roba da chiodi!" in favour of a much less colourful but semantically more strictly accurate "Creperai quando sentirai," the Italian *crepare* literally meaning "to burst," while the idiomatic *crepare dalle risa* colloquially means "to die laughing." The German Repe, the Ando of the Solomon Islands, the French Seine, the Scottish Tirry, and the New Zealand Rai all unobtrusively flow through Schenoni's very aquatic rendering.

His version of 1996, "O qualunque cosa fosse che hanno trescato di affermare che tontò con quei due" renders as an approximate surface reading "or whatever it was the three of them conspired to insinuate that he foolishly tried to do with those two," where "trescato" implies both "to conspire" (*trescare*) and "three" (*tre*), while "tontò" implies

---

5 The essay is not translated by Schenoni, but taken from Nemi D'Agostino's translation of Wilson's *The Wound and the Bow* (1947) as *La ferita e l'arco* (Milan: Garzanti, 1956).

both "tried" (*tentò*) and "foolishly" (*tonto*). The English river Foss puts in a discreet appearance. Oddly, and presumably inadvertently, in the phrase "con quei due" ("with those two") the demonstrative adjective "quei" is masculine rather than feminine, presenting Italian readers with an additional layer of textual obscurity to negotiate. Schenoni's revised version of 2001 duly corrects the slip, employing the feminine form "quelle" and thus restoring the femininity of "those two" ("quelle due"), while adding an aquatic German *Quelle* ("spring, well").

As for the park in question, Schenoni's "Fistolpark," employing the obsolete Italian expression *fistolo* ("fiend, devil"), suggests the quasi-diabolical nature of HCE's transgression, while also suggesting an oblique reference to the Polish river Vistula. While Schenoni's rendering does indeed evoke a "fiendish" park for Italian readers, however, Joyce's implied reference to the Phoenix Park (rather than any other "fiendish" park) is almost entirely obscured.

From Schenoni's 2001 closing lines of I.8 (*FW* 215.31–5, 216.3–5):

Non riesco a sentire con l'acque bisbiglie di. Le mormoricchianti acque di. Pipistrelli volicchianti, il parlottare dei topi campagnoli. Ho! Non sei tonnat'a pedone? Chi è Thom Malone?[6] Non riesco a sentire con il parlottare dei pipistrelli, con tutte le liffeggianti acque di. Ho, parla salvaci! I miei oossuti piedi non si mooseòvono. Mi sento vecchia come quell'elmlontano olmo. Una storia spifferata di Shaun o di Shem? ... Dimmel, dimmel, dimmel olmo! Notte Notte! Dimmi il detto di stelo e sasso. Accanto alle fiumeggianti acque di, alle quaelavaganti acque di. Notte!

Schenoni's speaker cannot manage (*riuscire*) to hear (*sentire*) because of the "whispering waters" ("l'acque bisbiglie") that "murmur" (*mormorare*) and "mumble" (*mormorare*) and "grumble" (*mormorare*) as they "doze" (*dormicchiare*) and "nibble" (*mordicchiare*) away at the riverbank. Bats (*pipistrelli*) are flying to and fro (*volare* "to fly"), and one hears the whispering (*parlottare*) and muttering (*parlottare*) of the field mice ("topi campagnoli").

As for Thom Malone, Schenoni changes his mind as to the best rendering. His "Ho! Non sei tornat'a casa?" in his 1996 rendering recruits the Zimbabwean river Nata in asking "Haven't you gone back home?" In this earlier version the misheard question elicits the confusedly inappropriate answer "Che roba mancava?" ("*What* stuff was missing?"). In his 2001 version, Schenoni invokes the aid of the German Tonna and Japanese Onna as well as the Zimbabwean Nata in a punning variation

---

6 In 1996 Schenoni has "Ho! Non sei tornat'a casa? Che roba mancava?"

of the opening question: "Non sei tonnat'a pedone," literally, "Haven't you gone back (*tornata*) on foot?" The phrase *a pedone* ("as a pedestrian, on foot") elicits, perhaps not entirely convincingly, even though presumably with a trisyllabic Italian pronunciation, the counterquestion "Chi è Thom Malone?" ("Who is Thom Malone?").

Whoever Thom Malone may be, the speaker still can't manage (*riuscire*) to hear (*sentire*) with the whispering (*parlottare*) and muttering (*parlottare*) of the bats (*pipistrelli*) and the liffeying waters. Her "Ho, parla, salvaci!" invites the river itself (Chinese *ho*) to speak (*parla* "speak") and save us. My feet ("i miei piedi"), she says, are "oosuti," playing as in the original on the German Oos, are "bony" (*ossuti*) and "will not move" (*non si muòvono*), playing now on the American Moose as "non si mooseòvono." She feels as old as "quell'elmlontano olmo," the adjective conflating Italian *quello* ("that, yonder"), German *Quelle* ("well"), English *elm*, Italian *lontano* ("distant"), and the Ghanaian river Tano. The "tale told" is now a "storia spifferata" (a "story blurted out") about Shaun or Shem.

Schenoni's triple "dimmel" plays on the /l/ and /m/ of *elm* and *olmo*, adds the English Mel to the Turkish Dim, and retains the original rhythm. His "Dimmi il detto di stelo e sasso" adheres closely to Joyce's original English, though "stelo e sasso" for "stem or stone" loses the echo of "Shem or Shaun." The "rivering waters," swollen by the affluence of the Brazilian Rio Canto (*accanto a* "beside"), are quite literally "fiumeggianti acque," the invented *fiumeggiare* based on *fiume* ("river") and, humorously, the existing verb *fiammeggiare* ("to blaze"), while the "hitherandthithering waters" are "quaelavaganti acque," waters that wander (*vagare* "to wander") here (*qua*) and wander there (*là*).[7]

6 Dutch

Bindervoet and Henkes's Dutch Wake (2002)

Dutch appeared for the first time among the languages of the macro-textual *Wake* in April 2002, when a complete and highly praised Dutch translation by Erik Bindervoet and Robbert-Jan Henkes, handsomely bound and with the original text on facing pages, appeared in Amsterdam, published by Athenaeum/Polak & Van Gennep. Bindervoet, born in 1962 in the northern Dutch town of Oostzaan, and Henkes, born in the same year in the southern Dutch city of Eindhoven, reportedly met as students of history at the University of Amsterdam – allegedly on

7 On Schenoni's 2001 rendering of *ALP*, see Livorni (2004).

the occasion of a student occupation of one of the university buildings. They began their joint labours on *FW* in the mid-nineties, in their early thirties, and spent the next seven years on the task. They both live in Amsterdam.

It has been observed that Bindervoet and Henkes initially "seemed quite unlikely candidates to tackle a job that had put off so many before them," since by that time they "had hardly any experience as English translators" (van der Weide 2003, 625). This lack was quickly made good, for having made a start with *FW*, the energetic duo subsequently, among many and multifarious other endeavours, translated *Hamlet*, *King Lear*, *A Portrait of the Artist as a Young Man*, *Ulysses*, *Dubliners*, *Pomes Penyeach* – and, in passing, the complete lyrics of both the Beatles and Bob Dylan.

Having been refused permission by Stephen Joyce to describe their rendering as a translation rather than an adaptation, the Dutch translators conflate *vertaling* ("translation") and *herhaling* ("repetition") in punningly calling it a *hertaling*, a "re-languaging," thus contributing a new term to the Dutch language. In interviews, they also refer to it as a "dutchification." The unchanged title *Finnegans Wake*, meanwhile, allows for being read as either a reductive Dutch "Finnegan's Wake," singular and funereal, or an untranslated original title readable as immediately suggesting the essential untranslatability of Joyce's text.

Bindervoet and Henkes render the opening lines (*FW* 3.1–3) as follows:

> rivierein langst de Eva en Adam van zwier van strand naar bocht van baai brengt ons via een commodius vicus van recirculatie terug naar Howth Kasteel en Immelanden.

Here "rivierein" conflates *rivier* ("river") and *rennen* ("to run"), while the element *rein* suggests not only a river that is "clean, pure, chaste" but also provides an echo of the river Rhine as an appropriately international and intercultural European avatar of Anna Livia. The fact that the various names of the Rhine – German *Rhein*, French *Rhin*, Dutch *Rijn* – share their etymological origins with the Irish noun *rith* ("run"), all of them deriving from an Indo-European root **rei-*, is a pleasingly appropriate translingual serendipity. Jack van der Weide also points out that *rivierein* is the seventeenth-century spelling of *refrein*, the refrain of a song or a poem, already adumbrating one of the central concepts, namely, "the same anew," while the combination of Dutch *revier* and German *ein* also designates the river in question as "river number one" (2003, 626). The river flows "langst de Eva en Adam," conflating

Dutch *langs* ("along") and the suggestion that the flow of this river will provide a very long story (*langst* "longest") indeed. From an alliterative "swerve (*zwier*) of shore (*strand*) to bend (*bocht*) of bay (*baai*)," echoing Joyce's iambic tetrameter, we are brought "via een commodius vicus van recirculatie" back (*terug*) to "Howth Kasteel en Immelanden," the term "immelanden" suggesting "surrounding territories," thus "environs."

As the rendering of "Howth Castle and Environs" suggests, a notable peculiarity of Bindervoet and Henkes's rendering is the substitution of the initials HKI for HCE throughout – an expedient made necessary by the infrequency with which words in Dutch begin with the letter *c*. HCE thus appears variously as "Humfried Kimpanszoon Ierwicker" ("Humphrey Chimpden Earwicker") and "Hier Komt Iedereen" ("Here Comes Everybody") and "Hebbet Kinders Inallehoekengaten" ("Haveth Childers Everywhere") among many other formulations. While the change from HCE to HKI has the negative effect of disrupting the overt relationship to the British politician H.C.E. Childers, generally credited with having provided HCE with his initials, and the associated textual links, the new combination, pronounced /haka'i:/, can claim the advantage of gesturing towards the Dutch verb *hakkelen* ("to stammer, to stutter"), a feature associated throughout the text in every language with the egregious HCE. Anna Livia Plurabelle retains her original name.

Their rendering of the opening page continues as follows (*FW* 3.4–10):

Heer Tristram, violaat d'amores, vannover de korte zee, was passencore weeromgekeerd uit Noord-Armorica deeszijds 't schierlijk eilandje van Klein-Europa voor het widervuren van zijn gepenisoleerde oorlog: noch hadden topzooiers rotshopen aan de Oconee-stroom zichcelverlei gecumulleerd naar Laurenslands gorgio's wijl ze gehelenal de tijd hun worpelingen verdubbelinden: noch bluisbalgde een stem vanuit de vuurte miesje miesje tot tauftauf giezijtpitriek:

Among noticeable features here, the Dutch rendering avoids direct reference to an isthmus, scraggy or otherwise, preferring to speak instead of a "schierlijk eilandje," literally, an "almost islet," playing on the Dutch term *schiereiland* ("peninsula"). Joyce's "wielderfight" becomes a Dutch "widervuren," which succeeds in combining German *wieder* ("again") and *wider* ("against"), Dutch *weer* ("again"), Dutch *vuren* ("to fire," as of a gun), and German *weiterführen* ("to continue"). There is also the suggestion of German *Widder* ("ram," the animal), translingually evoking the second syllable of Tristram's name as well as his sexual drive. The "gepenisoleerde oorlog" includes the war (*oorlog*), the penis (*penis*), and isolation (*geïsoleerd*, "isolated") but also reveals the shadow of a hidden "isol ... de."

The opening lines of I.8 (*FW* 196.1–7, 9–11) are rendered as follows:

O / vertel me alles over / Anna Livia! Ik wil alles horen / over Anna Livia. Nou, je kent Anna Livia? Ja natuurlijk, Anna Livia kennen we allemaal. Vertel me alles. Vertel me nu. Je lacht je dood asje het hoort. Nou, weet je nog, diem khabbir met z'n ongein en toen hij je weet wel wat deed. ... Of tweet niet wat drie trachtten te zien wat hij triochtte te duon in het Vreeslix Park.

In a particularly aquatic rendering, the washerwoman's "vertel me alles" ("tell me all") initially evokes the English Ver, Indian Tel, American Elm, and Russian Alle. "You'll die when you hear" becomes "Je lacht je dood asje het hoort," literally, "you'll laugh yourself to death when you (*als je*) hear it," a promise enlivened by fluvial evocations of the German Ach, Indian Dood, and Russian Asje rivers. The old cheb, after an opening "Nou, weet je nog" ("Well, you know") that evokes the Chinese Nu, Laotian Ou, and South African Vet rivers, is remodelled as an old *khabbir*, his identity suggested by the appearance of the letters KHI.

The epithet is triply and interlingually offensive to its victim, conflating a taboo epithet for a Black African (English *kaffir*), a Muslim epithet for an unbeliever (Arabic *kāfir*), and an impolite colloquialism for a boor (Dutch *kuffer*), thus succinctly passing less than favourable judgment on our hero's foreign origins, lack of religion, and lack of manners. He is further described as "met z'n ongein," roughly, "involved in a funny business (*ongein*) of some sort," a rendering that offers a comfortable home to four separate rivers from near and far, the Dutch Diem, Laotian Kha, Indian Habb, Australian Birrie, and Dutch Gein. The further comment, "en toen hij je weet wel wat deed," evoking Joyce's English "well" and the Scottish river Dee, is a pertinent reminder (or suggestion) that we " know well what he did."

As to the dubious events in the park, "Of tweet niet wat drie trachtten te zien wat hij triochtte te duon" suggests, roughly, "Or I don't know what the three (*drie*) of them were trying to see that he was trying to do," where "tweet" conflates, as well as the South African river Vet, *ik weet* ("I know") and *twee* ("two"), "triochtte" conflates Dutch *trachten* ("to try") and English *trio*, and "te duon" conflates the Dutch *doen* ("to do") and the English *duo*. The three watchers in this version appear at this point to be more interested in just spying on the old cheb than in constructing rumours to be spread abroad about him. The "Fiendish park," meanwhile, becomes the "Vreeslix Park," a "frightful" (*vreselijk*) place, a place to inspire "fear" (*vrees*), its new name, meanwhile, appropriately for the aquatic context, also evoking the Rees River of New Zealand and the Reese River of Nevada.

The final paragraph of I.8 includes lines (*FW* 215.31–5, 216.3–5) rendered as follows:

> Kannie horen met de wateren van. De klaterende wateren van. Vlederende muizen, veldmuizen klatsen klets. Ho! Moet je nou niet alles gaan? Welke Thom Malaan? Kannie horen met die klats van kleermuizen, al die liffiënde wateren van. Ho, klets beware ons! Krijg me voos niet moos. Ik voel me zo oud als gindse olm. Een verhaal verteld door Shaun of Shem? ... Vertel, vertel, vertel me, olm! Nacht nacht! Vertelmeverhaal van stam of steen. Langs de rivierende wateren van, hier-en-ginderende wateren van. Nacht!

Here the washerwoman can't hear with the clattering and splashing (*klaterend*) waters, while bats (*vleermuizen*) flitter and fieldmice (*veldmuizen*) talk (*kletsen*) nonsense (*klets*). Her question "Moet je nou niet alles gaan?" ("Don't you have to go now?") elicits the response "Welke Thom Malaan?," conflating "Malone," the Indian river Malan, and the German Lahn. "Klets beware ons" ("May this rubbishy chit-chat save us"), for "Krijg me voos niet moos," roughly, "My rotten (*voos*) foot (*voet*) is gathering neither moss (*mos*) nor money (*moos*)." All this, and a potential tale of stem (*stam*) or stone (*steen*), beside the rivering (*rivierende*) waters of, the "here-and-yondering" (*hier-en-ginderende*) waters.

The final page of the *Wake* in the Dutch rendering includes the following passage (*FW* 627.34–628.4):

> Ik ga heen. O bitter einde! Ik glip weg voor ze op zijn. Ze zullen het nooit zien. Of weten. Of me missen. En 't is oud en oud is 't erg en oud is 't erg en moe keer ik terug naar jou, mijn koude vader, mijn koude gekke vader, mijn koude gekke varige vader, tot de aanblik dichtbij al van zijn omvang alleen al, de moylen en moylen ervan, dreunendreinend, me zeezilt zoutziek maakt en ik me in jouw armen stort, mijn enige.

Dirk Van Hulle (2015, 3) has high praise for the Dutch *Wake* as being essentially not just a translation but also an overt *continuation* of Joyce's *Work in Progress*, in that it pays systematic attention to textual losses that have occurred throughout the highly complicated genetic history of the actual text of *FW*. A notable feature of the translation is that it is followed by no fewer than twenty-eight pages of such losses, "transmissional departures," as the translators call them, from the generally accepted original text. The last and most cited item in this list involves the final line of Joyce's text (*FW* 628.15–16), rewritten in Dutch as "Al weg al leen *al loren* al laatst al liefd al langs de" (emphasis added), translating "A way a lone *a lost* a last a loved a long the" (emphasis added), restoring the long-lost phrase "a lost" that had disappeared, for undetermined reasons, at some early point in the textual history. The final sentence of Bindervoet and Henkes's rendering thus provides a striking justification of Van Hulle's assertion that the Dutch text is not just a translation but also a continuation of Joyce's *Work in Progress*.[8]

The apparently indefatigable translators subsequently extended their *Wakean* endeavours to include a lively and entertaining 250-page quasi-encyclopedic commentary (in Dutch), their *Finnegancyclopedie* (2005), which includes, among much else, a substantial account (185–203) of no fewer than twenty-nine different translation methods they had found it appropriate to employ (and occasionally to avoid).

7 Korean

Kim's Korean Wake: P'inegan ŭi kyŏngya *(2002)*

The year 2002 in fact saw two new complete renderings of *FW*, for not only did Bindervoet and Henkes's Dutch version appear in Amsterdam, but a complete Korean translation by Chong-keon Kim of Korea University, whose rendering of *ALP* had appeared in 1985 already, was also published in Seoul, South Korea. It appeared under the title 피네간의經夜 and was reissued a decade later, substituting Korean characters for the two concluding Chinese characters, as 피네간의 경야 (Kim 2012a). Both of these titular renderings are romanized as *P'inegan ŭi kyŏngya*: the three characters 피네간 transliterate as "P'inegan," 의 is "ŭi," and the two final characters, whether the Chinese 經夜 or the Korean 경야, transliterate as "kyŏngya." Finnegan becomes "P'inegan" since the letter *f* does not occur in Korean and is replaced in foreign words and names by an aspirated *p*; "ŭi" is a possessive particle, the equivalent of an English apostrophe, and "kyŏngya" is the normal Korean term for "wake." The title thus literally means "Finnegan's wake," in the funeral sense, though the cultural implications are different, in

---

8 On Bindervoet and Henkes's Dutch rendering, see Evenhuis (2002), Van Hulle (2002, 2015), van der Weide (2003), Bindervoet and Henkes (2005). For a listing of some twenty further reviews in Dutch, see also *James Joyce Quarterly* 41 (2003/2004): 197–8.

that the Korean funereal custom involves staying all night at the house of the mourner but without the festive character of an Irish wake.[9] In Chinese (rather than Korean) the two final Chinese characters translate as *hīng* ("through") and *yè* ("night") respectively, thus suggesting a "nightwatch."

Younghee Kho reports that Chong-keon Kim in his 2002 rendering of *FW* incorporated Chinese characters at various points in an attempt to capture as many aspects as possible of Joycean polysemy. "The use of Chinese letters arises from Kim's view that its oppositional character to Korean can form a complementary relationship with the latter. The ideographic nature of Chinese characters, he claims, makes it possible to explain homonyms and what they create in the mixture of meanings and sounds" (Kho 2015, 450), while the Korean language, which is essentially phonetic, would be inadequate if the *Wake* were translated into Korean only. One example cited by Kho is the phrase "all thim liffeying waters of" (*FW* 215.33–4), where, in order to suggest what he calls an "exegetical" rendering of "liffeying," Kim includes the three Chinese characters 生跳葉 (meaning "living," "leaping," and "leafy," respectively) immediately after the corresponding Korean word, 리피 ("lipi," which is to say, "Liffey"). The advantage of such a method, in principle, is that the "exegetical" translation can capture multiple connotations and thus convey multiple and maximally polysemous meanings at the same time.[10]

Kho suggests, however, that in practice the use of Chinese characters was in at least one sense counterproductive, in that it made Kim's rendering inaccessible to many Korean readers – for, "in present-day Korea, younger generations are no longer generally educated in reading and writing Chinese or otherwise exposed to the language" (2015, 450). Kho reports that unlike the media sensation later caused in China by Congrong Dai's 2012 rendering of I.1–8, Kim's 2002 translation met with relatively little response among Korean readers. Kim published a revised version of the translation in 2012 (2012a), accompanied in this case by a separate volume of annotations (2012b), and in 2015 published an abridged and simplified version modelled after Charles and Mary Lamb's *Tales from Shakespeare* and incorporating only a reduced number of Chinese-based neologisms (Kho 2015, 451).

---

9 On Kim's Korean rendering, see Chun (2004), Jones (2004), Kim (2004), Kho (2015). The discussion of the Korean title here is greatly indebted to Younghee Kho of the Seoul National University of Science and Technology, in personal correspondence. On Kim's incorporation of Chinese characters in his Korean translation overall, see Kho (2015).

10 See also Kim (1990).

In an account of the Fifth Biennial International Korean James Joyce Conference at Chonnam University in November 2012, Shelly Brivic reports that "the most magnificent feature of the conference was Chongkeon Kim, a robust octogenarian who made frequent and striking comments from the floor. Professor Kim had just published a complete Korean translation of *Finnegans Wake*, accompanied by a book of notes longer than the *Wake*" (2011, 602).[11] Kim's monumental translation of Joyce's complete works, from *Dubliners* to *FW*, appeared in two large volumes in 2013.

8 Portuguese

Schüler's Portuguese Wake: Finnicius Revém *(2003)*

The foremost Portuguese contribution to the expanding universe of *FW* had for more than forty years been the likewise expanding collection of brief excerpts translated by the brothers Haroldo and Augusto de Campos in its first form as early as 1957. That situation was to change dramatically in 1999, with the appearance of the first volume (*FW* I.1) of Donaldo Schüler's complete, bilingual, and award-winning Portuguese rendering of *FW*, which appeared complete in five volumes in 2003.

Schüler (born 1932), poet, critic, and emeritus professor of Greek at the Federal University of Rio Grande do Sul in Pôrto Alegre, Brazil, is regarded as one of that country's most prominent intellectual figures. A translator of Homer's *Odyssey* as well as of Plato, Aeschylus, Euripedes, and Sophocles, he went on to publish his complete and richly annotated Portuguese rendering of *FW* in 2003. It appeared under the evocative title *Finnicius Revém*, borrowed, in an overt act of homage to its original coiners, from the Brazilian Campos brothers (1962, 13). The translated title can be read as combining "Finn" and a Latin quasi-comparative *finnicius* ("a thing even more Finn"), with attendant suggestions of "finishes" and "Phoenicians" (Portuguese *fenícios*) and "phoenix" (*fénix*), not to mention an "end" (Latin *finis*, Portuguese *fim*), all of which "comes again" (Portuguese *revém*) as if in a "dream" (French *rêve*). The invented name *Finnicius* also suggests the Brazilian personal name *Vinicius*, evoking a Brazilian *vinho* ("wine") in at least partial substitution for the Irish whiskey that brings an ever-thirsty Tim Finnegan back from the dead.

---

11   The reference here is to Kim (2012a and 2012b).

Schüler reported to interviewers that he took just four years to complete the translation, aiming to translate just one page a day, Monday to Friday (Oliveira et al. 2019, 296). The complete rendering likewise appeared in Pôrto Alegre over a four-year period: volume one (*FW* I.1) in 1999; volume two (*FW* I.2–4) in 2000; volume 3 (*FW* I.5–8) in 2001; volume 4 (*FW* II) in 2002; and volume 5 (*FW* III and IV) in 2003, in which year the complete translation appeared, partially revised, in five handsome matching paperback volumes, with the original text on the facing page in each case.[12]

Schüler renders the opening lines (*FW* 3.1–3) as follows:

> rolarriuanna e passa por Nossenhora d'Ohmem's roçando a praia, beirando ABahia reconduz-nos por commódios cominhos recorrentes de vico ao de Howth Castelo Earredores.

Here the translator chooses as his opening word an expansive "rolarriuanna," not only conflating *rolar* ("to roll, flow, run") and *rio* ("river") but also immediately establishing the identity of the river and Anna Livia Plurabelle – while simultaneously evoking the Arriu Nere or Black River of Catalonia. As du Bouchet (1962) and Lavergne (1982) extend the boundaries of Dublin on the Liffey to include Paris on the Seine, so Schüler's adventurous rendering "e passa por Nossenhora d'Ohmem's" extends those boundaries even further to include the Brazilian metropolis of São Paulo on the Rio Tietê. The name of that river reportedly and serendipitously means "river of truth" in the local indigenous language, Tupi. A well-known church in São Paulo, meanwhile, one discovers, is devoted to the popular cult of Nossa Senhora do Ó ("Our Lady of the Sigh"), the unusual epithet reportedly deriving from a series of prayers to the Virgin offered during Advent that all begin with the invocation "O," popularly understood by the devout as being a sigh of veneration.

Combining *Ó* and the noun *homem* ("man, humankind"), Schüler's version suggests proleptically that ALP is both alpha and omega and that Anna Livia, Our Lady of the Liffey, will also emerge as Our Lady of Humankind. Since Portuguese *homem* also translates Hebrew *adam* ("man"), we thus have both Adam and Eve subsumed in the Blessed Virgin Mary, while the unnecessary and ungrammatical apostrophe in "Ohmem's" reminds us both of the presence of the apostrophe in

---

12 On Schüler's Portuguese rendering, see Galvão (1999), Amarante (2003a, 2009, 2019), Schüler (2005, 2010), Torres and Furlan (2010), Paret-Passos (2014, 2015), Amaral (2019), Oliveira et al. (2019).

"Eve and Adam's" and the absence of the apostrophe in *Finnegans Wake* (O'Neill 2013, 45).

The phrase "roçando a praia, beirando ABahia" once again incorporates a transatlantic reference to Brazilian geography: the port city of Bahia is located eight hundred miles north of Rio de Janeiro and is situated, like Dublin, on a picturesque bay. The religious note introduced by the reference to the church of Nossa Senhora do Ó in the previous phrase is continued here: the city of Bahia is officially named São Salvador da Bahia ("Saint Saviour of the Bay"), and the bay on which it stands is the Bahia de Todos os Santos ("All Saints Bay"). Schüler's version literally has the river "brushing against (*roçando*) the strand (*a praia*), skirting (*beirando*) the bay (*a baía*)." The phrase *beirando a baía* provides the basis for a triple pun: *beirando* ("skirting") generates, by way of a series of translingual puns, the Portuguese noun *aba*, which means both the "skirts" (of a tailcoat, for example) and the "coast around a port"; the Old Irish *aba* ("river"), and the Sardinian *aba* ("water"); the noun *baía*, formerly spelled *bahia*, evoking the port city of the same name; and the irregularly capitalized feminine article *a* in "ABahia" once again evoking the presence of ALP, alpha in "ABahia" as she was omega in "Nossenhora d'Ohmem's" (O'Neill 2013, 50). The course of the river "reconduz-nos por commódios cominhos recorrentes de vicó," taking us back by commodious "roads (*caminhos*) that return," courtesy of Commodus and Vico, to Howth Castle and Environs.

Schüler's rendering of the opening page continues as follows (*FW* 3.4–10):

> Sir Tristrão, violeiro d'amores, d'além do mar encapelado, não tinha passancorado reveniente de Norte Armórica a estas bandas do istmo escarpado da Europa Menor para o virolento conflito de penisoldada guerra: nem as pétreas bolotas de Sawyer ao longo do Oconee caudaloso se tinham seggsagerado ao território laurenciano da Geórgia enquanto se dublinavam em mamypapypares o tempo todo: nem avoz do fogo rebellava mim-She, mim-She ao tauftauf do pautripedrícioquetués:

Schüler's Sir Tristrão, whose name combines those of Tristan (Tristão) and Tristram, voyages "d'além do mar encapelado" ("from beyond the swelling sea"), a sea that has "grown rough" (*encapelado*) and thus might also suggest stormy times ahead for Sir Tristrão. As in Anthony Burgess's 1975 Italian rendering, the Portuguese successfully plays on the verbs *passar* ("to pass") and *ancorar* ("to anchor") in "não tinha passancorado." The phrase "to wielderfight his penisolate war" has the Brazilian Tristan engaged in a "virolento conflito," a struggle both violent (*violento*) and virulent (*virulento*) in a "penisoldada guerra," emphasizing the presence of an embedded Portuguese Isolda, alias Iseult.

"Topsawyer's rocks" becomes "as pétreas bolotas de Sawyer," which retranslates literally as "the rocky acorns of Sawyer," incorporating Greek *pétra* and Latin *petra* ("rock") and their relationship to the name Peter – for Schüler sees Peter Sawyer rather than Tom as the more important referent. His use of *bolotas* ("acorns") for "rocks" overtly emphasizes the sexual connotation of Joyce's term, while also hinting (in colloquial Brazilian usage) that these acorns from which great oaks may grow are likely to lead not only to a "bunch" (*bolo*) of descendants but also a bunch of "trouble" (*bolo*).

One year after his five-volume *Finnicius Revém* appeared, the versatile Schüler also produced a highly abbreviated, very much simplified, and very loosely based children's version, *Finnício Riovém* (2004) – presumably the only children's version of the *Wake* in any language. Amusingly, the title improves further on the earlier title: the first word, *Finnício*, now includes not only "Finn" and *fim* ("end") but also *início* ("beginning"); while the second word, *riovém*, includes not only *revém* ("comes again") and thus by implication the suggestion of a French *rêve* ("dream"), but also *rio* ("river"), and thus Anna Livia Plurabelle, the eternal river that always returns in a commodius vicus of recirculation.

The first sentence of *Finnício Riovém*, moreover, is closely and interestingly based on the first sentence of *Finnicius Revém*. It reads:

> rolarriuanna e passa pelo parque de Eva e Adão, roçando a praia, beirando ABahia, reconduz-nos por cominhos recorrentes de Viço ao Homem do Castelocaveira Earredores.

Where the river of *Finnicius Revém* "passa por Nossenhora d'Ohmem's," in the later version it "passa pelo parque de Eva e Adão," passing neither by the church of "Eve and Adam's" nor by " Nossenhora d'Ohmem's," but by the "garden (*parque*) of Eve and Adam," suggesting at once the Garden of Eden, the fall of our first parents, and (at the expense of some small geographical displacement) the Phoenix Park (*parque*), the site of HCE's temptation and fall – however indeterminate – from grace.

The two versions of the phrase "to Howth Castle and Environs" are both striking. That of *Finnicius Revém* reads "ao de Howth Castelo Earredores" instead of the more normal word order *ao Castelo de Howth*, with the simple but surprisingly disruptive linguistic reversal effectively evoking the reversals of history, all too appropriate especially in the case of Howth. HCE's initials are saved by simply rewriting *e arredores* ("and environs") as "Earredores." The version of *Finnício Rio-vém*, though likewise retaining the initials HCE, reads "ao Homem do Castelocaveira Earredores." Here the "head" (Danish *hoved*) of Howth is transformed into a Portuguese *caveira* ("skull"), a term etymologically derived from the Latin *calvaria* (skull"), Howth Castle thus becomes Skull Castle, and HCE is transformed at least momentarily into Jesus Christ, the Man (*homem*) of Calvary, the "place of the skull," a culture hero notoriously also destroyed by the ignorance of the mob – but who rose again from the dead, as Finn was expected to do, and as Tim Finnegan appears to do.[13]

A striking characteristic of Schüler's version of *FW* is that, on several occasions, the translator uses specifically Brazilian references instead of Irish ones to extend the international reach of the *Wake*: thus "Nossenhora d'Ohmem's" for "Eve and Adam's," invoking a church in São Paulo rather than on Merchant's Quay (*FW* 3.1), or the reference to the northern city of Bahia, or "Dubelém" for Joyce's "Dubblenn" (*FW* 66.18), in this last case invoking both the Brazilian city of Belém and the biblical town of Bethlehem as well as the Irish city of Dublin. Such translatorial decisions certainly make an interesting contribution to a macrotextual *Wake* – as did du Bouchet's translation of "Eve and Adam's" to Paris with his rendering "Évant notre Adame" (*FW* 3.1).

Schüler's lively sense of fun, as demonstrated in his flamboyant treatment of names, can occasionally lead to distinctly extravagant results, as when he renders "Persse O'Reilly" as "Estour A. Tim Panos," literally, "pierces (*estoura*) eardrums (*timpanos*)" (*FW* 44.24) or "Hofed-ben-Edar" as "Coco-bem-Quisto," roughly, "Bladderhead the Wellbeloved" (*FW* 30.11), each of which is both clever and amusing but could certainly also be argued as distorting and damaging the overall original fabric of referential allusion. As against that, however, a macrotextual *Wake* is certainly flexible enough to accommodate such individual idiosyncrasies – which are of course entirely reminiscent of the translatorial liberties Joyce himself had no compunction about taking. At the very least, they contribute generously to the lots of fun to be had, in whatever linguistic version, at *Finnegans Wake*.

From Schüler's opening lines of *ALP* (*FW* 196.1–7, 9–11):

O / Conta-me tudo sobre / Ana Lívia! Quero ouvir tudo / sobre Ana Lívia. Be, conheces Ana Lívia? Açai, claro, todos conhecemos Ana Lívia.

---

13 My thanks to Dirce Waltrick do Amarante for kindly sending me a copy of *Finnício Riovém* as well as various other materials relating to Donaldo Schüler's work. On *Finnício Riovém*, see Amarante (2005; 2015, 85–8).

Conta-me tudo. Conta-me agora. É de morrer o que escutarás. Bem, sabes, quando o velho velhaco fez fiasco e fez o que fez. ... O que é que Tefé que tresandaram a descobrir o que ele doisdou de fazer no Fuscoix Parque.

Schüler's "Conta-me tudo" ("tell me all") evokes ("-ta-me") the English Tame, Thames (Portuguese *Tâmesis*), and Tud. The response "Yes, of course" becomes a rather extravagant "Açai, claro," where *açai* plays on *ah, sim* ("O yes") but literally refers to the tropical açai palm, whose name in the indigenous Tupi language of Brazil, referring to the watery fruit of the palm, reportedly means "weeps water," an aquatic reference immediately supported by the Brazilian Rio Claro. The old cheb who went futt is just "o velho velhaco" ("the old crook") who "fez fiasco" ("came a cropper") and "fez o que fez" ("did what he did"). As for whatever happened in the park, Schüler's "O que é que Tefé que tresandaram a descobrir o que ele doisdou de fazer" translates roughly as "Or whatever the devil (German *was Teufel* "what the devil") it was that the three (*três*) of them had in mind (*tresandar*) to reveal (*descobrir*) about what he was deciding (*decidir*) to do to the two (*dois*)." The dark deed was to take place, appropriately, in the "Fuscoix Parque," the Portuguese *fusco* meaning "dark."

From Schüler's final lines of *ALP* (*FW* 215.31–5, 216.3–5):

Não ouço com as correntes de! As lamuriantas corrientes de. Mor dentes mor cegos, res postas de rústicos ratos. Ho! Você ao solar não iria? Que solitária Maria? Não ouço com o mortelar de morcegos, as liffey-hiantes águas de. Ho, o verbo nos salve! As pernas emperram. Me sinto velha como aquele carvelho. Uma narrativa narrada de Shaun ou Shem? ... Fala-me, fala-me, fala-me, carvelha! Noite noite! Conta-me contos de Stem ou Stone. Junto às rio-revantes águas de, correntes-e-recorrentes águas de. Noite!

The washerwoman can't hear with the "correntes de" ("the currents of"), the "lamurientas corrientes," currents at once "moaning" (*lamuriante*) and "laughing" (*riente*). Bats (*morcegos*) are biting (*mordentes*), bats blind (*cegos*) and showing their teeth (*dentes*), eliciting responses (*resposta*) from fieldmice (*rústicos ratos*). "Você ao solar não iria?," she asks ("Why are you not going home?"), eliciting the puzzled response "Que solitária Maria?" (*What* lonely Maria?"). "O verbo nos salve" ("may words save us"), she exclaims, "As pernas emperram" ("My legs are going stiff"). And she feels "velha como aquele carvelho," as old (*velho*) not as that elm but as that oak tree (*carvalho*) over there. "Tell me (*fala-me*), old oak, old like myself ("carvelha"), tales of Stem or Stone, by the waters that come and go, flowing and reflowing" (*correntes-e-recorrentes*).

Lines (*FW* 627.34–628.4, 15–16), finally, from Schüler's rendering of the closing pages of the *Wake*:

> Estou de partida. Que amargo fim! Sorrateiramente partirei antes que acordem. Não vão me ver. Nem saber. Nem recordar-me. E é velha e velha é triste e velha é triste e exausta volto a ti, velhegélido pai, velhegélido indômito pai, meu velhegélido indômito, patético pai, até a mara vista da mera forma dele, as miolhas e miolhas dele, monotonando, me ressalgam, me ressacam e me arremesso, meu ínico, em teus braços. ... A via a lenta a leve a leta a long

Teixeira Filho (Portuguese, 2008)

A Portuguese version of *FW* I.1 by Afonso Teixeira Filho appeared, extensively annotated, in São Paulo, Brazil, in 2008 as part of a doctoral dissertation at the University of São Paulo entitled *A noite e as vidas de Renatos Avelar* (The night and the lives of Renatos Avelar). The translator explains that the name "Renatos Avelar," like "Finnegans Wake," uses thirteen letters; "Renatos," a plural form of the Italian given name Renato, as "Finnegans" is a plural form of "Finnegan," also conflates birth (Italian *nato* "born"), death (Greek *thanatos*), and rebirth (Italian *renato* "reborn"); while "Avelar," otherwise a not uncommon Portuguese surname, here conflates the Portuguese verb *a velar* ("to wake, to observe a vigil") and, contributing a more than usually idiosyncratic note, is also presented as a partial anagram of the name of Éamon de Valera, celebrated as father of the rebirth of the modern Irish state (2008, 202).

The tongue-in-cheek title, while undoubtedly both ingenious and jocular, as well as humorously domesticating for a Brazilian readership, has of course the associated effect of distracting readers from the dense knot of textual allusions associated with the names of both Tim Finnegan and his legendary Joycean avatar Finn MacCool. Donaldo Schüler's Portuguese *Finnicius Revém* (2003), which takes particular pleasure in humorously adjusting Joyce's names, sometimes to extravagant effect, may well have inspired Teixeira Filho's likewise extravagant title. As elsewhere, Hervé Michel's *Veillée Pinouilles* (2004) may also have had a liberating effect.

Teixeira Filho (2008, 159) renders the three-line incipit as follows:

> fluminente, eventando o riocurso adante, do desrumo da fraga até à orla da angra, reavida por um vicomodado recirculoso, devolutase para a colina de Howth, o Castelo e o Entorno.

Here the first word transforms the Liffey and Dublin into Brazil's Rio de Janeiro, a city whose own name is also that of a river, namely the "January River" (*rio de Janeiro*), named for its discovery in that month by sixteenth-century Portuguese mariners. Joyce's "riverrun" is rendered as "fluminente," conflating Latin *flumen* ("river"), Portuguese *fluir* ("to flow"), *ente* ("a being"), and the Brazilian Portuguese demonym *fluminense*, meaning "from the state of Rio de Janeiro." Brazilian readers who are soccer enthusiasts will be pleased to discover the only slightly adjusted name of the premier football club of the state, namely, Fluminense. This "river being," as if it were a mythological river goddess, is discovered pushing (*aventando*) the course of the river (*o rio-curso*) forward (*adiante*), while hospitably offering accommodation in passing to both Eve ("*even*tando") and Adam ("*adan*te").

The river's swerving (*desviarse* "to swerve") course (*rumo*) passes from the rocky crag (*fraga*) of the shore to the edge (*orla*) of the cove (*angra*) and, brought back to life (*reavivar* "to revive"; *vida* "life") by a convenient (*cômodo*) recirculating (*recirculoso*) vicus ("vico"), returns (*voltar* "to return") restored (*devoluto*) – and hibernicized once again – to the Hill (*colina*) of Howth, the Castle (*castelo*), and its Environs (*entorno*). Eve and Adam, though not necessarily Joyce's Eve and Adam's or Dublin's Adam and Eve's, are both present and correct, as are Commodus and Vico, while the river itself has changed hemispheres and become Brazilian rather than Irish. The "craggy" shore, meanwhile, is likewise clearly (and humorously) that of Rio de Janeiro with its dramatic 1,300-foot crag the Pão de Açúcar or Sugarloaf Mountain rather than the undramatic lowlands of Dublin's Liffey delta.

Teixeira Filho writes in personal correspondence of additional associations suggested in his rendering of the opening word. Since "riverrun" sounded, as it seemed to him, like the potential genitive case of a noun, as if suggesting "of the river," he decided to Latinize it. The resulting "fluminente," however, also incorporated the four elements of the philosophy of Empedocles: water is represented by *flumen* ("river" in Latin); air by *Luft* ("air" in German); fire by *lume* ("fire" in Portuguese); while earth is suggested by the concluding "-ente" as a necessary component of any *continente* ("continent").

Also in personal correspondence, Teixeira Filho writes that he specifically wanted to create a text that would sound as if it had been written in Portuguese originally, just as Joyce's Italian rendering of *ALP* sounded, and was intended to sound, as if originally composed in Italian. The puns and word games of the Portuguese rendering were in principle carefully designed to respect the natural historical process of word creation in Portuguese, the final text thus reading, the translator suggests, as if originally written in Old Portuguese – and since older terms are frequently conserved in rural speech, the text, he asserts, thus also displays a markedly oral character. Teixeira Filho also writes that his translation had very different concerns and criteria than Donaldo Schüler's, which, though very accurate, neglects in the younger translator's opinion both musicality and rhythm.[14]

Teixeira Filho's rendering of the opening page continues (*FW* 3.4–10):

Seo Tristão, violamor, de marilanda alenavara, inda se não havia arrevultado a passo ancora da Armórica do Norte, no magristmo da Eiropa Menor, aonde isolou-se forâneo ao quersoneso afuleimar-se em penoso prélio: nem tão sóia as fragas d'alta serra despenhar pelo regato Oconina amealhando-se ao gargalho do concelho laurenciano ao passo que dublicavam a gorjeta abeternamente: nem a chamejada voz a taufolegar mexe mexe a crendospadre espetrufara:

Amarante's Portuguese ALP *(2009)*

A second complete Portuguese version of *ALP* (following on Donaldo Schüler's rendering of 2001) appeared in 2009, by Dirce Waltrick do Amarante (born 1969) of the Federal University of Santa Catarina in Florianópolis, Brazil. The translation appears as the final part of a general discussion of *FW* and is preceded by the comment that in her translation she attempted to recreate the rhythm of the Portuguese text rather than simply reproducing Joyce's original rhythm, based in Joyce's case largely on monosyllables, common in English but less so in Portuguese. The result, she suggests, might be called a Brazilian or perhaps a Latin rhythm, a slower rhythm because of the predominance of longer words than in the original.[15]

Amarante renders the opening lines of *ALP* (*FW* 196.1–7, 9–11) as follows:

O / Me conta tudo sobre / Anna Livia! Quero saber tudo / sobre Anna Livia. Bem, conheces Anna Livia? Claro que sim, todo mundo conhece

---

14 My thanks to Afonso Teixeira Filho for kindly sending me an electronic copy of his dissertation.

15 "No meu ensaio de tradução, procurei recriar o ritmo do texto, e não reproduzir simplesmente o ritmo joyciano, baseado em monossílabos – comuns na língua inglesa, mas não no nosso idioma –; obtive assim um ritmo brasileiro, talvez latino, um ritmo mais lento, ao usar palavras mais longas do que as do original" (2009, 112). My thanks to Dirce Waltrick do Amarante for kindly sending me a copy of her translation.

Anna Livia. Me conta tudo. Me conta já. Cais dura se ouvires. Bem, sabes, quando o velho foolgado fallou e fez o que sabes. ... Seja lá o que quer que tenha sido eles teentaram doiscifrar o que ele trestou fazer no parque Fiendish.

Adding a metrical overlay on Joyce's opening delta, Amarante's "*O Me | conta | tudo | sobre | Anna | Livia!*" is readable as a rhythmical trochaic hexameter. Her "Me conta tudo" ("tell me all") introduces the Southeast Asian Mekong ("Me con-"), while "Bem" ("so") evokes the Australian Bemm and "Claro" the Brazilian Rio Claro. "You'll die when you hear" becomes "Cais dura se ouvires," literally, "You'll fall down stiff (*dura*) and dead, you'll be paralysed, when you hear," fluvially evoking the Portuguese Douro, French Ouve, and French Vire. The old cheb who went futt is now "o velho foolgado," a translingual "old fool" who is also a "lazy old devil" (*folgado*) who "fallou," which is to say, evoking the Irish river Allow, he simply "cracked up" (*falir* "to crack up"). What he actually did is "o que sabes" ("what you know").

Amarante's version of what happened in the park, "Seja lá o que quer que tenha sido eles teentaram doiscifrar o que ele trestou fazer," translates roughly as "Let it be (*seja lá*) whatever (*o que quer*) it may have been (*que tenha sido*) that they were trying (*tentar* 'to try') to make out (*decifrar* 'to decipher') that he was trying (*tratar* 'to try') to do," with references to both the three (*tres-tou*) and the two (*dois-cifrar*), as well as the English river Tees ("teentaram").

Lines (*FW* 215.31–5, 216.3–5) from Amarante's final paragraph of *ALP*:

Nouço com as agitadas águas de. As sussurrantes águas de. Alvoroçados morcegos, rumor farfalhado de ratos do campo. Ei! Não foste embora? Que Thom Aflora? Nãouço com o farfalhar dos morcegos, todas as liffyerrantes águas de. Ah, rumor nos livre! Moss pés criam limo. Me sinto tão velha como aquele olmo além. Um conto contado de Shaun e Shem? ... Me conta, me conta, olmo, me conta! Noite noite! Contaumconto de raiz ou rocha. Junto às ribeirinhas águas de, as correntesrecorrentes águas de. Noite!

Amarante's version here is unusually striking for its quietness, lacking any noisy bawk of bats or shriek or even squeak of mice. If the speaker can't hear, it is because of waters that are just restless (*agitadas*) and whispering (*sussurrantes*). Bats (*morcegos*) are quietly agitated (*alvoroçados*), fieldmice (*ratos do campo*) make no more than just a rustling (*farfalhado*) noise (*rumor*). "Não foste embora?" ("Haven't you gone away yet?"), she asks doubtfully, a question confusedly answered by

"Que Thom Aflora?" ("*What* Thom Aflora?"), her interlocutor having mistakenly heard the not uncommon Brazilian surname Aflora. "Ah, rumor nos livre!" ("Noise save us!"), she ejaculates, "moss pés criam limo," roughly, "My (*meus*) mossy feet (*pés*) are growing (*criam*) water-weeds (*limo*)." In a pleasing play on /l/ and /m/, she feels "tão velha como aquele olmo além" ("as old as yonder elm"), and craves a tale (*conto*), literally, "of root (*raiz*) or rock (*rocha*)." All of this by the rivering (*ribeirinhas*) waters of, the running and rerunning (*correntes-recorrentes*) waters of.

9 French

Michel's French Wake: Veillée Pinouilles *(2004)*

A complete online French translation of *FW* by Hervé Michel appeared in 2004 under the strikingly idiosyncratic title *Veillée Pinouilles*. Michel, born of French parents in 1950 in Casablanca, Morocco, returned with them as a twelve-year-old to Paris, where he briefly studied economics, sociology, and political science at Sciences Po before undertaking wide-ranging travels in Europe, the Americas, Africa, and the Middle East. After five further years studying Arabic in Casablanca, and subsequently graduating from the elite École Nationale d'Administration in Paris, he joined the French civil service in 1986. He served as a senior financial officer in the French Ministry of Defence from 1996 until his retirement in 2015 (Pyle 2017).

Michel first encountered *FW* in 1980, began translating it after years of preparation in 1997, published his first complete rendering online in 2004 – and extended the task indefinitely by continually refining and complexifying the translation over at least the next fifteen years. He reports having originally begun his translation by consulting Lavergne's rendering, but eventually stopped doing so – "not to say that it is unreadable or even not enjoyable, but it was of little use to me as anything but its own project" (Pyle 2017).

In 2016 Michel also published online *L'Illisible* (The unreadable), an adaptation of the Koran. By then, Michel had also become a member of the Collège de Pataphysique, a group of French writers and kindred spirits who vigorously keep alive the absurdist, provocatively subversive, and cheerfully antiserious tendencies promulgated and practised by Alfred Jarry (1873–1907), best known as the author of the satirical farce *Ubu Roi* (1896) and a precursor of both Surrealism and the Theatre of the Absurd. Jarry's *Gestes et opinions du Dr. Faustroll, pataphysicien* (1911) introduced his concept of pataphysics, defined as "the science of imaginary solutions." As Germaine Brée writes, "the spirit of dada still presides over the activities of the 'Collège de Pataphysique' founded in 1948 under his aegis" (1983, 173). Michel's whimsical approach to the task of rendering *FW* into French bears ample witness to his affinity with the pataphysical sympathies of such other writers in Jarry's wake as Raymond Queneau and Eugène Ionescu.

The traditional French title of *FW*, as reported, for example, by the French Wikipedia page for James Joyce in 2018, is *La veillée des Finnegan*, combining a funeral wake (*veillée*), an article (*des*) suggesting plurality, and the singular noun *Finnegan*. In spoken French, *Finnegan* and *Finnegans* are of course perfect homophones. Michel's rendering of Joyce's title, however, rejecting this far too easy option, already exuberantly celebrates the impossibility of translation in the case of *Finnegans Wake*. His quite extraordinary title *Veillée Pinouilles* (also referred to even more extraordinarily by the quasi-mathematical formulae $V\ i\pi\ n0$ and $\sqrt{i\pi n0}$) renames Finnegan as "Pinouille." Michel himself suggests in his online "Intraduction" [*sic*] the onomastic sequence involved in this process. First, humorously invoking a (non-existent) "Gaelic" etymology, the name Finnegan is asserted to derive from **finn-ogan*, allegedly meaning, or at any rate suggestive of, a "fine eye" (*fine oeil*).[16] In view of HCE's various failings, sexual, alcoholic, and miscellaneous, the invented **finn-ogan* then suggested the Italian *finocchio*, where *occhio* is indeed an "eye," but *finocchio* is not at all a "fine eye," but literally "fennel" and colloquially an insulting slang term for a male homosexual. *Finocchio* led in turn to *Pinocchio* (much given to lying), suggesting the noun *pinuche* (colloquial French for red wine), which evoked *Pinuche*, the nickname of a bumbling and occasionally inebriated policeman named Pinaud in a long-running popular French series of crime thrillers, which, allowing also for the onomastic presence of the Pinot grape, eventually led to the final term in a sliding eight-step onomastic series: *Finnegan* > **finn-ogan* > *finocchio* > *Pinocchio* > *pinuche* > *Pinot* > *Pinaud* > *Pinouille*.[17] Michel

---

16 To be boringly pedantic, the name Finnegan is actually an anglicization of the Irish *Ó Fionnagáin*, designating a descendant (*ó*) of an ancestor called *Fionnagán*, earlier *Finnacán*, a diminutive of *Finn*, meaning "fair-haired" (Ó Corráin and Maguire 1990, 13; Hanks et al. 2002, 216). The Irish language, in which "eye" is *súil*, is unhelpful in deciphering the hypothetical **finn-ogan*, which seems to owe more to Dutch *fijne ogen* and German *feine Augen*, both meaning "fine eyes," though both of very questionable relevance here.

17 César Pinaud was the bumbling assistant of police superintendent Antoine San-Antonio in a hugely popular series of crime thrillers by Frédéric Dard (1921-2000) that continued to appear in France for more than half a century, from 1949 to 2001. The San-Antonio series ran to no fewer than 175 volumes and sold 200 million copies;

provides a detailed online account of the ways in which variations of the name Pinouille in the text reflect Joyce's variations on the name Finnegan.[18]

One is also free to see the title as flamboyantly combining *veillée* as a (funeral) "wake"; mathematical *pi* as an ultimately indeterminable quantity; colloquial *pine* and also *pinouille* as doubly describing Finnegan as a "prick"; and colloquial *nouille* as describing him also as a "dope"; while the final *-s* both suggests a plural "Finnegans" and echoes the ungrammatical character of Joyce's final *-s*. Finnegan renamed as Pinouille is therefore by onomastic implication just a "stupid prick," the renaming suggesting in passing both his sexual misdemeanours and their associated lack of good sense, while the vinous echoes obliquely evoke both the proverbially alcoholic nature of an Irish wake and Tim Finnegan's almost fatal but ultimately revivifying love of the liquor.

Veillée Pinouilles is described on its decidedly baroque title page as an "intraduction et contraduction de *Finnegans Wake*," suggesting a translation (*traduction*) that will have some claim to be an introduction to the *Wake* but, like any other would-be translation of that text, will be essentially also a contradiction in terms. The overall endeavour is humorously ascribed to the efforts of one "Halphé Mihcel," which is to say, an Hervé Michel orthographically discombobulated by his extended translatorial dealings with ALP ("H*alph*é") and HCE ("Mi*hc*el") and their environs. The online URL (https://sites.google.com/site/finicoincequoique) offers another punning interlingual version of the title, "finicoince quoique," presenting a fairly recognizable "Finnegans," although (*quoique)* suggesting a protagonist perhaps already *fini* ("finished"), perhaps *coincé* ("stuck") in some *coin* ("corner") at what may be a heavily disguised wake ("quoique") – or, then again (*quoique*), may be something else altogether. In a word, "Quoiquoiquoiquoiquoiquoiquoiq!" (*FW* 195.6).[19]

---

the prolific Dard was the author of almost 300 novels and theatre pieces altogether (Anon. 2019). My thanks to Hervé Michel for drawing my attention in personal correspondence to the San-Antonio connection.

18   See https://sites.google.com/site/finicoincequoique/themes/finnegan.

19   Michel amusingly comments in his "Intraduction" that Donaldo Schüler's Portuguese title *Finnicius Revém* at least identifies the translated text "perhaps less radically than if it had been called *The Katzenjammer Kids: Pim Pam Poum.*" The acerbic comment is presumably intended ironically, given Michel's own hardly unremarkable title.

Michel renders the opening lines (*FW* 3.1–3) as follows in his 2016 revision:

> riverron, passe t'Eve n'Adam, de littorale sûre anse à la baie ondonnée nous ramène par un commodius vicus de recirculation à Howth Castel et Environs.

Here the opening "riverron" presents a quasi-French pronunciation of the original "riverrun," while also suggesting *nous verrons* ("we shall see"), *nous nous reverrons* ("we'll see each other again"), *nous errons* ("we go astray"), and, for good measure, the Vietnamese river Ron. The interlingual phrase "passe t'Eve n'Adam" simply incorporates a colloquial English "past Eve 'n' Adam," while also nodding, as Joyce's original is readable as doing, to the name "Stephen." The river in question "brings us back" (*nous ramène*) quite unproblematically by "un commodius vicus de recirculation" to "Howth Castel et Environs." Its course "from swerve of shore to bend of bay" proves to be rather more remarkable, however, even though apparently passing on one level just from a "littorale sûre," a "sure shore," to a "baie ondonée," a "wave-filled (*ondulé*) bay (*baie*)" that also evokes the Russian river Don.

The uneasy presence of the noun *anse*, however, disrupts this apparently calm syntactic flow, even though also meaning a small "bay" or "cove." Its unexpected appearance is explained by Michel's statement in his "Intraduction" that he in fact initially heard the phrase "from swerve of shore to bend of bay" as subliminally implying also "from self-assured to abandoned being," thus indicating "sûre anse" and "baie ondonnée" as evoking *assurance* and *abandonné*, while allegedly suggesting a quasi-Lacanian reading of the opening lines as also meaning, by implication, "the course of life, having passed beyond the stories of a primordial couple, always takes us, for all its detours, calmly and quietly to the particular place where we are and its immediate environs."[20] It is of course the personal responsibility of Michel's reader

---

20 "J'ai entendu dans *from swerve of shore to bend of bay* les mots 'from self-assured to abandoned being', c'est-à-dire 'de sûr de soi à l'être abandonné', dans lequel on a la dualité de l'égo et de l'être exprimée en référence à la structure de bord du psychisme de la personne dont parlait Lacan, la rive de la rivière, la ligne droite de la conscience qui sépare la terre et l'eau, et les inclinations de l'étant. Avec la perception de ce complexe littéraire littéral sur le littoral latéral, nous pouvons tirer une interprétation de la première phrase de *Finnegans Wake* qui dirait: le cours de la vie, dépassées les histoires de couple primordial, par tous ses détours nous ramène toujours avec sa facilité simple et tranquille au lieu particulier où nous sommes et à sa proximité."

to decide whether this comment is to be taken completely seriously or (as one might perhaps not be too surprised by from a pataphysicist) as a parodic deconstruction either of the nature of his own translatorial undertaking or of the entire academic endeavour of deciphering and translingually re-enciphering the untranslatable *Finnegans Wake*.[21]

Michel's rendering of the opening page continues (*FW* 3.4–10):

Sir Tristram, violer d'amores transpirate la mer courte, était passencore réarrivé d'Armorique du Nord sur ce côté de l'isthme efflanqué d'Europe Mineure wieldrefatailler sa guerre pénisolée; ni ne s'étaient les rochers de topsawyer sur le cours de l'Oconee exaggéré autreux-mêmes aux gorgi-oses du Comté de Laurens tandis qu'ils allaient doublinnant leur pompe mandite en permernance: n'ora évoicé d'un feu pluce loin dessouflé mishe mishe pour tauf tauf de boue tuespêtrick:

From Michel's opening lines of *ALP* (*FW* 196.1–7, 9–11):

O / dis-moi tout sur / Anna Livia! Je veux tout entendre / sur Anna Livia. Et puits, tu connais Anna Livia? Oui, bien sûr, on connaît tous Anna Livia. Dis-moi tout. Dis moi là. Tu mourras quand t'orras. Et puits, tu sais, quand le vieux cheb devint futt et fit à ce qu'au tu sais. ... Quand que ce fil qu'ils trièrent de sortrir il tentroit à deux dans le parc Faunisc.

Michel's rendering is rich in fluvial evocations, including all of the Scottish Dee and Irish Moy ("dis-moi"), French Endre ("entendre"), Luxembourg's Sûr and Syr ("bien sûr"), the Irish Moyle ("moi là"), Belgian Our ("mourras"), and Scottish Orr ("t'orras"). "Et puits, tu connais Anna Livia?" plays on *et puis* ("and so") and the noun *puit* (a "well"). "You'll die when you hear" becomes a pair of rhyming anapaests, "Tu mourras quand t'orras," conflating *tu ouïras* ("you will hear") and the Scottish river Orr. What the old cheb who went futt got up to was, as you know, simply a fiasco ("fit à ce qu'au tu sais"). What happened in the park remains highly obscure. Very approximately: "whatever it was (*quoi que ce fût*), and when ("quand"), this yarn (*fil*) that the three ("tri-") were sorting out ("trièrent") and putting together (*sortir*), laughingly (*rire* "to laugh"), about what he was trying (*tentait*), watched by the three (*trois*), to do to the two (*deux*) in the Faunus Park," a location associated with the orgiastic sexual practices of mythological fauns and satyrs.

---

21 On Michel's French rendering, see Pyle (2015b, 2017).

From Michel's closing lines of *ALP* (*FW* 215.31–5, 216.3–5):

Peux pas entendre avec les eaux de. Les eaux chitteriantes de. Chauves
souris vitte lotantes, abauque lauquace de rats des champs. Ho! T'es pas
devenu adomiceul? Quel Thom Messeul? Peux pas entendre avec l'abauque des chauvesourdis, toutes thimeurées eaux liffeyantes de. Ho, élo-
quieux sauve nous! Mes fousses vont pas mousse. Je me sens aussi vieux
qu'orme d'yondre. Histoire à conter de Shaun ou Shem? ... Dis-moi, dis-
moi, dis-moi, orme! Nuit nuit! Dismoidit de chêne ou de chaux. Au bord
des riverrantes eaux de, des hésiteurisantes eaux de. Nuit!

The speaker can't hear with the noise of the chittering waters and
the bawk ("abauque") of bats (*chauve-souris*) and the bald (*chauve*)
mice (*souris*) and the fieldmice (*rats des champs*). "Haven't you gone
home (*domicile*) on your own (*seul*)," one washerwoman asks, and the
other, confusedly hearing the French surname Messeul, asks "Which
Thom Messeul?" The bats, still bawking, are now deaf (*sourd*) as well,
"chauvesourdis," while "thim" liffeying waters appear somehow tim-
orous (*timorées*), like the French river Eure, perhaps. "May eloquence
(*éloquence*), full of praise (*élogieux*), save us," the speaker exclaims, for
"Mes fousses vont pas mousse," roughly, "my crazy (*fou*) German *Füße*
won't move (*se mouvoir*), won't gather any moss (*mousse*)." A tale of
stem or stone, of living oak (*chêne*) or inanimate lime (*chaux*), would
help. And all of this by the rivering ("riverrantes") wandering (*errant*)
waters, the waters that come and go hesitantly (*hésitant*), as if they were
just visitors (*visiteurs*).

From Michel's closing lines of the *Wake* (*FW* 627.34–628.4, 15–16):

Je vais y passer. O fin amère! Je m'aurai ecslipé avant qu'issoient debupts.
Ils neverront jamais. Ni ne sauront. Ni ne me regretteront. Et c'est vieille
et vieille c'est triste et vieille c'est triste et usée que je m'en revais vers toi,
mon froid père, mon froid fou père, mon froid fol effrayant père, jusqu'à ce
que la simple vue de sa seule taille, les moyles et les moyles de ça, sanglu-
aglutants, me donnent le mal de sel et le sale de mer, et que je me rue, mon
uniment, dans tes bras. ... Je vais une voie seule ultime aimée le long de çt

In an interview, Hervé Michel specifically distances his own rendering from what he calls academic translations: "Academic translations
have the merit of being organized, as well as watching the gates of literary value, so the translator can safely play, within their circles, with
the gist of the pun, while outside these circles, it is just one enormous
hoax." Responding to the same interviewer's question as to how best to

approach *FW*, "I would advise that a reader approach *Finnegans Wake* like a work of art – a composition of sounds and colors, music and painting, to be listened to and looked at not like an abstract, but like the *Garden of Earthly Delights* by Hieronymous Bosch, painted by Georges Braque, with music by Olivier Messaien, words by James Joyce" (Pyle 2017). *Lots* of fun, in other words, at *Finnegans Wake*.

Michel's translatorial approach has been greeted with enthusiasm by at least two subsequent translators of the *Wake*. The Argentinian translator Marcelo Zabaloy, whose Spanish rendering appeared in 2016, is a particular admirer of Michel's "extraordinary" work: "What Hervé has done is to emulate the astonishment of the English-speaking reader in front of the book. He didn't straighten, dilute or thin difficulties; let nonsense be nonsense seems to be the key factor" (Pyle 2015b). In similar vein, the Turkish translator Umur Çelikyay, in the introduction to his *Finnegan'ın vahı* (2016), freely acknowledges the impact of Michel's approach, characterizing his own rendering similarly as a "counter-translation or vice-translation" of the untranslatable original, and asserting that the concept was inspired specifically by Michel's presentation of *Veillée Pinouilles* as a "contraduction," a combination of French *traduction* and *contradiction* (Bayramova 2016, 4).

Chassaing (French, 2005)

The independent Paris-based Joyce scholar Michel Chassaing was reportedly inspired to explore the world of the *Wake* by his discovery in 1995 of the French rendering of its closing pages by Philippe Sollers and Stephen Heath in 1973. Ten years later, in the framework of a detailed 140-page online study, he posted a substantial French translation of roughly eighty pages of excerpts from *FW*.[22]

His rendering of the opening three lines (*FW* 3.1–3), which dispenses with all accents, reads as follows:

> rivierune, past Eve and Adam's, de bande de berge en bord de baie, nous ramene par commodius vicus de recirculation a Howth Castle et ses Environs.

---

22 Chassaing rendered the following excerpts: *FW* 3.1–6.28, 15.12–18.20, 21.5–23.15, 24.3–26.24, 30.1–33.13, 69.5–74.19, 118.18–123.10, 142.30–143.28, 152.18–159.20, 184.11–186.18, 213.11–216.5, 219.1–221.17, 234.6–237.12, 304.5–305.5, 363.17–365.15, 383.1–386.11, 414.16–419.11, 427.9–428.27, 430.17–433.9, 454.8–455.29, 471.35–473.25, 530.31–533.3, 555.1–555.29, 572.19–576.17, 593.1–594.9, 604.22–606.12, 610.34–613.16, 626.4–628.16.

The opening "rivierune" closely echoes the original "riverrun" phonetically, conflating *rivière* and *rune* ("rune") while implying also the presence of the original "run." The river flows alliteratively from bound (*bande*) of bank (*berge*) to side (*bord*) of bay (*baie*). The remainder of the sentence takes advantage of the Latinate diction to stay very close to the original wording. Chassaing writes in his online commentary on these lines that "the river of writing (runes) flows since Adam and Eve (and like the Liffey in front of the church of Adam and Eve in Dublin) between its two banks (binary principle, the two lips) past the conveniences (the toilets that represent life here below, or Molly's chamber pot) following the cycles of Vico (Vico Road, and *vicus*, "village" in Latin, from the days of Commodus to our own day), then returns to Howth Castle (ternary principle, III, and HCE)."[23]

His translation continues (*FW* 3.4–10):

Sir Tristram, violeur d'amores, pardessus la courte mer, n'était paquencore réarrivé d'Armorique du Nord sur cette rugue côte d'Europe Mineure pour wiederbattre sa péniseulette guerre: ni les rochers de topsawyer près l'effluve Oconee ne s'étaient exagérés eux-autres vers les gorgées du Comté de Laurens pendant qu'ils allaient dublant leurs mombres tout le temps: ni évoix d'un éfeu n'avait déjà sousbénire mishe mishe pour tauftaufer TourbéPoitruc:

10 Japanese

Miyata's Japanese Wake: Fineganzu weiku *(2004)*

An abridged and simplified Japanese translation of *FW* by Kyoko Miyata (2004a), one of the few female translators of the *Wake*, appeared in Tokyo in 2004 as *Fineganzu ueiku*, offering those Japanese readers who had found Naoki Yanase's complete rendering of 1993 to be impenetrably difficult a more accessible entry to *FW*. Eishiro Ito (2004) quotes and discusses Miyata's rendering of the three-line opening phrase (*FW* 3.1–3), romanized as follows:

---

23   In Chassaing's French, which likewise dispenses with accents, "la riviere de l'ecriture (runes) coule depuis Adam et Eve (et comme la Liffey devant l'Eglise *Adam and Eve* a Dublin), entre ses 2 berges (principe binaire, les 2 levres), par les commodites (les toilettes qui representent l'ici-bas, ou le pot de chambre de Molly) suivant les cycles de Vico (Vico Road, et *vicus* : village en latin), depuis l'Antiquite de Commode jusqu'a nos jours, puis revient vers le chateau de Howth (principe trinitaire, III, et HCE)."

kawa wa nagareru Evu to Adamu-kyokai wo sugi, ko wo eaku kagan kara wankyoku suru, umi eto mukai, saijunkansuru kokochiyoi Vico Road no waki wo susumi, Howsu-jo to sono shuhen e warera wo tsuremodosu.

Ito points out that "kawa wa nagareru" is the "stream of a river"; that "Evu to Adamu-kyokai" is "the church of Eve and Adam"; and that any reference to Commodus is absent, while Vico appears as Dublin's Vico Road under its untranslated English name. HCE's initials disappear.

Eishiro Ito observes that these examples and more like them are part of a systematic strategy of normalization on this translator's part, for while Yanase's earlier Japanese rendering (1991, 1993) aims to transpose the original ambiguities and complexities into his own translated text as much as possible, Miyata attempts from the beginning to make the translation as semantically clear and as readable as possible for Japanese readers, including by the use of chapter introductions and summaries and numerous explanatory footnotes. Miyata's strategy is thus in principle similar to both Anthony Burgess's *Shorter Finnegans Wake* of 1966 and Victor Pozanco's abridged Spanish *Finnegans Wake* of 1993.[24]

Hamada (Japanese, 2008, 2009)

Tatsuo Hamada, born in 1935 in the city of Kochi, turned after a university career as a biologist and researcher in animal nutrition to intensive study of *FW*, including founding and editing the journal *Abiko Annual*, devoted exclusively to *FW* and published by his own private publishing company, the Abiko Literary Press, whose initials are those also of Anna Livia Plurabelle. In addition to several books on the *Wake*, he also worked over the next twelve years towards a complete Japanese rendering of it. In 2008, his rendering of *FW* I.2–4 and IV appeared in the *Abiko Annual*, and the following year, with the completion of Book I, saw his version of Books I and IV, which appeared in Abiko, near Tokyo, under the title (as romanized) *Fineganzu ueiku, pato 1 to 4*.

11 Catalan

Aixàs's Catalan ALP (2004)

Catalan had already entered the *Wake* universe in 1982, the Joyce centenary year, with a brief excerpt rendered by Josep-Miquel Sobré. In

---

24 On Miyata's Japanese rendering, see Ito (2004), Jones (2004), Miyata (2004b).

2004 a more substantial contribution appeared, namely, a complete Catalan translation of *ALP* by Marissa Aixàs. Her Catalan *ALP*, together with other excerpts (*FW* 8.8–10.24, 15.28–18.16, 182.30–186.18), was presented as part of a doctoral dissertation at the Universitat Autònoma de Barcelona, where Aixàs went on to teach in the Department of Translation and Interpretation.[25] Her rendering largely limits itself to a sustained attempt to recuperate the primary surface meaning of Joyce's text (O'Neill 2013, 289).

Aixàs's rendering of the opening lines of *ALP* (*FW* 196.1–7, 9–11) reads as follows: ·

Ω / Explica-ho tot / d'Anna Livia! Ho vull saber tot / d'Anna Livia. Bé, coneixes Anna Livia, oi? Si, és clar. Tots coneixem a l'Anna Livia. Explica-ho tot. Explica-ho ara mateix. Et tronxaràs quan ho sàpigues. Bé, saps quan el vellot es tornà boig i féu el que ja saps? ... O fos el que fos que intentaren traspunxar que temptegés fer al parc Fiendish.

Aixàs's employment of the Greek omega for Joyce's "O," though abandoning the immediate visual implications, succinctly affirms Anna Livia as both alpha and omega of the entire narrative, while playing on the fact that Greek *omega*, pronounced /o:/, literally means "big O." Catalan, in an example of textual serendipity, enables two quite unexpected aquatic references: since the Catalan pronoun *ho* ("it") is a homophone of the French *eau* and a homograph of the (romanized) Chinese noun *ho* ("river"), Aixàs's "Explica-ho tot" ("tell it all") invokes both French "water" and a Chinese "river" as well as the English Exe, Peruvian Ica, and Indian Tut. "You'll die when you hear" becomes "Et tronxaràs quan ho sàpigues," literally, "It will slice you up when you hear," colloquially, "You'll be flabbergasted when you hear." The old cheb is merely "the old geezer" ("el vellot"), who simply "es tornà boig" ("went crazy") and "féu el que ja saps" ("did what you already know"). The Indonesian river Ello ("vellot") puts in an appearance.

The Catalan version of what happened in the park departs from Joyce's English. While doubly evoking the English river Foss, and thus at least implicitly the two water-related girls also, her rendering avoids any more specific reference to either the three or the two: "O fos el que fos que intentaren traspunxar que temptegés fer," roughly, "Or whatever it may have been (*o fos el que fos*) that they intended (*que intentaren*) to spread abroad (*traspunxar*) that he was attempting (*temptejar* 'to try')

---

25   On Aixàs's Catalan rendering, see Aixàs (2007).

to do." The "Fiendish park" is domesticated rather minimally as a Catalan "parc Fiendish."

12 Irish

Titley (Irish, 2008)

Another new language appeared in the *FW* firmament in 2008, when an Irish version of the first six lines (*FW* 3.1–6) appeared, rendered by Alan Titley (born 1947), professor of Modern Irish at University College Cork. Titley's rendering might conceivably have had something of a bittersweet nostalgic appeal for Joyce, who had studied Irish for two years as a young man while a student at University College Dublin. The Irish language is a particularly difficult one in which to attempt to replicate or even approximate Wakean wordplay. Titley does an admirable job with his rendering of the three-line incipit:

> rithruthag na habhann thairis Aoife agus Ádhamhach, ó chuas an chuain go bogha na bá, á dtuairt sinn go timpeallach timthriallach leithreasúil ar ais go dtí Halla Cheann Éadair agus a bhfuil máguaird.

Here "rithruthag na habhann" incorporates two separate terms for the noun "run," namely, *rith* and *rothag*, while also providing two separate terms for "river," a clearly identifiable *abha* (genitive case *na habhann* "of the river") and an only dimly discernible *sruth* almost hidden in the eddies of *rith* and *rothag*. Eve and Adam are present as the Irish *Aoife* and *Ádhamh*, the adjectival form *Ádhamhach* implying something indefinitely related. The river moves alliteratively, and with pleasing retention of the original rhythm, from the "cove" (*cuas*) of the "strand" (*cuan*) to the "curve" (*bogha*) of the "bay" (*bá*). The Irish "á dtuairt sinn" plays on the homophones *tabhairt* ("to bring") and *tuairt* ("rush"), as in the phrase *de thuairt* ("at a rush"), thus suggesting "bringing us suddenly," while the rendering "go timpeallach timthriallach leithreasúil" refers to a process involving movement in a fashion at once "circular (*timpeallach*), circuitous (*timthriallach*), and privy (*leithreasúil*)," the final (and invented) adjective playing on *leisciúil* ("lazy") and, by implication, English *commode*, as in the everyday use of the noun *leithreas* ("toilet") to designate an Irish public convenience.

The process as described brings us *ar ais* ("back") *go dtí* ("to") "Halla Cheann Éadair agus a bhfuil máguaird." Titley's version transforms "Howth Castle and Environs" into "the hall (*halla*) of Howth (Irish *Beann Édair*) and its surroundings (*a bhfuil máguaird*, literally, 'what is round about')," while the transformation of *beann* into *ceann* ("head";

lenited form *cheann*) both recalls the Old Norse etymology of the name Howth (from *hǫfuð* "head") and allows for the adroit inclusion of HCE as HCÉ. *Beann Édair*, meanwhile, literally means the "headland (*beann*) of Édar," and by conflating the name of the eponymous Édar and the noun *éad* ("jealousy"), Titley ingeniously evokes the fatal jealousy of the aging and betrayed Finn mac Cumhaill in the iconic medieval tale of "The Pursuit of Diarmaid and Gráinne," one episode of which takes place on Howth Head.

While Vico and Commodus do not appear by name, Viconian recirculation is implied in *timpeallach* ("circular"), while Commodus is evoked by the humorous association with a commode. This latter solution is certainly readable as an oblique intertextual reference to Lavergne's likewise humorous evocation of Commodus – and thus constitutes a pleasing example of one translation playing primarily on another translation rather than on the original *Wake*.

Titley's rendering also includes the next three lines (FW 3.4–6), as follows:

Saír Throstam, feichidveibhlín na mionsearc ar an bhfarraige, a raibh brot a chroí fillte go hanraiththráthuil chun caoil chreagaigh na mionEorpa d'fhonn tréanthroid an chogaidh a eisfhearadh go leaidiniseach ...

Titley's Sir Tristram (*FW* 3.4) becomes "Saír Throstam," which imaginatively combines English *sir* and the Irish prefixes *saor-* ("noble") and *sár-* ("excellent, outstanding") to characterize a "Trostam" (the initial *th-* is a grammatical necessity after the prefix, but also plays interlingually on the English *thrust*) whose name is based on an Irish *trost* that means both "thrust" and "fall": an aristocratic superthruster urging his conquests à la Don Juan to "trust him" – and whose heroic risings (*trost*) are nonetheless inevitably followed, à la HCE, by a correspondingly unheroic fall (*trost*) (O'Neill 2013, 69).

Titley's rendering appears to be the only attempt to date to translate any part of *FW* into Irish.[26]

13 Finnish

Mutanen (Finnish, 2006, 2009)

Yet another new language entered the universe of *Wake* translations with the poet Miikka Mutanen's Finnish version of the opening pages

---

26 My thanks to Alan Titley for confirming this statement in personal correspondence.

published online in 2006 (*FW* 3.1–10.23), and continued (*FW* 10.24–15.28) in 2009, amounting to thirteen pages altogether. Born near the town of Polvijärvi in southern Finland, Mutanen is also the author of two volumes of poetry.

His Finnish rendering of the opening lines (*FW* 3.1–3) reads as follows:

> virtavie, ohi Eilvan ja Aatomun, heitseistä rannan kaareen seppellah-den, takaisin kiertää avarjen kulco modeus meidät Kuinks Linnaan ja Ympäröivaan.

Mutanen does not hesitate to impress his own translatorial personality on Joyce's text. The opening "virtavie" alliteratively and appropriately combines *virta* ("river") and *vie* ("run") in a single word, taking us "ohi Eilvan ja Aatomun," suggesting not only "past (*ohi*) Eve (*Eeva*) and Adam (*Aatami*)," but also "past yesterday (*eilen*) and morning (*aamun*) – and dust (*tomun*)," invoking the river also as that of the always inevitable passage of time, from yesterday to tomorrow and to the final inevitable dust to dust. "From swerve of shore to bend of bay" is rendered as "heitseistä rannan kaareen seppellahden," which appears to suggest, very approximately, "from rugged (?) shore (*ranta*) to curve (*kaari*) of bay (*lahti*), a curve like that of a wreath (*seppel*)." The invented "heitseistä," possibly suggesting ruggedness, appears to combine *heitää* ("to throw") and *seistä* ("to stand"), evoking something like a confusion of scattered rocks, perhaps, standing at bound (Swedish *hejd*) of shore (*ranta*). The course of the river "returns (*keirtää*) us (*meidät*) back (*takaisin*)" by a way (Latin *modus*) that is not just a "commodious" (*avarien*) one but an "amusing (Swedish *kul*) co-modeus" way to travel (*kulkea*) to "How-th" Castle (*linna*) and Environs (*ympäristö*). Likewise amusing, Howth is reconfigured as the Finnish adverb *kuinka* ("how") with a suffixed *-th*.

A Finnish reader might have considerable difficulty in recuperating the geographical Howth from the playful verbal reconstruction "Kuinks," and might certainly also have difficulties with "heitseistä," reflections respectively of the overall playfulness and sheer overall difficulty of the *Wake*. And while Eve and Adam are duly present, and Commodus doubly so, Vico is nowhere to be discovered, and HCE's presence is completely cloaked by the transmogrified initials of "Kuinks Linnaan ja Ympäröivaan."[27]

---

27 My thanks to Lauri Niskanen of the University of Helsinki for generous assistance with Finnish linguistic issues.

14 Hungarian

Bozai (Hungarian, 2007, 2008)

A Hungarian version of the opening pages (*FW* 3.1–5.12) by Ágota Bozai, another of the very few female translators of any part of *FW*, appeared in 2007. Bozai, born in the western Hungarian town of Siófok in 1965, is a novelist and translator who is working on a complete Hungarian rendering of *FW*, as of this writing reportedly more than half completed. The project began as part of a doctoral thesis at the School of English and American Studies at Eötvös Lorand University (ELTE) in Budapest, and the complete translation is planned to appear online in 2024.[28]

Bozai's 2007 version of the opening three lines (*FW* 3.1–3) reads as follows:

> folyófolyt az Éva és Ádám hajója mellett, a partkanyartól az öböl-bel felé farolva, elfele kanyarult, komótosan, Commodius viciosusan, az utca mentén visszakörforgat, visz Howth Castle és Eme-kastély-vidéke felé.

Here the opening "folyófolyt" conflates *folyó* ("river") and *folyt* ("flows"); Eve and Adam retain their Joycean order; Commodus and Vico are clearly identifiable; the "vicus" is "vicious" (Latin *viciosus*); and HCE's initials are preserved with some difficulty by the locution "Howth Castle és Eme-kastély-vidéke," with the original "Environs" rendered as "the country (*vidéke*) around this (*eme*) castle (*kastély*)."

Further excerpts from Bozai's continuing rendering appeared in the online journal *Kalligram* in 2008, including *FW* 3.1–3, 115.20–35, 213.29–216.5 (this excerpt translated with László Kuroli, a doctoral candidate at Eötvös Lorand University), and 627.1–628.16.

Bozai's rendering (Anon. 2013) includes the following lines (*FW* 628.16, 3.1–3) – and a revision of the opening lines:

> A vágy, a vég, a hév, a messzi, hosszú út, a hol a kor az élet // folyó folyt, haladt, maradt az Ádám-Éva mellett el, a partkanyartól az öböl-bel felé farolva, kanyarult komótosan, Commodius Vico-osusan, körfogat circulus vici párhuzamosan, vízavisz Howth Castle és Eme-kastélynak-vidéke felé.

---

28 My thanks to Ágota Bozai for confirming these details – and to Erika Mihálycsa of Babeş-Bolyai University in Romania for generous assistance here and elsewhere in matters Hungarian.

Here Joyce's Eve and Adam revert to the more traditional arrangement; Commodus is once again doubly present; and the once vicious vicus is no longer obviously vicious.

15 Spanish

Silva-Santisteban (Spanish, 2000)

Ricardo Silva-Santisteban's *James Joyce: Textos esenciales*, published in Lima in 2000, includes all his previous renderings (1982, 1988, 1991) as well as newly translated excerpts from "Shem the Penman," "The Ondt and the Gracehoper," and the closing pages, some thirty-six pages altogether, produced over a period of almost three decades (*FW* 3.1–4.17, 185.27–190.9, 196.1–216.5, 418.11–419.8, 619.20–628.16).[29]

Fanzone (Spanish, 2007)

An annotated Spanish version by the Argentinian translator Leandro Fanzone of selected excerpts (*FW* 159.6–18, 215.31–216.5, 627.34–628.16) appeared in 2007, posted initially on the Argentinian website Seikilos.[30] Lines (*FW* 215.31–5, 216.3–5) from Fanzone's final paragraph of *ALP*:

No escucho con las aguas murmurantes de. Murciélagos que revolotean, charla insolente de ratones de campo. ¡Eh! ¿Ya te fuiste a tu casa? ¿Qué Thom Malone? No escucho con el griterío de los murciélagos, con toda esa agua de. ¡Que el charlar nos salve! Mis pies no se mueven. Me siento tan vieja como aquel olmo. ¿Una historia sobre Shaun o Shem? ... ¡Contame, contame, contame, olmo! ¡La noche noche! Contame de tronco o piedra. Junto a las corrientes aguas de, las aguas que van y vienen de. ¡La noche!

From Fanzone's final lines of the *Wake* (*FW* 627.34–628.4, 15–16):

Me estoy muriendo. ¡Oh, amargo final! Me voy a escabullir antes que se levanten. Nunca verán. Ni sabrán. Ni me extrañarán. Y es viejo y viejo es triste y viejo es triste y cansador vuelvo a vos, mi frío y loco padre, mi frío, loco y temible padre, hasta que el ver de cerca sus ojos, millas y millas de padre, lamentándome, me marea y me precipita, a mí sola, a tus brazos. ... Un camino solitario al final, amado, junto al

---

29 My thanks to Ricardo Silva-Santisteban for kindly sending me an electronic copy of his collected renderings in *James Joyce: Textos esenciales*.

30 http://seikilos.com.ar/seikilos/traducciones.

Victoria (Spanish, 2007, 2008, 2009)

The poet and novelist Juan Díaz Victoria was born in 1969 in the Mexican city of Cuernavaca and graduated in communication studies from the Monterrey Institute of Technology. He reportedly first encountered the *Wake* in 2005 and almost immediately undertook the ambitious project of what would at that point have been a first complete Spanish translation, extensively annotated for Hispanophone readers (Vázquez 2017). Excerpts from the opening chapter, demonstrating also a planned process of in-text annotation, appeared in the Mexican journal *La jornada semanal* in June 2007 (*FW* 3.1–24) and online in 2008 (*FW* 4.18–5.12, 5.26–6.28), while a first version of the complete annotated translation of *FW* I.1 appeared online in 2009. Further revisions, to which we shall return, appeared in 2010 and 2016.

16 Danish

Laugesen's Danish ALP (2009)

A Danish translation of the opening pages of *ALP* (*FW* 196.1–201.4) by Peter Laugesen appeared in 2009, in Bergen, in the Norwegian literary journal *Vagant*.[31] His rendering of the opening sentences of *ALP* include the following lines (*FW* 196.1–7, 9–11):

> Å / fortæl mig alt om / Anna Livia! Jeg vil høre alt / om Anna Livia. Du kender vel Anna Livia? Ja, selvfølgelig, vi kender alle sammen Anna Livia. Fortæl mig alt. Fortæl mig nu. Du dør når du hør. Nå ja, så den gamle kæp gik frut og gjorde du ved nok hvad. ... Eller hvad det nu var den dans de troede at vide han truede med at træde i den Fjendske park.

Like Grut's Swedish *ALP* (2001), Laugesen's Danish version renders Joyce's opening "O" by "Å," also pronounced /o:/, thus likewise managing to incorporate ALP's own initial, Joyce's "O" in diacritical form, the delta suggested by the typographical shape of an upper-case *A*, the Swedish *å* ("river"), the Sumerian *a* ("water"), the French *eau* ("water"), and the several Western European rivers named Aa. "Fortæl mig alt" ("tell me all") includes an evocation of the English river Alt, shortly followed by the Russian Ende ("kender"), South American Sama ("sammen"), and Chinese Nu. The Danish "Du dør når du hør" pleasingly introduces an

---

31 My thanks to Peter Laugesen for kindly sending me an electronic copy of the relevant issue of *Vagant*.

unexpected rhyme to render "You'll die when you hear," and "the old cheb" is adroitly rendered as "den gamle kæp," literally "the old stick," while retaining an interlingual echo of the Czech river Cheb.

As for the complex sentence "Or whatever it was they threed to make out he thried to two in the Fiendish park," Laugesen's likewise complex rendering suggests, roughly, "Or whatever sort of a dance (*dans*) it was they thought (*troede*) they were discovering (*vide* 'to know') that he was threatening (*true* 'to threaten') to perform (*træde* 'to step') in the 'Fjendske park,'" where the park, once again as in Grut's Swedish, is a hostile (*fjendsk*) one in which one might well encounter an enemy (*fjend*). The three in the trees are discernible in the triple play on *troede*, *truede*, *træde* that evokes both *tre* ("three") and *træ* ("tree") – while the two (Danish *to*) girls are, unaccountably, now nowhere to be seen.

17 Polish

Malicki (Polish, 2001)

A Polish translation by Jacek Malicki of the opening four pages (*FW* 3.1–7.5) appeared online in 2001 (incorporating most of his 1996 rendering of *FW* 6.29–7.15), using the title *Przebudzenie Finnegana* (Finnegan's awakening), with no connotations of reviving or revival, only of ceasing to sleep.[32]

Malicki's rendering of the opening three lines reads as follows:

rzekabiegnie mimo Evy i Adamsa, od odchylenia brzegu do wygięcia zatoki, przynosząc nas przez obszerną wieśrecyrkulacji zpowrotem do Howth-Zamku i Otoczeń.

Here the opening "rzekabiegnie" effectively achieves a one-word conflation of the corresponding vocabulary elements, *rzeka* ("river") and *biegnie* ("runs"). Eve and Adam retain Joyce's revised order, while Commodus and Vico disappear, as do both alliteration and HCE's initials.

Łuba (Polish, 2003)

The Polish writer and translator Arkadiusz Łuba published a Polish rendering of selected excerpts from *FW* in 2003 in a volume entitled

---

32 Personal correspondence from Krzysztof Bartnicki.

Ślady (Traces), an anthology of his own translations.[33] Born in 1977 in Olsztyn in northeastern Poland, Łuba studied literature and drama in Olsztyn and Zurich and served for several years as editor of the Olsztyn literary and cultural magazine *Portret*. The 2003 renderings were reprinted in 2006, with slight differences, in his book *Okno na Joyce'a* (Window on Joyce), an introduction to *FW*.

---

33 Łuba's 2003 renderings (in order of appearance): *FW* 627.29–31, 278.13–18, 337.10–14, 112.9, 110.22–31, 111.5–24, 424.23–34, and an early draft of the last two pages, corresponding to *FW* 627.13-628.16. My thanks to Krzysztof Bartnicki for kindly researching the bibliographical details.

Chapter Nine

The 2010s

*1 Esperanto; 2 Italian; 3 Polish; 4 Chinese; 5 Japanese;
6 German; 7 Danish; 8 Dutch; 9 Greek; 10 Swedish;
11 Portuguese; 12 Finnish; 13 Romanian; 14 Serbian;
15 French; 16 Spanish; 17 Hebrew; 18 Turkish;
19 Norwegian; 20 Russian; 21 Slovenian; 22 Georgian;
23 Ancient Egyptian; 24 Latin*

The 2010s were by far the most productive decade in terms of the number of renderings of and from *FW* produced, involving no fewer than twenty-four separate languages altogether, of which Esperanto, Hebrew, Norwegian, Georgian, Ancient Egyptian, and Latin were new to the *FW* macrotext. No fewer than seven complete renderings of *FW* appeared, with at least four more well under way.

These major new appearances included Krzysztof Bartnicki's complete Polish *Wake* (2012); Congrong Dai's Chinese rendering of *FW* I.1–8 (2012); Tatsuo Hamada's complete Japanese *Wake* (2012, 2014); Friedhelm Rathjen's *Winnegans Fake* (2012); Eleftherios Anevlavis's complete Greek *Wake* (2013); Siniša Stojaković's Serbian rendering of *FW* I.1–8 (2014) followed by *FW* III.1–4 and IV (2017); Umur Çelikyay's Turkish translation of *FW* I.1–8 (2016) and *FW* II.1–4 (2017); Fuat Sevimay's complete Turkish *Wake* (2016); Marcelo Zabaloy's complete Spanish *Wake* (2016); Andrey Rene's Russian rendering of *FW* I.1–8 (2018) and *FW* II.1–4 (2019); Giuliano Mazza's complete Italian *Wake* (2018); Enrico Terrinoni and Fabio Pedone's Italian rendering of *FW* III.1–2 (2017) followed by *FW* III.3–4 and IV (2019), completing the Mondadori Italian *Wake* begun by Luigi Schenoni in the 1970s. A much abbreviated Portuguese rendering of *FW* by Dirce Waltrick do Amarante appeared in 2018, and a planned new Portuguese translation of *FW* by Eclair Antonio Almeida Filho was announced in 2015, but later indefinitely postponed.

In addition to this, renderings of individual chapters included *FW* II.3–4 in Italian by Luigi Schenoni (published posthumously in 2011); a separately published Dutch *ALP* by Erik Bindervoet and Robbert-Jan Henkes (2013); a Swedish rendering of *FW* I.1 by Bertil Falk (2013); German renderings of *FW* II.4 (2014) and I.2 (2015) by Friedhelm Rathjen; an Italian rendering of *FW* I.1 by Orlando Mezzabotta (2016); a new online Spanish *ALP* by Eduardo Lago (2016); a new French *ALP* by Philippe Blanchon (2016); an annotated Spanish version of *FW* I.1 by Juan Díaz Victoria (2016); and a Georgian *ALP* by Tamar Gelashvili (2018). A very free poetic transcreation of *FW* I.1 in Finnish by Hannu Helin appeared in 2013.

Briefer renderings appeared anonymously in Esperanto (Anon. 2010); in Italian by Orlando Mezzabotta (2010, 2017), by Vittorio Santangelo (2014), and by Luigi Marrozzini (2017); in Spanish by Juan Díaz Victoria (2010, 2016b); in German by Friedhelm Rathjen (2012); in Danish by Peter Laugesen (2012); in Portuguese by Caetano Galindo (2013, 2016, 2019), by Adriano Scandolara (2014), and by Vitor Alevato do Amaral (2019); in French by Marie Darrieussecq (2014), by Philippe Blanchon (2015), and by Ludivine Bouton-Kelly and Tiphaine Samoyault (2016); in Hebrew by Yehuda Vizan (2015); in Norwegian by Leif Høghaug (2016, 2017, 2018); and in Slovenian by Jure Godler (2018). Both Dutch (Bindervoet and Henkes) and French (Philippe Blanchon) renderings of Ogden's *ALP* appeared in 2013, and a reprint in book form of Juan Rodolfo Wilcock's 1961 Italian renderings appeared in 2016.

In June 2013 Ithys Press of Dublin published, with considerable fanfare, the slim volume *Finn's Hotel*, in a fine press limited edition of 180 copies in three separate issues, at prices ranging from €350 to €2,500. The volume consisted of ten short narrative pieces written by Joyce in 1923, edited and arranged by the independent Joyce scholar Danis Rose and with an introduction by Seamus Deane. Scholarly battle was quickly and fiercely engaged between those who, like Rose, considered these pieces to constitute a separate and long-lost Joyce work, and those who considered them to be merely drafts for what eventually became *FW* and thus never meant for separate publication. The details of the controversy are not relevant in the present context, but it is of relevance to the notion of an expanding *Wake* universe that translations in several languages quickly appeared: in Spanish by Pablo Ingberg (2013), in Italian by Ottavio Fatica (2013), in Greek by George-Icaros Babassakis (2014), in Portuguese by Caetano Galindo (2014), in German by Friedhelm Rathjen (2014), in Romanian by Mihai Miroiu (2014), and in Polish by Jerzy Jarniewicz (2015).

Among distinctly more unusual renderings, a series of intersemiotic transcreations of *FW* by Krzysztof Bartnicki appeared in Polish in 2012, 2014, and 2015; Orlando Mezzabotta posted on YouTube excerpts in Ancient Egyptian hieroglyphics in 2018; and a quasi-Latin *Wake* by Adam Roberts appeared online in 2019.

1 Esperanto

Anonymous (Esperanto, 2010)

The year 2010 saw something quite new in the world of *FW* translations, with an anonymous machine-translated rendering of the opening lines (*FW* 3.1–3) on the James Joyce page of the Esperanto Wikipedia:

> riverkuro pasinta Eva kaj tiu de Adamo, de turno de marbordo fleksi da golfo, alportas nin de kommodiusvikus de recirkulado reen al Howth Castle kaj Ĉirkaŭas.

This version, produced by the machine translator GramTrans, opens with "riverkuro," which not only manages to conflate the nouns *rivero* ("river") and *kuro* ("run"), but also self-reflexively hints at both the literary work (*verko*) we are reading and the activity needed to produce it (*verki* "to write"). It also invokes the Japanese river Kuro as a Far Eastern avatar of Anna Livia, and leaves readers to discover for themselves the fact that the Japanese adjective *kuro* ("black") shares its meaning with the Irish adjective *dubh*, an element retained in the name of the city of Dublin, home to Anna Livia's riverrun. Translingual serendipity is clearly not restricted to the products of human translators.

After this brilliant start, however, GramTrans quickly comes to grief with "pasinta Eva kaj tiu de Adamo," confusing the adjectival and prepositional meanings of the English "past" and thus producing a contextually meaningless "former (*pasinta*) Eve and former Adam's." The phrase "de turno de marbordo fleksi da golfo," successfully navigates the "turn" (*turno*) of the "coast" (*marbordo*), but comes to grief once again in misreading "to bend" as an infinitive (*fleksi* "to bend"), thus preventing it from ever reaching the "bay" (*golfo*). At any rate, the riverrun "brings us" (*alportas nin*) by a "kommodiusvikus de recirkulado," retaining Commodus and Vico, "back" (*reen*) to Howth Castle "and surroundings" (*kaj ĉirkaŭas*), where HCE's initials, now HCĈ, show signs of the struggle.

2 Italian

Mezzabotta (Italian, 2010)

The year 2010 also saw an example of technological innovation in the world of *FW* translations when Orlando Mezzabotta, professional actor and independent Joyce scholar, born in 1944 in Ancona, posted (and read) on YouTube an Italian rendering of the prankquean episode (*FW* 21.5–23.15).

The opening lines of the prankquean episode include the following (*FW* 21.5–6, 9–11):

> It was of a night, late, lang time agone, in an auldstane eld, when Adam was delvin and his madameen spinning watersilts, ... and Jarl van Hoother had his burnt head high up in his lamphouse, laying cold hands on himself.

Mezzabotta's complex and entertaining Italian rendering:

> Era una nowtthe, tan tatardi, tan tatan totem befan, più olmeno arrotata la petra, quando Adamo zappescava e la sua madamina eva lì che anna ffilava, ... e Jarl van Hoother, spentosi sole cima del suo faro di testa, s'impose da sole le mani freddelossa.

For Mezzabotta's narrator, who is affected by a stutter characteristic of HCE (as if HCE himself were in fact the narrator), it was a night (*notte*), identified as a night specifically on Howth ("nowtthe"), late (*tardi*) and a long time ago (*tanto tempo fa*), a night when one might not have been too surprised if some old hag (*befana*) of a witch (*befana*) were to appear, in which case the time (*tempo*) would be more pleasantly (*più ameno*) spent if one had at least (*almeno*) already cautiously sharpened (*arrotata*) one's weapon – however difficult that might turn out to be with one made of stone (*pietra*).

Mezzabotta's Italian Adam, meanwhile, was digging (*escavare* "to excavate") with his hoe (*zappa*), and his madamina, as Eva, was spinning (*filare* "to spin"), while as Anna she was a life-giving source of water (*annaffiare* "to sprinkle, to water, to wet"), anticipating the prankquean's later making "her wit" at the door of Jarl van Hoother's abode. Adam's choosing to use a hoe, a less than adequate implement for digging, humorously evokes Joyce's "Hootch is for husbandman handling his hoe" (*FW* 5.9) – thus also anticipating Jarl van Hoother's self-pleasuring manual activities. And Jarl van Hoother, indeed, had already translingually "spent" himself, "extinguished" (*spento*) himself, having (for all that "it was of a night") seen the sunshine (*sole*) on the top (*sulla cima*) of the head (*testa*) of his lighthouse (*faro*), while laying (*s'impose*) on himself, all by himself (*da solo*), bony (*ossa* "bones") hands that were susceptible to the cold (*freddoloso*).

Schenoni (Italian, 2011)

Luigi Schenoni died in his early seventies in 2008, working until the end of his life on the ongoing translation of the *Wake* that he had begun almost thirty-five years earlier. His Italian rendering of *FW* II.3–4 (*FW* 39–99) appeared posthumously in 2011, thus completing his translation of Books I and II, the first twelve of the seventeen chapters of the *Wake*.

Corinna del Greco Lobner wrote in a brief obituary that Schenoni's demise "marks an irreplaceable loss in Joycean circles. His monumental effort to translate *Finnegans Wake* into Italian ... initiated an experiment in linguistic metamorphosis many found amusing and most found exceptionally brilliant" (2008, 434).

Fatica (Italian, 2013)

An Italian translation of *Finn's Hotel* (2013) by Ottavio Fatica appeared in Rome in November 2013. Fatica, born in Perugia and for many years a resident of Rome, is a poet and translator, whose translations include works by Kipling, Byron, Melville, Le Fanu, Edward Lear, Conan Doyle, Elizabeth Bowen, Yeats, and Tolkien among many others – and also include Joyce's *The Cat and the Devil*.

Mezzabotta (Italian, 2016)

The particularly productive year 2016 saw an online Italian rendering of the opening chapter by Orlando Mezzabotta. While the impossibility of achieving anything other than a rewriting of Joyce's text is firmly stated in his introductory note, the result is a thoroughgoing attempt to reproduce in Italian the linguistic experimentation of the *Wake*. The rendering is described on its title page as a version in "finntaliano," an Italian adjusted to accommodate the demands of Joyce's Finneganian extravagances.

The point is immediately made by the complex title and subtitle. Readers are likely to assume that Mezzabotta's *Opfertuere: il primo capitol'ho?* suggests at one level "Overture: the first chapter," and may possibly also conclude that the disorienting question mark reflects the disorienting role of the apostrophe in Joyce's original title. In further layers of meaning, "Opfertuere" clearly plays on both Italian *ouverture* and German *Ouvertüre* ("overture"), while playing also on German *Opfer*, which may variously mean both an "offering" (as in the present translatorial offering) and a "victim" (as of the present translation). The fact that German *Ouvertüre* may also be written as *Ouvertuere* enables a further play on both Latin *tuere* ("to examine") and French *tuer* ("to kill"), with the conflation thus readable as modestly suggesting that the translatorial examination undertaken of Joyce's text may in fact just succeed in killing it. The subtitle, while indeed readable as meaning "the first chapter" (*il primo capitolo*), ends in a question mark that not only evokes an absent original apostrophe but also implies immediate doubt as to the relationship between translation and original, with the translator self-reflexively wondering, humorously, "L'ho capito?" ("Have I understood it?").

Mezzabotta's "finntalian" rendering of the opening three lines (*FW* 3.1–3):

> rivierra, passato Eva ed Adamo, deviando dalla costa e curvando alla baia,
> ci riporta lungo un commodio vicus di ricerchio finn ad Howth, Castello
> Edintorni.

The opening "rivierra" conflates French *rivière* ("river") and Italian *riviera* ("coast") and *errare* ("to wander, to err"). The wandering river, having passed (*passato*) Eve and Adam, swerving (*deviando*) from the shore (*costa*) and curving (*curvando*) to the bay (*baia*), brings us (*ci riporta*) by a commodious (*commodio*) vicus of recirculation (*cerchio* "circle") back as far as ("finn") Howth, Castle and Environs. The invented preposition *finn* conflates the Italian preposition *fin* or *fino* ("as far as") and the legendary Finn, while HCE's initials are preserved by writing *e dintorni* ("and environs") as a single word – repeating a strategy first employed in Italian by Luigi Schenoni in 1982. The intrusive comma in "Howth, Castello Edintorni" slightly changes the original meaning, bringing us back to "Howth, with its Castle and Environs."

The rendering continues (*FW* 3.4–10):

> Messer Tristrano, violator d'amorey, d'alamar d'Irlanda, non era puss'ancora viarrivato dall'Armorica del Nord acquiesta parte dell'estmo diarreupato dell'Europa Minore a manecciare e a battere l'asciaguirra penisolata:
> e lirocce di Toppe Assaier, prius al fiume Oconee, non si erano esarginate
> fino ai gorghigori smontuosi della Laurens County anche s'era un dublione sull'altro in mumpero sempre crosciante: né una voce diolontana e

peana di fuoco ammugghiava mi-scio mi-scio al distorbattezzatore tauf tauftauf tu sei pietrizzio:

To mention just four out of several intriguing points: "Sir Tristram" is here rendered as "Messer Tristrano," conflating *Tristan*, *Tristram,*and the adjective *strano* ("strange"); "violator d'amorey" includes, inter alia, Tristrano as violator associated with the historical Amory Tristram; Joyce's "passancore" is rendered by a conflation of the Italian adverb *ancora* ("again"), the Italian noun *ancora* ("anchor"), and, immediately deflating any expected romantic overtones, the colloquial English *pussy*; and the capitalized "Toppe Assaier" conflates "top sawyer," "Tom Sawyer," and the adverb *assai* ("plenty"). Plenty indeed.

Terrinoni and Pedone (Italian, 2017, 2019)

After Luigi Schenoni's death in 2008, and the posthumous publication in 2011 of the last volume he had eventually completed (*FW* II.3–4), the project was revived after some delay by the publisher Mondadori, and Enrico Terrinoni and Fabio Pedone were named as Schenoni's continuators. Enrico Terrinoni (born 1976) was a professor of English at the Università per Stranieri di Perugia and a translator already of works by Brendan Behan, James Stephens, Muriel Spark, Nathaniel Hawthorne, and B.S. Johnson – and, among others, the poet Michael D. Higgins, President of Ireland. Together with a colleague, Carlo Bigazzi, he had produced an award-winning Italian translation of *Ulysses* in 2012.

Mondadori commissioned Terrinoni, who had lived in Dublin for several years and completed undergraduate and graduate work at University College Dublin, and another colleague, Fabio Pedone (born 1976), a Rome-based translator, critic, and scholar of Italian studies, to undertake the task of finishing Schenoni's translation. Their rendering of *FW* III.1–2, begun in August 2014, appeared to general applause in January 2017, dedicated to the then recently deceased Italian Joyceans Umberto Eco and Rosa Maria Bollettieri Bosinelli, both of whom had enthusiastically championed the project. The translation, seventy pages long, is accompanied by the original in parallel text, approximately 150 pages of detailed annotations, and an afterword by Pedone on Joyce's influence on Italian literature.

Terrinoni humorously claimed in an interview that their rate of progress was "two lines per day, and that takes about five hours" (Kearns 2017b, 171). Unlike Schenoni, the new translators were able to take advantage of modern technology, including digital dictionaries, e-mail, and a variety of social-media platforms. Their collaboration was in fact conducted largely by e-mail, since Terrinoni's teaching took place in Perugia, Pedone's a couple of hours away in Rome. Terrinoni elsewhere observes that they took almost three years altogether to translate the seventy pages involved – an achievement, he estimates, that with any other text might have taken just seven days.

Their procedure, as reported, was in principle similar to that employed by Joyce and his collaborators in producing both the French and Italian renderings of *ALP*. Terrinoni and Pedone would translate individual passages separately, then each would revise the other's work, followed by "a long ping-pong of ideas, suggestions, and compromises," the result of which continually changed until the very end, their translation of the *Wake* inevitably involving, in Beckett's phrase, continuing to fail, but striving to fail better. For months they also resorted to the unusual strategy of having their own weekly column in the literary pages of a newspaper, *Pagina 99*, inviting interested readers to propose Italian renderings for particularly polyvalent phrases, a procedure that, happily, led frequently to previously unexpected translational solutions (Barina 2017).[1]

Franca Ruggieri writes that the translators "seem to have taken Joyce's self-translation as their main source of inspiration" (2015, 730).[2] She adds that "the Italian reader will rediscover a sense of humor that had been partially lost in the final volumes of the previous translation," namely, Schenoni's, whose final volumes "were indeed pioneering and masterful works in many respects, but they were carried out from a different perspective. While Schenoni aimed at reproducing the original more or less faithfully, particularly in regard to the 'linear' disposition of the elements of the sentence, this new work privileges the principle of semantic compensation" (Ruggieri 2015, 730–1). Ruggieri also comments on the "incredibly detailed collection of annotations," which she sees as an invaluable aid in attracting new Italian readers to

---

1 "Dopo aver affrontato separatamente ogni brano ed esserci poi revisionati a vicenda, abbiamo iniziato un lungo ping-pong di idee, proposte, compromessi: la versione finale ha continuato a cambiare fino all'ultimo, perché tradurre vuol dire provare e fallire, diceva Beckett, riprovare e fallire sempre meglio, ed è impossibile mettere la parola fine a un testo che in ogni parola condensa più significati, irradia allusioni sorprendenti, reinventa la lingua. Un testo che offre una sconfinata libertà interpretativa. Per mesi abbiamo tenuto una rubrica sul settimanale *Pagina 99*, chiedendo ai lettori di proporre la loro versione italiana di alcune frasi: sono emerse soluzioni inaspettate e spesso molto valide" (Barina 2017).
2 Despite the 2015 date, this volume of the *James Joyce Quarterly* did indeed appear *after* Terrinoni and Pedone's 2017 rendering.

Joyce's text.[3] She writes elsewhere that "the new Italian *Wake* surprisingly reads as very Italian. It is also extremely Joycean, with its echoes and reverberations, and a joyful semantic compensation which replaces Schenoni's philological adherence to the original. The translators' way of playing with words, while respecting the critical achievements of earlier *Wake* criticism, makes for a different type of fidelity, conducted in the spirit of Renato Poggioli, who once said that the translator has to be faithful, without seeming so" (2017, 2).

When Terrinoni and Pedone's rendering of *FW* III.1–2 appeared in January 2017, the publisher Mondadori announced with some justifiable fanfare that the final volume of the long-planned complete Italian *FW* would appear on 4 May 2019, marking the eightieth anniversary of the original appearance of *FW*. The volume, rendered by the same two translators, and including both *FW* III.3–4 and IV, duly appeared, even a few days ahead of time, before the end of April 2019. It carried a preface by the writer and semiotician Stefano Bartezzaghi, an introduction by Fabio Pedone, and a concluding essay by Enrico Terrinoni.

The complete Mondadori *Wake*, published over no less than a thirty-seven-year period (1982–2019), thus finally consisted of six volumes altogether, the first four translated by Luigi Schenoni, the last two by Terrinoni and Pedone: vol. 1, 1982 (I.1–4); vol. 2, 2001 (I.5–8); vol.3, 2004 (II.1–2); vol. 4, 2011 (II.3–4); vol. 5, 2017 (III.1–2); vol. 6, 2019 (III.3–4 and IV). The complete translation was finally reissued by Mondadori in 2019 in six handsome matching volumes. Each volume includes the parallel English text, a full critical apparatus, detailed glossaries, and extensive annotations.[4]

The final volume was greeted with great enthusiasm by Italian reviewers, the translators were highly praised for their ingenuity and imaginativeness, and the publishers were lauded for their courage in supporting the decades-long endeavour. One reviewer in particular greeted the appearance of the final volume of the Mondadori *Wake* in almost euphoric tones, tempered only slightly by awareness of the realities to which publishers are subject: "Seventeen years to write it, eighty to translate it, and maybe as long again to be able to understand in what language it is written, this most beautiful book in the world, the only one whose author and translator is always the next reader who opens it for the first time; even just to provide that pleasure makes it worth [the

___

3 On Terrinoni and Pedone's rendering of *FW* III.1–2, see Ruggieri (2015, 2017), Terrinoni (2016), Barina (2017), Kearns (2017b).

4 On the thirty-seven-year evolution of the Mondadori *FW*, see Gurrado (2019). For reactions to the final volume, see Gurrado (2019), Ricciardi (2019).

publisher's] while to take the risk that nobody at all may in fact actually read it" (Gurrado 2019).[5]

Terrinoni referred in various interviews to Pedone and himself as not just *traduttori* ("translators") but also as *straduttori*, a term that can mean both "non-translators," since the *Wake* is by common consent not amenable to translation, and also something like "extreme translators," reflecting their efforts (and those of Schenoni before them) to transpose Joyce's original into just one version of *"infinitaliana,"* an Italian that not only attempts to transfigure Finn and Finnegan but could conceivably continue to do so – failing again, failing better – in an infinite number of different variations.

From Terrinoni and Pedone's rendering of the final lines of the *Wake* (*FW* 627.34–628.4, 15–16):

> E sto svanendo. O fine amara! … ed io stanca ritorno a te, mio freddo padre, mio freddo folle padre pauroso, finché la vista vicina della sua mera statura, le sue moyglia e moyglia, mononieanante, mi dà il saldimare e mi marterra e io corro, mio unico, nelle tue braccia … L'a via l'un al fine amata a lungo l'

Mezzabotta's Italian ALP (2017)

Also in 2017, Orlando Mezzabotta posted (and read) on YouTube an Italian rendering of the opening and closing pages of *ALP* (*FW* 196.1–201.20, 215.11–216.5), the same pages as iconically translated into Italian by Joyce and Frank almost eighty years earlier. In an accompanying translator's note, Mezzabotta observes that he decided to transpose Joyce's text into a consciously synthetic northern Italian based on a variety of local dialects and with frequent use of regional colloquialisms. The rendering, as he acknowledges, is freer even than that of Joyce and Frank, while striving nonetheless to remain faithful to the structural and literary principles of Joyce's original text. The result is considerably more complex than that of Schenoni's version of *ALP*, and even Italian readers may well find its frequent carefully wrought obscurities particularly challenging.

---

5 "Diciassette anni per scriverlo, ottanta per tradurlo e chissà ancora quanti per riuscire a capire in che lingua sia scritto il libro più bello del mondo, l'unico il cui autore e traduttore è sempre il prossimo lettore che lo aprirà per la prima volta; pur di procurargli questo piacere, vale la pena di rischiare che non lo legga nessuno" (Gurrado 2019).

Mezzabotta's rendering of the opening sentences of *ALP* includes the following lines (*FW* 196.1–7, 9–11):

Contame, O, di', va: dime d'Anna Livia. Oglio saône tuteau d'Anna Livia. Beh, tu cagnossi Anna Livia? Sì, certo, tute canossiamo Anna Livia. Dime tutto, dime dèsso. Timorioarai a sentir! Alloira, tu lo sai il vicio spor-calzone quondam l'ondà in maona e ha fotto qual che fece. ... Occhiosa quei trebbia han tredito di dire che lui attrentato di fare alle due nel parco Diablinico.

Mezzabotta's complex, flamboyant, and generously fluvial rendering begins by playing in cheerful emulation of Lavergne's French on a like-wise quasi-Homeric invocation of the Muse, "Tell me (*conta-me*), O tell (*di'*), goddess (*diva*)," evoking in the process the American Raccoon, English Tame, Irish Ow, and Scottish Dee, followed ("dime d'Anna Livia") by the Turkish Dim, Dutch Diem, and American Dan. Unlike Joyce's own Italian, Mezzabotta preserves the aquatic pun on French *eau*, though dis-placing it from its originally central position. His complex continuation "Oglio saône tuteau d'Anna Livia" plays on "I want (*voglio*) the whole (*tutto*) story, the whole fluvial (French *eau* 'water') sound (*sono*) of Anna Livia," now incorporating the Italian Oglio, French Saône, and Indian Tut. "You'll die when you hear," responds the other washerwoman, "Ti morirai a sentir!," evoking the Spanish Orio, the Arai of Papua New Guinea, and, for good measure, the Timor Sea of Indonesia.

"Well," the tale begins robustly, "allora," incorporating the French Loire (*Loira* in Italian), "you know when the dirty (*sporco*) old prick (*ca-zzone*) of a scoundrel (*mascalzone*) had gone looking for pussy (*andò in mona*) and done (*fatto*) what he fucking (*fotto*) did (*fece*)." The English river Maun bears witness to this less than gentlemanly behaviour. "Or whatever (*o che cosa*) those three (*tre*) tormentors (*trebbiare* 'to torment') revealed (*tradito*) about what he had scandalously attempted (*attentato*) to do (*fare*) to the two (*due*) in the diabolical (*diabolico*) Dublin park." The three in the trees are revealed in both "trebbia" and "tredito," while the Italian river Trebbia and the English river Trent ("attrentato") flow quietly through the account.

Mezzabotta's likewise flamboyant rendering of the closing lines of *ALP* (*FW* 215.31–5, 216.3–5):

Non sento con le acque di. Le ciaccerinelle acque di. Pipistrel, nottolìo inpudende. Oh! Non sei ancora andata? Che sciura Rata? Non sento coi pipistrilli, le liffyumeggianti acque di. Dimenaddio ci scampi! Edera ed è ai miei piè! Vecchia mi sento come quell'olmo e tremo. Vento che conta del

Rolmolo e del Remo? ... Dime, dime, dimelolm. Notte not! Rockontolmi di steli e monti. Alcanto alle frusciacque di, le quinciequindi acque di. Not!

Here the washerwoman's "Non sei ancora andata?" ("Haven't you gone yet?") elicits the confused response in Milanese dialect "Che sciura Rata?" ("What Signora Rata?"). There's no hearing with the shrieks (*strilli*) of bats (*pipistrelli*) and the rivering (*fiumeggianti*) liffey-ing waters. "Tell me goodbye (*di me un addio*), and God save us (*Dio ci scampi*)! There is ivy (*edera*) on my feet (*piei*)! I feel as old as that elm (*olmo*) there, and I tremble (*tremo*). A wind (*vento*) that tells (*conta*) of *olmo*-Romulus and *tremo*-Remus? Rock on! Tell me a tale (*raccontame*) of stalks (*steli*) and stones (*monti*). By the rivering waters (*frusciacque*), the hither-and-thithering (*quinciequindi*) waters." Rivers evoked include the Irish Suir and Russian Ura ("sciura"), the English Rat, Romanian Rât, and Ukrainian Rata, as well as the German Notte, while the humorous interlingual "Rock on!" summons up the American river Rock.

Marrozzini (Italian, 2017)

An Italian translation of the closing lines (*FW* 627.33–628.16) by the independent scholar Luigi Marrozzini appeared in 2017, in the online journal *bis numero uno*.

Mazza's Italian Wake *(2018)*

A highly unexpected publishing event occurred in 2018, when to considerable general surprise, and without any advance publicity or promotional fanfare, the first complete Italian translation of *FW* quietly appeared – the work, however, *not* of Luigi Schenoni and his official continuators already mentioned but of the seventy-eight-year-old poet and novelist Giuliano Mazza. Born in 1940 in Parma, and self-educated, Mazza reportedly left Italy in search of work as a seventeen-year-old, finding employment first in Switzerland and subsequently in Germany, England, and finally Australia before eventually returning to Parma in 1975, after eighteen years away, and producing his first volume of poetry in 1980.[6]

Mazza's rendering appeared under the bilingual title *Finnegans Wake: La veglia di Finnegan*, the Italian title meaning "Finnegan's wake" in the funeral sense, following the example of Juan Rodolfo Wilcock's

---

6 On Mazza's Italian rendering, see Anon. (2018b). My thanks to Enrico Terrinoni for personal correspondence on Mazza's translation.

renderings of 1961 and 2016. The publisher of his translation, Abax Editrice, a small local Parmesan press that had also recently published two of Mazza's novels, thus cheekily succeeded in stealing a major march on Mondadori, by far the largest and most prestigious Italian publisher, whose projected complete Italian rendering, begun by Luigi Schenoni in the 1970s and continued after Schenoni's death by Enrico Terrinoni and Fabio Pedone, had long been advertised to appear in May 2019, celebrating with all due fanfare the eightieth anniversary of the original appearance of *FW*.

The two projects are clearly very different in their approach, however. Mazza's version is an essentially normalizing one, with an introduction by the translator and occasional explanatory footnotes along similar lines to Lavergne's, but lacking the extensive and systematic annotation that was characteristic first of Schenoni's renderings and subsequently even more intensively in evidence in the case of his continuators. Mazza's wholly unexpected rendering was greeted by at least one enthusiastic Italian reviewer as no less than a "titanic" endeavour, the work of a translator whose devotion to the task of producing the first complete Italian *Wake* was, the reviewer felt, almost religious in its intensity (Anon. 2018b).

Mazza's rendering of the three-line opening (*FW* 3.1–3) reads:

corso del fiume passato l'Adamo ed Eva, da deviazione di spiaggia a svolta di baia, ci riporta con un commodius vicus di ricircolazione di nuovo al Castello di Howth e Environs.

Mazza takes advantage of Joyce's Latinate diction to adhere very closely to the original text. The course (*corso*) of the river (*fiume*), having passed (*passato*) Adam and Eve's, from swerve (*deviazione*) of strand (*spiaggia*) to turn (*svolta*) of bay (*baia*) brings us (*ci riporta*) by a commodious vicus of recirculation once again (*di nuovo*) to Howth Castle and its untranslated Environs. The order of Joyce's Eve and Adam is reversed; Commodus and Vico are exactly as much in evidence as they were in the original; and HCE's initials survive as CHE.

Mazza's opening sentences of *ALP* include the following lines (*FW* 196.1–7, 9–11):

O / dimmi tutto / d'Anna Livia! Voglio sentir tutto / d'Anna Livia. Bene, conosci Anna Livia? Sì, certamente, conosciam tutti Anna Livia. Dimmi tutto. Ditemelo subito. Creperai quando lo sentirai. Bene, sai, quando il vecchio chebrero fu fotto e commise ciò che sai. ... O qualunque cosa fosse che treviarono da dar da intendere che lui trentò con quelle due nel parco Fienico.

Mazza's washerwoman, as always, wants to hear all about Anna Livia, and we all know Anna Livia, *certamente* ("certainly"). You will die (*creperai*) when you hear it (*quando lo sentirai*). So you know, when the drunken (*ebbro*) old (*vecchio*) cheb not only went futt but got fucked (*fu fotto*) and did (*commise*) what you know. Or whatever it was (*qualunque cosa fosse*) that the three (*tre*) were threshing out (*tribbiare*) to give people to understand (*dare da intendere*) that he was trying (*tentò*) to do with those two (*due*). The park where the event took place is now renamed the "parco Fienico," evoking both Phoenix (*Fenice*) and Finn – and, speculating mildly on Finn's putative non-Irish origins, "Finnish" (*finnico*), and finally, since it is a park after all, on the possibility of an eventual crop of "hay" (*fieno*). Rivers evoked include the Italian Erta ("certamente"), the Indian Sai ("bene, sai"), and the English Trent ("trentò") and Foss ("fosse"), while, for good measure, even Rome's Trevi Fountain ("treviarono") puts in an unexpected appearance.

From the final lines of *ALP* (*FW* 215.31–5):

Non riesco a udire con le acque di. Le ciangottanti acque di. Pipistrelli svolazzanti, ciance di topi di campagna. Ho. Non sei andata a dhome? Cosa c'entra Thom Malone? Non riesco a udire con le ciance dei pipistrelli, con tutte le liffeyriottose acque di. Ho, ci save il parodio! Le mie foossa non si mooschiano. Mi sento vecchia quanto quell'elmo lontano. Un 'conto cantato di Shaun e Shem?

The most intriguing item in this otherwise domesticating rendering is the question "Non sei andata a dhome?," translating "Are you not gone ahome?," where "dhome" is readable as playing not only on Joyce's "ahome" and on English *home*, but also on Albanian *dhomë* ("house, room") – and possibly even, for the amusement of northern Italian readers, on the name, as one discovers, of a local nightclub, "Dhome," its name in fact a surname of Indian origin. One can certainly see the point of the puzzled response, "Cosa c'entra Thom Malone?" ("What's Thom Malone got to do with it?").

3 Polish

Bartnicki's Polish Wake: Finneganów tren *(2012)*

A first complete, widely praised, and award-winning Polish translation of *FW*, by Krzysztof Bartnicki, appeared in Krakow on 29 February 2012, a leap-year offering. Bartnicki's renderings of *FW* I.1 and IV had already appeared in the journal *Literatura na Świecie* and of "The Mookse and the Gripes" (*FW* 152.4–159.3) in the journal *Przekładaniec*, both in 2005.

The multitalented Bartnicki, born in 1971 in Opole in southern Poland, is a translator, writer, lexicographer, musician, and composer as well as a highly regarded independent Joyce scholar. A graduate of the University of Wrocław, where he first encountered the *Wake* as a student of English, his translations from Polish to English earned him an early reputation as a translator of very difficult texts, including the concrete poetry of Stanisław Dróżdż (1939–2009) and the highly complex poetry of Bolesław Leśmian (1877–1937), widely considered, as in the case of *FW*, to be almost entirely untranslatable (Gliński 2012a). A practising technical translator, Bartnicki has also collaborated in the compilation of specialist Polish-English dictionaries of banking, economics, and other areas.

Bartnicki reportedly spent ten years, beginning in 1999, on his translation of *FW*, frequently tempted to abandon the often almost overwhelming undertaking, estimating his progress not in pages but in lines, sometimes just five or six lines a day (Gliński 2012a, 2012b). Rather surprisingly, the publication of the translation in 2012 caused a considerable popular stir in Poland in the mainstream press, including the appearance of a flurry of articles about Joyce's final text as well as various interviews with the book's translator. Given the degree of attention in the media and especially on the Internet, Bartnicki also soon became the target of very mixed social-media reactions ranging from enthusiastic praise on the part of some for his translatorial work to ridicule on the part of others for such an elitist and, allegedly, totally pointless endeavour (Gliński 2012a).

Evidently unsatisfied with merely translating *FW*, Bartnicki provided his rendering, entitled *Finneganów tren* (2012a), with *Finneganów bdyn* (2012b), a companion volume of textual variants and their Polish translations; followed that with a highly unusual treatise on translation theory and its relevance to *FW* under the humorously disorienting title *Fu wojny* (2012c); followed that with an intersemiotic rendering of the *Wake*, namely, a 133-page musical cryptogram, *Da Capo al Finne* (2012d); followed that with a further and much more complicated 372-page musical transposition entitled *F_nnegans a_e* (2014a); and followed that, finally (as one may perhaps assume), with *Finnegans Meet* (2015), a third intersemiotic "translation" in the form in this case of a Rolodex version of Joyce's text involving a rotary business card holder, compiled together with the Polish visual artist Marcin Szmandra.

Bartnicki refers to *Finneganów tren* not as a translation, but rather as a "polonization" (*spolszczenie*) of Joyce's text, conceived of as an intralingual rather than interlingual rendering, namely, from one dialect of Wakese, Joyce's Anglo-Wakese, to another, his own Polish-based Wakese (Wawrzycka 2016–17, 170). His title initially suggests "Finnegans' threne," in the sense of a threnody, a lament for the dead (Greek *thrênos* "dirge"). In modern Polish the ending *-ów* denotes a genitive plural, thus "Finnegans'." In earlier forms of the language, however, as Bartnicki explains in personal correspondence, the ending *-ów* denoted in the case of certain possessive adjectives a masculine singular (where in standard modern Polish *-owy* is used), thus implying "Finnegan's," and achieving an elegant conflation of singularity and plurality.

The term *tren* is potentially evocative for a Polish reader of one of the major highlights of Polish Renaissance literature, the *Treny* (1580; *Lamentations*) of the poet Jan Kochanowski (1530–84), written on the death of his daughter. A secondary connotation of *tren* is the "train" of a dress, especially of a wedding dress, swirling in the wake of its wearer like the wake of a moving ship. A third meaning, as also of English *train*, is the flamboyant tail plumage of a peacock. Both of these latter meanings suggest the lots of fun that may also be had, even despite the titular suggestion of lamentation. The archaic but less multiply evocative Polish noun *bdyn*, meanwhile, refers specifically to a funeral "wake," deriving from the verb *budzić* ("to wake, to awaken"). Wishing also to retain the complementary echo, Bartnicki employed the title *Finneganów bdyn* (2012b) for the accompanying compilation of textual variants and their Polish translation published simultaneously with his *Finneganów tren*.[7]

Finneganów tren appeared as the nineteenth volume in a book series published since 2003 by the publishing firm Ha!art, based in Krakow and operating as the publishing arm of the magazine *Ha!art*, reportedly considered to be one of the most influential new literary and cultural magazines in Poland. The series title, "Liberatura," employs a neologism coined by the Polish poet Zenon Fajfer in 1999 to describe "a type or genre of literature in which the text is integrated with the physical space of the book into a meaningful whole and in which all elements, from the graphic ones to the kind of paper (or other material) and the

---

7 My thanks to Krzysztof Bartnicki for personal correspondence including these and other linguistic explanations – and for kindly sending me a copy of *Finneganów tren* and the associated intersemiotic renderings. On *Finneganów tren*, see Bazarnik (2010, 2012), Gliński (2012a, 2012b), Bartnicki (2014b), Camurri (2016), Wawrzycka (2016–17), Kearns (2017a).

physical shape of the book, may contribute to its meaning" and thus result in "a harmonious union of literature and the book" (Fajfer 2008). *Finneganów tren* duly appeared in covers of exactly the same shade of brown with yellow lettering as had the original *Finnegans Wake* of 1939. It also had exactly the same number of pages, so that major narrative events that happen on particular pages of the 628-page source text happen on exactly the same pages of the translation. Since the Polish text has more words than the original, as John Kearns reports, it took the typesetters three months of kerning and compositing to arrange the text in such a way as to achieve this. As Kearns observes, *Finneganów tren* can thus be seen "as a work that expands the notion of translation to acknowledge a physical, structural relationship between the translated book and the original" (2017a, 100, 101). *Finneganów bdyn* also appeared in covers of exactly the same shades of brown and yellow.

Katarzyna Bazarnik, author of several publications on the concept of "liberature," also published a particularly positive article on Bartnicki's ongoing work, based on the prepublication excerpts that appeared in 2005. She observes that Bartnicki's methodological premises "include a conviction that inventing a counterpart of the multilingual 'Wakese' idiom constitutes a kind of intralingual translation, a respect for the uniqueness of the book's structure, and a dedication to the reconstruction of conceptual images evoked by the original." She discusses in detail several of the translatorial strategies employed ("to astonishing effect"), including "transplantation, phonetic equivalence, foreign-language substitution, proportional distortion, anticipatory reinforcement, and equivalent conceptual blending" (2010, 574, 681). Jolanta Wawrzycka, in a detailed and likewise enthusiastic review, characterizing the translation as "masterful," quotes Bartnicki's description of himself in a Polish-language interview as a "molecular translator," one who deliberately avoided consulting overarching critical works on the *Wake* until he had first attempted to render individual "letters, then morphemes, words, phrases, punctuation, paragraphs, etc." (Wawrzycka 2016–17, 172, 173).

Bartnicki's rendering of the opening three lines (*FW* 3.1–3) reads as follows:

> rzekibrzeg, postephując od Ewy i Adama, od wygięcia wybrzeża do zakola zatoki, zanosi nas znów przez commodius vicus recyrkulacji pod Howth Castle i Ekolice.

Here the opening "rzekibrzeg" conflates *rzeka* ("river") and *bieg* ("run, running"), but also *brzeg* ("bank, riverside"). The river is "following on" (*postephując*) from (*od*) "Ewy i Adama," and "od wygięcia wybrzeża do zakola zatoki," literally, and alliteratively, "from the bending (*wygięcia*) of the shore (*wybrzeż*) to the curve (*zakol*) of the bay (*zatoka*)," and it takes us (*zanosi nas*) once again (*znów*), and once again alliteratively, by (*przez*) a "commodius vicus recyrkulacji," back to "Howth Castle i Ekolice." The final "Ekolice" may be seen as humorously altering the initial letter of *okolice* ("environs") to the more appropriate letter needed for HCE's initials. It may also be taken to conflate *okolice* and *eko-*, in which case, Katarzyna Bazarnik suggests, the neologism may be seen as invoking "the primeval character of the landscape described in the opening, its natural, prelapsarian state still unaffected by man" (2010, 569).

The rendering in *Finneganów tren* of the *ALP* chapter is the second complete Polish translation of that text, following on Maciej Słomczyński's *ALP* of 1985. Bartnicki's opening sentences include the following lines (*FW* 196.1–7, 9–11):

> O / mów mi wszystko o / Annie Livii! Chcę slyszeć wszystko / o Annie Livii. Cóż, znasz Annę Livię? Jasna rzecz, wszyscy znamy Annę Livię. Wszystko mów. Mówże już. Umrzesz jak uslyszysz. No cóż, wiesz, jak starego rachebe zafuttły i zrobił no wiesz. ... Albo co oni tam trybowali wydumać co też trzymał w dwanadrzu w parku Fiendish.

ALP, river of rivers, is accompanied by at least nine other rivers and two lakes in Bartnicki's decidedly fluvial incipit. The river Mow of Papua New Guinea even puts in a triple appearance, while Slovenia's Jasna Lake is evoked by the claim that, "sure thing" (*jasna rzecz*), everybody knows Anna Livia. The Czech Cheb, Chilean Futa, and German Wiese flow through the reminder of how the old cheb (*starego rechebe*) went futt (*zafuttły*) and did what you know (*zrobił no wiesz*). And finally, the German Alb, English Tame, and English Tees, as well as the Canadian Feeny Lake, are present in "albo co" ("or whatever") it was "over there" (*tam*) that the three (*trzy*) in the trees (*drzewa*) were trying (*próbowali*) to invent (*wydumać*) regarding what else (*co też*) he was holding (*trzymał*) in store (*w zanadrzu*) for the two (*dwa*), as, for example, ideally in a double bed (*w dwanadrzu*), in the Fiendish park.

The closing paragraph of the *ALP* chapter includes the following lines (*FW* 215.31–5, 216.3–5):

> Nie słyszę u wód co rzek. Paplejącej wody że. Trzepot nietop, mysz z pól zwrot. Ho! A iść już nie miałas do dom? Co Tom Malone? Nietopłyszę przez trzepot ten, nie przez liffale nurtów ton. Ho, mówże, zbaw nas! Stoop nie zmuszę o krook. Czuję już wiek jak si wiąz. A czy mowa tu że Shem czy

Shaun? ... Mówcie, mówrzecz wiąźle mów! Noc noc! Mówże mi czystem czyston. U rzekających nurtów jej, nurtędyowędych rzeki jej. Noc!

Finally, for interested readers, the following, from Bartnicki's closing lines of the *Wake* (*FW* 627.34–628.4, 15–16):

Odpływam. Po gorzki kres! Ucieknę nim wstaną. Nigdy nie ujrzą. Nie poznają. Nie uschną po mnie. O starcze o starcze rozpacze o przez starcze rozpacze i przez męczenie do ciebie, mój chłodny ojcze, mój chłodny ojcze szaleńcze trwożący, aż po bliski widok mórz brzyma, mielkiego na mile, w moanotoanii, że szlamosmorska słonosłabła runę, mój jedyny, w twe ramionia. ... Ach w dal a ląd a los a lot a cel gdzie

Bartnicki's *Finneganów tren* as a work of both literature and "liberature" was far from being the end of the matter as far as Bartnicki's highly developed taste for literary experimentation was concerned. The accompanying *Finneganów bdyn* (2012b) consists of some 110 pages of meticulously recorded variants among the several editions of *FW* then available in print, with each variant duly translated into Polish. While this may appear on the face of it to be no more than a mere scholarly exercise, it also potentially, and quite deliberately, destabilizes the translation offered in *Finneganów tren* in that the translation could clearly have been at least subtly different in several hundreds of cases.

Finneganów tren gained Bartnicki an unusual degree of celebrity for a Polish translator, or indeed for most translators, and he made a considerable number of promotional appearances of different kinds, during which he reportedly made no secret of the personal cost of the ten years of concentrated translatorial work – or of his growing irritation over those years with both *FW* and its author (Gliński 2012a, Okulska 2018). His next endeavour, an overtly postmodern mystification, has been interpreted as a translator's parodic attempt to turn the tables on the author translated, putting both Joyce and the *Wake* firmly in their place. It takes the form of an ostensible treatise on translation and appeared under the deliberately disorienting title *Fu wojny* (2012c) – and clearly numbers Jorge Luis Borges, Flann O'Brien, and Umberto Eco among its spiritual progenitors.

The military theorist Karl von Clausewitz, who famously asserted in the 1830s that "war is the continuation of politics by other means," also figures among those progenitors, for *Fu wojny* begins with the assertion that "translation is the continuation of war by other means" (Okulska 2018, 82). It goes on to consider how to apply an (alleged) ancient Chinese treatise on the art of war to the attempt to translate *FW*. Joyce, the argument goes, evidently plagiarized some such ancient Chinese treatise, or a translation of it, in the course of producing *FW*. Bartnicki, for his part, allegedly found that ancient treatise, or an ancient translation of it, and (re)translated it – and in the process ended up translating the "original" *FW* that was later "rewritten" by the latecomer Joyce. One translation of the title *Fu wojny* – which one might of course refer to parenthetically as "*FW*" – might be "The *fu* of war," *fu* being an ancient Chinese poetic form of rhapsodically detailed description; another might be "Fu's War," describing the warfare between the (alleged) ancient translator Fu, otherwise known as Kufu, and the (alleged) ancient text 守靈, "otherwise known as *Finnegans Wake* by James Joyce." The Chinese graph is pronounced *shŏulíng* and means "(funeral) wake," while the name Kufu hints at the possibilities, martial and otherwise, of kung fu – which in its original meaning, as we are told, can refer to any discipline or skill (such as the art of translation) achieved through hard work and practice.[8]

Very shortly afterwards, in the wake of this exuberant *jeu d'esprit*, the enormously energetic Bartnicki went on to produce three separate intersemiotic "translations" of the *Wake*. The first of these was published in Warsaw under the title *Da Capo al Finne* (2012d). The title plays in this case on the familiar direction *da capo al fine*, frequently encountered in musical scores, directing the performer to repeat a particular passage "from beginning to end." Bartnicki's text quite literally (though with significant adjustment) repeats Joyce's original text from beginning to end in the form of a musical transfiguration, while the title playfully conflates the name of Finn, once the leader (Italian *capo*) of the Fianna, the legendary standing army of Irish heroes. Bartnicki's text, by implication, converts the original text of *FW* into a bare-bones musical score (lacking any indications of pitch, duration, tempo, or instrumentation) by deleting everything in the entire 628-page original text other than the first eight letters of the alphabet, namely, all A's, B's, C's, D's, E's, F's, G's, and H's, with these letters to be understood as representing the corresponding notes in the German (and Polish) system of musical notation and the result to be understood as a vast source of potential music.[9]

---

8 *Fu wojny* is currently available only in Polish; Jolanta Wawrzycka is not alone in considering it "in dire need of an English translation" (2016–17, 173n5). My (second-level) description of it here is based almost entirely on a detailed discussion (in German) by Inez Okulska (2018), supplemented by detailed linguistic commentary on the Chinese implications kindly provided once again by Krzysztof Bartnicki in personal correspondence.

9 In the German (and Polish) system of musical notation, H corresponds to B natural, while B corresponds to B-flat.

The resulting "score," after an introduction (in Polish), involves 122 closely printed pages, 122 undeviatingly regular textual blocks in an eight-point font, consisting of only these eight letters, mostly but not entirely in lower case, and without any spaces, punctuation, numerals, symbols, paragraph indents, or textual breaks of any sort. Bartnicki notes in his introduction that "*Da Capo al Finne* stores nearly 400,000 letters. This is a lot of music. It can be played in fragment or in whole, just as the *Wake* can be enjoyed in whole or bit by bit. In effect, this publication can be viewed as a set of many, many melodies, or as just one giant symphony" (2012c, 8).[10] Among the fragmentary melodies identified by Bartnicki himself and by various later enthusiasts are snippets from Haydn, Chopin, Paganini, Rachmaninoff, "Yankee Doodle," assorted Russian and Japanese folksongs, and movie themes from *The Godfather*, *Star Wars*, and *Harry Potter*.

While the musical implications here are of considerable interest, what is left of the original *literary* text, it need hardly be said, is much less than inspiring. The title and opening lines (*FW* 3.1–3), for example, are retrievable by the would-be literary reader only as a radically concise – and radically unreadable – sequence of the permitted letters:

FegaaeeaEeadAdafeefhebedfbabgbacdcfeccabacHhCaeadE.

Here "*Finnegans Wake*" becomes "Fegaae"; "riverrun" becomes just "e"; "past Eve and Adam's" becomes "aEeadAda"; "from swerve of shore to bend of bay" becomes "feefbedfba"; "brings us by a commodius vicus of recirculation" becomes "bgbacfecca"; and "back to Howth Castle and Environs" becomes "bacHhCaeadE."[11] Very little more than HCE's initials survives, other than a reference to German *Bach* ("stream") and, appropriately for the musical context, to Johann Sebastian Bach.

Bartnicki's next transcreational musical extravaganza, *F_nnegans a_e Suite in the Key of Ш*, published in Warsaw in 2014, is credited to James Joyce as "composer" and Krzysztof Bartnicki as "arranger." Here, once again, the entire text of the *Wake* – with the 628 pages of the original condensed in this case to 372 – is transformed by a system of musical notation. The system, however, is vastly more complicated than in *Da Capo al Finne*. Rather than deriving a minimal musical score exclusively from the musical values of the first eight letters of the alphabet, Bartnicki now employs, among many other special characters, not only

---

10 Quoted from an English translation by Bartnicki himself, sent in personal correspondence.

11 On *Da Capo al Finne*, see Gliński (2014), Evans et al. (2015, 695–7), Camurri (2016), Bugliaro (2017), Czarnecki (2017), Kearns (2017a).

those same letters (ABCDEFGH), but also the letters of the solfège set (DRMFSLT), the letters of the Indian sargam set (DGMNPRS), and the numerals of the Chinese *jianpu* notation system (1234567). Upper and lower cases now denote major and minor keys, respectively, while certain characters may or may not be underlined, to quite different potential effect. Significant possibilities exist for overlapping and intersecting musical (and music-related) meanings: *E* or *e* may thus refer to the note E, but *e* may also invoke the little finger in guitar notation. The note *e* may also occur to different effect as *é* or *è* or *ê* or *ɛ*; while HCE's siglum III may be read as E-flat (since the siglum is flat on its back) or as E-sharp (since the arms protrude upwards as three sharp spikes). Any attempt to describe the notational system in greater detail is far beyond the scope of the present work.[12]

The title and opening lines now emerge (quoted in slightly simplified form here) as:

F̲innegᴀns a̲ke̲ | | ri̲verrun, pa̲st Ev̲e and Adam's, fro̲m s erv̲e o̲f sho̲re to̲ bend of ba , bri̲ngs us b a co̲mmo̲dius̲ vi̲cus o̲f reci̲rculatio̲n bac̲k to̲ Ho̲ th Castle and Env̲iro̲ns.

The original *literary* text here is much more clearly discernible than it is in *Da Capo al Finne*, but the musical implications are much more complex. The letters *w* and *y*, not represented in any of the notational sets, thus disappear, replaced by spaces. The first word, "Finnegans," illustrates the complexity of the notational system by immediately presenting an alternate spelling of the titular "F_nnegans." The presence or absence of underlining immediately emerges as perhaps the most striking factor of the whole notational endeavour, suggesting an extraordinarily complex variety of possible musical effects. By virtue of the fact that some letters are underlined and others are not, that first word, for example, contains the relevant notes from the solfège set (F, E, S), and also the note *ni* from the Indian sargam set three times.

Bartnicki's explanatory notes (2014a, 382–3), moreover, indicate that the underlined group *ga* represents the Byzantine note *gá* (Fa in solfège) and the underlined group *ke* the Byzantine note *ké* (La in solfège) in the second word of the title. Limiting further explorations to just the next three words, we discover that, by virtue of underlining, *i* refers to the index finger in guitar notation, *v* indicates *sull'arco* (up bow), *pa* the Byzantine note *pá* (Re in solfège), and *v sull'arco* once again, while the frequently recurring *o* indicates an open string. And so on, in

---

12 On *F_nnegans a_e*, see Bartnicki (2014a, 373–90), Kearns (2017a, 105–9).

daunting detail, for 372 closely printed pages. Responding to a query if he considered the project playable, Bartnicki asserted in personal correspondence that it is indeed playable, "but since it is a conceptual piece, I do not think it ever will be."

In both of Bartnicki's musical transformations, the procedure "consists of rewriting Joyce's text faithfully with the omission of musically insignificant signs," an activity that "makes Joyce's text *as literature* absent from the perceptual stratum of the pieces: the text is entirely transformed into musical sounds" (Czarnecki 2017, 125, 130). Both transformations comment essentially on the degree to which readers and translators may make an untranslatable *FW* their own by means of their chosen system of personal transfiguration. Bartnicki states provocatively in his afterword to *F_nnegans a_e* that "*Finnegans Wake* does not exist" (given the multitude of textual variants that at this point share the same title) and that "Joyce's work is never his" (given the irrepressible variability of readers' reactions) (2014a, 373, 375). Derek Pyle puts the matter succinctly: "The central question lurking within Bartnicki's music is: Who can say what is or is not a valid way of reading, or otherwise entering, *Finnegans Wake*?" (Evans et al. 2015, 696).

The same question even more obviously applies to Bartnicki's third and even more extraordinary intersemiotic adventure, *Finnegans Meet* (2015). This time the "translation" is no longer in musical but in "verbovisual" terms, in the form, that is to say, of a Rolodex transformation of Joyce's text, involving a rotary business card holder, compiled together with the Polish visual artist Marcin Szmandra, whose page-by-page illustrations of *Finneganów tren* had been appearing online since 2012.[13] Instead of trying merely to illustrate fragments of the *Wake*, however, Bartnicki, the instigator of the project, suggested that each page of Joyce's text should be assigned its own calling card, identifying a particular person, name, or theme to serve as the textual subject of a business card. Each card thus carries a quasi-name, an ostensible address, and an ostensible telephone number that in fact refers to the appropriate page and line of the *Wake*. The concept, involving an extreme form of "liberature," involved having each card, in principle 628 of them, eventually being mounted in a two-column Rolodex, which would not only serve to evoke the circular structure of the novel, but would also demonstrate the highly aleatory relationship between the cards across the two columns.

---

13 For examples of Szmandra's work, see his personal blog *Finneganowizje* (https://finneganowizje.tumblr.com/).

Inez Okulska (2016, 67) aptly notes the similarity of the concept informing *Finnegans Meet* to that of Raymond Queneau's celebrated *Cent mille milliards de poèmes* (1961), a radically experimental work justifiably regarded as one of the classic examples of "liberature" (Fajfer 2008). Queneau's brilliantly conceived endeavour involves a set of ten sonnets, printed on card with each line on a separate strip and any line from any particular sonnet interchangeable with any corresponding line from the nine other sonnets. *Finnegans Meet*, as Okulska observes, operates in a fashion that is in principle strikingly similar, "since by randomly flipping the cards of the Rolodex, the user destabilizes the initial narrative setting and begins to create a new one of their own" (2016, 67). Bartnicki and Szmandra's jointly self-published project was completed in December 2015, presented physically in a number of public exhibitions in Poland, and offered to potential purchasers in a variety of formats – though mostly, for reasons of cost, without the rotary card holder. As in the case of *F_nnegans a_e*, it thus remains essentially a highly imaginative conceptual piece.[14]

Jarniewicz (Polish, 2015)

A Polish translation of *Finn's Hotel* (2013) by Jerzy Jarniewicz appeared in Warsaw in 2015. Jarniewicz (born 1958) had translated *A Portrait of the Artist as a Young Man* into Polish ten years earlier, in 2005.

4 Chinese

Dai's Chinese Wake: Fēnnígēn de shǒulíng yè *(2012)*

Considerably later than either Japanese or Korean, Chinese also joined the universe of *Wake* translations in 2012, when with enormous fanfare a Chinese version of *FW* I.1–8 by Congrong Dai, one of the few female translators of *FW*, appeared in Shanghai.[15] "More than fifty media outlets around the world reported the news" (Li and Cheng 2013, 121). Translating *FW* into Chinese clearly involves difficulties that may be ultimately insuperable: Anthony Burgess, for example, once asserted that Chinese "is a tongue incapable of admitting puns" (1982, 187). The difficulties begin, of course, with the title, which Dai renders as 芬尼根的守灵夜 (*Fēnnígēn de shǒulíng yè*). The first three graphs or characters

---

14 On *Finnegans Meet*, see Gliński (2015), Okulska (2016).

15 Li and Cheng note that the book, though bearing the date 2012, actually appeared only in January 2013 (2013, 127n10).

here (芬尼根, *fēn ní gēn*) individually mean "fragrant, Buddhist nun, root," and the difficulty of construing the meaning of the three together is a clue to the Chinese reader that they in fact transliterate a non-Chinese word or name. Here, combining as *Fēnnígēn*, they suggest a phonetic rendering of "Finnegan." The fourth graph (的, *de*) is a possessive marker similar to the apostrophe as used in normal English (though dispensed with in Joyce's own title). The last three graphs (守灵夜, *shǒulíng yè*) translate as "night vigil" (or, more darkly, "night deathwatch"). It is possible to render the title without the last graph (夜, *yè*), meaning "night," thus yielding "Finnegan's vigil," and Dai notes in her introduction that she considered leaving out that last character, since the original title does not explicitly mention a time of day, but eventually chose to add it to the title because "night" connotes not only finality but also the expectation of daybreak.[16] The term *shǒulíng* (守灵) by itself does not imply awakening or suggest resurrection or revival. *Fēnnígēn*, meanwhile, can be interpreted as either singular or plural, since Chinese nouns generally do not have singular and plural forms.[17]

Dai (born 1971) wrote her doctoral dissertation on *Ulysses*, has published extensively on *Finnegans Wake*, has translated several scholarly books from English into Chinese, and is a professor of comparative literature at Fudan University in Shanghai. She reportedly spent two years making detailed notes before translating a single word of the *Wake*. Writing in a progress report, after four years of work already, of the extraordinary difficulty involved in putting the *Wake* into Chinese, and having found that she needs three days to translate a single page and a fourth day to revise it, she admits that "I tend to feel as though I am in a nightmare that I am not sure I can endure" (2010, 585). One sympathizes: she began her actual rendering in 2006, and Book I appeared six years later, the 216 pages of Joyce's original having expanded more than threefold to 775 pages, more than half of them devoted to explanatory notes for Chinese readers certain to be completely puzzled (Dai 2013; Yun 2014).

Dai's rendering, contrary to all likely expectations, quickly became nothing short of a publishing sensation, largely due to promotional efforts on an extraordinary scale by the publisher Shanghai Renmin Chubanshe (Shanghai People's Publishing House). Dai herself reports that the success is also due, rather paradoxically, at least partly to the

---

16 In 2007 Dai published a preliminary study (in Chinese) on the difficulty of reading *FW*. The title of the study refers to *FW* as "*Fennigen de shou ling*," omitting the graph *yè*.

17 This account paraphrases an instructive discussion by Cordell Yee (2013).

fact that many Chinese readers, tired of undemanding mass-market fiction, "expect works to be difficult and they expect to have to spend time deciphering them" (2013, 1). Her translation therefore deliberately draws upon the format of ancient Chinese texts, such as expository writings on the Confucian classics, typically consisting of "the original text printed in a large font; the explanation or commentary printed in a medium font following the original word or sentence to be explained; the detailed explanation printed in a smaller font and put into two lines following the first explanation." Dai's rendering adopts a similar three-part format involving a facing-page arrangement: the main translated text in a large font on the left-hand page; other possible meanings following in a medium font the individual word or phrase to be explained; more detailed explanations or commentary presented on the right-hand page.

The similarity between the formats therefore gives the reader of the Chinese *Wake* a sense of the learned tradition, "implying that it too is to be highly respected and much researched. It also implies the existence of an 'industry' surrounding the text" and that the existence of this industry "implies a profound and enlightening knowledge to which literate readers must devote their time and patience." Dai concludes that the difficulty is entirely functional: "A difficult work like *Finnegans Wake* should not be translated into a popular fiction." The difficulty, for both translator and readers, is increased by the fact that while there are some seven thousand commonly used Chinese characters, even that number is quite inadequate for the complexity of Joyce's text, in dealing with which new Chinese characters need to be generated in order to render Joyce's often extravagant neologisms, "each component indicating one of the possible meanings that Joyce put into his portmanteau words" (Dai 2013, 1).[18] As to the actual number of characters employed in Dai's rendering of Book I, Li and Cheng, who praise the "lucid and melodious language" of the translation, report a total of eight hundred thousand, while estimating that the translation of the entire *Wake* would be likely to involve about two million (2013, 121, 127n10).

The translator's personal travails were obvious. Various sources recycle Dai's report that she often quarrelled with her husband – he wanted her to go to bed; she wanted to stay awake and translate – and was driven to distraction trying to balance the project with family obligations. "My body suffered from the work, working every night," she said. "I looked older than I should be. My eyes became dark, and

---

18   On Dai's Chinese rendering, see Dai (2010, 2013, 2015), Li and Cheng (2013), O'Sullivan and Yip (2013), He (2014), McGrath (2014), Yun (2014).

my skin wasn't that good either." Her responses when asked when the complete translation might be forthcoming reportedly include "May God give me the courage to finish it" and "Don't ask me. I don't know any more than you do" (McGrath 2014).

Congrong Dai reported in late 2019 that she had by then received so many invitations to give lectures and interviews that she had to ask her publisher to decline all of them. She also reported that the publisher had no copies at all of the translation left, the entire edition of eight thousand copies having completely sold out – and that she was indeed continuing to work on a complete and similarly annotated translation, having spent the intervening seven years on the endeavour. By then she expected Book II to appear by the end of 2020, and Books III–IV, in a third volume, at some later point.[19]

While the daunting scope of Dai's translatorial task is universally acknowledged and her courageous efforts to respond to it almost universally lauded by reviewers, Chu He has unsurprisingly observed in a detailed textual analysis that "annotations may do well to inform and explain, but they cannot provide Chinese readers with comparable aesthetic experiences. ... Chinese readers are told what wordplays are intended in Joyce's original words, but they don't feel the playfulness nor do they experience the fun at first hand in their own language" (2014, 2).

The following lines are a small part of a textual sample offered by Dai herself, first in Chinese characters (omitted here), then in Pinyin romanization, and finally in her own explanatory back-translation into English (2013, 1):

In Joyce's original:

Sir Tristram, violer d'amores, fr'over the short sea, had passencore rearrived from North Armorica on this side the scraggy isthmus of Europe Minor to wielderfight his penisolate war (*FW* 3.4–6)

Dai's Pinyin romanization:

tè lǐ sī tè lā mǔ jué shi, ài de tí qín shǒu, yuè guò ài er lán hǎi, hái méi yǒu, | zái cí jīng guò cóng bù liè tǎ ní bàn dǎo běi bù, chóng lái xiǎo ōu zhōu nà cēng cī bù qī de dì xiá, | jǐng bù | yī xī, zài dǎ tā de bàn dǎo zhàn zhēng

---

19 My thanks to Congrong Dai for providing this information in personal
    correspondence.

Dai's back-translation:

Sir Tristram, violist of love, over the Naut Short Sea, not yet / pass encore rearrived on the scraggy isthmus / Issy of Europe Minor from the North Armorica to fight again his peninsular war / isolate pen war / penis war

Sir Tristram's name, one notices, metamorphoses splendidly (at least for an English-language reader), acquiring no fewer than four extra syllables in the process, into a Pinyin "Telisitelamu" – or more accurately, "tè lǐ sī tè lā mǔ." Butt and Taff, meanwhile, later become "bā tè hé tà fū" (Dai 2013, 1).[20]

5 Japanese

Hamada's Japanese Wake: Fineganzu ueiku *(2012, 2014)*

Tatsuo Hamada's rendering of *FW* I.2–4 and IV appeared, as mentioned, in 2008 in the *Abiko Annual*, and the following year, with the completion of Book I, saw his version of Books I and IV, which appeared in Abiko, near Tokyo, under the title (as romanized) *Fineganzu ueiku, pato 1 to 4*. Books II and III appeared three years later (as *Fineganzu ueiku, pato 2 to 3*), bringing his complete rendering to its conclusion, in 2012. After a further two years, in October 2014, at the age of seventy-nine, Hamada published a 974-page revised version of his complete Japanese rendering of *FW*.

Hamada's renderings, however, despite his sustained efforts over more than a decade, are reported to have had little resonance in Japan; Eishiro Ito reports in personal correspondence that all of Hamada's books and translations were out of print as of March 2020, or at least unavailable either through Japanese bookstores or online.[21]

6 German

Rathjen's German Wake: Winnegans Fake *(2012)*

Friedhelm Rathjen's *Winnegans Fake* (2012b) is a rendering of more than 230 pages of excerpts from *FW*, published in his own self-published

---

20 Eishiro Ito (2004) notes that in Japanese Sir Tristram's name (romanized) likewise becomes a hexasyllabic "Torisutoramu" for both Naoki Yanase (1991) and Kyoko Miyata (2004).

21 My thanks to Eishiro Ito for kindly carrying out bibliographical research in Japan on this matter.

series, Edition ReJoyce.[22] Rathjen had begun translating excerpts from *FW* almost thirty years earlier, in 1984 (Rathjen 2012b, 7). *Winnegans Fake* contains all of his numerous previously published excerpts from *FW* other than those separately published in his *Geschichten von Shem und Shaun*, which also appeared in 2012.

The playful title *Winnegans Fake*, drawing on Joyce's own phrase "Wimmegame's fake" (*FW* 375.16–17), humorously makes the point that translators of *FW* may very well "win" some translational battles and will undoubtedly lose a great many more (such as, for example, not getting the first word or even the first letter of the first word of the title right), and however impressive their wins may be, they will also inevitably produce a *Wake* that is fake. *Winnegans Fake*, which has Joyce's original in parallel-text format, has numerous comments, is extensively annotated, and includes a bibliography of all German translations of and from *FW*. It appeared in 111 signed and numbered copies. For Fritz Senn, Rathjen's rendering "amounts to a fair, representative selection of the whole" (Senn 2013, 871), thus to at least some extent in the tradition of Burgess's *A Shorter Finnegans Wake* (1966). While Rathjen suggests in his preface that this collection is likely to be his last foray into German versions of *FW*, Senn expresses the hope that this translator's "commendable work in progress" (2013, 874) over the previous three decades will continue. Further renderings by Rathjen did in fact appear in 2012, 2014, 2015, and 2020.

Andreas Puff-Trojan reports a comment by Rathjen during an interview in 2012 on how he sees his own renderings: "I replace the English-language version by a German-language version, with the result that in my renderings you may very well still not understand anything, but you will be significantly better equipped to suspect what it is that you are not understanding. *Finnegans Wake*, meanwhile, is not a book to be understood, but rather one to be experienced."[23]

Rathjen (German, 2012, 2014, 2015)

In addition to *Winnegans Fake*, the year 2012 also saw a second significant *Wake* translation by Friedhelm Rathjen. Each of these two

---

22 The excerpts in question are: Book I: 3, 6, 11–13, 22–9, 30–47, 58, 92–3, 102–3, 104–11; Book II: 219–24, 229, 250, 257–9, 260–1, 276, 307–8, 316, 336–7, 342, 353, 371–82, 383–99; Book III: 410–12, 420–8, 433–40, 448–73, 483–527, 531–40, 555–63, 564–82, 582–90; Book IV: 627–8). On Rathjen's rendering, see Senn (2013).

23 "Ich ersetze also die englischsprachige Basis durch eine deutschsprachige, so dass Sie jetzt in meinen Fassungen zwar immer noch nichts verstehen mögen, aber deutlich besser erahnen können, was es ist, das Sie da nicht verstehen. *Finnegans Wake* ist im Übrigen kein Buch zum Verstehen, sondern eher eines zum Erleben" (Puff-Trojan 2012).

renderings was a result, to quote Fritz Senn, of "the long-awaited expiration of copyright" (2013, 871). *Geschichten von Shem und Shaun* (2012a), published in Berlin by Suhrkamp Verlag, is Rathjen's rendering of *Tales Told of Shem and Shaun*, and includes, with Joyce's original text on facing pages, "Der Mauchs und der Traufen" (7–23), "Die verdreck-teste Sacke die jemals hörbetrüben ward" (25–75), and "Der Aumvaise und der Gnadshoffer" (77–87), renderings respectively of "The Mookse and the Gripes" (*FW* 152–9), "The Muddest Thick That Was Ever Heard Dump" (*FW* 282–304), and "The Ondt and the Gracehoper" (*FW* 414–19).[24] These renderings were originally scheduled by the Suhrkamp Verlag to appear as early as 1992, but persistent copyright complications delayed their appearance by no less than twenty years. Rathjen's highly praised and award-winning translation of *A Portrait of the Artist as a Young Man* also appeared in 2012, the third German translation of that text, following on earlier renderings by Georg Goyert in 1926 and by Klaus Reichert in 1972.

A German translation by Rathjen of *Finn's Hotel* (2013) appeared in Frankfurt am Main in October 2014. In the same year he edited *Mamalujo: Drei Fassungen eines Kapitels aus Finnegans Wake*. The volume appeared in his series Edition ReJoyce in a limited edition of 111 signed and numbered copies. Designed to demonstrate for German readers three stages in the development of the Mamalujo chapter (II.4; *FW* 383–99), the volume presents, in Joyce's original English with Rathjen's translations on facing pages, first the two sketches of 1923 recently translated by him in his 2014 rendering of *Finn's Hotel*; then the first printed version of 1924, translated into German by Rathjen for the first time; and finally the version that appeared as *FW* II.4, first translated by Rathjen in Reichert and Senn's *Finnegans Wake Deutsch* (1989, 220–37).

In 2015 Rathjen edited *Earwicker: Fünf Fassungen eines Kapitels aus Finnegans Wake*. The volume appeared in his series Edition ReJoyce in a limited edition of 111 signed and numbered copies. Designed to demonstrate for German readers five stages in the development of the Earwicker chapter, the volume presents two sketches from 1923, printed versions from 1925 and 1927, and the final text of I.2 (*FW* 30–47), in English in each case with Rathjen's translations on facing pages. His translation of *FW* I.2 first appeared in Reichert and Senn's *Finnegans Wake Deutsch* (1989, 45–63).

---

24 On Rathjen's rendering, see Koch (2012), Puff-Trojan (2012).

7 Danish

Laugesen (Danish, 2012)

The Danish translation of the opening pages of *ALP* (*FW* 196.1–201.4) by Peter Laugesen that had appeared in 2009 in the Norwegian literary journal *Vagant* was reprinted without changes to the text in 2012 in Copenhagen in the Danish literary journal *Trappe Tusind*.[25]

8 Dutch

Bindervoet and Henkes's Dutch ALP *(2013)*

A separately published Dutch translation of *ALP* by Erik Bindervoet and Robbert-Jan Henkes appeared in an attractive small volume in Amsterdam in 2013, reprinted from their 2002 translation of *FW*, but with the addition of an extensive commentary (in Dutch) on the texual development of *ALP* – and including also "basic Dutch" ("basis nederlands") translations (88–9, 131–2) of Ogden's Basic English renderings of *FW* 213.11–34 and *FW* 215.31–216.5.[26]

Ogden's rendering of *FW* 215.31–5, 216.3–5:

No sound but the waters of. The dancing waters of. Winged things in flight, field-rats louder than talk. Ho! Are you not gone, ho! What Tom Malone? No sound but the noise of these things, the Liffey and all its waters of. Ho, talk safe keep us! There's no moving this my foot. I seem as old as that tree over there. A story of Shaun or Shem but where? ... Say it, say it, tree! Night night! The story say of stem or stone. By the side of the river waters of, this way and that way waters of. Night!

In Bindervoet and Henkes's "basic Dutch":

Geen geluid behalve de wateren van. De dansende wateren van. Gevleugelde dingen in volle vlucht, veldratten luider dan praten. Ho! Moet je nog niet gaan, ho! Welke Tammerlaan? Geen geluid behalve het lawaai van deze dingen de Liffey en al haar wateren van. Ho, veilig praten bewaar ons! Ik kan deze voet van me niet bewegen. Ik lijk wel zo oud als die

---

25 My thanks to Karl Emil Rosenbæk for kindly sending me an electronic copy of the relevant issue of *Trappe Tusind*.

26 My thanks to Erik Bindervoet and Robbert-Jan Henkes for kindly sending me a copy of their Dutch *ALP*.

boom daar. Een verhaal van Shaun of Shem maar waar? ... Zeg het, zeg
het, boom! Nacht nacht! Vertel me verhaal van stam of steen. Aan de kant
van de rivierwateren van, de deze kant an die kant op wateren van. Nacht!

An amusing touch here is the transformation of Tom Malone. As in
2002, the Dutch translators render the "Thom Malone" of *FW* I.8 as
"Thom Malaan," conflating "Malone," the Indian river Malan, and the
German Lahn. They render Ogden's "Tom Malone" as a humorously
incongruous "Tammerlaan," summoning up the fourteenth-century
Mongol conqueror Tamerlane – primarily in order to facilitate the four-
fold fluvial evocation of the English Tamar, German Ammer, Russian
Amur, and German Lahn.

9 Greek

Anevlavis's Greek Wake: I agrýpnia ton Fínnegan *(2013)*

A complete Greek translation of *FW* by Eleftherios Anevlavis appeared
in Athens in April 2013 under the title Η αγρύπνια των Φίννεγκαν
(*I agrýpnia ton Fínnegan*). Anevlavis, born in 1943 in the town of Liva-
deia in central Greece, and a retired specialist in internal medicine at
a major hospital in Athens, reportedly spent seven years on the translation.[27] Online advertisements for the book (which I have not seen)
indicate that the 628 pages of the original expand, more than doubling,
to no less than 1,608 pages in the Greek text. The title suggests a pluralized "Finnegans' wake" in the funeral sense, Modern Greek *agrýpnia*
meaning "wake, vigil."

Anevlavis's Greek incipit (FW 3.1–3), as quoted in an online review
(Politismou 2013), reads as follows:

ποταμορροή, πίσω από την εκκλησία της Εύας και του Αδάμ, από το
σκέρτσο της ακτής στον μυχό του κόλπου, μας γυρίζει με κόμοδο βικόκυκλο
επανακύκλησης πίσω στο Κάστρο του Χοθ και τα Περίχωρα.

potamorroí, píso apó tin ekklisía tis Évas kai tou Adám, apó to skértso
tis aktís ston mychó tou kólpou, mas gyrízei me kómodo vikókyklo epanakýklisis píso sto Kástro tou Choth kai ta Períchora.

Anevlavis's version, transliterated, suggests, roughly, "river (*potámi*)
flow (*roí*), behind (*píso apó*) the church (*tin ekklisía*) of Eve and Adam (*tis*

---

27 On Anevlavis's Greek rendering, see Politismou (2013).

Évas kai tou Adám) from the play of the shore (*apó to skértso tis aktís*) to the head of the bay (*ston mychó tou kólpou*), returns us (*mas gyrízei*) by a comfortable (*kómodo*) Vico-circle (*kyklo*) of recirculation (*epanakýklisis*) back to the (*píso sto*) Castle (*Kástro*) of Howth (*tou Choth*) and its environs (*kai ta Períchora*)." Both Commodus and Vico are clearly in evidence; Howth is strangely metamorphosed in the foreign alphabet; and HCE's initials disappear without trace – or at any rate are replaced by the word-initials of the phrase "Κάστρο του Χοθ και τα Περίχωρα." A question that immediately comes to mind is how the translator will handle the numerous appearances and evocations of HCE throughout the text.

Babassakis (Greek, 2014)

A Greek translation by George-Icaros Babassakis of *Finn's Hotel* (2013) appeared in Athens in March 2014. Babassakis, born in 1960, is a poet, writer, and translator, whose translations include works by Nabokov, Bukowski, Henry Miller, Joseph Conrad, Conan Doyle, and Agatha Christie. He lives in Athens.

10 Swedish

Falk (Swedish, 2013)

Bertil Falk, born in Stockholm in 1933, is a journalist, translator, prolific author of mystery novels, and a publisher. A lifelong *Finnegans Wake* enthusiast, in December 2013, at the age of eighty, he produced a Swedish rendering of *FW* I.1, privately published in just eighty-five numbered copies in the small town of Trelleborg, the southernmost town of Sweden, as a Christmas gift for business colleagues and friends (Engholm 2013). It appeared under the title *Finnegans likvaka*, "Finnegan's wake," *likvaka* literally meaning a "corpse (*lik*) watch (*vaka*)" but also a "vigil," and thus suggesting also the possibility of a new day. Falk's rendering humorously describes itself on the title page as "transformulerad til swensko," literally, "transformulated," and not quite to Swedish (*till svenska*) but to something close to Swedish, namely, "til swensko," just as Joyce's original is written not quite in English but in something close to English. As in the case of Stündel's German *Finnegans Wehg* (1993), the lack of an apostrophe in Falk's Swedish (as opposed to Joyce's English) title is necessarily reductive, producing an unambiguously singular "Finnegan's."

Falk published his rendering under his own private imprint Zen Zat (the name a punning interlingual combination of "Zen" and "then that"). He reports elsewhere (Falk 2008, 142) that over many years, purely as a hobby, he has in fact worked with translating most of the *Wake*, but that other than this opening chapter nothing has been published, nor are there any further publishing plans. *Finnegans likvaka* was subsequently recorded by the publisher BTJ's library service as a four-hour CD, read by David Zetterstad, for the Swedish Agency for Accessible Media (Myndigheten för tillgängliga media), which produces and distributes literature, newspapers, and periodicals in accessible format to persons with reading impairments.[28]

In an introduction to his translation (2013, 7–21), Falk modestly describes it as just a *"klacksparksversion,"* which is to say, a straightforward, uncomplicated, and normalizing rendering intended primarily for the interest of Swedish readers new to the *Wake*. His rendering of the opening lines (*FW* 3.1–3) reads:

> flodflöde, förbi Eva och Adams, från strandens sväng till buktens böj, för oss via en behändig ström av återcirkulering tillbaka till Howth Castle och Environs.

The opening one-word conflation here, "flodflöde," alliteratively combines *flod* ("river") and *flöda* ("to flow, to run"); the river still runs past (*förbi*) Eve (now a Swedish Eva) and Adam's, runs alliteratively once again from "curve" (*sväng*) of "shore" (*strand*) to "bend" (*böj*) of "bay" (*bukt*), and "leads us" (*för oss*) by a "convenient" (*behändig*) "current" or "stream" (*ström*) of "recirculation" (*återcirkulering*) back (*tillbaka*) to Howth Castle and Environs, the three capitalized nouns of the final phrase left untranslated. Commodus and Vico are both missing, while HCE's initials are thus retained intact. The phrase "från strandens sväng till buktens böj" echoes Joyce's original particularly effectively in terms of both closely corresponding alliteration and the pleasing retention of the iambic tetrameter rhythm.

11 Portuguese

Galindo (Portuguese, 2013)

A Portuguese translation of the prankquean vignette (*FW* 21.5–23.15) by Caetano Galindo, professor of linguistics and translation at the Federal University of Paraná in Curitiba, Brazil, appeared in 2013. In

---

28 My thanks to Bertil Falk for kindly sending me a copy of his translation and for responding to requests for information.

the same year Galindo (born 1973) published a first volume of short stories and won a prestigious Brazilian literary prize for his translation of *Ulysses*. He has also translated works by Charles Darwin, Thomas Pynchon, Tom Stoppard, David Foster Wallace, and J.D. Salinger.

> It was of a night, late, lang time agone, in an auldstane eld, when Adam was delvin and his madameen spinning watersilts, ... and Jarl van Hoother had his burnt head high up in his lamphouse, laying cold hands on himself (*FW* 21.5–6, 9–11).

Galindo's rendering:

> Heraduma noite, tarde, munto timplo atroz, numa antaiga erdade das perdas, quando Adão socavava e sua madãominha tessia cedas d'água ... e Conte Dom Cabeço metia a testada tostada benhalta no farol queimorava, impondo mão fria assi mesmo.

Galindo's "munto timplo atroz," suggesting *muito tempo atrás* ("a long time ago"), seems to reveal ominous tones of a "terrible temple" (*templo atroz*) in the world (*mundo*) of an *antiga idade das pedras*, an "old stone age," literally an "ancient age of stones," whose difference from our own is emphasized by the disorientating strangeness of the formulation "antaiga erdade das perdas." Galindo's Adam, a Portuguese Adão, was conscientiously digging (*covava*) and pounding (*socava*) away, while his "madãominha," a "madameen" created from a rib of Adão, was spinning (*tessia*) watersilks ("cedas d'água"). The most striking thing about Jarl van Hoother is his change of name to "Conte Dom Cabeço," turning him into an Italo-Portuguese "earl" (Italian *conte*, Portuguese *conde*) – and recording only his given name, since the honorific *Dom* is always used only with the given name. The name Dom Cabeço, meanwhile, is based on the Portuguese noun *cabeça* ("head"), thus playing on the assumed Old Norse origins of the name Howth as meaning "head."

Galindo (Portuguese, 2014)

Caetano Galindo's Portuguese rendering of *Finn's Hotel* (2013) appeared in São Paulo in June 2014.[29]

---

29 On Galindo's rendering, see Amarante (2015, 79–83).

Scandolara (Portuguese, 2014)

A Portuguese translation by Adriano Scandolara of the closing and opening lines of *FW* (626.29–628.16; 3.1–5.12) appeared in the online review *escamandro* in June 2014. Scandolara, born 1988 in Curitiba, Brazil, is a poet, translator of Shelley and Milton, and a teacher of English at the Federal University of Paraná in Curitiba.

His rendering of the opening three lines (*FW* 3.1–3):

> rivieras, passando Eva e Adão, da curva da costa à boca da baía, nos leva por um cômodo vico de recirculação de volta a Howth, Castelo e Entornos.

The opening word, "rivieras," is plural, following on from the final line "A via a sós a mor a fim a lém das." The plural is readable as implying, in the first word already, that Anna Livia is not just a single river but a representative of all rivers everywhere. The subject of the now completed sentence, as in most other versions, but more obviously so, is the singular noun phrase "a via" – where Joyce's indefinite article *a* in "a way" is translated (by being left alone) into the Portuguese definite article *a*. Joyce's alliteration is pleasingly replicated (though "bend of bay" becomes "the mouth of the bay"), Eve and Adam retain their Joycean order, Commodus and Vico are likewise retained, as are HCE's initials – though the final comma implies a reading not as "to Howth Castle and Environs" but rather "to Howth, with its Castle and Environs."

Amarante's Portuguese Wake *(2018)*

The year 2018 also saw a Portuguese rendering by Dirce Waltrick do Amarante, in the tradition of Anthony Burgess's *A Shorter Finnegans Wake* (1966), of a book-length series of excerpts illustrating just one possible narrative thread through *FW*. In 2019, the volume, entitled *Finnegans Wake (por um fio)*, literally, "*Finnegans Wake* (by a thread)," was awarded the Brazilian Boris Schnaiderman prize for excellence in translation.

Amarante's version of the opening three lines (*FW* 3.1–3) reads:

> correorrio, após Adão e Eva, da contornada costa à encurvada enseada, nos leva por um commodius vicus recirculante de volta para Howth Castle e Entornos.

Here "correorrio" is readable as conflating *rio* ("river"), *correr* ("to run"), and even a hint of *correio* ("postman"), as if already evoking the figure of Shaun the Post. The river runs "após Adão e Eva," literally, "after (*após*) Adam and Eve," reversing the original gendered reversal and readable as conflating the Dublin church and, more obviously, the biblical pair who lend it their name. The alliterative "contornada costa" precedes a rhyming "encurvada enseada," the alliteration continuing for the adjective *encurvada* ("curved") but stopping short of the noun *enseada* ("bay"). "Commodius vicus," treated as if it were Latin, remains untranslated, while HCE's initials are unproblematically retained by means of the conveniently available noun *entornos* ("surroundings, environs").[30]

Lines (*FW* 627.34–628.2, 15–16) from her (selective) rendering of the final page:

Estou esvaindo. Ó amargo fim! Escapulirei antes deles levantarem. Nunca verão. Nem saberão. Nem sentirão minha falta. E é velho e velho é triste e velho é triste e cansativo eu volto pra você, meu gélido pai, meu gélido e louco pai. ... Um caminho um só um último um amoroso por onde

Amaral (Portuguese, 2019)

A Portuguese translation by Vitor Alevato do Amaral (Amaral 2019, 154) of the opening lines of III.3 (*FW* 474.1–3) appeared online in an article on comparative Portuguese translations of *FW*:

Lowly, longly, a wail went forth. Pure Yawn lay low. On the mead of the hillock lay, heartsoul dormant mid shadowed landshape, brief wallet to his side, and arm loose [...]

Amaral's rendering:

Ligeiro, longo, um lamento elevou-se. Puro Yawn levemente aleitado. No limpo campo da colina aleitado, fundamente adormecido em meio à ensombrecida vista, sacola de epístolas ao lado, e braço desleixado [...]

Galindo (Portuguese, 2019)

A Portuguese translation of the Mutt and Jute dialogue (*FW* 15.29–18.30) by Caetano Galindo appeared in December 2019 in the Brazilian online journal *Qorpus*.

---

30 On Amarante's Portuguese rendering, see Amaral (2019), Amarante (2019).

12 Finnish

Helin (Finnish, 2013)

The Finnish poet Hannu Helin (1944–2015), from Helsinki, was the author of numerous collections of poems – including one collection in English with the distinctly Joycean title *Pomes penyho* (2009). In 2013, under the punning quasi-English title "Finnegans Sake," he contributed what he himself described, according to Lauri Niskanen, as just "one suggestion for a 'translation' of the first book of Finnegan" to a volume entitled *Mitä Finnegans Wake tarkoittaa?* (What does *Finnegans Wake* mean?), edited by Ville-Juhani Sutinen, published in Turku by Savukeidas, and consisting mostly of several academic essays, thus suggesting a latter-day Finnish variation on *Our Exagmination Round His Factification for Incamination of Work in Progress.*[31]

Helin's contribution is in fact a long poem of roughly the same length as *FW* I.1. The elastic term *translation* is stretched to an extreme in Helin's poem, an exercise in very free association, drawing on the actual text of *FW* only at several removes. The opening three lines (Helin 2013, 106), which one might naively have expected to demonstrate some degree of direct reference to *FW* 3.1–3, read as follows, in an energetic trochaic rhythm:

hullun härän sarvet ja förbe aaton l'hiver il court
riimut kutka stephen kirjaa mollyn virtsalla
kahden penkan ja huulten välissä yöastia tristram

Lacking all knowledge of Finnish, and simply working one's way through these lines with the word-for-word help of Google Translate, one discovers the following linguistic matrix:

hullun ["mad"] härän ["bovine"] sarvet ["the horns"] ja ["and"] förbe [Swedish *förbi*, German *vorbei* "past"] aaton [*aatto* "eve, vigil"] l'hiver [French *l'hiver* "winter"] il court [French *il court* "it runs, flows"] riimut [*runes*] kutka [*whose*] stephen kirjaa [*kirja* "book"] mollyn virtsalla [*urine*] kahden ["the two of them"] penkan [*penkka* "bank"] ja huulten ["lips"] välissä ["between"] yöastia ["commode"] tristram

---

31 My thanks to Lauri Niskanen of the University of Helsinki for drawing Helin's work to my attention, for detailed linguistic information on Finnish, and for a lively exchange of opinions on the most appropriate back-translation into English of the first three lines of *Finnegans Sake.*

A further step suggests something like the following:

like a mad (*hullun*) bull's (*härän*) horns (*sarvet*) and past (Swedish *förbi*)
Eve (*aatto* "eve") and Adam (*Aadam*), the winter (*l'hiver*) river ("-iver")
runs (*court*), runes (*riimut*) whose (*kutka*) Stephen writes (*kirja* "book") in
Molly's urine (*virtsalla*) between (*välissä*) two (*kahden*) banks (*penkka*) and
two lips (*huulten*), another Tristan, a commode (*yöastia*)

This in turn suggests the following as a roughly approximate
back-translation:

A mad bull's horns, the winter river runs past eve and adam,
runes whose stephen writes in molly's urine
between two banks, two lips, a tristram, a commode.

Here the mad bull's horns may be read as suggesting the swirling currents of a raging river, perhaps reminding us that an older
Irish name of the Liffey was *Ruirthech* ("swift, rapid"), perhaps also
evoking the early medieval Irish epic *Táin Bó Cuailnge* (*The Cattle
Raid of Cooley*) with its iconic culminating battle of two raging bulls,
the brown bull of Ulster and the white bull of Connacht, a taurine
anticipation of the fraternal strife of Shem and Shaun. Scraps of
foreign languages, French, Swedish, German, are borne along on
the flood, almost but not quite concealing the presence of Eve and
Adam.

Eve, already introduced by *aatto* ("eve"), is present once again ("-ive-")
in *l'hiver*, which also implicitly suggests both the river ("-iver") and
a wintry climate. Reversing the biblical creation of Eve from a rib of
Adam, here Adam (*Aadam*) is linguistically generated from the noun
aatto, which introduces Eve. The river's runes (*riimut*) go beyond the
immediate text of *FW* (in the second line already) to suggest a related
Joycean text in which a lower-case Stephen potentially plays the role
of Tristan to Molly's Isolde, Bloom's Mark. The flow of the river is
reflected in the flow of lower-case Molly's urine, in which the fluvial
runes have Stephen write his earthy runes, a combined flowing song
of two banks, two lips, celebrating the river and celebrating love. The
emperor Commodus is playfully suggested at an interlingual remove
by *yöastia*, a "commode," while there is no identifiable sign yet either of
Vico or of Howth Castle and Environs. Even swerve of shore and bend
of bay have likewise disappeared, subordinated to the rushing current
of the wintry Finnish river.

13 Romanian

Miroiu (Romanian, 2014)

A Romanian translation of *Finn's Hotel* (2014) by Mihai Miroiu, who also contributed a long introduction, appeared in Bucharest in 2014. Miroiu is also the translator of works by Virginia Woolf, Scott Fitzgerald, and Laurence Sterne among others, as well as of Joyce's *Stephen Hero*.

14 Serbian

Stojaković's Serbian Wake: Finegana buđenje *(2014, 2017)*

Siniša Stojaković, born in Belgrade, Serbia, in 1966, graduated from the University of Belgrade with a degree in mechanical engineering. Based in Belgrade, he is the webmaster of the *Finnegans Wake* website finwake.com. His Serbian rendering of *FW* I appeared in 2014, followed by *FW* III/IV (rather than *FW* II) in 2017, both volumes published by the Pasus publishing house in Belgrade. The 2017 volume of the Serbian "book of the dark" quizzically features a reproduction of Rembrandt's *Night Watch* on the front cover.

The opening lines (*FW* 3.1–3) in Stojaković's 2014 translation of *FW* I read as follows:

> rečnotrčkaranje kraj hrama Eve i Adama, od skretaja obale do zavoja zaliva, vodi nas komodnim začaranim krugom recirkulacije nazad do Zamka Hout i Krajolika.

This back-translates roughly as "river (*rečni*) running (*trčkaranje*) past (*kraj*) the church (*hram*) of Eve and Adam, from turn (*skret*) of shore (*obala*) to bend (*zavoj*) of bay (*zaliv*), leads us (*vodi nas*) by a *komodnim* vicious (*začaranim*) circle (*krug*) of recirculation (*recirkulacije*) back (*nazad*) to *Hout* Castle (*zamak*) and Environs (*krajolik*)." The opening "rečnotrčkaranje" is unusual among renderings in expanding the originally trisyllabic "riverrun" from three to six syllables. While the term *trčkaranje* specifically means "running with small steps," the linguistically unrelated term *karanje* means "scolding," suggesting a river hurrying along muttering and grumbling to itself. Eve and Adam's is specifically identified as a church (*hram*). The term *komodnim*, introducing Commodus, plays interlingually on Joyce's "commodius" and the Serbian *komoda* ("commode"). Vico is present at a translingual remove in the "vicious circle"; Howth is Serbianized as *Hout*, since Serbian lacks both the letter *w* and the sound *th*; and HCE's initials are radically altered.

The formulation as a whole raises two interesting questions concerning appropriate readerly response in the polyglot universe of *Finnegans Wake*. In modern Dutch, *hout*, like German *Holz*, means "wood" (the material); in Middle Dutch, *hout* also means "forest," thus arguably suggesting Howth Castle on its rocky headland as also surrounded by forest – and thus, all unbeknownst to the first-time reader, already introducing the pervasive relationship of tree and stone. As for *trč-karanje*, once again, *karanje* not only means "scolding," but, vulgarly, also means "fucking," thus arguably introducing also, in the very first word, the pervasive motif of sexuality – with attention arguably drawn to the connotation since "running" can also be translated in Serbian by *trčanje*, which lacks any potential sexual implication.

Interestingly, Siniša Stojaković, in personal correspondence on this last point, observes that a Serbian reader, aware that there is no such individual word as **trč*, would be quite unlikely to see the word *karanje* as at all present in the word *trčkaranje*. For a reader unfamiliar with (and thus untrammelled by) the expectations of Serbian linguistic norms, on the other hand, such a conceivable conflation immediately suggests itself, if only because of its obvious semantic unreasonableness, as a by no means atypical example of *Wakean* serendipity.[32]

15 French

Darrieussecq (French, 2014)

In 2014 the French novelist Marie Darrieussecq (born 1969 in the French Basque country) translated into French, under the title *Brouillons d'un baiser* (Drafts of a kiss), five very early sketches by Joyce, drafted in 1923, relating to the first kiss of Tristan and Isolde, which were largely incorporated eventually in *FW* II.4. The collection is edited by Daniel Ferrer, and Valérie Bénéjam declares both the translation and the editorial apparatus to be "works of outstanding value" (2015, 12).[33]

Dirk Van Hulle (2015, 3) quotes Darrieussecq's translation of the beginning of Isolde's version of the Lord's Prayer, the original "Howfar wartnevin alibithename" becoming "Norepère quiètesosseuc tonom soixantifié" (Darrieussecq 2014, 64–5).

---

32 My thanks to Siniša Stojaković both for kindly providing the opening lines and also for a stimulating linguistic discussion. On his Serbian rendering, see Đurić (2020, 169–70).

33 On Darrieussecq's rendering, see Killeen (2014), Bénéjam (2015), Van Hulle (2015), Oliveira (2018).

Blanchon's French ALP *(2016)*

Philippe Blanchon (born 1967), poet, essayist, and translator also of Ezra Pound and T.S. Eliot among others, published a French rendering of Ogden's Basic English *ALP* in 2013, followed in 2015 by a translation, with commentaries, of a selection of the poems in *FW*.

A complete French translation of *ALP* by Blanchon appeared as a separate volume in Toulon in 2016, also containing a French rendering of *FW* 627.6–628.16 and 3.1–8.8.[34]

An excerpt (*FW* 196.1–7, 9–11) from Blanchon's opening lines of *ALP*:

Ô/ dis-moi tout / d'Anna Livia! Je veux tout entendre / d'Anna Livia. Et bien, connais-tu Anna Livia? Oui, bien sûr, nous connaissons tous Anna Livia. Dis-moi tout. Dis-moi maintenant. De l'entendre tu en mourras de rire. Et bien, tu sais, quand le vieux patère s'est retiré et a fait ce que tu sais. ... Ou quoi que ce fût qu'ils pelotèrent, qu'ils essayèrent de découvrir qu'il fît dans le Fieffé Park.

Here the initial "Ô" (as in Jacques Aubert's edition of Beckett and Péron's *Anna Livia Pluratself*) not only retains Joyce's original opening "O" and its conflated symbolic potential but also succeeds, by means of the strategically placed circumflex, in conveying a humorously minimalist suggestion of a fluvial delta. "De l'entendre tu en mourras de rire" rather cautiously explains that Joyce's "You'll die when you hear" actually means only to die laughing. The "old cheb" who "went futt" loses both of his fluvial associations, becoming just an old geezer (*patère*) who withdrew (*s'est retiré*) from the rules of normal behaviour and did "what you know" (*ce que tu sais*). The final sentence in particular is very much a normalizing version of Joyce's complex formulation "Or whatever it was they threed to make out he thried to two in the Fiendish park" (*FW* 196.9–11). The reference to the fact that there were three watchers and two watched disappears in Blanchon's rendering, which limits itself to "whatever it was that they cobbled together (*qu'ils pelotèrent*), whatever it was that they tried to reveal (*découvrir*) that he did." The sexual connotation of the verb *peloter* is particularly appropriate in the context, meaning as it does not only to wind things (like wool, for example, or string) into a ball, thus figuratively to cobble a set of assumptions together, but also, colloquially, to grope someone

---

34 My thanks to Philippe Blanchon for kindly sending me a copy of his French rendering of *ALP*.

sexually. Whatever it was that HCE did, whether it involved lascivious use of hands or lascivious use of eyes, he did it in the "Fieffé Park," the adjective *fieffé* suggesting both that HCE was "incorrigible" and the "wretched" park nothing short of a disaster.

Lines (*FW* 215.31–5, 216.3–5) from Blanchon's final paragraph of *ALP*:

> Je ne peux entendre avec les eaux de. Les eaux murmurantes de. Flip-flappent les souris chauves, blablatent souris champêtres. Ho! N'es-tu pas rentré? Quel Thom Malone? Je ne peux entendre avec l'écho des souris, toutes les eaux liffeyantes de. Ho, dires nous sauvent! Mes pieds ne font plus un pas. Je me sens aussi vieille que l'orme là-bas. ... Orme, dis-moi, dis-moi, dis-moi! Conte-moi le conte de Chaume et Gemme. Près des eaux rivièrantes de, eaux allantdecidelàerrantes de. Nuit!

In these final lines, Blanchon's rendering works decidedly loosely but also effectively with Joyce's text, occasionally changing the meaning, occasionally choosing to embroider the original. His washerwoman can't hear with the waters of, the murmuring waters of, the flipflapping of bats (*souris chauves*), the vociferous blathering of fieldmice (*souris champêtres*). Her question "N'es-tu pas rentré?" ("Haven't you gone back yet?") elicits the bewildered and bewildering response "Quel Thom Malone?" ("Which Thom Malone?"). She still can't hear, though not because of Joyce's "bawk of bats," but rather because of the echoing racket of the mice ("l'écho des souris") and all the liffeying waters of. May God (*Dieu*) save us, she ejaculates, may our sayings (*dires*) save us, for her feet are refusing to take one single further step. Feeling as old as yonder elm (*orme*), she needs to rehear the story of straw (*chaume*) and gem (*gemme*), of stem and stone, of stone and stem, of Shaun and Shem. By the rivering waters of, the waters ebbing and flowing and coming and going from here (*de ci*) and from there (*de là*).

Bouton-Kelly and Samoyault (French, 2016)

A French rendering of the first four pages of *ALP* (*FW* 196.1–199.33) by Ludivine Bouton-Kelly (born 1971) of the University of Nantes and Tiphaine Samoyault (born 1968) of the Sorbonne also appeared in 2016, in the online literary journal *Drunken Boat*. Tiphaine Samoyault was previously one of the main translators, responsible for four separate chapters altogether, of Jacques Aubert's team-translated second French *Ulysses* (2004).

Their French rendering of the opening lines of *ALP* (*FW* 196.1–7, 9–11):

Ô / raconte-moi tout ce que tu sais sur / Anna Livia ! Je veux tout entendre sur Anna Livia. / Allô, tu la connais, Anna Livia ? Oui, bien sûr, tout le
monde connait Anna Livia. Raconte-moi tout. Raconte maintenant. Tu vas
être clouée sur place de ce que tu vas entendre. Allô, tu vois quand le vieux
cheb a futé et a fait ce que tu sais. ... Quoi que ce soit qu'ils trifouillèrent
pour savoir comment il troisa les deux dans Finnix park.

As in Blanchon's rendering (and as in Jacques Aubert's edition of
Beckett and Péron's *Anna Livia Pluratself*), the initial "Ô" not only retains Joyce's original opening "O" and its conflated symbolic potential
but also succeeds, by means of the strategically placed circumflex, in
conveying a minimalist suggestion of a fluvial delta. The speaker wants
to hear (*entendre*) "everything you know" (*tout ce que tu sais*) about Anna
Livia. "Allô," says the other washerwoman, conflating *alors* ("right")
and the Irish river Allow. "You'll be nailed to the spot (*clouée sur place*)
by what you're going to hear." The old cheb who went futt remains a
"vieux cheb," who "a futé," who went translingually futt – though perhaps just in a crafty (*futé*) way. What happened in the park is unclear,
"whatever it was (*quoi que ce soit*) that the three ("tri-") of them cobbled
together (*trifouillèrent*) in figuring out (*pour savoir*) how he made a three
(*trois*) of the two (*deux*), namely by joining them, for whatever purpose,
in a park whose name conflates the names Phoenix and Finn.

16 Spanish

Ingberg (Spanish, 2013)

A Spanish rendering by Pablo Ingberg of *Finn's Hotel* (2013) appeared in
Buenos Aires in 2013. Ingberg, born 1960 in Argentina, graduated from
the University of Buenos Aires with a degree in Classics and is active
as a poet, editor, and award-winning translator from Ancient Greek,
Latin, English, and Italian. Author of several books of poetry and a
novel, he has also translated more than ninety works by Shakespeare,
Sophocles, Sappho, Aristophanes, Virgil, Catullus – and, among many
others, Joyce, including *Portrait, Exiles, Giacomo Joyce*, and *The Cats of
Copenhagen*. He lives in Buenos Aires.

Victoria (Spanish, 2016)

Juan Díaz Victoria's Spanish renderings of excerpts from *FW* I.1 originally appeared, as mentioned, in the Mexican journal *La jornada semanal* in June 2007
(*FW* 3.1–24) and online in 2008 (*FW* 4.18–5.12, 5.26–6.28), while a first version

of the complete annotated translation of *FW* I.1 appeared online in 2009. A further revised and more heavily annotated version of two extracts from I.1 (*FW* 3.1–4.17, 8.9–10.23) appeared in the Mexican journal *Estudios* in 2010.

After yet further revision and corrections, and now including a lengthy introduction as well as roughly one thousand annotations, the complete rendering of the first chapter finally, after almost a decade of sustained work, appeared in book form in October 2016, published in Guadalajara by the Mexican publisher Ediciones Arlequín. The earlier renderings employed a limited number of very brief in-text notes in square brackets, each involving just a word or two; the 2010 rendering continued to employ this type of in-text note but also added numerous more detailed footnotes. Victoria's Spanish rendering of *FW* 279 also appeared in June 2016, and his rendering of the "Ballad of Persse O'Reilly" (*FW* 44.24–47.32) followed in November 2016.

Victoria opted for the title *Estela de Finnegan*, where the term *estela*, like the English *stela* (both derived from Latin *stela*), suggests a commemorative marker for Finnegan, gone but not forgotten, a monument to his memory. It also means a "wake" in the maritime sense, and is employed here, as the translator indicates (2009, 1), to highlight the fact that a translation, whatever its intentions, ambitions, and achievements, ultimately never has any choice but to follow in the wake of its original.[35]

Victoria's planned complete and heavily annotated Spanish *Wake* is reportedly still in vigorous progress. Meanwhile, however, the honour of producing the first complete Spanish translation of the *Wake* was not to go to Victoria. The Argentinian translator Marcelo Zabaloy, having finished a Spanish rendering of *Ulysses* in 2009, began his own translation of the *Wake* shortly afterwards. Edgardo Russo, the director at that time of the Cuenco de Plata publishing house in Buenos Aires, having previously been approached by Victoria, had initially shown some interest in publishing his annotated rendering of the first chapter – but eventually opted for publishing instead Marcelo Zabaloy's (unannotated) translation of the entire *Wake*, which duly appeared in June 2016 (Vázquez 2017), and to which we shall return. Victoria is reported to have greeted Zabaloy's rendering with enthusiasm as providing a welcome complement to his own ongoing labours as both translator and annotator.[36]

---

35 On Victoria's Spanish rendering, see Venegas (2008), Léon (2017), Vázquez (2017).

36 "Lo de Zabaloy es el mapa del *Finnegans wake* –afirma Díaz Victoria–, pues te brinda vistas de pájaro y coordenadas. Lo mío es una exploración del accidentado territorio de la novela: subiendo y bajando cordilleras, bebiendo del agua corriente que aparece en cualquier recodo, saboreando las bayas silvestres. ... Es como una visita guiada en el turismo de aventura, o la subida al Everest con *sherpa* incluido" (Vázquez 2017).

Victoria's rendering of the opening three lines (showing the footnote numbers here to illustrate the overall visual effect of the system of double annotation, but ignoring the relevant content) is as follows:

Correrrío,[2] pasados [la iglesia & la taberna de] Eva y Adán,[3] desde viraje de ribera hasta recodo de bahía, nos trae por un comodio[4] [vicio] cívico[5] de recirculación devuelt'a Howth Castel[6] y Enrededores.[7]

The opening one-word "correrrío" conflates *correr* ("to run") and *río* ("river") as well as hinting at *errar* ("to err, to wander, to go astray"). A pluralized past participle (*pasados*) indicates that the river has already passed either both Eve and Adam or, if we are guided by the parenthetical note, both the church and the tavern ostensibly of that name. The river, flowing from swerve (*viraje*) of shore (*ribera*) to bend (*recodo*) of bay (*bahía*), takes us (*nos trae*) by a process of recirculation (*recirculación*) that, evoking both Commodus and Vico, is both comfortable (*cómodo*) and civic minded (*cívico*), though conceivably (as noted in parentheses) also vicious (*vicio*), back (*de vuelta*) to a slightly hispanicized Howth Castle (*castillo*) and its environs (*enrededores*). HCE's initials are faithfully preserved.

Victoria's rendering, quoted here by way of further illustration, continues as follows (*FW* 3.4–10):

Sir [Almeric][8] Tristram[9] [Tristán],[10] violamores,[11] de sobre'l mar angosto, había no todavía [pasadotravez] vueltoarrivar desde Norte Armórica[12] a este lado del raquítico istmo d'Europa Menor par'empuñapelear su [aislada] guerra peneinsular:[13] ni [había] habido piedras[14] de [jonathan][15] altosawyer[16] por el riachuelo Oconee[17] exageradas ellasmismás hasta [ser] jorgios[18] [no gitanos] fabulosos del condado de Laurens mientras fueron dubliando su número[19] [de mendigos (má's y padres) ininteligibles huraños & tramposos] todo el tiempo: ni unavoz[20] de unfuego[21] [había] bramadicho mishe mishe [yo(soy)yo] para babautizar túerespetricio:[22]

The passages quoted here suggest that while the system of combined in-text and footnote annotation can undoubtedly be helpful to sufficiently enthusiastic Hispanophone readers new to Joyce's text, it can clearly also be at least initially very off-putting for others. Victoria's suggestion that his own heavily annotated rendering and Zabaloy's unannotated rendering may be seen as constituting a fruitfully complementary pair has much to recommend it.

Zabaloy's Spanish Wake *(2016)*

The first complete Spanish translation of *FW*, by Marcelo Zabaloy, appeared in Buenos Aires in June 2016 in an edition of two thousand copies, which sold out in five months (Razo 2019). Zabaloy, born in Bahía Blanca in Argentina in 1957 and originally a computer technician, became fascinated by Joyce's later work in the early 2000s. After first completing a Spanish translation of *Ulysses* in 2009 – the fourth Spanish translation of that text, which actually appeared only in 2015 – he spent a further seven years of work on the task of translating *FW*. His complete rendering of the *Wake*, reportedly containing some thirty thousand Spanish neologisms (Juristo 2017), appeared in Buenos Aires in 2016 from the prestigious publishing house El Cuenco de Plata, which had published his *Ulysses* the previous year. Zabaloy originally intended to produce an annotated rendering of *FW*, but eventually decided against doing so (Pyle 2015a).

Zabaloy reported in interviews that he had specifically avoided reading either Pozanco's abbreviated Spanish rendering of the *Wake* or García Tortosa's complex Spanish rendering of *ALP* while working on his own translation, choosing instead to compare the two existing French renderings (Lavergne's and Michel's) and to consult especially on a frequent basis with Hervé Michel, whose continuing revisions of his complete French rendering of *FW* had already been appearing online over the dozen years since 2004. The two men met in Paris in 2012, and Zabaloy reported while still working on his translation that he always had Michel's text at hand: "It is my reference, my main guide. What he dares to do I will follow, not always but almost always" (Pyle 2015b). Zabaloy began his complete *FW* translation by translating not the first but the eighth chapter, beginning, that is to say, with the fluvial pleasures of *ALP*. After translating the entire first book, he then translated the third and fourth, and finally the second (León 2016). As in the case of Bartnicki's 2012 Polish rendering of the *Wake*, the pagination of Zabaloy's Spanish corresponds to that of Joyce's original, thus facilitating readers who might like to compare the translation and the original.[37]

Spanish-language critics and reviewers, celebrating the appearance of the first complete Spanish rendering of the *Wake*, were for the most part

---

37 On Zabaloy's Spanish rendering, see Pyle (2015a, 2015b), Calero (2016), León (2016), Belda (2017), Juristo (2017), Vázquez (2017), Razo (2019). See also https://www.elcuencodeplata.com.ar/en_los_medios/595.

highly enthusiastic. Gonzalo León, in *La Capital*, considered its appearance a matter for national celebration (2016). Antonio Garrigues Walker, in the national newspaper *ABC*, calls the translation "very close to perfect" (2016).[38] Ismael Belda, in *Revista de Libros*, at least equally enthusiastic, calls its appearance an "extraordinary event" and the rendering "exceptional, miraculously exact, inspired," and even "incredible" (2017).[39]

One major point of criticism, however, as reportedly voiced especially by the Spanish critic and translator Eduardo Lago, was that the Spanish of Zabaloy's *Wake* is unambiguously that of a single national variety, namely, that of Argentina.[40] Some reviewers reported having encountered colloquial Argentinian expressions and turns of phrase that would allegedly be quite incomprehensible to Spanish speakers from Madrid or Peru or Chile or Guatemala (Juristo 2017). Lago therefore interestingly if somewhat quixotically proposed a future pan-Spanish team translation of Joyce's text that would at least in principle involve translators from each of the twenty-four national varieties and the multiple major regional varieties of Spanish.

There is, however, one obvious way in which Zabaloy's preferred use of the Spanish idioms and turns of expression of Argentina rather than those of other variants of Spanish is entirely defensible, for it can be argued that Zabaloy is in fact following a linguistic model provided by Joyce himself. Writing of Joyce's Italian rendering of *ALP*, Serenella Zanotti has pointed out that the language Joyce clearly wanted his washerwomen to speak is closer to Triestine than it is to standard Italian or any of its other dialects (2001, 423), and she aptly observes in this context that his continued predilection for the Triestine form of Italian is similar to his predilection for the Dublin form of English (2002, 303–4). Arguably, Zabaloy's pervasive use of Argentinian Spanish rather than an internationally standard Spanish is not only an appropriate domesticating device for a particular readership but is also correspondingly reflective of Joyce's pervasive use of a base of Irish English rather than standard English throughout *FW*.

Zabaloy's rendering of the opening lines (*FW* 3.1–3) reads as follows:

> riverrante, pasando Eva y Adán, de curva ribereña a codo de bahía, nos trae por un comodioso vicus de recirculación de vuelta a Howth Castle y Environs.

---

38   "una labor muy cercana a lo perfecto" (Garrigues Walker 2016).

39   "esta excepcional traducción, milagrosamente exacta e inspirada, que sin duda constituye un evento extraordinario. Increíble, amigos y amigas" (Belda 2017).

40   See León (2016), Juristo (2017), Vázquez (2017).

The first word is perhaps the most interesting one here, the opening "riverrante" combining the Joycean "riverrun" and a Spanish *errante* ("wandering, straying"), reminiscent of the opening two words of Lavergne's 1982 French rendering, where "riverrun" becomes "erre revie," suggesting a combination of a recomposed *rivière* and the French verb *errer* ("to rove, wander, stray"). Zabaloy's river is in the process of "passing (*pasando*) Eve and Adam," from "curve" (*curva*) of "shore" (*ribera*) to the "elbow" (*codo*) of the "bay" (*bahía*), and it "carries us" (*nos trae*) "back" (*de vuelta*) to an untranslated Howth Castle and Environs by a "comodioso vicus de recirculación," where the Latinate diction of Joyce's text at this point allows for a very minimal degree of translation in the Romance language that is Spanish.

Zabaloy's opening sentences of *ALP* include the following lines (*FW* 196.1–7, 9–11):

¡Oh / cuéntame todo sobre / Anna Livia! Quiero oírlo todo / sobre Anna Livia. Bien, ¿conoces a Anna Livia? Sí, claro, todos conocemos a Anna Livia. Cuéntame todo. Cuéntame ya. Te morirás cuando lo escuches. Cuando el viejo chebón se volvió futt e hizo lo que ya sabes. ... O lo que sea que tresataron de distinguir de lo que tradó de a dos hacer en el parque Fiendish.

A generous selection of fluvial references here includes the English Tame (*cuéntame*), Ugandan Ivi (*Livia*), Brazilian Claro (*claro*), and the Ando (*cuando*) of the Solomon Islands. "You'll die (*te morirás*)," says one washerwoman to the other, "when you hear it (*cuando lo escuches*)," namely, how the old cheb, the old (*viejo*) bastard (*cabrón*), went futt and did (*hizo*) what you already (*ya*) know. Or whatever it may have been (*lo que sea*) that the three (*tres*) of them were trying (*trataron*) to grasp (*distinguir*) that he was trying (*trató*) to do to the two (*dó-, dos*) in the Fiendish park, its epithet left untranslated.

From the final lines of Zabaloy's *Wake* (*FW* 627.34–628.4, 15–16):

Me estoy desvaneciendo. ¡Oh final amargo! Voy a deslizarme antes que se levanten. Nunca lo verán. Ni ahora. Ni me extrañarán. Y es viejo y viejo es triste y viejo es triste y cansada regreso a ti, mi frío padre, mi frío y loco padre, mi fiero padre loco y frío, hasta la inminente visión de la eminente dimensión de él, las moilleas y moilleas del mismo, gimoanando, me vuelve limomarina y saliñorante y me apuro, único mío, a tus brazos. ... Una vía una sola una última una amada una larga

Lago's Spanish ALP (2016)

A complete online Spanish translation of *ALP* by Eduardo Lago, in progress in more than twenty bilingual instalments since March 2013, reached its final instalment in June 2016. Lago, born in Madrid in 1954 and a long-term resident of New York, is a Spanish novelist, translator, and critic. A faculty member at Sarah Lawrence College in New York, his translations include works by Henry James, John Barth, Sylvia Plath, Christopher Isherwood, and many others. In 2001 he published an award-winning comparative study of the three Spanish versions of *Ulysses* in existence at that time.[41]

Lago's rendering of *ALP*, presented online somewhat idiosyncratically to accompany a diary of his travels from March 2013 to June 2016, adopts in general an approach comparable to that of Víctor Pozanco, feeling free to translate Joyce's text quite loosely, overtly aiming in many passages to convey what is taken to be the general sense of the text rather than attempting more stringently to convey also the stylistic effects involved. At least one critic finds the overall result "excellent" (Belda 2017). The translation is presented in each instalment in two columns, with Joyce's original text on the left and Lago's version on the right, and with each column consisting eventually of more than six hundred numbered short phrases, with Joyce's longer sentences divided into shorter phrases where deemed appropriate for the rather unusual translational purposes.

Lago's rendering of the opening sentences of *ALP* includes the following lines (*FW* 196.1–7, 9–11):

O / de Anna Livia / lo quiero saber todo / de Anna Livia ¡cuéntamelo todo! Y bien: ¿conoces a Anna Livia? Sí, por supuesto, todas conocemos a Anna Livia. Cuéntamelo todo. Cuéntamelo ya. Cuando lo oigas es que te mueres. Bien ya sabes que cuando el Cheb llegó a viejo y se secó hizo lo que sabes. ... O lo que anduvieran intrenzando medrar en su afán por hacer de un tres un dos en el parque del fénix maligno.

Here the rendering overtly aims to suggest the perceived spirit of Joyce's text rather than attempting to reproduce in Spanish its style and tone. The order of the opening two sentences is reversed to "I want

---

41 *Ulysses* was translated into Spanish by José Salas Subirat in 1945, by José Maria Valverde in 1976, and by Francisco García Tortosa and María Luisa Venegas in 1999. Lago's study, *El íncubo de lo imposible*, appeared in 2001. *Ulysses* was subsequently translated into Spanish for a fourth time by Marcelo Zabaloy in 2015.

to know all about Anna Livia, tell me all about Anna Livia." Joyce's "You'll die when you hear" is similarly adjusted to "When you hear it (*cuando lo oigas*) you're going to die (*es que te mueres*)." As for the old cheb, "you know that when the Cheb got old (*llegó a viejo*) and all dried up (*y se secó*) he did what you know (*hizo lo que sabes*)." The Cheb is capitalized possibly to draw attention to the presence of HCE's initials as well as evoking the particular Czech river. The final sentence in the passage quoted here becomes, much more obscurely than in the original, and at a considerable remove, roughly: "Or whatever it was they were plotting and planning (*trenzar* "to plait") to spread about (*medrar* "to flourish") in their eagerness (*en su afán*) to make a two (*dos*) out of a three (*tres*) in the park of the wicked (*maligno*) phoenix (*fénix*)." The general sense here appears to suggest the anticipated degree of confusion the old Cheb is likely to cause in the fiendish (*maligno*) Phoenix Park, with the nature of the confusion to be caused left unmentioned, despite the reference to a three and a two.

The final sentences of Lago's *ALP* include the following lines (*FW* 215.31–5, 216.3–5):

No alcanzo a escuchar las aguas del. Las gorjeantes aguas del. Murciélagos titiritando, ratones de campo contando guarradías. ¡Joé! ¿Que no estás Casasolo? ¿Qué Tomás Solo? Con tanta cháchara murciélaga no oigo, todo atal lifeando aguas del. ¡Jo, habla salva nos! Ni fus ni mus. Me siento más viejo que ese olmo. ¿Un cuento que habla de Shaun o de Shem? ... ¡Alta a mí, y dime, y dime, olmo! ¡Noche Noche! Talacuéntame de tallo o piedra. Junto a las aguas riberrías del, acacullando aguas del. ¡Noche!

Once again, though in this case less flamboyantly, the rendering overtly aims to suggest, rather loosely, the general spirit rather than attending more closely to textual detail. Rather than being prevented from hearing by the waters, Lago's washerwoman cannot in fact manage (*alcanzar* "to manage") to hear (*escuchar*) the waters themselves, the gurgling (*gorjear* "to gurgle") waters of the. Bats (*murciélagos*) appear to give the impression of shivering (*titiritar* "to shiver") in trembling flight, while fieldmice (*ratones de campo*) may or may not "bawk talk" while apparently engaged in telling (*contando*) smutty stories (*guarradías*). "Hey, you're not Casasolo?" the washerwoman surprisingly exclaims, possibly misspeaking the recorded name Casasola – and eliciting the puzzled response "What Tomás Solo?," thus also providing a translingual pun on "Tom alone (*solo*)." She can't hear with so much bat-chattering (*cháchara murciélaga*) and all the liffeying waters. "Talk (*habla*) save us," she exclaims, and, surprisingly once again, "neither *fus* nor *mus*" – the latter a conflation of "My foos won't moos" and the Spanish phrase *ni fu ni fa* ("neither one thing nor the other"). She feels not just as old as that elm over there, but in fact older (*más viejo*) than it. A tale that tells (*que habla*) of Shaun or Shem? "Come on (*alta a mí*), and tell me, and tell me, elm, tell me (*cuéntame*) a tale of stem (*tallo*) or stone (*piedra*)," by the rivering waters of (*ribera* "riverside"), the hither-andthithering waters of, waters flowing hither (*acá*) and flowing thither (*acullá*).[42]

17 Hebrew

Vizan (Hebrew, 2015)

Yehuda Vizan, born in Yehud, Israel, in 1985, is an Israeli poet, novelist, editor, translator, and critic. He studied English at Tel Aviv University and is the editor of the Tel Aviv literary journal *Dehak*, which he founded in 2011. His numerous translations include works by T.S. Eliot, Virginia Woolf, H.G. Wells, William Faulkner, and many others – as well as Joyce's *The Cat and the Devil* (in 2012) and *The Cats of Copenhagen* (in 2013).

Vizan had mentioned in a 2012 online interview that his fellow Israeli poet and translator Ronen Sonis of the Hebrew University of Jerusalem was planning to translate some excerpts from *FW* for *Dehak*. Sonis having eventually withdrawn from the project, however, Vizan himself translated the three excerpts in question, namely *FW* 196–7, 627–8, and 44–5. To date, this is still the only Hebrew rendering of any part of the *Wake*.[43]

The opening lines of *ALP* (*FW* 196.1–7, 9–11) in Vizan's rendering, as transliterated:

Oh / sapri li al hakol al / Ana Liviya! Ani rotse lishmoah hakol al / Ana Liviya. Uvchen, at makirah et Ana Liviya? Ken, kamuvan, kulanu makirim et Ana Liviya. Sapri li hakol. Sapri li achshav. At tamuti kshetishmeii. Uvchen, at yodaat, kshehazaken halach kaput veahsah at yodaat mah. ... Oh ma sheze lo haya shehem nisu laahsot shehu nisah lahasot begnyochani.[44]

---

42 On Lago's Spanish rendering of *ALP*, see Vázquez (2017).

43 My thanks to Yehuda Vizan for kindly providing me with electronic copies of these excerpts. The Hebrew renderings are available online at https://library.osu.edu /projects/hebrew-lexicon/99995-files/99995008/99995008-005/99995008-005 -140-143.pdf.

44 My thanks to Na'ama Haklai of Queen's University in Kingston, Canada, for kindly providing the transliteration.

Once again, even a complete lack of Hebrew does not prevent an enterprising reader from taking part in Joyce's fluvial game and rediscovering one of the main stylistic features of *ALP*, namely, the continual evocation of rivers: the Sape ("sapri") of the Solomon Islands, the Togolese Anie ("Ani"), Ghanaian Mo ("lishmoah"), Romanian Mag ("makirah"), Indian Ken ("Ken"), Burmese Mu ("kamuvan"), French Aa ("yodaat"), South East Asian Ma ("mah"), American Niss ("nisu"), and Romanian Beg ("begnyochani").

18 Turkish

Erkmen (Turkish)

Nevzat Erkmen, translator of the first Turkish *Ulysses* in 1996, reportedly began work in 1998 on a planned complete Turkish translation of *FW*. Born in Izmir in 1931, Erkmen completed MA and PhD degrees in pedagogy at New York University. Specializing initially in marketing and management, he worked for Coca-Cola in the USA and later also in Turkey, where he opened several Coca-Cola factories and served as a board member of several companies. Having developed an interest in psychoanalysis, Eastern philosophies (Zen, yoga, Taoism), and mind games of various sorts, he founded the Söz publishing house in 1983, which specialized in puzzles, crosswords, and mathematical brain-teasers. In 1995 he founded the Turkish Club of Intelligence Games and was also a founding member of the World Puzzle Federation, serving for several years as coach of the Turkish team at the annual World Puzzle Championships (Anon. 2020a, 2020b).

He also translated a number of books both from English to Turkish (Jack Kerouac, Carlos Castaneda) and from Turkish to English, and his award-winning translation of *Ulysses* was widely celebrated, winning the Turkish Translator of the Year award – and the unusual accolade of a public letter of congratulations from the then president of Ireland, Mary Robinson. Erkmen was reported in *The Irish Times* in November 1996 as looking forward to his next Joycean challenge: "I will buy a little hut overlooking the Black Sea, and as I look at the waves of the Black Sea I will eat my fish, drink my raki, and start translating *Finnegans Wake*" (Connolly 1996).

Reportedly begun in 1998, that translation was listed twenty years later on the website of Yapı Kredi Yayınları, the publisher of his Turkish *Ulysses*, as still in progress. No anticipated publication date was announced by the publisher at that time; and no excerpts from the translation had appeared at any time – or have appeared subsequently.

Reportedly still continuing to work on the translation, as well as on a book of his experiences translating both *Ulysses* and *FW*, Erkmen died in Istanbul in April 2020, at the age of eighty-nine, a victim of the global Covid-19 pandemic (Anon. 2020a, 2020b). As of this writing, the publisher Yapı Kredi Yayınları has given no indication as to whether it might be considered feasible to publish any part or all of Erkmen's unfinished rendering in some form.[45]

Instead of the anticipated Turkish *Wake* in Nevzat Erkmen's translation, the year 2016 witnessed a publishing event that would have been distinctly unusual in any language, namely, the appearance of a further two competing Turkish translations, the first a rendering of *FW* I.1–8 by Umur Çelikyay in January of that year, the second a complete rendering of *FW* by Fuat Sevimay, which appeared later in the same year. Both renderings appeared in Istanbul: Çelikyay's shorter rendering from the publisher Aylak Adam, under the title *Finneganın vahı*; Sevimay's complete rendering from the publisher Sel Yayıncılık, under the title *Finnegan Uyanması*. Halila Bayramova notes that this surge of interest in Turkey was at least partly due to the much-awaited expiration of copyright on *FW* in 2012 (2016, 4).

Çelikyay's Turkish Wake: Finneganın vahı *(2016, 2017)*

Umur Çelikyay's title, *Finneganın vahı*, literally means "Finnegan's woe," but where the noun *vah* both means "woe" and suggests an interlingual echo of the English "wake" (Fenge 2016, 2; Bayramova 2016, 5). Both *-nın* and *-ı* are grammatically appropriate possessive suffixes.

According to a review by Halila Bayramova (and in her translation), Çelikyay states in his introduction to *Finneganın vahı* that it is a "counter-translation or vice-translation (Turkish *terscüme*)" of the untranslatable original, and that this translational concept was inspired by Hervé Michel's presentation of *Veillée Pinouilles* as a "contraduction," a combination of French *traduction* and *contradiction*. The term *terscüme* is a punning neologism based on the standard Turkish *tercüme* ("translation"), and Muhammed Baydere notes that it also suggests such concepts as "'inverse translation' or 'contrary translation,' among other possibilities. In addition, the translator intentionally presents himself as a 'Turkicizer,' as opposed to a 'translator'" (2018, 92). Çelikyay writes, in Bayramova's translation: "From the beginning, we have approached

<hr>

45 My thanks to Zeynep Atayurt Fenge of the University of Ankara for investigating whether Yapı Kredi Yayınları might have any plans for publishing Erkmen's unfinished rendering.

this work more as an attempt at literary Turkicization rather than a translation. The text at hand should be regarded as a possible Turkish version of *Finnegans Wake*, i.e., one of its many potential adaptations." Çelikyay, a faculty member at Koç University in Istanbul, "though not from an immediate Joycean background," has been "involved in the art of translation for approximately thirty years, for twenty-five of which he has also been teaching in different universities in Turkey" (Bayramova 2016, 4).

His ambition throughout, Çelikyay writes, is "to replicate Joyce's polysemy as well as the flavor, strangeness, and eccentricity of the original text" (Bayramova 2016, 4). His endeavours are assisted by the fact that the Turkish language belongs to an agglutinative language family, which thus offers multiple opportunities for wordplay. Zeynep Atayurt Fenge similarly observes that the translation "displays a notable accomplishment in tackling the verbal diversity of the text through a vigorous use of the agglutinative characteristics of the target language" (2016, 2). A comparison of the original and Çelikyay's rendering nonetheless makes it "clear that most of the solutions adopted for translation challenges in *Finneganın vahı* are arbitrary and contingent upon the scope and flexibility of the target language" (Bayramova 2016, 5). His translation is not accompanied by any facing-page version of the original text and also avoids any annotations or commentaries, thus leaving his readers to face the target-language text with as little assistance as readers of the Joycean original had and have (Bayramova 2016, 5; Fenge 2016, 2).[46]

Çelikyay's rendering of the opening lines (*FW* 3.1–3) reads as follows:

> ırmakgüzergâhı, Havva ve Adem'in oradan geçip, kıyı kıvrımından koy dönemecine, elverişli bir köy yolundan yeniden dolaşarak, gerisingeri Howth Kalesi ve Civarları'na getiriyor bizi. (qtd. Ekici 2016)

This suggests, roughly, according to a Turkish colleague consulted, "the river (*ırmak*) in its course (*güzergâh*) on past Eve and Adam's (*Havva ve Adem'in oradan geçip*), from swerve (*kıvrımından*) of shore (*kıyı*) to bend (*dönemeci*) of bay (*koy*), brings us (*getiriyor bizi*) circling back (*dolaşarak*) along a (*bir*) convenient (*elverişli*) village road (*köy yolu*) right back again (*gerisingeri*) to Howth Castle (*kale*) and environs (*civarlar*)." The "village road" is a back road deriving its existence from Joyce's "vicus," which in Latin means both "street" and "village." Çelikyay's "bir

---

46 On Çelikyay's Turkish rendering, see Genç (2015), Bayramova (2016), Ekici (2016), Fenge (2016), Baydere (2018).

köy" is "a village," which adroitly manages to suggest Vico ("bi-kö-")
as well as *vicus* ("village"), while his "köy yolu" ("village road") evokes
vicus as "street" and thus also Dublin's Vico Road. Joyce's "commodius" vicus becomes merely a "convenient" one, while HCE's initials
become unrecognizable as HKC in the sequence "gerisingeri Howth
Kalesi ve Civarları'na."[47]

Çelikyay's 2016 rendering of Book I was followed by a second volume containing Book II in October 2017, while a third volume containing Books III and IV was expected as of this writing to appear in the
early 2020s.[48]

Sevimay's Turkish Wake: Finnegan Uyanması *(2016)*

After graduating from Marmara University in Istanbul with a degree
in business and working in industry as a sales manager for two decades, Fuat Sevimay (born 1972) began writing merely as a spare-time
occupation, thinking of it as no more than a change of pace from professional concerns (Pyle and Jewell 2016). Unexpectedly, however, he
quite quickly became not only an award-winning novelist but also an
award-winning writer of short stories, while also translating Italo Svevo
from Italian. Having turned his attention to Joyce, he first translated the
Occasional, Critical, and Political Writing, then *Portrait*, and finally began
in early 2014 to undertake a complete Turkish translation of *FW*.[49]

In Sevimay's title, *Finnegan Uyanması* (Finnegans waking), the use
of the name "Finnegan" is consciously ungrammatical. "By rendering
'Finnegan' without the possessive or plural suffix (*-nın* and *-lar*, respectively), Sevimay echoes the obscurity of the original by creating
a structure that permits either meaning" (Fenge 2017, 2). *Uyanması*
("someone's awakening") includes both *uyanma* ("awakening") and
anma ("commemoration"), the latter suggesting a sense of remembrance (Fenge 2017, 2). Sevimay's translation was originally advertised
to appear as *Finnegans vakası* (Bayramova 2016, 4), where the noun *vaka*
means "case" (as in "the case of Finnegan") and suggests an interlingual
echo of the English "wake." The possessive suffix *-sı* is grammatically
necessary, while "Finnegans" rather than "Finnneganın" is as grammatically incorrect in Turkish as it may be taken to be in English.

---

47 My thanks to Duru Güngör for detailed assistance with the Turkish text.
48 My thanks to Umur Çelikyay for reporting this information in personal
    correspondence.
49 On Sevimay's Turkish rendering, see Genç (2015), Ekici (2016), Pyle and Jewell
    (2016), Fenge (2017).

Zeynep Atayurt Fenge once again refers to the specific significance of agglutinative effects in Turkish: the translator's "use of the agglutinative characteristics of Turkish epitomises Sevimay's lingual creativity and emphasises the ways in which his work speaks to the spirit of the original. He has sought to create a translation that is semantically and phonetically faithful to the original, incorporating many of its ambiguities and, at the same time, revealed the suitability of the Turkish language as a vehicle to express the idiosyncrasies of Joyce's style" (2017, 2).

Sevimay's Turkish rendering of the opening lines (*FW* 3.1–3) reads:

> nehiryatağında, Havva ile Âdem'i geçip sahilin keskin ucunda körfeze kıvrılır, emrisakin ve yılankavikusvari bir döngüyle bizi yine Howth Cebelhisarı ve Efradına ulaştırır. (qtd. Ekici 2016)

The same helpful Turkish colleague consulted reads that rendering as follows: "the river in its course (*nehir yatağı* "riverbed"), past Eve and Adam's (*Havva ile Âdem'i geçip*), bends (*kıvrılır*) into the bay (*körfeze*) at the sharp (*keskin*) end (*ucunda*) of the shore (*sahilin*), brings (*ulaştırır*) us (*bizi*) again (*yine*) by a tranquil (*sakin*) and serpentine (*yılan* "serpent") circuit (*döngüyle*) to the mountain (*cebel*) castle (*hisar*) of Howth and its inhabitants (*efradi*)." Sevimay combines *yılankavi* ("serpentine, sinuous") and "vikusvari," the latter combining in turn Joyce's "vicus" and *Vicovari* ("in Viconian style"). An archaic "cebelhisar" rather than Çelikyay's more modern *kale* ("castle") retains the (admittedly rather less than mountainous) hill of Howth while providing HCE with his second initial. *Efradi* ("inhabitants"), finally, completing HCE's initials, plays on *etrafi* ("environs"), the playfully unnecessary substitution effectively making the point in the opening sentence already that language in *Finnegans Wake* is always entirely malleable – and never to be taken for granted.[50]

Fuat Sevimay subsequently translated *Ulysses* into Turkish (2019), a third version in that language, following on Nevzat Erkmen's and Armağan Ekinci's translations of that work in 1996 and 2012, respectively.[51]

---

50 My thanks to Duru Güngör once again for generous and detailed help with the Turkish text.

51 My thanks to Zeynep Atayurt Fenge for reporting this information in personal correspondence.

19 Norwegian

Høghaug (Norwegian, 2016, 2017, 2018)

Leif Høghaug (born 1974), poet, novelist, and Norwegian translator of *The Communist Manifesto*, reported in an interview of 2 December 2016 with the Oslo weekly newspaper *Morgenbladet* (Lien 2016) that he had recently, turning from Marx to Joyce, begun work on a complete Norwegian translation of *FW*, having first conceived of the project in 1993. A first excerpt from his rendering (*FW* 3.1–10.24) appeared with an introduction in the December 2016 issue of the journal *Vinduet* (The window), followed by renderings in other journals of *FW* 13.33–19.19 and *FW* 44.22–47.29 in 2017 and of *FW* 169.1–174.4 in 2018.[52]

Høghaug's opening lines (*FW* 3.1–3) of the 2016 version read as follows:

> rinnælvrenn, post Evtan Adams, frå sjøleg sveng te bøyan bog, tek oss gjønni eit commodjøns vekkossattbruk bachatt te Howth Castle og Emlanda.

Here "rinnælvrenn," conflating Old Norse *rinna* ("to run, flow"), Norwegian *elv* ("river"), and Norwegian *renne* ("to run, flow"), suggests "runriverrun," while conserving the original rhythm and alliteration; "post Evtan Adams" conflates English *past* and Latin *post*, suggests both "past Eve and Adam's" and "after Eve and Adam's," while "Evtan" conflates "Eva," *eftan* ("evening"), and Old English *eft* ("again"); "frå sjøleg sveng" suggests a swerve, curve, or swing ("sveng"), where "sjøleg," a "sea-like" shore, becomes an adjective, in order to preserve the original rhythm and alliteration, while also alliterating interlingually with *shore*; "te bøyan bog" suggests a curved (*bøye* "to bend") bay (Swedish *bukt*), once again conserving the original rhythm and alliteration, while suggesting in passing possible interlingual puns on Danish *bog* (the "book" that is *FW*) and the source of the Liffey in an Irish bog.

Continuing, "tek oss" suggests "takes us"; while "gjønni" suggests a variant of *gjennom* ("via") and an oblique reference to Vico's first given name, Giovanni; "commodjøns" is "commodious," while also suggesting both Commodus and *komediens* ("comedy's") presence;

---

52 My thanks to Leif Høghaug for kindly providing me with electronic copies of these excerpts and for discussing linguistic details of his renderings.

"vekkossattbruk" conflates Vico, *ekko* ("echo"), and *sattbruk* ("intended use") to suggest "recirculation," while "vekk oss" echoes "tek oss" and also suggests "wake us," thus invoking one of the implications of the title, namely, awakening; "bachatt" conflates English *back*, Norwegian *att* ("back, again"), and German *Bach* ("stream"), invoking the opening Norwegian *elv* ("river") once again; and so "te Howth Castle og Emlanda," where *omlanda* ("surroundings, environs") becomes "Emlanda" to generate the initials HCE. Eve and Adam, Commodus and Vico, Howth Castle and Environs and HCE are all present and correct, while swerve of shore and bend of bay are interestingly and alliteratively modulated.

Leif Høghaug notes in personal correspondence that the adjective "sjøleg" also contains a "secret message"to himself, namely, that *sjøl eg* means "even I," humorously suggesting that "even I (the translator) can do this sort of thing."

Høghaug's rendering continues (*FW* 3.4–10):

Sir Tristram, violer d'amores, fr'over brottsjøen, hadd veiencore attkømmin frå Nord-Armorica førr hin side af Vetleuropas røffe hæljøy at wielderkjemp sin penisolatkrig: ei hell hadd tomståylers knaus via Oconeerørsla opphopa damsa te Laurens Countys gorgioar der dei uavlateleg sytte førr døbling ta mumpera sine: ell ovnfrårøyst bålsende moshe moshe te duptdupt duestpetrus:

20 Russian

Rene's Russian Wake: Na pomine Finneganov *(2016, 2017, 2018, 2019)*

The most substantial Russian contribution to date was made in these years by Andrey Rene, born in 1985, a graduate in physics, and a resident of Moscow, who began making notes for a complete Russian *Wake* in 2011 and whose online translation of *FW* I.1–2 and the opening pages of *ALP* (*FW* 196.1–201.20) appeared in 2016. His extended rendering of *FW* I.1–4 and I.7–8 appeared the following year, online and with extensive commentary, and in 2018 his complete translation of *FW* I.1–8 appeared both in book form (without commentary) and online (with extensive commentary, running to 6,300 notes in 1,666 pages) under the title На помине Финнеганов (*Na pomine Finneganov*). *FW* II.1–4 appeared both in book form (without commentary) and online (with extensive commentary) in December 2019. Andrey Rene notes in a Facebook post that his online version of *FW* I–II covers some 3,000 pages, and that the online version of *FW* II.3, for example, contains 436 pages, including 100 pages of text and 320 of annotations, as well as an extensive bibliography.

The traditional Russian translation of the title *Finnegans Wake* is *Pominki po Finneganu* ("Finnegan's wake" in a funeral sense), as also used by Konstantin Belyaev (2000). Rene's title *Na pomine Finneganov*, a pleasing trochaic tetrameter, refers to plural Finnegans, thus implying "at the Finnegans' wake" or "at the wake of the Finnegans." It also plays on the interrelationship of the nouns *pomin* ("prayer for the dead") and *pominki* ("wake"), the verb *pomint'* ("to remember"), and the colloquial phrase *lyogok na pomine*, the equivalent of "talk of the devil," implying "and he's sure to appear."[53] The title thus also implies something like "Praying for the Finnegans" and, more expansively, even something like "Praying for the Finnegans we remember, wake or no wake – and, by the same token, talk of the devil, we'll probably see them back again."[54]

The name Andrey Rene, meanwhile, is a pseudonym, playing humorously inter alia on the name of the five-hundred-pound, seven-foot tall French professional wrestler André René Rousimoff (1946–93), known (appropriately in the context of a translation involving the man-mountain HCE) as André the Giant. It is a pleasing coincidence in the *FW* context that Rousimoff, who grew up near the French village of Ussy-sur-Marne, north of Paris, was fond of telling people how he was occasionally given a ride to school in the 1950s by none other than Samuel Beckett, who had owned a small country home near Ussy since 1952 (Cronin 1996, 399, 416) – and whom we have already encountered as one of the very first translators of *FW*, specifically of the opening pages of *ALP*.

---

53 Andrey Rene observes in personal correspondence that *lyogok na pomine*, colloquially "talk of the devil," literally means "quick on remembrance," while *i v pomine net* means "there's no trace." In both of these cases the archaic *pomin* means "remembering," though only in these specific phrases; in modern Russian "to remember" is *vspominat'* while *pominat'* means both "to pray for" and "to feast for the dead." On Rene's translation in general, see Alexandrova (2020, 169–78).

54 Andrey Rene confirms, once again in personal correspondence, that *Finneganov* cannot be read as an adjectival form in his chosen title, unlike in Henri Volokhonsky's (first) title *Iz Finneganova Weik*: the prepositional construction with *na* would require the adjectival form *Finneganovom*. The only form common to both noun and adjective is *Finneganov*, which is a plural noun in the genitive case or an adjective in the nominative case. My thanks to Andrey Rene for his continued patience in providing detailed clarification of these linguistic intricacies.

Rene's three-line incipit (*FW* 3.1–3) reads:

рекутопия, после здания Евы и Адама, уйдя от берега, найти чтоб устья изгиб, принесёт нас по разомкнутому прочному круговику назад к границам и Замку-на-Взгорье.

rekutopiya, posle zdaniya Yevy i Adama, uydya ot berega, nayti chtob ust'ya izgib, prinesët nas po razomknutomu prochnomu krugoviku nazad k granitsam i Zamku-na-Vzgor'ye.

This rendering suggests something like the following: "the Utopian (*utopiya*) river (*reka*), past (*posle*) the house (*zdaniye*) of Eve and Adam (*Yevy i Adama*), leaving (*uydya*) the shore (*bereg*) in order (*chtob*) to find (*nayti*) the curve (*izgib*) of its mouth (*ust'ya*), brings us (*prinesët nas*) by (*po*) a broad (*razomknut* "open") and continuing (*prochnom*) process of circulation (*krug* "circle"; *krugovorot* "circulation") back (*nazad*) to the environs (*granitsa*) and Castle-on-the-Hill (*Zamku-na-Vzgor'ye*)." Rene's river flows in Utopia (*utopiya*), an imaginary place in some imaginary version of Dublin, where everything, it may initially appear, is as perfect as it once was in the Garden of Eden – though the possibility of drowning (*utop, utoplen*) is evoked as a reminder that even Edenic Utopias may have their challenges too. Mention of a *prochniy krug*, a "continuing circle," similarly implies the related possibility of a *porochniy krug*, a "vicious circle."

Commodus disappears except in the echoes of *-om-* in *razomknut* and *prochnom*, but Vico appears, only slightly and humorously disguised (*krugo-viku*), as a participant in a round robin (*po-krugovoy*), an event suggesting an early evocation of circularity, since a round robin is not only a tournament in which each competitor plays in turn against every other but may also imply a series or sequence of events, as in "a round robin of inconclusive talks." The name of Howth disappears, and since the letter *h* is rarely found in Russian, *Vzgor'ye* ("hill") is used for "Howth" here and throughout. HCE's Russian initials are thus established as GZV, and remain so throughout Rene's rendering. The noun *granitsa* means variously "precinct, environs, skirts."

Rene's rendering of Part I later provides a striking example of translingual serendipity when Shem and Shaun become Шем ("Shem") and Шон ("Shon"), respectively. Serendipitously, that is to say, the Cyrillic letter Ш (*sha*) mirrors in both cases Joyce's siglum (Ш) for their progenitor HCE, flat on his back, supinely (and inevitably) defeated by the next generation – "HCE interred in the landscape," as Joyce wrote to Harriet Weaver on 31 May 1927 (*L* 1, 254).

Rene's opening of the *ALP* chapter includes the following lines (*FW* 196.1–7, 9–11):

О,

расскажите же мне всё

про Анну Ливви! Я хочу услышать всё

про Анну Ливви. В смысле, вы же знаете Анну Ливви. Да, конечно, мы все знаем Анну Ливви. Расскажите же мне всё. Расскажите сейчас же. Вы умрёте, когда услышите. В смысле, вы же знаете, когда старая чуда пошёл крахом, свершилось вы сами знаете штоф. ... Что бы там они ни стремились обнаружить, что он треуспел надворить в том Теникс-парке.

O, / rasskazhite zhe mne vsë / pro Annu Livvi! Ya khochu uslyshat' vsë / pro Annu Livvi. V smysle, vy zhe znayete Annu Livvi. Da, konechno, my vse znayem Annu Livvi. Rasskazhite zhe mne vsë. Rasskazhite seychas zhe. Vy umrëte, kogda uslyshite. V smysle, vy zhe znayete, kogda staraya chuda poshël krakhom, svershilos' vy sami znayete shtof. ... Chto by tam oni ni stremilis' obnaruzhit', chto on treuspel nadvorit' v tom Teniks-parke.

Here the request to hear all ("uslyshat' vsë") about Anna Livia is responded to with the promise "Vy umrëte, kogda uslyshite," a quite literal "You'll die when you hear." The old cheb who went futt becomes the "staraya chuda," the old so-and-so, literally, "the old marvel," who "poshël krakhom" ("went crash") and did the "shtof" you all know about ("svershilos' vy sami znayete"). As to events in the park, the final sentence suggests "No matter what they were trying (*stremilis'*) to discover (*obnaruzhit'*) about whatever it was he managed (*treuspel*) to do (*nadvorit'*)" in that shadowy park whose name conflates the name Phoenix and the noun *teni* ("shadows"). The presence of the three (*tri*) is suggested in "treuspel," that of the two (*dva*) in "nadvorit'."

Fomenko (Russian, 2017)

Boriana Alexandrova (2020, 144) reports a 2017 Russian rendering of *FW* 593.1–595.30 by Elena Genyevna Fomenko in the course of a scholarly analysis of the difficulties and practical considerations of translating the *Wake* into a Slavic language.

21 Slovenian

Godler (Slovenian, 2018)

Slovenian made a second appearance in the *FW* universe in January 2018, when the Slovenian writer, composer, and television actor Jure Godler (born 1984) posted and read on YouTube a Slovenian rendering of *FW* 4.18–6.12 under the title *Finneganovo bdenje*.

22 Georgian

Gelashvili's Georgian ALP (2018)

In 2017 Tamar Gelashvili, a faculty member at Tbilisi State University in Georgia, translated *Giacomo Joyce*, with a commentary, into Georgian, and in 2018 the Universal Publishing House of Georgia (Gamomcemloba universali) published her Georgian rendering of *ALP* (*FW* I.8), with a commentary, and with Joyce's English on facing pages. Although all of Joyce's other major works already exist in Georgian translation, some in multiple versions, this was the first Georgian rendering of any part of *FW*.

Her rendering of *FW* 196.1–11 in Georgian script:

ოჰ

მომიყევი ყველაფერი

ანა ლივიაზე! ყკუცლაყკური მსურს ვიცოდე

ანა ლივიაზე! იცნობ ანა ლივიას? რა თქმა უნდა, ჩვენ ყველანი ვიცნობთ ანა ლივიას, ყველაფერი მითხარი. ახლავე მითხარი. მოკვდები როცა გაიგებ. ისედაც იგი იმ ზებრუცუნამ რა გააკეთა. ჰოდა რომ ვიცი გააგრძელე მოყოლა. ფრთხილად იყავი არ გაიწუწო. დაიკაპიწე სახელოები და ალაპარაკდი. ჰოდა კიდევ ნუ გამჭყლიტავ შენი უკანალით – შეჩერდი ! – როდესაც დაიხრები. რაც არ უნდა ყოფილიყო ისინი ცდილობდნენ მიეჩქმალათ მისი საქციელი ბორონიქსის პარკში. ზებერი მძორი. ერთი შეხედე მის პერანგს!

And as transliterated:

Oh / momikhevi khvelaperi / ana liviaze! khvelaperi msurs vicode / ana liviaze! icnob ana livias? ra tkma unda, chven khvela vicnobt ana livias, khvelaperi mitkhari. akhlave mitkhari. mokvdebi roca gaigeb. isedac ici im bebrutsunam ra gaaketa. hoda rom vici gaagrdzele mokola. prtkhilad ikhavi ar gaitsutso. daikapitse sakheloebi da alaparakdi. hoda kidev nu gamchkhlitav sheni ukanalit – shecherdi ! – rodesac daixrebi. rac ar unda kopilikho isini cdilodnen miechkmalat misi sakcieli boroniksis parkshi. beberi mdzori. erti shekhede mis perangs![55]

The Georgian language is the main one of four Kartvelian or South Caucasian languages, which do not belong to the Indo-European family of languages. Georgian grammar is consequently very different from that of most European languages and, as we are told, has many distinct features, such as split ergativity and a polypersonal verb agreement system. Georgian is agglutinative, uses postpositions instead of prepositions, has seven noun cases, no grammatical gender, and no articles. The alphabet currently most widely used, known as the *mkhedruli* ("military") alphabet, makes no distinction between upper and lower case. Given a vocabulary that is also extremely different from that of most European languages (other than in the case of a number of borrowings from Russian), translating in general and translating Joycean wordplay in particular can clearly pose some particularly difficult challenges.[56]

While many readers will thus, like the present writer, be almost entirely lost as to the finer points of what may be going on in the translation, even a non-Georgian reader is quickly able to identify numerous pleasing instances of river names. The Fijian Momi and Canadian Eve rivers can thus clearly be seen to put in early appearances ("momikhevi"), followed in quick succession by the American Ela and Turkish Peri ("khvelaperi"), the Luxembourg Sûre and Syr ("msurs"), the Portuguese Ave ("akhlave"), and the American Rock ("roca"). A particularly pleasing fluvial note is translingually sounded in the phrase "ra tkma unda," literally, "What do you want?" (as in French *Que voulez-vous?*), and thus colloquially meaning "of course" – but where the Georgian verb *unda* not only means "to want" but is also a serendipitous homonym of the Latin noun *unda*, meaning a "wave."

---

55 My thanks to Tamar Gelashvili for kindly sending me an electronic copy of her Georgian rendering of *FW* 196.1–11, for providing the transliteration, and for helpfully responding to linguistic enquiries.

56 For a discussion of some specific difficulties, see Gelashvili (2020a).

23 Ancient Egyptian

Mezzabotta (Ancient Egyptian hieroglyphics, 2018)

In 2018, Orlando Mezzabotta continued his playful Joycean experimentation by posting (and reading) on YouTube "*FW* Doublends Jined," a transposition of the closing and opening pages (*FW* 628.15–16; 3.1–3) into Ancient Egyptian hieroglyphics (2018a), involving *inter alia multa* the transposition of the title *Finnegans Wake*:

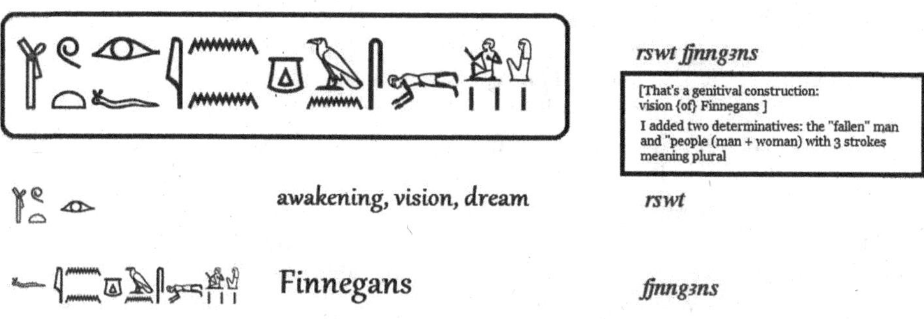

The hieroglyphic title is transliterated, Mezzabotta proposes, as *rswt fjnngens* and suggests, ambiguously, either a singular "Finnegan's awakening" or a plural "Finnegans' awakening" – or, in either case, the "dream" or "vision" of such an awakening. The singular Finnegan is represented in his fallen and apparently moribund state in the second-last glyph of the titular cartouche, while the final glyph evokes the plural Finnegans who are encouraged to respond to the titular call to awaken.

In subsequent personal correspondence, Mezzabotta proposed a significant further improvement, involving the replacement of *rswt* by glyphs transliterated as *weg*, an expression phonetically similar to "wake" and, serendipitously, the name in ancient Egypt of a festival of death and resurrection honouring Osiris. The title as adjusted would now suggest the death, wake, and resurrection of both a singular Finnegan and simultaneously of all those Finnegans, male and female, who are urgently encouraged to awaken.[57] Joyce would undoubtedly have approved.

In the same year, the irrepressible Mezzabotta also provided a brief transposition of the opening and closing lines of *ALP* into Ancient

---

57 My thanks to Orlando Mezzabotta for his detailed responses to various enquiries on matters hieroglyphic.

Egyptian hieroglyphics, posted (and read) once again on YouTube (2018b). His accompanying editorial note: "I couldn't help it!"

24 Latin

Roberts's (quasi-)Latin Wake: Pervigilium Finneganis *(2019)*

Adam Roberts, born in London in 1965, studied English and Classics at Aberdeen and Cambridge, and as of 2019 was a professor of English at Royal Holloway, University of London. According to his webpage, he was the author to that date of "twelve science fiction novels, eight parodies, two novellas, a collection of short stories and various other things." These latter now came to include *Pervigilium Finneganis*, which appeared in February 2019, humorously announcing itself to be the world's first complete translation of *FW* into Latin. Roberts cheerfully admits in his introduction, however, that the "translated" text is less in Latin than in "cod-Latin," quasi-Latin, where most of the individual words are indeed Latin words one might find in a dictionary but their combinations and grammatical interactions are far from anything one might think of as meaningful Latin discourse.

The "translated" text is the result of a sentence-by-sentence transposition of *FW* rendered by Google Translator, previously and subsequently manipulated by Roberts. Since Google Translator needs first to recognize the input text as words and phrases in its existing database, failing which the output merely repeats the input, Roberts describes the process involved as necessarily beginning with his "rewriting Joyce's original into a rough 'regular English' approximation, perhaps by writing out his portmanteaus to make explicit multiple puns; running this through Google Translator and then recombining the resulting cod-Latin in various ways." In other words, as he writes, "the machine translates, and I translate the machine."

He expands on the matter in an associated online blog: "So I had to fix up both text and translation, and it was this process, rather than any fetishisation of a Latin *Wake* as such, that interested me; like one of those avant garde composers who works with prepared pianos. It's text and machine and the intriguing stuff that comes out the far side."[58] Roberts's long and interesting introduction cheerfully discusses "the absurdity of the project and the balance of authenticity and fakery in the result," and wittily sums up the endeavour as a whole: "Translating *Finnegans Wake*

---

58   amechanicalart.blogspot.com/2019/02/pervigilium-finneganis.html. In an online comment on this blog, Hervé Michel applauds the experiment and observes that his own *Veillée Pinouilles* was essentially attempting the same procedure in French.

into Latin is a project neither serious nor plausible. But that's only fitting, for *Finnegans Wake* is itself not a serious or plausible work."

The title parodically reflects that of the *Pervigilium Veneris*, a possibly fourth-century Latin poem of unknown authorship, celebrating the arrival of spring and new life under the beneficent influence of the goddess Venus. Its title is variously translated as "The Vigil of Venus" or "The Eve of Venus." The *pervigilium* of Roberts's title, as he notes, refers also to the vigil or wake observed as part of Roman funerary practice, pointing thus "towards the ultimate sleep of death on the one hand and towards vigilance and wakefulness on the other." One notes that the modern colloquialism *perv*, as in *pervert*, also resonates in the context of HCE's dubious activities in the Phoenix Park.

The three-line incipit (*FW* 3.1–3) is rendered as follows:

flumenflue, transitum Eva et Adae, declinationem ab litore ad flectere lauri, commodius ab nobis facit Houuthi vicus de castro et recirculus ad circumstant.

This result already illustrates the concept of working with a prepared piano: *flumen* is indeed "river," but *flue*, while preserving the alliteration, is an imperative, thus "river, run!"; *transitum* is a noun ("passing") rather than a preposition; *Eva* is a nominative case, while *Adae* is a genitive; the original "to bend of bay" is rendered by the infinitive *flectere* ("to bend"); and *lauri* is the genitive case of *laurus*, which is indeed a "bay," but only as referring to the tree of the same name. And so on, the sometimes bizarrely unpredictable but nonetheless linguistically related results recalling the anonymous 2010 machine-generated translation of the same lines into Esperanto, as already discussed.

Roberts writes in his blog: "Obviously it's a kind of joke, and the joke depends both upon its pointlessness and its egregiousness." And as to why the experiment needed to be expanded to include the entire 628-page *Wake*: "I might have just floated the idea, and maybe translated a few pages; but if a thing's worth doing, it's worth doing well, and that counts double if a thing was never worth doing in the first place. I feel Joyce would agree with me here."[59]

Roberts's version of the opening lines of *ALP* (*FW* 196.17, 09–11), for general delectation – and "Youll 'die quo auditis":

O / indica mihi / Annam Liviam! Cupio audire omnia / Annam Liviam. Scis Annam? Bene, scitis Petrus comite Livia! Et quidem scimus Anna deṣit.

---

59 My thanks to Adam Roberts for kindly providing me with an electronic copy of his complete rendering.

Narra mihi omnia. Nunc autem dic mihi. Youll 'die quo auditis. Bene, scitis, quando vetus cheb abiit, et fecit futt quid nosti melius. ... Aut quisquod semper fuit, ut filum ex duobus in se est thried Modela Est parco.

And, for further delectation, his (and Google Translator's) rendering of the final lines of the *Wake* (*FW* 627.34–628.4, 15–16):

O finis amarum! Et auferetur ante lapsum nimium est. Et numquam videam. Nec scire. Mihi non diiset. Et illud antiquum et vetus est tristis et senex est tristis consocians defecit, ego vadam ad te, mea frigus Pater, mea frigus ad insaniam convertunt Pater, mea frigus ad insaniam convertunt mediocris Pater, usque ad circa visus est ipsa magnitudo eius, et stadiorum millia stadiorum est illud trepidi vehit mare salsissimum aegra ruere facit unicam meam in sinum tuum. ... A sola est via ad diu in novissimis enim dilexit ille

Chapter Ten

The 2020s

*1 Portuguese; 2 German; 3 Georgian; 4 Chinese; 5 Danish;
6 Serbian; 7 Spanish; 8 Russian; 9 Turkish; 10 Finnish;
11 Norwegian; 12 Hungarian; 13 Arabic*

It may seem premature to devote an entire chapter to a decade that has only just begun. The point of this final chapter, however, is to suggest just how vigorous and vibrant the international translatorial interest in *Finnegans Wake* continues to be. The year 2020 saw significant renderings from the *Wake* in Portuguese, German, and Georgian, and further activity was announced in a dozen languages, including promised new complete renderings of *Finnegans Wake* in no fewer than nine different languages, namely, Portuguese, Georgian, Chinese, Serbian, Russian, Turkish, Finnish, Norwegian, and Hungarian.

1 Portuguese

Oliveira (Portuguese, 2020)

A Portuguese translation of *FW* I.5 by Leide Daiane de Almeida Oliveira appeared in March 2020 as part of her doctoral dissertation at the Federal University of Santa Catarina in Florianópolis, Brazil. Her rendering includes the opening lines (*FW* 104.1–5):

In the name of Annah the Allmaziful, the Everliving, the Bringer of Plurabilities, haloed be her eve, her singtime sung, her rill be run, unhemmed as it is uneven! / Her untitled mamafesta memorialising the Mosthighest has gone by many names at disjointed times.

Oliveira's version:

Em nome de Annah a Allmisericordiosa, a Eviterna, a Provedora de Plurabilidades, alabada seja sua véspera, venha a nós o seu canto, seu rio corra à
vontade, sem cabeceira como nascéu! / Sua mamafesta não-titulada mem-
oralizando o Muitoaltíssimo foi conhecida por muitos nomes em tempos
desconjuntados.[1]

Amarante (Portuguese, early 2020s?)

Dirce Waltrick do Amarante confirms in personal correspondence that
she is planning a Portuguese rendering of "The Ondt and the Gracehoper" to appear under the title "A Seegraça e a Foulmiga" (São Paulo:
Iluminuras) in the early 2020s.

Amarante et al. (Portuguese, early 2020s?)

Dirce Waltrick do Amarante confirms in personal correspondence that
she is coordinating and editing a complete Portuguese team translation
of *FW* (São Paulo: Iluminuras), expected to appear in the early 2020s
under the title *Finnegans rivolta* and involving eleven different translators altogether: Afonso Teixeira Filho (I.1–3), Vinícius Alves (I.4), Daiane Oliveira (I.5), Luis Henrique Garcia Ferreira (I.6–7), Dirce Waltrick
do Amarante (I.8, IV), Fedra Rodriguez (II.1–2), André Cechinel (II.3–4),
Aurora Bernardini (III.1–2), Vitor Alevato do Amaral (III.3), Tarso do Amaral (III.4), Andréa Buch Bohrer (*FW* 619–28). The volume is to be illustrated by Sérgio Medeiros. Very surprisingly, no fewer than three of the
members of this team – Luis Henrique Garcia Ferreira, Afonso Teixeira
Filho, and Vinícius Alves – are reportedly also engaged in separate complete renderings of *Finnegans Wake*, likely to appear later in the 2020s.

Garcia Ferreira (Portuguese, 2020s?)

Luis Henrique Garcia Ferreira confirms in personal correspondence
that in addition to his involvement (*FW* I.6–7) in Dirce Waltrick do Amarante's ongoing team translation, *Finnegans rivolta*, he is also at work
on his own complete Portuguese rendering of *Finnegans Wake*, planned
to appear later in the 2020s.

---

1 My thanks to Daiane Oliveira for kindly sending me an electronic copy of her
   rendering.

Teixeira Filho (Portuguese, 2020s?)

Afonso Teixeira Filho confirms in personal correspondence that in addition to his involvement (*FW* I.1–3) in Dirce Waltrick do Amarante's ongoing team translation, *Finnegans rivolta*, he is also at work as of this writing on his own complete Portuguese rendering of *Finnegans Wake*, planned to appear under the title *Renatos Avelar* later in the 2020s.

Alves (Portuguese, 2020s?)

In addition to his involvement (*FW* I.4) in Dirce Waltrick do Amarante's ongoing team translation, *Finnegans rivolta*, Vinícius Alves confirms in personal correspondence that he is at work as of this writing on his own complete Portuguese rendering of *Finnegans Wake*, to be published by Kotter Editorial in Curitiba, Brazil, later in the 2020s. A writer and translator, Alves has translated works of Lewis Carroll, Edward Lear, and Edgar Allan Poe, as well as Joyce's *Pomes Penyeach* (under the title *Pomas penicada*).

Galindo (Portuguese, 2020s?)

Caetano Galindo confirms in personal correspondence that his complete Portuguese rendering of *FW* is planned to appear, under the untranslated original title, in the early 2020s
The opening lines (*FW* 3.1–3) of Galindo's planned translation have been reported (Amaral 2019, 160) as follows:

Ribeiranda, em pós de Eva e de Adão, do encolho da costa à dobrada baía, nos devolve por comódico vico recirculatório a Howth, seu Castelo Ealredores.

Here the river (*ribeira*) runs (*anda*) past (*em pós de*) both Eve and Adam, from the swerve (*encolho*) of coast (*costa*) to the bend (*dobrada*) of bay (*baía*) and brings us back (*nos devolve*) by a commodious (*comódico*) and recirculatory way (*vico*) to Howth, with its Castle and Environs. The opening "ribeiranda" closely echoes the original "riverrun"; the river brings us "past both Eve and Adam" rather than "past Eve and Adam's"; the alliteration linking swerve of shore and bend of bay is carefully preserved; we are brought back to Howth, "with its Castle and Environs"; and HCE's initials are preserved by combining *e alredores* ("and environs") as "Ealredores."

Almeida Filho (Portuguese)

In September 2015 a projected new Portuguese rendering of *FW* by Eclair Antonio Almeida Filho (born 1974), a professor of translation studies at the University of Brasilia, was announced in Brazilian newspapers, to be published by Lumme Editor of São Paulo, possibly under some variation on the tentative working title *Vigília/Incelença/Elegia para Finnegan*.[2] The triple working title, primarily intended to emphasize a strong Brazilian element in the translated text, conflates the concepts of vigil, elegy, and *incelença*, a traditional folk genre of mourning song performed during funerals in certain rural areas of Brazil. As director of a team of graduate students, Almeida Filho produced Portuguese renderings of *Epiphanies* in 2014 and of both *Giacomo Joyce* and *Pomes Penyeach* in 2015, published bilingually in all three cases by Lumme Editor. Further Joycean translations were envisaged, to culminate with at least a partial rendering of *FW*. Due to pressure of other academic work, however, the proposed rendering had to be indefinitely postponed.[3]

2 German

Rathjen (German, 2020)

In April 2020 the apparently indefatigable Friedhelm Rathjen published, once again in his series Edition ReJoyce, the volume *James Joyce jongliert: Genese und Konzeption von Finnegans Wake*, a general introduction to *FW* for German readers, including numerous extended excerpts from his own previous *Wake* translations in his volumes *Winnegans Fake* (2012), *Mamalujo* (2014), *Earwicker* (2015), and his German rendering of *Finn's Hotel* (2014).

Blumenbach (German, 2020s?)

Ulrich Blumenbach confirms in personal correspondence that negotiations are under way with Suhrkamp Verlag in Frankfurt for a complete German rendering of *FW*.

---

2 The announcements appeared in the *Folha de S. Paulo* of 5 September 2015 and in the journal *Época* of 9 October 2015.

3 My thanks to Eclair Antonio Almeida Filho for helpful explanations in personal correspondence – and for confirmation of the necessary postponement.

3 Georgian

Gelashvili (Georgian, 2020)

Tamar Gelashvili's Georgian rendering of *FW* I.1–8 appeared in October 2020, published by Printgeo in Tbilisi. This is a single-language edition, unaccompanied by Joyce's original, and appears in Georgian script only, supplemented by brief commentaries and concluding notes, also in Georgian. Each chapter is introduced by an illustration prepared by the translator.

Gelashvili, in personal correspondence, reports the following rendering of the opening three lines (*FW* 3.1–3), which she also kindly transliterates:

მდინარის დინება, ჩაუვლი ევას და ადამს, ნაპირიდან ყურემდე, შემდეგ მოჯადოებული წრეზე ტრიალი ისევ უკან გვაბრუნებს ჰოუთის კოშკთან და მის შემოგარენთან.

mdinaris dineba, chauvlis evas da adams, napiridan kuremde, shemdeg
mojadoebul tsreze triali isev ukan gvabrunebs houtis koshktan da mis
shemogarentan.

The rendering here opens strongly with the formulation "mdinaris dineba," which, doubling the number of Joyce's original three syllables, is at least triply fluvial, for *dineba* means "flow, stream" and *mdinaris* is the genitive case of the noun *mdinare* ("river"), while the homonymous adjective *mdinare* means "flowing, running." Eve and Adam retain their Joycean order, while the alliteration of swerve of shore and bend of bay disappears, as do both Commodus and Vico, victims in all cases of the linguistic restrictions imposed by the Georgian language. Howth Castle and Environs becomes "houtis koshktan da mis shemogarentan," where readers may or may not realize retrospectively that HCE's first two Georgian initials are suggested as present in "houtis koshktan" – while Shem, unexpectedly, is also not only present but doubly so ("shemdeg," "shemogarentan").

Generating the initials HCE proved to be a major translational challenge throughout. In rendering "Haveth Childers Everywhere," for example, Gelashvili found that since few words begin with either *h* or *ch* in Georgian, she needed to employ a relatively complicated strategy: for the first initial, it was convenient that the verb *khola* ("to have") has a archaic form *hkhola*; "Childers," more of a challenge, becomes an invented "Chvipuldersebi," combining elements of *chvip* (an archaic form for "small child") and *bavshvebi* ("children") enfolding the original letters *-lder-*; while "Everywhere" is rendered by the noun *ertiasad* ("a lot"), serendipitously containing the elements *erti* ("one") and *asi* ("hundred"), and thus suggesting indefinite expansion, familial and spatial alike. HCE as "Hkhola Chvipuldersebi Ertiasad" in this case, after considerable translatorial effort, thus preserves his original initials.[4]

Gelashvili (Georgian, 2020s?)

Tamar Gelashvili confirms in personal correspondence that she plans a complete Georgian rendering of the *Wake* to appear later in the 2020s.

4 Chinese

Dai (Chinese, 2020s?)

In early August 2020 Congrong Dai spoke with an online translation studies group led by James Elkins of the School of the Art Institute of Chicago. She reportedly commented that despite the enormous sales success of her rendering of Book I, the Chinese educational system not only fails to accommodate translation projects but actually discourages them. She reiterated that her health had suffered in translating Book I, and that it continued to do so in translating Book II, which she had just finished and which was expected to appear in the early 2020s. Work on Book III was under way, and Books III–IV were expected to appear in a third volume at some later date in the 2020s.[5]

Dai confirmed that she had changed her approach with Book II, opting to streamline her translation by presenting only one clear meaning for each word, while letting the footnotes and commentaries discuss additional meanings. To the suggestion that her rendering of Book I is more in the spirit of the original, in that it interrupts and slows reading, she observed that Chinese readers' overall reaction to her earlier rendering persuaded her that a more simplified and essentially reductive approach was necessary. She confirmed, however, that the printed format would remain the same as in her previous translation, with its elaborate structure of footnotes, glosses, and facing-page commentaries still designed to remind Chinese readers of traditional editions of

---

4 My thanks to Tamar Gelashvili for her detailed explanation on this point in personal correspondence.

5 My thanks to Congrong Dai for confirming this information in personal correspondence.

Confucian classics, thus implying that *FW* deserves the same sustained and respectful attention. It appears that the Chinese *Wake* will therefore be unusual in this differential approach to Books I and II.[6]

5 Danish

Laugesen (Danish, 2020s?)

Peter Laugesen confirms in personal correspondence that he is continuing to work on renderings especially of the three chapters *FW* I.1, I.8, and IV, one or more of them likely to appear in print at some point in the 2020s.[7]

6 Serbian

Stojaković (Serbian, 2020)

Siniša Stojaković's Serbian rendering of *FW* II appeared in April 2020, thus bringing his complete translation of *FW* to a conclusion. A fully revised version coordinating the details of the three volumes of the complete Serbian Wake, which began with *FW* I in 2014 and continued with III/IV in 2017 and finally II in 2020, is expected to appear by the mid-2020s, published in Belgrade, as before, by Pasus, under the title *Finegana buđenje*, literally, "Finnegan's awakening."[8]

7 Spanish

Victoria (Spanish, 2020s?)

Juan Díaz Victoria reports in personal correspondence that *FW* I.1, I.2, I.8, and II.2, including some three thousand footnotes altogether, are expected to appear in Peru in the early 2020s, published in Lima by Colmena Editores. His planned complete Spanish rendering of the *Wake* is reportedly in vigorous progress. It has been estimated, based on his renderings to date, that the final version might have to include as many as twenty thousand footnotes (Léon 2017).

---

6 My thanks to James Elkins for providing this information in personal correspondence.

7 My thanks to Peter Laugesen for providing this information in personal correspondence.

8 For an account (in Serbian) of insights gained and headaches generated while producing his complete rendering, see Stojaković (2019).

8 Russian

Rene (Russian, 2020s?)

Andrey Rene reports in personal correspondence that having completed *FW* I–II, and with work well under way on *FW* III–IV, he expects his complete Russian translation of *FW* to appear both online and in book form in the early 2020s.

9 Turkish

Çelikyay (Turkish, 2020s?)

Umur Çelikyay reports in personal correspondence that with *FW* I–II already in print, he expects his complete Turkish translation of *FW* to appear in the early 2020s.

10 Finnish

Lindholm (Finnish, 2020s?)

Lauri Niskanen reported in the Finnish online journal *Suomen Kuvalehti* (The Finnish magazine) on Bloomsday 2019 that the translator Juhani Lindholm was planning to undertake a complete Finnish rendering of *Finnegans Wake*, to be published by the Tammi publishing house of Helsinki. Lindholm (born 1951 in Helsinki) is an award-winning translator who has translated, among others, Shakespeare, Ian McEwan, Michael Ondaatje, Daniel Defoe, Emily Brontë, Herman Melville, David Foster Wallace – and *Gravity's Rainbow* by Thomas Pynchon.

Päivi Koivisto-Alanko of the Tammi publishing house confirms that Tammi has an agreement with Lindholm for a translation of *Finnegans Wake*, the expected date of publication being tentatively the early 2020s. A complete translation is planned; no excerpts have as yet appeared anywhere; and the translated title has not yet been discussed.[9]

Lauri Niskanen writes in personal correspondence: "I asked Lindholm if and how he thought *Finnegans Wake* could be translated, and he answered, freely translated: 'If it can be understood, it can be translated. It's just a question of how you understand it.'"

---

9 My thanks to Päivi Koivisto-Alanko for providing this information in personal
   correspondence.

11 Norwegian

Høghaug (Norwegian, 2020s?)

Leif Høghaug confirms in personal correspondence that his complete Norwegian translation of *FW* is expected to appear in the early 2020s, published by Det Norske Samlaget in Oslo and retaining the original title, *Finnegans Wake* – the lack of an apostrophe simultaneously suggesting to a Norwegian reader a grammatically correct "Finnegan's wake."

12 Hungarian

Bozai (Hungarian, 2020s?)

Ágota Bozai confirms in personal correspondence that her complete Hungarian rendering of *FW* is expected to appear online in the mid-2020s.

13 Arabic

Taha (Arabic)

Finally, there is the strange case of the Arabic *FW* – if we can even assume that it did in fact once exist. The Egyptian Joyce scholar Taha Mahmoud Taha (1929–2002) translated *Ulysses* into Arabic in 1982, and in the same year he published a long article on Arabic and Koranic elements in *FW*. As for a possible Arabic translation of *FW*, the Palestinian scholar of Irish literary studies Suheil Badi Bushrui had written in the early 1980s that an Arabic rendering of the *Wake* was essentially unthinkable, for literary Arabic is the language of the Koran: "It is therefore sacred, and for anyone to destroy its conventions, as Joyce does in *Finnegans Wake* to the English language, would seem like sacrilege on a massive scale. ... The question then is how is an Arab to invent a new language and still maintain absolute loyalty to that vehicle of expression which he regards as the absolute standard, and the integrity of whose style, structure, and rhetoric he is bound by faith to safeguard and preserve" (1982, 233–4). It was therefore all the more interesting that two decades later, in 2002, in the online weekly edition of the influential Egyptian newspaper *Al-Ahram*, an anonymous newspaper obituary of Taha Mahmoud Taha indicated, without any further details, that in addition to his translation of *Ulysses* he had in fact also completed an Arabic translation of *FW* (Anon. 2002).

Ten years later still, the Egyptian writer Maher Battuti reported on-line that Taha had confirmed to him, in personal correspondence in the 1980s, that he was working on a *FW* translation. Battuti also reports having read a confirmation in the magazine *Al-Arabi* that Taha had indeed translated *FW*. He reports that the magazine even carried an illustration of the (intended?) cover – but that he was subsequently unable to locate any copy of the translation itself (Battuti 2012). Nor has any further trace of it, to my present knowledge, emerged over the intervening years. Interviewed by Tatsuo Hamada in 2014, the Lebanese-American Joyce scholar Aida Yared, whose work focuses on the Arabian aspects and sources of Joyce's works, was unaware of the existence of any Arabic rendering of *FW* – although, she adds: "It would be beautiful in Arabic, because Arabic is a very rich language with an enormous vocabulary, and therefore the possibility of very nuanced renderings" (Hamada 2014b, 139).

Battuti reports that Taha originally intended to use the title مأتم آلفينيجانانت. "But it seems that eventually he returned to the safer transliteration of فينيجانز ويك " (Battuti 2012). The original provisional title given here, مأتم آلفينيجانانت, *ma'aatem alfinegaanaat*, is doubly plural, as if suggesting "Finnegans' wakes." There is no exact equivalent in the Arabic Muslim tradition of a funeral wake, however, the deceased being typically prepared for burial with only family members in attendance, after which a funeral ceremony or *ma'tam* takes place to accompany the actual burial. The plural *ma'aatem* thus translates not as "wakes" but as "funeral ceremonies" or "memorial ceremonies." The title to which Taha reportedly reverted, فينيجانز ويك, is a phonetic transliteration of the English title, *Finnegans* [فينيجانز] *Wake* [ويك].[10]

---

10 My thanks to Amal Eldiaby at Queen's University in Kingston, Canada, for linguistic and cultural information.

Conclusion

The nine decades covered in the preceding survey may, as already suggested, be roughly divided into three periods: the early years (1930s–1960s), the middle years (1970s–1990s), and what we may not unreasonably call the boom years (2000s–2020s).

Other than Joyce's own iconic partial French and Italian renderings of *ALP*, the four decades of the early years thus saw in print, among a number of more modest contributions, one very early complete Czech *ALP* (Weatherall, Procházka, and Hoffmeister 1932); three decades later some forty pages of excerpts in Italian by Juan Rodolfo Wilcock (1961), followed by four chapters in French, *FW* I.1 and IV by André du Bouchet (1962), *FW* I.7 and I.1 by Philippe Lavergne (1967, 1968); and some ten pages of excerpts in German by Arno Schmidt (1969). The opening chapter, *FW* I.1, could by 1968 already be read in two different French versions, by du Bouchet (1962) and Lavergne (1968), respectively.

The three decades of the middle years (1970s–1990s) of our survey saw a marked increase in translatorial activity, resulting inter alia in three complete renderings of *FW*, in French (Lavergne 1982), German (Stündel 1993), and Japanese (Yanase 1991, 1993), and an abridged Spanish rendering (Pozanco 1993). About a quarter of the original text also appeared in German translations by various hands (Reichert and Senn 1989) and some forty pages in Russian translation (Volokhonsky 1996–9). The first four chapters, in addition, appeared in Italian (Schenoni 1982b), the first three in Japanese (Suzuki et al. 1971), the first two in Galician (Pagán 1993), the first chapter in Portuguese (Schüler 1999), the sixth in German (Horn 1989), and the seventh also in German (Reichert et al. 1989). The first chapter could be read by the end of the 1990s in eight separate renderings in six different languages: French (twice), German, Japanese (twice), Italian, Galician, and Portuguese. These middle years also saw eight complete versions of *ALP*, three in German (Goyert 1970, Hildesheimer 1970, Wollschläger 1970), one in Japanese (Osawa et al. 1982), one in Polish (Słomczyński 1985), one in Korean (Kim 1985), and two in Spanish (Silva-Santisteban 1991, García Tortosa 1992). In addition, Joyce and Frank's original Italian *ALP*, purged of Settanni's emendations, appeared in print for the first time in 1979, while Beckett and Péron's original French *ALP* also finally appeared in print, likewise for the first time, in 1985.

The first two decades of what I am calling the boom years (2000s–2020s) have seen a greatly accelerated expansion of the *FW* universe, as measured by the number of published renderings. These years have seen no fewer than twelve further complete renderings of *FW*, in Dutch (Bindervoet and Henkes 2002), Korean (Kim 2002), Portuguese (Schüler 2003), French (Michel 2004), Polish (Bartnicki 2012), Greek (Anevlavis 2013), Japanese (Hamada 2014), Spanish (Zabaloy 2016), Turkish (Sevimay 2016), Italian (Mazza 2018; Schenoni, Terrinoni, and Pedone 2019), and quasi-Latin (Roberts 2019). Among these, Michel's rendering was a second complete French version and Hamada's a second complete Japanese version. In addition, the boom years have seen nine further complete versions of *ALP*, in Swedish (Grut 2001), Catalan (Aixàs 2004), Japanese again (Miyata 2004a, somewhat abbreviated), Portuguese again (Amarante 2009), Chinese (Dai 2012), French again (Blanchon 2016), Spanish again (Lago 2016), Turkish again (Çelikyay 2016), and Russian (Rene 2017).

The expanding universe of *Finnegans Wake* shows no signs of slowing its multilingual expansion in the 2020s and beyond. Other than the Mondadori Italian rendering (Schenoni, Terrinoni, and Pedone 2019), the eightieth anniversary of the original appearance of *FW* is also expected to be marked in the early 2020s by a second complete Brazilian Portuguese rendering, sixteen years after the appearance of Donaldo Schüler's Portuguese translation of 2003. The new rendering is planned as a team effort, coordinated and edited by Dirce Waltrick do Amarante and involving eleven different translators – no fewer than three of whom, as mentioned (Teixeira Filho, Garcia Ferreira, Alves), are already also reported to be involved in their own ongoing complete renderings of *FW*. Yet another complete Brazilian Portuguese rendering of *FW*, by Caetano Galindo, is likewise expected to appear in the early 2020s, as are complete renderings in Russian (by Andrey Rene), Norwegian (by Leif Høghaug), German (by Ulrich Blumenbach), Georgian (by Tamar Gelashvili), and Hungarian (by Ágota Bozai), as well as a second Turkish version (by Umur Çelikyay), and at a slightly later date a complete Chinese rendering (by Congrong Dai). Japanese can already boast two complete renderings of *FW* (Yanase 1993, Hamada 2014) and one abridged version (Miyata 2004a); Italian can boast two complete renderings (Mazza 2018; Schenoni, Terrinoni, and Pedone 2019), French likewise has two separate complete renderings, Philippe Lavergne's in 1982 and Hervé Michel's in 2004 (the latter with multiple subsequent and continuing revisions). Other than Japanese, no language can so far boast three different *Wakes* – though Portuguese, as mentioned, seems as of this writing to be well on the way to having no fewer than *six* complete renderings within the present decade.

To summarize, and if all of the currently projected complete translations actually come to fruition as planned, there could be as many as an amazing twenty-nine complete translations of the untranslatable *Finnegans Wake* by the end of the 2020s. Sixteen complete translations of *FW* currently exist in thirteen different languages altogether: French (Lavergne 1982; Michel 2004), German (Stündel 1993), Japanese (Yanase 1993; Hamada 2012), Dutch (Bindervoet and Henkes 2002), Korean (Kim 2002), Portuguese (Schüler 2003), Polish (Bartnicki 2012), Greek (Anevlavis 2013), Spanish (Zabaloy 2016), Turkish (Sevimay 2016), Italian (Mazza 2018; Schenoni, Terrinoni, and Pedone 2019), quasi-Latin (Roberts 2019), and Serbian (Stojaković). At least thirteen further complete renderings have been announced as under way for anticipated publication in the 2020s, in Portuguese (Amarante et al.; Galindo; Teixeira Filho; Garcia Ferreira; Alves), Norwegian (Høghaug), Finnish (Lindholm), Russian (Rene), Turkish (Çelikyay), German (Blumenbach), Hungarian (Bozai), Georgian (Gelashvili), and Chinese (Dai).

H.G. Wells famously wondered who on earth James Joyce must have thought he was to demand so much of a reader's precious few years of life in attempting to deal with the *Wake*. How much more might translators of Joyce's entire text wonder. But translators of the untranslatable *Wake* are clearly a very special breed – and clearly given to heroic endeavour. Luigi Schenoni, for example, began working on a planned complete Italian translation of *FW* in 1973 and continued to work on it until his death thirty-five years later, by which time he had completed just twelve of the seventeen chapters. Nevzat Erkmen began work on a planned complete Turkish rendering in 1998 and continued to work on it until his death in 2020 – it is still unclear how much of his rendering he had completed. Ricardo Silva-Santisteban produced his first Spanish rendering of an excerpt from *FW* in 1971 and his latest (to date) in 2000, almost thirty years later. Friedhelm Rathjen began translating the *Wake* in 1984 and was continuing his labours more than thirty-five years later. Times to complete renderings vary widely, of course, and among other translators, Dieter Stündel's German rendering took seventeen years to complete, Krzysztof Bartnicki's Polish ten years, Naoki

Yanase's Japanese seven and a half, Bindervoet and Henkes's Dutch, Marcelo Zabaloy's Spanish, and Eleftherios Anevlavis's Greek each took seven years, while Donaldo Schüler's Portuguese took just four years. Congrong Dai, meanwhile, spent eight years translating just Part I, while Masayoshi Osawa and his team worked for at least fifteen years on translating a complete Japanese *ALP* (1982). At the other end of the durational spectrum is Adam Roberts's *Pervigilium Finneganis*, which, as he cheerfully reports, took him more than a week, "but not much more" (2019).

Finnegans Wakes illustrates the multiple ways in which the ultimately untranslatable text is, paradoxically, extended and enriched by its cumulative renderings, which together with Joyce's original can be seen, to repeat the point, as constituting an ever-expanding *FW* universe. Earlier renderings (and some later ones) tend to be essentially explanatory, usually involving attempted normalization and a focus on what appears to the translator to be the primary plotline. As opposed to such explanatory readings – Lavergne's, for example – that attempt primarily to recapitulate the narrative, there is Krzysztof Bartnicki's description of himself as a "molecular translator," one who deliberately avoided consulting any overarching critical works on the *Wake* until he had first attempted to render individual "letters, then morphemes, words, phrases, punctuation, paragraphs, etc." (Wawrzycka 2016–17, 172, 173).

Some translators make extensive use of annotations. Lavergne's version, for example, includes more than six hundred footnotes. Schenoni's Italian rendering is likewise accompanied by a very large number of systematic annotations – as are, to varying degrees, Alberte Pagán's Galician rendering (1993), Afonso Teixeira Filho's Spanish version (2008), and Andrey Rene's Russian translation (2018), this last including particularly extensive and meticulous notes. In a sense, explanatory rewritings such as Lavergne's are themselves a form of detailed extended annotation. Annotations, for their part, can of course both enhance and reduce readerly pleasure.

In a similarly explanatory mode, some translators endeavour to produce a shorter *FW*, whose common implicit ambition is clearly to demonstrate the real heart of the matter. Though preceded by Juan Rodolfo Wilcock in Italian (1961) and André du Bouchet in French (1962), Anthony Burgess's *A Shorter Finnegans Wake* (1966) played a key role in this particular approach, leading the way for relatively extended translated variants in several languages, including by Víctor Pozanco in Spanish (1993), Kyoko Miyata in Japanese (2004a), Friedhelm Rathjen in German (2012), and Dirce Waltrick do Amarante in Portuguese (2018).

Taking a very different approach, other translators, especially more recent translators, enthusiastically accept the untranslatability of the text not only as a given but also as a liberating invitation to translatorial play rather than explanation or normalization – thus essentially following the example of Joyce's Italian *ALP* in attempting to produce not a would-be replication of the text but a continuation of it. Bindervoet and Henkes thus write of a Dutchification rather than a translation, Michel of a *contraduction*, Bartnicki of a Polonization, Çelikyay of a Turkicization, Laugesen of a Danishing, Falk of a transformulation "til swensko," Rathjen of *Eindeutschungen* ("Germanizings") resulting in what will inevitably be a *Winnegans Fake*. Several more recent renderings in this particular mode emulate Joyce's own game of unrelenting complexification: examples among many would include Hervé Michel's cheerfully arbitrary onomastic series from Finnegan to Pinouille or Orlando Mezzabotta's extravagantly convoluted title of his Italian rendering of the opening chapter, *Opfertuere: il primo capitol'ho?* – not to mention his linguistic adventures in Ancient Egyptian hieroglyphics. Michel's employment of pataphysicist free association in his *Veillée Pinouilles* has thus proven to be particularly influential among later translators such as Marcelo Zabaloy in Spanish or Umur Çelikyay in Turkish. Adam Roberts's concept of his quasi-Latin rendering as being like a version produced on a prepared piano found enthusiastic approval from Hervé Michel, who declared that this was exactly how he saw his own French rendering as functioning. Umberto Eco's paradoxical suggestion resonates that while *FW* may indeed be untranslatable, in some ways it may also be the *easiest* of texts to translate.

Whatever the particular translational approach adopted, various renderings of *FW* are printed with the original text on facing pages, thus allowing for (and inviting) a comparative reading. These include, for example, Schenoni's Italian (1982), Bindervoet and Hankes's Dutch (2002), and Schüler's Portuguese (2003). While, by implication, the translation is thus readable in all such cases as a detailed running commentary on the original, the reverse procedure is also available. A comparison by Emily Cersonsky (2011) of Joyce's original and Stündel's German rendering of 1993, treating both texts as essentially independent, is a good illustration of the possibilities offered by an approach of this kind, whatever the quality of the particular translation involved. In the case of editions that do not include a facing-page version of the original text, the target-language reader is faced with a quite different challenge, the same challenge as faced Joyce's original reader of *FW*, namely, to make unaided sense of the dauntingly complex text. Examples here include Lavergne's French (1982), Yanase's Japanese (1993),

Kim's Korean (2002), Bartnicki's Polish (2012), Dai's Chinese (2012), and Çelikyay's Turkish (2016).

As for *Wake* translators themselves, as a group they constitute an intriguing phenomenon in many ways. In terms of age, for example, they so far range from those born in the 1880s (Joyce himself, Goyert) to those born in the 1980s (Rene in Russian, Scandolara in Portuguese, Vizan in Hebrew), and very likely one or two from the 1990s already.

In terms of professional background, quite a few, unsurprisingly, were or are active or retired members of university departments either of English (Reichert, Füger, Enzensberger, Roberts) or of translation studies (Aixàs, Amarante, Çelikyay) – or, in some cases, of Ancient Greek (Schüler) or Irish (Titley) or philosophy (Ogden, Lourenço). Goyert was a German secondary-school teacher, as well as a professional translator. Schenoni worked initially as a technical and commercial translator. Mario Monteforte was a prominent Guatemalan politician.

Several translators began their Joycean career with a rendering originally undertaken as part of a master's or doctoral dissertation (Aixàs, Bozai, Teixeira Filho, Amarante, Oliveira). Many were already or would shortly become published poets (du Bouchet, Nishiwaki, Silva-Santisteban, Laugesen) or novelists (Butor, Hildesheimer, Wollschläger, Burgess, Mazza) or dramatists (Hildesheimer) or all three (Beckett). Hildesheimer originally planned a career as a painter, Wollschläger and Burgess each originally planned a career as a musician. Only Beckett appears to have subsequently been a recipient of the Nobel Prize, though Nishiwaki was reportedly nominated several times.

Schüler, a professional classicist, has also translated widely from Ancient Greek to Portuguese, Goyert also from French to German, Silva-Santisteban from French to Spanish, Lindholm from Swedish to Finnish. Volokhonsky's first attempted translation from English to Russian was, very bravely, *Finnegans Wake*. Mezzabotta transposed excerpts from the *Wake* into Ancient Egyptian hieroglyphics, and Roberts transposed the entire *Wake* into Latin, or, at any rate, quasi-Latin.

A striking feature is how many *Wake* translators have scientific rather than literary backgrounds: Wilcock graduated in civil engineering, for example, Stojaković in mechanical engineering, Volokhonsky in biochemistry, Hamada in biology, Rene in physics. Lavergne was a telecommunications engineer, Zabaloy was originally a computer technician, Anevlavis is a medical doctor. Among other professional backgrounds, Stündel is a journalist, as was Grut; Sevimay is a former sales executive; Erkmen was a marketing and management executive; Michel is a retired French civil servant; and Mezzabotta is a professional actor. Among other interests, Lavergne was fascinated by mathematics, numerology, parapsychology, and astrology; Erkmen was fascinated by psychology, Eastern philosophies, and mind games of various sorts, and was eventually a founder of the World Puzzle Federation.

Another noticeable feature is the relative dearth of female translators. The first rendering by a woman of any part of the *Wake* was that of Maria Weatherall with the very early Czech *ALP* of 1932; the second, by Ingeborg Horn in German, followed only more than half a century later, in 1989. Another decade elapsed before the 2000s saw Marissa Aixàs's Catalan *ALP* and Kyoko Miyata's abbreviated Japanese *Wake*, both in 2004, then the first excerpts of Ágota Bozai's ongoing Hungarian *Wake* in 2007, and Dirce Waltrick do Amarante's Portuguese *ALP* in 2009. The following decade saw Book I of Congrong Dai's Chinese *Wake* in 2012, and a French rendering of the opening pages of *ALP* by Ludivine Bouton-Kelly and Tiphaine Samoyault in 2016. Dai and Bozai both aim to produce complete versions in due course, the first complete rendering in Chinese and in Hungarian, respectively. Redressing the gender imbalance somewhat further, seven of the seventeen chapters of Amarante's anticipated Portuguese team rendering of the *Wake*, expected to appear in the early 2020s, have been assigned to female translators.

Stündel's German rendering was greeted with great fanfare as a media event, but critical reception was far less rapturous. Yanase's Japanese, Bartnicki's Polish, and Dai's Chinese were all received with great enthusiasm, while Kim's Korean, Hamada's Japanese, and Rene's ongoing Russian version have generated disappointingly little reaction among potential target-language readers. Bartnicki and Dai both reported finding the translational experience little short of traumatic. Schenoni, on the other hand, found it exhilarating, while Słomczyński, based on his rendering of *ALP*, considered the task essentially to present no great problem. Translators may of course also have their individual translatorial quirks, such as Lavergne's determination in French to find Irish explanations for as many textual oddities and obscurities as possible; Schüler's flaunted onomastic playfulness in Portuguese; Stündel's equally flaunted process of unrelenting verbal deformation combined with lower-body extravagances; and Bartnicki's flamboyant trio of intersemiotic transpositions.

Given all of this, it is perhaps unsurprising that a certain number of myths have circulated concerning *Wake* translators. It has variously been reported, for example, that Yanase's Japanese version of the *Wake* in fact needed three separate translators, after the first disappeared and the second went mad (McGrath 2014, Yun 2014, Bugliaro 2017). Other *Wake* myths include the colourful legend of Luigi Schenoni's protracted survival on copious supplies of pasta provided by a conveniently available aunt and Dieter Stündel's claim to have invented fifty thousand new German words in his rendering.

As for the individual languages into which the *Wake* has been rendered, partially or in full, one would almost certainly not have expected Czech, for example, to have been the first language to boast a complete rendering of *ALP* – which in 1932 was the most substantial translation in any language from what would eventually become the *Wake*. It would be almost three decades before renderings in Italian by Wilcock and in French by du Bouchet produced a greater number of pages from the *Wake*. In more recent years, the *Wake* has been rendered in part or in whole into all the major and many of the minor European languages, with the exception (so far) of Icelandic, Basque, Ukrainian, Bulgarian, Irish (other than the six lines translated by Alan Titley in 2008), and the other Celtic languages.

Among languages that one might perhaps not necessarily have expected to appear in the *Wake* universe at all are Catalan (Aixàs), Galician (Pagán), Hungarian (Bíró, Bozai), Finnish (Mutanen, Helin, Lindholm), Serbian (Stojaković), Slovak (Kot 1965), Croatian (Šoljan (1978), Slovenian (Skubic 2000, Godler 2018), and Georgian (Gelashvili 2018). The sudden prominence of Turkish in 2016 was both an unexpected and an intriguing development. Languages of the Iberian Peninsula are in general well represented, but in Portuguese, for example, Brazil is increasingly prominent while Portugal is notably absent with the sole exception of Manuel Lourenço's rendering more than half a century ago of the opening page (1968). Norwegian was completely absent in the *Wake* macrotext before a 2016 rendering of the opening pages by Leif Høghaug, whose advertised complete translation in progress now seems likely to make Norwegian the main *Wake* language of Scandinavia, though briefer renderings existed at an earlier point in both Swedish and Danish. Japanese, Korean, and more recently Chinese have been prominent among Asian languages. Perhaps the most unexpected language to have put in an appearance so far, other than Ancient Egyptian, Esperanto, and Latin, is the South American indigenous language Guarani (Medeiros 1999).

There is also a sizeable group of complete translations that might have been, ghost translations that never actually came to fruition. The Russian translator Henri Volokhonsky referred in 2003 to an Albanian translation (Alexandrova 2015, 146) – but he was obviously very vague as to what translations of the *Wake* there might be other than his own, and no Albanian translation seems in fact to exist. Whether or not an Arabic rendering exists remains an intriguing puzzle (Battuti 2012). In the 1940s Ivan Goll was rumoured to be working on a complete German *Wake*, but it seems to have remained at the rumour stage. Adolf Hoffmeister may or may not have continued to work on a longer or even a complete Czech rendering in the 1940s. The suggestion that Philippe Soupault, Raymond Queneau, Samuel Beckett, and others were engaged in a French rendering in the mid-forties was a fascinating one, but the plan led nowhere. André du Bouchet, Salvador Elizondo, Arno Schmidt, and Maciej Słomczyński all considered the possibility of a complete rendering, in French, Spanish, German, and Polish, respectively, during the 1960s, but in each case the plan was abandoned. Other complete renderings reportedly planned but subsequently abandoned include those in Italian by Anthony Burgess in the 1970s, in Spanish by Román Buenaventura in the 1980s, and in Swedish by Jan Östergren also in the 1980s. Eclair Antonio Almeida Filho's planned Portuguese rendering has more recently been indefinitely postponed, and Nevzat Erkmen died in 2020 before finishing the Turkish translation on which he had been working for two decades. A Romanian rendering was advertised in the 1990s (Oţoiu 2004, 203), but it appears never to have actually been undertaken.

One final question that suggests itself, but will remain unanswered here, is which language or languages might be considered the most potentially productive in which to undertake a translation of or from the *Wake*. The ability to generate puns and other forms of wordplay would of course be entirely crucial. Nino Frank initially objected to Joyce's planned Italian rendering of *ALP* on the grounds that Italian, in his opinion, does not lend itself to puns, and certainly not to Joycean puns. Joyce, aiming to extend the boundaries of Italian as he had already extended those of English (Ellmann 1982, 632), triumphantly demonstrated that Italian was perfectly capable of doing so, and such later Italian translators as Schenoni, Mezzabotta, and Schenoni's continuators Terrinoni and Pedone have very competently continued the demonstration. The Irish language is likewise generally considered to be not at all amenable to the generation of puns, and a fortiori of Joycean puns – but Alan Titley's adroit rendering of just half a dozen lines once again proves the contrary. It is widely accepted that Chinese does not lend itself to puns in any European sense of the concept, and the same appears to be true for Japanese and Korean – but translators in all three of these languages have devised a variety of ingenious compensatory mechanisms. Reviewers of recent Turkish *Wake* translations have written of the particular pun-producing advantages of Turkish as an agglutinative language. Other agglutinative languages such as Hungarian, Finnish, Japanese, and Korean may well share those advantages. Maciej Słomczyński, meanwhile, claimed that Polish would actually have afforded Joyce far more scope for polysemous play than mere English ever did – and Naoki Yanase made a very similar claim for Japanese.

Jacques Aubert went on record in 1967 as wondering if any further, and inevitably failed, attempts to translate *FW* should really be undertaken at all. To which, more than half a century later, one can only respond, Certainly they should, and the more the better! The early reviewer's amusing quip that Lavergne's French rendering was undoubtedly a labour of love, "but so was the monster for Frankenstein" (Benstock and Benstock 1985, 231), essentially asks the same question. Amusing, certainly, but the more such textual monsters we have, even allowing for wide and inevitable differences in translational quality, the richer and more varied the *Wake* macrotext becomes. For the ever-expanding macrotext of *Finnegans Wake* enables not just a corresponding increase but an exponential increase in the ever-expanding pleasures of the *Wake* universe. And while there is certainly lots of fun to be had at *Finnegans Wake*, there is undoubtedly, to repeat a claim implicitly reiterated throughout the present work, even more fun to be had at a macrotextual *Wake*.

Postscript

Too late to be considered in detail in the present volume, a seventeenth complete translation of *FW* appeared in September 2021, Bertil Falk's Swedish *Finnegans likvaka* (Landsbro, Sweden: Aleph Bokförlag). Born in 1933, Falk began working on the preliminary stages of this rendering as early as 1954 – and completed it in April 2021, no less than sixty-six years later. The first chapter already appeared as a separate publication in 2013 (see pp. 277–8 above and 336 below). With the appearance of the complete Swedish *FW*, the number of complete translations of *ALP* has now, as of late 2021, reached thirty-six (cf. p. 346).

Likewise too late to be considered in detail, Andrey Rene's complete Russian translation of *FW* appeared in October 2021 under the title *На помине Финнеганов (Na pomine Finneganov)*. Print version Krakow: Rideró IT Publishing; online version, extensively annotated (in Russian), at http://samlib.ru/r/rene_a/(and see pp. 320, 324 above). Rene's rendering, on which he worked for ten years, is the eighteenth complete translation of *FW* to appear.

Daniel Sénécot's complete French rendering of *FW*, dated 2006–2014 after its final line, appeared online in 2021 at finnfanfun@free.fr, under the title *Finnfanfun, une lecture parisienne du* Finnegans Wake *de James Joyce*. Earlier online versions may also have appeared, but are no longer accessible. The idiosyncratic title promises Joyce's primordial giant Finn's fans lots of fun, while evoking both the Marvel Comics giant dragon Fin Fang Foom and the "Fee fie fo fum" of Jack's beanstalk giant. Sénécot's rendering is the nineteenth complete translation of *FW* and the thirty-seventh of *ALP* to appear.

Appendix 1: Translators, Titles, Texts

Readers' difficulties with *Finnegans Wake*, and most especially would-be translators' difficulties, begin with the title already, provocatively lacking as it does the apostrophe expected by most readers. Richard Ellmann wrote in the first edition of his Joyce biography that Joyce's planned title "was to be *Finnegans Wake*, the apostrophe omitted because it meant both the death of Finnegan and the resurgence of all Finnegans" (1959, 556). In the second edition, twenty-three years later, he more inclusively lists the most striking features of the title planned by Joyce as being that "*Finnegans Wake* contained the *double entendres* of wake (funeral) and wake (awakening or resurrection), as well as of Fin (end) and again (recurrence)" (1982, 597). Indeed, as Fargnoli and Gillespie crisply phrase it, the title *Finnegans Wake* "implies the plurality of identity and the polarity of opposites" (1995, 76). While all of these comments are perfectly accurate, however, they are still far from being the whole story, especially when it comes to translation.[1]

To begin with, why might a hypothetical reader entirely new to Joyce assume that there *was* in fact a missing apostrophe? The title, after all, can be read as a perfectly grammatical English statement that some group of people called "Finnegan" wake, possibly from sleep, possibly from inertia, possibly even from death. For most readers, however, Joyce's title does indeed suggest "Finnegan's wake," certainly for those readers who remember the comic nineteenth-century music-hall song "Finnegan's Wake," in which a drunken Irish builder's labourer, Tim Finnegan, falls from a ladder, apparently to his death, but who revives

---

1　An earlier discussion of the title *Finnegans Wake* was delivered as an invited lecture at the Federal University of Santa Catarina in Florianópolis, Brazil, in June 2019, and subsequently appeared, together with a Portuguese translation, in the online journal *Qorpus* (O'Neill 2019).

when accidentally splashed with whiskey in the course of his wake. A *wake*, meanwhile, as helpfully defined by the *Oxford English Dictionary*, is "the watching (especially by night) of relatives and friends beside the body of a dead person from death to burial, or during a part of that time; [also] the drinking, feasting, and other observances incidental to this. Now chiefly Anglo-Irish or with reference to Irish custom."

The title, however, could obviously also imply a wake not just for a single Finnegan but for a plurality of Finnegans, a plural "Finnegans' wake." It could also be taken as a call addressed to all Finnegans currently asleep ("Finnegans, wake!") as well as already anticipating the success of that call, as all "Finnegans" do indeed "wake." A reference is also suggested to the legendary Irish hero Finn mac Cumhaill (Joyce's Finn MacCool), dead and buried for centuries but destined in folklore to come back to life again in Ireland's hour of greatest need. And perhaps that hour is even already at hand, for "Finn again's wake," employing a now obsolete sense of the adjective *wake* rather than the noun *wake*, suggests that Finn is indeed once again "wake," namely, awake. And many critics have noted that while French *fin* means "end," Latin *negans* means "denying," thus punningly suggesting that what may appear to be an end may in reality be not just an end but also a new beginning. Finn's legendary return will accordingly be reflected by the circular structure of Joyce's text, its unfinished final sentence on page 628 concluded by its opening words on page 3.

The flauntedly challenging title thus plays – and all, apparently, for want of an inconspicuous apostrophe – on singularity and plurality, nouns and verbs, grammatical correctness and all other fixed categories, certainty and uncertainty, history and legend, stasis and change. In so doing it immediately throws down the interpretive gauntlet: the text, like the title that introduces it, will clearly be reconstructable (if at all) only by the most vigorous co-constructive efforts of its readers – preceded, of course, where appropriate, by the vigorous co-constructive efforts of its translators. Variations on the title that are helpfully provided in the text of *Finnegans Wake* itself include, among others, "Finn again's weak" (*FW* 93.35–6), "Wimmegame's fake" (*FW* 375.16–17), "Quinnigan's Quake" (*FW* 497.1), and "the Phoenican wakes" (*FW* 608.32) – as well as, somewhat further afield, "pinnacle's peak" (*FW* 70.13), "jibberweek's joke" (*FW* 565.14), and "for Fullacan's sake" (*FW* 531.26).

So what is a beleaguered would-be translator (acting as if translation were possible) supposed to make of all this? Joyce's missing apostrophe liberates a spectacular vein of possible meanings in its various translations, the degree of complexity of which has tended to increase with the years. To summarize, translators have a good dozen quite different understandings to choose from as a preliminary basis for rendering Joyce's extremely slippery title. The result will only rarely capture more than two or three of the implications of Joyce's extravagantly polysemous challenge to the translator's art – other than the fact that any title containing the word *Finnegans* (and there are those that do not) can also be taken to include potential reference to the hero Finn, to French *fin*, to English *again*, and to Latin *negans*. Translators' interpretive options include the following.[2]

Option 1: Assume that since the title is clearly untranslatable, it is best left untranslated.

Various translators, understandably, choose to treat the title as untranslatable: thus, to name just a few examples, Lavergne's French (1982), Schenoni's Italian (1982), Bindervoet and Henkes's Dutch (2002), Zabaloy's Spanish (2016). How does a reader who is a speaker (perhaps even a monoglot speaker) of the relevant target language react to this title? Certainly, the foreignness, the otherness of the text is advertised from the start. Also perhaps the notion that the title, which has by now acquired international cult status, is "already translated." This assumption, however, involves introducing the translated text by an overtly foreign element, one that is potentially even more immediately disorienting in the target language than in the original.

Option 2: Assume the grammatically correct sentence "Finnegans wake," where "wake" is a verb and "Finnegans" its plural subject, suggesting that Finnegans of all sorts (whoever they may be) wake up from sleep, or inertia, or even death.

The missing apostrophe is a warning shot across the bows of new readers – except, of course, for those readers who see the title as grammatically a perfectly correct sentence. A new reader previously unacquainted both with Joyce's text and with the existence of the music-hall song "Finnegan's Wake" would in principle have no reason *not* to assume this option. Despite this, however, no translator in any language appears to have chosen this titular option.

Option 3: Assume "Finnegan's wake," suggesting a funeral vigil for somebody called Finnegan.

This variant, undoubtedly the most generally popular, teasingly appears at one point in the text itself, reincorporating the missing titular

---

2 The various titles mentioned in appendix 1 are in almost all cases discussed in greater detail in the relevant main entry above.

apostrophe, as "lovesoftfun at Finnegan's Wake" (*FW* 607.16) – where the reference is clearly both to the music-hall song and to Joyce's own text. Many renderings in various languages choose to go with this option, but we can limit ourselves here to considering just a few examples that introduce some interesting implications.

The title of Dieter Stündel's 1993 German rendering, *Finnegans Wehg*, conflates a rhyming echo of the English *wake* with German *Weh* ("woe") and *Weg* ("way"), with perhaps a faint echo of German *wecken* ("to wake someone up"). Strikingly, since German, unlike English, does not use an apostrophe to signal a genitive case, the lack of an apostrophe in the German (as opposed to Joyce's) title does not involve any element of textual play, but is merely reductive, producing an unambiguously singular "Finnegan's." The neologism *Wehg* might also be seen as jocularly referring to the translator's own "woe" as he struggles to find a "way" through the dense thickets of Joyce's text. Umur Çelikyay's Turkish rendering of Book I in 2016 adopts a similar titular strategy to Stündel. This version appeared as *Finneganın vahı*, "Finnegan's woe," where the noun *vah* both means "woe" and suggests an interlingual echo of the English "wake" (Fenge 2016, 2; Bayramova 2016, 5), while the possessive markers *-nın* and *-ı* indicate an unambiguously singular "Finnegan's." Bertil Falk's 2013 Swedish rendering of the opening chapter employs the unambiguously funeral title *Finnegans likvaka*, "Finnegan's wake," literally, Finnegan's "corpse (*lik*) watch (*vaka*)." As in the case of Stündel's version, the lack of an apostrophe is again merely reductive, definitely indicating a singular "Finnegan's."

Moving further afield linguistically, the first three chapters of the *Wake* appeared in 1971 in a Japanese team translation led by Yukio Suzuki under the title *Finnegan tetsuya-sai*, the title implying "Finnegan's wake," with the English noun *wake* rendered as "staying up all night (*tetsuya*)." Chong-keon Kim's Korean rendering of *Finnegans Wake* appeared in 2002 under the title (as romanized) *P'inegan ŭi kyŏngya*. Here "Finnegan" becomes "P'inegan" since the letter *f* does not occur in Korean and is replaced in foreign words and names by an aspirated *p*; "ŭi" is a possessive particle, and "kyŏngya" is the normal Korean term for "wake." The title thus literally means "Finnegan's wake," in a funeral sense – but different cultural implications are introduced, in that the Korean wake custom involves staying all night at the house of the mourners, while the festive character of an Irish wake is absent.

Option 4: Assume a plural "Finnegans' wake," suggesting a funeral vigil for at least two Finnegans.

André du Bouchet's 1957 French rendering of selected excerpts appeared as "Les veilles des Finnegans," a pluralized "Finnegans' wake," the plural *veilles* even suggesting plural obsequies for plural Finnegans,

"Finnegans' wakes." The title of Alberte Pagán's 1993 Galician translation of the first two chapters as *Velório de Finnegans* also literally suggests a plural "Finnegans' wake," a funeral wake for plural Finnegans, but plays on the fact that *Finnegans Wake* is frequently referred to in Spanish as "el *Finnegans*," much as English-speaking readers refer to "the *Wake*." Eleftherios Anevlavis's 2013 Greek *I agrýpnia ton Fínnegan* (*Η αγρύπνια των Φίννεγκαν*) is similarly a pluralized "Finnegans' wake," a funeral wake for plural Finnegans.

Between 1996 and 1999 Henri Volokhonsky translated into Russian some forty pages of excerpts from the *Wake* in a literary journal under the title *Iz Finneganova Weika* (*Из Финнеганова Уэйка*). Here, given the word order, as I am informed by Russian colleagues, *Finneganov* functions adjectivally, thus, roughly, "From a Finneganian Wake," and the title is consequently readable as referring to either a singular "Finnegan's Wake" or a plural "Finnegans' Wake." A collected edition of the same excerpts appeared in book form in 2000 as *Weik Finneganov* (*Уэйк Финнеганов*), where, given the new word order, the nominal rather than adjectival function of *Finneganov* is now primary and the title thus a singular "Finnegan's Wake" – but with the adjectival meaning ("A Finneganian Wake") even still resonating to imply also the possibility of a plural "Finnegans' wake." Thanks to this particular idiosyncrasy of Russian grammar, Volokhonsky is thus able to achieve a pleasing combination of singularity and plurality.

Moving far afield linguistically once again, in 2012 a Chinese version of Book I by Dai Congrong appeared. Dai renders the title as *Fēnnígēn de shǒulíng yè* (芬尼根的守灵夜). The first three Chinese characters of the title (芬尼根) individually mean "fragrant, nun, root," and the difficulty of construing the meaning of the three together is a clue that they transliterate a non-Chinese word or name. Here, combining as *Fēnnígēn*, they suggest a phonetic rendering of "Finnegan" – either singular or plural, since Chinese nouns generally do not have singular and plural forms. The fourth character [的, *de*] is a possessive marker similar to the apostrophe as used in English, and the last three characters [守灵夜, *shǒulíng yè*] translate as "night deathwatch." Dai notes in her introduction that she considered leaving out the last character (夜, *yè*), meaning "night," since the original title does not explicitly mention a time of day, but eventually chose to include it because "night" connotes not only finality but also the expectation of daybreak (Yee 2013).

Option 5: Assume "Finnegan's wake," suggesting a maritime metaphor, as in the wake of a ship.

While André du Bouchet's 1957 French rendering of selected excerpts is unambiguous as to the funeral context, as we have seen, his earlier translation of excerpts, published in 1950 as "Dans le sillage de

Finnegan," is equally unambiguously maritime in sense, suggesting following in: "in Finnegan's wake, in the wake of Finnegan."

In an interesting variation on this option, Juan Díaz Victoria's 2009 Spanish translation of the opening chapter uses the title *Estela de Finnegan*. The term *estela*, like the English *stela* (both derived from Latin *stela*), suggests a commemorative marker for Finnegan, gone but not forgotten, a monument to his memory. It also means a "track" or "trail" or "wake" in the maritime sense, and is employed here, as the translator indicates (Victoria 2009, 1), to highlight the fact that a translation, whatever its intentions, ambitions, and achievements, ultimately never has any choice but to follow in the wake of its original.

Option 6: Assume a plural "Finnegans' wake," likewise suggesting a maritime metaphor, and following in the collective wake of more than one Finnegan.

I am not aware of any translator having chosen this option.

Option 7: Assume the command or exhortation "Finnegans, wake!," a call to all Finnegans to wake up, to stop sleeping, presumably to undertake some unspecified action.

Again, I am not aware of any translator having chosen this option.

Option 8: Assume "Finnegan's awake," he is neither sleeping nor dead.

This understanding of the title involves not the noun *wake* but the now obsolete adjective *wake*, as listed in the *Oxford English Dictionary*, meaning *awake*. A number of translators thus opt for a singular Finnegan who either wakes or is already awake: Jozef Kot's 1965 Slovak version of the opening two pages uses the title "Finnegannovo prebúdzanie," literally, "Finnegan's awakening," and Roberto Sanesi's 1982 Italian rendering of a single page uses the title "Il risveglio di Finnegan," also literally, "Finnegan's awakening," though in Italian allowing also for "Finnegan's revival," as if from the dead. Endre Bíró's 1992 Hungarian *Finnegan ébredése* translates excerpts from, literally, "Finnegan's awakening," and Jacek Malicki's 2001 Polish rendering of excerpts uses the title *Przebudzenie Finnegana*, again literally, "Finnegan's awakening" (from sleep).

Option 9: Remembering the same obsolete adjectival usage of "wake," assume "Finnegans awake," involving at least two Finnegans who are neither sleeping nor dead.

A complete Turkish translation by Fuat Sevimay appeared in 2016 as *Finnegan Uyanması*, where the noun *uyanma* means "awakening" and "Finnegan" is consciously ungrammatical. The noun *uyanması*, with the singular possessive suffix *-sı* literally means "his awakening." But by employing the name "Finnegan" without an appropriate possessive suffix, whether singular or plural (*-nın* or *-lar*, respectively), Sevimay "echoes the obscurity of the original by creating a structure that permits either meaning" (Fenge 2017, 2). *Uyanma* also includes the noun *anma* ("commemoration"), thus suggesting a sense of remembrance (Fenge 2017, 2), Finnegan remembered.

Option 10: Assume "Finn again's (a)wake," implying that Finn MacCool is once again awake, as legend predicted.

I am not aware of any translator having taken up this option – but Joyce himself was pleased to receive an early review of *Finnegans Wake* from Helsinki, where clearly, as he puns on two separate occasions in correspondence, "the Finn again wakes" (*L* 3, 463, 466).

Option 11: Assume, as in option 1, that the original title should remain untranslated, but transliterate it into the relevant target language.

In one sense this is the same as leaving the title untranslated, but new and potentially interesting cultural resonances may very well come into play. Three separate Japanese translations, for example (Yanase 1993, Miyata 2004, Hamada 2012), appeared under the transliterated title *Fineganzu ueiku* (フィネガンズ・ウェイク). A Japanese wake, however, as I am informed, is not called a *ueiku* (ウェイク) but a *tsuya* (通夜), literally, "passing the night," and the ceremonial formalities and social conventions involved are quite different from those of an Irish wake. Similarly, a newspaper obituary of the Egyptian Joyce scholar Taha Mahmoud Taha recorded in 2002 that he had also completed an Arabic translation of the *Wake*. This translation does not seem ever to have actually appeared, but its intended title is recorded as having been a phonetic transliteration of the English title, *Finnegans Wake* (فينيجانز ويك) (Battuti 2012). Once again, however, there is no equivalent in the Arabic Muslim tradition of an Irish funeral wake, the deceased being typically prepared for burial with only family members in attendance, after which a *ma'tam* or "funeral ceremony" takes place to accompany the actual burial. Unlike a traditional Irish wake, alcohol plays no part in either of these ceremonial occasions.

Option 12: Assume none of the above, and rewrite the title altogether.
This final option allows for more uninhibited use of the principle that *Finnegans Wake* cannot in fact be translated but can only be rewritten. In many ways this is the most interesting of the available options – and the results are certainly the most adventurous.

Donaldo Schüler's evocative 2003 Portuguese title, *Finnicius Revém*, is borrowed, in an act of homage to its original coiners, from the Brazilian brothers Augusto and Haroldo de Campos, whose Portuguese rendering of excerpts from the *Wake* appeared in book form in 1962 as *Panaroma do Finnegans Wake* but employed the phrase "Finnicius Revém" as an internal title (1962, 13). That title, as used by Schüler, can be read as combining "Finn" and suggestions of "Phoenicians" (Portuguese *fenícios*) and Phoenix (Portuguese *fénix*), not to mention an "end" (French *fin*, Portuguese *fim*, Latin *finis*, English *finish*), all of which "comes again" (Portuguese *revém*) as if in a "dream" (French *rêve*), reflecting Joyce's own reported statement that one of the many things he wanted to convey in the *Wake* was what goes on in the mind of a dreamer. The invented name *Finnicius*, while evoking Finn MacCool, also suggests the Brazilian personal name *Vinícius*, evoking a Brazilian *vinho* ("wine") in at least partial substitution for the Irish whiskey that brings an ever-thirsty Tim Finnegan back from the dead.

The playful title of a subsequent children's book by Schüler, meanwhile, loosely based on elements of the *Wake*, *Finnício Riovém* (2004), actually improves further on his earlier title. The first word, *Finnício*, now includes *início* ("beginning") as well as *fim* ("end"), Finn, and "Phoenician"; while *riovém* includes not only *revém* ("comes again") and thus by implication the suggestion of a French *rêve* ("dream"), but also *rio* ("river"), and thus Anna Livia Plurabelle, the iconic river that flows through Joyce's text from its non-beginning to its non-end.

One year later than Schüler's five-volume rendering, Hervé Michel's 2004 French rendering of the title overtly flaunts the impossibility of translation rather than rewriting in the case of *Finnegans Wake*. His highly idiosyncratic online *Veillée Pinouilles* (also referred to by the quasi-mathematical formulas $V\ i\pi\ n0$ and $\sqrt{i\pi}^{n0}$) renames Finnegan as "Pinouille." Michel himself describes in his online introduction the process of free association that led to the name: the name *Finnegan* suggested to him the term *finocchio* (an Italian slang term for a male homosexual), which suggested the puppet *Pinocchio*, which suggested *pinuche* (colloquial French for red wine), which eventually led to *Pinouille*. The title as a whole is readable as flamboyantly combining *veillée* as a funeral "wake"; mathematical *pi* (3.14159 ...) as a finally indeterminable quantity; colloquial French *pine* (for *pénis* "penis") describing the renamed Finnegan as a "prick"; and colloquial French *nouille* describing him also as a "stupid dope"; while the final *-s* both suggests a plural "Finnegans" and echoes the overtly ungrammatical character of Joyce's final *-s*. The echo of the French Pinot grape evokes the proverbially alcoholic nature of an Irish wake. Michel's title thus retains the concept of a funeral wake (*veillée*) but entirely rewrites Joyce's use of "Finnegans" and abandons its multiple associations and implications by a process of almost entirely unrelated free association. The intention here is clearly to provide a similarity of reading experience for a French readership, but the most obvious similarity between the two titles is in fact the shared willingness to play flamboyantly on the possibilities of language.

Another flamboyantly opaque rendering of the title is Afonso Teixeira Filho's *A noite e as vidas de Renatos Avelar* ("The night and the lives of Renatos Avelar"), employed as the title of his 2008 Portuguese rendering of the first chapter. "Renatos Avelar," like "Finnegans Wake," uses thirteen letters. "Renatos" is explained by the translator as conflating birth (Italian *nato* "born"), death (Greek *thanatos*), and rebirth (Italian *renato* "reborn"), while "Avelar," otherwise a not uncommon Portuguese surname, here conflates the Portuguese verb *velar* ("to wake, to observe a vigil") and, contributing a highly idiosyncratic note, a partial anagram of the name of Éamon de Valera (1882–1975), former revolutionary and later president of Ireland, here presented as father to the rebirth of the Irish state (2008, 202). The tongue-in-cheek title has of course the associated effect of directing its potential readers away from the dense knot of textual allusions associated with the names of both Tim Finnegan and his legendary avatar Finn MacCool. It also raises in particularly graphic form, as in the case of Hervé Michel's *Veillée Pinouilles*, an inescapable initial question for any literary translator, namely, the degree to which it is legitimate or desirable to ring extravagant titular changes, however clever, on the original title of a literary work – not, of course, that *Finnegans Wake* is just any literary work.

The title of Krzysztof Bartnicki's complete 2012 Polish translation, *Finneganów tren*, suggests a "funeral lament" (a *tren*, from Greek *thrênos*, a "funeral lament") for either a singular Finnegan or for plural Finnegans. In modern Polish the ending *-ów* denotes a genitive plural; in earlier forms of the language, however, the ending *-ów* denoted in the case of certain possessive adjectives a masculine singular (where in standard modern Polish *-owy* is used), thus a singular "Finnegan's," achieving an elegant combination of singularity and plurality.

For a Polish reader the term *tren* is evocative of one of the major highlights of Polish Renaissance literature, namely, the *Treny* (*Lamentations*) of the sixteenth-century poet Jan Kochanowski, written in 1580 on the death of his daughter. A secondary connotation of *tren* is the "train" of a dress, especially of a wedding dress, flowing in the wake of its wearer like the wake of a ship. A third meaning of Polish *tren*, as also of English *train*, is the flamboyant tail plumage of a peacock. Both of these latter meanings suggest the lots of fun that may also be had at Finnegan's translated wake, even despite lamentation. The archaic but less multiply evocative Polish noun *bdyn*, meanwhile, refers specifically to a funeral "wake." Wishing to retain the complementary echo, Bartnicki parodically employed the title *Finneganów bdyn* for a compilation of textual variants published simultaneously with *Finneganów tren*.

Andrey Rene's online Russian translation-in-progress began to appear in 2016 under the title *Na pomine Finneganov* (На помине Финнеганов). The traditional Russian translation of the title *Finnegans Wake* is *Pominki po Finneganu*, "Finnegan's wake" in the funeral sense. Rene explains in personal correspondence that his own title *Na pomine Finneganov* plays on the interrelationship of the nouns *pomin* ("prayer for the dead") and *pominki* (a funeral "wake"), the verb *pomint'* ("to remember"), and the colloquial phrase *legok na pomine*, the equivalent of "talk of the devil," implying "and he's sure to appear." The title thus suggests more narrowly something like "Praying for Finnegan," and more broadly something like "Praying for Finnegan as we remember him – and, wake or no wake, we'll probably see him back again, resurrected."

The latest translated title of the *Wake*, as of this writing, is that of Adam Roberts's *Pervigilium Finneganis* (2019), a rendering in quasi-Latin, compiled in collaboration with Google Translate, and essentially a literary joke, as Roberts cheerfully acknowledges. The title parodically reflects that of the anonymous Latin poem, possibly datable to the fourth century, *Pervigilium Veneris* (The vigil of Venus), celebrating the imminent arrival of spring and the rebirth of nature under the beneficent influence of the goddess. As Roberts notes, however, a *pervigilium* was also the vigil or wake observed as part of Roman funerary practice, thus permitting his parodic title to refer simultaneously both to death and to rebirth. The modern colloquialism *perv*, as in *pervert*, also resonates in the context of HCE's dubious activities in the Phoenix Park.

The German translator Friedhelm Rathjen deserves to be given the last word. The playful title of his 2012 collection of excerpts in German translation is *Winnegans Fake*, drawing on Joyce's own phrase "Wimmegame's fake" (*FW* 375.16–17) and humorously making the point that translators of *Finnegans Wake* may very well "win" some translational battles and will undoubtedly lose a great many more (such as, for example, not getting even the first word – or even the first letter – of the title right), and however impressive their wins may turn out to be, they will also inevitably produce a *Wake* that is fake. Rathjen's title, while clearly also a joke, is a particularly interesting one in that while it is certainly no longer Joyce's title, and certainly also not in any sense a translation, the playful exchange of the two word initials makes clear that it should be *read* as a translation – while simultaneously acknowledging that *any* attempt to translate Joyce's final text, beginning with the title, will inevitably remain merely a would-be translation.

Among related Wakean titles, renderings of (or from) *Anna Livia Plurabelle* have in most cases involved only relatively minor variations on that title: Joyce's own French team translation of 1931 used the title "Anna Livie Plurabelle," punningly suggesting the Liffey, interlingually, as the river of "life" (*la vie*) as well as the river named Life /ˈlɪfə/ in Irish. His Italian rendering of 1940 opted rather differently for "Anna Livia Plurabella," French *belle* becoming Italian *bella*, both forms meaning "beautiful" but *bella* also allowing for a Latin plural *bella* meaning "wars" and thus allowing for a play on Vico's *pia et pura bella*, the religious wars of his heroic age, holy wars both "pure" and "pious." The title *Anna Livia Plurabella* had in fact already been employed in the very early complete Czech rendering (Weatherall, Procházka, and Hoffmeister 1932), of which Joyce will almost certainly have been sent a copy by Adolf Hoffmeister, as it would later be in Georg Goyert's German, of which Joyce reportedly received a copy in 1933. The same variation recurs more recently also in Mario Grut's Swedish *Anna Livia Plurabella* (2001). Almost all other renderings have preferred to stay with the original *Anna Livia Plurabelle*.

The one more adventurous early exception among titles of *ALP* was Beckett and Péron's "Anna Lyvia Pluratself," completed in 1930 but first published only in 1985, which gestures reflexively towards the act of translation itself by demonstratively transposing "Livia" into "Lyvia" as well as augmenting the Liffey by adding not only New Zealand's river Lyvia but also, by the suggestion of a lengthened vowel, the Irish Lee, English Lea, and Chinese Li. Its flaunted strangeness also suggests an Anna with a problematically compound personality, sometimes almost "plural," sometimes almost "itself," very likely a puzzle (German *Rätsel*) even to itself, resulting perhaps in bouts of secret weeping (Latin *plorat* "she weeps") no doubt about things both many (Latin *plura*) and variable, Virgil's tears of things. While Jacques Aubert published the translation under this title in 1985, Beckett himself had evidently lost his enthusiasm as early as 1930 for the extravagant titular variation, for the corrected proofs of his and Péron's rendering for the journal *Bifur* show that he eventually abandoned it and carefully, letter by letter, restored Joyce's original title (O'Neill 2018, 23).

An at least equally flamboyant titular variation, and one that would very likely have won Joyce's amused approval, is that of the more recent Italian rendering by Orlando Mezzabotta (2017), posted on YouTube under the cover title *Anna Livia Plurabelle* and the textual title *Arna Livia Risciaquata*. The latter, extending the resonances of the text primarily for the amusement of Italian readers, is a playful allusion to the nineteenth-century Italian literary eminence Alessandro Manzoni (1785–1873), whose classic novel *I promessi sposi* (*The Betrothed*) first appeared in 1827. Fifteen years later, in 1842, Manzoni reissued his novel in a linguistically revised form, having announced that he now wished to contribute to the development of a standardized Italian literary language by purifying his own earlier vocabulary, "washing" it in the purer waters of Dante's Florentine Tuscan. As he phrased it himself, he wished to "risciaquare i panni in Arno," literally, "to rinse the clothes in the Arno." Mezzabotta consequently morphed *Anna* into *Arna* as a mock feminine of Florence's river Arno, with the title *Arna Livia Risciaquata* thus suggesting an "Anna Livia rinsed in the Arno."[3] The metaphor, emphasizing ALP's fluvial identity, is very appropriate also for the activity of the chattering washerwomen rinsing Anna Livia's clothes in the Liffey – but only at the obvious and fairly serious cost of abandoning ALP's original titular initials as well as the whole cluster of resonances generated by Joyce's original "Plurabelle."

In Eleftherios Anevlavis's Greek rendering of *FW* (2013), meanwhile, the character ALP becomes Άννα Λίβια Πολυόμορφη (Anna Lívia Polyómorfi), an Anna Livia not only very (Modern Greek *polý*) beautiful (*ómorfi*), and a Plurabelle of many (Ancient Greek *polý-*) beauties (*omorfiés*), but also an Anna Livia who is essentially polymorphous (*polýmorfi*), an ever-flowing ALP of ever-changing form, ever-changing identity, who nonetheless, unchanging in perennial change, retains her original initials. In Andrey Rene's Russian (2017), ALP, while likewise retaining her initials, becomes Анна Ливви Присеребрённая (Anna Livvi Priserebronnaya), in this guise suggesting an Anna Livia "silvered" (*poserebronnaya*) by the ever-changing glintings and glimmerings of reflected light on the ripples of the flowing river.

Finally, Orlando Mezzabotta's extraordinarily complex title for his 2016 Italian rendering of *FW* I.1 – *Opfertuere: il primo capitol'ho?* – certainly also deserves honourable mention. Mezzabotta's rendering is described on its title page as a version in "finntaliano," an Italian adjusted to accommodate the demands of Joyce's Finneganian extravagances.

---

3 Personal correspondence from Orlando Mezzabotta.

The suggested meaning is at one level, as already discussed, fairly obviously "Overture: the first chapter," and we may possibly also conclude that the disorienting final question mark reflects the disorienting role of the apostrophe in Joyce's original title. The subtitle, while readable as suggesting merely "the first chapter" (*il primo capitolo*), ends in a question mark that not only evokes an absent original apostrophe but also implies immediate doubt as to the relationship between translation and original, with the translator self-reflexively wondering, albeit humorously, "L'ho capito?" ("Have I understood it?"). It is a question that resonates powerfully for any reader of *Finnegans Wake* – in any language.

Appendix 2: Anna Livia Plurilingual

Of the individual chapters of the *Wake*, the most popular with translators has always been the eighth chapter (I.8), previously published separately in book form in 1928 as *Anna Livia Plurabelle*.

As of the beginning of the 2020s, sixteen complete translations of *Finnegans Wake* existed in thirteen different languages altogether: French (Lavergne 1982, Michel 2004), German (Stündel 1993), Japanese (Yanase 1993, Hamada 2012), Dutch (Bindervoet and Henkes 2002), Korean (Kim 2002), Portuguese (Schüler 2003), Polish (Bartnicki 2012), Greek (Anevlavis 2013), Spanish (Zabaloy 2016), Turkish (Sevimay 2016), Italian (Mazza 2018; Schenoni, Terrinoni, and Pedone 2019), quasi-Latin (Roberts 2019), and Serbian (Stojaković, 2020).

As of the same date, and including the versions in the complete renderings of *Finnegans Wake* listed above, there existed thirty-five complete versions of *ALP* (in **bold** below) and a further thirty-four partial or fragmentary versions of *ALP*, in twenty-six different languages altogether, distributed across languages as follows:

1	French *ALP*s	Joyce et al. 1931, Butor 1948, Coeuroy 1962, **Lavergne 1982**, Beckett and Péron 1985, **Michel 2004**, Chassaing 2005, **Blanchon 2016**, Bouton-Kelly and Samoyault 2016
2	Italian *ALP*s	Joyce and Settanni 1940, Wilcock 1961, Bernardini 1964, Joyce and Frank 1979, **Schenoni 1996**, **Schenoni 2001**, Santangelo 2014, Mezzabotta 2017, **Mazza 2018**
3	German *ALP*s	Senn 1961, Hildesheimer 1969, **Goyert 1970**, **Hildesheimer 1970**, **Wollschläger 1970**, **Stündel 1993**

4 Spanish *ALP*s   Castro and Blanco 1982, **Silva-Santisteban 1991,
                          García Tortosa 1992**, Pozanco 1993, Fanzone
                          2007, **Lago 2016, Zabaloy 2016**
5 Portuguese *ALP*s   Campos and Campos 1957, Luft 1989, **Schüler
                          2001, Amarante 2009**
6 Northern *ALP*s   Danish (Laugesen 2009), Dutch (**Bindervoet and
                          Henkes 2002**), Swedish (**Grut 2001**)
7 Eastern *ALP*s   Czech (**Weatherall, Procházka, and
                          Hoffmeister 1932**), Greek (**Anevlavis 2013**),
                          Hungarian (Szentkuthy 1975, Bíró 1992), Polish
                          (Strzetelski 1959, Krasińska 1984, **Słomczyński
                          1985, Bartnicki 2012**), Romanian (Biberi 1965,
                          Antip 1996, Milesi 1998), Russian (Belyaev
                          2000, **Rene 2017**), Serbian (Anon. 1956,
                          Stojaković 2014)
8 Asian *ALP*s   Chinese (**Dai 2012**), Georgian (**Gelashvili 2018**),
                          Hebrew (Vizan 2015), Japanese (Nishiwaki 1933,
                          **Osawa 1982, Yanase 1991, Miyata 2004,
                          Hamada 2012**), Korean (**Kim 1985**), Turkish
                          (**Sevimay 2016, Çelikyay 2016**)
9 Other *ALP*s   Basic English (Ogden 1931), Catalan (**Aixàs
                          2004**), Galician (Rodríguez 1969), quasi-
                          Latin (**Roberts 2019**) – and Ancient Egyptian
                          hieroglyphics (Mezzabotta 2018b)

In addition, and not included in the above figures, the following ten
new complete *ALP*s were also announced as expected to appear in the
2020s as chapter I.8 of new renderings of *FW*:

10 Anticipated *ALP*s   Spanish (**Victoria**), Portuguese (**Amarante,
                          Galindo, Teixeira Filho, Garcia Ferreira,
                          Alves**), Finnish (**Lindholm**), Norwegian
                          (**Høghaug**), German (**Blumenbach**), Hungarian
                          (**Bozai**)

Bibliography

Joyce's works are cited parenthetically in the text by the abbreviations listed in section 1 below. The annotation "bilingual" in section 2 indicates that the translation is accompanied, usually on a facing page, by the original text.

1 Works by James Joyce

ALP Anna Livia Plurabelle. Introduction by Padraic Colum. New York: Crosby Gaige, 1928; London: Faber and Faber, 1930. Corresponds to *FW* 196–216.

– *Tales Told of Shem and Shaun*. Preface by C.K. Ogden. Paris: Black Sun Press, 1929. Corresponds to *FW* 152–9, 282–304, 414–19.

– *Haveth Childers Everywhere*. Paris: Babou and Kahane; New York: Fountain Press, 1930. Corresponds to *FW* 532–54.

– *Two Tales of Shem and Shaun*. London: Faber and Faber, 1932. Corresponds to *FW* 152–9, 414–19.

– *The Mime of Mick, Nick and the Maggies*. The Hague: Servire Press, 1934. Corresponds to *FW* 219–59.

– *Storiella As She Is Syung*. London: Corvinus Press, 1937. Corresponds to *FW* 260–75, 304–8

FW Finnegans Wake. London: Faber and Faber; New York: Viking Press, 1939. Introduction by John Bishop. Harmondsworth, UK: Penguin, 1999.

FW2 The Restored Finnegans Wake. Edited by Danis Rose and John O'Hanlon. London: Penguin, 2012.

FW3 Finnegans Wake. Edited by Robbert-Jan Henkes, Erik Bindervoet, and Finn Fordham. Oxford: Oxford University Press, 2012.

– *Finn's Hotel*. Edited by Danis Rose. Introduction by Seamus Deane. Dublin: Ithys Press. 2013.

L 1 The Letters of James Joyce, vol. 1. Edited by Stuart Gilbert. London: Faber, 1957.

L 2/3 The Letters of James Joyce, vols. 2 and 3. Edited by Richard Ellmann. London: Faber; New York: Viking, 1966.

SI Scritti italiani. 1979. Edited by Gianfranco Corsini and Giorgio Melchiori. Milan: Mondadori. Includes "Anna Livia Plurabella," translated by James Joyce and Nino Frank, 197–214.

U Ulysses. Paris: Shakespeare & Co., 1922; New York: Random House, 1934; London: Bodley Head, 1936. Edited by Hans Walter Gabler with Wolfhard Steppe and Claus Melchior. New York: Random House/Vintage Books, 1986.

2 Other Works Cited

Ackerley, C.J., and S.E. Gontarski. 2006. *The Faber Companion to Samuel Beckett: A Reader's Guide to His Works, Life, and Thought*. London: Faber and Faber.

Ahrens, Kristina. 2017. "Georg Goyert und *Anna Livia Plurabelle*: Über die (Un-)Möglichkeiten einer Übersetzung von James Joyces *Finnegans Wake*." In Barlach et al. 2017, 35–50.

Aixàs, Marissa. 2004. *Estudi del joc de paraules en* Anne Livia Plurabelle: *Anàlisi contrastiva de traduccions i proposta pròpia de versió*. Diss. Universitat Autònoma de Barcelona. Includes Catalan version of *FW* 8.8–10.24; 15.28–18.16; 182.30–186.18; 196.1–216.5.

Aixàs, Marissa. 2007. "The Process of Transposing Anna Livia Plurabelle into Catalan: Some Reflections and Considerations." In *Joyce and/in Translation*, edited by Rosa Maria Bollettieri Bosinelli and Ira Torresi, 143–8. Rome: Bulzoni Editore.

Alexandrova, Boriana. 2015. "Wakeful Translations: An Initiation into the Russian Translations of *Finnegans Wake*." *Joyce Studies Annual*: 128–67.

– 2020. "Multilingualism in Translation: The Russian *Wake*(s) in Context." In *Joyce, Multilingualism, and the Ethics of Reading*, 129–98. Palgrave Studies in Modern European Literature. Cham: Palgrave Macmillan.

Allen, Kim. 2000. "Beckett, Joyce, and Anna Livia: The Plurability of Translating *Finnegans Wake*." In *Translation Perspectives XI: Beyond the Western Tradition*, edited by Marilyn Gaddis Rose, 427–35. Binghampton, NY: Center for Translation Research.

Amaral, Vitor Alevato do. 2019. "A Bahia se revém: Considerações sobre a tradução de *Finnegans Wake*." *Revista da Anpoll* (Florianópolis) 1, no. 50: 152–64. https://doi.org/10.18309/anp.v1i50.1332.

Amarante, Dirce Waltrick do. 2001. *A terceira margem do Liffey: Uma aproximação ao* Finnegans Wake. Florianópolis (Brazil): Dissertação de Mestrado, Universidade Federal de Santa Catarina.

– 2003a. "A tradução antropofágica de *Finnegans Wake*." *Cult* (São Paulo) 6 (72): 18–20.

– 2003b. "The Language and Translation of *Finnegans Wake*." *ABEI Journal* no. 5: 321–7.

– 2005. "Para as crianças de todas as idades." *DC Cultura* 15 January 2005, 14–15.
– 2009. *Para ler Finnegans Wake de James Joyce*. São Paulo: Editora Iluminuras. Includes Portuguese version of *FW* 196.1–216.5.
– 2015. *James Joyce e seus tradutores*. São Paulo: Editora Iluminuras.
– 2018. *Finnegans Wake (por um fio)* [*FW*, excerpts: Portuguese]. São Paulo: Editora Iluminuras. Bilingual.
– 2019. "*Finnegans Wake*: Uma tentativa de travessia em português." *Qorpus* (Florianópolis, Brazil) 9, no. 3: 78–89. https://qorpuspget.paginas.ufsc.br /arquivo/.
Anevlavis, Eleftherios [Ελευθέριος Ανευλαβής], trans. 2013. *Η αγρύπνια των Φίννεγκαν* [I agrýpnia ton Fínnegan] [*FW*: Greek]. Athens: Kaktos.
Anon, trans. 1931. "Considerații despre Anna Livia Plurabelle." *Cuvântul* (Bucharest), 7/2352 (6 November 1931): 2.
– trans. 1956. "Anna Livia Plurabelle" [*ALP*, excerpt: Serbian]. *Mlada kultura* (Belgrade) 5, May 1956, 49–50.
– 1968. "Joyce-Übersetzung: Wsch! Ne Möwe." *Der Spiegel* 22, 15 January 1968, 104.
– trans. 1986. "Sandhyas! Sandhyas! Sandhyas!" [*FW* 593–4: Serbian]. *Delo* (Belgrade), September–October 1986, 32–3.
– 2002. "Joyce's Monk." *Al-Ahram Weekly Online* 583 (25 April–1 May 2002). http://weekly.ahram.org.eg/Archive/2002/583/cu7.htm.
– 2004. "*Finnegans Wake* in Japanese." http://www.honco.net/japanese/04 /page4.html.
– 2007. "Liana Burgess." Obituary. *Telegraph*, 5 December 2007. https://www .telegraph.co.uk/news/obituaries/1571513/Liana-Burgess.html.
– 2009. "Finnegans Wake." Wikipedia. Czech. 25 March 2009. Includes Czech translation of *FW* 3.1–3.
– 2010. "Finnegans Wake." Wikipedia. Esperanto. 4 March 2010. Includes Esperanto translation of *FW* 3.1–3.
– 2013. "*Finnegan ébredése*" [FW, excerpts: Hungarian]. Wikipedia. Hungarian. 23 November 2013. Includes renderings by Ágota Bozai (FW 628.15–16; 3.1–3) and Endre Bíró (FW 170.9–174.4).
– 2017. "Maciej Słomczyński." Wikipedia. 23 November 2017.
– 2018a. "Endre Bíró." Wikipedia. 30 March 2018.
– 2018b. "*Finnegans Wake*: Quel sogno intraducibile finalmente tradotto." *Gazzetta di Parma*, 4 November 2018. https://www.gazzettadiparma.it/news /cultura/549202/finnegans-wake-quel-sogno-intraducibile-finalmente -tradotto.html.
– 2018c. "Henri Volokhonsky." Wikipedia. 6 November 2018.
– 2019. "San-Antonio (série)." Wikipédia. 4 November 2019.
– 2020a. "First Translator of Joyce's *Ulysses* into Turkish Nevzat Erkmen Dies of Covid-19." BIA News Desk, Istanbul. 16 April 2020. http://bianet.org

/english/print/223055-first-translator-of-joyce-s-ulysses-into-turkish
-nevzat-erkmen-dies-of-covid-19.

– 2020b. "Nevzat Erkmen (1931–2020)." *Biyografya*. April 2020. https://www
.biyografya.com/biyografi/14806.

– 2020c. "Counts of Castell." Wikipedia. 17 July 2020.

Antip, Felicia. 1996. "Să ne jucăm de-a Joyce." *Lettre Internationale* (Bucharest),
18, 82–8. Includes Romanian translation of *ALP* (83–8).

Antolín Rato, Mariano. 1994. Review of *Finnegans Wake*. Translated by Víctor
Pozanco. *El mundo*. 29 January 1994. http://www.abretelibro.com/foro
/viewtopic.php?f=19&t=41204.

Attridge, Derek, ed. 1990. *The Cambridge Companion to James Joyce*. Cambridge:
Cambridge University Press.

Attridge, Derek, and Daniel Ferrer, eds. 1984. *Post-Structuralist Joyce: Essays
from the French*. Cambridge: Cambridge University Press.

Aubert, Jacques. 1965. Review (erroneously attributed to Fritz Senn) of
Finnegans Wake. French translation by André du Bouchet (1962). *James Joyce
Quarterly* 3: 81–2.

– 1967. "*Finnegans Wake*: Pour en finir avec les traductions?" *James Joyce
Quarterly* 4 (3): 217–22.

– 1982. "Un texte impossible et peu présentable: La traduction intégrale de
Finnegans Wake." *Le Monde* (Paris), 10 December 1982, 23.

– 1985. Introduction to "Anna Lyvia Pluratself." Translated by Samuel Beckett
and Alfred Péron. In *James Joyce*, edited by Jacques Aubert and Fritz Senn,
417–18. Paris: Editions de l'Herne.

Aubert, Jacques, and Fritz Senn. 1985. *James Joyce*. Paris: Éditions de l'Herne.

Babassakis, George-Icaros (Γιώργος-Ίκαρος Μπαμπασάκης), trans. 2014. Το
Κονάκι του Φιν [*Finn's Hotel*: Greek]. Athens: Psichogios Publications.

Bacigalupo, Massimo. 2009. "La lingua di Finnegan: James Joyce saggista e
poeta italiano." In *Scrittori stranieri in lingua italiana dal Cinquecento a oggi:
Convegno internazionale di studi, Padova*, 20–1 March 2009, edited by Furio
Brugnolo, 361–73. Padua: Unipress.

Bair, Deirdre. 1978. *Samuel Beckett: A Biography*. New York: Harcourt Brace
Jovanovich.

Banta, Melissa, and Oscar A. Silverman, eds. 1987. *James Joyce's Letters to Sylvia
Beach, 1921–1940*. Bloomington: Indiana University Press.

Banville, John. 2003. *Prague Pictures: Portrait of a City*. London: Bloomsbury.

Barina, Antonella. 2017. "Cinque ore al giorno per tre anni, se tradurre è
un'impresa." *Repubblica* 13 January 2017. http://www.gennarocucciniello
.it/gc/james-joyce-finnegans-wake-viaggio-al-termine-del-900/.

Barlach, Kerstin, Hannah Breuer, Carolin Brinkhoff, and Miriam Prellwitz,
eds. 2017. *Georg Goyert: Sein Leben und seine Übersetzungen*. Berlin: Christian
A. Bachmann Verlag.

Bartnicki, Krzysztof, trans. 2004. *Finneganów tren*: księga I, rozdział I; księga IV [*FW* I.1 and IV: Polish]. *Literatura na Świecie* 7–8: 5–31, 69–105.

– trans. 2005. "*Finneganów tren*: Bajka o Mooksie i Gripowronie" ["The Mookse and the Gripes": Polish]. *Przekładaniec* 13, no. 2/14, no. 1 (2004/2005): 156–71. *FW* 152.4–159.23.

– trans. 2012a. *Finneganów tren* [*FW*: Polish]. Krakow: Korporacja Ha!art.

– 2012b. *Finneganów bdyn*. Krakow: Korporacja Ha!art.

– 2012c. *Fu wojny*. Krakow: Korporacja Ha!art.

– 2012d. *Da Capo al Finne*. Warsaw: Sowa.

– 2014a. *F_nnegans a_e: Suite in the Key of III*. Warsaw: Sowa.

– 2014b. *Finnegans Ware*. YouTube. 6:32 minutes. Posted 16 June 2014. https://www.youtube.com/watch?v=ONHfwKg74tY.

– 2015. With Marcin Szmandra. *Finnegans Meet*. Opole (Poland): Self-published.

Bašić, Sonja. 2004. "The Reception of James Joyce in Croatia." In *The Reception of James Joyce in Europe*, edited by Geert Lernout and Wim Van Mierlo, 178–86. Vol. 1 of 2 vols. London: Thoemmes Continuum.

Bataillard, Pascal. 2014. "Joyce & Fargue: Au titre de l'amitié." *Ludions: Bulletin de la Société des Lecteurs de Léon-Paul Fargue* no. 14: 241–57.

Battuti, Maher. 2012. "Battuti's Review: *Finnegans Wake*." 30 May 2012. https://www.goodreads.com/review/show/339557069.

Baydere, Muhammed. 2018. "A New (Mis)Conception in the Face of the (Un)Translatable: '*Terscüme*'." *transLogos* 1 (1): 92–120. https://dergipark.org.tr/en/download/article-file/606831. https://doi.org/10.29228/transLogos.1/1.10.

Bayramova, Halila. 2016. Review of Umur Çelikyay's *Finneganın vahı* [*FW*: Turkish]. *James Joyce Literary Supplement* 30 (2): 4–5.

Bazarnik, Katarzyna. 1999. "O polskich przekładach Finnegans Wake." In *Wokół Jamesa Joyce'a*, edited by Katarzyna Bazarnik and Finn Fordham, 194–204. Krakow: Universitas.

– 2010. "A Polish Translation of *Finnegans Wake* in Progress." *James Joyce Quarterly* 47: 567–77. https://doi.org/10.1353/jjq.2010.0002.

– 2012. "Finnegansowe ABC." https://www.dwutygodnik.com/artykul/3256-finnegansowe-abc.html.

– 2017. "A Stylometric Enquiry in Polish Translations of *Finnegans Wake*." Unpublished paper delivered at the Fourteenth International Conference on English and American Literature and Culture held in April 2017 in Krakow, Poland.

Beach, Sylvia. 1980. *Shakespeare and Company*. 1956. Lincoln: University of Nebraska Press.

Beck, Harald, trans. 1986. "Incipit opus progrediens" [*FW*, excerpt: German]. *Bargfelder Bote* 104–6 (July 1986): 44–5. *FW* 3.1–5.29.

– trans. 1987. "*Finnegans Wake* 5.29ff." [German]. *Bargfelder Bote* 110–12 (January 1987): 54. *FW* 5.29–7.6.

– trans. 1989. "I.1 (Der Anfang)" [*FW* 3.1–11.28: German]. In *Finnegans Wake Deutsch: Gesammelte Annäherungen*, edited by Klaus Reichert and Fritz Senn, 27–35. Frankfurt: Suhrkamp.

Beckett, Samuel. 1929. "Dante ... Bruno . Vico .. Joyce." *transition* 16–17 (June 1929): 242–53.

– 1972. "Dante ... Bruno . Vico .. Joyce." In *Our Exagmination Round His Factification for Incamination of Work in Progress*, by Samuel Beckett et al., 3–22. 1929. London: Faber and Faber.

Beckett, Samuel, and Alfred Péron, trans. 1985. "Anna Lyvia Pluratself." Edited by Jacques Aubert. In *James Joyce*, edited by Jacques Aubert and Fritz Senn. Paris: Editions de l'Herne, 418–22; rpt. Bosinelli 1996: 153–61. Corresponds to *FW* 196.1–201.21.

Beckett, Samuel, Alfred Perron [*sic*], Yvan Goll, Eugène Jolas, Paul Léon, Adrienne Monnier, Philippe Soupault, and James Joyce, trans. 1931. "Anna Livie Plurabelle" [*ALP*, excerpts: French]. *Nouvelle Revue Française* 19, no. 212 (1 May 1931): 633–46; rpt. Bosinelli 1996: 3–29. Corresponds to *FW* 196–201, 215–16. Cited as Joyce et al. 1931.

Begnal, Michael H., and Fritz Senn. 1974. *A Conceptual Guide to* Finnegans Wake. University Park: Pennsylvania State University Press.

Belda, Ismael. 2017. "Lectores contra el monstruo: el periplo de *Finnegans Wake*." *Revista de Libros*, 8 March 2017. https://www.revistadelibros.com/articulo_imprimible.php?art=5347&t=articulos.

Belyaev, Konstantin. 2000. "*Pominki po Finneganu*: Apologiya perevoda." *Soyuz Pisatelei* (Kharkov, Ukraine). Includes Russian translation of *FW* 196.1–6, 209.18–212.19. http://sp-issues.narod.ru/2/index.htm.

Bendelli, Giuliana. 2014. "Sanesi tra le prime versioni italiane di *Finnegans Wake*." *Autografo* 52: 149–64.

Bénéjam, Valérie. 2015. "Joyce's Draft of a Kiss." *James Joyce Literary Supplement* 29 (2): 12–14.

Benet, Juan. 1971. "Prólogo." In *El Ulises de James Joyce*, by Stuart Gilbert, 1–24. Bilbao: Siglo XXI de España.

Bennett, Arnold. 1929. Review of *Anna Livia Plurabelle*, by James Joyce. *Evening Standard*, 19 September 1929, 7.

Benstock, Bernard. 1965. *Joyce-again's Wake: An Analysis of* Finnegans Wake. Seattle: University of Washington Press.

– ed. 1985a. *Critical Essays on James Joyce*. Boston: G.K. Hall.

– 1985b. *James Joyce*. New York: Ungar.

Benstock, Shari, and Bernard Benstock. 1985. Review of *Finnegans Wake*, translated by Philippe Lavergne (1982). *James Joyce Quarterly* 22: 231.

Bernardini, Piero, trans. 1964. *James Joyce*, by Richard Ellmann (1959). Italian translation. Milan: Feltrinelli.

– trans. 1982. *James Joyce*, by Richard Ellmann (1982). Italian translation. Milan: Feltrinelli.

Biberi, Ion. 1935. "James Joyce." *Revista Fundaţiilor Regale* (Bucharest) 5: 392–406.

– 1965. "Monologul interior la James Joyce." *Secolul 20* (Bucharest) 2: 117–32.

Bindervoet, Erik, and Robbert-Jan Henkes, trans. 2002. *Finnegans Wake* [Dutch]. Amsterdam: Querido. Bilingual.

– 2005. *Finnegancyclopedie*. Amsterdam: Athenaum–Polak & Van Gennep.

– trans. 2013. *Anna Livia Plurabelle* [Dutch]. Amsterdam: Rainbow.

Bíró, Endre, trans. 1964. "Szemelvények a *Finnegans Wake*-ből" [*FW*, excerpts: Hungarian]. *Híd* 28.11 (1964): 1241–56. Rpt. in *Magyar Műhely* (Paris), September 1973: 9–59 and June 1979: 22–9. Includes excerpts from *FW* 8–10, 169–95, 196–216, 627–8.

– trans. 1992. *Finnegan ébredése (részletek)* [*FW*, excerpts: Hungarian]. Budapest: Holnap Kiadó. Includes excerpts from *FW* 8–10, 35, 152–9, 169–95, 196–216, 226, 261–2, 414–21, 499–501, 627–8.

Bishop, John. 1986. *Joyce's Book of the Dark:* Finnegans Wake. Madison: University of Wisconsin Press.

Blanchon, Philippe, trans. 2013. *Anna Livia Plurabelle* [French translation from Ogden's Basic English]. Toulon: La Termitière. 12 pp.

– trans. 2015. *Les poèmes du Wake et commentaires* [Poems from *FW*: French]. Toulon: Éditions La Nerthe.

– trans. 2016. *Anna Livia Plurabelle* [French]. Toulon: Éditions La Nerthe. Also contains French translation of *FW* 627.6–628.16 and 3.1–8.8.

Blumenbach, Ulrich. 1990. "Üb-Errsetzungen aus dem Anglo-Wakischen ins Germano-Wakische: Untersuchungen zum Problem der Übersetzbarkeit von James Joyces *Finnegans Wake*." Wissenschaftliche Hausarbeit zur Ersten Staatsprüfung für das Amt des Studienrats. MA thesis, Free University of Berlin.

– 1998. "A Bakhtinian Approach towards Translating *FW*." In *Images of Joyce*, edited by Clive Hart et al., 645–9. Gerrards Cross, UK: Colin Smythe. 2:

– and Reinhard Markner, trans. 1989. "Anna Livias Monolog" [*FW* 619.20–628.16: German]. In *Finnegans Wake Deutsch: Gesammelte Annäherungen*, edited by Klaus Reichert and Fritz Senn, 262–70. Frankfurt: Suhrkamp.

Bockelmann, Eske. 2002. "Die kesse Wehr: James Joyce übersetzt." *Neue Rundschau* 113 (1): 177–85. Review of *Finnegans Wehg*, German translation by Dieter Stündel (1993).

Bosinelli, Rosa Maria Bollettieri. 1987. "Joyce e la traduzione: Rifacimenti italiani di *Finnegans Wake*." *Lingua e stile* (Bologna) 22: 515–38.

– 1990. "Beyond Translation: Italian Re-Writings of *Finnegans Wake*." *Joyce Studies Annual* 1: 142–61.

– ed. 1996. *Anna Livia Plurabelle di James Joyce*. Introduction by Umberto Eco. Scrittori tradotti da scrittori, 8. Turin: Einaudi. Includes 1928 and 1939 texts of *ALP*; Joyce et al. (1931); Joyce and Frank (1979); Ogden (1932); Beckett and Péron (1985); and Schenoni (1996).

– 1998a. "Introduction: Anna Livia Plurabelle's Sisters." In *Transcultural Joyce*, edited by Karen R. Lawrence, 173–8. Cambridge: Cambridge University Press.

– 1998b. "Anna Livia's Italian Sister." In *Transcultural Joyce*, edited by Karen R. Lawrence, 193–8. Cambridge: Cambridge University Press.

– 2000. "Joyce on the Turrace of Babbel." In *Classic Joyce: Joyce Studies in Italy* 6, edited by Franca Ruggieri. Roma: Bulzoni, 417–29.

– 2001. "Joyce Slipping across the Borders of English: The Stranger in Language." *James Joyce Quarterly* 38: 395–409.

Bouton-Kelly, Ludivine, and Tiphaine Samoyault. 2016. "Translating James Joyce." *Drunken Boat* 24. https://d7.drunkenboat.com/db24/outranspo /ludivine-bouton-kelly. Includes French translation of *FW* 196.1–199.33.

Bowker, Gordon. 2011. *James Joyce: A Biography*. London: Weidenfeld and Nicolson.

Bozai, Ágota, trans. 2007. "*Finnegans Wake*: Részlet James Joyce regényéből" (Excerpt from James Joyce's novel). *Litera* 16 June 2007. http://www.litera. hu/hirek/finnegans-wake. Includes Hungarian translation of *FW* 3.1–5.12.

– 2008. "Translation in Progress: A *Finnegans Wake* fordítása." *Kalligram* 17 (6): 24–30. Includes Hungarian translation of *FW* 3.1–3, 115.20–35, 213.29–216.5 (with László Kuroli), 627.1–628.16. http://www.kalligramoz.eu/Kalligram /Archivum/2008/XVII.-evf.-2008.-junius-Joyce/Joyce/Translation-in -Progress-a-Finnegans-Wake-forditasa.

Brée, Germaine. 1983. *Twentieth-Century French Literature*. Translated by Louise Guiney. Chicago: University of Chicago Press.

Brivic, Shelly. 2011. "'Hybrid Joyce': The Fifth Biennial International Korean James Joyce Conference, Chonnam National University, Kwangju, Korea, 10–11 November 2012." *James Joyce Quarterly* 48: 601–2.

Broch, Hermann. 1936. *James Joyce und die Gegenwart*. Vienna: Herbert Reichert Verlag.

Brown, Richard. 1991. "News from Poland." *James Joyce Broadsheet* 35: 4.

Budgen, Frank. 1972. *James Joyce and the Making of* Ulysses. Oxford: Oxford University Press.

Buenaventura, Román. 1993. "El libro de nunca acabar." *El Mundo*, 8 February 1993, 46.

Bugliaro, Matteo. 2017. "*Finnegans Wake* – James Joyce e J. Rodolfo Wilcock." *Piego di Libri*. http://www.piegodilibri.it/recensioni/finnegans-wake -james-joyce/.

Burgess, Anthony, ed. 1966. *A Shorter Finnegans Wake*. London: Faber and
Faber.

– 1970. "Bless Thee Bottom." *Times Literary Supplement*, 18 September 1970,
1024–5.

– 1972. "Letter from Europe." *The American Scholar* 41, no. 1 (1971–72):
139–42.

– 1973. *Joysprick: An Introduction to the Language of James Joyce*. London: André
Deutsch.

– 1975. "Writing in Rome (pHorbiCEtta)." *Times Literary Supplement*,
31 October 1975, 1296. Includes Italian translation of *FW* 3.1–14.

– 1982. *Here Comes Everybody: An Introduction to James Joyce for the Ordinary
Reader*. Revised edition. London: Hamlyn Paperbacks. Originally published
London: Faber and Faber, 1965.

Burneo, Cristina. 2004. "¿Traducir *Finnegans Wake*?" *Kipus: Revista andina de
letras* 18: 19–26.

Bushrui, Suheil Badi. 1982. "Joyce in the Arab World." In *James Joyce: An
International Perspective*, edited by Suheil Badi Bushrui and Bernard
Benstock, 232–49. Gerrards Cross, UK: Colin Smythe; Totawa, NJ: Barnes
and Noble.

Butor, Michel. 1948. "Petite croisière préliminaire à une reconnaisance de
l'archipel Joyce." *La vie intellectuel* 16 (5): 104–35. Rpt. in *Répertoire: Etudes
et conférences 1948–1959*, by Michel Butor, 195–218. Paris: Les Editions
de Minuit, 1960. Includes translation of *FW* 3.1–3, 196.1–7, 215.34–216.5,
419.5–8.

– 1957. "Esquisse d'un seuil pour Finnegan." *La Nouvelle Revue Française* n.s.
5 (60): 1033–53. Rpt. in *Répertoire: Etudes et conférences 1948–1959*, by Michel
Butor, 219–33. Paris: Les Editions de Minuit, 1960. Rpt. in *Finnegans Wake*,
by André du Bouchet, 7–28. Paris: Gallimard, 1962.

– 1967. "La traduction, dimension fondamentale de notre temps." *James Joyce
Quarterly* 4 (3): 215–16.

Calero, César G. 2016. "¿Alguien dijo que el *Finnegans Wake* era intraducible?"
El mundo (Buenos Aires), 27 July 2016. http://www.elmundo.es/cultura
/2016/07/22/5790a6db46163fe33e8b4658.html.

Campbell, Joseph, and Henry Morton Robinson. 1961. *A Skeleton Key to
Finnegans Wake*. 1944. New York: Viking Press.

Campos, Augusto de, and Haroldo de Campos, trans. 1957. [*FW*, excerpts:
Portuguese]. *Jornal do Brasil* (São Paulo) 15 September 1957; 29 December
1957. Seven fragments from *FW* 3, 159, 196, 214–16, 556, 561, 627–8.

– trans. 1962. *Panaroma do Finnegans Wake* [*FW*, excerpts: Portuguese]. São
Paulo: Comissão de Literatura do Conselho Estadual de Cultura. Eleven
fragments from *FW* 3, 143, 159, 189, 196, 214–16, 226, 556, 559, 561, 627–8.
Bilingual.

– trans. 1971. *Panaroma do Finnegans Wake* [*FW*, excerpts: Portuguese]. Second edition. São Paulo: Perspectiva. Sixteen fragments from *FW* 3, 13, 143, 157–9, 182–4, 189–90, 196, 202, 206–7, 214–16, 226, 244, 556, 559, 561, 627–8.

– trans. 2001. *Panaroma do Finnegans Wake* [*FW*, excerpts: Portuguese]. Fourth edition. São Paulo: Perspectiva. Twenty-two fragments from *FW*.

Campos, Haroldo de, trans. 1999. "Dois fragmentos de *Finnegans Wake*, transcriados de Haroldo de Campos." In *Joyce Revém*, edited by Marcelo Tápia, 30–5. São Paulo: Editora Olavobrás/Associação Brasileira de Estudos Irlandeses. *FW* 292, 449.

Camurri, Edoardo. 2016. "La guida di un poeta ingegnere nel labirinto di Joyce." *Il Foglio*. 2 February 2016. https://www.ilfoglio.it/gli-inserti -del-foglio/2016/02/02/news/la-guida-di-un-poeta-ingegnere-nel-labirinto -di-joyce-92210/.

Carnero González, José. 1992. "Anna Livia Plurabelle." *Revista Alicantina de Estudios Ingleses* 5: 245–8. https://doi.org/10.14198/raei.1992.5.19-2.

Castelain, Daniel, trans. 1964. "Un itinéraire pour *Finnegans Wake*: Tentative de traduction fragmentaire." *Two Cities* (Paris) 9: 35–40. Includes French translation of excerpts from *FW* 3, 44, 169–71, 384, 627–8.

Castro, Enrique, and Beatriz Blanco, trans. 1982. *James Joyce*. By Richard Ellmann. 1982. Spanish translation. Barcelona: Anagrama Editorial.

Celati, Gianni. 1972. "Da *Finnegans Wake*: Elaborazioni sul tema visita al museo Wellington: Traduzioni di linguaggi inventati." *Il Caffè* 19 (3–4): 26–9. Includes Italian translation of *FW* 8.9–10.24.

Çelikyay, Umur, trans. 2016. *Finneganın vahı* [*FW* I.1–8: Turkish]. Istanbul: Aylak Adam.

– trans. 2017. *Finneganın vahı: II kitap* [*FW* II.1–4: Turkish]. Istanbul: Aylak Adam.

Cersonsky, Emily. 2011. "Reconsidering a *Wehg* Less Traveled: Another Look at Stündel's German *Finnegan*." *Joyce Studies Annual* 2011: 191–201. https:// doi.org/10.1353/joy.2011.0024.

Chassaing, Michel, trans. 2005. *Finnegans Wake de James Joyce*. [Includes French translations of *FW* 3.1–6.28, 15.12–18.20, 21.5–23.15, 24.3–26.24, 30.1–33.13, 69.5–74.19, 118.18–123.10, 142.30–143.28, 152.18–159.20, 184.11–186.18, 213.11–216.5, 219.1–221.17, 234.6–237.12, 304.5–305.5, 363.17–365.15, 383.1–386.11, 414.16–419.11, 427.9–428.27, 430.17–433.9, 454.8–455.29, 471.35– 473.25, 530.31–533.3, 555.1–555.29, 572.19–576.17, 593.1–594.9, 604.22–606.12, 610.34–613.16, 626.4–628.16]. http://riverrun.free.fr/ traduction.pdf.

Chastaing, Maxime, Armand Jacob, and Arthur Watt, trans. 1951. "Tentatives pour une traduction de *Finnegans Wake*." *Roman* (Saint-Paul, Alpes Maritimes) 3 (June 1951): 270–1. Includes French translation of *FW* 627.9–628.16.

Chitarroni, Luis, and C.E. Feiling, trans. 1992. "Anna Livia Plurabelle" [*FW* 196.1–199.12, 215.31–216.5]. *Conjetural: Revista Psicoanalítica* 24. Special issue: *James Joyce. Versiones de "Anna Livia Plurabelle."* Buenos Aires: Ediciones Sitio. 31–4. www.conjetural.com.ar/revistas/24.pdf.

Chun, Eun-Kyung. 2004. "On the Untranslatability of *Finnegans Wake*: With an Example of a Korean Translation by Kim Chong-keon." *James Joyce Journal* 10 (2): 173–90.

Coeuroy, André, trans. 1962. *James Joyce*. By Richard Ellmann. 1959. French translation. Paris: Gallimard.

Conley, Tim. 2012. "'Avec hésitance': Lavergne's Footnotes and Translations of *Finnegans Wake*." *Scientia Traductionis* 12: 20–35. http://dx.doi.org /10.5007/1980-4237.2012n12p20.

– 2017. *Useless Joyce: Textual Functions, Cultural Appropriations*. Toronto: University of Toronto Press.

Connolly, John. 1996. "Molly Bloom Says Yes beneath the Crescent Moon." *Irish Times* (online edition), 1 November 1996.

Coromines, Joan. 2012. *Breve diccionario etimológico de la lengua castellana*. Madrid: Editorial Gredos.

Cortanze, Gérard de. 1983. "Le *Finnegans Wake* de Philippe Lavergne, ou les contorsions de la Sibylle." *Europe: Revue Littéraire Mensuelle* (Paris) 649 (May 1983): 179–86.

Costanzo, W.V. 1971. "The French Version of *Finnegans Wake*: Translation, Adaption, Recreation." *James Joyce Quarterly* 9: 225–36.

Crémieux, Benjamin. 1929. "Le règne des mots." *Candide* 14 November 1929, 3.

Crispi, Luca, and Sam Slote, ed. 2007. *How Joyce Wrote* Finnegans Wake: *A Chapter-by-Chapter Genetic Guide*. Madison: University of Wisconsin Press.

Cronin, Anthony. 1996. *Samuel Beckett: The Last Modernist*. London: HarperCollins.

Curtin, Adrian. 2009. "Hearing Joyce Speak: The Phonograph Recordings of 'Aeolus' and 'Anna Livia Plurabelle' as Audiotexts." *James Joyce Quarterly* 46: 269–84. https://doi.org/10.1353/jjq.0.0134.

Ćwiąkała, Jadwiga. 1971. "Joyce in Poland." *James Joyce Quarterly* 9: 93–8.

Czarnecki, Jan. 2017. "*Musica textualis*: Word-Made Music in Prose as a Philosophical Problem." PhD dissertation. Università degli Studi di Padova.

Dai, Congrong. 2007. *Zi you zhi shu: Fennigen de shou ling jie du*. Liu dian xue shu. Shanghai: Shang hai ren min chu ban she [Shanghai People's Publishing House].

– 2010. "A Chinese Translation of *Finnegans Wake*: The Work in Progress." *James Joyce Quarterly* 47: 579–88. https://doi.org/10.1353/jjq.2010.0006.

– trans. 2012. *Fēnnígēn de shǒulíng yè* [*FW* I.1–8: Chinese]. Shanghai: Shang hai ren min chu ban she [Shanghai People's Publishing House].

– 2013. "The Chinese Giant Wakes to Finnegans." *James Joyce Broadsheet* 94: 1.

– 2015. "Advancing Cross-Cultural Understanding through Experimental Literary Translation: Chinese Translation of *Finnegans Wake* in China." *Fudan Journal of the Humanities and Social Sciences* 8, no. 3 (September 2015): 335–46. https://doi.org/10.1007/s40647-015-0079-6.

Dante Alighieri. 1982. *The Divine Comedy of Dante Alighieri: Inferno*. Translated by Allen Mandelbaum. Toronto: Bantam Books.

Darrieussecq, Marie, trans. 2014. *Brouillons d'un baiser: Premiers pas vers* Finnegans Wake. Edited by Daniel Ferrer. Bilingual. Paris: NRF/Gallimard.

Debons, Pierre-André. 1983. *"Finnegans Wake* enfin traduit." *Samedi Littéraire* 1 January 1983, iii.

Del Pozzo, Silvia. 1982. "Il labirinto violato." *Panorama* 31 May 1982, 153–6.

Diacono, Mario. 1961. "A James Joyce's mamafesta: By the stream of Zemzem under Zigzag Hill." *La Tartaruga* 1961. Rpt. as "Da *Finnegans Wake* di James Joyce, traduzione 107–108," Naples: Colonnese Editore, 1970. Rpt. under original title in *Joyce Studies in Italy* 2, edited by Clara de Petris. Rome: Bolzoni, 1988. 195–6. Includes Italian translation of *FW* 107.8–108.36.

Diament, Henri. 1996. "Gallic Joys of Joyce: On Translating Some Names in *Finnegans Wake* into French." *Names: A Journal of Onomastics* (DeKalb, IL) 44 (2): 83–104. https://doi.org/10.1179/nam.1996.44.2.83.

Ding, Zhenqi. 1998. "Translations of the Title of *Finnegans Wake*." *Journal of WuXi Normal College* 1: 40–3. In Chinese.

Drews, Jörg. 1977. "Work after the *Wake*, or: A First Look at the Influence of James Joyce on Arno Schmidt." *Bargfelder Bote* 19 (February 1977): 3–14.

– 1993. "Parforce-Ritt zur Unsterblichkeit, oder In ein teutsches Modell vergossen." Review of *Finnegans Wehg*, German translation by Dieter Stündel (1993). *Neue Deutsche Literatur* 41: 147–55.

– 1998. "'Anything Goes' Is My Device? Some Remarks on Dieter H. Stündel's German Version of *Finnegans Wake*." In *A Collideorscape of Joyce: Festschrift for Fritz Senn*, edited by Ruth Frehner and Ursula Zeller, 427–35. Dublin: Lilliput Press.

du Bouchet, André, trans. 1950. "Dans le sillage de Finnegan" [*FW*, excerpts: French]. *L'Âge Nouveau* (Paris) 45 (January 1950): 24–8. Excerpts from *FW* 619, 624, 625–8. Bilingual.

– trans. 1957. "Les veilles des Finnegans" [*FW*, excerpts: French]. *Nouvelle Revue Française* ns 5, no. 60 (December 1957): 1054–64. Includes an introduction, "Lire *Finnegans Wake*?" (1054–5) and fragments from *FW* 604–28.

– trans. 1962. *Finnegans Wake* [Excerpts: French]. Fragments adaptés par André du Bouchet. Introduction de Michel Butor. Suivis de "Anna Livia Plurabelle." Paris: Gallimard. Includes slightly abbreviated renderings of *FW* IV and I.1; also Joyce's 1931 team translation of *ALP*.

– trans. 2003. *Lire Finnegans Wake?* Fontfroide (France): Fata Morgana. Includes slightly abbreviated renderings of *FW* IV and I.1.

Đurić, Mina M. 2020. "Immanent Polyglossia of *Ulysses*: South Slavic Context Born Retranslated." In *Retranslating Joyce for the 21st Century*, edited by Jolanta Wawrzycka and Erika Mihálycsa, 165–78. Leiden; Boston: Brill Rodopi.

Eco, Umberto. 1978. "Come si dice in italiano tumptytumtoes?" *L'Espresso* 24 (28 May 1978): 74–83.

– 1989. *The Aesthetics of Chaosmos: The Middle Ages of James Joyce*. Translated by Ellen Esrock. Cambridge, MA: Harvard University Press.

– 1996. "Ostrigotta, ora capesco." In *Anna Livia Plurabelle di James Joyce*, edited by Rosa Maria Bollettieri Bosinelli, v–xxix. Turin: Einaudi.

– 2001. *Experiences in Translation*. Translated by Alastair McEwen. Toronto: University of Toronto Press.

Egri, Péter. 1967. "James Joyce's Works in Hungarian Translation." *James Joyce Quarterly* 4 (3): 234–36.

Eichhorn, Thomas. 2015. "Das Übersetzen und Arno Schmidt." *Bargfelder Bote* 389–90: 3–16.

Ekici, Armağan. 2016. "Finneganın Vahı Vakası." *K24* 7 (January 2016). http://t24.com.tr/k24/yazi/finnegans-wake,523.

Elizondo, Salvador, trans. 1962. "La primera página de *Finnegans Wake*" [*FW* 3.1–24: Spanish]. *S.Nob* 20 June 1962: 14–16. Rpt. in his *Teoría del infierno y otros ensayos*. Mexico, DF: El Colegio Nacional, Ediciones del Equilibrista, 1992, 155–62. Rpt. *Casa del tiempo* 89 (June 2006): 53–6.

Ellmann, Richard. 1959. *James Joyce*. New York: Oxford University Press.

– 1982. *James Joyce*. New and revised edition. New York: Oxford University Press.

Engholm, Ahrvid. 2013. "Ordrik bok i begränsad utgåva." *DAST Magazine*, 17 November 2013. http://www.dast.nu/artikel/ordrik-bok-i-begransad-utgava.

Enzensberger, Christian, et al., trans. 1985. "Aus 'Glugg's Confession'" [*FW*, excerpt: German]. *Protokolle* 1: 103–6. [*FW* 241.1–26]

Epstein, Edmund Lloyd. 2009. *A Guide through* Finnegans Wake. Gainesville: University Press of Florida.

Esslin, Martin. 1969: *The Theatre of the Absurd*. Second edition. Garden City, NY: Anchor Books.

Evans, Ollie, Christa-Maria Lerm Hayes, and Derek Pyle. 2015. "Joyce Smithy: A Curated View of Joyce in Visual Art, Music, and Performance (2016)." *James Joyce Quarterly* 52: 693–706.

Evenhuis, Arend. 2002. "Terug naar de rivierbron." *Trouw*, 5 April 2002. http://www.trouw.nl/tr/nl/5009/Archief/article/detail/2580457/2002/04/05/Terug-naar-de-rivierbron.dhtml.

Fajfer, Zenon. 2008. "A Brief Comment for the Foreign Reader of Liberature." Translated by Katarzyna Bazarnik. https://www.slideshare.net/mik _krakow/zenon-fajfer-a-brief-comment-for-the-foreign-reader-of-liberature.

Falk, Bertil. 2008. *Litterära solitärer: Essäer*. Lund: BTJ Förlag.

– trans. 2013. *Finnegans likvaka, bok 1 Föräldrarnas bok: kapitel 1 Finnegans fall* [*FW* I.1: Swedish]. Trelleborg, Sweden: Zen Zat.

– trans. 2014. *Finnegans likvaka, bok 1* [*FW* I.1: Swedish]. CD-Rom, play time 04:07:47. Read by David Zetterstad. Lund: BTJ.

Fanzone, Leandro, trans. 2007. "Fragmentos de *Finnegans Wake*, de James Joyce" [*FW*, excerpts: Spanish]. *Seikilos* (Buenos Aires), 8 November 2007. http://picholoco.tripod.com/sitebuildercontent/sitebuilderfiles /fiineganswake.pdf. [*FW* 159.6–18, 215.31–216.5, 627.34–628.16.]

Fargnoli, A. Nicholas, and Michael Patrick Gillespie. 1995. *James Joyce A to Z: An Encyclopedic Guide to His Life and Work*. London: Bloomsbury.

Fatica, Ottavio, trans. 2013. *Finn's Hotel* [Italian]. Rome: Gallucci.

Federici, Fabrizio. 1982. "Un viaggio al limite del linguaggio." *Avanti!* 27 July 1982, 8.

Feiling, C.E., trans. 1992. "Anna Livia Plurabelle: La noche simplificada." *Conjetural: Una Revista Psicoanalítica* 24: 83–5. [Ogden's *ALP*: Spanish] www.conjetural.com.ar/revistas/24.pdf.

Fenge, Zeynep Atayurt. 2016. Review of Umur Çelikyay's *Finneganın vahı*. *James Joyce Broadsheet* 105: 2.

– 2017. Review of Fuat Sevimay's *Finneganın Uyanması*. *James Joyce Broadsheet* 107: 2.

Ferrer, Daniel, and Jacques Aubert. 1998. "Anna Livia's French Bifurcations." In *Transcultural Joyce*, edited by Karen R. Lawrence, 179–86. Cambridge: Cambridge University Press.

Fomenko, Elena G. 2017. "Proba perevoda na russkiy yazyk finala 'Pominok po Finneganu' Dzheimsa Dzhoisa." *Naukoviy Visnik Mizhnarodnogo Gumanitarnogo Universitetu, Filologiya* 2 (29): 124–8. Includes Russian translation of *FW* 593.1–595.30.

Fordham, Finn. 2007a. *Lots of Fun at* Finnegans Wake: *Unravelling Universals*. Oxford: Oxford University Press.

– 2007b. "'The End'; 'Zee End': Chapter I.1." In *How Joyce Wrote* Finnegans Wake: *A Chapter-by-Chapter Genetic Guide*, edited by Luca Crispi and Sam Slote, 462–81. Madison: University of Wisconsin Press.

Frank, Nino. 1949. "Souvenirs sur James Joyce." *La Table Ronde* (Paris) 23 (November 1949), 1671–93.

– 1967. "L'ombre qui avait perdu son homme." In *Memoire brisée*, 26–94. Paris: Calmann-Lévy.

– 1979. "The Shadow That Had Lost Its Man." In *Portraits of the Artist in Exile: Recollections of James Joyce by Europeans*, edited by Willard Potts, 74–105. Seattle: University of Washington Press.

Franke, Damon. 2008. "The ABCs of ALP: Basic English and *Finnegans Wake*." In *Modernist Heresies: British Literary History, 1883–1924*, 201–7. Columbus: Ohio State University Press.

Frehner, Ruth, and Ursula Zeller, eds. 1998. *A Collideorscape of Joyce: Festschrift for Fritz Senn*. Dublin: Lilliput Press.

Friberg, Georg, and Gösta Friberg. 1987. "James Joyce: Ur *Finnegans Wake*." *Lyrikvännen* 34 (2–3): 106–8.

Fried, Erich, trans. 1978. "Werkstatt *Finnegans Wake*, 4. My Remembrandts." Unpublished radio broadcast, 18 April 1978. Includes translation of *FW* 403–4 with extensive commentary.

– trans. 1985. "Eine Übersetzung aus *Finnegans Wake*" [*FW*, excerpt: German]. *Protokolle* 1: 107–20. [*FW* 403.1–404.3]

Friedman, Max M. 2010. "'Kubla Khan' in *Finnegans Wake*." *James Joyce Quarterly* 47: 643–5.

Füger, Wilhelm, trans. 1983. "*Finnegans Wake* (German)" [*FW* 4.18–5.5: German]. *James Joyce Broadsheet* 12 (October 1983): 3.

Fuld, Werner. 1993. "Kein Weg zu Finnegan." *Frankfurter Allgemeine Zeitung*, 5 October 1993. Review of Dieter Stündel's German *Finnegans Wehg* (1993).

Galindo, Caetano, trans. 2013. "Um fragmento de *Finnegans Wake*" [*FW* 21–3: Portuguese]. *Folha de S. Paulo*. 24 November 2013. http://www1.folha.uol .com.br/ilustrissima/2013/11/1374886-um-fragmento-de-finnegans-wake .shtml.

– trans. 2014. *Finn's Hotel* [Portuguese]. São Paulo: Companhia das Letras.

– trans. 2016. "James Joyce: do *Finnegans Wake*" [*FW* 104.1–107.35: Portuguese]. *Circuladô: Tradução como Criação e Crítica* (São Paulo) 4 (5): 65–70. http:// www.casadasrosas.org.br/crhc/arquivos/revista-circulado-ed5.pdf.

– trans. 2019. "Juto & Muto (um excerto do *Finnegans Wake*)" [*FW* 15.29–18.30: Portuguese]. *Qorpus* (Florianópolis, Brazil) 9 (3): 151–7. https://qorpuspget .paginas.ufsc.br/arquivo/.

Galvão, Walnice Nogueira. 1999. "A mitopoética de Joyce." *Biblioteca Folha*. http://www2.folha.uol.com.br/biblioteca/1/22/1999111401.html.

García Tortosa, Francisco, trans., 1992, with Ricardo Navarrete Franco and José Maria Tejedor Cabrera. *Anna Livia Plurabelle* [*FW* 196.1–216.5: Spanish]. Edited by Francisco García Tortosa. Madrid: Ediciones Cátedra. Bilingual.

– 1993. "Difícil, pero no ilegible." *El mundo* 17 February 1993, 48.

– 1998. "The Spanish Translation of *Anna Livia Plurabelle*." In *Transcultural Joyce*, edited by Karen R. Lawrence, 208–12. Cambridge: Cambridge University Press.

Garrigues Walker, Antonio. 2016. "Una lectura de *Finnegans Wake*, de James Joyce." *ABC* (Madrid), 25 November 2016. https://www.elcuencodeplata .com.ar/en_los_medios/666.

Gelashvili, Tamar, trans. 2018. *Finnegans Wake, Book 1, Chapter VIII* [Georgian]. Tbilisi: Gamomcemloba universali. Bilingual.

– 2020a. "Transforming Shem into Shermadin: Some Difficulties of Translating Chapter VII of *Finnegans Wake*." In *James Joyce Translations and Studies in Georgia*, edited by Manana Gelashvili.Tbilisi: Dzavapoligraph.

– 2020b. *Finnegans Wake, Book I* [FW I.1–8: Georgian]. Tbilisi: Printgeo.

Genç, Kaya. 2015. "Finneganın Vahı." *London Review of Books: LRB* blog 21 December 2015. https://www.lrb.co.uk/blog/2015/december/finneganin-vahi.

Gerber, Richard. 1971. "James Joyce, *Anna Livia Plurabelle*." *Neue Rundschau* 82 (3): 570–3.

Gillet, Louis. 1979. "The Living Joyce." In *Portraits of the Artist in Exile: Recollections of James Joyce by Europeans*, edited by Willard Potts, 170–204. Seattle: University of Washington Press.

Glaister, Dan. 1993. "Caught up in Babel's Wake." *The Guardian*, 11 March 1993.

Gliński, Mikołaj. 2012a. "The Strange Case of Translating *Finnegans Wake* into Polish." *Culture.pl*, 27 March 2012. http://culture.pl/en/article/the-strange-case-of-translating-finnegans-wake-into-polish.

– 2012b. "Krzysztof Bartnicki." *Culture.pl*, 15 September 2012. https://culture.pl/en/artist/krzysztof-bartnicki.

– 2014. "Secret Code in Joyce's *Finnegans Wake* Cracked." *Culture.pl*, 28 January 2014. https://culture.pl/en/article/secret-code-in-joyces-finnegans-wake-cracked.

– 2015. "*Finnegans Wake* Rolodexed." *Culture.pl* 8 June 2015. http://culture.pl/en/article/finnegans-wake-rolodexed.

Godler, Jure, trans. 2018. "*Finneganovo bdenje*" [FW 4.18–6.12: Slovenian]. YouTube. 4:20 minutes. Posted 9 January 2018. https://www.youtube.com/watch?v=4CX8dPH0x38.

Goldmann, Márta. 2006. "Belated Reception: James Joyce's Work in Hungary." *Comparative Critical Studies* 3 (3): 227–48. http://muse.jhu.edu/journals/comparative_critical_studies/v003/3.3goldman.pdf.

Gooding, Mel. 2001. "Roberto Sanesi." Obituary. *The Guardian*, 13 February 2001. https://www.theguardian.com/news/2001/feb/13/guardianobituaries.books1.

Gordon, John. 1986. *Finnegans Wake: A Plot Summary*. Syracuse, NY: Syracuse University Press.

Goyert, Georg, trans. 1927. *Ulysses* [German]. Basel, Zurich: Rhein-Verlag.

– trans. 1946. "Anna Livia Plurabella" [FW 196–8, 213–16: German]. *das silberboot* (Salzburg) 2 (8): 139–41. Also appeared in *Die Fähre* (Munich) 1, no. 6 (1946): 337–40.

– trans. 1970. "Anna Livia Plurabella" [ALP: German]. *Anna Livia Plurabelle*, edited by Klaus Reichert and Fritz Senn, 141–66. Frankfurt: Suhrkamp. Rpt. *Finnegans Wake Deutsch: Gesammelte Annäherungen*. Edited by Klaus Reichert and Fritz Senn. Frankfurt: Suhrkamp, 1989. 159–77.

Gramigna, Giuliano. 1982. "Il libro millelingue parla italiano." *Corriere della Sera*, 27 June 1982, 11.

Greve, Jacob. 1999. "[-Fin(negans Wa)ke-]: Titlen som gåde." *Passage* 33: 46–52. http://ojs.statsbiblioteket.dk/index.php/passage/article/view/1950/1742.

Greve, Jacob, and Steen Klitgård Povlsen. 2004. "The Reception of James Joyce in Denmark." In *The Reception of James Joyce in Europe*, edited by Geert Lernout and Wim Van Mierlo, 1: 111–28. 2 vols. London: Thoemmes Continuum.

Grisi, Francesco. 1982. "Tradurre Joyce: Un'arte difficile." *Il Borghese* 33 (26 December 1982): 1063–4.

Grmela, Josef. 2004. "The Czech Reception of Irish Literature: The 1930s." *THEPES* (University of Masaryk) 2: 36–42.

Grut, Mario, trans. 2001. *Anna Livia Plurabella* [*ALP*: Swedish]. Lund: Ellerström. *FW* 196.1–216.5.

– trans. 2002. *Maran och gracehoppet* [*FW* 414.22–419.8: Swedish]. Lund: Ellerström.

Gumucio, Alfonso. 2011. "Los 100 de Mario Monteforte." Posted 6 September 2011. http://gumucio.blogspot.com/2011/09/los-100-de-mario-monteforte.html.

Gurrado, Antonio. 2019. "*Finnegans Wake* finalmente torna in libreria." *Il Foglio* (Rome), 4 May 2019. https://www.ilfoglio.it/cultura/2019/05/04/news/finnegans-wake-finalmente-torna-in-libreria-252780/.

Halper, Nathan. 1967. "Joyce and *Anna Livia*." *James Joyce Quarterly* 4: 223–8.

Hamada, Tatsuo, trans. 2008. Japanese translation of *FW* I.2–4 and IV. *Abiko Annual* 27: 8–131.

– trans. 2009. *Fineganzu ueiku, pato 1 to 4* [*FW* I.1–8 and IV: Japanese]. Abiko (Japan): Abiko Literary Press.

– trans. 2012. *Fineganzu ueiku, pato 2 to 3* [*FW* II and III: Japanese]. Abiko (Japan): Abiko Literary Press.

– trans. 2014a. *Fineganzu ueiku* [*FW*: Japanese]. Abiko (Japan): Abiko Literary Press.

– 2014b. *How to Read* Finnegans Wake? *Why to Read* Finnegans Wake? *What to Read in* Finnegans Wake? Edited by C. George Sandulescu and Lidia Vianu. Joyce Lexicography. Vol. 78. Bucharest: Contemporary Literature Press.

Hanks, Patrick, Flavia Hodges, A.D. Mills, and Adrian Room, ed. 2002. *The Oxford Names Companion*. Oxford: Oxford University Press.

Harman, Mark. 2019. "More Borgesian than Borges?: Joyce, Borges, and Translation." *ABEI Journal* 21 (1): 63–8.

Hart, Clive. 1985. "The Elephant in the Belly: Exegesis of *Finnegans Wake*." In *Critical Essays on James Joyce*, edited by Bernard Benstock, 111–20. Boston: G.K. Hall.

– 1962. *Structure and Motif in* Finnegans Wake. London: Faber and Faber.

Hart, Clive, and Fritz Senn, ed. 1968. *A Wake Digest*. Sydney: Sydney University Press.

Haselberg, Peter von. 1978. "Werkstatt *Finnegans Wake*, 5" [*FW* 593: German]. Unpublished radio broadcast, Norddeutscher Rundfunk, 11 July 1978.

Hatherly, Ana, E.M. de Melo e Castro, António Aragão, and Alberto Pimentol. 1982. *Joyciana*. Lisbon: &etc. Includes Hatherly's collection of 23 poems, *Ana viva e plurilida*, based on *FW* 628.8–16, 3.1–3.

Haugen, Karin. 2005. "Språk mot samfunnet." *Klassekampen*, 22 August 2005. http://www.klassekampen.no/7678/article/item/null/sprak-mot -samfunnet.

Hawtree, Christopher. 2007. "Liana Burgess." Obituary. *The Guardian*, 15 December 2007. https://www.theguardian.com/news/2007/dec/15 /guardianobituaries.booksobituaries.

Hayman, David. 1990. *The* Wake *in Transit*. Ithaca, NY: Cornell University Press.

He, Chu. 2014. "Hit or Miss? The Chinese Translation of *Finnegans Wake*." *James Joyce Literary Supplement* 28 (2): 2–3.

Heath, Stephen, and Philippe Sollers. 1973. "Joyce in Progress." *Tel Quel* 54: 4–24. Includes (19–24) French translation of *FW* 593.1–594.9, 596.34–598.16, 626.35–628.16.

Helin, Hannu. 2013. "Finnegans Sake." In *Mitä* Finnegans Wake *tarkoittaa?*, edited by Ville-Juhani Sutinen, 106–33. Turku: Savukeidas.

Henkes, Robbert-Jan. 2017. "How Works in Progress Grew." Review of *James Joyce's* Work in Progress: *Pre-Book Publications* of Finnegans Wake, by Dirk Van Hulle. *James Joyce Broadsheet* 107: 1.

Herms, Uwe, trans. 1977. "Werkstatt *Finnegans Wake*, 2. It's Phoenix, dear." Unpublished radio broadcast, 13 December 1977. Includes German translation of excerpts from *FW* 17, 18, 66, 68, with extensive commentary.

– trans. 1985. "'It's Phoenix, dear!'" [*FW*, excerpts: German]. *Protokolle* 1: 121–35. [*FW* 17, 18, 66, 68]

Hess, Albert W., Klaus Reichert, and Karl H. Reichert, trans. 1961. *James Joyce*. By Richard Ellmann. 1959. German translation. Zurich: Rhein-Verlag. Rpt. Frankfurt am Main: Suhrkamp, 1978.

Higginson, Fred H. 1960. *Anna Livia Plurabelle: The Making of a Chapter*. Minneapolis: University of Minnesota Press.

Hildesheimer, Wolfgang, trans. 1969. "Übersetzung und Interpretation einer Passage aus *Finnegans Wake* von James Joyce." In *Interpretationen: James Joyce, Georg Büchner. Zwei Frankfurter Vorlesungen*, 7–29. Frankfurt: Suhrkamp. [*FW* 196.1–197.33: German]

– trans. 1970. "Anna Livia Plurabelle" [German] In *Anna Livia Plurabelle*, edited by Klaus Reichert and Fritz Senn, 65–97. Frankfurt: Suhrkamp. Rpt. *James Joyce: Gesammelte Gedichte / Anna Livia Plurabelle*. Frankfurt am Main: Suhrkamp, 1981. 231–77. Rpt. *Finnegans Wake Deutsch: Gesammelte*

Annäherungen. Edited by Klaus Reichert and Fritz Senn. Frankfurt: Suhrkamp, 1989. 178–97.

– 2006. "Über Arno Schmidt als Übersetzer und Interpret von *Finnegans Wake*." *Bargfelder Bote* 288–9 (March 2006): 11–14.

Hirata, Hosea. 2014. *The Poetry and Poetics of Nishiwaki Junzaburo: Modernism in Translation*. Princeton: Princeton University Press.

Hoffmeister, Adolf. 1979. "Portrait of Joyce." In *Portraits of the Artist in Exile: Recollections of James Joyce by Europeans*, edited by Willard Potts, 127–36. Seattle: University of Washington Press.

Hoffmeister, Adolf, and Vladimír Procházka, trans. 1930–1. "James Joyce: Anna Livia Plurabella." *Literární noviny* 5, no. 9 (1930–1): 4. Includes Czech translation of *FW* 197.16–199.10.

Høghaug, Leif, trans. 2016. "Frå 'riverrun' til 'rinnælvrenn': *Finnegans Wake* på norsk." *Vinduet* (4): 85–93. Includes Norwegian translation of *FW* 3.1–10.24.

– trans. 2017a. "James Joyce, *Finnegans Wake*. Første bok, første kapittel, 13.33–19.19" [*FW* 13.33–19.19: Norwegian]. *Mellom* (2): 1–6.

– trans. 2017b. "To songar frå James Joyce si verd." *Syn og Segn* (2): 88–91. Includes Norwegian translation of "The Ballad of Persse O'Reilly" (*FW* 44.22–47.29).

– trans. 2018. "Penneknekt Shem og postmann Shaun." *Billedkunst* (5): 1–7. Includes Norwegian translation of *FW* 169.1–174.4.

Holland, John. 2010. "Scares of all knotknow." *Psychanalyse* 19: 5–13.

Holmes, M.E. 2011. "Nino Frank, from Dada to Film Noir." https:// rememberninofrank.org/?jjj=1581283424791.

Horn, Ingeborg, trans. 1989. "Shem, Shaun: Quisquiquock" [I.6; *FW* 126–68: German]. In *Finnegans Wake Deutsch: Gesammelte Annäherungen*, edited by Klaus Reichert and Fritz Senn, 73–115. Frankfurt: Suhrkamp.

Hrách, Tomáš, trans. 2000. [*FW* 74.16–19, 177.31–178.7, 188.9–24, 189.28–190.9, 201.5–6, 627.33–628.16: Czech]. In *Kánon západní literatury*, by Harold Bloom, translated by Ladislav Nagy and Martin Pokorný, 439–46. Prague: Prostor.

Ingberg, Pablo, trans. 2013. *Finn's Hotel* [Spanish]. Buenos Aires: Losada.

Ionescu, Arleen. 2004. "Inter-War Romania: Misinterpreting Joyce and Beyond." In *The Reception of James Joyce in Europe*, edited by Geert Lernout and Wim Van Mierlo, 1: 214–18. 2 vols. London: Thoemmes Continuum.

– 2012. "Joyce's Reception in Romania, 1935–1965." *Joyce Studies Annual*: 277–86.

– 2014a. "From Translation to Re-Creation: The Cases of *Ulysses* and *Finnegans Wake* in Romanian." *Joyce Studies Annual*: 196–214.

– 2014b. *Romanian Joyce: From Hostility to Hospitality*. Frankfurt am Main: Peter Lang.

Iribarren, Teresa. 2004. "The Reception of James Joyce in Catalonia." In *The Reception of James Joyce in Europe*, edited by Geert Lernout and Wim Van Mierlo, 2: 445–54. 2 vols. London: Thoemmes Continuum.

Ito, Eishiro. 2004. "Two Japanese Translations of *Finnegans Wake* Compared: Yanase (1991–1993) and Miyata (2004)." *James Joyce Journal* 10 (2): 117–52. http://p-www.iwate-pu.ac.jp/~acro-ito/Joycean_Essays/FW_2JapTranslations.html.

Jarniewicz, Jerzy, trans. 2015. *Hotel Finna* [*Finn's Hotel*: Polish]. Warsaw: Wydawnicza Foksal.

Jauffret, Régis. 1982. "Entretien avec le traducteur de *Finnegans Wake*: Joyce mode d'emploi," *Le Monde* 3 December 1982, 21. https://www.lemonde.fr/archives/article/1982/12/03/entretien-avec-le-traducteur-de-finnegans-wake-joyce-mode-d-emploi_3109350_1819218.html.

Jauslin, Kurt, trans. 1989. "I.1 (Der Anfang)" [*FW* 3.1–5.29: German]. In *Finnegans Wake Deutsch: Gesammelte Annäherungen*, edited by Klaus Reichert and Fritz Senn, 36–8. Frankfurt: Suhrkamp.

Jolas, Eugene. 1948. "My Friend James Joyce." In *James Joyce: Two Decades of Criticism*, edited by Seon Givens, 3–18. New York: Vanguard Press.

Jolas, Maria. 1949. "Traduttore ... Traditore?" In *A James Joyce Yearbook*, edited by Maria Jolas, 171–8. Paris: Transition Press.

Jones, Ellen Carol. 2004. "'An apogean humanity of beings created in varying forms': The 2004 International Conference on James Joyce and the Humanities, Seoul, South Korea, November 2004." *James Joyce Quarterly* 41 (1/2)(2003/2004): 15–22.

Josipović, Sandra. 2011. "The Reception of James Joyce's Work in Twentieth-Century Serbia." In *Censorship across Borders: The Reception of English Literature in Twentieth-Century Europe*, edited by Catherine O'Leary and Alberto Lázaro, 93–104. Newcastle upon Tyne: Cambridge Scholars Publishing.

Joyce et al. 1931. See Beckett, Samuel, Alfred Perron [*sic*], Ivan Goll, Eugene Jolas, Paul Léon, Adrienne Monnier, Philippe Soupault, and James Joyce, trans. 1931.

Joyce, James, and Ettore Settanni, trans. 1940. "Anna Livia Plurabella; I fiumi scorrono." *Prospettive* (Rome) 4, no. 2 (15 February 1940): 13–15; 4.11–12 (15 December 1940): 14–16. *FW* 196.1–201.20, 215.11–216.5. Rpt. in *James Joyce e la prima versione italiana del* Finnegan's [*sic*] Wake. By Ettore Settanni. Venezia: Edizioni del Cavallino, 1955; rpt. as "Anna Livia Plurabella." Edited by Jacqueline Risset. *Tel Quel* (Paris) 55 (1973): 59–62; rpt. *Carte segrete* 31 (1976): 27–40.

Joyce, James, and Nino Frank, trans. 1979. "Anna Livia Plurabella. Passi di *Finnegans Wake* tradotti da James Joyce e Nino Frank, 1938" [*ALP*, excerpts: Italian]. Edited by Jacqueline Risset. In *Scritti italiani*. By James Joyce. Edited by Gianfranco Corsini and Giorgio Melchiori. Milan: Mondadori, 1979. 216–33; rpt. Bosinelli 1996: 3–29. *FW* 196.1–201.20, 215.11–216.5.

Juristo, Juan Ángel. 2017. "Joycemaquia: Versiones argentinas versus españoles." *Cuadernos hispanoamericanos*, 1 March 2017. https://

cuadernoshispanoamericanos.com/joycemaquia-versiones-argentinas
-versus-espanolas/.

Kearns, John. 2017a. *"Finneganów tren, Da Capo al Finne, and Finnegans _ake*:
Krzysztof Bartnicki, Translation and Authorship." In *Authorizing Translation*,
edited by Michelle Woods, 96–113. *IATIS Yearbook*. London: Routledge.

– 2017b. Interview with Enrico Terrinoni. *Translation Ireland* 20 (1): 169–85.

Kho, Younghee. 2015. Review of *Tales from Finnegans Wake*, by Chong-keon
Kim (Seoul: Amunhaksa Books, 2015). *James Joyce Quarterly* 52: 449–52.

Killeen, Terence. 2014. Review of *Brouillons d'un baiser*, edited by Daniel Ferrer,
translated by Marie Darrieussecq (Paris: NRF/Gallimard, 2014). *James Joyce
Quarterly* 51: 727–31.

Kim, Chong-keon, trans. 1985. [*ALP*: Korean]. Seoul: Jeong-eumsa.

– 1990. "Joycean Study in Korea." *James Joyce Quarterly* 27 (1990): 465–72.

– trans. 2002. 피네간의 經夜 [*FW*: Korean]. Seoul: Bumwoosa.

– 2004. "On the Korean Translation of *Finnegans Wake*." *James Joyce Journal* 10.2
(2004): 153–72.

– 2011. "Reading the Title of *Finnegans Wake*." *James Joyce Journal* 17 (1): 5–25.
In Korean with English abstract.

– trans. 2012a. 피네간의 경야 [*FW*: Korean]. Seoul: Korea University Press.

– 2012b. [Finnegans Wake: *Annotations*]. Seoul: Korea University Press.

– trans. 2013. [Complete Works of James Joyce: Korean]. 2 vols. Seoul: Korea
University Press.

– trans. 2015. 피네간의 경야 이야기 [*Tales from* Finnegans Wake]. Seoul:
Amunhaksa Books.

Kirkup, James. 2001. "Obituary: André du Bouchet." *The Independent*
(London). http://findarticles.com/p/articles/mi_qn4158/is_20010424/ai
_n14387657/print.

Kitcher, Philip. 2007. *Joyce's Kaleidoscope: An Invitation to* Finnegans Wake.
Oxford: Oxford University Press.

Knowlson, James. 1996. *Damned to Fame: The Life of Samuel Beckett*. London:
Bloomsbury.

Knuth, Leo. 1972. "The *Finnegans Wake* Translation Panel at Trieste." *James
Joyce Quarterly* 9: 266–9.

Koch, Manfred. 2012. "Glücklich in Kannitverstan." *Neue Zürcher Zeitung*,
15 December 2012. https://www.nzz.ch/gluecklich-in-kannitverstan
-1.17891135.

Kosta, Peter. 2013. "Mehrdeutigkeit und Humor in der Übersetzung."
Zeitschrift für Slavistik 58 (3): 297–324.

Kot, Jozef, trans. 1965. "Finnegannovo prebúdzanie" [*FW*, excerpt: Slovak].
Slovenské pohľady 81 (10): 86–7. FW 3.1–5.4.

Krasińska, Ewa, trans. 1984. *James Joyce*. By Richard Ellmann. 1982. Polish
translation. Krakow: Wydawnictwo Literackie.

Królikowski, Adam, trans. 1998a. "*Finnegans Wake* (1)." *Magazyn Literacki* (Warsaw) 1: 91–2 [*FW* 3.1–24: Polish].

– trans. 1998b. "*Finnegans Wake* (2)." *Magazyn Literacki* (Warsaw) 2–3: 139 [*FW* 4.1–17: Polish].

– trans. 1998c. "*Finnegans Wake* (3)." *Magazyn Literacki* (Warsaw) 4: 55 [*FW* 4.18–5.12: Polish].

– trans. 1999a. "*Finnegans Wake* (4)." *Magazyn Literacki* (Warsaw) 1: 58 [*FW* 5.13–29: Polish].

– trans. 1999b. "*Finnegans Wake* (5)." *Magazyn Literacki* (Warsaw) 2: 62 [*FW* 5.29–6.12: Polish].

– trans. 1999c. "*Finnegans Wake* (6)." *Magazyn Literacki* (Warsaw) 3: 61 [*FW* 6.13–28: Polish].

Laederach, Jürg. 1995. "Der nette Herr Finnegan als Hirnmasseur: Zu Dieter Stündels Joyce-Übersetzung." In *Eccentric. Kunst und Leben: Figuren der Seltsamkeit*, by Jürg Laederach, 141–4. Frankfurt am Main: Suhrkamp, 1995.

Lago, Eduardo, trans. 2016. "Anna Livia Plurabelle" [Spanish]. http://www .enriquevilamatas.com/eduardolago/AnnaLiviaPlurabelle.html.

Laman, Barbara. 2007. "ALP Goes to Germany." In *Joyce and/in Translation*, edited by Rosa Maria Bollettieri Bosinelli and Ira Torresi, 135–41. Rome: Bulzoni Editore.

Lamborghini, Leónidas, trans. 1992. "Anna Livia Plurabelle" [*FW* 196.1– 198.16: Spanish]. *Conjetural: Revista Psicoanalítica* 24: 35–7. Special issue: *James Joyce. Versiones de "Anna Livia Plurabelle."* Buenos Aires: Ediciones Sitio. www.conjetural.com.ar/revistas/24.pdf.

Larriera, Sergio, et al. 2017. "*Anna Livia Plurabelle*: Versiones del último párrafo." Círculo Lacaniano James Joyce. Madrid, 2017. http://www .cilajoyce.com/sites/default/files/documentos/2017_LVI-Larriera-et-al _traducciones.pdf.

Laugesen, Peter, trans. 1997. *ALP-Traum*. Copenhagen: Edison Theatre. Printed program for a theatre performance based on *FW* 618–28 in Danish translation, at the Betty Nansen Theatre in Copenhagen.

– 1999. "Vågn op igen, Finn!" *Passage* 33: 35–7. Includes two different Danish versions of *FW* 171.12–28. http://dx.doi.org/10.7146/pas.v14i33.1954.

– trans. 2009. "Fra *Finnegans Wake*. Af James Joyce." [*FW* 196.1–201.4: Danish]. *Vagant* (Bergen) 1: 66–70.

– trans. 2012. "Anna Livia: Uddrag fra *Finnegans Wake*" [*FW* 196.1–201.4: Danish]. *Trappe Tusind: Tidsskrift for litteraturvidenskab* (Copenhagen) January 2012, 64–8.

Lavergne, Philippe, trans. 1967. "Shem" [*FW* I.7: French]. *Tel Quel* 30 (Summer 1967): 67–89. FW 169.1–195.6.

– trans. 1968. "*Finnegans Wake*." [*FW* I.1: French]. *Change* 1, no. 1 (Spring 1968). FW 3.1–29.36.

– trans. 1982. *Finnegans Wake* [French]. Paris: Gallimard.

Lawrence, Karen R., ed. 1998. *Transcultural Joyce*. Cambridge: Cambridge University Press.

León, Gonzalo. 2016. "Traducir lo intraducible." *La Capital*, 11 September 2016. https://www.elcuencodeplata.com.ar/en_los_medios/610.

– 2017. "El hombre que anota a Joyce, una entrevista a Juan Díaz Victoria." https://revistapenultima.com/entrevista-a-juan-diaz-victoria-traductor-del-finnegans/.

Lernout, Geert. 2007. "The Beginning: Chapter I.1." In *How Joyce Wrote* Finnegans Wake: *A Chapter-by-Chapter Genetic Guide*, edited by Luca Crispi and Sam Slote, 49–65. Madison: University of Wisconsin Press.

Lernout, Geert, and Wim Van Mierlo, ed., 2004. *The Reception of James Joyce in Europe*. London: Continuum.

Levin, Harry. 1960. *James Joyce: A Critical Introduction*. 1941. New York: New Directions.

Li Weiping and Cheng Huijuan. 2013. "A Portrait of the Artist as a Literary Giant: Thirty Years of Joyce Scholarship in China." *James Joyce Quarterly* 51: 119–28.

Lien, Marius. 2016. "Frihet under ansvar: Intervju med Leif Høghaug." *Morgenbladet*, 2 December 2016. https://morgenbladet.no/boker/2016/12/frihet-under-ansvar.

Livorni, Ernesto. 2004. Review of Luigi Schenoni's Italian translation of *Finnegans Wake: Libro Primo V-VIII*. *James Joyce Literary Supplement* 18.1 (2004): 9–10.

Lobner, Corinna del Greco. 1986. "Anna Livia Plurabella: La lavandaia antabecedariana di James Joyce." *Rivista di Studi Italiani* (Toronto) 4 (1): 84–91.

– 1989. *James Joyce's Italian Connection: The Poetics of the Word*. Iowa City: University of Iowa Press.

– 1994. Review of *Anna Livia Plurabelle*. Translated by Francisco García Tortosa. 1992. *James Joyce Quarterly* 31 (3): 400–3.

– 1999. "The Italian Joyce." *James Joyce Quarterly* 36: 37–9.

– 2008. "Luigi Schenoni, 1935–2008." *James Joyce Quarterly* 45 (3–4): 434–5.

Lo Pinto, Luca. 2013. "Diaconia: Una conversazione con Mario Diacono." *Doppiozero*, 18 February 2013. https://www.doppiozero.com/materiali/interviste/diaconia.

Lorenz, Sabine. 1991. "On the Im?possibility of Translating *Finnegans Wake*." In *Interculturality and the Historical Study of Literary Translations*, edited by Harald Kittel and Armin Paul Frank, 111–19. Berlin: Erich Schmidt.

Loukopoulou, Eleni. 2013. "Upon Hearing James Joyce: The *Anna Livia Plurabelle* Gramophone Disc (1929)." In *The Aesthetics of Matter: Modernism, the Avant-Garde and Material Exchange*, edited by Sarah Posman et al., 118–27. Berlin: Walter de Gruyter.

Lourenço, Manuel. 1968. "*Finnegans Wake*, I, 3." *O tempo e o modo* (Lisbon) 57/58: 243–4. [*FW* 3.1–24: Portuguese].

Łuba, Arkadiusz, trans. 2003. "*Finnegans Wake* (fragmenty)" [Polish: excerpts]. In *Ślady. Antologia przekładów Arkadiusza Łuby*, 159–64. Olsztyn: Portret.

– 2006. *Okno na Joyce'a*. Olsztyn: WBP.

Luft, Lya, trans. 1989. *James Joyce*. By Richard Ellmann. 1982. Portuguese translation. São Paulo: Editora Globo.

Malicki, Jacek, trans. 1996. "Przebudzenie Finnegana." *Gnosis* 9. [*FW* 6.29–7.15, 306.11–308.36]. https://www.gnosis.art.pl/numery/gn09_joyce _przebudzenie_finnegana.htm.

– trans. 2001. "Czytanie Joyce'a *Przebudzenie Finnegana*." Includes Polish translation of FW 3.1–7.5. www.fototapeta.art.pl/2001/jmmgp.php.

Mambrini, Simona. 1998. "Il linguaggio in traduzione: *Finnegans Wake*." In *Fin de Siècle and Italy*, edited by Franca Ruggieri, 189–212. Joyce Studies in Italy, 5. Rome: Bulzoni.

Mandelbaum, Allen, trans. 1982. *The Divine Comedy of Dante Alighieri: Inferno*. Toronto: Bantam Books.

Mánek, Bohuslav. 2004. "The Czech and Slovak Reception of James Joyce." In *The Reception of James Joyce in Europe*, edited by Geert Lernout and Wim Van Mierlo, 1: 187–97. 2 vols. London: Thoemmes Continuum.

Marrozzini, Luigi, trans. 2017. "James Joyce, *Finnegans Wake*." *bis numero uno* (December 2017). Includes Italian translation of *FW* 627.33–628.16. www .edizionibis.it.

Masoliver, Joan Ramón, ed. 1982. *James Joyce en el seus millors escrits*. Barcelona: Miquel Arimany.

Mazza, Giuliano, trans. 2018. *Finnegans Wake: La veglia di Finnegan*. Lemignano, Parma: Abax Editrice.

McArthur, Tom. 1992. "Basic English." In *The Oxford Companion to the English Language*, edited by Tom McArthur, 107–9. Oxford: Oxford University Press.

McCarthy, Patrick A., ed. 1992. *Critical Essays on James Joyce's* Finnegans Wake. New York: G.K. Hall.

– 2007. "Making Herself Tidal: Chapter I.8." In *How Joyce Wrote* Finnegans Wake: *A Chapter-by-Chapter Genetic Guide*, edited by Luca Crispi and Sam Slote, 163–80. Madison: University of Wisconsin Press.

McGrath, Andrew. 2014. "The Challenge of Translating *Finnegans Wake*." https://www.mhpbooks.com/the-challenge-of-translating-finnegans-wake/.

McHugh, Roland. 2016. *Annotations to* Finnegans Wake. 4th ed. Baltimore: Johns Hopkins University Press.

McKenzie, John L. 1965. *Dictionary of the Bible*. New York: Collier Macmillan.

McMurren, Blair. 2002. "Anna Livia and her Septuagint." In "James Joyce and the Rhetoric of Translation." DPhil thesis. University of Oxford. 361–82. https://ora.ox.ac.uk/objects/uuid:41fd0bc5-acc9-406f-b5e3-e21021470f92.

Medeiros, Sérgio, trans. 1999. "Husamenta" [*FW* 189.28–190.9: Guarani].
Unpublished handout distributed on Bloomsday 1999 at the University of
São Paulo, Brazil.

Meister, Guido G., trans. 1960. *James Joyce in Selbstzeugnissen und
Bilddokumenten.* By Jean Paris. Hamburg: Rowohlt. Includes (156) German
rendering of *FW* 627–8.

Meltz, Raphaël. 2003. "James Joyce et Jean-Yves Lafesse." *Le Tigre*, 2 January
2003. http://www.le-tigre.net/James-Joyce-et-Jean-Yves-Lafesse.html.

Mezzabotta, Orlando. 2010. "*Finnegans Wake*: The Prankquean" [*FW* 21.5–
23.15: Italian] YouTube. 11:25 minutes. Posted 28 October 2010. https://
www.youtube.com/watch?v=fq97QXBiv-Y.

– trans. 2016. *Opfertuere: Finnegans Wake: il primo capitol'ho?* [*FW* I.1: Italian].
Ilmiolibro e-book. https://ilmiolibro.kataweb.it/libro/narrativa/245920
/opfertuere/.

– trans. 2017. *Anna Livia Plurabelle* [*FW* 196.1–201.21, 215.11–216.5: Italian].
YouTube. 27:12 minutes. Posted 13 March 2017. https://www.youtube
.com/watch?v=RXtKZNbeHUY.

– trans. 2018a. *FW Doublends Jined* [*FW* 628.15–16; 3.1–3: Ancient Egyptian
hieroglyphics]. YouTube. 1:37 minutes. Posted 23 September 2018. https://
www.youtube.com/watch?v=MkdV_KNScnI&feature=youtu.be.

– trans. 2018b. *Anna Livia Hieroglyphwake* [*FW* 196.1–9; 216.3–5: Ancient
Egyptian hieroglyphics]. YouTube. 1:58 minutes. Posted 13 October 2018.
https://youtu.be/yQnsNtQFWnE.

Michel, Hervé, trans. 2004. *Veillée Pinouilles* [*FW*: French]. Continually revised
online. https://sites.google.com/site/finicoincequoique/.

Mihálycsa, Erika. 2012. "Horsey Women and Arse-temises: Wake-ing *Ulysses*
in Translation." In *Why Read Joyce in the 21st Century?*, edited by Franca
Ruggieri and Enrico Terrinoni, 79–91. Joyce Studies in Italy 13. Rome:
Edizioni Q.

Milaneschi, Francesca. 2019. "Beckett traducteur de Joyce: *Anna Lyvia
Pluratself.*" *Revue italienne d'études françaises* 9. http://journals.openedition
.org/rief/3020.

Milesi, Laurent. 1985. "L'idiome Babélien de *Finnegans Wake*." In *Génèse de
Babel: Joyce et la Création*, edited by Claude Jacquet, 155–215. Paris: Éditions
du Centre National de la Recherche Scientifique.

– 1996. "*Finnegans Wake*: The Obliquity of Trans-lations." In *Joyce in the
Hibernian Metropolis: Essays*, edited by Morris Beja and David Norris, 279–
89. Columbus: Ohio State University Press.

– 1998. "ALP in Roumanian (with Some Notes on Roumanian in *Finnegans
Wake* and in the Notebooks)." In *Transcultural Joyce*, edited by Karen R.
Lawrence, 199–207. Cambridge: Cambridge University Press. Includes
Romanian version of *FW* 213.11–216.5.

– ed. 2003. *James Joyce and the Difference of Language*. Cambridge: Cambridge University Press.

– 2004. "Joyce, Language, and Languages." In *Palgrave Advances in James Joyce Studies*, edited by Jean-Michel Rabaté, 144–61. London: Palgrave Macmillan.

Mink, Louis O. 1978. *A* Finnegans Wake *Gazetteer*. Bloomington: Indiana University Press.

Mirkowicz, Tomasz, trans. 1982. "*Finnegans Wake* (sześć pierwszych akapitów)" [*FW* 3.1–5.12: Polish]. *Literatura na Świecie* 8 (August 1982): 352–3.

Miroiu, Mihai, trans. 2014. *Hanul lui Finn* [*Finn's Hotel*: Romanian]. Bucharest: Editura Rao.

Mitchell, Breon. 1976. *James Joyce and the German Novel 1922–33*. Athens: Ohio University Press.

Miyata, Kyoko, trans. 2004a. *Shoyaku Finneganzu ueiku* [*FW*, Japanese; abridged]. Tokyo: Shueisha.

– 2004b. "Translating *Finnegans Wake*." *James Joyce Journal* 10 (2): 257–60.

Monnier, Adrienne. 1925. "James Joyce: From Work in Progress." Introduction by Adrienne Monnier. *Le Navire d'Argent* 2, no. 5 (October 1925): 59–74.

Monteforte Toledo, Mario. 1974. "*Finnegans Wake*: Presentación y algunas páginas." *La cultura en México: Suplemento de Siempre!* (Mexico, DF) no. 662, 16 October 1974.

– 1982. "Finnegans Wake." *El guacamayo y la serpiente* (Cuenca, Ecuador) 22 (April 1982): 3–17.

Mooney, Sinéad. 2011. "'Becquettant les crocs' and 'Transluding from the Otherman': 'Anna Lyvia Pluratself'." In *A Tongue Not Mine: Beckett and Translation*, 42–7. Oxford: Oxford University Press.

Morales Ladrón, Marisol. 2004. "Joycean Aesthetics in Spanish Literature." In *The Reception of James Joyce in Europe*, edited by Geert Lernout and Wim Van Mierlo, 2: 434–44. 2 vols. London: Thoemmes Continuum.

Mutanen, Miikka, trans. 2006. "James Joyce: *Finnegans Wake*, 3–10" [*FW* 3.1–10.23: Finnish]. http://fwsuomi.freehostia.com/3.htm. Posted 18 May 2006.

– trans. 2009. "James Joyce: *Finnegans Wake*, 10–15" [*FW* 10.24–15.28: Finnish]. http://fwsuomi.freehostia.com/3.htm.Posted 16 April 2009.

Nestrovski, Arthur. 1990. "'Mercius (de seu mesmo)': Notes on a Brazilian Translation." *James Joyce Quarterly* 27 (3): 473–7. Includes Portuguese translation of *FW* 193.31–195.6.

– 1998. "Fragmento: Mamafesta" [*FW* 104.1–112.27]. *Folha de São Paulo*, 16 June 1998. https://www1.folha.uol.com.br/fsp/ilustrad/fq16069808.htm.

Nishiwaki, Junzaburo, trans. 1933. "Anna Livia Plurabelle." In *Joyce shishu* [Joyce's Poems; selections from the poems and from *ALP*: Japanese]. Tokyo: Daiichi-shobo. *FW* 196.1–19, 213.11–216.5.

Niskanen, Lauri A. 2019. "'Hear, hear!' eli 'Kuulkaahan, kuulkaahan!' – Näin James Joycen tekstit ovat kääntyneet suomeksi." *Suomen Kuvalehti*. 16 June 2019. https://suomenkuvalehti.fi/jutut/kulttuuri/kirjat/hear-hear-eli-kuulkaahan-kuulkaahan-nain-james-joycen-tekstit-ovat-kaantyneet-suomeksi/.

Ó Corráin, Donnchadh, and Fidelma Maguire. 1990. *Irish Names*. Dublin: Lilliput Press.

Ogden, C.K., trans. 1922. *Tractatus Logico-Philosophicus*. By Ludwig Wittgenstein. London: Routledge and Kegan Paul.

– 1930. *Basic English: A General Introduction with Rules and Grammar*. London: K. Paul, Trench, Trubner & Co.

– trans. 1931. "Anna Livia Plurabelle in Basic." *Psyche* 12, no. 2 (October 1931): 92–5. *FW* 213.11–216.5.

– 1932a. "James Joyce's Anna Livia Plurabelle in Basic English." *transition* 21 (March 1932): 259–62; rpt. Bosinelli 1996: 141–50. *FW* 213.11–216.5.

– 1932b. "Notes in Basic English on the *Anna Livia Plurabelle* Record." *Psyche* 12, no. 4 (April 1932): 86–95.

Okuhara, Takashi. 2000. "Translating *Finnegans Wake* into Japanese." *Studies in the Humanities* (Senshu University), no. 84: 1–10. https://www.academia.edu/9803438/Translating_Finnegans_Wake_into_Japanese.

Okulska, Inez. 2016. "From Intersemiotic Translation to Tie-in Products, or Transmedial Storytelling as a Translation Strategy." *Forum of Poetics* (Fall 2016): 58–69.

– 2018. "*Fu wojny* als translatorische Mystifikation." In *Wer hat's geschrieben, wer übersetzt? Autor- und Übersetzerschaft als kontingente Rollen*, 75–84. Reihe Thematicon, vol. 32. Berlin: Logos.

Oliveira, Leide Daiane de Almeida. 2018. Review of *Brouillons d'un baiser*, edited by Daniel Ferrer, translated by Marie Darrieussecq (Paris: NRF/Gallimard, 2014). *Ilha do Desterro* (Florianopolis, Brazil) 71, no. 2 (May/August 2018). http://dx.doi.org/10.5007/2175-8026.2018v71n2p255.

– 2020. *A teoria da epifania e seus ecos em* Finnegans Wake*: A palavra em laténcia e o gesto da tradução*. Doctoral dissertation, Federal University of Santa Catarina, Florianópolis. Includes translation of *FW* I.5.

Oliveira, Leide Daiane de Almeida, Larissa Ceres Lagos, and Giovana Beatriz Manrique Ursini. 2019. "Entrevista com Donaldo Schüler." *Cadernos de Tradução* (Florianópolis) 39 (2): 294–304. https://doi.org/10.5007/2175-7968.2019v39n2p294.

O'Neill, Patrick. 1974. "Zettel's Traum." *A Wake Newslitter* 11 (3): 52–4.

– 2005. *Polyglot Joyce: Fictions of Translation*. Toronto: University of Toronto Press.

– 2013. *Impossible Joyce: Finnegans Wakes*. Toronto: University of Toronto Press.

– 2016. "Beckett, Péron, Joyce, and the Strange Case of the French *ALPs*." *Qorpus* (Florianópolis, Brazil), no. 21 (June 2016). https://qorpuspget. paginas.ufsc.br/arquivo/.

– 2018. *Trilingual Joyce: The Anna Livia Variations*. Toronto: University of Toronto Press.

– 2019. "Translators, Titles, Texts: Reading the First Two Words of *Finnegans Wake*." *Qorpus* 9 (3): 15–29. With Portuguese translation, "Tradutores, títulos, textos: A leitura das duas primeiras palavras de *Finnegans Wake*," by Vitor Alevato do Amaral and Isabela Martins (29–44). https://qorpuspget. paginas.ufsc.br/arquivo/.

Ors, J. 2010. "*Finnegans Wake*: El libro de Joyce que las editoriales no se atreven a traducir." *La Razón*. 10 July 2010. http://www.larazon.es /historico/1991-el-libro-sin-traducir-de-james-joyce-SLLA_RAZON_282965.

Osawa, Masayoshi, and Junnosuke Sawasaki, trans. 1968. Selections. *Sekai Bungaku Zenshuu* 35 [Selected works of world literature, vol. 35]. Tokyo: Shueisha. Includes *FW* 206.29–207.20, 418.10–419.8, 627.34–628.16.

Osawa, Masayoshi, Kyoko Ono, Shigeru Koike, Junnosuke Sawasaki, and Kenzo Suzuki, trans. 1970–2. "Anna Livia Plurabelle." *Kikan Paedeia* [Paedeia quarterly], nos. 7–11, 13, 15. Tokyo: Takeuchi-shoten. *FW* 196.1–208.5. Serialized in seven numbers of the journal.

Osawa, Masayoshi, Kyoko Ono, Shigeru Koike, Junnosuke Sawasaki, Kenzo Suzuki, and Motoi Toda, trans. 1978. "Fineganzu weiku yori 5-hen" [Five pieces from *Finnegans Wake*: Japanese]. *Sekai no Bungaku* [World literature] (Tokyo: Shueisha) 1. Includes *FW* 169.1–170.24, 206.29–207.20, 418.10–419.8, 593.1–18, 627.34–628.16.

– trans. 1982. *Anna Livia Plurabelle. Bungei-zasshi Umi* [Umi literary magazine] (December 1982): 288–305.

Osawa, Masayoshi, Shigeru Koike, Junnosuke Sawasaki, and Motoi Toda, trans. 1966. "Shem the Penman." *Kikan Sekai-Bungaku* [World literature quarterly] (Tokyo) 2: B1–12. *FW* 169.1–170.24.

O'Sullivan, Carol. 2006. "Joycean Translations of *Anna Livia Plurabelle*: 'It's translation, Jim, but not as we know it'." In *Italian Culture: Interactions, Transpositions, Translations*, edited by Cormac Ó Cuilleanáin, Corinna Salvadori, and John Scattergood, 175–82. Dublin: Four Courts Press.

O'Sullivan, Michael, and Oi Lin Irene Yip. 2013. Review of Chinese translation of *Finnegans Wake* by Congrong Dai. *James Joyce Quarterly* 50: 1095–9.

Oțoiu, Adrian. 2004. "'*Le sens du pousser*': On the Spiral of Joyce's Reception in Romania." In *The Reception of James Joyce in Europe*, edited by Geert Lernout and Wim Van Mierlo, 1: 198–213. 2 vols. London: Thoemmes Continuum.

Pagán, Alberte, trans. 1993. *Contos contados de Finnegan e HCE (Velório de Finnegans, I.1–2)* [*FW* I.1–2: Galician]. Juncalinho (Cape Verde): Morabeza. http://albertepagan.eu/wp-content/uploads/2013/12/contos-contados -de-finnegan-e-hce.pdf.

– 2000. *A voz do trevón: Unha aproximación a* Finnegans Wake. Santiago de Compostela: Laiovento. Includes most of the Galician translation of *FW* I.1–2 from Pagán 1993.

Papetti, Maria Viola. 1988. "'Mollilivia Bloodrabella' sulle orme di Joyce." Joyce Studies in Italy, 2. Rome: Bulzoni, 1988. 111–14.

Paret-Passos, Marie-Hélène. 2014. "De *Finnegans Wake à Finnicius revém*: Approche génétique des cahiers de travail d'un traducteur." *Genesis* 38: 69–83.

– 2015. "Les cahiers de travail d'un traducteur: Analyse d'un traduire-écrire: Donaldo Schüler traducteur de James Joyce." *Linguistica Antverpiensia, New Series: Themes in Translation Studies* 14: 54–71.

Paris, Václav. 2017. "Anna Livia Plurabella česká." *Litikon* 2 (1): 102–13.

Parks, Gerald. 1992. "Blotty Words for Dublin: An Excursus around the Translation of *Finnegans Wake* by Luigi Schenoni." In *SSLM Miscellanea*, 197–206. Trieste: Università degli Studi di Trieste, Scuola Superiore di Lingue Moderne per Interpreti e Traduttori.

Pilling, John. 2006. *A Samuel Beckett Chronology*. London: Palgrave Macmillan.

Politismou, Arkheio. 2013. «Η αγρύπνια των Φίννεγκαν» του Τζόυς, σε ελληνική μετάφραση. *I Kathimerini*, 13 May 2013. http://www.kathimerini.gr/38756 /article/politismos/arxeio-politismoy/h-agrypnia-twn-finnegkan-toy -tzoys-se-ellhnikh-metafrash.

Potts, Willard, ed. 1979. *Portraits of the Artist in Exile: Recollections of James Joyce by Europeans*. Seattle: University of Washington Press.

Pozanco, Víctor, trans. 1993. *Finnegans Wake* [Spanish]. Barcelona: Editorial Lumen. Abridged and simplified.

Price, Brian L. 2009. "A Portrait of the Mexican Artist: Elizondo and Joyce." *20th Century Mexican Literature* (blog). 7 July 2009. https://mexlit.wordpress .com/2009/07/07/a-portrait-of-the-mexican-artist-elizondo-and-joyce/.

Puff-Trojan, Andreas. 2012. "Ein Mammutprojekt." *Literarische Welt*, 16 June 2012. https://www.welt.de/print/die_welt/literatur/article106609842 /Ein-Mammutprojekt.html.

Pyle, Derek. 2015a. "If I did that shamething it was on pure poise." Interview with Marcelo Zabaloy. Part 1. *Massachusetts Review*, 4 September 2015. http://massreview.org/node/467.

– 2015b. "ef you now what eye mint." Interview with Marcelo Zabaloy. Part 2. *Massachusetts Review*, 4 September 2015. https://www.massreview.org /node/469.

– 2017. "Translating *Finnegans Wake*: An Interview with Hervé Michel." *Asymptote*, 6 March 2017. http://www.asymptotejournal.com /blog/2017/03/06/translating-finnegans-wake-an-interview -with-herve-michel/.

Pyle, Derek, and Sarah Jewell. 2016. "In Conversation with Fuat Sevimay, Turkish Translator of *Finnegans Wake*." *Asymptote*, 14 January 2016. http://

www.asymptotejournal.com/blog/2016/01/14/in-conversation
-with-fuat-sevimay/.

Quigley, Megan. 2004. "Justice for the 'Illstarred Punster': Samuel Beckett and
Alfred Péron's Revisions of 'Anna Lyvia Pluratself'." *James Joyce Quarterly*
41: 469–87.

– 2015. "A Dream of International Precision: James Joyce, Ludwig
Wittgenstein, and C.K. Ogden." In *Modernist Fiction and Vagueness:
Philosophy, Form, and Language*, 103–46. Cambridge: Cambridge University
Press.

Rabaté, Jean-Michel. 1983. "Translating *Finnegans Wake*." *James Joyce Broadsheet*
12 (October 1983): 2.

Rathjen, Friedhelm, trans. 1989. [FW excerpts: German]. In *Finnegans Wake
Deutsch: Gesammelte Annäherungen*. Edited by Klaus Reichert and Fritz Senn.
Frankfurt: Suhrkamp, 44, 45–63, 124–31, 220–37, 256–61, 275. Includes *FW*
3.1–14; 30.1–47.32; 152.15–159.18; 383.1–399.36; 414.16–419.10; 627.24–628.16.

– trans. 1992a. "Die Alimente der Gehomantie." *Schreibheft: Zeitschrift für
Literatur* 39 (May 1992): 3–8. *FW* 282.1–287.17.

– 1992b. "Schämes Scheuss wirrdeutscht: Anmerkungen zur Übersetzung von
Finnegans Wake." *Merkur* (Stuttgart) 46 (5): 407–14.

– 1993. "*Finnegans Wake*, plattgemacht." *Konkret* (September 1993): 52–5.

– trans. 1994. *Joyce für Jedermann*. German translation of *Here Comes Everybody*.
By Anthony Burgess. 1965. 2nd ed. 1982. Frankfurt am Main: Frankfurter
Verlagsanstalt. Rpt. Frankfurt am Main: Suhrkamp Taschenbuch Verlag,
2004.

– trans. 1995a. "Whas war dhaas?: Bettszene, erste Stellung (*Finnegans Wake*
III.iv)." *Griffel: Magazin für Literatur und Kritik* 1 (June 1995): 69–76. *FW*
555.1–563.36.

– trans. 1995b. *Der Mauchs und der Traufen: Eine Fabel aus* Finnegans Wake.
Unterreit: Antinous Presse. Limited edition (125 copies). Rpt. from Reichert
and Senn (1989: 124–31).

– 1995c. "Quadratur des Kreises: Zur Übersetzung von *Finnegans Wake* ins
Deutsche." *Griffel: Magazin für Literatur und Kritik* 1 (June 1995): 65–8.

– 1998. "On Translating Names, Titles and Quotations: Ten Practitioners'
Rules Derived from and Applied to German Renderings of *Ulysses* and
Finnegans Wake." In *A Collideorscape of Joyce: Festschrift for Fritz Senn*, edited
by Ruth Frehner and Ursula Zeller, 407–26. Dublin: Lilliput Press.

– 1999. "Sprakin sea Djoytsch? *Finnegans Wake* into German." *James Joyce
Quarterly* 36 (4): 905–16.

– 2005. "Re: Joyce, germanlooking: Vom Verdicken und Verdünnen." In *Dritte
Wege: Kontexte für Arno Schmidt und James Joyce*, 31–45. Scheeßel: Edition ReJoyce.

– 2009. "Quadratur des Kreises: Zur Übersetzung von *Finnegans Wake* ins
Deutsche." In *Quadratur des Kreises: Zum Übersetzen*, 127–39. Scheeßel:

Edition ReJoyce. Expanded from *Griffel: Magazin für Literatur und Kritik* 1 (June 1995): 65–8.

– 2010. "Nöö, Euer Maddetät! Überlegungen zu Status und Theorie der Schmidtschen *Finnegans-Wake*-Übersetzungen und ein Gegenentwurf." In *Bargfeld Transfer: Studien zu Arno Schmidt als Übersetzer und Transformator*, 123–43. Scheeßel: Edition ReJoyce. Reprinted from *Zettelkasten* 10 (1991): 197–229.

– ed. and trans. 2012a. *Geschichten von Shem und Shaun / Tales Told of Shem and Shaun*. Bilingual. Frankfurt: Suhrkamp. Corresponds to *FW* 152–9, 282–304, 414–19.

– ed. and trans. 2012b. *Winnegans Fake* [*FW*, excerpts: German]. Südwesthörn: Edition ReJoyce. Limited edition of 111 numbered copies. Includes German translation of excerpts from *FW* 3, 6, 11–13, 22–9, 30–47, 58, 92–3, 102–11, 219–24, 229, 250, 257–9, 260–1, 276, 307–8, 316, 336–7, 342, 353, 371–99, 410–12, 420–8, 433–40, 448–73, 483–527, 531–40, 555–90, 627–8. Bilingual.

– trans. 2014a. *Finn's Hotel* [German]. Frankfurt: Suhrkamp.

– ed. and trans. 2014b. *Mamalujo: Drei Fassungen eines Kapitels aus Finnegans Wake* [*FW* II.4 and two earlier versions: German]. Südwesthörn: Edition ReJoyce. Limited edition of 111 numbered copies. Bilingual.

– ed. and trans. 2015a. *Earwicker: Fünf Fassungen eines Kapitel aus Finnegans Wake* [*FW* I.2 and four earlier versions: German]. Südwesthörn: Edition ReJoyce. Limited edition of 111 numbered copies. Bilingual.

– 2015b. "Joyce, erdwärts gekehrt: Neue Details zu Genese und Verwertung von Schmidts *Finnegans-Wake* Übersetzungen." *Bargfelder Bote* 389–90 (May 2015): 17–30.

– 2019. "*Finnegans Wake*, erdwärts gekehrt: Schlüsselsuche und Übersetzungsversuche 1960/61." In *Die Höllenschmiede: Arno Schmidt zerschlossert James Joyce*, 57–82. Südwesthörn: Edition ReJoyce.

– 2020a. *Die Schlüsselschmiede: Materialien zu Arno Schmidts Joyce-Rezeption.* Südwesthörn: Edition ReJoyce.

– 2020b. *James Joyce jongliert: Genese und Konzeption von* Finnegans Wake*– Eine Einführung mit Textbeispielen*. Südwesthörn: Edition ReJoyce.

Razo, Praxedis. 2019. "*Finnegans Wake* en un espejo." *La Razón* (Mexico), 15 June 2019. https://www.elcuencodeplata.com.ar/en_los_medios/666.

Reichert, Klaus. 1972. "*Finnegans Wake*: Zum Problem einer Übersetzung. Der Wildschütz." *Neue Deutsche Rundschau* 83 (1): 165–9.

– 1989a. "Nacht Sprache: Zur Einführung." In *Finnegans Wake Deutsch: Gesammelte Annäherungen*, edited by Klaus Reichert and Fritz Senn, 7–20. Frankfurt: Suhrkamp.

– trans. 1989b. "Anna Livias Monolog" [*FW* 619.20–620.2; 626.35–628.16: German]. In *Finnegans Wake Deutsch: Gesammelte Annäherungen*, edited by Klaus Reichert and Fritz Senn, 271–3. Frankfurt: Suhrkamp.

– 1989c. *Vielfacher Schriftsinn: Zu* Finnegans Wake. Frankfurt: Suhrkamp.

– 1989d. "Soft Morning, City." In *Vielfacher Schriftsinn: Zu* Finnegans Wake. By Klaus Reichert. Frankfurt: Suhrkamp. 52–69. Includes German translation of *FW* 619.20–620.2, 626.35–628.16.

– "Anna Livia Plurabelle." In *Vielfacher Schriftsinn: Zu* Finnegans Wake, 70–95. Frankfurt: Suhrkamp.

Reichert, Klaus, and Fritz Senn, eds. 1970. *Anna Livia Plurabelle*. Intro. Klaus Reichert. Frankfurt: Suhrkamp. Includes Wolfgang Hildesheimer, "Anna Livia Plurabelle" (65–97); Hans Wollschläger, "Anna Livia Plurabelle, parryotphrosed myth brockendootsch" (99–133); and Georg Goyert, "Anna Livia Plurabella" (141–66). Also includes *FW* 196–216, Joyce et al. 1931, and Ogden 1932.

– eds. 1987. *James Joyce, Werkausgabe in sechs Bänden* [Collected works, study edition: German]. 6 vols. Frankfurt: Suhrkamp, 1987. [1] *Dubliner*, translated by Dieter E. Zimmer (1969); [2] *Stephen der Held. Ein Porträt des Künstlers als junger Mann*, translated by Klaus Reichert (1972); [3] *Ulysses*, translated by Hans Wollschläger (1975); [4] *Kleine Schriften*, translated by Hiltrud Marschall and Klaus Reichert (1974); [5] *Gesammelte Gedichte* [6] *Finnegans Wake* (original text).

– eds. 1989. *Finnegans Wake Deutsch: Gesammelte Annäherungen* [*FW*, selections: German]. Translated by various. Frankfurt: Suhrkamp. Cited as *FWD*.

Reichert, Klaus, et al., trans. 1989. "Shem the Penman" [*FW* 169.1–195.6: German]. In *Finnegans Wake Deutsch: Gesammelte Annäherungen*, edited by Klaus Reichert and Fritz Senn, 132–58. Frankfurt: Suhrkamp.

Reisinger, Tamara. 2015. "*Work in Progress*: Der Aspekt der Unübersetzbarkeit am Beispiel der Übersetzungen von James Joyces *Finnegans Wake*." MA thesis, University of Vienna. http://othes.univie.ac.at/37796/1/2015-05-28 _0904246.pdf.

Rene, Andrey, trans. 2016. На помине Финнеганов [*Na pomine Finneganov*] [*FW* I.1–2 and 196.1–201.20: Russian]. http://samlib.ru/r/rene_a/.

– trans. 2017. На помине Финнеганов [*Na pomine Finneganov*] [*FW* I.1–4, 7–8: Russian]. http://samlib.ru/r/rene_a/.

– trans. 2018. На помине Финнеганов: Книга 1 [*Na pomine Finneganov: Kniga 1*] [*FW* I.1–8]. Krakow: Rideró IT Publishing. Print version (without annotations), 298 pp. Online version extensively annotated, approx. 1,300 pp., at http://samlib.ru/r/rene_a/.

– trans. 2019. На помине Финнеганов [*Na pomine Finneganov: Kniga 2*] [*FW* II.1–4: Russian]. Krakow: Rideró IT Publishing. http://samlib.ru /r/rene_a/.

Reynolds, Mary. 1981. *Joyce and Dante: The Shaping Imagination*. Princeton: Princeton University Press.

Ricciardi, Caterina. 2019. "Proviamo di districarci nella lingua verticale di *Finnegans Wake*." *Il manifesto*, 30 June 2019. https://ilmanifesto.it/proviamo -a-districarci-nella-lingua-verticale-di-finnegans-wake/.

Richards, I.A., and C.K. Ogden. 1923. *The Meaning of Meaning: A Study of the Influence of Language upon Thought and of the Science of Symbolism*. London: Kegan Paul.

Risset, Jacqueline. 1973. "Joyce traduit par Joyce." *Tel Quel* 55: 47–62.

– ed. 1979. "Anna Livia Plurabella. Passi di *Finnegans Wake* tradotti da James Joyce e Nino Frank, 1938." In *Scritti italiani*, edited by Gianfranco Corsini and Giorgio Melchiori, 216–33. Milan: Mondadori.

– 1984. "Joyce Translates Joyce." Translated by Daniel Pick. *Comparative Criticism* 6: 3–21.

Roberts, Adam, trans. 2019. *Pervigilium Finneganis* [FW: Latin]. Kindle Edition: Ancaster Books.

Rodríguez, Leopoldo. 1969. "Impresións encol do *Finnegans Wake* de James Joyce." *Grial* 26: 475. Includes Galician translation of FW 215.31–216.5.

Rombi, Elisabetta. 1987. "La riproliferazione del senso: *Anna Livia Plurabelle* nell'italiano di James Joyce." *Il Lettore di Provincia*, April-May 1987: 50–60.

Rosado, Benjamín. 2016. "Ramón Buenaventura: 'Traducir es leer profundamente'." *El mundo*, 3 November 2016. https://www.elmundo.es /cultura/2016/11/03/581b8c18e2704e49288b460f.html.

Ruggieri, Franca. 2015. Review of Enrico Terrinoni and Fabio Pedone's Italian *Finnegans Wake*, III.1–2. *James Joyce Quarterly* 52: 730–3.

– 2017. Review of Enrico Terrinoni and Fabio Pedone's Italian *Finnegans Wake*, III.1–2. *James Joyce Broadsheet* 107: 2.

Sailer, Susan Shaw. 1999. "Universalizing Languages: *Finnegans Wake* Meets Basic English." *James Joyce Quarterly* 36: 853–68.

Sanesi, Roberto, trans. 1982. "Il risveglio di Finnegan." *Nuova Rivista Europea* 4 (29–30): 21–4 [FW 593.1–595.29: Italian].

– trans. 1983. *Il risveglio di Finnegan*. Milan: Severgnini [FW 593.1–595.29: Italian]

Santangelo, Vittorio, trans. 2014. *James Joyce*. By Richard Ellmann. 1982. Italian translation. Rome: Castelvecchi.

Scandolara, Adriano, trans. 2014. "James Joyce, *Finnegans Wake*." *Escamandro*, 16 June 2014. [FW 626.29–628.16; 3.1–5.12: Portuguese]. https:// escamandro.wordpress.com/2014/06/16/james-joyce-finnegans-wake/.

Schenoni, Luigi, trans. 1974. "Specimen Translation of *Finnegans Wake* 4.18–5.4 into Italian." *James Joyce Quarterly* 11: 405.

– trans. 1976. "The Prankquean, *FW* 21.05–23.15" [Italian]. *A Wake Newslitter* n.s. 13 (2): 36–8.

382   Bibliography

- trans. 1977a. "Mutt & Jute"; "O foenix culprit" [*FW* 15.29–18.16, 23.16–29.36: Italian]. *Carte segrete* 11 (35): 36–47.
- trans. 1977b. "Qui viene ognuno." *La Serpe* 23, no. 4 (December 1977): 17–18 [*FW* 30.1–32.19: Italian].
- trans. 1978a. "Dal *Finnegans Wake* di James Joyce." *Paragone* 338 (April 1978): 98–105. [*FW* 35.1–42.16: Italian].
- trans. 1978b. "Grande mascherattore." *Tuttolibri*, 6 May 1978: 12–13 [*FW* 35.1–36.34: Italian].
- trans. 1978c. [*FW* 3.1–10: Italian] *L'Espresso*, 28 May 1978, 79.
- trans. 1979a. "Il musovoleo willingdone: James Joyce, *Finnegans Wake*, 8.09–10.23: A Translation in Progress." *Stanford Italian Review* 1 (1): 163–9.
- trans. 1979b. "*Finnegans Wake* 55.03–62.25" [Italian] *Carte segrete* 13 (45–6): 21–36.
- trans. 1982a. "*Finnegans Wake* Translated into Italian." *James Joyce Broadsheet*, 7 February 1982: 4. [*FW* 85.20–86.31: Italian].
- trans. 1982b. *Finnegans Wake: H.C.E.* [*FW* I.1–4: Italian]. Introduction by Giorgio Melchiori. Bibliography by Rosa Maria Bosinelli. Milan: Mondadori. Bilingual.
- 1984. "Dai *Dubliners* a *Finnegans Wake*: Problemi di traduzione." *Annali della Facoltà di Lingue dell'Università di Bari*, 117–32.
- 1986. "Is There One Who Understands Me?" In *Myriadmindedman: Jottings on Joyce*, edited by Rosa Maria Bosinelli, Paola Pugliatti, and Romana Zacchi, 255–61. Bologna: Università di Bologna. Includes Italian translation of *FW* 627.9–628.16.
- trans. 1990. "Traduzione di *Finnegans Wake* I.5, 104.01–112.27." *Il Piccolo Hans* 64 (1989–90).
- trans. 1991. "Conciliar suonsenso e senso suono: Una traduzione di *FW* 117.09–125.23." In *Names and Disguises*, edited by Carla De Petris, 125–41. Joyce Studies in Italy, 3. Rome: Bulzoni.
- trans. 1996. "Anna Livia Plurabelle" [Italian]. In *James Joyce*, Anna Livia Plurabelle, edited by Rosa Maria Bollettieri Bosinelli, 87–139. Turin: Einaudi. Bilingual. *FW* 196.1–216.5.
- trans. 1999. "*Finnegans Wake*: Book I, Chapter 7 (*FW* 169.01–171.28)." *James Joyce Quarterly* 36: 43–5.
- trans. 2001a. *Finnegans Wake: Libro Primo I–IV*. Milan: Mondadori. *FW* I.1–4. Bilingual.
- trans. 2001b. *Finnegans Wake: Libro Primo V–VIII*. Milan: Mondadori. *FW* I.5–8. Bilingual.
- 2003. "Una lunga storiella." In *Romantic Joyce*, edited by Franca Ruggieri, 217–25. Joyce Studies in Italy, 8. Rome: Bulzoni.
- trans. 2004a. *Finnegans Wake: Libro Secondo I–II*. Milan: Mondadori. *FW*, II.1–2. Bilingual.

– 2004b. "Intorno a Joyce." *Transfinito: International Webzine*, November 2004. http://www.transfinito.it/_archivio/letteratura/schenoni1.htm.

– trans. 2011. *Finnegans Wake: Libro Secondo III–IV*. Milan: Mondadori. *FW*, II.3–4. Bilingual.

Schenoni, Luigi, Enrico Terrinoni, and Fabio Pedone, trans. 2019. *Finnegans Wake* [Italian]. Milan: Mondadori.

Schmidt, Arno. 1960. "Das Geheimnis von *Finnegans Wake*." *Die Zeit* nos. 49–51 (2, 9, and 16 December 1960).

– 1961. "Kaleidoskopische Kollidier-Eskapaden." *Konkret* no. 20 (20 October 1961). Rpt. *Der Triton mit dem Sonnenschirm: Großbritannische Gemütsergetzungen*. Karlsruhe: Stahlberg, 1969. 292–320.

– 1969. "Der Triton mit dem Sonnenschirm: Überlegungen zu einer Lesbarmachung von *Finnegans Wake*." In *Der Triton mit dem Sonnenschirm: Großbritannische Gemütsergetzungen*,194–253. Karlsruhe: Stahlberg. Originally delivered as a radio lecture, 10 November 1961. The volume also includes German translations of *FW* 63–4, 175, 182–4, 244–5, 259, 403–6.

– trans. 1984. "Übersetzung ins Deutsche sowie Anmerkungen und Nachwort von Arno Schmidt." Facsimile of original typescript, published to accompany *Arno Schmidts Arbeitsexemplar von Finnegans Wake by James Joyce*. Zurich: Haffmans, 1984. Rpt. Reichert and Senn (1989: 276–319).

– 2006. *Finnegans Wake von James Joyce*. Frankfurt am Main: Edition der Arno Schmidt Stiftung im Suhrkamp Verlag, 2006. CD recording (20 min. 10 sec) of Schmidt reading from "Der Triton mit dem Sonnenschirm" (1969). Originally broadcast 10 November 1961 by Süddeutscher Rundfunk.

Schönmetzler, Klaus J., trans. 1987a. "*... ein sitzam Saeculi Phoenis*": Sechs deutsche Annäherungen an Finnegans Wake *von James Joyce* [*FW*, excerpts: German]. Bad Aibling: privately published. *FW* 3.1–5.29, 152.16–159.18, 169.1–175.28, 383.1–384.32, 414.16–415.22, 605.4–606.12, 626.20–628.16.

– trans. 1987b. "Here's another version of ..." [*FW*, excerpt: German]. *Bargfelder Bote* 113–114: 24–5. *FW* 3.1–6.1.

Schönwiese, Ernst. 1986. "Erinnerungen an Hermann Broch." *Literatur und Kritik* 21: 412–15.

Schotter, Jesse. 2010. "Verbivocovisuals: James Joyce and the Problem of Babel." *James Joyce Quarterly* 48: 89–109.

Schrödter, Wolfgang, trans. 1989. "I.1 (Der Anfang)" [*FW* 3.1–4.17: German]. In *Finnegans Wake Deutsch: Gesammelte Annäherungen*, edited by Klaus Reichert and Fritz Senn, 39–43. Frankfurt: Suhrkamp.

Schüler, Donaldo, trans. 1999. *Finnicius Revém: Livro I, Capítulo 1* [*FW* I.1: Portuguese]. Pôrto Alegre, Brazil: Ateliê Editorial.

– trans. 2000. *Finnicius Revém: Livro I, Capítulos 2–4* [*FW* I.2–4: Portuguese]. Pôrto Alegre, Brazil: Ateliê Editorial.

– trans. 2001. *Finnicius Revém: Livro I, Capítulos 5–8* [*FW* I.5–8: Portuguese]. Pôrto Alegre, Brazil: Ateliê Editorial.

– trans. 2002. *Finnicius Revém: Livro II, Capítulos 1–4* [*FW* II.1–4: Portuguese]. Pôrto Alegre, Brazil: Ateliê Editorial.

– trans. 2003. *Finnicius Revém* [*FW*, Portuguese]. Pôrto Alegre, Brazil: Ateliê Editorial. 5 vols. Bilingual. Includes vol. 1 (*FW* I.1), 1999; vol. 2 (*FW* I.2–4), 2000; vol. 3 (*FW* I.5–8), 2001; vol. 4 (*FW* II.1–4), 2002; vol. 5 (*FW* III.1–4; IV), 2003.

– 2004. *Finnício riovém*. Rio de Janeiro: Lamparina.

– 2005. "A alquimià da tradução." *Irish Studies in Brazil*, edited by Munira H. Mutran and Laura P.Z. Izarra, 247–60. Pesquisa e Crítica, 1. São Paulo: Associação Editorial Humanitas.

– 2010. "Donaldo Schüler em torno à tradução e o *Finnegans Wake*." *Scientia Traductionis* no. 8: 300–11. http://www.periodicos.ufsc.br/index.php /scientia/index.

Schulte, Adolf. 1990. "Der Übersetzer Georg Goyert (1882–1966)." *Jahrbuch für Orts- und Heimatkunde in der Grafschaft Mark* 88: 85–96.

Senn, Fritz. 1967a. "The Issue is Translation." *James Joyce Quarterly* 4: 163–4.

– 1967b. "Resolution." James Joyce Quarterly 4: 216.

– 1967c. "The Tellings of the Taling." *James Joyce Quarterly* 4: 229–33.

– 1978a. "Werkstatt *Finnegans Wake*, 6." Unpublished radio broadcast, Norddeutscher Rundfunk, 28 November 1978. Includes German translation of *FW* 176–7.

– 1978b. "'Entzifferungen und Proben': *Finnegans Wake* in der Brechung von Arno Schmidt." *Bargfelder Bote* 27 (February 1978): 3–14; rpt. Senn 1983, 261–77.

– 1983. *Nichts gegen Joyce: Joyce versus Nothing: Aufsätze 1959–1983*. Edited by Franz Cavigelli. Zürich: Haffmans Verlag.

– 1984. *Joyce's Dislocutions: Essays on Reading as Translation*. Edited by John Paul Riquelme. Baltimore: Johns Hopkins University Press.

– 1993. "'Wehg' zu Finnegan? Dieter Stündel's Übertragung von *Finnegans Wake*." *Neue Zürcher Zeitung*, 10–11 July 1993: 59–60.

– 1995a. *Inductive Scrutinies: Focus on Joyce*. Edited by Christine O'Neill. Dublin: Lilliput Press.

– 1995b. "*Finnegans Wehg*: Dieter Stündel's German Translation of *Finnegans Wake*." *James Joyce Broadsheet* 40: 3.

– 1998. "ALP Deutsch: 'ob überhaupt möglich?'" In *Transcultural Joyce*, edited by Karen R. Lawrence, 187–92. Cambridge: Cambridge University Press.

– 2007. *Joycean Murmoirs: Fritz Senn on James Joyce*. Edited by Christine O'Neill. Dublin: Lilliput.

– 2013. Review of *Winnegans Fake*, translated by Friedhelm Rathjen. *James Joyce Quarterly* 50 (3): 870–4.

Sergeev, Andrey, trans. 1977. "Ballada o Khukho O'V'orttkke" ["The Ballad of Persse O'Reilly" (*FW* 44.22–47.29): Russian]. In *Zapadnoevropeiskaia poeziia XX veka*. Moscow: Khudozhestvennaia literatura. Rpt. http://www.vekperevoda.com/1930/sergeev.htm.

Settanni, Ettore. 1933. "Aria di Joyce." In *Romanzo e romanzieri d'oggi*, 55–61. Naples: Alfredo Guida.

– 1937. *Les hommes gris*. Translated by Adeline E. Auscher. Paris: Éditions Rieder.

– 1939. *Amour conjugale*. Paris: Éditions Rieder.

– 1940. "Nota su Finnegan's [*sic*] Wake." *Prospettive* 4, no. 2 (15 February 1940): 12.

– 1955. *James Joyce e la prima versione italiana del* Finnegan's [*sic*] Wake. Venezia: Edizioni del Cavallino.

Sevimay, Fuat, trans. 2016. *Finnegan Uyanması* [*FW*: Turkish]. Istanbul: Sel Yayıncılık.

Silva-Santisteban, Ricardo, trans. 1971. "La última página de *Finnegans Wake*." *Creación y crítica* 2 (February 1971): 1–4. *FW* 626–8.

– trans. 1982. "Anna Livia Plurabelle" [Excerpts: Spanish]. *Cielo abierto* (Lima) 7 (April-June 1982): 25–8. *FW* 196.1–197.17, 213.11–216.5.

– trans. 1988. *Anna Livia Plurabelle y otros textos del Finnegans Wake*. Lima: Privately published. *FW* 3.1–5.29, 196.1–197.17, 213.11–216.5, 626–8.

– trans. 1991. "Anna Livia Plurabelle" [*FW* 196.1–216.5: Spanish]. *Biblioteca de México* (Mexico, DF) 3–4: 36–43.

– trans. 2000. *James Joyce: Textos esenciales*. Lima: Adobe Editores [includes renderings of *FW* 3.1–4.17, 185.27–190.9, 196.1–216.5, 418.11–419.8, 619.20–628.16].

Silver, Marc, and Luca Torrealta. 1983. "La traduzione trovata: Intervista a Luigi Schenoni." *Quindi*, January 1983, 20–1.

Skubic, Andrej E., trans. 2000. "Finneganovo bdenje (izbor)" [*FW* (selections): Slovenian]. In *James Joyce: Poezija in kratka proza* [Poetry and selected prose], edited by Aleš Pogačnik. Ljubljana: DZS. Includes *FW* 30.1–34.29, 380.6–382.27, 604.28–606.7, 611.4–612.15, 615.12–619.19.

Słomczyński, Maciej, trans. 1972. *James Joyce: Utwory poetyckie. Poetical Works*. Kraków: Wydawnictwo Literackie. 54–6, 57–8. Includes Polish rendering of *FW* 44–7, 398–9.

– trans. 1973. "*Anna Livia Plurabelle*. Fragmenty" [Polish]. *Literatura na Świecie* 5 (May 1973): 42–53. *FW* 196–202, 215–16.

– trans. 1985. *Anna Livia Plurabelle* [Polish]. Kraków: Wydawnictwo Literackie. *FW* 196.1–216.5.

– trans. 1996. "Ostatnia strona *Finnegans Wake*" [*FW*, closing page: Polish]. *Studium: Pismo literacko-artystyczne* 4 (Summer 1996): 130–1.

Slote, Sam. 2019. "*Finnegans Wake*, however basically translated." *Translation Studies* 12:78–88. https://www.tandfonline.com/doi/full/10.1080/1478170 0.2019.1593237.

Smirnov, Dmitry, trans. 2003. "Tri kvarka dlya mastera Marka" [*FW* 383.1–14: Russian]. In *James Joyce: Stikhotvoreniya* [Collected poems], edited by G. Kruzhkov. Moscow: Raduga.

Sobré, Josep-Miquel [Josep Miquel Sobrer], trans. 1982. [*FW* 538.18–539.8: Catalan]. In *James Joyce en el seus millors escrits*, edited by Joan Ramón Masoliver, 80–2. Barcelona: Miquel Arimany. Also in *El Eco de Sitges*, 31 December 1982.

Šoljan, Nada, trans. 1978. "Bdijenje Finnegana" [Brief excerpts from *FW*: Croatian]. *Zbornik Trećeg programa Radio Zagreba* (Proceedings of Radio Zagreb's third program, Zagreb) 2: 314–22.

Sollers, Philippe. 1982. "*Finnegans Wake* de Joyce, version française." *Libération* 26 November 1982, 22.

Sonnemann, Ulrich, trans. 1978. "Werkstatt *Finnegans Wake*, 3. Das Finneganwunder oder Die Ausgießung des Heiligen Geistes." Unpublished radio broadcast, Norddeutscher Rundfunk, 28 November 1978. Includes translation of *FW* 429–30, 431.

– trans. 1995. "Das Finneganwunder oder Die Ausgießung des Heiligen Geistes. Zwei Absätze aus *Finnegans Wake*. Kommentierter Übersetzungsversuch." In *Müllberge des Vergessens. Elf Einsprüche*. By Ulrich Sonnemann, edited by Paul Fiebig, 63–78. Stuttgart: Metzler. Includes translation of *FW* 429–30, 431.

Soupault, Philippe. 1931. "A propos de la traduction d'*Anna Livia Plurabelle*." *Nouvelle Revue Française* 36: 633–6.

– 1943. *Souvenirs de James Joyce*. Algiers: Charlot.

– 1979. "James Joyce." In *Portraits of the Artist in Exile: Recollections of James Joyce by Europeans*, edited by Willard Potts, 108–18. Seattle: University of Washington Press.

Stephens, Christopher. 2000. "The Joyceful Life." *Kansai Time Out* (Kobe, Japan), June 2000, 22.

Stella, Rachel. 2011. "Hommage à Jean Fanchette." *Revue des Revues* 46. https://jeanfanchette.wordpress.com/two-cities/.

Stojaković, Siniša, trans. 2014. *Finegana buđenje: Knjiga I* [*FW* I: Serbian]. Belgrade: Pasus.

– trans. 2017. *Finegana buđenje: Knjiga III i IV* [*FW* III–IV: Serbian]. Belgrade: Pasus.

– 2019. *Rezana građa, vol. 1: Uvidi i ogledi tokom prevodenja 'Finegana Buđenja' Džemsa Džojsa*. Belgrade: Pasus.

– trans. 2020. *Finegana buđenje: Knjiga II* [*FW* II: Serbian]. Belgrade: Pasus.

Stoltefuß, Helmut, trans. 1989. "Humphrey Chimpden Earwicker" [*FW* 30.1–38.8: German]. In *Finnegans Wake Deutsch: Gesammelte Annäherungen*, edited by Klaus Reichert and Fritz Senn, 64–72. Frankfurt: Suhrkamp.

Strzetelski, Jerzy, trans. 1959. "Noc opłakiwania Finnegana (Urywki)" [*ALP*, excerpts: Polish]. *Twórczość* 15 (December 1959): 62–4. Includes *FW* 196.1–197.4, 198.9–14, 206.35–207.11, 215.31–216.5.

Stündel, Dieter H., trans. 1989a. "Mamalujo" [II.4; *FW* 383–99: German]. In *Finnegans Wake Deutsch: Gesammelte Annäherungen*, edited by Klaus Reichert and Fritz Senn, 238–55. Frankfurt: Suhrkamp.

– trans. 1989b. "Anna Livias Monolog" [*FW* 619.20–620.2, 628.6–16: German]. In *Finnegans Wake Deutsch: Gesammelte Annäherungen*, edited by Klaus Reichert and Fritz Senn, 274.Frankfurt: Suhrkamp.

– trans. 1992. "Finnegans Wehg: Kainnäh ÜbelSätzZung des Wehrkess fun Schämes Scheuß." *Schreibheft: Zeitschrift für Literatur* 39 (May 1992): 143–56. Includes translation of *FW* 309–21.

– trans. 1993. *Finnegans Wehg: Kainnäh ÜbelSätzZung des Wehrkess fun Schämes Scheuß* [*FW*: German]. Darmstadt: Häusser (large format edition). Frankfurt am Main: Zweitausendeins, 1993 (paperback). Bilingual.

Sullam, Sara. 2017. "Un lungo viaggio verso la notte: Delle (s)fortune di *Finnegans Wake* in Italia." *Alfabeta2: Speciale James Joyce*. 11 March 2017: 6. https://www.alfabeta2.it/2017/03/11/speciale-james-joyce/.

Suzuki, Yukio. 1983. "The Japanese Translation of *Finnegans Wake*." *James Joyce Broadsheet* no.12 (October 1983): 2.

Suzuki, Yukio, Ryo Nonaka, Koichi Konno, Kayo Fujii, Tazuko Nagasawa, and Naoki Yanase, trans. 1971. *Finnegan tetsuya-sai sono-1* [*FW* I.1–3: Japanese]. Tokyo: Toshishuppansha.

Svevo, Italo. 2011. *Un sodalizio creativo*. La parola salvata. Recco: Le Mani.

Szczerbowski, Tadeusz. 2000. *Anna Livia Plurabelle po polsku*: Finnegans Wake *Jamesa Joyce'a ks. I, rozdz. 8*. Kraków: Wydawnictwo Naukowe Akademii Pedagogicznej.

Szentkuthy, Miklós, trans. 1975. [*FW* 628.16, 3.1–3, 215.31–216.5: Hungarian.] In Naganowski, Egon. 1975. *Joyce*. Hungarian translation by Irén Fejér. Budapest: Gondolat. 142, 158.

Taha, Taha Mahmoud. 1982. "Arabic and Quranic Allusions in *Finnegans Wake*." *Kruispunt*, 21 (85): 85–107.

Teixeira Filho, Afonso. 2008. *A noite e as vidas de Renatos Avelar: Considerações sobre a tradução do primeiro capítulo de* Finnegans Wake *de James Joyce*. Doctoral diss. Universidade de São Paulo. Includes annotated Portuguese translation of *FW* I.1.

Terrinoni, Enrico. 2016. "Translating the 'Plutiple': Awakening Joyce in Finnitalian." *Translation and Literature* 25, no. 2 (July 2016): 213–21.

Terrinoni, Enrico, and Fabio Pedone, trans. 2017. *Finnegans Wake: Libro Terzo I–II*. Milan: Mondadori. *FW* III.1–2. Bilingual.

– trans. 2019. *Finnegans Wake: Libro III, capitoli 3 e 4. Libro IV*. Milan: Mondadori. *FW* III.3–4 and IV. Bilingual.

Titley, Alan. 2008. "An Seoigheach sa Ghaeilge." In *Aistriú Éireann*, edited by Charlie Dillon and Ríóna Ní Fhrighil, 108–19. Belfast: Queen's University Press. Includes Irish translation of opening lines (*FW* 3.1–6).

Toledo, Alejandro. 2003. "Las traducciones del *Finnegans Wake*." http:// www.eloceanodelcaos.com/traducfinnegans.html.

Topia, André. 1990. "*Finnegans Wake*: La traduction parasitée." *Palimpsestes: Revue de traduction* 4: 45–61. https://doi.org/10.4000/palimpsestes.602.

Torres, Marie-Hélène, and Mauri Furlan. 2010. "Donaldo Schüler em torno a tradução e o *Finnegans Wake*." *Scientia Traductionis* (Florianópolis) 8: 313–24.

Triesch, Manfred. 1968. *Ein Mann in Dublin namens Joyce*. German translation of *Here Comes Everybody*. By Anthony Burgess. 1965. Bad Homburg: Gehlen.

Urbánek, Zdeněk. 1966. "A dále tedy: Prekladatelovy hodiny s Joycem." *Světová literatura* (Prague) 11 (1): 199–202.

van der Weide, Jack. 2003. Review of *Finnegans Wake*, Dutch translation by Erik Bindervoet and Robbert-Jan Henkes. Amsterdam: Athenaeum/Polak & Van Gennep, 2002. *James Joyce Quarterly* 40: 625–9.

Van Hulle, Dirk. 2002. "*Finnegans Wake* en andere vertalingen." *Filter: Tijdschrift over Vertalen* 9 (3): 25–32. http://www.tijdschrift-filter.nl/jaargangen /2002/93/finnegans-wake-en-andere-vertalingen-25-32-abstract.aspx.

– 2004. "The Manner of Meaning: Ogden and Beckett Translating Joyce." *BELL: Belgian Journal of English Language and Literature* 2: 75–84.

– 2007. "Dame Plurabelle: Joyce's Art of Decomposition and Recombination." In *Joyce in Trieste: An Album of Risky Readings*, edited by Sebastian D.G. Knowles, Geert Lernout, and John McCourt, 87–101. Gainesville: University Press of Florida.

– 2015. "The *Wake* in Progress: Translation, Edition, Genesis." *James Joyce Broadsheet* 100 (February 2015): 3.

– 2016. *James Joyce's* Work in Progress: *Pre-Book Publications of* Finnegans Wake. Abingdon: Routledge.

Van Laere, François. 1968. "Les traducteurs français devant *Finnegans Wake*." *Revue des Langues Vivantes* (Liège) 34: 126–33.

Vázquez, Cristian. 2017. "*Finnegans Wake*: Las traducciones del libro intraducible." *Letras libres* (Mexico, DF), 16 July 2017. https://www .letraslibres.com/espana-mexico/revista/ finnegans-wake-las-traducciones -del-libro-intraducible.

Venegas, Ricardo. 2008. "La traducción como apropiación." *La jornada semanal* (Mexico, DF), 30 November 2008. https://www.jornada.com .mx/2008/11/30/sem-leer.html.

Verdin, Simonne. 1979. "Tradlire Joyce." *Courrier du Centre International d'Études Poétiques* (Brussels): 15–25. Includes French translation of excerpts from *FW* 627–8.

Versteegen, Heinrich. 1998. "Translating *FW*: Translatability and the Translator's Personality." In *Images of Joyce*, edited by Clive Hart et al., 2: 698–707. 2 vols. Gerrards Cross, UK: Colin Smythe.

Vichnar, David. 2020. "The Fabulous Artificer, the Architect, and the Roadminder: On Retranslating Aloys Skoumal's Czech *Ulysses*." In *Retranslating Joyce for the 21st Century*, edited by Jolanta Wawrzycka and Erika Mihálycsa, 148–64. Leiden, Boston: Brill Rodopi.

Victoria, Juan Díaz, trans. 2007. "Estela de Finnegan (una versión anotada)" *FW* 3.1–24: Spanish. *La jornada semanal* (Mexico, DF), 17 June 2007. https://www.jornada.com.mx/2007/06/17/sem-victoria.html.

– trans. 2008. "Retrato de Finnegan" [*FW* 4.18–5.12, 5.26–6.28]. *La jornada semanal* (Mexico, DF), 3 August 2008. https://www.jornada.com.mx/2008/08/03/sem-james.html.

– trans. 2009. *Estela de Finnegan: Un ensayo de traducción* (FW 1.1) [*FW* I.1: Spanish]. Mexico, DF: Lulu. http://www.lulu.com/product/file-download/estela-de-finnegan.

– trans. 2010. "Traducción anotada de dos fragmentos de *Finnegans Wake*" [*FW* 3.1–4.17, 8.9–10.23: Spanish]. *Estudios* 92 (8): 81–98.

– trans. 2016a. *Estela de Finnegan: Una lectura anotada del primer capítulo de Finnegans Wake de James Joyce* [*FW* I.1]. Guadalajara: Ediciones Arlequín.

– trans. 2016b. "La confissyón" [*FW* 279: Spanish]. *Revista C2*, 16 June 2016. https://www.revistac2.com/la-confissyon/.

– trans. 2016c. "La balada de Persse O'Reilly" [*FW* 44.24–47.32: Spanish]. *Casa del Tiempo* 34 (November 2016): 3–6. http://www.uam.mx/difusion/casadeltiempo/34_nov_2016/casa_del_tiempo_eV_num_34_03_06.pdf.

Villanueva, Darío. 1993. "Anna Livia Plurabelle." *ABC Literario*, 22 January 1993, 7.

Vizan, Yehuda, trans. 2015. [Three fragments from *Finnegans Wake*; *FW* 196–7, 627–8, 44–5: Hebrew]. *Dehak* 5: 140–3. https://library.osu.edu/projects/hebrew-lexicon/99995-files/99995008/99995008-005/99995008-005-140-143.pdf.

Volkov, Solomon. 1998. *Conversations with Joseph Brodsky: A Poet's Journey Through the Twentieth Century*. New York: Simon and Schuster.

Volokhonsky, Henri, trans. 1996–9. Из Финнеганова Уэйка (*Iz Finneganova Weika*) [*FW* 3.1–171.28, excerpts: Russian]. *Mitin Zhurnal* 53 (1996): 138–46; 54 (1997): 244–7; 55 (1997): 204–11; 56 (1998): 295–300; 57 (1999): 452–62; 58 (1999): 295–304.

– trans. 2000. *Weik Finneganov* [*FW* 3.1–171.28, excerpts: Russian]. Tver (Russia): Kolonna Publications. http://www.james-joyce.ru/works/anri-volhonskiy-text.htm.

Vouvé, Solange. 1985. "Aux limites du langage, aux limites de la traduction: *Finnegans Wake*." *Texte* (Toronto) 4: 209–21.

Washuus, Dorte. 2015. "Det sprog, man drømmer i." *Kristeligt Dagblad*, 8 May 2015. https://www.kristeligt-dagblad.dk/kultur/det-sprog-man -droemmer-i.

Wawrzycka, Jolanta W. 2004a. "The Reception of James Joyce in Poland." In *The Reception of James Joyce in Europe*, edited by Geert Lernout and Wim Van Mierlo, 1: 219–29. 2 vols. London: Thoemmes Continuum.

– 2004b. "Joyce *en slave* / Joyce Enclave: The Joyce of Maciej Słomczyński – A Tribute." In *Twenty-First Joyce*, edited by Ellen Carol Jones and Morris Beja, 137–56. Gainesville: University Press of Florida.

– 2016–17. Review of *Epifanie*, trans. Adam Poprawa (Wrocław: Biuro Literackie, 2016) and *Finneganów tren*, trans. Krzysztof Bartnicki (Kraków: Korporacja Ha!art, 2012). *James Joyce Quarterly* 54 (2016–17): 167–76.

Wawrzycka, Jolanta, and Erika Mihálycsa, eds. 2020. *Retranslating Joyce for the 21st Century*. European Joyce Studies 30. Leiden: Brill Rodopi.

Weatherall, Maria, Vladimír Procházka, and Adolf Hoffmeister, trans. 1932. *Anna Livia Plurabella: Fragment: Díla v zrodu* [*ALP*: Czech] / *Anna Livia Plurabella: Fragment: Work in Progress*. Afterword by Adolf Hoffmeister. Prague: Odeon. Rpt. *Dialog* (Prague) 1 (1965): 48–68. New edition Liberec: Dauphin, 1996. Bilingual. *FW* 196–216.

Weninger, Robert. 1982. *Arno Schmidts Joyce-Rezeption*. Frankfurt: Lang.

– 1984. *The Mookse and the Gripes. Ein Kommentar zu James Joyces Finnegans Wake*. München: edition text + kritik. Includes (210–18) German translation of *FW* 152.15–159.18, rpt. *Finnegans Wake Deutsch: Gesammelte Annäherungen*. Edited by Klaus Reichert and Fritz Senn. Frankfurt: Suhrkamp, 1989. 116–23.

– 1985. "An den Grenzen der Sprache. Bemerkungen zur (Un-) Übersetzbarkeit von *Finnegans Wake* mit einer Kostprobe: 'Der Muhkus und Der Trauben'." *Protokolle* 1: 85–102.

– 2012. *The German Joyce*. Gainesville: University Press of Florida.

Wilcock, J. Rodolfo, trans. 1961. "Frammenti scelti da *La veglia di Finnegan*" [*FW*, excerpts: Italian]. *Tutte le opere di James Joyce*, edited by Giacomo Debenedetti, 1125–74. 3 vols. Milan: Mondadori, 1961. Includes *FW* 3.1–20, 33.14–34.4, 104.1–109.36, 112.9–27, 169.1–170.9, 179.9–32, 182.30–184.10, 185.14–26, 187.28–188.19, 189.28–191.4, 196.1–24, 206.29–207.14, 219.1– 222.17, 249.5–33, 258.19–259.10, 306.7–308.27, 384.6–20, 543.13–545.22, 558.26–559.31, 572.7–575.7, 599.25–606.12, 626.33–628.16.

– trans. 2016. *Finnegans Wake* [Italian]. Edited by Eduardo Camurri. Macerata: Giometti & Antonello. Bilingual.

Winkler, Willi. 1993. "Ordspindelvaev." *Die Zeit*, 29 October 1993, 74. Review of *Finnegans Wehg*, German trans. by Dieter Stündel (1993).

Wollschläger, Hans, trans. 1970. "Anna Livia Plurabelle, parryotphrosed myth brockendootsch" [*ALP*: German]. In *Anna Livia Plurabelle*, edited by Klaus Reichert and Fritz Senn, 99–133. Frankfurt: Suhrkamp. Rpt. *James Joyce: Gesammelte Gedichte / Anna Livia Plurabelle*. Frankfurt am Main: Suhrkamp, 1981. 279–329. Rpt. *Finnegans Wake Deutsch: Gesammelte Annäherungen*. Edited by Klaus Reichert and Fritz Senn. Frankfurt: Suhrkamp, 1989. 198–219.

Woods, Michelle, trans. 2005. "The Game of Evenings: Adolf Hoffmeister and James Joyce." *Granta 89: The Factory* (Spring 2005). Online Edition. Translation (from Czech) of Hoffmeister's account of an interview (in French) with Joyce in Paris in August 1930, originally published in the Czech literary magazine *Rozpravy aventina* over two issues in 1930–1. https://granta.com/the-game-of-evenings/.

– 2012. "Framing Translation: Adolf Hoffmeister's Comic Strips, Travelogues, and Interviews as Introductions to Modernist Translations." *Translation & Interpreting Studies* 7 (1): 1–18.

Yanase, Naoki, trans. 1991. *Finneganzu ueiku I–II* [*FW* I–II: Japanese]. Tokyo: Kawade shobo shinsa.

– trans. 1993. *Fineganzu ueiku III–IV* [*FW* III–IV: Japanese]. Tokyo: Kawade shobo shinsha.

– trans. 2004. *Finneganzu ueiku* [*FW*: Japanese]. Paperback ed. in 3 vols. *FW* I, II, III/IV. Tokyo: Kawade shobo shinsa.

Yee, Cordell D.K. 2013. Review of Congrong Dai's *Fennigen de shouling ye* (2012). *James Joyce Quarterly* 51: 204–10.

Yun, Sheng. 2014. "Short Cuts." *London Review of Books* 36, no. 7 (3 April 2014): 24. https://www.lrb.co.uk/v36/n07/-shengyun/short-cuts.

Zabaloy, Marcelo, trans. 2016. *Finnegans Wake* [Spanish]. Buenos Aires: El Cuenco de Plata.

Zanotti, Serenella. 2001. "An Italianate Irishman: Joyce and the Languages of Trieste." *James Joyce Quarterly* 38: 411–30.

– 2002. "L'italiano di Joyce nell'auto-traduzione di *Anna Livia Plurabelle*." In *Eteroglossia e plurilinguismo letterario*, vol. 2, *Plurilinguismo e letteratura*, edited by Furio Brugnolo and Vincenzo Orioles, 277–307. Rome: Editrice Il Calamo.

– 2004. "L'italiano di Joyce nell'auto-traduzione di *Anna Livia Plurabelle*." In *Joyce in Italy / L'italiano in Joyce*, by Serenella Zanotti, 144–78. Rome: Aracne.

– 2006. "The Translator's Visibility: The Italian Translations of *Finnegans Wake*." *MediAzioni* no. 2. http://www.mediazioni.sitlec.unibo.it/.

– 2013. "Un chiacchiericcio assurdo e bislacco: The Italian Translation of *Anna Livia Plurabelle*." In *Italian Joyce: A Journey through Language and Translation*, by Serenella Zanotti, 70–3. Bologna: Bononia University Press.